MICROECONOMIC THEORY

BASIC PRINCIPLES *and* EXTENSIONS

Seventh Edition

MICROECONOMIC THEORY

BASIC PRINCIPLES *and* EXTENSIONS

Seventh Edition

WALTER NICHOLSON
Amherst College

THE DRYDEN PRESS

Harcourt Brace College Publishers

Fort Worth   Philadelphia   San Diego   New York   Orlando   Austin   San Antonio

Toronto   Montreal   London   Sydney   Tokyo

Publisher	George Provol
Acquisitions Editors	Emily Barrosse and Gary Nelson
Product Manager	Kathleen Sharp
Developmental Editor	Anita Fallon
Project Editor	Sandy Walton
Art Director	Jeanette Barber
Production Manager	Lois West

ISBN: 0-03-024474-9

Library of Congress Catalog Card Number: 97-67941

Address for Orders
The Dryden Press, 6277 Sea Harbor Drive, Orlando, FL 32887-6777
1-800-782-4479

Address for Editorial Correspondence
The Dryden Press, 301 Commerce Street, Suite 3700, Fort Worth, TX 76102

Web Site Address
http://www.hbcollege.com

Printed in the United States of America

7 8 9 0 1 2 3 4 5 6   039   9 8 7 6 5 4 3 2 1

The Dryden Press
Harcourt Brace College Publishers

To Kate, David, Tory, Paul, and Brad

THE DRYDEN PRESS SERIES IN ECONOMICS

MARLOW
Public Finance: Theory and
Practice

NICHOLSON
Intermediate Microeconomics and
Its Application
Seventh Edition

NICHOLSON
Microeconomic Theory:
Basic Principles and Extensions
Seventh Edition

PUTH
American Economic History
Third Edition

RAGAN AND THOMAS
Principles of Economics
*Second Edition (also available in
Micro and Macro paperbacks)*

RAMANATHAN
Introductory Econometrics with
Applications
Fourth Edition

RUKSTAD
Corporate Decision Making in the
World Economy: Company Case
Studies

RUKSTAD
Macroeconomic Decision Making
in the World Economy: Text and
Cases
Third Edition

SAMUELSON AND MARKS
Managerial Economics
Second Edition

SCARTH
Macroeconomics: An Introduction
to Advanced Methods
Third Edition

STOCKMAN
Introduction to Economics
*(also available in Micro and Macro
paperbacks)*

WALTON AND ROCKOFF
History of the American Economy
Eighth Edition

WELCH AND WELCH
Economics: Theory and Practice
Sixth Edition

YARBROUGH AND YARBROUGH
The World Economy:
Trade and Finance
Fourth Edition

PREFACE

The seventh edition of *Microeconomic Theory: Basic Principles and Extensions* is intended to provide students with a comprehensive and accessible summary of modern microeconomics. As in previous editions, this is accomplished by including intuitive explanations of the principal results and by stressing the mathematical structure that is common to many problems in microeconomics. The primary goal of the present edition has been to do some pruning to a text that had become a bit long while adding new material, especially on game theory, that has been incorporated into the economists' standard tool kit in recent years.

Major changes that have been incorporated into this edition include:

NEW TO THE SEVENTH EDITION

- A new introductory chapter on game theory that presents most of the basic concepts earlier in the book (Chapter 10) so that they may be used selectively elsewhere;

- An extended chapter on game theoretic models of pricing in markets with few sellers (Chapter 20). The presentation of this material has been expanded to include simple discussions of both dynamic and Bayesian games;

- Many new, worked-out examples that provide detailed guidance on how students might proceed in solving problems;

- Significantly expanded and reworked "Extensions" that provide a link between microeconomic theory and applied empirical work. Each extension now includes discussions of a variety of empirical studies so that students can better appreciate how the theory is used in practice;

- Revised student aids, including: (1) brief answers to the queries that accompany each example; (2) answers to the odd-numbered problems in the text; and (3) a complete glossary.

All of the ancillaries for the text have also been thoroughly updated for this new edition. These include:

- The comprehensive *Workbook* by David Stapleton;
- The graphing and spreadsheet computer-oriented ancillary by Tod Porter and Teresa Riley;
- The *Solutions Manual and Test Bank* that is available to instructors at no charge.

The Dryden Press will provide complimentary supplements or supplement packages to those adopters qualified under our adoption policy. Please contact your sales representative to learn how you may qualify. If as an adopter or potential user you receive supplements you do not need, please return them to your sales representative or send them to:

Attn: Returns Department
Troy Warehouse
465 South Lincoln Drive
Troy, MO 63379

Because some of the most useful improvements to the text and its ancillaries have come from suggestions by users, I would appreciate receiving any feedback about whether this new edition is achieving its goals. E-mail has become my primary mode of communication (wenicholson@amherst.edu), though I still read old-fashioned correspondence. My home page for this book, http://www.amherst.edu/~econ/wen/microtheo.html, is still under construction, but will eventually provide worthwhile browsing—as does the Amherst College Economics Home Page.

ACKNOWLEDGMENT

I am indebted to all of the economists who have taken the opportunity to make suggestions about how this book might be improved over its many editions. Especially helpful were a series of detailed reviews of the Sixth Edition that I relied on in developing the Seventh. These were prepared by:

- David Black, University of Delaware
- Ronald E. Deiter, Iowa State University
- Gabriel Fuentes, Loyola University
- Barnali Gupta, Miami University
- Jon D. Harford, Cleveland State University
- Jack Osman, San Francisco State University
- Kislaya Prasad, Florida State University
- Richard Saba, Auburn University
- Joel L. Schrag, Emory University

- Joaquim Silvestre, University of California-Davis
- Pankaj Tandon, Boston University

Although I have not always followed the advice I was given, I did learn a lot from these reviews and will probably come to regret those ideas I have not adopted.

The list of Amherst students who have helped me with this book gets even longer. This year Jordan Milev '98 helped me assemble the empirical illustrations in the new extensions for the book. He joins Mark Bruni, Adrian Dillon, David Macoy, Tatyana Mamut, Katie Merrell, and Jeff Rodman in sharing responsibility for various pieces of the book as it stands today. I am also grateful to the many Amherst students who, in using the book, have pointed out where I have been especially wrong-headed.

Happi Kramer of Word-for-Word typed most of the manuscript for this edition and its *Solutions Manual*. She did a great job of keeping things organized when chaos threatened. The staff at The Dryden Press did its usual professional job in bringing this book to publication in seemingly effortless fashion. Sandy Walton deserves special praise for her handling of all phases of the book's production. Anita Fallon was a great help in spurring me onward in this edition and keeping me on schedule. The copyediting by Leon Unruh caught many of my errors and I thank Jeanette Barber for developing a very nice, compact design. Thanks go to Lois West for her efforts in the production process. Emily Barrosse, acquisition editor at Dryden, was very supportive of this edition, and I appreciate all of her assistance.

The thanks due my family remain as important for this edition as for the many previous ones. Special thanks go to Susan as we enter our thirtieth year together for giving up most of her favorite reading places to the clutter of unreadable manuscript. Neither Kate, David, Tory, nor Paul have yet seen fit to use this book for their edification. Nor has the latest member of our family, my son-in-law Brad. He is welcome to the family, nevertheless. Perhaps all these potential customers are saving this book for retirement reading.

Walter Nicholson
Amherst, Massachusetts
July 1997

ABOUT THE AUTHOR

Walter Nicholson is the Ward H. Patton Professor of Economics at Amherst College. He received his B.A. in mathematics from Williams College and his Ph.D. in economics from the Massachusetts Institute of Technology. Professor Nicholson's primary research interests focus on the econometric analysis of labor market policies. He is also the author of *Intermediate Microeconomics and Its Application,* Seventh Edition (The Dryden Press, 1997). He and his wife, Susan, live in Amherst, Massachusetts.

CONTENTS

PART II CHOICE AND DEMAND 67

PART IV   PRODUCTION AND SUPPLY   287

CHAPTER 11   PRODUCTION FUNCTIONS   289

CHAPTER 12   COSTS   322

CHAPTER 13   PROFIT MAXIMIZATION AND SUPPLY   363

PART V PERFECT COMPETITION 397

PART VII   PRICING IN INPUT MARKETS   633

CHAPTER 21   FIRMS' DEMANDS FOR INPUTS   635

CHAPTER 22   LABOR SUPPLY   666

CHAPTER 23   CAPITAL   690

PART VIII LIMITS OF THE MARKET 727

INTRODUCTION

This part consists of two chapters that provide some background for the study of microeconomic theory. Chapter 1 describes the general approach used in microeconomics, with particular attention to showing how economists devise and verify simple models of economic activity. Some of the philosophical issues involved in the construction of economic models, together with an analysis of how "good" models might be differentiated from "bad" ones, are also discussed.

Chapter 2 has a mathematical orientation. It describes several methods that can be used to solve maximization (and minimization) problems. Because many economic models start with the assumption that economic agents (individuals, firms, government agencies, and so forth) are seeking the maximum value of something, given their limited resources, such problems provide a major focus for this book. The mathematical techniques introduced in Chapter 2 will be used repeatedly in later chapters to derive implications about economic behavior.

CHAPTER 1

ECONOMIC MODELS

This book illustrates how models of markets are developed and used by economists to explain the pricing of goods and services. Its goal is to provide students with a strong foundation for their later work in both theoretical and applied fields in economics. This first chapter is largely philosophical in nature. It looks at the role of modeling in science and reviews a bit of the history of economics. The chapter also provides a first opportunity to illustrate how some familiar economic models are constructed using simple mathematics. A brief overview of the book's major themes provides a concluding section to the chapter.

THEORETICAL MODELS

A modern economy is a very complicated place. Thousands of firms engage in producing millions of different goods. Millions of individuals work in all sorts of occupations and make decisions about which of these goods to buy. Somehow all of these actions must be coordinated. Take peanuts, for example. They must be harvested at the right time; they must be shipped to processors who turn them into peanut butter, peanut oil, peanut brittle, and numerous other peanut delicacies. These processors, in turn, must make certain that their products arrive at thousands of retail outlets in the proper quantities to meet individual demands.

Since it would be impossible to describe such features of an economy in complete detail, economists have chosen to abstract from the vast complexities of the real world and to develop rather simple models that capture the "essentials." Just as a road map proves to be helpful, even though it does not record every house or every blade of grass, economic models of, say, the market for peanuts are also very useful even though they do not record every minute feature of the peanut economy. In this book we shall be studying the most widely used economic models. We shall see that, even though they make heroic abstractions from the true complexities of the real world, they nonetheless capture certain features that are common to all economic activities.

The use of models is widespread in both the physical and social sciences. In physics, the notion of a "perfect" vacuum or an "ideal" gas is an abstraction that permits scientists to study real-world phenomena in simplified settings. In chemistry, the idea of an atom or a molecule is in actuality a very simplified model of the structure of matter. Architects use mock-up models to plan buildings. Television repairers refer to wiring diagrams to locate problems. So too, economists have developed their models as aids to understanding economic issues. These portray the way individuals make decisions, the way firms behave, and the way in which these two groups interact to establish markets.

VERIFICATION OF ECONOMIC MODELS

Of course, not all models prove to be "good." For example, the earth-centered model of planetary motion devised by Ptolemy was eventually disregarded because it proved incapable of explaining accurately how the planets move around the sun. An important purpose of scientific investigation is to sort out the "bad" models from the "good." Two general methods have been used for verifying economic models in this way: (1) a direct approach, which seeks to establish the validity of the basic assumptions on which a model is based; and (2) an indirect approach, which attempts to confirm validity by showing that a simplified model correctly predicts real-world events. To illustrate the basic differences in the two approaches, let's briefly examine a model that we will use extensively in later chapters of this book—the model of a firm that seeks to maximize profits.

The Profit-Maximization Model

The model of a firm seeking to maximize profits is obviously a simplification of reality. It ignores the personal motivations of a firm's managers and does not treat personal conflicts among them. It assumes that profits are the only relevant goal of a firm; other possible goals, such as obtaining power or prestige, are treated as unimportant. The simple model also assumes that a firm has sufficient information about its costs and the nature of the market to which it sells to be able to discover what its profit-maximizing decisions actually are. Most real-world firms, of course, do not have this information readily available. Yet, such shortcomings in the model are not necessarily serious. No model can describe reality exactly. The real question is whether this simple model has any claim to being a good one.

Testing Assumptions

One test of the model of a profit-maximizing firm investigates its basic assumption: Do firms really seek maximum profits? Economists have examined this question by sending questionnaires to executives asking them to specify what goals they pursue. The results of such studies have been varied. Businesspeople often mention goals other than profits or claim they only do "the best they can" given their limited information. On the other hand, most respondents also mention a strong "interest" in profits and express the view that profit maximization is an appropriate goal. Testing the profit-maximizing model by testing its assumptions therefore has provided inconclusive results.

Testing Predictions

Some economists, most notably Milton Friedman, deny that a model can be tested by inquiring into the "reality" of its assumptions.[1] They argue that all theoretical models are based on "unrealistic" assumptions; the very nature of theorizing demands that we make certain abstractions. These economists conclude that the only way to determine the validity of a model is to see whether it is capable of explaining and predicting real-world events. The ultimate test of an economic model comes when it is confronted with data from the economy itself.

Friedman provides an important illustration of that principle. He asks what kind of a theory one should use to explain the shots expert pool players will make. He argues that the laws of velocity, momentum, and angles from theoretical classical physics would be a suitable model. Pool players shoot shots *as if* they followed these laws. But if we ask players whether they understand the physical principles behind the game of pool, most will undoubtedly answer that they do not. Nonetheless, Friedman argues, the physical laws provide very accurate predictions and therefore should be accepted as appropriate theoretical models of how pool is played by experts.

A test of the profit-maximization model, then, would be provided by trying to predict the behavior of real-world firms by assuming that these firms behave *as if* they were maximizing profits. If these predictions are reasonably in accord with reality, we may accept the profit-maximization hypothesis. The fact that firms respond to questionnaires by disclaiming any precise attempt at profit maximization is no more damaging to the validity of the basic hypothesis than are pool players' disclaimers of knowledge of the laws of physics. Rather, the ultimate test of either theory is its ability to predict *real-world events*.

Importance of Empirical Analysis

The primary concern of this book is the construction of theoretical models. But the ultimate goal of such models is to learn something about the real world. Although the inclusion of a lengthy set of applied examples would

---

[1] See M. Friedman, *Essays in Positive Economics* (Chicago: University of Chicago Press, 1953), chap. 1. For an alternative view stressing the importance of using "realistic" assumptions, see H. A. Simon, "Rational Decision Making in Business Organizations," *American Economic Review* 69, no. 4 (September 1979): 493–513.

needlessly expand an already bulky book,[2] the Extensions included at the end of many chapters are intended to provide a transition between the theory presented here and the ways in which that theory is actually applied. Each Extension is accompanied by a brief discussion of a real-world application that shows how the theory works in practice. It is hoped these Extensions provide both some life to what might otherwise be relatively dry theory and some encourgement to students to pursue applied economics on their own.

GENERAL FEATURES OF ECONOMIC MODELS

The number of economic models in current use is, of course, very large. Specific assumptions used and the degree of detail provided vary greatly depending on the problem being addressed. The types of models employed to explain the overall level of economic activity in the United States, for example, must be considerably more aggregated and complex than those that seek to interpret the pricing of Arizona strawberries. Despite this variety, however, practically all economic models incorporate three common elements: (1) the *ceteris paribus* (other things the same) assumption; (2) the supposition that economic decision-makers seek to optimize something; and (3) a careful distinction between "positive" and "normative" questions. Because we will use these elements throughout this book, it may be helpful at the outset to describe briefly the philosophy behind each of them.

The *Ceteris Paribus* Assumption

As is the case in most sciences, models used in economics attempt to portray relatively simple relationships. A model of the market for wheat, for example, might seek to explain wheat prices with a small number of quantifiable variables, such as wages of farmworkers, rainfall, and consumer incomes. This parsimony in model specification permits the study of wheat pricing in a simplified setting in which it is possible to understand how the specific forces operate. Although any researcher will recognize that many "outside" forces (presence of wheat diseases, changes in the prices of fertilizers or of tractors, or shifts in consumer attitudes about eating bread) affect the price of wheat, these other forces are held constant in the construction of the model. It is important to recognize that economists are *not* assuming that other factors do not affect wheat prices, but rather, such other variables are assumed to be unchanged during the period of study. In this way the effect of only a few forces can be studied in a simplified setting. Such *ceteris paribus* (other things equal) assumptions are used in all economic modeling.

Use of the *ceteris paribus* assumption does pose some difficulties for the empirical verification of economic models from real-world data. In other

---

[2] For an intermediate level text containing an extensive set of real-world applications see W. Nicholson, *Microeconomics Theory and Its Application,* 7th ed. (Fort Worth: The Dryden Press, 1997).

sciences such problems may not be so severe because of the ability to conduct controlled experiments. For example, a physicist who wishes to test a model of the force of gravity would probably not do so by dropping objects from the Empire State Building. Experiments conducted in that way would be subject to too many extraneous forces (wind currents, particles in the air, variations in temperature, and so forth) to permit a precise test of the theory. Rather, the physicist would conduct experiments in a laboratory, using a partial vacuum in which most other forces could be controlled or eliminated. In this way the theory could be verified in a simple setting, without needing to consider all the other forces that affect falling bodies in the real world.

With a few notable exceptions, economists have not been able to conduct controlled experiments to test their models. Instead, economists have been forced to rely on various statistical methods to control for other forces when testing their theories. Although these statistical methods are in principle as valid as the controlled experiment methods used by other scientists, in practice they raise a number of thorny issues. For that reason, the limitations and precise meaning of the *ceteris paribus* assumption in economics are subject to somewhat greater controversy than in the laboratory sciences.

Optimization Assumptions

Many economic models start from the assumption that the economic actors being studied are rationally pursuing some goal. We briefly discussed such an assumption previously when investigating the notion of firms maximizing profits. Other examples that we will encounter in this book include consumers maximizing their own well-being (utility), firms minimizing costs, and government regulators attempting to maximize public welfare. Although, as we will show, all of these assumptions are somewhat controversial, all have won widespread acceptance as good starting places for developing economic models. There seem to be two reasons for this acceptance. First, the optimization assumptions are very useful for generating precise, solvable models. That primarily results from the ability of such models to draw on a variety of mathematical techniques suitable for optimization problems that would not otherwise be available. Many of these techniques, together with the logic behind them, are reviewed in Chapter 2. A second reason for the popularity of optimization models concerns their apparent empirical validity. As some of our Extensions show, such models seem to be fairly good at explaining reality. In all, then, optimization models have come to occupy a prominent position in modern economic theory.

Positive-Normative Distinction

A final feature of most economic models is the attempt to differentiate carefully between "positive" and "normative" questions. So far we have been concerned primarily with *positive* economic theories. Such "scientific" theories take the real world as an object to be studied, attempting to explain those economic phenomena that are observed. Positive economics seeks to determine how resources are *in fact* allocated in an economy. A somewhat different use of economic theory is *normative,* taking a definite stance about what *should be* done. Under the heading of normative analysis, economists have a great deal to say about how resources *should be* allocated. For example, an economist engaged in positive analysis might investigate why and how the American health care industry uses the quantities of capital, labor, and land that are currently devoted to providing medical services. The economist might also choose to measure the costs and benefits of devoting even more resources to health care. But when economists advocate that more resources *should* be allocated to health, they have implicitly moved into normative analysis.

Some economists believe that the only proper economic analysis is positive analysis. Drawing an analogy with the physical sciences, they argue that "scientific" economics should concern itself only with the description (and possibly prediction) of real-world events. To take moral positions and to plead for special interests are considered to be outside the competence of an economist acting as an economist. Other economists, however, believe strict application of the positive-normative distinction to economic matters is inappropriate. They believe that the study of economics necessarily involves the researchers' own views about ethics, morality, and fairness. According to these economists, searching for scientific "objectivity" in such circumstances is hopeless. Despite this ambiguity, this book adopts a mainly positivist tone, leaving normative concerns to the student.

DEVELOPMENT OF THE ECONOMIC THEORY OF VALUE

Although economic activity has been a central feature of all societies, it is surprising that these activities were not studied in any detail until fairly recently. For the most part, economic phenomena were treated as a basic aspect of human behavior that was not sufficiently interesting to deserve specific attention. It is, of course, true that individuals have always studied economic activities with a view toward making some kind of personal gain. Roman traders were certainly not above making profits on their transactions. But investigations into the basic nature of these activities did not begin in any depth until the eighteenth century.[3] Since this book is about economic theory as it stands today, not about the history of economic thought, our discussion of the evolution of economic theory will be brief. Only one area of economic study will be examined in its historical setting: the *theory of value.*

---

[3] For a detailed treatment of early economic thought, see the classic work by J. A. Schumpeter, *History of Economic Analysis* (New York: Oxford University Press, 1954), pt. II, chaps. 1, 2, and 3.

The theory of value, not surprisingly, concerns the determinants of the "value" of a commodity. The study of this subject is at the center of modern microeconomic theory and is closely intertwined with the subject of the allocation of scarce resources for alternative ends. The logical place to start is with a definition of the word *value*. Unfortunately, the meaning of this term has not been consistent throughout the development of the subject. Today we regard "value" as being synonymous with the "price" of a commodity.[4] Earlier philosopher-economists, however, made a distinction between the market price of a commodity and its value. The term "value" was then thought of as being in some sense synonymous with "importance," "essentiality," or (at times) "godliness." Since "price" and "value" were separate concepts, they could differ, and most early economic discussions centered on these divergences. For example, St. Thomas Aquinas believed value to be divinely determined. Since prices were set by humans, it was possible for the price of a commodity to differ from its value. A person accused of charging a price in excess of a good's value was guilty of charging an "unjust" price. For example, St. Thomas believed the "just" rate of interest to be zero. Any lender who demanded a payment for the use of money was charging an unjust price and could be—and often was—prosecuted by church officials.

Early Economic Thought

During the latter part of the eighteenth century, philosophers began to take a more "scientific" approach to economic questions. The publication of *The Wealth of Nations* by Adam Smith (1723–1790) in the eventful year 1776 is generally considered the beginning of modern economics. In his vast, all-encompassing work, Smith laid the foundation for thinking about market forces in an ordered and systematic way. Still, Smith and his immediate successors, such as David Ricardo (1772–1823), continued to distinguish between value and price. To Smith, for example, the value of a commodity meant its "value in use," whereas the price represented its "value in exchange." The distinction between these two concepts was illustrated by the famous water-diamond paradox. Water, which obviously has great value in use, has little value in exchange (it has a low price); diamonds are of little practical use but have a great value in exchange. The paradox with which early economists struggled derives from the observation that some very "useful" items have low prices whereas certain "nonessential" items have high prices.

The Founding of Modern Economics

---

[4] This is not completely true when "externalities" are involved and a distinction must be made between private and social value (see Chapter 24).

Labor Theory of Exchange Value

Neither Smith nor Ricardo ever satisfactorily resolved the water-diamond paradox. The concept of value in use was left for philosophers to debate, while economists turned their attention to explaining the determinants of value in exchange (that is, to explaining relative prices). One obvious possible explanation is that exchange values of goods are determined by what it costs to produce them. Costs of production are primarily influenced by labor costs—at least this was so in the time of Smith and Ricardo—and therefore it was a short step to embrace a labor theory of value. For example, to paraphrase an example from Smith, if catching a deer takes twice the number of labor-hours as catching a beaver, then one deer should exchange for two beavers. In other words, the price of a deer should be twice that of a beaver. Similarly, diamonds are relatively costly because their production requires substantial labor input.

But how does that explanation of exchange value apply to other productive resources? How do payments for rent and for capital equipment enter into the determination of price? Ricardo answered this problem with an ingenious analysis. He argued that the cost of using capital could also be regarded as labor costs, with the labor being invested some years ago at the time the machines were produced. In this way, any capital cost could ultimately be traced back to some primary labor input. Ricardo disposed of rent by theorizing that rent is not a determinant of price (see Ricardo's analysis of rent in Chapter 15). Therefore, we are left with a pure labor theory of value: The relative price of two commodities is determined by the direct and indirect labor inputs used in each good.

To students with even a passing knowledge of what we now call the *law of supply and demand,* Ricardo's explanation must seem strange. Didn't he recognize the effects of demand on price? The answer to this question is both "yes" and "no." He did observe periods of both rapidly rising and rapidly falling prices and attributed such changes to demand shifts. However, he regarded such changes as abnormalities that produced only a temporary divergence of market price from labor value. Because he had not really solved the paradox of value in use, he was unwilling to assign demand any more than a transient role in determining exchange value. Rather, Ricardo believed long-run exchange values were determined solely by labor costs of production.

The Marginalist Revolution

Between 1850 and 1880, economists became increasingly aware that to construct an adequate alternative to Ricardo's theory of value, they had to come to grips with the paradox of value in use. During the 1870s several economists proposed that it is not the total usefulness of a commodity that helps to determine its exchange value, but rather the usefulness of the *last unit consumed.* For example, water is certainly very useful—it is necessary for all life. But, because water is relatively plentiful, consuming one more pint (*ceteris paribus*) has a relatively low value to people. These "marginalists" redefined the concept of value in use from an idea of overall usefulness to one of marginal, or incremental, usefulness—the usefulness of an *additional unit of a commodity*. The concept of the demand for an incremental unit of output was now contrasted to Ricardo's analysis of production costs in order to derive a comprehensive picture of price determination.[5]

The clearest statement of these marginal principles was presented by the English economist Alfred Marshall (1842–1924) in his *Principles of Economics*, published in 1890. Marshall showed that demand and supply *simultaneously* operate to determine price. As Marshall noted, just as you cannot tell which blade of a scissors does the cutting, so too you cannot say that either demand or supply alone determines price. That analysis is illustrated by the famous Marshallian cross shown in Figure 1.1. In the diagram the quantity of a good purchased per period is shown on the horizontal axis, and its price appears on the vertical axis. The curve *DD* represents the quantity of the good demanded per period at each possible price. The curve is negatively sloped to reflect the marginalist principle that as quantity increases, people are willing to pay less and less for the last unit purchased. It is the value of this last unit that sets the price for all units purchased. The curve *SS* shows how (marginal) production costs rise as more output is produced. This reflects the increasing cost of producing one more unit as total output expands. In other words, the upward slope of the *SS* curve reflects increasing marginal costs, just as the downward slope of the *DD* curve reflects decreasing marginal value. The two curves intersect at P^*, Q^*. This is an *equilibrium* point—both buyers and sellers are content with the quantity being traded and the price at which it is traded. If one of the curves should shift, the equilibrium point would shift to a new location. Thus price and quantity are simultaneously determined by the joint operation of supply and demand.

Marshallian Supply-Demand Synthesis

Marshall's model resolves the water-diamond paradox. Prices reflect both the marginal evaluation that demanders place on goods and the marginal costs

Paradox Resolved

---

[5] Ricardo had earlier provided an important first step in marginal analysis in his discussion of rent. Ricardo theorized that as the production of corn increased, land of inferior quality would be used and this would cause the price of corn to rise. In his argument Ricardo implicitly recognized that it is the marginal cost—the cost of producing an additional unit—that is relevant to pricing. Notice that Ricardo implicitly held other inputs constant when discussing diminishing land productivity; that is, he employed one version of the *ceteris paribus* assumption.

FIGURE 1.1

THE MARSHALLIAN SUPPLY-DEMAND CROSS

Marshall theorized that demand and supply interact to determine the equilibrium price (P^*) and the quantity (Q^*) that will be traded in the market. He concluded that it is not possible to say that either demand or supply alone determines price or therefore that either costs or usefulness to buyers alone determines exchange value.

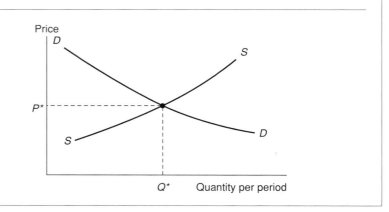

of producing the goods. Viewed in this way, there is no paradox. Water is low in price because it has both a low marginal value and a low marginal cost of production. On the other hand, diamonds are high in price because they have both a high marginal value (because people are willing to pay quite a bit for one more) and a high marginal cost of production. This basic model of supply and demand lies behind much of the analysis presented in this book. As a starting point, let's look at a very simple mathematical representation of Marshall's ideas. Later, we will be delving more deeply into the fundamental aspects of economic behavior that lie behind Marshall's curves.

EXAMPLE 1.1

SUPPLY-DEMAND EQUILIBRIUM

Although graphical presentations are adequate for some purposes, economists often use algebraic representations of their models both to clarify their arguments and to make them more precise. As a very elementary first example, suppose we wished to study the market for peanuts and, on the basis of statistical analysis of historical data, concluded that the quantity of peanuts demanded each week (Q—measured in bushels) depended on the price of peanuts (P—measured in dollars per bushel) according to the equation

$$\text{quantity demanded} = Q_D = 1000 - 100P. \qquad (1.1)$$

Since this equation for Q_D contains only the single independent variable P, we are implicitly holding constant all other factors that might affect the demand for peanuts. Equation 1.1 indicates that, if other things do not change, at a price of $5 per bushel people will demand 500 bushels of peanuts, whereas at a price of $4 per bushel they will demand 600 bushels. The negative coefficient for P in Equation 1.1 reflects the marginalist principle that a lower price will cause people to buy more peanuts.

To complete this simple model of pricing, suppose that the quantity supplied of peanuts also depends on price:

$$\text{quantity supplied} = Q_S = -125 + 125P. \qquad (1.2)$$

Here the positive coefficient of price also reflects the marginal principle that a higher price will call forth increased supply—primarily because it permits firms to incur higher marginal costs of production without incurring losses on the additional units produced.

Equilibrium Price Determination

Equations 1.1 and 1.2 therefore reflect our model of price determination in the market for peanuts. An equilibrium price can be found by setting quantity demanded equal to quantity supplied:

$$Q_D = Q_S \qquad (1.3)$$

or

$$1000 - 100P = -125 + 125P \qquad (1.4)$$

or

$$225P = 1125 \qquad (1.5)$$

so,

$$P^* = 5. \qquad (1.6)$$

At a price of $5 per bushel, this market is in equilibrium—at this price people want to purchase 500 bushels, and that is exactly what peanut producers are willing to supply. This equilibrium is pictured graphically as the intersection of D and S in Figure 1.2.

Shifts in Demand Yield a New Equilibrium

Assuming the model portrayed by Equations 1.1 and 1.2 accurately reflects the peanut market, the only way to explain a new price-quantity equilibrium is by hypothesizing that either the supply or the demand curve has shifted. Without such a shift, the model would continue to "predict" a price of $P = \$5$ and a quantity of $Q = 500$.

FIGURE 1.2

CHANGING SUPPLY-DEMAND EQUILIBRIA

The initial supply-demand equilibrium is illustrated by the intersection of D and S ($P^* = 5$, $Q^* = 500$). When demand shifts to $Q_{D'} = 1450 - 100P$ (denoted as D'), the quilibrium shifts to $P^* = 7$, $Q^* = 750$.

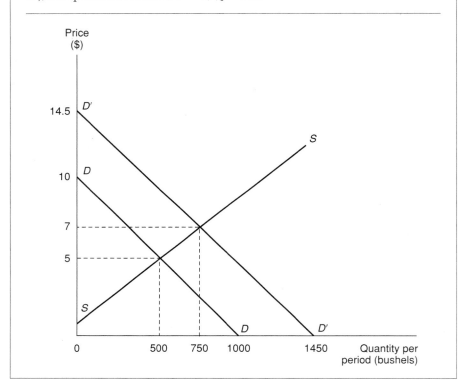

One way to incorporate a shift into our simple model is to assume that the demand for peanuts increases to

$$Q'_D = 1450 - 100P. \tag{1.7}$$

As Figure 1.2 shows, this new demand curve (labeled D'D') represents a parallel shift outward of the old demand—at every price 450 more bushels of peanuts are demanded than was the case for the old demand. In this case, Marshall's model predicts that both the equilibrium price and quantity for peanuts will rise as Figure 1.2 illustrates. We can find an explicit algebraic solution, as before, by setting quantity demanded equal to quantity supplied:

$$Q'_D = 1450 - 100P =$$
$$Q_S = -125 + 125P \tag{1.8}$$

or

$$225P = 1575 \tag{1.9}$$
$$P^* = 7 \tag{1.10}$$

and

$$Q'_D = Q_S = 750. \tag{1.11}$$

This new solution illustrates Marshall's scissors analogy—the new price-quantity equilibrium is determined by the forces of both demand and supply. Although demand has increased by 450 bushels at any given price, the rise in price brought about by this shift causes a movement upward along the new demand curve and therefore reduces quantity demanded below what would have been chosen at the old price of $5. Only by using information from the supply curve is it possible to compute the new equilibrium price and the final effect on the quantity of peanuts produced (which only increases by 250 bushels to a total of 750 bushels).

QUERY: If the price of peanuts had stayed at $5 (say, because of government regulation), how many bushels would be demanded? How many supplied? What do you think would happen in this situation?

General Equilibrium Models

Although the Marshallian model is an extremely useful and versatile tool, it is a *partial equilibrium model,* looking at only one market at a time. For some questions this narrowing of perspective gives valuable insights and analytical simplicity. For other, broader questions such a narrow viewpoint may prevent the discovery of important interrelations among markets. To answer more general questions we must have a model of the whole economy that suitably mirrors the interrelationships among various markets and various economic agents. The French economist Leon Walras (1831–1910), building on a long Continental tradition in such analysis, created the basis for modern investigations into those broad questions. His method of representing the economy by a large number of simultaneous equations forms the basis for an understanding of the interrelationships implicit in *general equilibrium* analysis. Walras recognized that one cannot talk about a single market in isolation; what is needed is a model that permits the effects of a change in one market to be followed through other markets.

For example, suppose that the price of peanuts were to increase. Marshallian analysis would seek to understand the reason for this increase by looking at conditions of supply and demand in the peanut market. General equilibrium analysis would look not only at that market but also at repercussions in other markets. A rise in the price of peanuts would cause increased costs for peanut butter makers, which would, in turn, affect the supply curve for peanut butter. Similarly, the rising price of peanuts might mean higher land prices for peanut farmers, which would affect the demand curves for all products that they buy. The demand curves for automobiles, furniture, and trips to Europe would all shift out, and that might create additional incomes for the providers of those products. Consequently, the effects of the initial increase in demand for peanuts eventually would spread throughout the economy. General equilibrium analysis attempts to develop models that permit us to examine such effects in a simplified setting. Several models of this type are described in Part V of this text.

Production Possibility Frontier

Here we briefly introduce general equilibrium models by using another graph you should remember from introductory economics—the *production possibility frontier*. This graph shows the various amounts of two goods that an economy can produce using its available resources during some period (say, one week). Because the production possibility frontier shows two goods, rather than the single good in Marshall's model, it is used as a basic building block for general equilibrium models.

Figure 1.3 shows the production possibility frontier for two goods, food and clothing. The graph illustrates the supply of these goods by showing the combinations that can be produced with this economy's resources. For example, 10 pounds of food and 3 units of clothing could be produced, or 4 pounds of food and 12 units of clothing. Many other combinations of food and clothing could also be produced. The production possibility frontier shows all of them. Combinations of food and clothing outside the frontier cannot be produced because not enough resources are available. The production possibility frontier reminds us of the basic economic fact that resources are scarce—there are not enough resources available to produce all we might want of every good.

This scarcity means that we must choose how much of each good to produce. Figure 1.3 makes clear that each choice has its costs. For example, if this economy produces 10 pounds of food and 3 units of clothing at point *A*, producing 1 more unit of clothing would "cost" 1/2 pound of food—increasing the output of clothing by 1 unit means the production of food would have to decrease by 1/2 pound. Economists would say that the *opportunity cost* of 1 unit of clothing at point *A* is 1/2 pound of food. On the other hand, if the economy initially produces 4 pounds of food and 12 units of clothing at point *B*, it would cost 2 pounds of food to produce 1 more unit of clothing. The opportunity cost of 1 more unit of clothing at point *B* has

FIGURE 1.3

PRODUCTION POSSIBILITY FRONTIER

The production possibility frontier shows the different combinations of two goods that can be produced from a certain amount of scarce resources. It also shows the opportunity cost of producing more of one good as the amount of the other good that cannot then be produced. The opportunity cost at two different levels of clothing production can be seen by comparing points A and B.

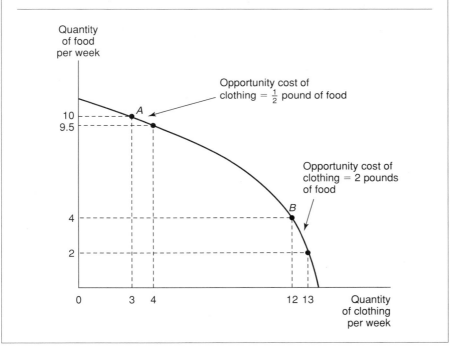

increased to 2 pounds of food. Because more units of clothing are produced at point B than at point A, both Ricardo's and Marshall's ideas of increasing incremental costs suggest that the opportunity cost of an additional unit of clothing will be higher at point B than at point A. This effect is just what Figure 1.3 shows.

The production possibility frontier provides two general equilibrium results that are not clear in Marshall's supply and demand model of a single market. The first result is that producing more of one good means producing less of another good because resources are scarce. Economists often (perhaps too often!) use the expression "there is no such thing as a free lunch" to explain that every economic action has opportunity costs. The second result shown by the production possibility frontier is that these opportunity costs depend on how much of each good is produced. The frontier is like a supply curve for two goods—it shows the opportunity cost of producing more of one good as the decrease in the amount of the second good. The production possibility frontier is therefore a particularly useful tool for studying several markets at the same time. Before leaving this concept for now, let's examine a simple algebraic example which offers our first opportunity to use calculus.

EXAMPLE 1.2

A PRODUCTION POSSIBILITY FRONTIER

Suppose the production possibility frontier for two goods (X and Y) is given by

$$2X^2 + Y^2 = 225. \tag{1.12}$$

A graph of this production possibility frontier would have the shape of a quarter ellipse and would resemble the frontier shown in Figure 1.3. Some points on the frontier include ($X = \sqrt{112.5} = 10.6$, $Y = 0$), ($X = 10$, $Y = 5$), ($X = 5$, $Y = \sqrt{175} = 13.2$), and ($X = 0$, $Y = 15$). There are infinitely many such points that satisfy Equation 1.12. To find the slope of the frontier at any point, we can solve for Y,

$$Y = \sqrt{225 - 2X^2} \tag{1.13}$$

and then differentiate (see Chapter 2) to obtain

$$\frac{dY}{dX} = \frac{1}{2}(225 - 2X^2)^{-1/2} \cdot (-4X)$$

$$= \frac{-4X}{2Y} = \frac{-2X}{Y}. \tag{1.14}$$

Hence, at $X = 10$, $Y = 5$, the slope is $-2(10)/5 = -4$, and the opportunity cost of producing 1 more unit of X is a decrease in Y production of 4 units. At $X = 5$, $Y = \sqrt{175}$, the opportunity cost of X is $-2(5)/\sqrt{175} = -0.76$—when less X is produced, it has a lower opportunity cost in terms of the number of units of Y that must be foregone in order to produce 1 more unit of X. At many places in this text, we will calculate slopes in this way using the technique of differentiation to illustrate the trade-offs inherent in most economic problems.

QUERY: Use your calculator together with Equation 1.13 to show that the slope of this function is indeed approximately -4 at the point ($X = 10$, $Y = 5$). That is, calculate how much Y can be produced if $X = 9.99$ or if $X = 10.01$. Why does your calculator permit you to calculate only an approximate value for the slope at the point ($X = 10$, $Y = 5$)?

Welfare Economics

In addition to their use in examining positive questions about how the economy operates, the tools used in general equilibrium analysis have also been applied to the study of normative questions about the social desirability of various economic arrangements. Although such questions were a major focus of the great eighteenth- and nineteenth-century economists (Smith, Ricardo, Marx, Marshall, and so forth), perhaps the most significant advances in their study were made by the British economist Francis Y. Edgeworth (1848–1926) and the Italian economist Vilfredo Pareto (1848–1923) in the early years of the twentieth century. These economists helped to provide a precise definition for the concept of "economic efficiency" and to demonstrate the conditions under which markets will be able to achieve that goal. By clarifying the relationship between the allocation of resources and the pricing of resources, they provided some support for the idea, first enunciated by Adam Smith, that properly functioning markets provide an "invisible hand" that helps allocate resources efficiently. Parts V and VIII of this book focus on some of these welfare issues.

MODERN DEVELOPMENTS INCLUDED IN THIS BOOK

Research activity in economics expanded rapidly in the years following World War II. A major purpose of this book is to summarize much of this research. By illustrating how economists have tried to develop models to explain increasingly complex aspects of economic behavior, I hope the reader will be in a better position to recognize both the power of the tools that have been devised and some of the unanswered questions that remain. Three specific theoretical developments that provide the foundation for much of this book are highlighted: (1) clarifying the basic behavioral assumptions about individual and firm behavior; (2) devising new tools to study markets; and (3) incorporating uncertainty and imperfect information into economics.

The Foundations of Economic Models

A major postwar development in microeconomic theory has been the clarification and formalization of the basic assumptions that are made about individuals and firms. A major landmark in this development was the 1947 publication of Paul Samuelson's *Foundations of Economic Analysis*, in which the author (the first American Nobel Prize winner in economics) laid out a number of models of optimizing behavior.[6] Samuelson demonstrated the importance of basing behavioral models on well-specified mathematical postulates so that various optimization techniques from mathematics could be applied. The power of his approach made it inescapably clear that mathematics had become an integral part of modern economics. In Chapter 2 of this book we review some of the most widely used mathematical techniques.

New Tools for Studying Markets

A second feature that has been incorporated into this book is the presentation of a number of new tools for explaining market equilibria. These include techniques for describing pricing in single markets such as increasingly sophisticated models of monopolistic pricing or models of the strategic relationships among firms that use game theory. They also include general equilibrium tools for exploring relationships among many markets simultaneously. As we shall see, all of these new techniques help to provide a more complete and realistic picture of how markets operate.

The Economics of Uncertainty and Information

A final major theoretical advance during the postwar period was the incorporation of uncertainty and imperfect information into economic models. Some of the basic assumptions used to study behavior in uncertain situations were originally developed in the 1940s in connection with the theory of games. Later developments showed how these ideas could be used to explain why individuals tend to be adverse to risk and how they might gather information in order to reduce the uncertainties they face. In this book, problems of uncertainty and information enter the analysis on many occasions.

Computers and Empirical Analysis

One final aspect of the postwar development of microeconomics should be mentioned—the increasing use of computers to analyze economic data. As computers have become more able to handle large amounts of information and carry out complex mathematical manipulations, economists' ability to test their theories has dramatically improved. Whereas previous generations had to be content with rudimentary tabular or graphical analyses of real-world data, today's economists have available a wide variety of sophisticated techniques and machine-readable data with which to develop appropriate tests of their models. To examine these techniques and some of

---

[6] Paul A. Samuelson, *Foundations of Economic Analysis* (Cambridge, Mass.: Harvard University Press, 1947).

their limitations would be beyond the scope and purpose of this book. However, Extensions at the end of most chapters are intended to help you get started on reading some of these applications.

SUMMARY

This chapter has provided some background on how economists approach the study of the allocation of resources. Much of the material discussed here should be familiar to you—and that's the way it should be. In many respects, the study of economics represents acquiring increasingly sophisticated tools for addressing the same basic problems. The purpose of this book (and, indeed, of most upper-level books on economics) is to provide you with more of these tools. As a starting place, this chapter reminded you of the following points:

- Economics is the study of how scarce resources are allocated among alternative uses. Economists seek to develop simple models to help understand that process. Many of these models have a mathematical basis because the use of mathematics offers a precise shorthand for stating the models and exploring their consequences.

- The most commonly used economic model is the supply-demand model first thoroughly developed by Alfred Marshall in the latter part of the nineteenth century. This model shows how observed prices can be taken to represent an equilibrium balancing of the production costs incurred by firms and the willingness of demanders to pay for those costs.

- Marshall's model of equilibrium is only "partial"—that is, it looks only at one market at a time. To look at many markets together requires that we develop an expanded set of general equilibrium tools.

- Testing the validity of an economic model is perhaps the most difficult task economists face. Occasionally, a model's validity can be appraised by asking whether it is based on "reasonable" assumptions. More often, however, models are judged by how well they can explain economic events in the real world.

SUGGESTED READINGS

On Methodology

Boland, Lawrence E. "A Critique of Friedman's Critics." *Journal of Economic Literature* (June 1979): 503–522.
Good summary of criticisms of positive approaches to economics and of the role of empirical verification of assumptions.

Caldwell, Bruce J. "Clarifying Popper." *Journal of Economic Literature* (March 1991): 1–33.
Examines philosophical notions of the "falsifyability" of scientific theories (as presented by Karl Popper) and

whether such an approach is appropriate to economics. Concludes that the approach is useful especially in combination with Friedman's focus on predictability.

Friedman, Milton. "The Methodology of Positive Economics." In *Essays in Positive Economics*, pp. 3–43. Chicago: University of Chicago Press, 1953.
Basic statement of Friedman's positivist views.

Harrod, Roy F. "Scope and Method in Economics." *Economic Journal* 48 (1938): 383–412.
Classic statement of appropriate role for economic modeling.

Hausman, David M., and Michael S. McPherson. "Taking Ethics Seriously: Economics and Contemporary Moral Philosophy." *Journal of Economic Literature* (June 1993): 671–731.
Argues strongly that economists should be concerned with ethical questions both because ethics may influence the behavior of economic actors and because moral principles may be needed to determine the relevance of findings from positive economics.

McCloskey, Donald N. *If You're So Smart: The Narrative of Economic Expertise.* Chicago: University of Chicago Press. 1990.
Discussion of McCloskey's view that economic persuasion depends on "rhetoric" as much as on "science." For an interchange on this topic see also the articles in The Journal of Economic Literature, *June 1995.*

Nagel, Ernest. "Assumptions in Economic Theory." *American Economic Review* (May 1963): 211–219.
Thoughts on economic methods by a philosopher.

Primary Sources on the History of Economics
Edgeworth, F. Y. *Mathematical Psychics.* London: Kegan Paul, 1881.
Initial investigations of welfare economics, including rudimentary notions of economic efficiency and the contract curve.

Marshall, A. *Principles of Economics.* 8th ed. London: Macmillan & Co., 1920.
Complete summary of neoclassical view. A long-running, popular text. Detailed mathematical appendix.

Marx, K. *Capital.* New York: Modern Library, 1906.
Full development of labor theory of value. Discussion of "transformation problem" provides a (perhaps faulty) start for general equilibrium analysis. Presents fundamental criticisms of institution of private property.

Ricardo, D. *Principles of Political Economy and Taxation.* London: J. M. Dent & Sons, 1911.
Very analytical, tightly written work. Pioneer in developing careful analysis of policy questions, especially trade-related issues. Discusses first basic notions of marginalism.

Smith, A. *The Wealth of Nations.* New York: Modern Library, 1937.
First great economics classic. Very long and detailed, but Smith had the first word on practically every economic matter. This edition has helpful marginal notes.

Walras, L. *Elements of Pure Economics.* Translated by W. Jaffé. Homewood, Ill.: Richard D. Irwin, 1954.
Beginnings of general equilibrium theory. Rather difficult reading.

Secondary Sources on the History of Economics
Blaug, Mark. *Economic Theory in Retrospect.* 5th ed. Cambridge: Cambridge University Press, 1996.
Very complete summary stressing analytical issues. Excellent "Readers' Guides" to the classics in each chapter.

Heilbroner, Robert L. *The Worldly Philosophers.* 6th ed. New York: Simon and Schuster, 1987.
Fascinating, easy-to-read biographies of leading economists. Chapters on Utopian Socialists and Thorstein Veblen highly recommended.

Keynes, John M. *Essays in Biography.* New York: W. W. Norton, 1963.
Essays on many famous persons (Lloyd George, Winston Churchill, Leon Trotsky) and on several economists (Malthus, Marshall, Edgeworth, F. P. Ramsey, and Jevons). Shows the true gift of Keynes as a writer.

Schumpeter, J. A. *History of Economic Analysis.* New York: Oxford University Press, 1954.
Encyclopedic treatment. Covers all the famous and many not-so-famous economists. Also briefly summarizes concurrent developments in other branches of the social sciences.

CHAPTER 2

THE MATHEMATICS
OF OPTIMIZATION

$\mathbf{M}$any economic models start with the assumption that an agent is seeking to find the optimal value of some function. For consumers that function measures the utility provided by their purchases; for firms it measures their profits. But, in both cases, the formal, mathematical aspects of the solution are identical. In this chapter we examine the mathematics common to all such problems. For those familiar with multivariable calculus, this chapter will be largely in the nature of a review. For those who are familiar only with some concepts from basic calculus, this chapter should provide enough background to get started on looking at the ways in which calculus is used to construct microeconomic models. More generally, the chapter is intended to provide a reference that may be useful as these various mathematical concepts are encountered later in the text.

Let's start with a simple example. Suppose that a manager of a firm desires to maximize[1] the profits received from selling a particular good. Suppose also that the profits (π) received depend only on the quantity (q) of the good sold. Mathematically,

MAXIMIZATION OF A FUNCTION OF ONE VARIABLE

$$\pi = f(q). \tag{2.1}$$

Figure 2.1 shows a possible relationship between π and q. Clearly, to achieve maximum profits, the manager should produce output q^*, which yields profits π^*. If a graph such as that of Figure 2.1 were available, this would seem to be a simple matter to be accomplished with a ruler.

---

[1] In this chapter we will generally explore maximization problems. A virtually identical approach would be taken to study minimization problems.

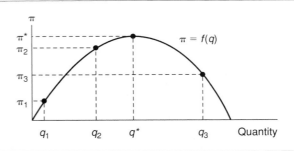

FIGURE 2.1

HYPOTHETICAL RELATIONSHIP BETWEEN QUANTITY
PRODUCED AND PROFITS

If a manager wishes to produce the level of output that maximizes profits, q^*
should be produced. Notice that at q^*, $d\pi/dq = 0$.

Suppose, however, as is more likely, the manager does not have such an
accurate picture of the market. He or she may then try varying q to see where
a maximum profit is obtained. For example, by starting at q_1, profits from
sales would be π_1. Next, the manager may try output q_2, observing that profits
have increased to π_2. The commonsense idea that profits have increased in
response to an increase in q can be stated formally as

$$\frac{\pi_2 - \pi_1}{q_2 - q_1} > 0 \quad \text{or} \quad \frac{\Delta\pi}{\Delta q} > 0, \tag{2.2}$$

where the Δ notation is used to mean "the change in" π or q. As long as $\Delta\pi/\Delta q$
is positive, profits are increasing and the manager will continue to increase
output. For increases in output to the right of q^*, however, $\Delta\pi/\Delta q$ will be
negative, and the manager will realize that a mistake has been made if he or
she continues to expand q.

Derivatives As you probably know, the limit of $\Delta\pi/\Delta q$ for very small changes in q
is called the *derivative* of the function, $\pi = f(q)$, and is denoted by $d\pi/dq$
or df/dq or $f'(q)$. More formally, the derivative of a function $\pi = f(q)$ at the
point q_1 is defined as

$$\frac{d\pi}{dq} = \frac{df}{dq} = \lim_{h \to 0} \frac{f(q_1 + h) - f(q_1)}{h}. \tag{2.3}$$

Notice that the value of this ratio obviously depends on the point q_1 that is chosen.

A notational convention should be mentioned: Sometimes one wishes to note explicitly the point at which the derivative is to be evaluated. For example, the evaluation of the derivative at the point $q = q_1$ could be denoted by

$$\left.\frac{d\pi}{dq}\right|_{q = q_1} \tag{2.4}$$

Value of the Derivative at a Point

At other times one is interested in the value of $d\pi/dq$ for all possible values of q, and no explicit mention of a particular point of evaluation is made.

In the example of Figure 2.1,

$$\left.\frac{d\pi}{dq}\right|_{q = q_1} > 0,$$

whereas

$$\left.\frac{d\pi}{dq}\right|_{q = q_3} < 0.$$

What is the value of $d\pi/dq$ at q^*? It would seem to be 0, since the value is positive for values of q less than q^* and negative for values greater than q^*. The derivative is the slope of the curve in question; this slope is positive to the left of q^* and negative to the right of q^*. At the point q^*, the slope of $f(q)$ is 0.

This result is quite general. For a function of one variable to attain its maximum value at some point, the derivative at that point (if it exists) must be 0. Hence, if a manager could estimate the function $f(q)$ from some sort of real-world data, it would be theoretically possible to find the point where $df/dq = 0$. At this optimal point (say q^*), it would be the case that

$$\left.\frac{df}{dq}\right|_{q = q^*} = 0. \tag{2.5}$$

First-Order Condition for a Maximum

An unsuspecting manager could be tricked, however, by a naïve application of this rule alone. For example, suppose that the profit function looks like that shown in either Figure 2.2a or 2.2b. If the profit function is that shown in Figure 2.2a, the manager, by producing where $d\pi/dq = 0$, will choose point q_a^*. This point in fact yields minimum, not maximum, profits for the manager. Similarly, if the profit function is that shown in Figure 2.2b, the manager will

Second-Order Conditions

FIGURE 2.2

**TWO PROFIT FUNCTIONS THAT GIVE MISLEADING RESULTS
IF THE FIRST DERIVATIVE RULE IS APPLIED UNCRITICALLY**

In (a) the application of the first derivative rule would result in point q_a^* being chosen. This point is in fact a point of minimum profits. Similarly, in (b) output level q_b^* would be recommended by the first derivative rule, but this point is inferior to all outputs greater than q_b^*. This demonstrates graphically that finding a point at which the derivative is equal to 0 is a necessary, but not a sufficient, condition for a function to attain its maximum value.

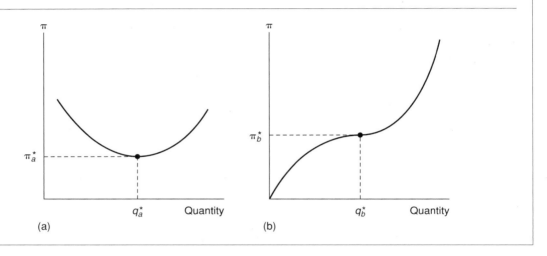

(a) (b)

choose point q_b^*, which, although it yields a profit greater than that for any output lower than q_b^*, is certainly inferior to any output greater than q_b^*. These situations point up the mathematical fact that $d\pi/dq = 0$ is a *necessary* condition for a maximum, but not a *sufficient* condition. To ensure that the chosen point is indeed a maximum point, a second condition must be imposed.

Intuitively, this additional condition is clear: The profit available by producing either a bit more or a bit less than q^* must be smaller than that available from q^*. If this is not true, the manager can do better than q^*. Mathematically, this means that $d\pi/dq$ must be greater than 0 for $q < q^*$ and must be less than 0 for $q > q^*$. Therefore, at q^*, $d\pi/dq$ must be decreasing. Another way of saying this is that the derivative of $d\pi/dq$ must be negative at q^*.

Second Derivatives   The derivative of what is already a derivative is called a *second derivative* and is denoted by

$$\frac{d^2\pi}{dq^2} \text{ or } \frac{d^2f}{dq^2} \text{ or } f''(q).$$

The additional condition for q^* to represent a (local) maximum is therefore

$$\left.\frac{d^2\pi}{dq^2}\right|_{q=q^*} = f''(q)\Big|_{q=q^*} < 0, \tag{2.6}$$

where the notation is again a reminder that this second derivative is to be evaluated at q^*.

Hence, although Equation 2.5 ($d\pi/dq = 0$) is a necessary condition for a maximum, that equation must be combined with Equation 2.6 ($d^2\pi/dq^2 < 0$) to ensure that the point is a local maximum for the function. Equations 2.5 and 2.6 together are therefore sufficient conditions for such a maximum. Of course, it is possible that by a series of trials the manager may be able to decide on q^* by relying on market information rather than on mathematical reasoning (remember Friedman's pool player analogy). In this book we shall be less interested in how the point is discovered than in its properties and how the point changes when conditions change. A mathematical development will be very helpful in answering these questions.

Here are a few familiar rules for taking derivatives. We will use these at many places in this book.

Rules for Finding Derivatives

1. If b is a constant, then

$$\frac{db}{dx} = 0.$$

2. If a and b are constants and $b \neq 0$, then

$$\frac{dax^b}{dx} = bax^{b-1}.$$

3. $\dfrac{d \ln x}{dx} = \dfrac{1}{x}$,

   where $\ln$ signifies the logarithm to the base e ($= 2.71828$).

4. $\dfrac{da^x}{dx} = a^x \ln a$ for any constant a.

   A particular case of this rule is $de^x/dx = e^x$.

Now suppose that $f(x)$ and $g(x)$ are two functions of x and that $f'(x)$ and $g'(x)$ exist. Then

5. $\dfrac{d[f(x) + g(x)]}{dx} = f'(x) + g'(x)$.

6. $\dfrac{d[f(x) \cdot g(x)]}{dx} = f(x)g'(x) + f'(x)g(x)$.

7. $\dfrac{d\left(\dfrac{f(x)}{g(x)}\right)}{dx} = \dfrac{f'(x)g(x) - f(x)g'(x)}{[g(x)]^2}$,

provided that $g(x) \neq 0$.

Finally, if $y = f(x)$ and $x = g(z)$ and if both $f'(x)$ and $g'(z)$ exist, then

8. $\dfrac{dy}{dz} = \dfrac{dy}{dx} \cdot \dfrac{dx}{dz} = \dfrac{df}{dx} \cdot \dfrac{dg}{dz}$.

This result is called the *chain rule*. It provides a convenient way for studying how one variable (z) affects another variable (y) solely through its influence on some intermediate variable (x).

EXAMPLE 2.1

PROFIT MAXIMIZATION

Suppose that the relationship between profits (π) and quantity produced (q) is given by

$$\pi = 1{,}000q - 5q^2. \tag{2.7}$$

A graph of this function would resemble the parabola shown in Figure 2.1. The value of q that maximizes profits can be found by applying Rule 2 for finding derivatives:

$$\frac{d\pi}{dq} = 1{,}000 - 10q = 0 \tag{2.8}$$

so

$$q^* = 100. \tag{2.9}$$

At $q = 100$, Equation 2.7 shows that profits are 50,000—the largest value possible. If, for example, the firm opted to produce $q = 50$, profits would be 37,500. At $q = 200$, profits are precisely zero.

That $q = 100$ is a "global" maximum can be shown by noting that the second derivative of the profit function is −10 (see Equation 2.8). Hence, the rate of increase in profits is always decreasing—up to $q = 100$ this rate of increase is still positive, but beyond that point it becomes negative. In this example, $q = 100$ is the only local maximum value for the function π. With more complex functions, however, there may be several such maxima.

QUERY: Suppose the firm's output, q, depended only on labor input, L, according to $q = 2\sqrt{L}$. What would be the profit-maximizing level of labor input? Does this agree with the previous solution? [*Hint:* you may wish to solve this problem by substitution or by using the chain rule.]

Economic problems seldom involve functions of a single variable only. Most goals of interest to economic agents depend on several variables, and trade-offs must be made among these variables. For example, the *utility* an individual receives from activities as a consumer depends on the amount of each good consumed. For a firm's *production function*, the amount produced depends on the quantity of labor, capital, and land devoted to production. In these circumstances this dependence of one variable (y) on a series of other variables ($x_1, x_2, \ldots, x_n$) is denoted by

$$y = f(x_1, x_2, \ldots, x_n). \qquad (2.10)$$

FUNCTIONS OF SEVERAL VARIABLES

We are interested in the point at which y reaches a maximum and how an economic agent might find that point. It is again convenient to picture this agent as changing the variables at his or her disposal (the x's) in order to locate a maximum. Unfortunately, for a function of several variables, the idea of *the* derivative is not well defined. Just as in climbing a mountain the steepness of ascent depends on which direction you go, so does the slope (or derivative) of the function depend on the direction in which it is taken. Usually, the only directional slopes of interest are those that are obtained by increasing one of the x's while holding all the other variables constant (the analogy of mountain climbing might be to measure slopes only in a north-south or east-west direction). These directional slopes are called *partial derivatives.* The partial derivative of y with respect to (that is, in the direction of) x_1 is denoted by

Partial Derivatives

$$\frac{\partial y}{\partial x_1} \text{ or } \frac{\partial f}{\partial x_1} \text{ or } f_{x_1} \text{ or } f_1 .$$

It is understood that in calculating this derivative all of the other x's are held constant. Again it should be emphasized that the numerical value of this slope depends on the value of x_1 and on the (preassigned) values of $x_2, \ldots, x_n$.

A somewhat more formal definition of the partial derivative is

$$\frac{\partial f}{\partial x_1}\bigg|_{\overline{x}_2,\ldots,\overline{x}_n} = \lim_{h\to0}\frac{f(x_1 + h,\overline{x}_2,\ldots,\overline{x}_n) - f(x_1,\overline{x}_2,\ldots,\overline{x}_n)}{h}, \qquad (2.11)$$

where the notation is intended to indicate that $x_2,\ldots,x_n$ are all held constant at the preassigned values $\overline{x}_2,\ldots,\overline{x}_n$ so that the effect of changing x_1 only can be studied. Partial derivatives with respect to the other variables $(x_2,\ldots,x_n)$ would be calculated in a similar way.

Partial Derivatives and the *Ceteris Paribus* Assumption

In Chapter 1 we described the way in which economists use the *ceteris paribus* assumption in their models to hold constant a variety of outside influences so that the particular relationship being studied can be explored in a simplified setting. Partial derivatives are a precise mathematical way of representing this approach; that is, they show how changes in one variable affect some outcome when other influences are held constant—exactly what economists need for their models. For example, Marshall's demand curve shows the relationship between price (P) and quantity (Q) demanded when other factors are held constant. Using partial derivatives, we could represent the slope of this curve by $\partial Q/\partial P$ to indicate the *ceteris paribus* assumptions that are in effect. The fundamental law of demand—that price and quantity move in opposite directions when other factors do not change—is therefore reflected by the mathematical statement "$\partial Q/\partial P < 0$." Again, the use of a partial derivative serves as a reminder of the *ceteris paribus* assumptions that surround the law of demand.

Calculating Partial Derivatives

It is easy to calculate partial derivatives. The calculation proceeds as for the usual derivative by *treating $x_2,\ldots,x_n$ as constants* (which indeed they are in the definition of a partial derivative). Consider the following examples:

1. If $y = f(x_1, x_2) = ax_1^2 + bx_1x_2 + cx_2^2$,
   then

$$\frac{\partial f}{\partial x_1} = f_1 = 2ax_1 + bx_2$$

   and

$$\frac{\partial f}{\partial x_2} = f_2 = bx_1 + 2cx_2.$$

Notice that $\partial f/\partial x_1$ is in general a function of both x_1 and x_2 and therefore its value will depend on the particular values assigned to these variables. It also depends on the parameters a, b, and c, which do not change as x_1 and x_2 change.

2. If $y = f(x_1, x_2) = e^{ax_1 + bx_2}$,
   then

$$\frac{\partial f}{\partial x_1} = f_1 = ae^{ax_1 + bx_2}$$

and

$$\frac{\partial f}{\partial x_2} = f_2 = be^{ax_1 + bx_2}.$$

3. If $y = f(x_1, x_2) = a \ln x_1 + b \ln x_2$,
   then

$$\frac{\partial f}{\partial x_1} = f_1 = \frac{a}{x_1}$$

and

$$\frac{\partial f}{\partial x_2} = f_2 = \frac{b}{x_2}.$$

Notice here that the treatment of x_2 as a constant in the derivation of $\partial f/\partial x_1$ causes the term $b \ln x_2$ to disappear upon differentiation because it does not change when x_1 changes. In this case, unlike our previous examples, the size of the effect of x_1 on y is independent of the value of x_2. In other cases the effect of x_1 on y will depend on the level of x_2.

Second-Order Partial Derivatives

The partial derivative of a partial derivative is directly analogous to the second derivative of a function of one variable and is called a *second-order partial derivative*. This may be written as

$$\frac{\partial(\partial f/\partial x_i)}{\partial x_j}$$

or more simply as

$$\frac{\partial^2 f}{\partial x_j \partial x_i} = f_{ij}. \tag{2.12}$$

For the examples above:

1. $\dfrac{\partial^2 f}{\partial x_1 \partial x_1} = f_{11} = 2a$

$f_{12} = b$

$f_{21} = b$

$f_{22} = 2c$.

2. $f_{11} = a^2 e^{ax_1 + bx_2}$

$f_{12} = abe^{ax_1 + bx_2}$

$f_{21} = abe^{ax_1 + bx_2}$

$f_{22} = b^2 e^{ax_1 + bx_2}$.

3. $f_{11} = \dfrac{-a}{x_1^2}$

$f_{12} = 0$

$f_{21} = 0$

$f_{22} = \dfrac{-b}{x_2^2}$.

Young's Theorem   These examples illustrate the mathematical result that, under quite general conditions, the order in which partial differentiation is conducted to evaluate second-order partial derivatives does not matter. That is,

$$f_{ij} = f_{ji} \tag{2.13}$$

for any pair of variables x_i, x_j. This result is sometimes called "Young's theorem." For an intuitive explanation of the theorem, we can return to our mountain-climbing analogy. In this example the theorem states that the gain in elevation a hiker experiences depends on the directions and distances traveled, but not on the order in which these occur. That is, the gain in altitude is independent of the actual path taken as long as the hiker proceeds from one set of map coordinates to another. He or she may, for example, go one mile north, then one mile east or proceed in the opposite order by going one mile east first, then a mile north. In either case, the gain in elevation is the same since in both cases the hiker is moving from one specific place to another. In later chapters we will make quite a bit of use of this result because it provides a very convenient way of showing some of the predictions that economic models make about behavior.

Using partial derivatives, we can now discuss the maximization of functions of several variables. To understand the mathematics used in solving this problem, an analogy to the one-variable case is helpful. In this one-variable case, we can picture an agent varying x by a small amount, dx, and observing the change in y (call this dy). This change is given by

MAXIMIZATION OF FUNCTIONS OF SEVERAL VARIABLES

$$dy = f'(x) \, dx. \qquad (2.14)$$

The identity in Equation 2.14 then records the fact that the change in y is equal to the change in x times the slope of the function. This formula is equivalent to the *point-slope* formula used for linear equations in basic algebra. As before, the necessary condition for a maximum is that $dy = 0$ for small changes in x around the optimal point. Otherwise, y could be increased by suitable changes in x. But since dx does not necessarily equal 0 in Equation 2.14, $dy = 0$ must imply that at the desired point, $f'(x) = 0$. This is another way of obtaining the first-order condition for a maximum that we already derived.

Using this analogy it is possible to envision the decisions made by an economic agent who must choose the levels of several variables. Suppose that this agent wishes to find a set of x's that will maximize the value of $y = f(x_1, x_2, \ldots, x_n)$. The agent might consider changing only one of the x's, say x_1, while holding all the others constant. The change in y (that is, dy) that would result from this change in x_1 is given by

$$dy = \frac{\partial f}{\partial x_1} \, dx_1 = f_1 dx_1.$$

This says that the change in y is equal to the change in x_1 times the slope measured in the x_1 direction. Using the mountain analogy again, this would say that the gain in altitude a climber heading north would achieve is given by the distance northward traveled times the slope of the mountain measured in a northward direction.

If all the x's are varied by a small amount, the total effect on y will be the sum of effects such as that shown above. Therefore the total change in y is defined to be

Total Differential

$$dy = \frac{\partial f}{\partial x_1} \, dx_1 + \frac{\partial f}{\partial x_2} \, dx_2 + \cdots + \frac{\partial f}{\partial x_n} \, dx_n$$

$$= f_1 dx_1 + f_2 dx_2 + \cdots + f_n dx_n. \qquad (2.15)$$

This expression is called the *total differential* of f and is directly analogous to the expression for the single-variable case given in Equation 2.14. The equation is intuitively sensible: The total change in y is the sum of changes brought about by varying each of the x's.[2]

First-Order Condition for a Maximum

A necessary condition for a maximum (or a minimum) of the function $f(x_1, x_2, \ldots, x_n)$ is that $dy = 0$ for any combination of small changes in the x's. The only way this can happen is if at the point being considered

$$f_1 = f_2 = \cdots = f_n = 0. \tag{2.16}$$

A point where Equations 2.16 hold is called a *critical point*. Equations 2.16 are the necessary conditions for a local maximum. To see this intuitively, note that if one of the partials (say, f_i) were greater (or less) than 0, then y could be increased by increasing (or decreasing) x_i. An economic agent then could find this maximal point by finding the spot where y does not respond to very small movements in any of the x's. This is an extremely important result for economic analysis. It says that any activity (that is, the x's) should be pushed to the point where its "marginal" contribution to the objective (that is, y) is 0. To stop short of that point would fail to maximize y.

Second-Order Conditions

Again, however, the conditions of Equations 2.16 are not sufficient to ensure a maximum. This can be illustrated by returning to an already overworked analogy: All hilltops are (more or less) flat, but not every flat place is a hilltop. A second-order condition similar to Equation 2.6 is needed to ensure that the point found by applying Equations 2.16 is a local maximum. Intuitively, for a local maximum, y should be decreasing for any small changes in the x's away from the critical point. As in the single-variable case, this necessarily involves looking at the second-order partial derivatives of the function f. These second-order partials must obey certain restrictions (analogous to the restriction that was derived in the single-variable case) if the critical point

---

[2] The total differential in Equation 2.15 also can be used to demonstrate the chain rule as it applies to functions of several variables. Suppose that $y = f(x_1, x_2)$ and that $x_1 = g(z)$ and $x_2 = h(z)$. If all these functions are differentiable, it is possible to calculate the effects of a change in z on y. The total differential of y is

$$dy = f_1 dx_1 + f_2 dx_2.$$

Dividing this equation by dz gives

$$\frac{dy}{dz} = f_1 \frac{dx_1}{dz} + f_2 \frac{dx_2}{dz} = f_1 \frac{dg}{dz} + f_2 \frac{dh}{dz}.$$

Hence, calculating the effect of z on y requires calculating how z affects both of the determinants of y (that is, x_1 and x_2). If y depends on more than two variables, an analogous result holds. This result acts as a reminder to be rather careful to include all possible effects when calculating derivatives of functions of several variables.

found by applying Equations 2.16 is to be a local maximum. Later in this chapter we will look at certain types of functions that obey these restrictions.

EXAMPLE 2.2

FINDING A MAXIMUM

Suppose that y is a function of x_1 and x_2 given by

$$y = -(x_1 - 1)^2 - (x_2 - 2)^2 + 10 \qquad (2.17)$$

or

$$y = -x_1^2 + 2x_1 - x_2^2 + 4x_2 + 5.$$

For example, y might represent an individual's health (measured on a scale of 0 to 10), and x_1 and x_2 might be daily dosages of two life-saving drugs. We wish to find values for x_1 and x_2 that make y as large as possible. Taking the partial derivatives of y with respect to x_1 and x_2 and applying the necessary conditions given by Equations 2.16 yields

$$\frac{\partial y}{\partial x_1} = -2x_1 + 2 = 0$$

$$\frac{\partial y}{\partial x_2} = -2x_2 + 4 = 0 \qquad (2.18)$$

or

$$x_1^* = 1$$

$$x_2^* = 2.$$

The function is therefore at a critical point when $x_1 = 1$, $x_2 = 2$. At that point, $y = 10$ is the best health status possible. A bit of experimentation should provide convincing evidence that this is the greatest value y can have. For example, if $x_1 = x_2 = 0$, then $y = 5$, or if $x_1 = x_2 = 1$, then $y = 9$. Values of x_1 and x_2 larger than 1 and 2, respectively, reduce y because the negative quadratic terms in Equation 2.17 become large. Consequently, the point found by applying the necessary conditions is in fact a local (and global) maximum.[3]

QUERY: Suppose y took on a fixed value (say, 5). What would the relationship implied between x_1 and x_2 look like? How about for $y = 7$? Or $y = 10$? (These graphs are *contour lines* of the function and will be examined in more detail in Chapter 3. See also Problem 2.7.)

---

[3] More formally, the point $x_1 = 1$, $x_2 = 2$ is a local maximum because the function described by Equation 2.17 is concave (see our discussion later in this chapter).

Although mathematical equations are often written with a "dependent" variable (y) as a function of one or more independent variable(s) (x), this is not the only way to write such a relationship. As a trivial example, the equation

$$y = mx + b \tag{2.19}$$

can also be written as

$$y - mx - b = 0 \tag{2.20}$$

or, even more generally, as

$$f(x, y, m, b) = 0 \tag{2.21}$$

where this functional notation indicates a relationship between x and y that also depends on the slope (m) and intercept (b) parameters of the function, which do not change. Functions written in the form given by Equations 2.20 and 2.21 are sometimes called implicit functions because the relationships between the variables and parameters are implicitly present in the equation rather than being explicitly calculated as, say, y as a function of x and the parameters m and b.

Often it is a simple matter to translate from implicit functions to explicit ones. For example, the implicit function

$$x + 2y - 4 = 0 \tag{2.22}$$

can easily be "solved" for x as

$$x = -2y + 4 \tag{2.23}$$

or for y as

$$y = \frac{-x}{2} + 2. \tag{2.24}$$

Derivatives from Implicit Functions

Often, for purposes of economic analysis, equations such as 2.23 or 2.24 are more convenient to work with because the effect of x on y (or vice versa) is readily apparent; it is much easier to calculate dy/dx from Equation 2.24 than from Equation 2.22, for example. In many circumstances, however, it is helpful to compute derivatives directly from implicit functions without solving for one of the variables. For example, the implicit function $f(x, y) = 0$ has a total differential of $0 = f_x dx + f_y dy$ so

$$\frac{dy}{dx} = -\frac{f_x}{f_y}. \tag{2.25}$$

Hence, the derivative dy/dx can be found as the negative of the ratio of the partial derivatives of the implicit function, providing $f_y \neq 0$.

~~~~~~

EXAMPLE 2.3

A PRODUCTION POSSIBILITY FRONTIER—AGAIN

In Example 1.2 we examined a production possibility frontier for two goods
of the form

$$2x^2 + y^2 = 225 \tag{2.26}$$

or, written implicitly,

$$f(x, y) = 2x^2 + y^2 - 225 = 0. \tag{2.27}$$

Hence,

$$f_x = 4x,$$

$$f_y = 2y$$

and, by Equation 2.25, the opportunity cost trade-off between x and y is

$$\frac{dy}{dx} = \frac{-f_x}{f_y} = \frac{-4x}{2y} = \frac{-2x}{y}, \tag{2.28}$$

which is precisely the result we obtained earlier, with considerably less work.

QUERY: Why does the trade-off rate between x and y depend only on the ratio
of x to y, but not on the "size of the economy" as reflected by the 225 constant?

Implicit Function Theorem

It may not always be possible to solve implicit functions of the form $g(x, y) = 0$
for unique explicit functions of the form $y = f(x)$. Mathematicians have
analyzed the conditions under which a given implicit function can be solved
explicitly with one variable being a function of other variables and various
parameters. Although we will not investigate these conditions here, they
involve requirements on the various partial derivatives of the function that
are sufficient to ensure that there is indeed a unique relationship between the
dependent and independent variables.[4] In many economic applications,
these derivative conditions are precisely those required to ensure that the
second-order conditions for a maximum (or a minimum) hold. Hence, in
these cases, we will assert that the *implicit function theorem* holds and that it
is therefore possible to solve explicitly for trade-offs such as those reflected
in Equation 2.25.

---

[4] For a detailed discussion of the implicit function theorem in various contexts, see Carl P. Simon
and Lawrence Bloom, *Mathematics for Economists* (New York: W. W. Norton Inc., 1994) chap. 15.

THE ENVELOPE THEOREM

One major application of the implicit function theorem, which will be used at many places in this book, is called the *envelope theorem*; it concerns how the optimal value for a particular function changes when a parameter of the function changes. Because many of the economic problems we will be studying concern the effects of changing a parameter (for example, the effects that changing the market price of a commodity will have on an individual's purchases), this is a type of calculation we will frequently make. The envelope theorem often provides a nice shortcut.

A Specific Example

Perhaps the easiest way to understand the envelope theorem is through an example. Suppose y is a function of a single variable (x) and a parameter (a) given by

$$y = -x^2 + ax. \tag{2.29}$$

For different values of the parameter a, this function represents a family of inverted parabolas. If a is assigned a specific value, Equation 2.29 is a function of x only, and the value of x that maximizes y can be calculated. For example, if $a = 1$, $x^* = \frac{1}{2}$ and, for these values of x and a, $y = \frac{1}{4}$ (its maximal value). Similarly, if $a = 2$, $x^* = 1$ and $y^* = 1$. Hence, an increase of 1 in the value of the parameter a has increased the maximum value of y by 3/4. In Table 2.1, integral values of a between 0 and 6 have been used to calculate the optimal values for x and the associated values of the objective function y. Notice that as a increases, the maximal value for y also increases. This is also illustrated

TABLE 2.1

OPTIMAL VALUES OF y AND x FOR ALTERNATIVE VALUES OF a IN $y = -x^2 + ax$

VALUE OF a	VALUE OF x^*	VALUE OF y^*
0	0	0
1	$\frac{1}{2}$	$\frac{1}{4}$
2	1	1
3	$\frac{3}{2}$	$\frac{9}{4}$
4	2	4
5	$\frac{5}{2}$	$\frac{25}{4}$
6	3	9

in Figure 2.3, which shows that the relationship between a and y^* is quadratic. Now we wish to calculate how y^* changes as the parameter a changes.

The envelope theorem states that there are two equivalent ways we can make this calculation. First, we can calculate the slope of the function in Figure 2.3 directly. To do so, we must solve Equation 2.29 for the optimal value of x for any value of a:

A Direct, Time-Consuming Approach

$$\frac{dy}{dx} = -2x + a = 0;$$

FIGURE 2.3

ILLUSTRATION OF THE ENVELOPE THEOREM

The envelope theorem states that the slope of the relationship between y^* (the maximum value of y) and the parameter a can be found by calculating the slope of the auxiliary relationship found by substituting the respective optimal values for x into the objective function and calculating $\partial y / \partial a$.

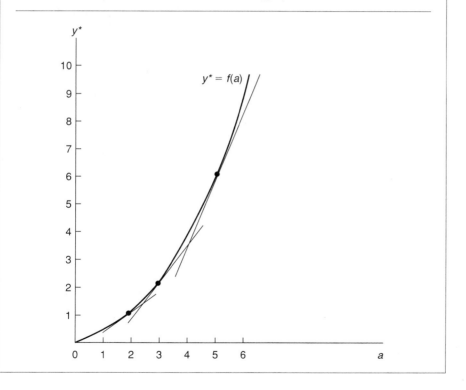

hence,

$$x^* = \frac{a}{2}.$$

Substituting this value of x^* in Equation 2.29 gives

$$y^* = -(x^*)^2 + a(x^*)$$

$$= -\left(\frac{a}{2}\right)^2 + a\left(\frac{a}{2}\right)$$

$$= -\frac{a^2}{4} + \frac{a^2}{2} = \frac{a^2}{4},$$

and this is precisely the relationship shown in Figure 2.3. From the previous equation, it is easy to see that

$$\frac{dy^*}{da} = \frac{2a}{4} = \frac{a}{2} = x^* \tag{2.30}$$

and, for example, at $a = 2$, $x^* = 1$, and $dy^*/da = 1$. That is, at $a = 2$ an increase of a by 1 increases y^* also by 1. Table 2.1 verifies that fact (remembering that in the case of derivatives, we are dealing with only small changes rather than the discrete changes reflected in the table).

The Envelope Shortcut Arriving at this result was a bit complicated. We had to find the optimal value of x for each value of a and then substitute this value for x^* into the equation for y. In more general cases this may be quite burdensome since it requires repeatedly maximizing the objective function. The envelope theorem, providing an alternative approach, states that for small changes in a, dy^*/da can be computed by holding x constant *at its optimal value* and simply calculating $\partial y/\partial a$ from the objective function directly. Substituting x^* in Equation 2.29 gives

$$y^* = -(x^*)^2 + ax^* \tag{2.31}$$

and

$$\frac{\partial y^*}{\partial a} = x^*. \tag{2.32}$$

This is precisely the result obtained earlier. The reason that the two approaches yield similar results is illustrated in Figure 2.3. For $x = x^*$ the linear relationship between y^* and a given by Equation 2.31 is tangent to the y^* curve at the specified value of a. Hence, at that point the equations have the same slope. This result is quite general, and we will use it at several places in this book to simplify our results. To summarize, the envelope theorem states that the change in the optimal value of a function with respect to a parameter of that function can be found by partially differentiating the objective function while holding x (or several x's) constant at its optimal value. That is,

$$\frac{dy^*}{da} = \frac{\partial y}{\partial a}\ \{x = x^*\,(a)\}, \tag{2.33}$$

where the notation provides a reminder that $\partial y/\partial a$ must be computed at that value of x that is optimal for the particular value of the parameter a being examined.

An analogous envelope theorem holds for the case where y is a function of several variables. Suppose that y depends on a set of x's ($x_1, \ldots, x_n$) and on a particular parameter of interest, say, a,

Many-Variable Case

$$y = f(x_1, \ldots, x_n, a). \tag{2.34}$$

Finding an optimal value for y would consist of solving n first-order equations of the form

$$\partial y/\partial x_i = 0 \qquad (i = 1, \ldots, n), \tag{2.35}$$

and a solution to this process would yield optimal values for these x's (x_1^*, $x_2^*, \ldots, x_n^*$) that would implicitly depend on the parameter a. Assuming the second-order conditions are met, the implicit function theorem would apply in this case and assure that we could solve each x_i^* explicitly as a function of the parameter a:

$$x_1^* = x_1^*\,(a)$$
$$x_2^* = x_2^*\,(a)$$
$$\vdots \tag{2.36}$$
$$x_n^* = x_n^*\,(a).$$

Substituting these functions into our original objective (Equation 2.34) yields an expression in which the optimal value of y (say, y^*) depends on the parameter a both directly and indirectly through the effect of a on the x^*'s.

$$y^* = f[x_1^*(a), x_2^*(a), \ldots, x_n^*(a), a]$$

Differentiating this expression with respect to a yields

$$\frac{dy^*}{da} = \frac{\partial f}{\partial x_1} \cdot \frac{dx_1}{da} + \frac{\partial f}{\partial x_2} \cdot \frac{dx_2}{da} \cdots + \frac{\partial f}{\partial x_n} \cdot \frac{dx_n}{da} + \frac{\partial f}{\partial a}. \tag{2.37}$$

But, because of the first-order conditions in Equation 2.35, all of these terms except the last are equal to 0 if the x's are at their optimal values. Hence, again we have the envelope result:

$$\frac{dy^*}{da} = \frac{\partial f}{\partial a}. \tag{2.38}$$

Changes in the optimal value of y brought about by changing the parameter can be calculated directly from the original function through partial differentiation since all the x's are assumed to be adjusted to their optimal values.

EXAMPLE 2.4

THE ENVELOPE THEOREM: HEALTH STATUS REVISITED

Earlier, in Example 2.2, we examined the maximum values for the health status function

$$y = -(x_1 - 1)^2 - (x_2 - 2)^2 + 10 \tag{2.39}$$

and found that

$$x_1^* = 1 \atop x_2^* = 2 \tag{2.40}$$

and

$$y^* = 10.$$

Suppose now we use the arbitrary parameter a instead of the constant 10 in Equation 2.39. Here a might represent a measure of the best possible health for a person, but this value would obviously vary from person to person. Hence,

$$y = -(x_1 - 1)^2 - (x_2 - 2)^2 + a. \tag{2.41}$$

In this case the optimal values for x_1 and x_2 do not depend on a (they are always $x_1^* = 1$, $x_2^* = 2$), so at those optimal values we have

$$y^* = a \tag{2.42}$$

and

$$\frac{dy^*}{da} = 1. \tag{2.43}$$

People with "naturally better health" will have concomitantly higher values for y^*, providing they choose x_1 and x_2 optimally. But this is precisely what the envelope theorem indicates since

$$\frac{dy^*}{da} = \frac{\partial f}{\partial a} = 1 \tag{2.44}$$

from Equation 2.41. Increasing the parameter a simply increases the optimal value for y^* by an identical amount (again, assuming the dosages of x_1 and x_2 are correctly chosen).

QUERY: Suppose we focused instead on the optimal dosage for x_1 in Equation 2.39—that is, suppose we used a general parameter, say, b, instead of 1. Explain in words and using mathematics why $\partial y^*/\partial b$ would necessarily be zero in this case.

So far we have focused our attention on finding the maximum value of a function without restricting the choices of the x's available. In most economic problems not all values for the x's are permissible, however. In many situations it is required, for example, that all the x's be positive. This would be true for the problem faced by the manager choosing output to maximize profits; a negative output would have no meaning. In other instances the x's may be constrained by different economic considerations. For example, in choosing the items to consume, an individual is not able to choose any quantities desired. Rather, choices are constrained by the amount of purchasing power available; that is, by the budget constraint. Such constraints may lower the maximum value for the function we are seeking to maximize. Because we are not able to choose freely among all the x's, y may not be as large as it can be. The constraints would be said to be "nonbinding" if we could obtain the same level of y with or without imposing the constraint.

CONSTRAINED MAXIMIZATION

One method for solving constrained maximization problems is the *Lagrangian multiplier method,* which involves a clever mathematical trick that also turns out to have a useful economic interpretation. The rationale of this method is quite simple, although no rigorous presentation will be attempted here.[5] In a prior section the necessary conditions for a local maximum were discussed. It was shown that at the optimal point all the partial derivatives of f must be 0. There are therefore n equations ($f_i = 0$ for $i = 1, \ldots, n$) in n unknowns (the x's). Generally, these equations can be solved for the optimal x's. When the x's are constrained, however, there is at least one additional equation (the constraint) but no additional variables. The set of equations therefore is overdetermined. The Lagrangian technique introduces an additional variable (the Lagrangian multiplier), which not only helps to solve the problem at hand (since there are now $n + 1$ equations in $n + 1$ unknowns) but also has an interpretation that is useful in a variety of economic circumstances.

Lagrangian Multiplier Method

---

[5] For a detailed presentation, see A. K. Dixit, *Optimization Economic Theory,* 2nd ed. (Oxford: Oxford University Press, 1990).

The Formal Problem

More specifically, suppose that we wish to find the values of $x_1, x_2, \ldots, x_n$ that maximize

$$y = f(x_1, x_2, \ldots, x_n), \tag{2.45}$$

subject to a constraint that permits only certain values of the x's to be used. A general way of writing that constraint is

$$g(x_1, x_2, \ldots, x_n) = 0, \tag{2.46}$$

where the function[6] g represents the relationship that must hold among all the x's.

First-Order Conditions

The Lagrangian multiplier method starts with setting up the expression

$$\mathcal{L} = f(x_1, x_2, \ldots, x_n) + \lambda g(x_1, x_2, \ldots, x_n), \tag{2.47}$$

where λ is an additional variable that is called the Lagrangian multiplier. Later we shall interpret this new variable. First, however, notice that when the constraint holds, $\mathcal{L}$ and f have the same value [since $g(x_1, x_2, \ldots, x_n) = 0$]. Consequently, if we restrict our attention only to values of the x's that satisfy the constraint, finding the constrained maximum value of f is equivalent to finding a critical value of $\mathcal{L}$. Let us proceed then to do so, treating λ also as a variable (in addition to the x's). From Equation 2.47 the conditions for a critical point are

$$\frac{\partial \mathcal{L}}{\partial x_1} = f_1 + \lambda g_1 = 0$$

$$\frac{\partial \mathcal{L}}{\partial x_2} = f_2 + \lambda g_2 = 0$$

$$\cdot$$
$$\cdot$$
$$\cdot$$

$$\frac{\partial \mathcal{L}}{\partial x_n} = f_n + \lambda g_n = 0$$

$$\frac{\partial \mathcal{L}}{\partial \lambda} = g(x_1, x_2, \ldots, x_n) = 0. \tag{2.48}$$

---

[6] As we pointed out earlier, any function of $x_1, x_2, \ldots, x_n$ can be written in this implicit way. For example, the constraint $x_1 + x_2 = 10$ could be written $10 - x_1 - x_2 = 0$. In later chapters we shall usually follow this procedure in dealing with constraints.

Equations 2.48 are then the conditions for a critical point for the function $\mathscr{L}$. Notice that there are $n + 1$ equations (one for each x and a final one for λ) in $n + 1$ unknowns. The equations can generally be solved for $x_1, x_2, \ldots, x_n$, and λ. Such a solution will have two properties: (1) the x's will obey the constraint since the last equation in 2.48 imposes that condition; and (2) among all those values of x's that satisfy the constraint, those that also solve Equations 2.48 will make $\mathscr{L}$ (and hence f) as large as possible. The Lagrangian multiplier method therefore provides a way to find a solution to the constrained maximization problem we posed at the outset.[7]

The solution to Equations 2.48 will usually differ from that in the unconstrained case (see Equations 2.16). Rather than proceeding to the point where the marginal contribution of each x is 0, Equations 2.48 require us to "stop short" because of the constraint. Only if the constraint were ineffective (in which case, as we show below, λ would be 0) would the constrained and unconstrained equations (and their respective solutions) agree. These marginal conditions have economic interpretations in many different situations.

Of course, Equations 2.48 are only necessary conditions for a maximum. There are also second-order conditions that must be checked to ensure that the solution calculated is indeed a local maximum. These conditions are examined briefly later in this chapter.

So far we have used the Lagrangian multiplier (λ) only as a mathematical "trick" to arrive at the solution we wanted. In fact, that variable also has an important economic interpretation, which will be central to our analysis at many points in this book. To develop this interpretation, rewrite the first n equations in 2.48 as

Interpretation of the Lagrangian Multiplier

$$\frac{f_1}{-g_1} = \frac{f_2}{-g_2} = \cdots = \frac{f_n}{-g_n} = \lambda. \qquad (2.49)$$

In other words, at the maximum point, the ratio of f_i to g_i is the same for every x_i. But the numerators in Equations 2.49 are simply the marginal contributions of each x to the function f. They show the *marginal benefit* that one more unit of x_i will have for the function we are trying to maximize (that is, for f).

---

[7] Strictly speaking, these are the necessary conditions for an interior local maximum. In some economic problems, it is necessary to amend these conditions (in fairly obvious ways) to take account of the possibility that some of the x's may be on the boundary of the region of permissible x's. For example, if all the x's are required to be nonnegative, it may be that the conditions of Equations 2.48 will not hold exactly, since these may require negative x's. We shall not detail the ways in which these conditions must be modified to take account of such problems, although some of these modifications will be hinted at throughout the book.

A complete interpretation of the denominators in Equations 2.49 is probably best left until we encounter these ratios in actual economic applications. There we will see that these usually have a "marginal cost" interpretation. That is, they reflect the added burden on the constraint of using slightly more x_i. As a simple illustration, suppose that the constraint required that total spending on x_1 and x_2 (say) be given by a fixed dollar amount, F. Hence, the constraint would be $p_1 x_1 + p_2 x_2 = F$ (where p_i is the per unit cost of x_i). Using our present terminology, this constraint would be written in implicit form as:

$$g(x_1, x_2) = F - p_1 x_1 - p_2 x_2 = 0. \tag{2.50}$$

In this situation, then

$$-g_i = p_i \tag{2.51}$$

and the derivative $-g_i$ does indeed reflect the per unit, marginal cost of using x_i. Practically all of the optimization problems that we will encounter in later chapters have a similar interpretation for the derivatives of the constraints.

Lagrangian Multiplier as a Benefit-Cost Ratio

Now we can give Equations 2.49 an intuitive interpretation. They indicate that, at the optimal choices for the x's, the ratio of the marginal benefit of increasing x_i to the marginal cost of increasing x_i should be the same for every x. To see that this is an obvious condition for a maximum, suppose that it were not true: Suppose that the "benefit-cost ratio" were higher for x_1 than for x_2. In this case slightly more x_1 should be used in order to achieve a maximum. This can be shown by considering employing additional x_1 but giving up enough x_2 to keep g (the constraint) constant. Hence, the marginal cost of the additional x_1 used would equal the cost saved by using less x_2. But since the benefit-cost ratio (the amount of benefit per unit of cost) is greater for x_1 than for x_2, the additional benefits from using more x_1 would exceed the loss in benefits from using less x_2. The use of more x_1 and appropriately less x_2 would then increase y since x_1 provides more "bang for your buck." Only if the marginal benefit–marginal cost ratios are equal for all the x's will there be a local maximum, one in which no small changes in the x's can increase the objective. Concrete applications of this basic principle are developed in many places in this book. The result is a fundamental one for the microeconomic theory of optimizing behavior.

The Lagrangian multiplier (λ) can also be interpreted in the light of this discussion. λ is the common benefit-cost ratio for all the x's. That is,

$$\lambda = \frac{\text{marginal benefit of } x_i}{\text{marginal cost of } x_i} \tag{2.52}$$

for every x_i. If the constraint were relaxed slightly, it would not matter exactly which x is changed (indeed, all the x's could be altered), since, at the margin, each promises the same ratio of benefits to costs. The Lagrangian multiplier then provides a measure of how such an overall relaxation of the constraint would affect the value of y. λ in essence assigns a "shadow price" to the constraint. A high λ indicates that y could be increased substantially by relaxing the constraint, since each x has a high benefit-cost ratio. A low value of λ, on the other hand, indicates that there is not much to be gained by relaxing the constraint. If the constraint is not binding at all, λ will have a value of 0, thereby indicating that the constraint is not restricting the value of y. In such a case, finding the maximum value of y subject to the constraint would be identical to finding an unconstrained maximum. The shadow price of the constraint is zero. This interpretation of λ can also be shown using the envelope theorem as we describe later in this chapter.

Duality

The previous discussion indicates that there is a clear relationship between the problem of maximizing a function subject to constraints[8] and the problem of assigning values to constraints. This reflects what is called the mathematical principle of "duality": Any constrained maximization problem has associated with it a dual problem in constrained *minimization* that focuses attention on the constraints in the original ("primal") problem. For example, to jump a bit ahead of our story, economists assume that individuals maximize their utility, subject to a budget constraint. This is the consumer's primal problem. The dual problem for the consumer is to minimize the expenditure needed to achieve a given level of utility. Or, a firm's primal problem may be to minimize the total cost of inputs used to produce a given level of output, whereas the dual problem is to maximize output for a given cost of inputs purchased. Many similar examples will be developed in later chapters. Each illustrates that there are always two ways to look at any constrained optimization problem. Sometimes taking a frontal attack by analyzing the primal problem can lead to greater insights. In other instances the "back door" approach of examining the dual problem may be more instructive. Whichever route is taken, the results will generally, though not always, be identical, so that the choice made will mainly be a matter of convenience.

---

[8] The discussion in the text concerns problems involving a single constraint. In general, one can handle m constraints ($m < n$) by simply introducing m new variables (Lagrangian multipliers) and proceeding in an analogous way to that discussed above.

EXAMPLE 2.5

CONSTRAINED MAXIMIZATION: HEALTH STATUS YET AGAIN

Let's return once more to our (perhaps far-fetched) health maximization problem. As before, the individual's goal is to maximize

$$y = -x_1^2 + 2x_1 - x_2^2 + 4x_2 + 5,$$

but now assume that choices of x_1 and x_2 are constrained by the fact that he or she can only tolerate one drug dose per day. That is,

$$x_1 + x_2 = 1 \qquad (2.53)$$

or

$$1 - x_1 - x_2 = 0.$$

Notice that the original optimal point $(x_1 = 1, x_2 = 2)$ is no longer attainable because of the constraint on possible dosages: other values must be found. To do so we first set up the Lagrangian expression:

$$\mathscr{L} = -x_1^2 + 2x_1 - x_2^2 + 4x_2 + 5 + \lambda(1 - x_1 - x_2). \qquad (2.54)$$

Differentiation of $\mathscr{L}$ with respect to x_1, x_2, and λ yields the following necessary condition for a constrained maximum:

$$\frac{\partial \mathscr{L}}{\partial x_1} = -2x_1 + 2 - \lambda = 0$$

$$\frac{\partial \mathscr{L}}{\partial x_2} = -2x_2 + 4 - \lambda = 0 \qquad (2.55)$$

$$\frac{\partial \mathscr{L}}{\partial \lambda} = 1 - x_1 - x_2 = 0.$$

Equations 2.55 can now be solved for the optimal values of x_1, x_2, and λ. Using the first and second equations gives

$$-2x_1 + 2 = \lambda = -2x_2 + 4$$

or

$$x_1 = x_2 - 1. \qquad (2.56)$$

Substitution of this value for x_1 into the constraint 2.53 yields the solution:

$$x_2 = 1$$
$$x_1 = 0. \qquad (2.57)$$

In words, if this person can tolerate only one dose of drugs, he or she should opt for taking only the second. By using either of the first two equations, it is easy to complete our solution by showing that

$$\lambda = 2. \qquad (2.58)$$

This, then, is the solution to the constrained-maximum problem. If $x_1 = 0$, $x_2 = 1$, then y takes on the value 8. Constraining the values of x_1 and x_2 to sum to 1 has reduced the maximum value of health status, y, from 10 to 8.

QUERY: Suppose this individual could tolerate two dosages per day. Would you expect y to increase? Would increases in tolerance beyond three dosages per day have any effect on y?

EXAMPLE 2.6

OPTIMAL FENCES AND CONSTRAINED MAXIMIZATION

Suppose a farmer had a certain length of fence, P, and wished to enclose the largest possible rectangular area. What shape area should the farmer choose? This is clearly a problem in constrained maximization. To solve it, let x be the length of one side of the rectangle and y be the length of the other side. The problem then is to choose x and y so as to maximize the area of the field (given by $A = x \cdot y$), subject to the constraint that the perimeter is fixed at $P = 2x + 2y$.

Setting up the Lagrangian expression as in Equation 2.47 gives

$$\mathcal{L} = x \cdot y + \lambda(P - 2x - 2y), \tag{2.59}$$

where λ is an unknown Lagrangian multiplier. The first-order conditions for a maximum are

$$\frac{\partial \mathcal{L}}{\partial x} = y - 2\lambda = 0$$

$$\frac{\partial \mathcal{L}}{\partial y} = x - 2\lambda = 0 \tag{2.60}$$

$$\frac{\partial \mathcal{L}}{\partial \lambda} = P - 2x - 2y = 0.$$

The three equations in 2.60 must be solved simultaneously for x, y, and λ. The first two equations say that $y/2 = x/2 = \lambda$, showing that x must be equal to y. They also imply that x and y should be chosen so that the ratio of marginal benefits to marginal cost is the same for both variables. The benefit (in terms of area) of one more unit of x is given by y (area is increased by $1 \cdot y$), and the marginal cost (in terms of perimeter) is 2 (the available perimeter is reduced by 2 for each unit that the length of side x is increased). The maximum conditions then state that this ratio should be equal for each of the variables.

Since we have shown that $x = y$, we can use the constraint to show that

$$x = y = \frac{P}{4}, \tag{2.61}$$

and because $y = 2\lambda$,

$$\lambda = \frac{P}{8}. \qquad (2.62)$$

Interpretation of the Lagrangian Multiplier. If the farmer were interested in knowing how much more field could be fenced by adding an extra yard of fence, the Lagrangian multiplier suggests that he could find out by dividing the present perimeter by 8. Some specific numbers might make this clear. Suppose that the field currently has a perimeter of 400 yards. If the farmer has planned "optimally," the field will be a square with 100 yards ($= P/4$) on a side. The enclosed area will be 10,000 square yards. Suppose now that the perimeter (that is, the available fence) were enlarged by one yard. Equation 2.62 would then "predict" that the total area would be increased by approximately 50 ($= P/8$) square yards. That this is indeed the case can be shown as follows: Since the perimeter is now 401 yards, each side of the square will be 401/4 yards. The total area of the field is therefore $(401/4)^2$, which, according to the author's calculator, works out to be 10,050.06 square yards. Hence, the "prediction" of a 50-square-yard increase that is provided by the Lagrangian multiplier proves to be remarkably close. As in all constrained maximization problems, here the Lagrangian multiplier provides useful information about the implicit value of the constraint.

Duality. The dual of this constrained maximization problem is that for a given area of a rectangular field, the farmer wishes to minimize the fence required to surround it. Mathematically, the problem is to minimize

$$P = 2x + 2y, \qquad (2.63)$$

subject to the constraint

$$A = x \cdot y. \qquad (2.64)$$

Setting up the Lagrangian expression

$$\mathcal{L}^D = 2x + 2y + \lambda^D(A - x \cdot y) \qquad (2.65)$$

(where the D denotes the dual concept) yields the following first-order conditions for a minimum:

$$\frac{\partial \mathcal{L}^D}{\partial x} = 2 - \lambda^D \cdot y = 0$$

$$\frac{\partial \mathcal{L}^D}{\partial y} = 2 - \lambda^D \cdot x = 0 \qquad (2.66)$$

$$\frac{\partial \mathcal{L}^D}{\partial \lambda^D} = A - x \cdot y = 0.$$

Solving these equations as before yields the result:

$$x = y = \sqrt{A}. \tag{2.67}$$

Again, the field should be square if the length of fence is to be minimized. The value of the Lagrangian multiplier in this problem is

$$\lambda^D = \frac{2}{y} = \frac{2}{x} = \frac{2}{\sqrt{A}}. \tag{2.68}$$

As before, this Lagrangian multiplier indicates the relationship between the objective (minimizing fence) and the constraint (needing to surround the field). If the field were 10,000 square yards, as we saw before, a fence 400 yards long would be needed. Increasing the field by one square yard would require about .02 more yards of fence ($= 2/\sqrt{A} = 2/100$). The reader may wish to fire up his or her calculator to show this is indeed the case—a fence 100.005 yards on each side will exactly enclose 10,001 square yards. Here, as in most duality problems, the value of the Lagrangian in the dual is simply the reciprocal of the value for the Lagrangian in the primal problem. Both provide the same information, although in somewhat different form.

QUERY: An implicit constraint here is that the farmer's field be rectangular. If this constraint were not imposed, what shape field would enclose maximal area? How would you prove that?

The envelope theorem, which we discussed previously in connection with unconstrained maximization problems, also has important applications in constrained maximization problems. Here we will provide only a brief presentation of the theorem. Later in the text a number of applications will be illustrated.

ENVELOPE THEOREM IN CONSTRAINED MAXIMIZATION PROBLEMS

Suppose we seek the maximum value of

$$y = f(x_1 \ldots x_n; a), \tag{2.69}$$

subject to the constraint

$$g(x_1 \ldots x_n; a) = 0, \tag{2.70}$$

where we have made explicit the dependence of the functions f and g on some parameter, a. As we have shown, one way to solve this problem is to set up the Lagrangian expression

$$\mathcal{L} = f(x_1 \ldots x_n; a) + \lambda g(x_1 \ldots x_n; a) \tag{2.71}$$

and solve the first-order conditions (see Equations 2.48) for the optimal values $x_1^* \ldots x_n^*$. Alternatively, it can be shown that

$$\frac{dy^*}{da} = \frac{\partial \mathcal{L}}{\partial a} (x_1^* \ldots x_n^*; a). \tag{2.72}$$

That is, the change in the maximal value of y that results when the parameter a changes (and all the x's are recalculated to new optimal values) can be found by partially differentiating the Lagrangian expression (Equation 2.71) and evaluating the resultant partial derivative at the optimal point.[9] Hence, the Lagrangian expression plays the same role in applying the envelope theorem to constrained problems as does the objective function itself in unconstrained problems (see Equation 2.38). As a simple exercise the reader may wish to show that this result holds for the problem of fencing a rectangular field described in Example 2.6.[10]

MAXIMIZATION WITHOUT CALCULUS

Not all economic maximization problems can be solved using the calculus methods outlined above. For example, the manager of a firm may not know its profit function exactly but may only be able to approximate parts of it by straight lines. This situation is illustrated in Figure 2.4a. Here q^* is clearly the quantity that produces maximum profits, but this point cannot be found by calculus methods since $d\pi/dq$ does not exist[11] at q^*. Some other method must be found in order to locate a point such as q^* systematically.

A second example of the failure of traditional calculus methods is illustrated in Figure 2.4b. Here the manager can produce only integral units of q—it makes no sense to produce $4\frac{1}{3}$ cars. In this case again $d\pi/dq$ is not defined at q^*—calculus will not provide a systematic method for finding q^*.

Specific mathematical "programming" techniques have been developed for dealing with problems such as those illustrated in Figure 2.4. The example illustrated in 2.4a is an extremely simple case of a problem that can be solved by "linear programming" methods; that illustrated in 2.4b can be solved by

---

[9] For a more complete discussion, see Eugene Silberberg, *The Structure of Economics*, 2d ed. (New York: McGraw-Hill Book Company, 1990).

[10] For the primal problem the perimeter P is the parameter of principal interest here. By solving for the optimal values of x and y and substituting into the expression for the area (A) of the field, it is easy to show that $dA/dP = P/8$. Differentiation of the Lagrangian expression (Equation 2.59) yields $\frac{\partial \mathcal{L}}{\partial P} = \lambda$ and, at the optimal values of x and y, $\frac{dA}{dP} = \frac{\partial \mathcal{L}}{\partial P} = \lambda = \frac{P}{8}$. The envelope theorem in this case then offers further proof that the Lagrangian multiplier can be used to assign a shadow price to the constraint.

[11] To see this, note that the slope of $f(q)$ changes very abruptly at q^*.

FIGURE 2.4

**POSSIBLE PROFIT FUNCTIONS FOR WHICH THE CALCULUS
MAXIMIZATION TECHNIQUES WOULD BE INAPPROPRIATE**

In (a), calculus methods would not succeed in finding that level of output that
yields maximum profits (q^*) since the derivative is not defined at such a point.
Similarly, in (b) the manager may choose only integral values for q. In this case
the small changes required to apply calculus reasoning cannot be made. In
order to find either of these maximum points, various kinds of "programming"
techniques must be used.

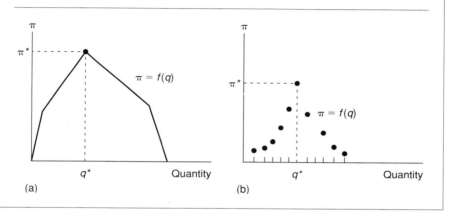

"integer programming" methods.[12] These techniques provide powerful tools
for solving constrained maximization problems and have proved extremely
useful in analyzing difficult real-world situations. In this book, however, we
shall be concerned primarily with calculus methods of solving constrained
maximization problems. This choice is made both for simplicity and because
calculus methods and programming techniques have numerous similarities.
Most economically interesting aspects of programming techniques are
illustrated by the calculus methods.

So far our discussion of optimization has focused primarily on necessary
("first-order") conditions for finding a maximum. That is indeed the practice
we will follow throughout much of this book because, as we shall see, most

**SECOND-ORDER
CONDITIONS**

---

[12] For a simple discussion of these methods, see Michael D. Intriligator, "Mathematical
Programming with Applications to Economics," in K. J. Arrow and M. D. Intriligator, eds.,
Handbook of Mathematical Economics, vol. 1 (Amsterdam, North Holland, 1981).

economic problems involve functions for which the second-order conditions for a maximum are also satisfied. In this section we give a brief analysis of the connection between second-order conditions for a maximum and the related curvature conditions that functions must have to ensure that these hold. The economic rationale for these conditions will be discussed throughout the text.

Functions of One Variable

First we consider the case in which our objective, y, is a function of only a single variable, x. That is,

$$y = f(x). \tag{2.73}$$

A necessary condition for this function to attain its maximum value at some point is that

$$\frac{dy}{dx} = f'(x) = 0 \tag{2.74}$$

at that point. To ensure that the point is indeed a maximum, we must have y decreasing for movements away from it. We already know (by Equation 2.74) that for small changes in x, the value of y does not change; what we need to check is whether or not y is increasing before that "plateau" is reached and declining thereafter. We have already derived an expression for the change in y (dy), which is given by the total differential:

$$dy = f'(x)\, dx. \tag{2.75}$$

What we now require is that dy be decreasing for small increases in the value of x. The differential of Equation 2.75 is given by:

$$d(dy) = d^2y = \frac{d\,[f'(x)\,dx]}{dx} \cdot dx = f''(x)\, dx \cdot dx = f''(x)\, dx^2. \tag{2.76}$$

But

$$d^2y < 0$$

implies that

$$f''(x)\, dx^2 < 0 \tag{2.77}$$

and since dx^2 must be positive (since anything squared is positive), we have

$$f''(x) < 0 \tag{2.78}$$

as the required second-order condition. In words, this condition requires that the function f have a concave shape at the critical point (contrast Figures 2.1 and 2.2). Similar curvature conditions will be encountered throughout this section.

EXAMPLE 2.7

PROFIT MAXIMIZATION AGAIN

In Example 2.1 we considered the problem of finding the maximum of the function

$$\pi = 1{,}000q - 5q^2. \tag{2.79}$$

The first-order condition for a maximum requires

$$\frac{d\pi}{dq} = 1{,}000 - 10q = 0 \tag{2.80}$$

or

$$q^* = 100. \tag{2.81}$$

The second derivative of the function is given by

$$\frac{d^2\pi}{dq^2} = -10 < 0, \tag{2.82}$$

and hence Equation 2.78 is satisfied. The point $q^* = 100$ obeys the sufficient conditions for a local maximum.

QUERY: Here the second derivative is not only negative at the optimal point, but it is always negative. What does that imply about the optimal point? How should the fact that the second derivative is a constant be interpreted?

As a second case we consider y as a function of two independent variables:

$$y = f(x_1, x_2). \tag{2.83}$$

Functions of Two Variables

A necessary condition for such a function to attain its maximum value is that its partial derivatives in both the x_1 and the x_2 directions be 0. That is,

$$\frac{\partial y}{\partial x_1} = f_1 = 0$$

$$\frac{\partial y}{\partial x_2} = f_2 = 0. \tag{2.84}$$

A point that satisfies these conditions will be a "flat" spot on the function (a point where $dy = 0$) and therefore will be a candidate for a maximum. To ensure that the point is a local maximum, y must diminish for movements in any direction away from the critical point: In pictorial terms there is only one way to leave a true mountaintop, and that is to go down.

An Intuitive Argument

Before describing the mathematical properties required of such a point, an intuitive approach may be helpful. If we consider only movements in the x_1 direction, the required condition is clear: The slope in the x_1 direction (that is, the partial derivative f_1) must be diminishing at the critical point. This is simply an application of our discussion of the single-variable case, and it shows that for a maximum, the second partial derivative in the x_1 direction must be negative. An identical argument holds for movements only in the x_2 direction. Hence, we have shown that both own second partial derivatives (f_{11} and f_{22}) must be negative for a local maximum. In our mountain analogy, if attention is confined only to north-south or east-west movements, the slope of the mountain must be diminishing as we cross its summit—the slope must change from positive to negative.

The particular complexity that arises in the two-variable case involves movements through the initial point that are not solely in the x_1 or in the x_2 directions (say, movements from northeast to southwest). In such cases the own second-order partial derivatives do not provide complete information about how the slope is changing near the critical point. Conditions must also be placed on the cross-partial derivative ($f_{12} = f_{21}$) to ensure that dy is decreasing for movements through the critical point in any direction. As we shall see, those conditions amount to requiring that the own second-order partial derivatives be sufficiently large so as to counterbalance any possible "perverse" cross-partial derivatives that may exist. Intuitively, if the mountain falls away steeply enough in the north-south and east-west directions, relatively minor failures to do so in other directions can be compensated for.

A Formal Analysis

We now proceed to make these points more formally. What we wish to discover are the conditions that must be placed on the second partial derivatives of the function f to ensure that d^2y is negative for movements in any direction through the critical point. Recall first that the total differential of the function is given by

$$dy = f_1\, dx_1 + f_2\, dx_2. \qquad (2.85)$$

The differential of that function is given by

$$d^2y = (f_{11}\, dx_1 + f_{12}\, dx_2)\, dx_1 + (f_{21}\, dx_1 + f_{22}\, dx_2)\, dx_2 \qquad (2.86)$$

or

$$d^2y = f_{11}\, dx_1^2 + f_{12}\, dx_2\, dx_1 + f_{21}\, dx_1\, dx_2 + f_{22}\, dx_2^2. \qquad (2.87)$$

Since, by Young's theorem, $f_{12} = f_{21}$, we can arrange terms to get

$$d^2y = f_{11}\, dx_1^2 + 2 f_{12}\, dx_1\, dx_2 + f_{22}\, dx_2^2. \qquad (2.88)$$

For Equation 2.88 to be unambiguously negative for any change in the x's (that is, for any choices of dx_1 and dx_2), it is obviously necessary that f_{11} and f_{22} be negative. If, for example, $dx_2 = 0$, then

$$d^2y = f_{11}\, dx_1^2 \qquad\qquad (2.89)$$

and $d^2y < 0$ implies

$$f_{11} < 0. \qquad\qquad (2.90)$$

An identical argument can be made for f_{22} by setting $dx_1 = 0$. If neither dx_1 nor dx_2 is 0, we then must consider the cross partial, f_{12}, in deciding whether or not d^2y is unambiguously negative. Relatively simple algebra can be used to show that the required condition is[13]

$$f_{11}f_{22} - f_{12}^2 > 0. \qquad\qquad (2.91)$$

Concave Functions

Intuitively, what Equation 2.91 requires is that the own second partial derivatives (f_{11} and f_{22}) be sufficiently large that the outweigh any possible perverse effects from the cross-partial derivatives ($f_{12} = f_{21}$). Functions which obey such a condition are called *concave functions*. In three dimensions, such functions resemble inverted teacups. This image makes it clear that a flat spot on such a function is indeed a true maximum since the function always slopes downward from such a spot. More generally, concave functions have the property that they always lie below any plane that is tangent to them—the plane defined by the maximum value of the function is simply a special case of this property.[14]

---

[13] The proof proceeds by adding and subtracting the term $(f_{12}dx_2)^2/f_{11}$ to Equation 2.88 and factoring. But this approach is only applicable to this special case. A more easily generalized approach that uses matrix algebra recognizes that Equation 2.88 is a "Quadratic Form" in dx_1 and dx_2 and that Equations 2.90 and 2.91 amount to requiring that the Hessian matrix

$$\begin{bmatrix} f_{11} & f_{12} \\ f_{21} & f_{22} \end{bmatrix}$$

be "negative definite." In particular, Equation 2.91 requires that the determinant of the Hessian be positive. For a discussion, see Carl P. Simon and Lawrence Bloom, *Mathematics for Economists* (New York: W. W. Norton, 1994), chap. 16.

[14] Generalization of these properties to more than three dimensions is relatively straightforward. For a succinct treatment, see Peter Berck and Knut Sydsaeter, *Economists' Mathematical Manual*, 2nd ed. (Berlin: Springer-Verlag, 1993), chap. 12.

EXAMPLE 2.8

SECOND-ORDER CONDITIONS: HEALTH STATUS FOR THE LAST TIME

In Example 2.2 we considered the health status function

$$y = f(x_1, x_2) = -x_1^2 + 2x_1 - x_2^2 + 4x_2 + 5. \tag{2.92}$$

The first-order conditions for a maximum are:

$$f_1 = -2x_1 + 2 = 0$$
$$f_2 = -2x_2 + 4 = 0 \tag{2.93}$$

or

$$x_1^* = 1$$
$$x_2^* = 2. \tag{2.94}$$

The second-order partial derivatives for Equation 2.92 are

$$f_{11} = -2$$
$$f_{22} = -2 \tag{2.95}$$
$$f_{12} = 0.$$

These derivatives clearly obey Equations 2.90 and 2.91, so both necessary and sufficient conditions for a local maximum are satisfied.[15]

QUERY: Describe the concave shape of the health status function and indicate why it has only a single global maximum value.

Constrained Maximization
As a final case, consider the problem of choosing x_1 and x_2 to maximize

$$y = f(x_1, x_2), \tag{2.96}$$

subject to the linear constraint

$$c - b_1 x_1 - b_2 x_2 = 0 \tag{2.97}$$

(where c, b_1, b_2 are constant parameters in the problem). This problem is of a type that will be frequently encountered in this book and is a special case of the constrained maximum problems that we examined earlier. There we

---

[15] Notice that Equations 2.95 obey the sufficient conditions not only at the critical point but also for all possible choices of x_1 and x_2. That is, the function is concave. In more complex examples this need not be the case: The second-order conditions need only be satisfied at the critical point for a local maximum to occur.

showed that the first-order conditions for a maximum may be derived by setting up the Lagrangian expression

$$\mathcal{L} = f(x_1, x_2) + \lambda(c - b_1 x_1 - b_2 x_2). \tag{2.98}$$

Partial differentiation with respect to x_1, x_2, and λ yields

$$f_1 - \lambda b_1 = 0$$
$$f_2 - \lambda b_2 = 0 \tag{2.99}$$
$$c - b_1 x_1 - b_2 x_2 = 0.$$

These equations can in general be solved for the optimal values of x_1, x_2, and λ. To ensure that the point derived in that way is a local maximum, we must again examine movements away from the critical points by using the "second" total differential already presented in Equation 2.88:

$$d^2 y = f_{11}\, dx_1^2 + 2 f_{12}\, dx_1\, dx_2 + f_{22}\, dx_2^2. \tag{2.100}$$

Now, however, not all possible small changes in the x's are permissible. Only those values of x_1 and x_2 that continue to satisfy the constraint can be considered valid alternatives to the critical point. To examine such changes, we must calculate the total differential of the constraint (Equation 2.97):

$$- b_1\, dx_1 - b_2\, dx_2 = 0 \tag{2.101}$$

or

$$dx_2 = -\frac{b_1}{b_2}\, dx_1. \tag{2.102}$$

This equation shows the relative changes in x_1 and x_2 that are allowable in considering movements from the critical point. To proceed further on this problem, we need to use the first-order conditions. The first two of these imply

$$\frac{f_1}{f_2} = \frac{b_1}{b_2}, \tag{2.103}$$

and combining this result with Equation 2.102 yields

$$dx_2 = -\frac{f_1}{f_2}\, dx_1. \tag{2.104}$$

We now substitute this expression for dx_2 in Equation 2.100 to demonstrate the conditions that must hold for $d^2 y$ to be negative:

$$d^2 y = f_{11}\, dx_1^2 + 2 f_{12}\, dx_1 \left(-\frac{f_1}{f_2}\, dx_1\right) + f_{22}\left(-\frac{f_1}{f_2}\, dx_1\right)^2 \tag{2.105}$$

$$= f_{11}\, dx_1^2 - 2 f_{12}\frac{f_1}{f_2}\, dx_1^2 + f_{22}\frac{f_1^2}{f_2^2}\, dx_1^2.$$

Combining terms and putting each over a common denominator gives

$$d^2y = (f_{11}f_2^2 - 2f_{12}f_1f_2 + f_{22}f_1^2)\frac{dx_1^2}{f_2^2}. \tag{2.106}$$

Consequently, for $d^2y < 0$ it must be the case that

$$f_{11}f_2^2 - 2f_{12}f_1f_2 + f_{22}f_1^2 < 0. \tag{2.107}$$

Quasi-Concave Functions

Although Equation 2.107 appears to be little more than an inordinately complex mass of mathematical symbols, in fact the condition is quite an important one. It characterizes a set of functions termed *quasi-concave functions.* These have the property that the set of all points for which such a function takes on a value greater than any specific constant is a convex set (that is, any two points in the set can be joined by a line contained completely within the set too). Many economic models are characterized by such functions and, as we will see in considerable detail in Chapter 3, in these cases the condition for quasi-concavity has a relatively simple economic interpretation. Problems 2.9 and 2.10 examine two specific quasi-concave functions that we will frequently encounter in this book.[16]

EXAMPLE 2.9

SECOND-ORDER CONDITIONS FOR THE FENCES PROBLEM

To demonstrate the second-order conditions in the constrained case, we will examine the fencing problem analyzed in Example 2.6. In formal terms that problem required that we maximize

$$A = f(x, y) = xy \tag{2.108}$$

subject to the constraint

$$P - 2x - 2y = 0. \tag{2.109}$$

---

[16] Again, the mathematical conditions for quasi-concavity are best stated using matrix algebra. For a concise summary, see Peter Berck and Knut Sydsaeter, *Economists' Mathematical Manual*, 2nd ed. (Berlin: Springer-Verlag, 1993), chap. 12.

Setting up the Lagrangian expression,

$$\mathcal{L} = xy + \lambda(P - 2x - 2y),\qquad (2.110)$$

yields the following necessary conditions for a maximum:

$$\frac{\partial \mathcal{L}}{\partial x} = y - 2\lambda = 0$$

$$\frac{\partial \mathcal{L}}{\partial y} = x - 2\lambda = 0 \qquad (2.111)$$

$$\frac{\partial \mathcal{L}}{\partial \lambda} = P - 2x - 2y = 0.$$

Solving these for the optimal values of x, y, and λ yields

$$x^* = y^* = \frac{P}{4}$$

$$\lambda = \frac{P}{8}. \qquad (2.112)$$

Second-Order Conditions. To examine the second-order conditions, we compute

$$f_1 = f_x = y$$
$$f_2 = f_y = x$$
$$f_{11} = f_{xx} = 0 \qquad (2.113)$$
$$f_{12} = f_{xy} = 1$$
$$f_{22} = f_{yy} = 0.$$

Making the appropriate substitutions in Equation 2.107, we have

$$0 \cdot x^2 - 2 \cdot 1 \cdot y \cdot x + 0 \cdot y^2 = -2xy. \qquad (2.114)$$

Since x and y are both positive in this problem, the second-order conditions for a local constrained maximum are satisfied.

QUERY: What does the function $f(x,y)$ look like? Does it have a global maximum value? For a fixed value for f, what is the shape of the function's contour lines?

SUMMARY

Despite the formidable appearance of some parts of this chapter, this is not a book on mathematics. Rather, the intention here was to gather together a variety of tools that will be used to develop economic models throughout the remainder of the text. Material in this chapter will then be useful as a handy reference.

One way to summarize the mathematical tools introduced in this chapter is by stressing again the economic lessons that these tools illustrate:

- Using mathematics provides a convenient, shorthand way for economists to develop their models. Implications of various economic assumptions can be studied in a simplified setting through the use of such mathematical tools.

- The mathematical concept of the derivatives of a function is widely used in economic models because economists are often interested in how marginal changes in one variable affect another variable. Partial derivatives are especially useful for this purpose because they are defined to represent such changes when all other factors are held constant. In this way, partial derivatives incorporate the *ceteris paribus* assumption found in most economic models.

- The mathematics of optimization is an important tool for the development of models that assume that economic agents rationally pursue some goal. In the unconstrained case, the first-order conditions state that any activity that contributes to the agent's goal should be expanded up to the point at which the marginal contribution of further expan-

sion is 0. In mathematical terms, the first-order condition for an optimum requires that all partial derivatives be 0.

- Most economic optimization problems involve constraints on the choices agents can make. In this case the first-order conditions for a maximum suggest that each activity be operated at a level at which the ratio of the marginal benefit of the activity to its marginal cost is the same for all activities actually used. This common marginal benefit–marginal cost ratio is also equal to the Lagrangian multiplier, which is often introduced to help solve constrained optimization problems. The Lagrangian multiplier can also be interpreted as the implicit value (or shadow price) of the constraint.

- The implicit function theorem is a useful mathematical device for illustrating the dependence of the choices that result from an optimization problem on the parameters of that problem (for example, market prices). The envelope theorem is useful for examining how these optimal choices change when the problem's parameters (prices) change.

- The first-order, marginal conditions developed in this chapter are necessary conditions only for a maximum or minimum. Ensuring that a true maximum or minimum has been attained requires checking second-order conditions that describe the curvature of the function being optimized. Often these curvature conditions will have useful economic implications.

PROBLEMS

2.1

For each of the following functions of one variable, determine all local maxima and minima and indicate points of inflection (where $f'' = 0$):
a. $f(x) = 4x^3 - 12x$
b. $f(x) = 4x - x^2$
c. $f(x) = x^3$

2.2

If we cut four congruent squares out of the corners of a square piece of cardboard 12 inches on a side, we can fold up the four remaining flaps to obtain a tray without a top. What size squares should be cut in order to maximize the volume of the tray? (See figure.)

2.3

The height of a ball t seconds after it is thrown straight up is $-\frac{1}{2}gt^2 + 40t$ (where g is the acceleration due to gravity).

a. If $g = 32$ (as on the earth), when does the ball reach a maximum height? What is that height?

b. If $g = 5.5$ (as on the moon), when does the ball reach a maximum height and what is that height? Can you explain the reasons for the difference between this answer and the answer for part (a)?

c. In general, develop an expression for the change in maximum height for a unit change in g. Explain why this value depends implicitly on the value of g itself.

2.4

Taxes in Oz are calculated according to the formula

$$T = .01I^2,$$

where T represents thousands of dollars of tax liability and I represents income measured in thousands of dollars. Using this formula, answer the following questions:

a. How much tax do individuals with incomes of $10,000, $30,000, and $50,000 pay? What are the average tax rates for these income levels? At what income level does tax liability equal total income?

b. Graph the tax schedule for Oz. Use your graph to estimate marginal tax rates for the income levels specified in part (a). Also show the average tax rates for these income levels on your graph.

c. Marginal tax rates in Oz can be estimated more precisely by calculating tax owed if persons with the incomes in part (a) get one more dollar. Make this computation for these three income levels.

Compare your results by calculating the marginal tax rate function using calculus.

2.5

Suppose $U = (x,y) = 4x^2 + 3y^2$.

a. Calculate $\partial U/\partial x$, $\partial U/\partial y$.

b. Evaluate these partial derivatives at $x = 1$, $y = 2$.

c. Write the total differential for U.

d. Calculate dy/dx for $dU = 0$—that is, what is the implied trade-off between x and y holding U constant?

e. Show $U = 16$ when $x = 1$, $y = 2$.

f. In what ratio must x and y change to hold U constant at 16 for movements away from $x = 1$, $y = 2$?

g. More generally, what is the shape of the $U = 16$ contour line for this function? What is the slope of that line?

2.6

Suppose that $f(x,y) = xy$. Find the maximum value for f if x and y are constrained to sum to 1. Solve this problem in two ways: by substitution and by using the Langrangian multiplier method.

2.7

Suppose a firm's total revenues depend on the amount produced (q) according to the function

$$TR = 70q - q^2.$$

Total costs also depend on q:

$$TC = q^2 + 30q + 100$$

a. What level of output should the firm produce in order to maximize profits ($TR - TC$)? What will profits be?

b. Show that the second-order conditions for a maximum are satisfied at the output level found in part (a).

c. Does the solution calculated here obey the "marginal revenue equals marginal cost" rule? Explain.

2.8

Show that if $f(x_1,x_2)$ is a concave function, it is also a quasi-concave function. Do this by comparing Equation 2.107 (defining quasi-concavity) to Equation 2.88 (defining concavity). Can you give an intuitive reason for this result? Is the converse of the statement true? Are quasi-concave functions necessarily concave?

2.9

One of the most important functions that we will encounter in this book is the Cobb-Douglas function:

$$y = (x_1)^\alpha (x_2)^\beta$$

where α and β are positive constants that are each less than one.

a. Show that this function is quasi-concave using a "brute force" method by applying Equation 2.107.

b. Show that the Cobb-Douglas function is quasi-concave by showing that the any contour line of the form $y = c$ (where c is any positive constant) is convex and therefore that the set of points for which $y > c$ is a convex set.

c. Show that if $\alpha + \beta > 1$ then the Cobb-Douglas function is not concave (thereby illustrating that not all quasi-concave functions are concave).

2.10

Another function that we will encounter often in this book is the "power function"

$$y = x^\delta$$

where $0 \leq \delta \leq 1$ (at times we will also examine this function for cases where δ can be negative too, in which case we will use the form $y = x^\delta / \delta$ to ensure that the derivatives have the proper sign).

a. Show that this function is concave (and therefore also, by the result of problem 2.8, quasi-concave). Notice that the $\delta = 1$ is a special case and that the function is "strictly" concave only for $\delta < 1$.

b. Show that the multivariate form of the power function

$$y = f(x_1, x_2) = (x_1)^\delta + (x_2)^\delta$$

is also concave (and quasi-concave). Explain why, in this case, the fact that $f_{12} = f_{21} = 0$ makes the determination of concavity especially simple.

c. One way to incorporate "scale" effects into the function described in part b is to use the monotonic transformation

$$g(x_1, x_2) = y^\gamma = [(x_1)^\delta + (x_2)^\delta]^\gamma$$

where γ is a positive constant. Does this transformation preserve the concavity of the function? Is g quasi-concave?

SUGGESTED READINGS

Berck, Peter, and Knut Sydsaeter. *Economists' Mathematical Manual*, 2nd ed. Berlin: Springer-Verlag, 1993.
An indispensable tool for mathermatical review. Contains 32 chapters covering most of the mathematical tools that economists use. Discussions are very brief, so this is not the place to encounter new concepts for the first time.

Dixit, A. K. *Optimization in Economic Theory*, 2nd ed. New York: Oxford University Press, 1990.
A complete and modern treatment of optimization techniques. Uses relatively advanced analytical methods.

Intriligator, Michael D. *Mathematical Optimization and Economic Theory.* Englewood Cliffs, NJ: Prentice-Hall, 1971.
Comprehensive treatment of maximization techniques, including several "programming" methods applicable when calculus methods are not appropriate.

Mas-Colell, Andreu, Michael D. Whinston, and Jerry R. Green. *Microeconomic Theory.* New York: Oxford University Press, 1995.

Encyclopedic treatment of mathematical microeconomics. Extensive mathematical appendices cover relatively high-level topics in analysis.

Samuelson, Paul A. *Foundations of Economic Analysis.* Cambridge, MA: Harvard University Press, 1947. Mathematical Appendix A.
A basic reference. Mathematical Appendix A provides an advanced treatment of necessary and sufficient conditions for a maximum.

Silberberg, Eugene. *The Structure of Economics: A Mathematical Analysis.* 2d ed. New York: McGraw-Hill Book Company, 1990.
A mathematical microeconomics text that stresses the observable predictions of economic theory. The text makes extensive use of the envelope theorem.

Simon, Carl P., and Lawrence Bloom. *Mathematics for Economists.* New York: W. W. Norton, 1994.
A very useful text covering most areas of mathematics

relevant to economists. Treatment is at a relatively high level. Two topics discussed better here than elsewhere are differential equations and basic point-set topology.

Sydsaeter, Knut. *Topics in Mathematical Analysis for Economists.* New York: Academic Press, 1981.
An advanced mathematical text that provides detailed discussions of the mathematical intricacies of maximization techniques.

Taylor, Angus E., and W. Robert Mann. *Advanced Calculus.* 3d ed. New York: John Wiley, 1983, pp. 183–195.
A comprehensive calculus text with a good discussion of the Lagrangian technique.

Thomas, George B., and Ross L. Finney. *Calculus and Analytic Geometry.* 8th ed. Reading, MA: Addison-Wesley Publishing Co., 1992.
Basic calculus text with excellent coverage of differentiation techniques.

CHOICE AND DEMAND

In Part II we will investigate the economic theory of choice. One final goal of this examination is to develop the notion of market demand in a formal way so that this concept can be used in later sections of the text. A more general goal of the part is to illustrate the theory that economists use to explain how individuals make choices in a wide variety of contexts.

Part II begins with a description of the way economists model individual preferences, which are usually referred to by the formal term "utility." Chapter 3 shows how economists are able to conceptualize utility in a mathematical way. Particularly important is the development of "indifference curves," which show the various exchanges that individuals are willing to make voluntarily.

The utility concept is next used in Chapter 4 to illustrate the theory of choice. The fundamental hypothesis of the chapter—the first economic example of an optimization hypothesis that we have encountered—is that individuals who are faced with limited incomes will make economic choices in such a way as to achieve as much utility as possible. Chapter 4 uses both mathematical and intuitive analyses to indicate the insights that this hypothesis provides about economic behavior.

Chapters 5 and 6 then use the model of utility maximization to investigate how individuals will respond to changes in their circumstances. Chapter 5 is primarily concerned with responses to changes in the price of a commodity, an analysis that leads directly to the demand curve notion. Chapter 6 continues this type of analysis and applies it to developing an understanding of demand relationships among different goods.

Finally, Chapter 7 uses the material from Chapters 3–6 to derive the familiar market demand curve for a commodity. By developing this curve from the basic economic theory of choice, this chapter offers a fairly complete understanding of the factors that determine the location of the curve and the factors that might cause it to shift to a new position. The chapter also introduces the notion of elasticity as a way to measure the responsiveness of market demand to changes in various economic parameters such as income and prices. Such elasticities are widely used in empirical studies of market responses in the real world.

CHAPTER 3

PREFERENCES AND UTILITY

In this chapter we look at the way in which economists characterize individuals' preferences. We begin with a fairly abstract discussion of the "preference relation" but quickly turn to the economists' primary tool for studying individual choices—the utility function. We look both at some general characteristics of such a function and at a few simple examples of specific utility functions that we will encounter throughout this book.

AXIOMS OF RATIONAL CHOICE

One way to begin an analysis of individuals' choices is to state a basic set of postulates, or axioms, that characterize "rational" behavior. Although a number of sets of such axioms have been proposed, all have similarities in that they begin with the concept of "preference": When an individual reports that "A is preferred to B," it is taken to mean that all things considered, he or she feels better off under situation A than under situation B. This preference relation is assumed to have three basic properties:

I. *Completeness:* If A and B are *any* two situations, the individual can always specify exactly one of the following three possibilities:
    1. "A is preferred to B,"
    2. "B is preferred to A," or
    3. "A and B are equally attractive."
    Individuals are consequently assumed not to be paralyzed by indecision: They completely understand and can always make up their minds about the desirability of any two alternatives. The assumption also rules out the possibility that the individual can report both that A is preferred to B and that B is preferred to A.
II. *Transitivity:* If an individual reports that "A is preferred to B" and that "B is preferred to C," then he or she must also report that "A is preferred to C."

This assumption states that the individual's choices are internally consistent. Such an assumption can be subjected to empirical study. Generally, such studies conclude that a person's choices are indeed transitive, but that conclusion must be modified in cases where the individual may not fully understand the consequences of the choices he or she is making. Since, for the most part, we will assume choices are fully informed (but see the discussion of uncertainty in Part III and elsewhere), the transitivity property seems an appropriate assumption to make about preferences.

III. *Continuity:* If an individual reports "A is preferred to B," then situations suitably "close to" A must also be preferred to B.

This rather technical assumption is required if we wish to analyze individuals' responses to relatively small changes in income and prices. The purpose of the assumption is to rule out certain kinds of discontinuous, knife-edge preferences that pose problems for a mathematical development of the theory of choice. Assuming continuity does not seem to run the risk of missing types of economic behavior that are especially important in the real world.

UTILITY

Given the assumptions of completeness, transitivity, and continuity, it is possible to show formally that people are able to rank in order all possible situations from the least desirable to the most.[1] Following the terminology introduced by the nineteenth-century political theorist Jeremy Bentham, economists call this ranking *utility.*[2] We also will follow Bentham by saying that more desirable situations offer more utility than do less desirable ones. That is, if a person prefers situation A to situation B, we would say that the utility assigned to option A, denoted by $U(A)$, exceeds the utility assigned to B, $U(B)$.

Nonuniqueness of Utility Measures

We might even attach numbers to these utility rankings. But these numbers will not be unique. Any set of numbers we arbitrarily assign that accurately reflects the original preference ordering will imply the same set of choices. It makes no difference whether we say that $U(A) = 5$ and $U(B) = 4$ or that $U(A) = 1,000,000$ and $U(B) = 0.5$. In either case the numbers imply that A is

[1] These properties and their connection to representation of preferences by a utility function are discussed in detail in Andreu Mas-Colell, Michael D. Whinston, and Jerry R. Green, *Microeconomic Theory* (New York: Oxford University Press, 1995).

[2] J. Bentham, *Introduction to the Principles of Morals and Legislation* (London: Hafner, 1848).

preferred to B. In technical terms, our notion of utility is defined only up to an order-preserving ("monotonic") transformation.[3] Any set of numbers that accurately reflects a person's preference ordering will do. Consequently, it makes no sense to ask "how much more is A preferred than B?" since that question has no unique answer. Surveys that ask people to rank their "happiness" on a scale of 1 to 10 could just as well use a scale of 7 to 1,000,000. About all that can be hoped for is that a person who reports he or she is a "6" on the scale one day and a "7" on the next day is indeed happier on the second day. Utility rankings are therefore like the ordinal rankings of restaurants or movies using one, two, three, or four stars. They simply record the relative desirability of commodity bundles.

This lack of uniqueness in the assignment of utility numbers also reflects the conclusion that it is not possible to compare utilities between people. If one person reports that a steak dinner provides a utility of "5" and another reports that the same dinner offers a utility of "100," we cannot say which individual values the dinner more since they could be using very different scales. Similarly, we have no way of measuring whether a move from situation A to situation B provides more utility to one person or to another. Nonetheless, as we will see, economists can say quite a bit about utility rankings by examining what people voluntarily choose to do.

The *Ceteris Paribus* Assumption

Because *utility* refers to overall satisfaction, such a measure clearly is affected by a variety of factors. A person's utility is affected not only by his or her consumption of physical commodities but also by psychological attitudes, peer group pressures, personal experiences, and the general cultural environment. Although economists do have a general interest in examining such influences, usually a narrowing of focus is necessary. Consequently, a common practice is to devote attention exclusively to choices among quantifiable options (for example, the relative quantities of food and shelter bought, the number of hours worked per week, or votes among specific taxing formulas) while holding constant the other things that affect behavior. This *ceteris paribus* (other things being equal) assumption is invoked in all economic analysis of utility-maximizing choices so as to make the analysis of choices manageable within a simplified setting.

---

[3] We can denote this idea mathematically by saying that any numerical utility ranking (U) can be transformed into another set of numbers by the function F providing that F(U) is order preserving. This can be assured if $F'(U) > 0$. For example, the transformation $F(U) = U^2$ is order preserving as is the transformation $F(U) = ln\ U$. At some places in the text and problems, we may find it convenient to make such transformations in order to make a particular utility ranking easier to analyze.

Utility from Consumption of Goods

As an important example of the *ceteris paribus* assumption, consider the individual's problem of choosing, at a single point in time, among n consumption goods $X_1, X_2, \ldots, X_n$. We shall assume that the individual's ranking of these goods can be represented by a utility function of the form:

$$\text{utility} = U(X_1, X_2, \ldots, X_n; \text{other things}), \tag{3.1}$$

where the X's refer to the quantities of the goods that might be chosen and the "other things" notation is used as a reminder that many aspects of individual welfare are being held constant in the analysis.

Quite often it is easier to write Equation 3.1 as

$$\text{utility} = U(X_1, X_2, \ldots, X_n) \tag{3.2}$$

or, if only two goods are being considered,

$$\text{utility} = U(X, Y), \tag{3.2'}$$

where it is clear that everything is being held constant (that is, outside the frame of analysis) except the goods actually referred to in the utility function. It would be tedious to remind you at each step what is being held constant in the analysis, but it should be remembered that some form of the *ceteris paribus* assumption will always be in operation.

Arguments of Utility Functions

The utility function notation is used to indicate how an individual ranks the particular arguments of the function being considered. In the most usual case, the utility function (Equation 3.2) will be used to represent how an individual ranks certain bundles of goods that are available at one point in time. On occasion it will be useful to use other arguments in the utility function, and it is best to clear up certain conventions at the outset. For example, it may be useful to talk about the utility an individual receives from real wealth (W). Therefore we shall use the notation:

$$\text{utility} = U(W). \tag{3.3}$$

Unless the individual is a rather peculiar Scrooge-type of person, wealth in its own right gives no direct utility. Rather, it is only when wealth is spent on consumption goods that any utility results. For this reason Equation 3.3 will be taken to mean that the utility from wealth is in fact derived by spending that wealth in such a way as to yield as much utility as possible.

Two other arguments of utility functions will be used in later chapters. In Chapter 22 we shall be concerned with the individual's labor-leisure choice and will therefore have to consider the presence of leisure in the utility function. A function of the form

$$\text{utility} = U(C, H) \tag{3.4}$$

will be used. Here C represents consumption and H represents hours of nonwork time (that is, leisure) during a particular time period.

In Chapter 23 we shall be interested in the individual's consumption decisions in different time periods. In that chapter we shall use a utility function of the form

$$\text{utility} = U(C_1, C_2), \tag{3.5}$$

where C_1 is consumption in this period and C_2 is consumption in the next period. By changing the arguments of the utility function, therefore, we will be able to focus on specific aspects of an individual's choices in a variety of simplified settings.

In summary then, we start our examination of individual behavior with the following definition:

DEFINITION

Utility Individuals' preferences are assumed to be represented by a utility function of the form

$$U(X_1, X_2, \ldots, X_n), \tag{3.6}$$

where $X_1, X_2, \ldots, X_n$ are the quantities of each of n goods that might be consumed in a period. This function is unique only up to an order-preserving transformation.

Economic Goods

In this representation the X's are taken to be "goods"—that is, whatever economic quantities they represent, we assume that more of any particular X_i during some period is preferred to less. We assume this is true of every good, be it a simple consumption item such as a hot dog or a complex aggregate such as wealth or leisure. We have pictured this convention for a two-good utility function in Figure 3.1. There, all consumption bundles in the shaded area are preferred to the bundle X^*, Y^* because any bundle in the shaded area provides more of at least one of the goods. By our definition of "goods," then, bundles of goods in the shaded area are ranked more highly than X^*, Y^*. Similarly, bundles in the area marked "worse" are clearly inferior to X^*, Y^* since they contain less of at least one of the goods and no more of the other. Bundles in the two areas indicated by question marks are difficult to compare to X^*, Y^* because they contain more of one of the goods and less

FIGURE 3.1

MORE OF A GOOD IS PREFERRED TO LESS

The shaded area represents those combinations of X and Y that are unambiguously preferred to the combination X^*, Y^*. *Ceteris paribus*, individuals prefer more of any good rather than less. Combinations identified by "?" involve ambiguous changes in welfare since they contain more of one good and less of the other.

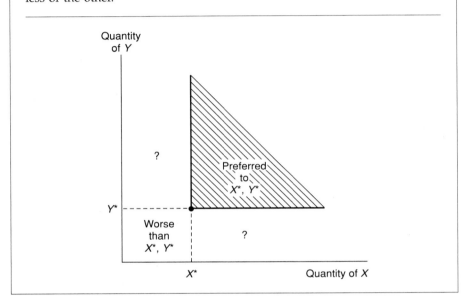

of the other. As we will see, movements into these areas involve trade-offs between the two goods.

TRADES AND SUBSTITUTION

Most economic activity involves voluntary trading between individuals. When someone buys, say, a loaf of bread, he or she is voluntarily giving up one thing (money) for something else (bread) that is of greater value. To examine this kind of voluntary transaction, we need to develop a formal apparatus for illustrating trades in the utility function context.

Indifference Curves and the Marginal Rate of Substitution

To discuss such voluntary trades, it is easiest first to develop the idea of an *indifference curve*. In Figure 3.2 the curve U_1 represents all the alternative combinations of X and Y for which an individual is equally well off (remember again that all other arguments of the utility function are being

FIGURE 3.2

A SINGLE INDIFFERENCE CURVE

The curve U_1 represents those combinations of X and Y from which the individual derives the same utility. The slope of this curve represents the rate at which the individual is willing to trade X for Y while remaining equally well off. This slope (or, more properly, the negative of the slope) is termed the *marginal rate of substitution*. In the figure the indifference curve is drawn on the assumption of a diminishing marginal rate of substitution.

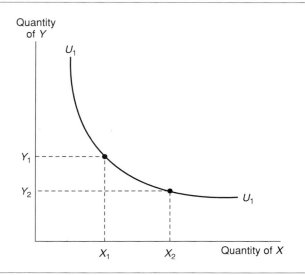

held constant). The individual is equally happy consuming, for example, either the combination of goods X_1, Y_1 or the combination X_2, Y_2. This curve representing all the consumption bundles that the individual ranks equally is called an *indifference curve:*

DEFINITION

Indifference Curve An *indifference curve* (or, in many dimensions, indifference surface) shows a set of consumption bundles among which the individual is indifferent. That is, the bundles all provide the same level of utility.

The slope of the indifference curve in Figure 3.2 is negative, showing that if the individual is forced to give up some Y, he or she must be compensated by an additional amount of X to remain indifferent between the two bundles of goods. The curve is also drawn so that the slope increases as X increases (that is, the slope starts at negative infinity and increases toward 0). This is a graphical representation of the assumption that individuals become progressively less willing to trade away Y to get more X. In mathematical terms, this slope diminishes as X increases. Hence, we have the following definition:

DEFINITION

Marginal Rate of Substitution The negative of the slope of an indifference curve (U_1) at some point is termed the *marginal rate of substitution (MRS)* at that point. That is,

$$MRS = -\left.\frac{dY}{dX}\right|_{U = U_1} \tag{3.7}$$

where the notation indicates that the slope is to be calculated along the U_1 indifference curve.

The slope of U_1 and the MRS therefore tell us something about the trades this person will voluntarily make. At a point such as X_1, Y_1, the person has quite a lot of Y and is willing to trade away a significant amount to get one more X. The indifference curve at X_1, Y_1 is therefore rather steep. This is a situation where the person has, say, many hamburgers (Y) and little to drink with them (X). This person would gladly give up a few burgers (say, 5) to quench his or her thirst with one more drink.

At X_2, Y_2, on the other hand, the indifference curve is flatter. Here this person has quite a few drinks and is willing to give up relatively few burgers (say, 1) to get another soft drink. Consequently, the MRS diminishes between X_1, Y_1 and X_2, Y_2. The changing slope of U_1 shows how the particular consumption bundle available influences the trades this person will freely make.

Indifference Curve Map

In Figure 3.2 only one indifference curve was drawn. The X, Y quadrant, however, is densely packed with such curves, each corresponding to a different level of utility. Since every bundle of goods can be ranked and yields some level of utility, each point in Figure 3.2 must have an indifference curve passing through it. Indifference curves are similar to contour lines on a map in that they represent lines of equal "altitude" of utility. In Figure 3.3 several indifference curves are shown to indicate that there are infinitely many in the plane. The level of utility represented by these curves increases as we move in a northeast direction—the utility of curve U_1 is less than that of U_2, which

FIGURE 3.3

THERE ARE INFINITELY MANY INDIFFERENCE CURVES IN THE *X-Y* PLANE

There is an indifference curve passing through each point in the *X-Y* plane. Each of these curves records combinations of *X* and *Y* from which the individual receives a certain level of satisfaction. Movements in a northeast direction represent movements to higher levels of satisfaction.

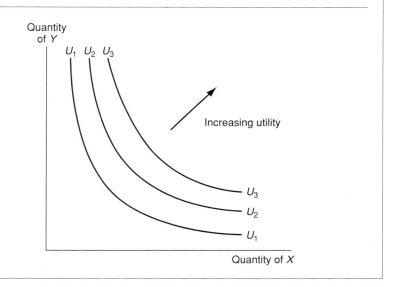

is less than that of U_3. This is because of the assumption made in Figure 3.1: More of a good is preferred to less. As was discussed earlier, there is no unique way to assign numbers to these utility levels. All the curves show is that the combinations of goods on U_3 are preferred to those on U_2, which are preferred to those on U_1.

Indifference Curves and Transitivity

As an exercise in examining the relationship between consistent preferences and the representation of preferences by utility functions, consider the following question: Can any two of an individual's indifference curves intersect? Two such intersecting curves are shown in Figure 3.4. We wish to know if they violate our basic axioms of rationality. Using our map analogy, there would seem to be something wrong at point *E*—there "altitude" is equal to two different numbers, U_1 and U_2. But no point can be both 100 and 200 feet above sea level.

FIGURE 3.4

**INTERSECTING INDIFFERENCE CURVES
IMPLY INCONSISTENT PREFERENCES**

Combinations A and D lie on the same indifference curve and therefore are equally desirable. But the axiom of transitivity can be used to show that A is preferred to D. Hence, intersecting indifference curves are not consistent with rational preferences.

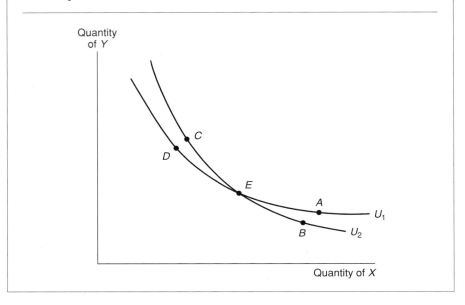

To proceed formally, let us analyze the bundles of goods represented by points A, B, C, and D. By the assumption of nonsatiation, "A is preferred to B" and "C is preferred to D." But the individual is equally satisfied with either B or C (they lie on the same indifference curve), so the axiom of transitivity implies that A must be preferred to D. But that cannot be true, since A and D are on the same indifference curve and are by definition regarded as equally desirable. Hence, the axiom of transitivity shows that indifference curves cannot intersect. We therefore should always draw indifference curve maps as they appear in Figure 3.3.

**Convexity of
Indifference
Curves**

An alternative way of stating the principle of a diminishing marginal rate of substitution uses the mathematical notion of a convex set. A set of points is said to be *convex* if any two points within the set can be joined by a straight line that is contained completely within the set. The assumption of a

FIGURE 3.5

**THE NOTION OF CONVEXITY AS AN ALTERNATIVE
DEFINITION OF A DIMINISHING *MRS***

In (a) the indifference curve is *convex* (any line joining two points above U_1 is also above U_1). In (b) this is not the case, and the curve shown here does not everywhere have a diminishing *MRS*.

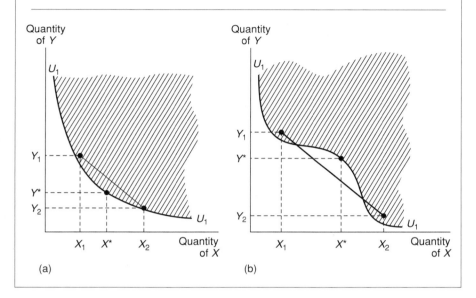

(a)

(b)

diminishing *MRS* is equivalent to the assumption that all combinations of X and Y, which are preferred to or indifferent to a particular combination X^*, Y^*, form a convex set.[4] This is illustrated in Figure 3.5a, where all combinations preferred to or indifferent to X^*, Y^* are in the shaded area. Any two of these combinations—say, X_1, Y_1 and X_2, Y_2—can be joined by a straight line also contained in the shaded area. In Figure 3.5b this is not true. A line joining X_1, Y_1 and X_2, Y_2 passes outside the shaded area. Therefore, the indifference curve through X^*, Y^* in 3.5b does not obey the assumption of a diminishing *MRS*, since the set of points preferred or indifferent to X^*, Y^* is not convex.

[4] This definition is equivalent to assuming that the utility function is quasi-concave. Such functions were discussed in Chapter 2, and we shall return to examine them in the next section. Sometimes the term *strict quasi-concavity* is used to rule out the possibility of indifference curves having linear segments. We generally will assume strict quasi-concavity but in a few places will indicate the complications posed by linear portions of indifference curves.

FIGURE 3.6

BALANCED BUNDLES OF GOODS ARE PREFERRED TO EXTREME BUNDLES

If indifference curves are convex (if they obey the assumption of a diminishing *MRS*), then the line joining any two points that are indifferent will contain points preferred to either of the initial combinations. Intuitively, balanced bundles are preferred to unbalanced ones.

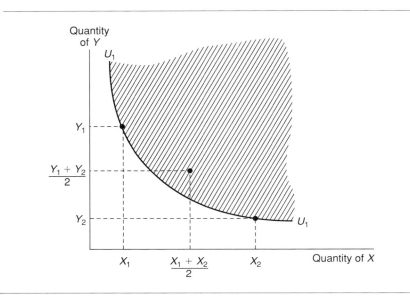

Convexity and Balance in Consumption

By using the notion of convexity, we can show that individuals prefer some balance in their consumption. Suppose that an individual is indifferent between the combination X_1, Y_1 and X_2, Y_2. If the indifference curve is strictly convex, then the combination $(X_1 + X_2)/2, (Y_1 + Y_2)/2$ will be preferred to either of the initial combinations.[5] Intuitively, "well-balanced" bundles of commodities are preferred to bundles that are heavily weighted toward one commodity. This is illustrated in Figure 3.6. Since the indifference curve is assumed to be convex, all points on the straight line joining (X_1, Y_1) and (X_2, Y_2) are preferred to these initial points. This therefore will be true of the point $(X_1 + X_2)/2, (Y_1 + Y_2)/2$, which lies at the midpoint of such a line. Indeed, any proportional combination of the two indifferent bundles of goods will be

---

[5] In the case in which the indifference curve has a linear segment, the individual will be indifferent among all three combinations.

preferred to the initial bundles, since it will represent a more balanced combination. Thus, strict convexity is equivalent to the assumption of a diminishing *MRS*. Both assumptions rule out the possibility of an indifference curve being straight over any portion of its length.

EXAMPLE 3.1

UTILITY AND THE *MRS*

Suppose a person's ranking of hamburgers (Y) and soft drinks (X) could be represented by the utility function

$$\text{utility} = \sqrt{X \cdot Y}. \tag{3.8}$$

An indifference curve for this function is found by identifying that set of combinations of X and Y for which utility has the same value. Suppose we arbitrarily set utility equal to 10. Then the equation for this indifference curve is

$$\text{utility} = 10 = \sqrt{X \cdot Y}. \tag{3.9}$$

Since squaring this function is order preserving, the indifference curve is also represented by

$$100 = X \cdot Y, \tag{3.10}$$

which is easier to graph. In Figure 3.7 we show this indifference curve—it is a familiar rectangular hyperbola. One way to calculate the *MRS* is to solve Equation 3.10 for Y,

$$Y = 100/X, \tag{3.11}$$

and then we use the definition (Equation 3.7):

$$MRS = -dY/dX \text{ (along } U_1) = 100/X^2. \tag{3.12}$$

This derivation shows that for a point such as A on the indifference curve with a lot of hamburgers (say, $X = 5$, $Y = 20$), the slope is steep so the *MRS* is high:

$$MRS \text{ at } (5, 20) = 100/X^2 = 100/25 = 4. \tag{3.13}$$

Here the person is willing to give up 4 hamburgers to get 1 more soft drink. On the other hand, at B where there are relatively few hamburgers (here $X = 20$, $Y = 5$), the slope is flat and the *MRS* is low:

$$MRS \text{ at } (20, 5) = 100/X^2 = 100/400 = 0.25. \tag{3.14}$$

Now he or she will only give up one-quarter of a hamburger for another soft drink.

FIGURE 3.7

INDIFFERENCE CURVE FOR UTILITY = $\sqrt{X \cdot Y}$

This indifference curve illustrates the function $10 = U = \sqrt{X \cdot Y}$. At point A (5, 20), the MRS is 4, implying that this person is willing to trade $4Y$ for an additional X. At point B (20, 5), however, the MRS is 0.25, implying a greatly reduced willingness to trade.

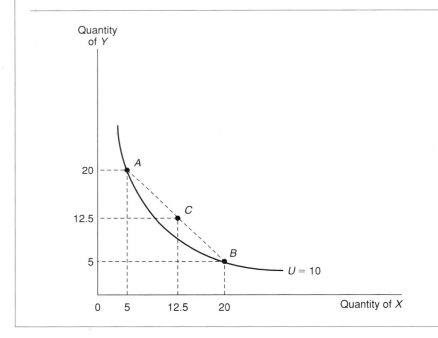

Notice also how convexity of the indifference curve U_1 is illustrated by this numerical example. Point C is midway between points A and B—at C this person has 12.5 hamburgers and 12.5 soft drinks. Here utility is given by

$$\text{utility} = \sqrt{X \cdot Y} = \sqrt{(12.5)^2} = 12.5, \qquad (3.15)$$

which clearly exceeds the utility along U_1 (which was assumed to be 10).

QUERY: From our derivation here, it appears that the MRS depends only on the quantity of X consumed. Why is this misleading? How does the quantity of Y implicitly enter into Equations 3.13 and 3.14? (See also Example 3.2.)

A somewhat more mathematical derivation of the *MRS* concept proceeds directly from the utility function itself. This derivation is helpful both for providing additional intuition about what the concept means and for illustrating how the *MRS* can be computed in specific examples.

AN ALTERNATIVE DERIVATION

Suppose that an individual ranks goods by a utility function of the form

Marginal Utility

$$\text{utility} = U(X_1, X_2, \ldots, X_n), \tag{3.16}$$

where $X_1, X_2, \ldots, X_n$ are the amounts of each of n goods X consumed. By the marginal utility of good X_1, we mean the function

$$\textbf{marginal utility of } X_1 = MU_{X_1} = \frac{\partial U}{\partial X_1}. \tag{3.17}$$

The marginal utility of X_1 is the extra utility obtained from slightly more X_1 while holding the amount of all other commodities constant. Obviously, the value of the marginal utility depends on the point at which the partial derivative is to be evaluated—it depends on how much $X_1, X_2, \ldots, X_n$ the individual is currently consuming. It also depends on the particular scale used to measure utility. Hence, the concept is not measurable in any unique way.

We can write the total differential of U as

$$dU = \frac{\partial U}{\partial X_1} dX_1 + \frac{\partial U}{\partial X_2} dX_2 + \cdots + \frac{\partial U}{\partial X_n} dX_n \tag{3.18}$$
$$= MU_{X_1} dX_1 + MU_{X_2} dX_2 + \cdots + MU_{X_n} dX_n.$$

Equation 3.18 says that the extra utility obtainable from slightly more X_1, $X_2, \ldots, X_n$ is simply the sum of the additional utility provided by each of these increments. Again, this value depends on how utility is measured.

Now consider changing only the level of two goods, X and Y, so as to keep the individual indifferent (that is, $dU = 0$). By Equation 3.18

Deriving the *MRS*

$$dU = 0 = \frac{\partial U}{\partial X} dX + \frac{\partial U}{\partial Y} dY = MU_X \, dX + MU_Y \, dY. \tag{3.19}$$

Notice that all other goods are held constant, hence dU is only affected by changing the quantities of the two goods in question. This is the same approach used in the development of indifference curves in the previous section.

Rearranging terms a bit gives

$$-\left.\frac{dY}{dX}\right|_{U=\text{constant}} = \frac{MU_X}{MU_Y} = \frac{\partial U/\partial X}{\partial U/\partial Y}, \tag{3.20}$$

where the notation is a reminder that Y and X are constrained to change so as to hold the level of utility constant.[6] But Equation 3.20 is simply the definition of the *MRS* given in Equation 3.7. Hence, the result of this section is that the marginal rate of substitution (of X for Y) is equal to the ratio of the marginal utility of X to the marginal utility of Y. That conclusion makes intuitive sense. Suppose that the marginal utility of an extra soft drink were 4 utils and that of an extra hamburger were 2 utils. Then the *MRS* (of soft drinks for hamburgers) should be 4 utils/2 utils = 2. The individual can trade two hamburgers for one extra soft drink and remain equally well off: The loss of hamburgers reduces utility by 4 utils, whereas the gain of a soft drink raises utility by 4 utils. Notice also that the units of utility measure (what we have, for lack of a better name, termed a util) drop out when constructing the *MRS*. This result is quite general—the *MRS* is independent of how utility is measured even though marginal utility itself is not.[7]

Diminishing Marginal Utility and the *MRS*

In Chapter 1 we described how the assumption of diminishing marginal utility was used by Marshall to solve the water-diamond paradox. Marshall theorized that it is the marginal valuation that an individual places on a good that determines its value: It is the amount that an individual is willing to pay for one more pint of water that determines the price of water. Since it might be thought that this marginal value declines as the quantity of water that is consumed increases, Marshall showed why water has a low exchange value. Intuitively, it seems clear that the assumption of the decreasing marginal utility of a good is related to the assumption of a decreasing *MRS*; both concepts seem to refer to the same commonsense idea of an individual becoming relatively satiated with a good as more of it is consumed. Unfortunately, the two concepts are quite different. (See Problem 3.7.) Technically, the assumption of a diminishing *MRS* is equivalent to requiring that the utility function be quasi-concave. This requirement is related in a

---

[6] Holding utility constant creates an implicit relationship between X and Y. Equation 3.20 shows how this implicit relationship can be differentiated. More formally, if $U(X, Y) - U_1 = 0$ is the implicit function for the indifference curve U_1, then $dY/dX = -U_x/U_y$. This method of differentiation is sometimes called the *implicit function rule* (see the discussion in Chapter 2).

[7] More formally, let $F(U)$ be any arbitrary order-preserving transformation of U (that is, $F'(U) > 0$). Then for the transformed utility function

$$MRS = \frac{\partial F/\partial X}{\partial F/\partial Y} = \frac{F'(U)\partial U/\partial X}{F'(U)\partial U/\partial Y}$$

$$= \frac{\partial U/\partial X}{\partial U/\partial Y},$$

which is the *MRS* for the original function U—the fact that the $F'(U)$ terms cancel out shows that the *MRS* is independent of how utility is measured.

rather complex way to the assumption that each good encounters diminishing marginal utility (that is, that f_{ii} is negative for each good).[8] But that is to be expected since the concept of diminishing marginal utility is not independent of how utility itself is measured, whereas the convexity of indifference curves is indeed independent of such measurement.

EXAMPLE 3.2

MARGINAL UTILITY AND THE *MRS*

In Example 3.1 we assumed that the utility provided by hamburgers (Y) and soft drinks (X) was given by

$$\text{utility} = U(X, Y) = \sqrt{X \cdot Y} = X^{.5}Y^{.5}. \tag{3.21}$$

Hence, the marginal utility from an additional soft drink is

---

[8] We have shown that if utility is given by $U = f(X, Y)$, then

$$MRS = \frac{f_X}{f_Y} = \frac{f_1}{f_2} = -\frac{dY}{dX}.$$

The assumption of a diminishing *MRS* means that $dMRS/dX < 0$, but

$$\frac{dMRS}{dX} = \frac{f_2(f_{11} + f_{12} \cdot dY/dX) - f_1(f_{21} + f_{22} \cdot dY/dX)}{f_2^2}.$$

Using the fact that $f_1/f_2 = -dY/dX$, we have

$$\frac{dMRS}{dX} = \frac{f_2[f_{11} - f_{12}(f_1/f_2)] - f_1[f_{21} - f_{22}(f_1/f_2)]}{f_2^2}.$$

Combining terms and recognizing that $f_{12} = f_{21}$ yields

$$\frac{dMRS}{dX} = \frac{f_2 f_{11} - 2f_1 f_{12} + (f_{22}f_1^2)/f_2}{f_2^2},$$

or, multiplying numerator and denominator by f_2,

$$\frac{dMRS}{dX} = \frac{f_2^2 f_{11} - 2f_1 f_2 f_{12} + f_1^2 f_{22}}{f_2^3}.$$

If we assume that $f_2 > 0$ (that marginal utility is positive), then the *MRS* will diminish provided that

$$f_2^2 f_{11} - 2f_1 f_2 f_{12} + f_1^2 f_{22} < 0.$$

Notice that diminishing marginal utility ($f_{11} < 0$ and $f_{22} < 0$) will not ensure this inequality. One must also be concerned with the f_{12} term. That is, one must know how decreases in Y affect the marginal utility of X. In general it is not possible to predict the sign of that term.

The condition required for a diminishing *MRS* is precisely that discussed in Chapter 2 to ensure that the function f is strictly quasi-concave. The condition shows that the necessary conditions for a maximum of f subject to a linear constraint are also sufficient. We will use this result in Chapter 4 and elsewhere.

$$\text{marginal utility} = MU_X = \partial U/\partial X = .5X^{-.5}Y^{.5}. \tag{3.22}$$

Notice that marginal utility declines as X increases and that, as is generally the case, the marginal utility for good X also depends on the amount of Y consumed. In this particular case the marginal utility from extra soft drinks (X) increases as the number of hamburgers (Y) increases, but that need not always be so.

The marginal utility for hamburgers is calculated in a similar way:

$$MU_Y = \partial U/\partial Y = .5X^{.5}Y^{-.5}. \tag{3.23}$$

Now we can use Equation 3.20 to calculate the *MRS*:

$$MRS = -\frac{dY}{dX}\bigg|_{U = \text{constant}} = \frac{MU_X}{MU_Y} = \frac{.5X^{-.5}Y^{.5}}{.5X^{.5}Y^{-.5}} = \frac{Y}{X}. \tag{3.24}$$

As before, at the point $X = 5$, $Y = 20$, Equation 3.24 shows that the *MRS* is 4.0, whereas at the point $X = 20$, $Y = 5$ it is 0.25.

Notice here that a monotonic transformation of this utility function does not affect the *MRS*. Suppose, for example, we used the natural logarithm of utility

$$ln\ (U) = ln\ (X^{.5}Y^{.5}) = .5(ln\ X) + .5(ln\ Y). \tag{3.25}$$

Hence:

$$MU_X = .5/X$$
$$MU_Y = .5/Y \tag{3.26}$$

and, as before,

$$MRS = \frac{MU_X}{MU_Y} = \frac{Y}{X}. \tag{3.27}$$

Frequently, using an appropriate transformation can make it much easier to solve problems involving utility functions. In cases where the units of measurement are meaningful (as for production functions—see Chapter 11), such an approach would be inappropriate, however.

QUERY: In what units is the *MRS* measured? Explain why Equation 3.24 is consistent in that each entry in it is measured as hamburgers foregone per extra soft drink consumed.

EXAMPLES OF UTILITY FUNCTIONS

Individuals' rankings of commodity bundles and the utility functions implied by these rankings are unobservable. All we can learn about people's preferences must come from the behavior we observe when they respond to changes in income, prices, and other factors. It is nevertheless useful to examine a few of the forms particular utility functions might take, both because such an examination may offer some insights into observed behavior and (more to the point) because understanding the properties of such functions can be of some help in solving problems. Here we will examine four specific examples of utility functions for two goods. Indifference curve maps for these functions are illustrated in the four panels of Figure 3.8. As should be visually apparent, these cover quite a few possible shapes. Even greater variety is possible once we move to functions for three or more goods, and some of these possibilities are mentioned in later chapters.

Figure 3.8a shows the familiar shape of an indifference curve. One commonly used utility function that generates such curves has the form

Cobb-Douglas Utility

$$\text{utility} = U(X, Y) = X^{\alpha}Y^{\beta}, \tag{3.28}$$

where α and β are positive constants.

In Examples 3.1 and 3.2, we studied a particular case of this function for which $\alpha = \beta = 0.5$. The more general case presented in Equation 3.28 is termed a *Cobb-Douglas utility function* after two researchers who used such a function for their detailed study of production relationships in the U.S. economy (see Chapter 11). In general, the relative sizes of α and β indicate the relative importance of the two goods to this individual. Since utility is unique only up to a monotonic transformation, it is often convenient to assume $\alpha + \beta = 1$.

The straight-line indifference curves in Figure 3.8b are generated by a utility function of the form

Perfect Substitutes

$$\text{utility} = U(X, Y) = \alpha X + \beta Y, \tag{3.29}$$

where, again, α and β are positive constants. That the indifference curves for this function are straight lines should be readily apparent: Any particular curve can be calculated by setting $U(X, Y)$ equal to a constant that, given the linear form of the function, clearly specifies a straight line. The linear nature of these indifference curves gave rise to the term *perfect substitutes* to describe the implied relationship between X and Y. Because the *MRS* is constant (and equal to α/β) along the entire indifference curve, our previous notions of a diminishing *MRS* do not apply in this case. A person with these preferences would be willing to give up the same amount of Y to get one more X no matter how much X was being consumed. Such a situation might describe the relationship between different brands of what is essentially the same product. For example, many people (including the author) don't care where they buy gasoline. A gallon of gas is a gallon of gas in spite of the best efforts of the Exxon and Mobil advertising departments to convince me otherwise. Given this fact, I am always willing to give up 10 gallons of Exxon in exchange for 10 gallons of Mobil because it doesn't matter to me which I use or where I got my

FIGURE 3.8

EXAMPLES OF UTILITY FUNCTIONS

The four indifference curve maps illustrate alternative degrees of substitutability of X for Y. The
Cobb-Douglas and CES functions (drawn here for
relatively low substitutability) fall between the
extremes of perfect substitution (panel b) and no
substitution (panel c).

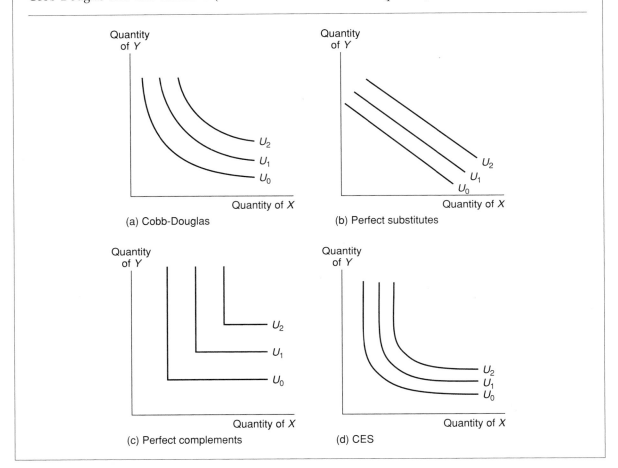

(a) Cobb-Douglas

(b) Perfect substitutes

(c) Perfect complements

(d) CES

last tankful. Indeed, as we will see in the next chapter, one implication
of such a relationship is that I will buy all my gas from the least expensive
seller. Since I don't experience a diminishing *MRS* of Exxon for Mobil,
I have no reason to seek a balance among the gasoline types I use.

A situation directly opposite to the case of perfect substitutes is illustrated by the L-shaped indifference curves in Figure 3.8c. These preferences would apply to goods that "go together"—coffee and cream, peanut butter and jelly, or cream cheese and lox would be familiar examples. The indifference curves shown in Figure 3.8c imply that these pairs of goods will be used in the fixed proportional relationship represented by the vertices of the curves. A person who prefers 1 ounce of cream with 8 ounces of coffee will want 2 ounces of cream with 16 ounces of coffee. Extra coffee without cream is of no value to this person, just as extra cream would be of no value without coffee. Only by choosing the goods together can utility be increased.

Perfect Complements

These concepts can be formalized by examining the mathematical form of the utility function that generates these L-shaped indifference curves:

$$\text{utility} = U(X, Y) = \min\ (\alpha X, \beta Y). \tag{3.30}$$

Here α and β are positive parameters, and the operator "min" means that utility is given by the smaller of the two terms in the parentheses. In the coffee-cream example, if we let ounces of coffee be represented by X and ounces of cream by Y, utility would be given by

$$\text{utility} = U(X, Y) = \min\ (X, 8Y). \tag{3.31}$$

Now 8 ounces of coffee and 1 ounce of cream provide 8 units of utility. But 16 ounces of coffee and 1 ounce of cream also provide only 8 units of utility because min $(16, 8) = 8$. The extra coffee without cream is of no value as shown by the horizontal section of the indifference curves for movement away from a vertex—utility does not increase when only X increases (with Y constant). Only if coffee and cream are both doubled (to 16 and 2, respectively) will utility increase to 16.

More generally, neither of the two goods in Equation 3.30 will be in excess only if

$$\alpha X = \beta Y. \tag{3.32}$$

Hence,

$$Y/X = \alpha/\beta, \tag{3.33}$$

which shows the fixed proportional relationship between the two goods that must occur if choices are to be at the vertices of the indifference curves.

The three specific utility functions illustrated so far are all special cases of the more general constant elasticity of substitution function (CES), which takes the form:

CES Utility

$$\text{utility} = U(X, Y) = \frac{X^\delta}{\delta} + \frac{Y^\delta}{\delta} \tag{3.34}$$

when $\delta \neq 0$ and

$$\text{utility} = U(X, Y) = \ln X + \ln Y \tag{3.35}$$

when $\delta = 0$. It is obvious that the case of perfect substitutes (Equation 3.29) corresponds to $\delta = 1$ in Equation 3.34 and that the Cobb-Douglas[9] case corresponds to $\delta = 0$ in Equation 3.35. Less obvious is that the case of fixed proportions (Equation 3.30) corresponds to $\delta = -\infty$ in Equation 3.34, but that result can also be shown using a limits argument.

The use of the term "elasticity of substitution" for this function derives from the notion that the possibilities illustrated in Figure 3.8 correspond to various values for the substitution parameter, σ, which for this function is given by $\sigma = 1/(1 - \delta)$. For perfect substitutes then $\sigma = \infty$, and the fixed proportions case has $\sigma = 0$.[10] Because the CES function allows us to explore all of these cases, and many cases in between, it will prove quite useful for illustrating the degree of substitutability present in various economic relationships.

The specific shape of the CES function illustrated in panel d of Figure 3.8 is for the case, $\delta = -1$: That is,

$$\text{utility} = -X^{-1} - Y^{-1} = -\frac{1}{X} - \frac{1}{Y}. \tag{3.36}$$

For this situation, $\sigma = \frac{1}{1-\delta} = \frac{1}{2}$, and as the graph shows, these sharply curved indifference curves apparently fall between the Cobb-Douglas and fixed proportion cases. The negative signs in Equation 3.36 may seem strange, but the marginal utilities of both X and Y are positive and diminishing, as would be expected. This explains why δ must appear in the denominators in Equation 3.34. In the particular case of Equation 3.36, utility increases from $-\infty$ (when $X = Y = 0$) toward 0 as X and Y increase. This is an odd utility scale, perhaps, but perfectly acceptable.

EXAMPLE 3.3

HOMOTHETIC PREFERENCES

All of the utility functions described in Figure 3.8 are "homothetic"—that is, the marginal rate of substitution for these functions depends only on the *ratio*

---

[9] The CES function could easily be generalized to allow for differing weights to be attached to the two goods. Since the main use of the function is to examine substitution questions, we will usually not make that generalization. In many of the applications of the CES function, we will also omit the denominators of the function since these constitute only a scale factor.

[10] The elasticity of substitution concept is discussed in more detail in Chapter 11.

of the amounts of the two goods, not on the total quantities of the goods. This fact is obvious for the case of the perfect substitutes (when the MRS is the same at every point) and the case of perfect complements (where the MRS is infinite for $Y/X > \alpha/\beta$, undefined when $Y/X = \alpha/\beta$, and zero when $Y/X < \alpha/\beta$. For the Cobb-Douglas function, the MRS can be found by calculating the marginal utilities

$$MU_X = \frac{\partial U}{\partial X} = \alpha X^{\alpha-1} Y^{\beta}$$

$$MU_Y = \frac{\partial U}{\partial Y} = \beta X^{\alpha} Y^{\beta-1}$$

(3.37)

and then taking the ratio of these two terms,

$$MRS = \frac{MU_X}{MU_Y} = \frac{\alpha X^{\alpha-1} Y^{\beta}}{\beta X^{\alpha} Y^{\beta-1}} = \frac{\alpha}{\beta}(Y/X),$$

(3.38)

which clearly depends only on the ratio Y/X. Showing that the CES function is also homothetic is left as an exercise (see Problem 3.10).

The importance of homothetic functions is that in such a situation, one indifference curve is much like another. Slopes of the curves depend only on the ratio Y/X, not on how far the curve is from the origin. Indifference curves for higher utility are simple copies of those for lower utility. Hence, we can study the behavior of an individual who has homothetic preferences by looking only at one indifference curve or at a few nearby curves without fearing that our results would change at very different levels of utility.

QUERY: How might you define homothetic functions geometrically? What would the locus of all points with a particular MRS look like on an individual's indifference curve map?

EXAMPLE 3.4

NONHOMOTHETIC PREFERENCES

Although all of the indifference curve maps in Figure 3.8 exhibit homothetic preferences, this need not always be true. Consider the utility function

$$utility = U(X, Y) = X + \ln Y.$$

(3.39)

Now good Y exhibits a diminishing marginal utility:

$$MU_Y = \partial U/\partial Y = 1/Y,$$

but for X marginal utility is constant:

$$MU_X = \partial U/\partial X = 1.$$

Hence,

$$MRS = MU_X/MU_Y = Y.$$

The *MRS* diminishes as the quantity chosen of *Y* decreases, but it is independent of the quantity of *X* consumed. Since *X* has a constant marginal utility, a person's willingness to give up *Y* to get one more unit of *X* only depends on how much *Y* he or she has. Contrary to the homothetic case, then, a doubling of *X* and *Y* doubles the *MRS* here rather than leaving it unchanged.

QUERY: What does the indifference curve map for the utility function in Equation 3.39 look like? Can you think of any situations that might be described by such a function?

Generalizations to More Than Two Goods

All of these specific utility functions can easily be generalized to many goods. For example, a many-good Cobb-Douglas function might be written as

$$\text{utility} = U(X_1, X_2, \ldots, X_n) = X_1^{\beta_1} X_2^{\beta_2} \ldots X_n^{\beta_n},$$

or a many-good case of perfect substitutes might be written as

$$\text{utility} = U(X_1, X_2, \ldots, X_n) = \beta_1 X_1 + \beta_2 X_2 + \cdots + \beta_n X_n,$$

where for both cases the β's are all positive constants. Notions of indifference surfaces and marginal rates of substitution can also be discussed for these functions using the definitions we already have. Some of the problems in this and later chapters ask students to make use of such many-good functions.

SUMMARY

In this chapter we have described the way in which economists formalize individuals' preferences about the goods they choose. We drew several conclusions about such preferences that will play a central role in our analysis of the theory of choice in the following chapters:

- If individuals obey certain basic behavioral postulates in their preferences among goods, they will be able to rank all commodity bundles, and that ranking can be represented by a utility function. In

making choices, individuals will behave as if they were maximizing this function.

- Utility functions for two goods can be illustrated by an indifference curve map. Each indifference curve contour on this map shows all the commodity bundles that yield a given level of utility.

- The negative of the slope of an indifference curve is defined to be the marginal rate of substitution (*MRS*). This shows the rate at which an individual would willingly give up an amount of one good (*Y*) if he or she were compensated by receiving one more unit of another good (X).

■ The assumption that the MRS decreases as X is substituted for Y in consumption is consistent with the notion that individuals prefer some balance in their consumption choices. If the MRS is always decreasing, individuals will have strictly convex indifference curves.

■ A few simple functional forms can capure important differences in individuals' preferences for two (or more) goods. Here we examined the Cobb-Douglas function, the linear function (perfect substitutes), the fixed proportions func-

tion (perfect complements), and the CES function (which includes the other three as special cases).

■ The MRS can also be represented as the ratio of the marginal utility of one good to that of another good. Although the marginal utility concept itself is not especially useful (because it can be affected by how utility is measured), it is quite helpful in deriving the MRS in some cases. Because the MRS itself is the ratio of marginal utilities, it is not affected by the way in which utility is measured. In formal terms, utility functions will be (strictly) quasi-concave.

PROBLEMS

3.1
Laidback Al derives utility from 3 goods: music (M), wine (W), and cheese (C). His utility function is of the simple linear form

$$\text{utility} = U(M, W, C) = M + 2W + 3C.$$

a. Assuming Al's consumption of music is fixed at 10, determine the equations for the indifference curves for W and C for $U = 40$ and $U = 70$. Sketch these curves.
b. Show that Al's MRS of wine for cheese is constant for all values of W and C on the indifference curves calculated in part (a).
c. Suppose Al's consumption of music increases to 20. How would this change your answers to parts (a) and (b)? Explain your results intuitively.

3.2
Suppose the utility function for two goods, X and Y, has the Cobb-Douglas form

$$\text{utility} = U(X, Y) = \sqrt{X \cdot Y}.$$

a. Graph the $U = 10$ indifference curve associated with this utility function.
b. If $X = 5$, what must Y equal to be on the $U = 10$ indifference curve? What is the MRS at this point?
c. In general, develop an expression for the MRS for this utility function. Show how this can be inter-

preted as the ratio of the marginal utilities for X and Y.
d. Consider a logarithmic transformation of this utility function:

$$U' = \log U$$

where log is the logarithmic function to base 10. Show that for this transformation the $U' = 1$ indifference curve has the same properties as the $U = 10$ curve calculated in parts (a) and (b). What is the general expression for the MRS of this transformed utility function?

3.3
Georgia always eats hot dogs in a bun together with 1 oz. of mustard. Each hot dog eaten in this way provides 15 units of utility, but any other combination of hot dogs, buns, and mustard is worthless to Georgia.
a. Explain the nature of Georgia's utility function and indicate the form of her indifference curve map.
b. Suppose hot dogs cost $1, buns cost $.40, and mustard costs $.10 per ounce. Show how Georgia's utility can be represented by the total amount of money she spends on these three items.
c. How would your answer to part (b) change if the price of hot dogs rose to $1.50?

3.4
For each of the following expressions, state the formal

assumption that is being made about the individual's utility function:

a. It (margarine) is just as good as the high-priced spread (butter).
b. Peanut butter and jelly go together like a horse and carriage.
c. Things go better with Coke.
d. Popcorn is addictive—the more you eat, the more you want.
e. Mosquitoes ruin a nice day at the beach.
f. A day without wine is like a day without sunshine.
g. It takes two to tango.

3.5

Graph a typical indifference curve for the following utility functions and determine whether they have convex indifference curves (that is, whether they obey the assumption of a diminishing *MRS*):

a. $U = 3X + Y$.
b. $U = \sqrt{X \cdot Y}$.
c. $U = \sqrt{X^2 + Y^2}$.
d. $U = \sqrt{X^2 - Y^2}$.
e. $U = X^{2/3} Y^{1/3}$.
f. $U = \log X + \log Y$.

3.6

In footnote 8 of Chapter 3, we showed that in order for a utility function for two goods to have a strictly diminishing *MRS* (that is, to be strictly quasi-concave), the following condition must hold:

$$f_2^2 f_{11} - 2f_1 f_2 f_{12} + f_1^2 f_{22} < 0.$$

Use this condition to check the convexity of the indifference curves for each of the utility functions in Problem 3.5. Describe any shortcuts you discover in this process.

3.7

Consider the following utility functions:

a. $U(X, Y) = XY$.
b. $U(X, Y) = X^2 Y^2$.
c. $U(X, Y) = \ln X + \ln Y$.

Show that each of these has a diminishing *MRS*, but that they exhibit constant, increasing, and decreasing marginal utility, respectively. What do you conclude?

3.8

Example 3.3 shows that the *MRS* for the Cobb-Douglas function

$$U(X, Y) = X^\alpha Y^\beta$$

is given by

$$MRS = \frac{\alpha}{\beta} (Y/X).$$

a. Does this result depend on whether $\alpha + \beta = 1$? Does this sum have any relevance to the theory of choice?
b. For commodity bundles for which $Y = X$, how does the *MRS* depend on the values of α and β? Develop an intuitive explanation of why if $\alpha > \beta$, $MRS > 1$. Illustrate your argument with a graph.
c. Suppose an individual obtains utility only from amounts of X and Y that exceed minimal subsistence levels given by X_0, Y_0. In this case,

$$U(X, Y) = (X - X_0)^\alpha (Y - Y_0)^\beta.$$

Is this function homothetic? (For a further discussion, see the extensions to Chapter 4.)

3.9

Two goods have independent marginal utilities if

$$\frac{\partial^2 U}{\partial Y \partial X} = \frac{\partial^2 U}{\partial X \partial Y} = 0.$$

Show that if we assume diminishing marginal utility for each good, then any utility function with independent marginal utilities will have a diminishing *MRS*. Provide an example to show that the converse of this statement is not true.

3.10

a. Show that the CES function

$$\alpha \frac{X^\delta}{\delta} + \beta \frac{Y^\delta}{\delta}$$

is homothetic. How does the *MRS* depend on the ratio Y/X?
b. Show that your results from part (a) agree with Example 3.3 for the case $\delta = 1$ (perfect substitutes) and $\delta = 0$ (Cobb-Douglas).
c. Show that the *MRS* is strictly diminishing for all values of $\delta < 1$.
d. Show that if $X = Y$, the *MRS* for this function depends only on the relative sizes of α and β.

e. Calculate the *MRS* for this function when $Y/X = .9$ and $Y/X = 1.1$ for the two cases $\delta = .5$ and $\delta = -1$. What do you conclude about the extent to which the *MRS* changes in the vicinity of $X = Y$? How would you interpret this geometrically?

SUGGESTED READINGS

Barten, Anton P., and Volker Böhm. "Consumer Theory." In K. J. Arrow and M. D. Intriligator, eds. *Handbook of Mathematical Economics.* Vol. II. Amsterdam: North-Holland Publishing Co., 1982.
Sections 4–6 have a concise statement of the relationship between preference ordering and utility.

Katzner, Donald W. *Static Demand Theory.* New York: The Macmillan Company, 1970. Chaps. 2 and 3.
Theoretical treatment of preferences and of the conditions under which preferences can be represented by a utility function.

Kreps, David M. *A Course in Microeconomic Theory.* Princeton, NJ: Princeton University Press, 1990.
Chapter 1 covers preference theory in some detail. Good discussion of quasi-concavity.

Kreps, David M. *Notes on the Theory of Choice.* London: Westview Press, 1988.
Good discussion of the foundations of preference theory.

Most of the focus of the book is on utility in uncertain situations.

Mas-Colell, Andreu, Michael D. Whinston, and Jerry R. Green. *Microeconomic Theory.* New York: Oxford University Press, 1995.
Chapters 2 and 3 provide a detailed development of preference relations and their representation by utility functions.

Marshall, A. *Principles of Economics.* 8th ed. London: Macmillan & Co., Ltd., 1920. Chaps. I–IV. Book III.
Early basic text. Still a very readable and interesting treatment of consumer theory.

Stigler, G. "The Development of Utility Theory." *Journal of Political Economy* 59, pts. 1–2 (August/ October 1950): 307–327, 373–396.
A lucid and complete survey of the history of utility theory. Has many interesting insights and asides.

EXTENSIONS

Special Preferences

The utility function concept is a quite general one that can be adapted to a large number of special circumstances. Discovery of ingenious functional forms that reflect the essential aspects of some problem can provide a number of insights that would not be readily apparent with a more literary approach. Here we look at three aspects of preferences that economists have tried to portray with special functional forms: (1) quality; (2) habits and addictions; and (3) second-party preferences.

E3.1 Quality

Because many consumption items differ widely in quality, economists have an interest in incorporating such differences into models of choice. One approach is simply to regard items of different quality as totally separate goods that are relatively close substitutes. But this approach can be unwieldy because of the large number of goods involved. An alternative approach focuses on quality as a direct item of choice. Utility might in this case be reflected by

$$\text{Utility} = U(q, Q) \qquad \text{(i)}$$

where q is the quantity consumed and Q is the quality of that consumption. Although this approach permits some examination of quality-quantity trade-offs, it encounters difficulty when the quantity consumed of a commodity (e.g., wine) consists of a variety of qualities. Quality might then be defined as an average (see Theil, 1982), but that approach may not be appropriate when the quality of new goods is changing rapidly (as in the case of personal computers, for example). A more general approach (originally suggested by Lancaster, 1971) focuses on a well-defined set of attributes of goods and assumes that those attributes provide utility. If a good q provides two such attributes, a_1 and a_2, then utility might be written as

$$\text{Utility} = U[q, a_1(q), a_2(q)] \qquad \text{(ii)}$$

and utility improvements might arise either because this individual chooses a larger quantity of the good or because a given quantity yields a higher level of valuable attributes.

Personal Computers

This is the practice followed by economists who study demand in such rapidly changing industries as personal computers. In this case it would be clearly incorrect to focus only on the quantity of personal computers purchased each year, since new machines are much better than old ones (and, presumably, provide more utility). For example, Berndt, Griliches, and Rappaport (1995) find that personal computer quality has been rising about 30 percent per year over a relatively long period of time primarily because of improved attributes such as faster processors or better hard drives. A person who spends, say, $2,000 for a personal computer today buys much more utility than did a similar consumer 5 years ago.

E3.2 Habits and Addiction

Because consumption occurs over time, there is the possibility that decisions made in one period will affect utility in later periods. Habits are formed when individuals discover they enjoy using a commodity in one period and this increases their consumption in subsequent periods. An extreme case is addiction (be it to drugs, cigarettes, or Marx Brothers movies) where

past consumption significantly increases the utility of present consumption. One way to portray these ideas mathematically is to assume that utility in period t depends on consumption in period t and on the total of all prior consumption of the habit-forming good (say X):

$$\text{Utility} = U_t(X_t, Y_t, S_t) \qquad \text{(iii)}$$

where $S_t = \sum_{i=1}^{\infty} X_{t-i}$.

This approach has been used by Stigler and Becker (1977) to explain why individuals develop tastes for activities such as playing golf or attending operas and by Becker and Murphy (1988), who used these ideas to explain the binges of drug addicts and why cold turkey strategies may be required to control addiction.

Cigarettes

Use of the most important applications of this approach has been to the study of cigarette smoking. For example, Becker, Grossman, and Murphy (1994) show current cigarette consumption depends importantly on past consumption. Hence, policies intended to affect smoking must pay careful attention to the dynamics of the situation. The authors show, for example, that cigarette taxes may have a much larger effect on consumption over the long term than they do immediately. The belief that such consumption is determined by a utility function such as that in Equation iii also provides a strong rationale for adopting policies that discourage smoking by children.

E3.3 Second Party Preferences

Individuals clearly care about the well-being of other individuals. Phenomena such as making charitable contributions or making bequests to children cannot be understood without recognizing the interdependence that exists among people. Such preferences can be incorporated into the utility function of person i say, by

$$\text{Utility} = U_i(X_i, Y_i, U_j), \qquad \text{(iv)}$$

where U_j is the utility of someone else.

If $\partial U_i/\partial U_j > 0$ this person will engage in altruistic behavior, whereas if $\partial U_i/\partial U_j < 0$ he or she will demonstrate the malevolent behavior associated with envy. The usual case of $\partial U_i / \partial U_j = 0$ is then simply a middle ground between these alternative preference types. Gary Becker has been a pioneer in the study of these possiblities and has written on a variety of topics, including the general theory of social interactions (1976) and the importance of altruism in the theory of the family (1981).

Evolutionary Biology and Genetics

Biologists have suggested a particular form for the utility function in Equation iv, drawn from the theory of genetics. In this case

$$\text{Utility} = U_i (X_1, Y_i) + \sum_j r_j U_j \qquad \text{(v)}$$

where r_j measures closeness of the genetic relationship between person i and person j. For parents and children, for example, $r_j = .5$, whereas for cousins $r_j = .125$. Bergstrom (1996) describes a few of the conclusions about evolutionary behavior that biologists have drawn from this particular functional form.

References

Becker, Gary S. *The Economic Approach to Human Behavior.* Chicago: The University of Chicago Press, 1976.

———. *A Treatise on the Family.* Cambridge, MA: Harvard University Press, 1981.

Becker, Gary S., Michael Grossman, and Kevin M. Murphy. "An Empirical Analysis of Cigarette Addiction." *American Economic Review* (June 1994): 396–418.

Becker, Gary S., and Kevin M. Murphy. "A Theory of Rational Addiction." *Journal of Political Economy* (August 1988): 675–700.

Bergstrom, Theodore C. "Economics in a Family Way." *Journal of Economic Literature* (December 1996): 1903–1934.

Berndt, Erst R., Zvi Griliches, and Neal J. Rappaport. "Econometric Estimates of Price Indexes for Personal Computers in the 1990s." *Journal of Econometrics* (July 1995): 243–268.

Lancaster, Kelvin J. *Consumer Demand: A New Approach.* New York: Columbia University Press, 1971.

Stigler, George J., and Gary S. Becker. "De Gustibus Non Est Disputandum." *American Economic Review* (March 1977): 76–90.

Theil, Henri. "Qualities, Prices, and Budget Enquiries." *Review of Economic Studies* (April 1952): 129–147.

CHAPTER 4

UTILITY MAXIMIZATION AND CHOICE

In this chapter we will examine the basic model of choice that econo-mists use to explain individuals' behavior. That model assumes that individuals who are constrained by limited incomes will behave as if they were using their purchasing power in such a way as to achieve the highest utility possible. That is, individuals are assumed to behave as if they maximized utility subject to a budget constraint. Although the specific applications of this model are quite varied, as we will show, all of them are based on the same fundamental mathematical model, and all arrive at the same general conclusion: In order to maximize utility, individuals will choose bundles of commodities for which the rate of trade-off among those commodities (the *MRS*) reflects the commodities' market prices. Market prices convey information about opportunity costs to individuals, and this information plays an important role in affecting the choices actually made.

Utility Maximization and Lightning Calculations

Before starting our formal study of the theory of choice, it may be appropriate to dispose of two complaints noneconomists often make about the approach we will take. First is the charge that no real person can make the kinds of "lightning calculations" required for utility maximization. According to this complaint, when moving down a supermarket aisle, people just grab what is available with no real pattern or purpose to their actions. Economists are not persuaded by this complaint. They doubt that people behave randomly (everyone, after all, is bound by some sort of budget constraint), and they view the lightning calculation charge as misplaced. Recall, again, Friedman's pool player. He or she also cannot make the lightning calculations required to plan a shot according to the laws of physics, but those laws still predict the player's behavior. So too, as we shall see, the utility-maximization model predicts many aspects of behavior even though no one carries around a computer with his or her utility function programmed into it. To be precise, economists assume that people behave *as if* they made such calculations, so the complaint that the calculations cannot possibly be made is irrelevant.

Altruism and Selfishness

A second complaint against our model of choice is that it appears to be extremely selfish—no one, according to this complaint, has such solely self-centered goals. Although economists are probably more ready to accept self-interest as a motivating force than are some other, more Utopian thinkers (Adam Smith observed, "We are not ready to suspect any person of being deficient in selfishness"[1]), this charge is also misplaced. Nothing in the utility-maximization model prevents individuals from deriving satisfaction from philanthropy or generally "doing good." These activities also can be assumed to provide utility. Indeed, economists have used the utility-maximization model extensively to study such issues as donating time and money to charity, leaving bequests to children, or even giving blood. One need not take a position on whether such activities are "selfish" or "selfless" since economists doubt people would undertake them if they were against their own best interests, broadly conceived.

AN INITIAL SURVEY

Before starting our formal study of the utility-maximization model, it may be useful to indicate where we are going. The general results of our examination can be stated succinctly:

OPTIMIZATION PRINCIPLE

Utility Maximization   In order to maximize utility, given a fixed amount of money to spend, an individual will buy those quantities of goods that exhaust his or her total income and for which the psychic rate of trade-off between any two goods (the *MRS*) is equal to the rate at which the goods can be traded one for the other in the marketplace.

That spending all one's income is required for utility maximization is obvious. Since extra goods provide extra utility (there is no satiation) and since there is no other use for income (there is no saving in this model), to leave any unspent would be to fail to maximize utility. Throwing money away is not a utility-maximizing activity.

---

[1] Adam Smith, *The Theory of Moral Sentiments* (1759; reprint, New Rochelle, NY: Arlington House, 1969), p. 446.

The condition specifying equality of trade-off rates requires a bit more explanation. Since the rate at which one good can be traded for another in the market is given by the ratio of their prices, this result can be restated to say that the individual will equate the *MRS* (of X for Y) to the ratio of the price of X to the price of Y (P_X/P_Y). This equating of a personal trade-off rate to a market trade-off rate is a result common to all individual utility-maximization problems (and to many other types of maximization problems). It will occur again and again throughout this text.

A Numerical Illustration   To see the intuitive reasoning behind this result, assume that it were not true that the individual had equated the *MRS* to the ratio of the prices of goods. Specifically, assume that the individual's *MRS* is equal to 1, that he or she is willing to trade 1 unit of X for 1 unit of Y and remain equally well off. Assume also that the price of X is $2 per unit and of Y is $1 per unit. It is easy to show in this case that the individual can be made better off. Give up 1 unit of X and trade it in the market for 2 units of Y. Only 1 extra unit of Y was needed to keep the individual as happy as before the trade—the second unit of Y is a net addition to well-being. Therefore, the individual's spending could not have been allocated optimally in the first place. A similar method of reasoning can be used whenever the *MRS* and the price ratio P_X/P_Y differ. The condition for maximum utility must be the equality of these two magnitudes.

THE TWO-GOOD CASE: A GRAPHICAL ANALYSIS   This discussion seems eminently reasonable, but it can hardly be called a proof. Rather, we must now show the result in a rigorous manner and, at the same time, illustrate several other important attributes of the maximization process. First, using a graphic approach, we illustrate utility maximization for the two-good case. We begin with an analysis of the budget constraint.

Budget Constraint   Assume that the individual has *I* dollars to allocate between good X and good Y. If P_X is the price of good X and P_Y is the price of good Y, then the individual is constrained by

$$P_X X + P_Y Y \leq I. \tag{4.1}$$

That is, no more than *I* can be spent on the two goods in question. This budget constraint is shown graphically in Figure 4.1. The individual can only afford to choose combinations of X and Y in the shaded triangle of the figure. If all of *I* is spent on good X, it will buy I/P_X units of X. Similarly, if all is spent on Y, it will buy I/P_Y units of Y. The slope of the constraint is easily seen to be $-P_X/P_Y$.

FIGURE 4.1

THE INDIVIDUAL'S BUDGET CONSTRAINT FOR TWO GOODS

Those combinations of X and Y that the individual can afford are shown in the shaded triangle. If, as we usually assume, the individual prefers more rather than less of every good, the outer boundary of this triangle is the relevant constraint where all of the available funds are spent either on X or on Y. The slope of this straight-line boundary is given by $-P_X/P_Y$.

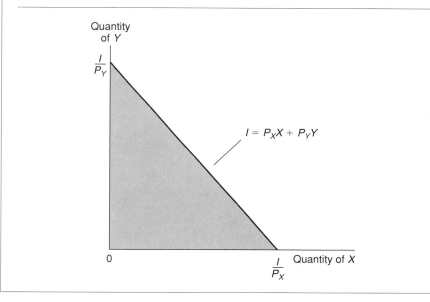

EXAMPLE 4.1

A BUDGET CONSTRAINT

Let's look at a very simple example. Suppose hamburgers (Y) sell for $1 each and soft drinks ($X$) cost $.25. If an individual has $2.00 to spend, the constraint (assuming all of the $2.00 is spent) would be

$$.25X + Y = 2.00$$

or

$$Y = -.25X + 2. \tag{4.2}$$

Here the Y-intercept shows that this person could buy 2 hamburgers with $2 providing $X = 0$. If the person buys 4 soft drinks, $Y = 1$ since he or she now has only $1 to spend on hamburgers. The coefficient of X here ($-.25$) shows that the *opportunity cost* of consuming one more soft drink is one-fourth of a hamburger.

QUERY: What would a budget constraint look like for three goods (say, X, Y, and Z)? If this equation is solved for Y, how should the coefficients of X and Z be interpreted?

First-Order Conditions for a Maximum

The budget constraint can be imposed on the individual's indifference curve map to show the utility-maximization process. Figure 4.2 illustrates this procedure. The individual would be irrational to choose a point such as A— he or she can get to a higher utility level just by spending some of the unspent portion of income. The assumption of nonsatiation implies that a person

FIGURE 4.2

A GRAPHICAL DEMONSTRATION OF UTILITY MAXIMIZATION

Point C represents the highest utility level that can be reached by the individual, given the budget constraint. The combination X^*, Y^* is therefore the rational way for the individual to allocate purchasing power. Only for this combination of goods will two conditions hold: All available funds will be spent; and the individual's psychic rate of trade-off (MRS) will be equal to the rate at which the goods can be traded in the market (P_X/P_Y).

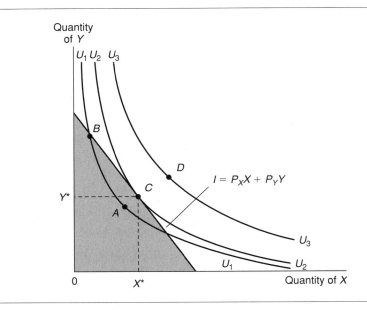

should spend all of his or her income in order to receive maximum utility from it. Similarly, by reallocating expenditures, the individual can do better than point B. Point D is out of the question because income is not large enough to purchase D. It is clear that the position of maximum utility is at point C, where the combination X^*, Y^* is chosen. This is the only point on indifference curve U_2 that can be bought with I dollars; no higher utility level can be bought. C is a point of tangency between the budget constraint and the indifference curve. Therefore at C,

$$\text{slope of budget constraint} = \frac{-P_X}{P_Y} = \text{slope of indifference curve}$$

$$= \frac{dY}{dX}\bigg|_{U = \text{constant}}$$

or

$$\frac{P_X}{P_Y} = -\frac{dY}{dX}\bigg|_{U = \text{constant}} = \text{MRS (of } X \text{ for } Y). \tag{4.3}$$

Our intuitive result is proved—for a utility maximum, all income should be spent and the MRS should equal the ratio of the prices of the goods. It is obvious from the diagram that if this condition is not fulfilled, the individual could be made better off by reallocating expenditures.

The tangency rule is only a necessary condition for a maximum. To see that it is not a sufficient condition, consider the indifference curve map shown in Figure 4.3. Here a point of tangency (C) is inferior to a point of nontangency (B). Indeed, the true maximum is at another point of tangency (A). The failure of the tangency condition to produce an unambiguous maximum can be attributed to the shape of the indifference curves in Figure 4.3. If the indifference curves are shaped like those in Figure 4.2, no such problem can arise. But we have already shown that "normally" shaped indifference curves result from the assumption of a diminishing MRS. Therefore, if the MRS is assumed to be diminishing, the condition of tangency is both a necessary and sufficient condition for a maximum.[2] Without this assumption one would have to be careful in applying the tangency rule.

Second-Order Conditions for a Maximum

The utility-maximization problem illustrated in Figure 4.2 resulted in an "interior" maximum, in which positive amounts of both goods were

Corner Solutions

---

[2] In mathematical terms, because the assumption of a diminishing MRS is equivalent to assuming quasi-concavity, the necessary conditions for a maximum subject to a linear constraint are also sufficient, as we showed in Chapter 2.

FIGURE 4.3

EXAMPLE OF AN INDIFFERENCE CURVE MAP FOR WHICH THE TANGENCY CONDITION DOES NOT ENSURE A MAXIMUM

If indifference curves do not obey the assumption of a diminishing *MRS*, not all points of tangency (points for which $MRS = P_X/P_Y$) may truly be points of maximum utility. In this example tangency point C is inferior to many other points, which can also be purchased with the available funds. In order that the necessary conditions for a maximum (that is, the tangency conditions) also be sufficient, one usually assumes that the *MRS* is diminishing; that is, the utility function is strictly quasi-concave.

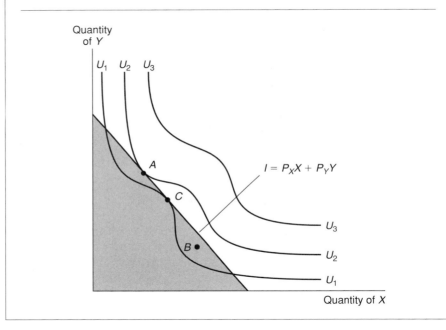

consumed. In some situations individuals' preferences may be such that they can obtain maximum utility by choosing to consume no amount of one of the goods. If someone does not like hamburgers very much, there is no reason to allocate any income to their purchase. This possibility is reflected in Figure 4.4. There utility is maximized at E, where $X = X^*$ and $Y = 0$—any point on the budget constraint where positive amounts of Y are consumed yields a lower utility than does point E. Notice that at E the budget constraint is not precisely tangent to the indifference curve U_2. Instead, at the optimal point the budget constraint is flatter than U_2, indicating that the rate at which X can be traded for Y in the market is lower than the individual's psychic trade-off

FIGURE 4.4

CORNER SOLUTION FOR UTILITY MAXIMIZATION

With the preferences represented by this set of indifference curves, utility maximization occurs at E, where 0 amounts of good Y are consumed. The first-order conditions for a maximum must be modified somewhat to accommodate this possibility.

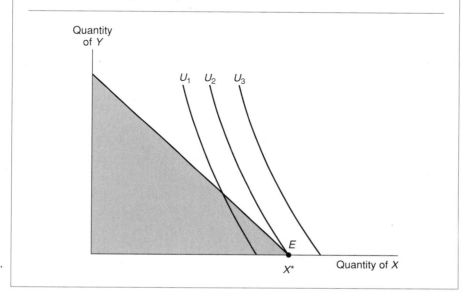

rate (the *MRS*). At prevailing market prices the individual is more than willing to trade away Y to get extra X. Because it is impossible in this problem to consume negative amounts of Y, however, the physical limit for this process is the X-axis, along which purchases of Y are 0. Hence, as this discussion makes clear, it is necessary to amend the first-order conditions for a utility maximum a bit to allow for corner solutions of the type shown in Figure 4.4. Following our discussion of the general n-good case, we will show how this can be accomplished.

THE *n*-GOOD CASE

The results derived graphically in the case of two goods carry over directly to the case of n goods. Again it can be shown that for an interior utility maximum, the *MRS* between any two goods must equal the ratio of the prices of these goods. However, because the case of n goods cannot be presented in a two-dimensional graph, we shall adopt a mathematical proof, which provides additional insights into the maximization assumption.

First-Order Conditions

When there are n goods to choose from, the individual's objective is to maximize utility from these n goods:

$$\text{utility} = U(X_1, X_2, \ldots, X_n), \tag{4.4}$$

subject to the budget constraint:[3]

$$I = P_1X_1 + P_2X_2 + \cdots + P_nX_n \tag{4.5}$$

or

$$I - P_1X_1 - P_2X_2 - \cdots - P_nX_n = 0. \tag{4.6}$$

Following the techniques developed in Chapter 2 for maximizing a function subject to a constraint, we set up the Lagrangian expression:

$$\mathcal{L} = U(X_1, X_2, \ldots, X_n) + \lambda(I - P_1X_1 - P_2X_2 - \cdots - P_nX_n). \tag{4.7}$$

Setting the partial derivatives of $\mathcal{L}$ (with respect to $X_1, X_2, \ldots, X_n$ and λ) equal to 0 yields $n+1$ equations representing the necessary conditions for an interior maximum:

$$\frac{\partial \mathcal{L}}{\partial X_1} = \frac{\partial U}{\partial X_1} - \lambda P_1 = 0$$

$$\frac{\partial \mathcal{L}}{\partial X_2} = \frac{\partial U}{\partial X_2} - \lambda P_2 = 0$$

$$\cdot$$
$$\cdot \tag{4.8}$$
$$\cdot$$

$$\frac{\partial \mathcal{L}}{\partial X_n} = \frac{\partial U}{\partial X_n} - \lambda P_n = 0$$

$$\frac{\partial \mathcal{L}}{\partial \lambda} = I - P_1X_1 - P_2X_2 - \cdots - P_nX_n = 0.$$

These $n+1$ equations can usually be solved for the optimal $X_1, X_2, \ldots, X_n$ and for λ (see Example 4.2 to be convinced that such a solution is possible).

Equations 4.8 are necessary but not sufficient for a maximum. The second-order conditions that ensure a maximum are relatively complex.

---

[3] Again, the budget constraint has been written as an equality here because, given the assumption of nonsatiation, it is clear that the individual will spend all available income.

However, the assumption of strict quasi-concavity (a diminishing *MRS* in the two-good case) is sufficient to ensure that any point obeying Equations 4.8 is in fact a true maximum.

Implications of First-Order Conditions

The first-order conditions represented by Equations 4.8 can be rewritten in a variety of interesting ways. For example, for any two goods, X_i and X_j, we have

$$\frac{\partial U/\partial X_i}{\partial U/\partial X_j} = \frac{P_i}{P_j}. \tag{4.9}$$

But previously it was shown that the ratio of the marginal utilities of two goods is in fact identical to the marginal rate of substitution between them. Therefore, the conditions for an optimal allocation of income become

$$MRS\ (X_i\ for\ X_j) = \frac{P_i}{P_j}. \tag{4.10}$$

This is exactly the result derived earlier in this chapter; in order to maximize utility, the individual should equate the psychic rate of trade-off to the market trade-off rate.

Interpreting the Lagrangian Multiplier

Another result can be derived by solving Equations 4.8 for λ:

$$\lambda = \frac{\partial U/\partial X_1}{P_1} = \frac{\partial U/\partial X_2}{P_2} = \cdots = \frac{\partial U/\partial X_n}{P_n} \tag{4.11}$$

or

$$\lambda = \frac{MU_{x_1}}{P_1} = \frac{MU_{x_2}}{P_2} = \cdots = \frac{MU_{x_n}}{P_n}.$$

This equation says that at the utility-maximizing point, each good purchased should yield the same marginal utility per dollar spent on that good. Each good therefore should have an identical (marginal) benefit to (marginal) cost ratio. If this were not true, one good would promise more "marginal enjoyment per dollar" than some other good, and funds would not be optimally allocated.

Although the reader is again warned against talking very confidently about marginal utility, what Equation 4.11 says is that an extra dollar should yield the same "additional utility" no matter which good it is spent on. The common value for this extra utility is given by the Lagrangian multiplier for the consumer's budget constraint (that is, by λ). Consequently, λ can be regarded as the marginal utility of an extra dollar of consumption expenditure (the marginal utility of "income").

One final way to rewrite the necessary conditions for a maximum is

$$P_i = \frac{MU_{x_i}}{\lambda} \qquad (4.12)$$

for every good i that is bought. This equation says that for every good that an individual buys, the price of that good represents his or her evaluation of the utility of the last unit consumed. The price obviously represents how much the individual is willing to pay for that last unit. In Chapter 5 (and elsewhere) we will make considerable use of this result when discussing the value of a good to a consumer and the "consumer surplus" received by some purchasers when they are able to buy a good for less than the maximum amount they would be willing to pay.

Corner Solutions   The first-order conditions of Equations 4.8 hold exactly only for interior maxima for which some positive amount of each good is purchased. When corner solutions (such as those illustrated in Figure 4.4) arise, the conditions have to be modified slightly.[4] In this case, Equations 4.8 become

$$\frac{\partial \mathcal{L}}{\partial X_i} = \frac{\partial U}{\partial X_i} - \lambda P_i \leq 0 \ (i = 1 \ldots n), \qquad (4.13)$$

and, if

$$\frac{\partial \mathcal{L}}{\partial X_i} = \frac{\partial U}{\partial X_i} - \lambda P_i < 0, \qquad (4.14)$$

then

$$X_i = 0. \qquad (4.15)$$

To interpret these conditions, we can rewrite Equation 4.14 as

$$P_i > \frac{\dfrac{\partial U}{\partial X_i}}{\lambda} = \frac{MU_{x_i}}{\lambda}. \qquad (4.16)$$

Hence, the optimal conditions are as before, except that any good whose price (P_i) exceeds its marginal value to the consumer (MU_{x_i}/λ) will not be purchased ($X_i = 0$). Thus, the mathematical results conform to the commonsense idea that individuals will not purchase goods that they believe are not worth the money. Although such corner solutions will not provide a major focus for our analysis in this book, the reader should

---

[4] Formally, these conditions are called the "Kuhn-Tucker" conditions for nonlinear programming. For a more complete explanation, see A. K. Dixit, *Optimization in Economic Theory*, 2nd ed. (New York: Oxford University Press, 1990).

keep in mind the possibilities for such solutions arising and the economic interpretation that can be attached to the optimal conditions in such cases.

EXAMPLE 4.2

COBB-DOUGLAS DEMAND FUNCTIONS

As we showed in Chapter 3, the Cobb-Douglas utility function is given by

$$U(X, Y) = X^\alpha Y^\beta, \tag{4.17}$$

where, for convenience, we assume $\alpha + \beta = 1$. We can now solve for the utility-maximizing values of X and Y for any prices (P_X, P_Y) and income (I). Setting up the Lagrangian expression

$$\mathcal{L} = X^\alpha Y^\beta + \lambda(I - P_X X - P_Y Y) \tag{4.18}$$

yields the first-order conditions

$$\frac{\partial \mathcal{L}}{\partial X} = \alpha X^{\alpha-1} Y^\beta - \lambda P_X = 0$$

$$\frac{\partial \mathcal{L}}{\partial Y} = \beta X^\alpha Y^{\beta-1} - \lambda P_Y = 0 \tag{4.19}$$

$$\frac{\partial \mathcal{L}}{\partial \lambda} = I - P_X X - P_Y Y = 0.$$

Taking the ratio of the first two terms shows that

$$\frac{\alpha Y}{\beta X} = \frac{P_X}{P_Y} \tag{4.20}$$

or

$$P_Y Y = \frac{\beta}{\alpha} P_X X = \frac{1-\alpha}{\alpha} P_X X, \tag{4.21}$$

where the final equation follows because $\alpha + \beta = 1$. Substitution of the first-order condition in Equation 4.21 into the budget constraint gives

$$I = P_X X + P_Y Y = P_X X + \frac{1-\alpha}{\alpha} P_X X = P_X X \left(1 + \frac{1-\alpha}{\alpha}\right) = \frac{1}{\alpha} P_X X; \tag{4.22}$$

solving for X yields

$$X^* = \frac{\alpha I}{P_X}; \tag{4.23}$$

and a similar set of manipulations would give

$$Y^* = \frac{\beta I}{P_Y}. \tag{4.24}$$

These results show that an individual whose utility function is given by Equation 4.17 will always choose to allocate α percent of his or her income to buying good X (that is, $P_X X/I = \alpha$) and β percent to buying good Y ($P_Y Y/I = \beta$). Although this feature of the Cobb-Douglas function often makes it very easy to work out simple problems, it does suggest that the function has limits in its ability to explain actual consumption behavior. Since the share of income devoted to particular goods often changes significantly in response to changing economic conditions, a more general functional form may provide insights not provided by the Cobb-Douglas function. We illustrate a few possibilities in Example 4.3.

Numerical Example. First, however, let's look at a specific numerical example for the Cobb-Douglas case. Suppose, as in Example 4.1, that X (soft drinks) sell for \$.25 and Y (hamburgers) sell for \$1.00 and that total income is \$2.00. Succinctly then, assume that $P_X = .25$, $P_Y = 1$, $I = 2$. Suppose also that $\alpha = \beta = 0.5$ so that this individual splits his or her income equally between these two goods. Now the demand Equations 4.23 and 4.24 imply

$$X^* = \alpha I/P_X = .5I/P_X = .5(2)/.25 = 4$$
$$Y^* = \beta I/P_Y = .5I/P_Y = .5(2)/1 = 1 \tag{4.25}$$

and, at these optimal choices,

$$\textbf{Utility} = X^{.5}Y^{.5} = (4)^{.5}(1)^{.5} = 2. \tag{4.26}$$

Notice also that we can compute the value for the Lagrangian Multiplier associated with this income allocation by using Equation 4.19:

$$\lambda = \alpha X^{\alpha-1}Y^{\beta}/P_X = .5(4)^{-.5}(1)^{.5}/.25 = 1. \tag{4.27}$$

This value implies that small changes in income yield about the same size changes in utility. For example, if income were to rise to $I = 2.1$ (with P_X and P_Y unchanged), Equations 4.23 and 4.24 predict that $X^* = 4.2$, $Y^* = 1.05$ and the new level of utility would be:

$$\textbf{Utility} = (4.2)^{.5}(1.05)^{.5} = 2.10 \tag{4.28}$$

which was predicted by the fact that $\lambda = 1$.

QUERY: Would a change in P_Y affect the quantity of X demanded in Equation 4.23? Explain your answer mathematically. Also develop an intuitive explanation based on the notion that the share of income devoted to good Y is a constant given by the parameter of the utility function, β.

EXAMPLE 4.3

CES DEMAND

To illustrate cases in which budget shares are responsive to economic circumstances, let's look at two specific examples of the CES function. First, assume $\delta = .5$ in the CES function. Then utility is given by:

$$U(X, Y) = X^{.5} + Y^{.5}. \tag{4.29}$$

Setting up the Lagrangian expression

$$\mathcal{L} = X^{.5} + Y^{.5} + \lambda(I - P_X - P_Y) \tag{4.30}$$

yields the following first order conditions for a maximum:

$$\partial\mathcal{L}/\partial X = .5X^{-.5} - \lambda P_X \quad = 0$$
$$\partial\mathcal{L}/\partial Y = .5Y^{-.5} - \lambda P_Y \quad = 0 \tag{4.31}$$
$$\partial\mathcal{L}/\partial\lambda = I - P_X X - P_Y Y) = 0.$$

Division of the first two of these shows that

$$(Y/X)^{.5} = P_X/P_Y. \tag{4.32}$$

By substituting this into the budget constraint and using some algebraic manipulation, it is fairly easy to derive the demand functions associated with this utility function:

$$X^* = I/P_X[1 + (P_X/P_Y)] \tag{4.33}$$

$$Y^* = I/P_Y[1 + (P_Y/P_X)]. \tag{4.34}$$

Price Responsiveness. In these demand functions notice that the share of income spent on, say, good X—that is, $P_X X/I = 1/[1 + (P_X/P_Y)]$—is not a constant, it depends on the price ratio P_X/P_Y. The higher is the relative price of X, the smaller will be the share of income spent on that good. In other words, the demand for X is so responsive to its own price that a rise in the price reduces total spending on X. That the demand for X is very price responsive can also be illustrated by comparing the exponent on P_X in the demand function given by Equation 4.33 (−2) to that from Equation 4.23 (−1). In Chapter 7 we will discuss this observation more fully when we examine the elasticity concept in detail.

CHOICE AND DEMAND

A CES Function with Less Substitutability. Alternatively, let's look at a demand function with less substitutability[5] than the Cobb-Douglas. If $\delta = -1$, the utility function is given by

$$U(X, Y) = -X^{-1} - Y^{-1} \tag{4.35}$$

and it is easy to show that the first-order conditions for a maximum require

$$Y/X = (P_X/P_Y)^{.5}. \tag{4.36}$$

Again, substitution of this condition into the budget constraint together with some algebra yields the demand functions

$$X^* = I/P_X[1 + (P_Y/P_X)^{.5}]$$
$$Y^* = I/P_Y[1 + (P_X/P_Y)^{.5}]. \tag{4.37}$$

That these demand functions are less price responsive can be seen in two ways. First, now the share of income spent on good X—$P_X X/I = 1/[1 + (P_Y/P_X)^{.5}]$—responds positively to increases in P_X. As the price of X rises, this individual cuts back only modestly on good X so total spending on that good rises. That the demand functions in Equations 4.37 are less price responsive than the Cobb-Douglas is also illustrated by the relatively small exponents of each good's own price (−.5) in Equations 4.37. Overall then, the CES function allows us to illustrate a wide variety of possible relationships between two goods.[6]

QUERY: Do changes in income affect expenditure shares in any of the CES functions discussed here? How is the behavior of expenditure shares related to the homothetic nature of this function?

INDIRECT UTILITY FUNCTION

Examples 4.2 and 4.3 illustrate the principle that it is often possible to manipulate the first-order conditions for a constrained utility-maximization problem to solve for the optimal values of $X_1, X_2, \ldots, X_n$. These optimal values in general will depend on the prices of all the goods and on the individuals' income. That is,

---

[5] One way to measure substitutability is by the elasticity of substitution, which for the CES function is given by $\sigma = 1/(1 - \delta)$. Here $\delta = .5$ implies $\sigma = 2$, $\delta = 0$ (the Cobb-Douglas) implies $\sigma = 1$, and $\delta = -1$ implies $\sigma = .5$.

[6] These relationships for the CES function are pursued in more detail in Problem 4.9 and in Extension E4.3.

$$X_1^* = X_1(P_1, P_2, \ldots, P_n, I)$$

$$X_2^* = X_2(P_1, P_2, \ldots, P_n, I)$$

.

.   (4.38)

.

$$X_n^* = X_n(P_1, P_2, \ldots, P_n, I).$$

In later chapters we will analyze in more detail this set of *demand functions*, which show the dependence of the quantity of each X_i demanded on $P_1, P_2, \ldots, P_n$ and I. Here we use the optimal values of the X's from Equations 4.38 to substitute in the original utility function to yield

$$\textbf{maximum utility} = U(X_1^*, X_2^*, \ldots, X_n^*)$$

$$= U[X_1^*(P_1, P_2, \ldots, P_n, I),$$

$$X_2^*(P_1, P_2, \ldots, P_n, I), \qquad (4.39)$$

$$\ldots X_n^*(P_1, P_2, \ldots, P_n, I)]$$

$$= V(P_1, P_2, \ldots, P_n, I).$$

In words, because of the individual's desire to maximize utility, given a budget constraint, the optimal level of utility obtainable will depend *indirectly* on the prices of the goods being bought and on the individual's income. This dependence is reflected by the indirect utility function V. If either prices or income were to change, the level of utility that can be attained would also be affected. Sometimes, in both consumer theory and in many other contexts, it is possible to use this indirect approach to study how changes in economic circumstances affect various kinds of outcomes, such as utility or (later in this book) firms' costs.

EXAMPLE 4.4

INDIRECT UTILITY FROM HAMBURGERS AND SOFT DRINKS

In our hamburger/soft drink example, we found (Equations 4.25 with $\alpha = \beta = 0.5$)

$$X^* = \frac{I}{2P_X}$$

$$\qquad (4.40)$$

$$Y^* = \frac{I}{2P_Y}.$$

Substituting these into the utility function gives

$$\textbf{maximum utility} = U(X^*, Y^*) = (X^*)^{.5}(Y^*)^{.5} \tag{4.41}$$

$$= \left(\frac{I}{2P_X}\right)^{.5}\left(\frac{I}{2P_Y}\right)^{.5}$$

$$= \frac{I}{2P_X^{.5}P_Y^{.5}}. \tag{4.42}$$

With $I = 2$, $P_X = .25$, and $P_Y = 1$, Equation 4.42 shows that maximum utility can be indirectly computed as

$$\textbf{maximum utility} = \frac{2}{2(.25)^{.5}(1)^{.5}} = 2, \tag{4.43}$$

which is the same value we derived from the direct utility function. More generally, notice in Equation 4.42 that increases in income raise (indirect) utility, whereas increases in either of the prices cause utility to fall. By stating utility as a function of such "outside forces" as prices and income, it is possible to study explicitly these forces' effects on well-being.

Lump Sum Principle.   The indirect utility concept is very useful for studying the impact of taxes on an individual's utility. For example, it is straightforward to illustrate the "lump sum" principle that general income taxes reduce utility to a smaller extent than do single commodity taxes that yield the same revenue to the government. In the present case, suppose the government were to adopt a $.50 income tax. Equation 4.43 shows that this would reduce the individual's indirect utility from 2.00 to 1.50. A soft drink tax of $.25 would raise the same revenues since Equation 4.25 shows that when P_X rises from $.25 to $.50 purchases fall to 2 soft drinks. Hence, tax collections are $.50 (= $.25 per drink times 2 soft drinks). With the soft drink sales tax, the individual's indirect utility is now

$$\textbf{maximum utility} = \frac{I}{2P_X^{.5}P_Y^{.5}} = \frac{2}{2(.50)^{.5}(1)^{.5}} = 1.41, \tag{4.44}$$

which falls short of utility under the income tax. The reason is that a soft drink tax alters individuals' choices in two ways—by reducing purchasing power and by changing relative prices. The income tax only has the first effect and is therefore less harmful. Additional material related to the lump sum principle is discussed in Problems 4.7 and 4.8.

QUERY: The indirect utility function in Equation 4.42 shows that a doubling of income and all prices leaves utility unchanged. Do you think that is a general property of indirect utility?

In Chapter 2 we pointed out that many constrained maximum problems have associated "dual" constrained minimum problems. For the case of utility maximization, the associated dual minimization problem concerns allocating income in such a way as to achieve a given utility level with the minimal expenditure. This problem is clearly analogous to the primary utility-maximization problem, but the goals and constraints of the problems have been reversed. Figure 4.5 illustrates this dual expenditure-minimization problem. There the individual must attain utility level U_2—this is now the constraint in the problem. Three possible expenditure amounts (E_1, E_2, and E_3) are shown as three "budget constraint" lines in the figure. Expenditure level E_1 is clearly too small to achieve U_2. Hence, it cannot solve the dual

EXPENDITURE MINIMIZATION

FIGURE 4.5

THE INDIVIDUAL'S DUAL EXPENDITURE-MINIMIZATION PROBLEM

The dual of the individual's utility-maximization problem is to attain a given utility level (U_2) with minimal expenditures. An expenditure level of E_1 does not permit U_2 to be reached, whereas E_3 provides more spending power than is strictly necessary. With expenditure E_2 the individual can just reach U_2 by consuming X^* and Y^*.

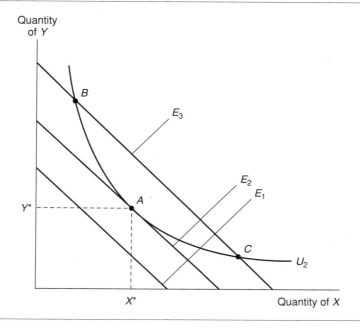

problem. With expenditures given by E_3, the individual can reach U_2 (at either of the two points B or C), but this is not the minimal expenditure level required. Rather, E_2 clearly provides just enough total expenditures to reach U_2 (at point A), and this is in fact the solution to the dual problem. By comparing Figures 4.2 and 4.5, it is obvious that both the primary utility-maximization approach and the dual expenditure-minimization approach yield the same solution (X^*, Y^*)—they are simply alternative ways of viewing the same process. Often the expenditure-minimization approach is more useful, however, because expenditures are directly observable, whereas utility is not.

A Mathematical More formally, the individual's dual expenditure-minimization problem is to
Statement choose $X_1, X_2, \ldots, X_n$ so as to minimize

$$\text{total expenditures} = E = P_1 X_1 + P_2 X_2 + \cdots + P_n X_n, \qquad (4.45)$$

subject to the constraint

$$\text{utility} = U_2 = U(X_1, X_2, \ldots, X_n). \qquad (4.46)$$

The optimal amounts of $X_1, X_2, \ldots, X_n$ chosen in this problem will depend on the prices of the various goods $(P_1, P_2, \ldots, P_n)$ and on the required utility level U_2. If any of the prices were to change or if the individual had a different utility "target," another commodity bundle would be optimal. This dependence can be summarized by an *expenditure function:*

DEFINITION

Expenditure Function   The individual's expenditure function shows the minimal expenditures necessary to achieve a given utility level for a particular set of prices. That is,

$$\text{minimal expenditures} = E(P_1, P_2, \ldots, P_n, U). \qquad (4.47)$$

This definition shows that the expenditure function and the indirect utility function are inverse functions of one another (compare Equations 4.39 and 4.47). Both depend on market prices but involve different constraints (income or utility). In the next chapter we will see how this relationship is quite useful in allowing us to examine the theory of how individuals respond to price changes, which may affect their well-being.

EXAMPLE 4.5

EXPENDITURE FUNCTION FOR HAMBURGERS AND SOFT DRINKS

Returning yet again to hamburgers and soft drinks, the individual's dual problem is to minimize

$$E = P_X X + P_Y Y \tag{4.48}$$

subject to

$$\text{utility} = \overline{U} = X^{.5} Y^{.5}, \tag{4.49}$$

where $\overline{U}$ is the utility target.

The Lagrangian expression for this problem is

$$\mathcal{L} = P_X X + P_Y Y + \lambda(\overline{U} - X^{.5} Y^{.5}), \tag{4.50}$$

and the first-order conditions for a minimum are

$$\frac{\partial \mathcal{L}}{\partial X} = P_X - .5\lambda X^{-.5} Y^{.5} = 0$$

$$\frac{\partial \mathcal{L}}{\partial Y} = P_Y - .5\lambda X^{.5} Y^{-.5} = 0 \tag{4.51}$$

$$\frac{\partial \mathcal{L}}{\partial \lambda} = \overline{U} - X^{.5} Y^{.5} = 0.$$

These can again be solved by moving the terms in λ to the right and dividing:

$$\frac{P_Y}{P_X} = \frac{.5\lambda X^{.5} Y^{-.5}}{.5\lambda X^{-.5} Y^{.5}} = \frac{X}{Y} \tag{4.52}$$

or

$$P_X X = P_Y Y, \tag{4.53}$$

which is precisely the same first-order condition we had before (see Equation 4.21 with $\alpha = \beta = .5$). Now, however, we wish to solve for expenditures as a function of P_X, P_Y, and U—that is, we wish to eliminate X and Y from Equation 4.48. This will give us the type of expenditure function we defined earlier in this section. Although the algebra here isn't difficult, it is important to keep this goal in mind since it is easy to become confused about whether you have found a solution or not. Substituting Equation 4.53 into the expenditure function yields

$$E = P_X X^* + P_Y Y^* = 2P_X X^* \tag{4.54}$$

so

$$X^* = \frac{E}{2P_X} \qquad (4.55)$$

and similarly,

$$Y^* = \frac{E}{2P_Y}. \qquad (4.56)$$

But, the utility target requires

$$\overline{U} = (X^*)^{.5}(Y^*)^{.5} \qquad (4.57)$$

so

$$\overline{U} = \left(\frac{E}{2P_X}\right)^{.5}\left(\frac{E}{2P_Y}\right)^{.5} = \frac{E}{2P_X^{.5}P_Y^{.5}}. \qquad (4.58)$$

Hence, we have the function

$$E = 2\overline{U}P_X^{.5}P_Y^{.5} \qquad (4.59)$$

as the minimum expenditure necessary to reach $\overline{U}$. If, as before, $\overline{U} = 2$, $P_X = .25$, and $P_Y = 1$, we have a required expenditure of

$$E = 2(2)(.25)^{.5}(1)^{.5} = 2. \qquad (4.60)$$

Notice this was the original value for income with which we started this problem. We know that this income level is indeed just sufficient to attain a utility level of 2. Of course, as the expenditure function in Equation 4.59 shows, a higher utility target would require greater expenditures. Similarly, an increase in P_X or P_Y would also require greater expenditures to attain a given utility target. Without such added expenditures, the utility target would have to be reduced—the individual would be worse off. Looked at in another way, the expenditure function shows how much extra purchasing power this person would need to compensate for a rise in the price of a good. In later chapters we will make some use of this property of the function.

QUERY: A doubling of P_X and P_Y in Equation 4.59 will precisely double the expenditures needed to reach $\overline{U}$. Technically, this function is "homogeneous of degree one" in the prices of the two goods (see footnote 1 in Chapter 5). Is this a property of all expenditure functions?

SUMMARY

In this chapter we examined the basic economic model of utility maximization subject to a budget constraint. Although we approached this problem in a variety of ways, all of these approaches lead to the same basic result:

- To reach a constrained maximum, an individual should spend all available income and should choose a commodity bundle such that the MRS between any two goods is equal to the ratio of those goods' market prices. This basic tangency will result in the individual equating the ratios of the marginal utility to market price for every good that is actually consumed. Such a result is common to most constrained optimization problems.

- The tangency conditions are only the first-order conditions for a constrained maximum, however. To ensure that these conditions are also sufficient, the individual's indifference curve map must exhibit a diminishing MRS. In formal terms, the utility function must be strictly quasi-concave.

- The tangency conditions must also be modified to allow for corner solutions in which the optimal level of consumption of some goods is zero. In this case, the ratio of marginal utility to price for such a good will be below the common marginal benefit–marginal cost ratio for goods actually bought.

- A consequence of the assumption of constrained utility maximization is that the individual's optimal choices will depend implicitly on the parameters of his or her budget constraint. That is, the choices observed will be implicit functions of all prices and income. Utility will therefore also be an indirect function of these parameters.

- The dual to the constrained utility-maximization problem is to minimize the expenditure required to reach a given utility target. Although this dual approach yields the same optimal solution as the primal constrained maximum problem, it also yields additional insight into the theory of choice. Specifically, this approach leads to expenditure functions in which the spending required to reach a given utility target depends on the goods' market prices.

PROBLEMS

4.1
Each day Paul, who is in third grade, eats lunch at school. He only likes Twinkies (T) and Orange Slice (S), and these provide him a utility of

$$\text{utility} = U(T, S) = \sqrt{TS}.$$

a. If Twinkies cost $.10 each and Slice costs $.25 per cup, how should Paul spend the $1 his mother gives him in order to maximize his utility?
b. If the school tries to discourage Twinkie consumption by raising the price to $.40, by how much will Paul's mother have to increase his lunch allowance to provide him with the same level of utility he

received in part (a)? How many Twinkies and cups of Slice will he buy now (assuming that it is possible to purchase fractional amounts of both of these goods)?

4.2
a. A young connoisseur has $300 to spend to build a small wine cellar. She enjoys two vintages in particular: an expensive 1987 French Bordeaux (W_F) at $20 per bottle and a less expensive 1993 California varietal wine (W_C) priced at $4. How much of each wine should she purchase if her utility is characterized by the following function?

$$U(W_F, W_C) = W_F^{2/3} W_C^{1/3}.$$

b. When she arrived at the wine store, our young oenologist discovered that the price of the 1987 French Bordeaux had fallen to $10 a bottle because of a decline in the value of the franc. If the price of the California wine remains stable at $4 per bottle, how much of each wine should our friend purchase to maximize utility under these altered conditions?

4.3

a. On a given evening J. P. enjoys the consumption of cigars (C) and brandy (B) according to the function

$$U(C, B) = 20C - C^2 + 18B - 3B^2.$$

How many cigars and glasses of brandy does he consume during an evening? (Cost is no object to J. P.)

b. Lately, however, J. P. has been advised by his doctors that he should limit the sum of brandy and cigars consumed to 5. How many glasses of brandy and cigars will he consume under these circumstances?

4.4

a. Mr. Odde Ball enjoys commodities X and Y according to the utility function

$$U(X, Y) = \sqrt{X^2 + Y^2}.$$

Maximize Mr. Ball's utility if $P_X = \$3$, $P_Y = \$4$, and he has $50 to spend.
Hint: It may be easier here to maximize U^2 rather than U. Why won't this alter your results?

b. Graph Mr. Ball's indifference curve and its point of tangency with his budget constraint. What does the graph say about Mr. Ball's behavior? Have you found a true maximum?

4.5

Mr. A derives utility from martinis (M) in proportion to the number he drinks:

$$U(M) = M.$$

Mr. A is very particular about his martinis, however: He only enjoys them made in the exact proportion of two parts gin (G) to one part vermouth (V). Hence, we can rewrite Mr. A's utility function as

$$U(M) = U(G, V) = \min\left(\frac{G}{2}, V\right).$$

a. Graph Mr. A's indifference curve in terms of G and V for various levels of utility. Show that regardless of the prices of the two ingredients, Mr. A will never alter the way he mixes martinis.

b. Calculate the demand functions for G and V.

c. Using the results from part (b), what is Mr. A's indirect utility function?

d. Calculate Mr. A's expenditure function; for each level of utility, show spending as a function of P_G and P_V.

4.6

a. Suppose that a fast-food junkie derives utility from three goods: soft drinks (X), hamburgers (Y), and ice cream sundaes (Z) according to the Cobb-Douglas utility function

$$U(X, Y, Z) = X^{.5}\, Y^{.5}\, (1 + Z)^{.5}.$$

Suppose also that the prices for these goods are given by $P_X = .25$, $P_Y = 1$, and $P_Z = 2$ and that this consumer's income is given by $I = 2$.

a. Show that for $Z = 0$, maximization of utility results in the same optimal choices as in Example 4.2. Show also that any choice that results in $Z > 0$ (even for a fractional Z) reduces utility from this optimum.

b. How do you explain the fact that $Z = 0$ is optimal here? (*Hint:* Think about the ratio MU_z/P_z.)

c. How high would this individual's income have to be in order for any Z to be purchased?

4.7

In Example 4.4 we used a specific indirect utility function to illustrate the lump sum principle that an income tax reduces utility to a lesser extent than a sales tax that garners the same revenue. Here you are asked to

a. Show this result graphically for a two-good case by showing the budget constraints that must prevail under each tax. (*Hint:* First draw the sales tax case. Then show that the budget constraint for an income tax that collects the same revenue must pass through the point chosen under the sales tax but will offer options preferable to the individual.)

b. Show that if an individual consumes the two goods in fixed proportions, the lump sum principle does not hold since both taxes reduce utility by the same amount.

c. Discuss whether the lump sum principle holds for the many-good case too.

4.8

The lump sum principle discussed in Example 4.4 can be applied to transfers, too, but in this case it may be easier to use expenditure functions.

a. Consider the expenditure function given by Equation 4.59 in Example 4.5. How much would it cost the government (in terms of extra expenditures for this person) to raise utility from 2.0 to 2.5 with unchanged prices? If the government wished to permit individuals to attain the same utility target by subsidizing the cost of hamburgers, what should the hamburger subsidy be? How much will such a subsidy cost the government?

b. Explain intuitively and with a graph why the income transfer in part (a) proves to be a lower cost way of raising utility than does the hamburger subsidy.

c. Is the lower cost of lump sum transfers a general result that applies to the many-good case as well?

4.9

The general CES utility function is given by

$$U(X, Y) = \frac{X^\delta}{\delta} + \frac{Y^\delta}{\delta}.$$

a. Show that the first-order conditions for a constrained utility maximum with this function require individuals to choose goods in the proportion

$$\frac{X}{Y} = \left(\frac{P_X}{P_Y}\right)^{\frac{1}{\delta - 1}}.$$

b. Show that the result in part (a) implies that individuals will allocate their funds equally between X and Y for the Cobb-Douglas case ($\delta = 0$) as we have shown before in several problems.

c. How does the ratio $P_X X/P_Y Y$ depend on the value of δ? Explain your results intuitively. (For further details on this function, see Extension E4.3.)

4.10

Suppose individuals require a certain level of food (X) to remain alive. Let this amount be given by X_0. Once X_0 is purchased, individuals obtain utility from food and other goods (Y) of the form

$$U(X, Y) = (X - X_0)^\alpha Y^\beta$$

where $\alpha + \beta = 1$.

a. Show that if $I > P_X X_0$ the individual will maximize utility by spending $\alpha(I - P_X X_0) + P_X X_0$ on good X and $\beta(I - P_X X_0)$ on good Y.

b. How do the ratios X/I and Y/I change as income increases in this problem? (See also Extension E4.2.)

SUGGESTED READINGS

Barten, A. P., and Volker Böhm. "Consumer Theory." In K. J. Arrow and M. D. Intriligator, eds., *Handbook of Mathematical Economics*. Vol. II. Amsterdam: North-Holland Publishing Company, 1982.
Sections 10 and 11 have compact summaries of many of the concepts covered in this chapter.

Deaton, A., and J. Muelbauer. *Economics and Consumer Behavior.* Cambridge: Cambridge University Press, 1980.
Section 2.5 provides a nice geometric treatment of duality concepts.

Hicks, J. R. *Value and Capital.* Oxford: Clarendon Press, 1946.

Chapter II and the Mathematical Appendix provide some early suggestions of the importance of the expenditure function.

Samuelson, Paul A. *Foundations of Economic Analysis.* Cambridge: Harvard University Press, 1947.
Chapter V and Appendix A provide a succinct analysis of the first-order conditions for a utility maximum. The appendix provides good coverage of second-order conditions.

Silberberg, E. *The Structure of Economics: A Mathematical Analysis.* 2d ed. New York: McGraw-Hill Book Company, 1990.

A useful, though fairly difficult, treatment of duality in consumer theory.

Theil, H. *Theory and Measurement of Consumer Demand.* Amsterdam: North-Holland Publishing Co., 1975. *Good summary of basic theory of demand together with implications for empirical estimation.*

Varian, H. R. *Microeconomic Analysis.* 3d ed. New York: W. W. Norton and Company, 1992. *Sections 7.3–7.4 summarize the relationships between utility functions and expenditure functions.*

EXTENSIONS

Utility Functions and Budget Shares

Because data on budget shares are readily available from studies of individuals' consumption patterns, they can be used to shed light on underlying preferences. Here we look at three specific utility functions and show they have been used to study budget shares. Throughout our discussion, we will consider only the two-good (X and Y) case, though most results are readily generalizable to many goods. Following customary notation, the share of income devoted to good $X(P_X X/I)$ will be denoted by s_X and $s_Y = 1 - s_X$.

Before beginning, the connection between budget shares and homothetic preferences should be mentioned. In Chapter 3 we showed that for homothetic utility functions, the *MRS* depends only on the ratio Y/X, not on the absolute levels of the goods. Since utility maximization requires $MRS = P_X/P_Y$ for homothetic functions, the price ratio will determine the ratio Y/X. Hence, the budget shares themselves will be determined solely by relative prices. If relative prices do not change, budget shares will not change even when income fluctuates. Our examples of homothetic functions (the Cobb-Douglas and the CES) illustrate this result, whereas the Linear Expenditure System shows why nonhomothetic functions may be preferable in some circumstances.

E4.1 Cobb-Douglas Utility

If the utility function has the Cobb-Douglas form

$$U(X, Y) = X^\alpha Y^\beta \tag{i}$$

then Example 4.2 showed that the demand functions are

$$X = \alpha I/P_X$$
$$Y = \beta I/P_Y \tag{ii}$$

Hence,

$$s_X = P_X X/I = \alpha$$
$$s_Y = P_Y Y/I = \beta \tag{iii}$$

and the budget shares are constant for all possible relative prices. Although this feature of the Cobb-Douglas is one reason for its popularity in the study of production (see Chapter 11), it does limit its suitability for the study of consumption. Budget shares in consumption do not appear to be constant under changing economic circumstances.

Food

Ever since the pioneering studies of Ernst Engel in the mid-nineteenth century, economists have been interested in the share of income that consumers devote to food purchases. Literally thousands of studies have confirmed that this share is indeed influenced by circumstances. Not only do food shares data exhibit Engel's Law ($\partial s_X/\partial I < 0$), but they also illuminate many other aspects of consumer behavior. For example, Hayashi (1995) shows that the share of income devoted to foods favored by the elderly is significantly larger in two-generation households in Japan than in one-generation households. Altruism appears to be a significant feature of extended families in Japan.

Development economists sometimes make a distinction between the share of income devoted to food and the share of income devoted to nutrients. In principle, nutrients' share of income might or might not follow Engel's Law for the poorest people in developed countries. If individuals choose increasingly nutrient-rich foods as their incomes rise, at the margin nutrients' share would exceed the share of food in total income. On the other hand, if individuals opt for nutrient-poor foods as income rises, the situation would be reversed. Behrman (1989) presents evidence that an individual's demand for an increasing variety of food as income rises may interfere with the ability of general economic improvement to raise the nutrient intake of poorest segments of the population.

E4.2 Linear Expenditure System

A generalization of the Cobb-Douglas function that incorporates the idea that certain minimal amounts of each good must be bought by the individual (X_0, Y_0) is the utility function

$$U(X, Y) = (X - X_0)^{\alpha}(Y - Y_0)^{\beta} \qquad \text{(iv)}$$

for values of $X \geq X_0$ and $Y \geq Y_0$ and again $\alpha + \beta = 1$.

Demand functions can be derived from this utility function in a way analogous to the Cobb-Douglas case by introducing the concept of supernumerary income (I^*), which represents the amount of purchasing power remaining after purchasing the minimum bundle

$$I^* = I - P_X X_0 - P_Y Y_0. \qquad \text{(v)}$$

Using this notation then, the demand functions are

$$X = (P_X X_0 + \alpha I^*)/P_X$$
$$Y = (P_Y Y_0 + \beta I^*)/P_Y \qquad \text{(vi)}$$

In this case, then, the individual spends a constant fraction of supernumerary income on each good once the minimum bundle has been purchased. Manipulation of Equation vi yields the share equations:

$$s_X = \alpha + (\beta P_X X_0 - \alpha P_Y Y_0)/I$$
$$s_Y = \beta + (\alpha P_Y Y_0 - \beta P_X X_0)/I, \qquad \text{(vii)}$$

which show that this demand system is not homothetic. Inspection of Equation vii shows the unsurprising result that the budget share of a good is positively related to the minimal amount of that good needed and negatively related to the minimal amount of the other good required. Because the notion of necessary purchases seems to accord well with real-world observation, this linear expenditure system (LES), which was first developed by Stone (1954), is widely used in empirical studies.

Traditional Purchases

One of the most interesting uses of the LES is to examine how its notion of necessary purchases change as conditions change. For example, Oczkowski and Philip (1994) study how access to modern consumer goods may affect the share of income that individuals in transitional economies devote to traditional local items. They show that villagers of Papua New Guinea reduce such shares significantly as outside goods become increasingly accessible. Hence, such improvements as better roads for moving goods provide one of the primary routes by which traditional cultural practices are undermined.

E4.3 CES Utility

In Chapter 3 we introduced the CES utility function

$$U(X, Y) = \frac{X^{\delta}}{\delta} + \frac{Y^{\delta}}{\delta} \qquad \text{(viii)}$$

for $\delta \leq 1$, $\delta \neq 0$. The primary use of this function is to illustrate alternative substitution possibilities (as reflected in the value of the parameter δ). Budget shares implied by this utility function provide a number of such insights. Manipulation of the first-order conditions for a constrained utility maximum with the CES function yield the share equations

$$s_X = 1/[1 + (P_Y/P_X)^K]$$
$$s_Y = 1/[1 + (P_X/P_Y)^K] \qquad \text{(ix)}$$

where $K = \delta/(\delta - 1)$.

The homothetic nature of the CES function is shown by the fact that these shared expressions depend only on the relative price ratio, P_X/P_Y. Behavior of the shares in response to changes in relative prices depends on the value of the parameter K. For the Cobb-Douglas case, $\delta = 0$ so $K = 0$ and

$s_X = s_Y = \frac{1}{2}$, as we have found in several examples. When $\delta > 0$, substitution possibilities are great and $K < 0$. In this case Equation ix shows that s_X and P_X/P_Y move in opposite directions. If P_X/P_Y rises, the individual substitutes Y for X to such an extent that s_X falls. Alternatively, if $\delta < 0$, substitution possibilities are limited, $K > 0$, and s_X and P_X/P_Y move in the same direction. In this case an increase in P_X/P_Y causes only minor substitution of Y for X, and s_X actually rises because of the relatively higher price of good X.

North American Free Trade

CES demand functions are most often used in large-scale computer models of general equilibrium (see Chapter 16) that economists use to evaluate the impact of major economic changes. Because the CES model stresses that shares respond to changes in relative prices, it is particularly appropriate for looking at innovations such as changes in tax policy or in international trade restrictions where changes in relative prices are quite likely. One important recent area of such research has been on the impact of the North American Free Trade Agreement for Canada, Mexico, and the United States. In general, these models find that all of the countries involved might be expected to gain from the agreement, but that Mexico's gains may be the greatest because it is experiencing the greatest change in relative prices. Kehoe and Kehoe (1995) present a number of computable equilibrium models that economists have used in these examinations.[7]

REFERENCES

Behrman, Jere R. "Is Variety the Spice of Life? Implications for Caloric Intake." *Review of Economics and Statistics* (November 1989): 666–672.

Green, H. A. *Consumer Theory.* London: The Macmillan Press, 1976.

Hyashi, Fumio. "Is the Japanese Extended Family Altruistically Linked? A Test Based on Engel Curves." *Journal of Political Economy* (June 1995): 661–674.

Kehoe, Patrick J., and Timothy J. Kehoe. *Modeling North American Economic Integration.* London: Klower Academic Publishers, 1995.

Oczkowski, E., and N. E. Philip. "Household Expenditure Patterns and Access to Consumer Goods in a Transitional Economy." *Journal of Economic Development* (June 1994): 165–183.

Stone, R. "Linear Expenditure Systems and Demand Analysis." *The Economic Journal* (September 1954): 511–527.

---

[7]The Research on the North American Free Trade Agreement is discussed in more detail in the Extensions to Chapter 16.

CHAPTER 5

INCOME AND SUBSTITUTION EFFECTS

In this chapter we will use the utility-maximization model to study how the quantity of a good that an individual chooses is affected by a change in that good's price. This examination will result in our being able to construct the individual's demand curve for the good. In the process we will provide a number of insights into the nature of this price response and into the kinds of *ceteris paribus* assumptions that lie behind most analyses of demand.

As we pointed out in Chapter 4, in principle it will often be possible to solve the necessary conditions of a utility maximum for the optimal levels of X_1, $X_2, \ldots, X_n$ (and λ, the Lagrangian multiplier) as functions of all prices and income. Mathematically, this can be expressed as n demand functions of the form

DEMAND FUNCTIONS

$$X_1^* = d_1(P_1, P_2, \ldots, P_n, I)$$

$$X_2^* = d_2(P_1, P_2, \ldots, P_n, I)$$

.

. $\qquad\qquad$ (5.1)

.

$$X_n^* = d_n(P_1, P_2, \ldots, P_n, I),$$

where we now use the functional notation d for the individual's "demand." Once we know the functions $d_1, d_2, \ldots, d_n$ and the values of $P_1, P_2, \ldots, P_n$ and I, (and if we assume preferences don't change) we can "predict" how much of each good the individual will buy. In later sections we shall be interested in what happens to the optimal amount of, say, X_1 when P_1 changes. We shall also investigate what happens to X_1 when income changes or (in Chapter 6) when the price of another good changes. Such questions involve the study of the derivatives of the demand functions; we are interested in comparing utility-maximization choices under alternative circumstances, and the demand functions provide a shorthand way for recording the results of this *comparative statics analysis*.

Homogeneity

One comparative statics "theorem" can easily be demonstrated here. If we were to double all prices and income (indeed, if we were to multiply them all by any positive constant), the optimal quantities demanded would remain unchanged. Doubling all prices and income changes only the units by which we count, not the "real" quantity of goods demanded. This result can be seen in a number of ways, although perhaps the easiest is through a graphic approach. Referring back to Figures 4.1 and 4.2, it is clear that if we double P_X, P_Y, and I, we shall not affect the graph of the budget constraint. Hence, X^*, Y^* will still be the combination that is chosen. $P_X X + P_Y Y = I$ is the same constraint as $2P_X X + 2P_Y Y = 2I$. Somewhat more technically, we can write this result as saying that for any good X_i,

$$X_i^* = d_i(P_1, P_2, \ldots, P_n, I) = d_i(tP_1, tP_2, \ldots, tP_n, tI) \qquad (5.2)$$

for any $t > 0$. Functions that obey the property illustrated in Equation 5.2 are said to be homogeneous of degree zero.[1] Hence, we have shown that individual *demand functions are homogeneous of degree zero in all prices and income*. Changing all prices and income in the same proportions will not affect the physical quantities of goods demanded. This result shows that individuals' demands will not be affected by a "pure" inflation during which all prices and incomes rise proportionally. They will continue to demand the same bundle of goods. Of course, if an inflation were not pure (that is, if some prices rose more rapidly than others), this would not be the case.

EXAMPLE 5.1

HOMOGENEITY

Homogeneity of demand is a direct result of the utility-maximization assumption. Demand functions derived from utility maximization will be homogeneous and, conversely, demand functions that are not homogeneous

---

[1] More generally, a function $f(X_1, X_2, \ldots, X_n)$ is said to be homogeneous of degree k if $f(tX_1, tX_2, \ldots, tX_n) = t^k f(X_1, X_2, \ldots, X_n)$ for any $t > 0$. The most common cases of homogeneous functions are $k = 0$ and $k = 1$. If f is homogeneous of degree zero, doubling all of its arguments leaves f unchanged in value. If f is homogeneous of degree 1, doubling all its arguments will double the value of f. We shall encounter functions homogeneous of degree 1 in Part IV.

cannot reflect utility maximization (unless prices enter into the utility function itself as they might for goods with snob appeal). If, for example, an individual's utility for food (X) and housing (Y) is given by

$$\text{utility} = U(X, Y) = X^{.3}Y^{.7}, \tag{5.3}$$

it is a simple matter (following the procedure used in Example 4.2) to derive the demand functions

$$X^* = \frac{.3I}{P_X}$$
$$\tag{5.4}$$
$$Y^* = \frac{.7I}{P_Y}.$$

These functions obviously exhibit homogeneity—a doubling of all prices and income would leave X^* and Y^* unaffected.

If the individual's preferences for X and Y were reflected instead by the CES function:

$$U(X, Y) = X^{.5} + Y^{.5}, \tag{5.5}$$

we showed in Example 4.3 that the demand fuctions are given by:

$$X^* = \left(\frac{1}{1 + P_X/P_Y}\right) \cdot \frac{I}{P_X}$$
$$\tag{5.6}$$
$$Y^* = \left(\frac{1}{1 + P_Y/P_X}\right) \cdot \frac{I}{P_Y}.$$

As before, both these demand functions are homogeneous of degree zero—a doubling of P_X, P_Y, and I would leave X^* and Y^* unaffected.

QUERY: Do the demand functions derived in this example assure that total spending on X and Y will exhaust the individual's income for *any combination* of P_X, P_Y, and I? Can you prove that this is the case?

As an individual's purchasing power rises, it is natural to expect that the quantity of each good purchased will also increase. This situation is illustrated in Figure 5.1. As expenditures increase from I_1 to I_2 to I_3, the quantity of X demanded increases from X_1 to X_2 to X_3. Also, the quantity of Y increases from Y_1 to Y_2 to Y_3. Notice that the budget lines I_1, I_2, and I_3 are all parallel, reflecting the fact that only income is changing, not the relative prices of X and Y. Since the ratio P_X/P_Y stays constant, the utility-

CHANGES IN INCOME

FIGURE 5.1

EFFECT OF AN INCREASE IN INCOME ON THE QUANTITIES OF X AND Y CHOSEN

As income increases from I_1 to I_2 to I_3, the optimal (utility-maximizing) choices of X and Y are shown by the successively higher points of tangency. Notice that the budget constraint shifts in a parallel way because its slope (given by $-P_X/P_Y$) does not change.

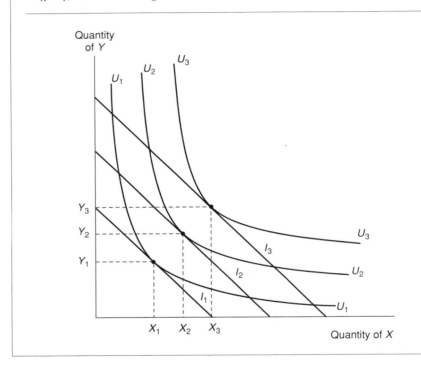

maximizing conditions also require that the *MRS* stay constant as the individual moves to higher levels of satisfaction. The *MRS* is therefore the same at point (X_3, Y_3) as at (X_1, Y_1).

Normal and Inferior Goods

In Figure 5.1, both X and Y increase as income increases—$\partial X/\partial I$ and $\partial Y/\partial I$ are both positive. This might be considered the usual situation, and goods that exhibit this property are called *normal goods* over the range of income change being observed.

For some goods, however, the quantity chosen may decrease as income increases in some ranges. Some examples of these goods might be rotgut

FIGURE 5.2

AN INDIFFERENCE CURVE MAP EXHIBITING INFERIORITY

In this diagram, good Z is inferior because the quantity purchased actually declines as income increases. Y is a normal good (as it must be if there are only two goods available), and purchases of Y increase as total expenditures increase.

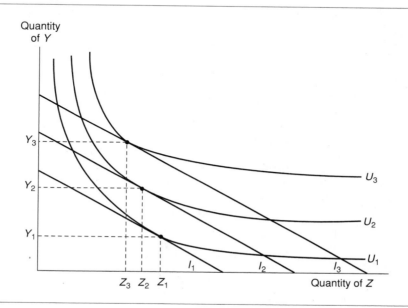

whiskey, potatoes, and secondhand clothing. A good Z for which $\partial Z/\partial I$ is negative is called an *inferior good.* This phenomenon is illustrated in Figure 5.2. In this diagram the good Z is inferior because for increases in income in the range shown, less of Z is actually chosen. Notice that indifference curves do not have to be "oddly" shaped to exhibit inferiority; the curves corresponding to goods Y and Z in Figure 5.2 continue to obey the assumption of a diminishing *MRS.* Good Z is inferior because of the way it relates to the other goods available (good Y here), not because of a peculiarity unique to it. Hence, we have developed the following definitions:

DEFINITION

Inferior and Normal Goods   A good X_i for which $\partial X_i/\partial I < 0$ over some range of income changes is an *inferior good* in that range. If $\partial X_i/\partial I \geq 0$ over some range of income variation, the good is a *normal,* or "noninferior," *good* in that range.

Engel's Law Since the eighteenth century, the relationship between income and the consumption of specific items has been studied extensively by economists. Most commonly, expenditure data are collected from a sample of families and are then classified by income levels (or by "social class") to see if any important regularities are visible. Probably the most widely referenced sample data are those used by the Prussian economist Ernst Engel in his original studies. An abbreviated set of these data, showing the average budgetary allocations made by a sample of 153 Belgian families in 1857, appears in Table 5.1.

From these data Engel drew what was perhaps the first empirical generalization about consumer behavior: The proportion of total expenditure devoted to food declines as income rises. In other words, food is a necessity whose consumption rises less rapidly than does income. That hypothesis has come to be known as "Engel's law," and it has been verified in hundreds of studies. It holds true not only within a particular geographic area but also across countries and continents: Cross-country comparisons show that, on the average, individuals in less-developed countries spend a larger percentage of their incomes on food than do individuals in the industrial economies. The percentage of income spent on food also tends to decline over time as incomes rise. For example, in nineteenth-century America, individuals spent nearly 50 percent of their incomes on food. Today that figure has fallen to below 20 percent. Indeed, Engel's law appears to be such a consistent empirical finding that some economists have suggested that the proportion of income spent on food might be a useful indicator of poverty. Families that

---

TABLE 5.1

PERCENTAGE OF TOTAL EXPENDITURES ON VARIOUS ITEMS BY BELGIAN FAMILIES IN 1857

	ANNUAL INCOME		
EXPENDITURE ITEM	$225–$300	$450–$600	$750–$1,000
Food	62.0%	55.0%	50.0%
Clothing	16.0	18.0	18.0
Lodging, light, and fuel	17.0	17.0	17.0
Services (education, legal, health)	4.0	7.5	11.5
Comfort and recreation	1.0	2.5	3.5
Total	100.0%	100.0%	100.0%

SOURCE: Adapted from A. Marshall, *Principles of Economics*, 8th ed. (London: Macmillan & Co., 1920), p. 97.

spend more than, say, 35 percent of their income on food might be regarded as "poor," whereas those who spend less than that percentage would not be so regarded.

The effect of a price change on the quantity of a good demanded is somewhat more complex to analyze than is the effect of a change in income. Geometrically, this is because changing a price involves changing not only the position of the budget constraint but also its slope. Consequently, moving to the new utility-maximizing choice entails not only moving to another indifference curve but also changing the MRS. When a price changes, therefore, two analytically different effects come into play. One of these is a *substitution effect*—even if the individual were to stay on the *same* indifference curve, consumption patterns would be allocated so as to equate the MRS to the new price ratio. A second effect, the *income effect,* arises because a price change necessarily changes an individual's "real" income—the individual cannot stay on the initial indifference curve but must move to a new one. We begin by analyzing these effects graphically. Then we will provide a mathematical development.

CHANGES IN A GOOD'S PRICE

Income and substitution effects are illustrated in Figure 5.3. The individual is initially maximizing utility (subject to total expenditures, I) by consuming the combination X^*, Y^*. The initial budget constraint is $I = P_X^1 X + P_Y Y$. Now suppose that the price of X falls to P_X^2. The new budget constraint is given by the equation $I = P_X^2 X + P_Y Y$ in Figure 5.3. It is clear that the new position of maximum utility is at X^{**}, Y^{**}, where the new budget line is tangent to the indifference curve U_2. The movement to this new point can be viewed as being composed of two effects. First, the change in the slope of the budget constraint would have motivated the individual to move to point B, even if choices had been confined to those on the original indifference curve U_1. The dashed line in Figure 5.3 has the same slope as the new budget constraint $(I = P_X^2 X + P_Y Y)$, but is drawn to be tangent to U_1 because we are conceptually holding "real" income (that is, utility) constant. A relatively lower price for X causes a move from X^*, Y^* to B if we do not allow the individual to be made better off as a result of the lower price. This movement is a graphic demonstration of the *substitution effect.* The further move from B to the optimal point X^{**}, Y^{**} is analytically identical to the kind of change exhibited earlier for changes in income. Because the price of X has fallen, the individual has a greater "real" income and can afford a utility level (U_2) that is greater than that which could previously be attained. If X is a normal good, the individual will demand more of it in response to this increase in purchasing

Graphical Analysis of a Fall in Price

FIGURE 5.3

DEMONSTRATION OF THE INCOME AND
SUBSTITUTION EFFECTS OF A FALL IN THE PRICE OF *X*

When the price of X falls from P_X^1 to P_X^2, the utility-maximizing choice shifts from X^*, Y^* to X^{**}, Y^{**}. This movement can be broken down into two analytically different effects: first, the substitution effect, involving a movement along the initial indifference curve to point B, where the MRS is equal to the new price ratio; and secondly, the income effect, entailing a movement to a higher level of utility, since real income has increased. In the diagram, both the substitution and income effects cause more X to be bought when its price declines. Notice that point I/P_Y is the same as before the price change. This is because P_Y has not changed. Point I/P_Y therefore appears on both the old and new budget constraints.

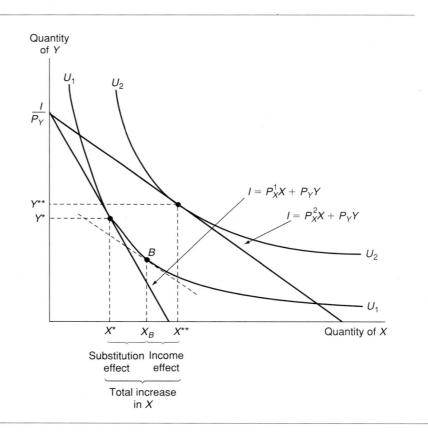

power. This observation explains the origin of the term *income effect* for the movement. Overall then, the result of the price decline is to cause more X to be demanded.

It is important to realize that the individual does not actually make a series of choices from X^*, Y^* to B and then to X^{**}, Y^{**}. We never observe point B; only the two optimal positions are reflected in the individual's behavior. However, the notion of income and substitution effects is analytically valuable because it shows that a price change affects the quantity of X that is demanded in two conceptually different ways. We will see how this separation offers major insights in the theory of demand.

Graphical Analysis of an Increase in Price

If the price of good X were to increase, a similar analysis would be used. In Figure 5.4 the budget line has been shifted inward because of an increase in the price of X from P_X^1 to P_X^2. The movement from the initial point of utility maximization (X^*, Y^*) to the new point (X^{**}, Y^{**}) can be decomposed into two effects. First, even if the individual could stay on the initial indifference curve (U_2), there would still be an incentive to substitute Y for X and move along U_2 to point B. However, because purchasing power has been reduced by the rise in the price of X, the individual must move to a lower level of utility. This movement is again called the income effect. Notice in Figure 5.4 that both the income and substitution effects work in the same direction and cause the quantity of X demanded to be reduced in response to an increase in its price.

Effects of Price Changes for Inferior Goods

So far we have shown that substitution and income effects tend to reinforce one another. For a price decline, both cause more of the good to be demanded, whereas for a price increase, both cause less to be demanded. Although this analysis is accurate for the case of normal (noninferior) goods, the possibility of inferior goods complicates the story somewhat. In this case, income and substitution effects work in opposite directions, and the total result of a price change is indeterminate. A fall in price, for example, will always cause an individual to tend to consume more of a good because of the substitution effect. But if the good is inferior, the increase in purchasing power caused by the price decline may cause less of the good to be bought. The result is therefore indeterminate—the substitution effect tends to increase the quantity of the inferior good bought, whereas the (perverse) income effect tends to reduce this quantity. Unlike the situation for normal goods, it is not possible here to predict exactly how the price change will affect the quantity chosen.

Giffen's Paradox

If the income effect of a price change is strong enough, the change in price and the resulting change in the quantity demanded could actually move in

FIGURE 5.4

DEMONSTRATION OF THE INCOME AND SUBSTITUTION EFFECTS OF AN INCREASE IN THE PRICE OF *X*

When the price of X increases, the budget constraint shifts inward. The movement from the initial utility-maximizing point (X^*, Y^*) to the new point (X^{**}, Y^{**}) can be analyzed as two separate effects. The substitution effect would be depicted as a movement to point B on the initial indifference curve (U_2). The price increase, however, would create a loss of purchasing power and a consequent movement to a lower indifference curve. This is the income effect. In the diagram, both the income and substitution effects cause the quantity of X to fall as a result of the increase in its price. Again, the point I/P_Y is not affected by the change in the price of X.

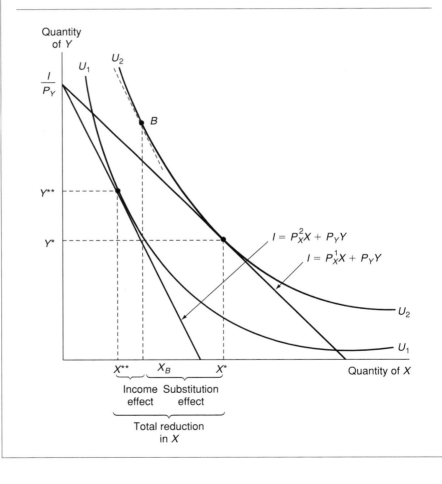

the same direction. Legend has it that the English economist Robert Giffen observed this paradox in nineteenth-century Ireland—when the price of potatoes rose, people reportedly consumed more of them. This peculiar result can be explained by looking at the size of the income effect of a change in the price of potatoes. Potatoes were not only inferior goods but also used up a large portion of the Irish people's income. An increase in the price of potatoes therefore reduced real income substantially. The Irish were forced to cut back on other luxury food consumption in order to buy more potatoes. Even though this rendering of events is historically implausible, the possibility of an increase in the quantity demanded in response to an increase in the price of a good has come to be known as *Giffen's paradox*.[2] Later we will provide a mathematical analysis of how Giffen's Paradox might occur.

Hence, our graphical analysis leads to the following conclusions:

A Summary

OPTIMIZATION PRINCIPLE

Substitution and Income Effects   The utility-maximization hypothesis suggests that for normal goods, a fall in the price of a good leads to an increase in quantity purchased because (1) the *substitution effect* causes more to be purchased as the individual moves *along* an indifference curve; and (2) the *income effect* causes more to be purchased because the price decline has increased the individual's purchasing power, thereby permitting movement to a *higher* indifference curve. When the price of a normal good rises, similar reasoning predicts a decline in the quantity purchased. For inferior goods, substitution and income effects work in opposite directions, and no definite predictions can be made.

So far we have shown that an individual's demand for a good (say, X_1) depends on his or her preferences and on all prices and income:

THE INDIVIDUAL'S DEMAND CURVE

$$X_1^* = d_1(P_1, P_2, \ldots, P_n, I). \tag{5.7}$$

---

[2] A major problem with this explanation is that it disregards Marshall's observation that both supply and demand factors must be taken into account when analyzing price changes. If potato prices increased because of the potato blight in Ireland, then supply should have become smaller, so how could *more* potatoes possibly have been consumed? Also, since many Irish people were potato farmers, the potato price increase should have increased real income for them. For a detailed discussion of these and other fascinating bits of potato lore, see G. P. Dwyer and C. M. Lindsey, "Robert Giffen and the Irish Potato," *American Economic Review* (March 1984): 188–192.

Frequently, it is convenient to graph X_1 as simply a function of its own price (P_1), with the understanding that all other prices and income are being held constant. To show the construction of such a graph, we assume that there are only two goods (X and Y) and that the demand function for good X is given by

$$X^* = d_X(P_X, P_Y, I). \tag{5.8}$$

Figure 5.5a shows utility-maximizing choices of X and Y as the individual is presented with successively lower prices of good X (while holding P_Y and I constant). It is assumed that the quantities of X chosen increase from X' to X'' to X''' as that good's price falls from P_X' to P_X'' to P_X'''. Such an assumption is in accord with our general conclusion that, except in the unusual case of Giffen's paradox, $\partial X/\partial P_X$ is negative.

In Figure 5.5b information about the utility-maximizing choices of good X is transferred to a *demand curve*, having P_X on the vertical axis and sharing the same horizontal axis as the figure above it. The negative slope of the curve again reflects the assumption that $\partial X/\partial P_X$ is negative. Hence, we may define an individual demand curve as follows:

DEFINITION

Individual Demand Curve   An *individual demand curve* shows the relationship between the price of a good and the quantity of that good purchased, assuming that all other determinants of demand are held constant.

The demand curve illustrated in Figure 5.5 stays in a fixed position only so long as all other determinants of demand remain unchanged. If one of these other factors does change, the curve may shift to a new position, as we now describe.

Shifts in the Demand Curve   Three basic factors were held constant in deriving the demand curve: (1) income; (2) prices of other goods (say, P_Y); and (3) the individual's preferences. If any of these were to change, the entire demand curve might shift to a new position. For example, if I were to increase, the curve would shift outward (provided that $\partial X/\partial I > 0$; that is, that the good is a "normal" good over this income range). More X would be demanded at *each* price. If another price, say, P_Y, were to change, the curve would shift inward or outward, depending precisely on how X and Y are related. In the next chapter we will examine that relationship in detail. Finally, the curve would shift if the individual's preferences for good X were to change. A sudden advertising blitz by the McDonald's Corporation might shift the demand for hamburgers outward, for example.

FIGURE 5.5

CONSTRUCTION OF AN INDIVIDUAL'S DEMAND CURVE

In (a) the individual's utility-maximizing choices of X and Y are shown for three different prices of X (P'_X, P''_X, and P'''_X). In (b) this relationship between P_X and X is used to construct the demand curve for X. The demand curve is drawn on the assumption that P_Y, I, and preferences remain constant as P_X varies.

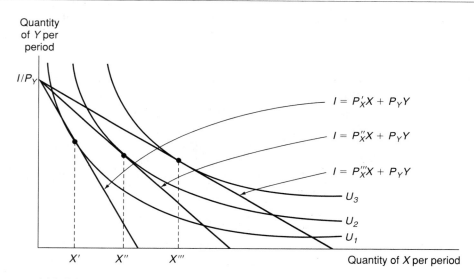

(a) Individual's indifference curve map

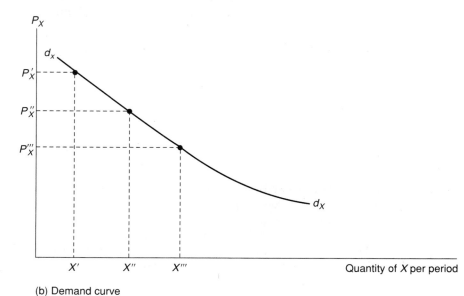

(b) Demand curve

As this discussion makes clear, one must remember that the demand curve is only a two-dimensional representation of the true demand function (Equation 5.7 or 5.8) and that it is stable only if other things in fact stay constant. It is important to keep clearly in mind the difference between a movement along a given demand curve caused by a change in P_X and a shift in the entire curve caused by a change in income, in one of the other prices, or in preferences. Traditionally, the term "an increase in demand" is reserved for an outward shift in the demand curve, whereas the term "an increase in the quantity demanded" refers to a movement along a given curve caused by a change in P_X.

EXAMPLE 5.2

DEMAND FUNCTIONS AND DEMAND CURVES

To be able to graph a demand curve from a given demand function, we must assume that the preferences that generated the function remain stable and that we know the values of income and other relevant prices. In the first case studied in Example 5.1, we found that

$$X = \frac{.3I}{P_X}$$

and (5.9)

$$Y = \frac{.7I}{P_Y}.$$

If preferences do not change and if this individual's income is $100, then these functions become

$$X = \frac{30}{P_X}$$

(5.10)

$$Y = \frac{70}{P_Y}$$

or

$$P_X X = 30$$

$$P_Y Y = 70,$$

which makes clear that the demand curves for these two goods are each rectangular hyperbolas. A rise in income would shift both of the demand curves outward. Notice also, in this case, that the demand curve for X is not shifted by changes in P_Y and vice versa.

For the second case examined in Example 5.1, the analysis is more complex. For good X, say, we know that

$$X = \left(\frac{1}{1 + P_X/P_Y}\right) \cdot \frac{I}{P_X} \qquad (5.11)$$

so to graph this in the P_X–X plane we must know both I and P_Y. If we again assume $I = 100$ and let $P_Y = 1$, Equation 5.11 becomes

$$X = \frac{100}{P_X^2 + P_X}, \qquad (5.12)$$

which, when graphed, would also show a general hyperbolic relationship between price and quantity consumed. In this case the curve would be relatively flatter because substitution effects are larger than in the Cobb-Douglas case. From Equation 5.11 we know that

$$\frac{\partial X}{\partial I} = \left(\frac{1}{1 + P_X/P_Y}\right) \cdot \frac{1}{P_X} > 0$$

and $\qquad (5.13)$

$$\frac{\partial X}{\partial P_Y} = \frac{I}{(P_X + P_Y)^2} > 0$$

so increases in I or P_Y would shift the demand curve for good X outward.

QUERY: How would the demand functions in Equations 5.10 change if $\alpha = \beta = 0.5$? Show that these demand functions predict the same X consumption at the point $P_X = 1$, $P_Y = 1$, $I = 100$ as does the Equation 5.11. Use a numerical example to show that the CES demand function is more responsive to an increase in P_X than is the Cobb-Douglas demand function.

In Figure 5.5 the individual's utility varies along the demand curve. As P_X falls, the individual is made increasingly better off as shown by the increase in utility from U_1 to U_2 to U_3. The reason this happens is that the demand curve is drawn on the assumption that nominal income and other prices are held constant; hence, a decline in P_X makes the individual better off by increasing his or her real purchasing power. Although this is the most common way to impose the *ceteris paribus* assumption in developing a demand curve, it is not the only way. An alternative approach holds the individual's *real* income (or utility) constant while examining reactions to changes in P_X. The derivation is illustrated in Figure 5.6. There we hold utility constant (at U_2) while successively reducing P_X. As P_X falls, the individual's nominal income is effectively reduced to prevent any increase in utility from occurring. In other words, the effects of the price change on purchasing power are "compensated" so as to constrain the individual to remain on U_2. Reactions to changing prices therefore include only substitution effects. If we

COMPENSATED DEMAND CURVES

FIGURE 5.6

CONSTRUCTION OF A COMPENSATED DEMAND CURVE

The curve h_X shows how the quantity of X demanded changes when P_X changes, holding P_Y and *utility* constant. That is, the individual's income is "compensated" so as to keep utility constant. Hence, h_X reflects only substitution effects of changing prices.

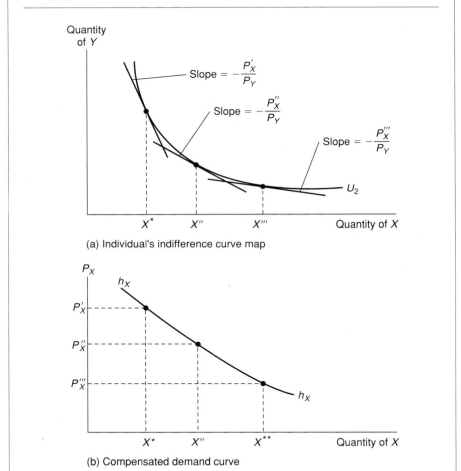

(a) Individual's indifference curve map

(b) Compensated demand curve

were instead to examine effects of increases in P_X, income compensation would be positive: The individual's income would have to be increased to permit him or her to stay on the U_2 indifference curve in response to the price rises. We can summarize these results as follows:

DEFINITION

Compensated Demand Curve A *compensated (or, Hicksian) demand curve* shows the relationship between the price of a good and the quantity purchased on the assumption that other prices *and utility* are held constant. The curve therefore illustrates only substitution effects. Mathematically, the curve is a two-dimensional representation of the *compensated demand function*

$$X^* = h_X(P_X, P_Y, U). \tag{5.14}$$

Relationship between Compensated and Uncompensated Demand Curves

This relationship between the two demand curve concepts we have developed is illustrated in Figure 5.7. At P_X'' the curves intersect, since at that price the individual's income is just sufficient to attain utility level U_2 (compare Figures 5.5 and 5.6). Hence, X'' is demanded under either demand concept. For prices below P_X'', however, the individual suffers a negative income compensation on the curve h_X to prevent an increase in utility from the lower price. Hence, assuming X is a normal good, less X is demanded at P_X''' along h_X than along the uncompensated curve d_X. Alternatively, for a price above P_X'' (such as P_X'), income compensation is positive, since the individual needs some help to remain on U_2. Hence, again assuming X is a normal good, at P_X' more X is demanded along h_X than along d_X. In general then, for a normal good, the compensated demand curve is somewhat less responsive to price changes than is the uncompensated curve because the latter reflects both substitution and income effects of price changes whereas the compensated curve reflects only substitution effects.

The choice between using compensated or uncompensated demand curves in economic analysis is largely a matter of convenience. In most empirical work uncompensated curves are used since the data on prices and nominal incomes needed to estimate them are readily available. In the Extensions to Chapter 7 we will describe some of these estimates and show how they might be employed for practical policy purposes. For some theoretical purposes, however, compensated demand curves are a more appropriate concept, since the ability to hold utility constant offers some advantages. Our discussion of "consumer surplus" in the final section of this chapter offers one illustration of these advantages.

EXAMPLE 5.3

COMPENSATED DEMANDS FOR HAMBURGERS AND SOFT DRINKS

In Example 3.1, we assumed that the utility function for hamburgers (Y) and soft drinks (X) was given by

FIGURE 5.7

COMPARISON OF COMPENSATED AND UNCOMPENSATED DEMAND CURVES

The compensated (h_X) and uncompensated (d_X) demand curves intersect at P''_X since X'' is demanded under each concept. For prices above P''_X, the individual's income is increased with the compensated demand curve, so more X is demanded than with the uncompensated curve. For prices below P''_X, income is reduced for the compensated curve, so less X is demanded than with the uncompensated curve. The curve d_X is flatter because it incorporates both substitution and income effects whereas the curve h_X reflects only substitution effects.

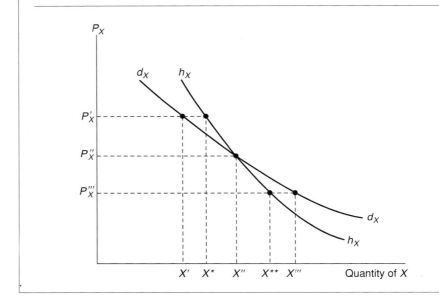

$$\text{utility} = U(X, Y) = X^{.5}Y^{.5}, \tag{5.15}$$

and in Example 4.2, we showed that we can calculate the Marshallian demand functions for such utility functions as

$$X = \frac{\alpha I}{P_X} = \frac{I}{2P_X}$$

$$Y = \frac{\beta I}{P_Y} = \frac{I}{2P_Y}. \tag{5.16}$$

Also, in Example 4.4, we calculated the indirect utility function by combining Equations 5.15 and 5.16 as

$$\text{utility} = V(I, P_X, P_Y) = \frac{I}{2P_X^{.5}P_Y^{.5}}. \tag{5.17}$$

To obtain the compensated demand functions for X and Y, we simply use Equation 5.17 to solve for I and then substitute this expression involving V into Equations 5.16. This permits us to interchange income and utility so that we may hold the latter constant as is required for the compensated demand concept. Making these substitutions yields

$$X = \frac{VP_Y^{.5}}{P_X^{.5}}$$

$$Y = \frac{VP_X^{.5}}{P_Y^{.5}}. \tag{5.18}$$

These are the compensated demand functions for X and Y. Notice that now demand depends on utility (V) rather than on income. Holding utility constant it is clear that increases in P_X reduce the demand for X—and this now reflects only the substitution effect (see Example 5.4 also).

Although P_Y did not enter into the uncompensated demand function for good X, it does enter into the compensated function—increases in P_Y shift the compensated demand curve for X outward. The two demand concepts agree at our initial point $P_X = .25$, $P_Y = 1$, $I = 2$, and $V = 2$—Equations 5.16 predict $X = 4$, $Y = 1$ at this point as do Equations 5.18. For $P_X > .25$ or $P_X < .25$, the demands differ under the two concepts, however. If, say, $P_X = 1$, the un-compensated functions (Equations 5.16) predict $X = 1$, $Y = 1$ whereas the compensated functions (Equations 5.18) predict $X = 2$, $Y = 2$. The reduction in X resulting from the rise in its price is smaller with the compensated demand function than it is with the uncompensated function because the former concept does not include the negative income effect arising from the price rise.

This example makes clear the different *ceteris paribus* assumptions inherent in the two demand concepts. With uncompensated demand, expenditures are held constant at $I = 2$ so the rise in P_X from .25 to 1 results in a loss of utility—in this case, utility falls from 2 to 1. In the compensated demand case, utility is held constant at $V = 2$. To keep utility constant, expenditures must rise to $E = 1(2) + 1(2) = 4$ in order to offset the effects of the price rise (see Equation 5.17).

QUERY: Are the compensated demand functions given in Equations 5.18 homogeneous of degree zero in P_X and P_Y if utility is held constant? Would you expect that to be true for all compensated demand functions?

A MATHEMATICAL DEVELOPMENT OF RESPONSE TO PRICE CHANGES

Up to this point we have largely relied on graphical devices to describe how individuals respond to price changes. Since additional insights are provided by a more mathematical approach, we will now pursue such an analysis. Our basic goal is to examine the partial derivative $\partial X/\partial P_X$; that is, how a *ceteris paribus* change in the price of a good affects its purchase. Later we take up the question of how changes in the price of one commodity affect purchases of another commodity.

Direct Approach

Our goal is to use the utility-maximization model to learn something about how the demand for good X changes when P_X changes; that is, we wish to calculate $\partial d_X/\partial P_X$. The direct approach to this problem makes use of the first-order conditions for utility maximization (Equations 4.8). Differentiation of these $n+1$ equations yields a new system of $n+1$ equations, which eventually can be solved for the derivative we seek.[3] Unfortunately, obtaining this solution is quite cumbersome and the steps required yield little in the way of economic insights. Hence, we will instead adopt an indirect approach that relies on the concept of duality. In the end, both approaches yield the same conclusion, but the indirect approach is much richer in terms of the economics it contains.

Indirect Approach

In order to begin our indirect approach,[4] we will assume there are only two goods (X and Y) and focus on the compensated demand function, $h_X(P_X, P_Y, U)$, introduced in Equation 5.14. We now wish to illustrate the connection between this demand function and the ordinary demand function, $d_X(P_X, P_Y, I)$. In Chapter 4 we introduced the notion of the expenditure function, which records the minimal expenditure necessary to attain a given utility level. If we denote this function by

$$\text{minimum expenditure} = E(P_X, P_Y, U), \tag{5.19}$$

then by definition,

$$h_X(P_X, P_Y, U) = d_X[P_X, P_Y, E(P_X, P_Y, U)]. \tag{5.20}$$

This conclusion was already introduced in connection with Figure 5.7, which showed that the quantity demanded is identical for the compensated and uncompensated demand functions when income is exactly what is needed to attain the required utility level. Equation 5.20 is obtained by inserting that expenditure level into the demand function, d_X. Now we can proceed by

---

[3] See, for example, Paul A. Samuelson, *Foundations of Economic Analysis* (Cambridge, Mass.: Harvard University Press, 1947), pp. 101–103.

[4] The following proof is adapted from Phillip J. Cook, "A 'One Line' Proof of the Slutsky Equation," *American Economic Review* 62 (March 1972): 139.

partially differentiating Equation 5.20 with respect to P_X and recognizing that P_X enters into the ordinary demand function in two places. Hence,

$$\frac{\partial h_X}{\partial P_X} = \frac{\partial d_X}{\partial P_X} + \frac{\partial d_X}{\partial E} \cdot \frac{\partial E}{\partial P_X}, \tag{5.21}$$

and rearranging terms,

$$\frac{\partial d_X}{\partial P_X} = \frac{\partial h_X}{\partial P_X} - \frac{\partial d_X}{\partial E} \cdot \frac{\partial E}{\partial P_X}. \tag{5.22}$$

The Substitution Effect

Consequently, the derivative we seek has two terms. We now examine each of these. Interpretation of the first term is straightforward: It is the slope of the compensated demand curve. But that slope represents movement along a single indifference curve—it is in fact what we called the "substitution effect" earlier. The first term on the right of Equation 5.22 is a mathematical representation of that effect.

The Income Effect

The second term in Equation 5.22 reflects the way in which changes in P_X affect the demand for X through changes in necessary expenditure levels (that is, changes in purchasing power). This term therefore reflects the income effect. The negative sign in Equation 5.22 shows the precise direction of the effect. For example, an increase in P_X increases the expenditure level necessary to attain a given utility level (mathematically, $\partial E/\partial P_X > 0$). But because nominal income is in fact held constant, these extra expenditures are not available, so X must be reduced to meet this shortfall. The extent of the reduction is given by $\partial d_X/\partial E$. On the other hand, if P_X falls, the minimum expenditure level required to attain a given utility falls too. The decline in X that would normally accompany such a fall in expenditures is precisely the amount that must be added back through the income effect (by subtracting a negative change in X) to account for the increase in X brought about by this increase in real purchasing power.

The Slutsky Equation

The relationships embodied in Equation 5.22 were first discovered by the Russian economist Eugen Slutsky in the late nineteenth century. A slight change in notation is required to state the result the way Slutsky did. First, we write the substitution effect as

$$\text{substitution effect} = \frac{\partial h_X}{\partial P_X} = \left.\frac{\partial X}{\partial P_X}\right|_{U = \text{constant}} \tag{5.23}$$

to indicate movement along an indifference curve. For the income effect we have

$$\text{income effect} = -\frac{\partial d_X}{\partial E} \cdot \frac{\partial E}{\partial P_X} = -\frac{\partial X}{\partial I} \cdot \frac{\partial E}{\partial P_X}, \tag{5.24}$$

since changes in income or expenditures amount to the same thing in the function d_X.

It is a relatively easy matter to show that

$$\frac{\partial E}{\partial P_X} = X. \tag{5.25}$$

Intuitively, a \$1 increase in P_X raises necessary expenditures by X dollars since \$1 extra must be paid for each unit of X purchased. A formal proof of this assertion, which relies on the envelope theorem (see Chapter 2), will be relegated to a footnote.[5]

By combining Equations 5.23–5.25 we can arrive at the following:

OPTIMIZATION PRINCIPLE

Slutsky Equation The utility-maximization hypothesis shows that the substitution and income effects arising from a price change can be represented by

$$\frac{\partial d_X}{\partial P_X} = \text{substitution effect} + \text{income effect}, \tag{5.26}$$

or

$$\frac{\partial d_X}{\partial P_X} = \frac{\partial X}{\partial P_X}\bigg|_{U\,=\,\text{constant}} - X\frac{\partial X}{\partial I}. \tag{5.27}$$

---

[5] Remember that the individual's dual problem is to minimize $E = P_X X + P_Y Y$, subject to $\overline{U} = U(X, Y)$. The Lagrangian expression for this problem is

$$\mathcal{L} = P_X X + P_Y Y + \lambda[\overline{U} - U(X, Y)],$$

and the envelope theorem applied to constrained minimization problems states that at the optimal point,

$$\frac{\partial E}{\partial P_X} = \frac{\partial \mathcal{L}}{\partial P_X} = X.$$

This is the result that was to be shown. The result, and similar ones that we will encounter in the theory of firms' costs, is sometimes called Shephard's lemma. Its importance in empirical work is that the *demand function* for good X can be found directly from the expenditure function by simple partial differentiation. The demand functions generated in this way will depend on $\overline{U}$, so they should be interpreted as compensated demand functions. In Example 4.5 we found that the expenditure function for hamburgers and soft drinks was

$$E = 2\,V P_X^{.5} P_Y^{.5}.$$

Partial differentiation of this expression with respect to P_X yields the compensated demand function in Equations 5.18. For a further discussion, see the extensions to this chapter.

The Slutsky equation allows us to give a more definitive treatment of the direction and size of substitution and income effects than was possible with only a graphic analysis. First, the substitution effect ($\partial X/\partial P_X|U = \text{constant}$) is always negative as long as the *MRS* is diminishing. A fall (rise) in P_X reduces (increases) P_X/P_Y, and utility maximization requires that the *MRS* fall (rise) too. But this can only occur along an indifference curve if X increases (or, in the case of a rise in P_X, decreases). Hence, insofar as the substitution effect is concerned, price and quantity must move in opposite directions. Equivalently, the slope of the compensated demand curve must be negative.[6] We will show this result in a somewhat different way in the next section.

The sign of the income effect ($-X\,\partial X/\partial I$) depends on the sign of $\partial X/\partial I$. If X is a normal good, $\partial X/\partial I$ is positive and the entire income effect, like the substitution effect, is negative. Thus for normal goods, price and quantity always move in opposite directions. For example, a fall in P_X raises real income, and because X is a normal good, purchases of X rise. Similarly, a rise in P_X reduces real income and purchases of X fall. Overall then, as we described previously using a graphic analysis, substitution and income effects work in the same direction to yield a negatively sloped demand curve. In the case of an inferior good, $\partial X/\partial I < 0$ and the two terms in Equation 5.27 would have different signs. It is at least theoretically possible that in this case the second term could dominate the first, lending to Giffen's paradox ($\partial d_X/\partial P_X > 0$).

EXAMPLE 5.4

A SLUTSKY DECOMPOSITION

The uncompensated and compensated demand functions for soft drinks were derived in Example 5.3 as

$$X = d_X(P_X, P_Y, I) = \frac{I}{2P_X} \tag{5.28}$$

and

$$X = h_X(P_X, P_Y, V) = \frac{VP_Y^{.5}}{P_X^{.5}}, \tag{5.29}$$

respectively. The effect of a change in P_X for the uncompensated function is found by differentiation of Equation 5.28:

---

[6] It is possible that substitution effects would be 0 if indifference curves have an L-shape (implying that X and Y are used in fixed proportions). Some examples are provided in the Chapter 5 problems.

$$\frac{\partial X}{\partial P_X} = \frac{\partial d_X}{\partial P_X} = \frac{-I}{2P_X^2}. \tag{5.30}$$

This is the left-hand side of the Slutsky equation (5.27). To arrive at the right-hand side, we calculate the slope of the compensated demand function:

$$\frac{\partial X}{\partial P_X}\bigg|_{U = \text{constant}} = \frac{\partial h_X}{\partial P_X} = \frac{-.5 \, VP_Y^{.5}}{P_X^{1.5}} \tag{5.31}$$

and then use the indirect utility functions (Equation 5.17) to eliminate V:

$$\frac{\partial X}{\partial P_X}\bigg|_{U = \text{constant}} = \frac{-I}{4P_X^2}. \tag{5.32}$$

The second part of the Slutsky decomposition is given by

$$-X\frac{\partial X}{\partial I} = -X\left(\frac{1}{2P_X}\right) = \frac{-I}{4P_X^2}. \tag{5.33}$$

Combining Equations 5.32 and 5.33 yields

$$\frac{\partial X}{\partial P_X} = \frac{\partial X}{\partial P_X}\bigg|_{U = \text{constant}} - X\frac{\partial X}{\partial I} = \frac{-I}{4P_X^2} - \frac{I}{4P_X^2} = \frac{-I}{2P_X^2}, \tag{5.34}$$

which agrees with the result calculated directly from the uncompensated demand function in Equation 5.30.

Our previous numerical example also illustrates the Slutsky decomposition. When soft drink prices rise from $P_X = .25$ to $P_X = 1$, uncompensated demand falls from $X = 4$ to $X = 1$. Of this decline, the reduction from $X = 4$ to $X = 2$ represents the substitution effect (movement along the compensated demand curve) whereas the fall from $X = 2$ to $X = 1$ reflects the income effect. For this example therefore, in proportional terms, the effects are of the same size.

QUERY: How does the fact that the income and substitution effects are of the same size in this example help explain why, with constant nominal income, the share of income spent on X and Y is independent of the prices of these goods?

REVEALED PREFERENCE AND THE SUBSTITUTION EFFECT

As we have seen, the principal unambiguous prediction that can be derived from the utility-maximization model is that the slope of the compensated demand curve (that is, the substitution effect of a price change) is negative. Our proof of this assertion relies on the assumption of a diminishing MRS and the related observation that with a diminishing MRS the necessary conditions for a utility maximum are also sufficient. To some economists, such reliance on a hypothesis about an unobservable utility function represented a weak foundation indeed on which to base a theory of demand. An alternative approach, which leads to the same result, was first proposed by Paul Samuelson in the late 1940s.[7] This approach, which Samuelson termed the *theory of revealed preference*, defines a principle of rationality that is based on observed behavior and then uses this principle to approximate an individual's utility function. In this sense, a person who follows Samuelson's principle of rationality behaves *as if* he or she were maximizing a proper utility function and exhibits a negative substitution effect. Because Samuelson's approach provides considerable additional insights into our model of consumer choice, we will briefly examine it here.

The principle of rationality in the theory of revealed preference is as follows: Consider two bundles of goods, A and B. If at some prices and income level, the individual can afford both A and B but chooses A, we say that A has been "revealed preferred" to B. The principle of rationality states that under any different price-income arrangement, B can never be revealed preferred to A. If B is in fact chosen at some price-income configuration, it must be because the individual cannot afford A. The principle is illustrated in Figure 5.8. Suppose that when the budget constraint is given by I_1, point A is chosen, even though B also could have been purchased. A then has been revealed preferred to B. If for some other budget constraint, B is in fact chosen, it must be a case such as that represented by I_2—where A could not have been bought. If B were chosen when the budget constraint is I_3, this would be a violation of the principle of rationality, since with I_3 both A and B can be bought. With budget constraint I_3 it is likely that some point other than either A or B, say, C, will be bought. Notice how this principle uses observable reactions to alternative budget constraints to rank commodities rather than assuming the existence of a utility function itself.

Graphical Approach

Using the principle of rationality, we can now show why the substitution effect must be negative (or zero). Suppose that an individual is *indifferent* between two bundles, C (composed of X_C and Y_C) and D (composed of X_D and Y_D). Let P_X^C, P_Y^C be the prices at which bundle C is chosen and P_X^D, P_Y^D be the prices at which bundle D is chosen.

Negativity of the Substitution Effect

Since the individual is indifferent between C and D, it must be the case that when C was chosen, D cost at least as much as C:

$$P_X^C X_C + P_Y^C Y_C \leq P_X^C X_D + P_Y^C Y_D. \qquad (5.35)$$

---

[7] Paul A. Samuelson, *Foundations of Economic Analysis* (Cambridge, Mass.: Harvard University Press, 1947).

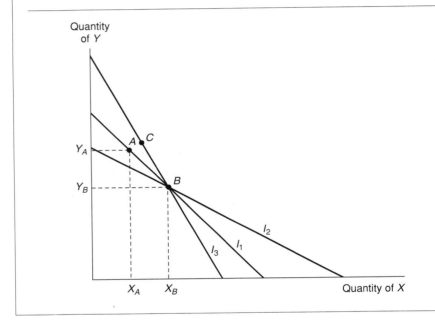

FIGURE 5.8

DEMONSTRATION OF THE PRINCIPLE OF RATIONALITY IN THE THEORY OF REVEALED PREFERENCE

With income I_1 the individual can afford both points A and B. If A is selected, A is revealed preferred to B. It would be irrational for B to be revealed preferred to A in some other price-income configuration.

A similar statement holds when D is chosen:

$$P_X^D X_D + P_Y^D Y_D \leq P_X^D X_C + P_Y^D Y_C. \tag{5.36}$$

Rewriting Equations (5.35) and (5.36) gives

$$P_X^C(X_C - X_D) + P_Y^C(Y_C - Y_D) \leq 0 \tag{5.37}$$

$$P_X^D(X_D - X_C) + P_Y^D(Y_D - Y_C) \leq 0. \tag{5.38}$$

Adding these together we get

$$(P_X^C - P_X^D)(X_C - X_D) + (P_Y^C - P_Y^D)(Y_C - Y_D) \leq 0. \tag{5.39}$$

Now suppose that only the price of X changes; assume that $P_Y^C = P_Y^D$. Then

$$(P_X^C - P_X^D)(X_C - X_D) \leq 0. \tag{5.40}$$

But Equation 5.40 simply says that price and quantity move in the opposite direction when utility is held constant (remember, bundles C and D are equally attractive). This is precisely a statement about the nonpositive nature of the substitution effect:

$$\left.\frac{\partial X}{\partial P_X}\right|_{U \,=\, \text{constant}} \leq 0. \tag{5.41}$$

We have arrived at the result by an approach that requires neither the existence of a utility function nor the assumption of a diminishing MRS.

Mathematical Generalization

Generalizing the revealed preference idea to n goods is straightforward. If at prices P_i^0, bundle X_i^0 is chosen and bundle X_i^1 is also affordable, then

$$\sum_{i=1}^{n} P_i^0 X_i^0 \geq \sum_{i=1}^{n} P_i^0 X_i^1 ; \tag{5.42}$$

that is, bundle 0 has been "revealed preferred" to bundle 1. Consequently, at the prices that prevail when bundle 1 is bought (say, P_i^1), it must be the case that X_i^0 is more expensive:

$$\sum_{i=1}^{n} P_i^1 X_i^0 > \sum_{i=1}^{n} P_i^1 X_i^1 . \tag{5.43}$$

Although this initial definition of revealed preference focuses on the relationship between two bundles of goods, the most often used version of the basic principle requires a degree of transitivity for preferences among an arbitrarily large number of bundles. This is summarized by the following "strong" axiom:

DEFINITION

Strong Axiom of Revealed Preference The *strong axiom of revealed preference* states that if commodity bundle 0 is revealed preferred to bundle 1, and if bundle 1 is revealed preferred to bundle 2, and if bundle 2 is revealed preferred to bundle 3, . . . , and if bundle $K - 1$ is revealed preferred to bundle K, *then* bundle K cannot be revealed preferred to bundle 0 (where K is any arbitrary number of commodity bundles).

Most other properties that have been developed using the concept of utility can be proved using this revealed preference axiom instead. For example, it is an easy matter to show that demand functions are homogeneous of degree zero in all prices and income. It therefore is apparent that the revealed preference axiom and the existence of "well-behaved" utility functions are somehow equivalent conditions. That this is in fact the case was first shown by H. S. Houthakker in 1950. Houthakker showed that a set of indifference curves can always be derived for an individual who obeys the strong axiom of revealed preference.[8] Hence, this axiom provides a quite general and believable foundation for utility theory based on relatively simple comparisons among alternative budget constraints. This approach is widely used in the construction of price indices and for a variety of other applied purposes.

CONSUMER SURPLUS

An important problem in applied economics is to develop a monetary measure of the gains or losses that individuals experience as a result of price changes. For example, as we will show in Part VI, if sellers of a commodity are relatively few in number, they may be able to raise the market price of the commodity in order to obtain greater profits. To put a monetary cost on this distortion, we need some way of evaluating the welfare loss that consumers experience from the price rise. Similarly, some inventions cause the price of products to fall dramatically (consider the invention of the electronic chip, for example), and in this case we might wish to evaluate how much consumers gain. In order to make such calculations, economists have developed the concept of *consumer surplus*, which permits welfare gains or losses to be estimated from knowledge of the market demand curve for a product. In this section we will show how these calculations are made; we will then use the consumer surplus notion in several places later in the text.

Consumer Welfare and Expenditure Functions

In Chapter 4 we developed the concept of the expenditure function as a way of recording the minimum expenditure necessary to achieve a desired level of utility given the prices of various goods. We denoted this function as

$$\text{expenditure} = E(P_X, P_Y, U_0), \tag{5.44}$$

where U_0 is the "target" level of utility that is sought. One way to evaluate the welfare cost of a price increase (say, from P_X^0 to P_X^1) would be to compare the expenditures required to achieve U_0 under these two situations:

$$\text{expenditures at } P_X^0 = E_0 = E(P_X^0, P_Y, U_0) \tag{5.45}$$

$$\text{expenditures at } P_X^1 = E_1 = E(P_X^1, P_Y, U_0), \tag{5.46}$$

so the loss in welfare would be measured as the increase in needed expenditures. Thus,

---

[8] H. S. Houthakker, "Revealed Preference and the Utility Function," *Economica* 17 (May 1950): 159–174.

$$\text{welfare change} = E_0 - E_1. \tag{5.47}$$

Since $E_1 > E_0$, this change would be negative, indicating that the price rise makes this person worse off. On the other hand, if P_X fell, E_0 would exceed E_1 and the individual would experience a welfare gain. Knowledge of the expenditure function is therefore sufficient to make the kind of calculations we need.

We can make further headway in this problem by using the envelope theorem result (see footnote 5 of this chapter) that the derivative of the expenditure function with respect to P_X yields the compensated demand function, h_X:

A Graphical Approach

$$\frac{dE\ (P_X, P_Y, U_0)}{dP_X} = h_X(P_X, P_Y, U_0). \tag{5.48}$$

In words, the change in necessary expenditures brought about by a change in P_X is given by the quantity of X demanded. For evaluating this change in expenditures over a "large" price change (from P_X^0 to P_X^1), we must integrate Equation 5.48:

$$\text{change in expenditures} = \int_{P_X^0}^{P_X^1} dE = \int_{P_X^0}^{P_X^1} h_X(P_X, P_Y, U_0)\,dP_X \tag{5.49}$$

The integral in Equation 5.49 has a graphical interpretation—it is the area to the left of the compensated demand curve (h_X) between P_X^0 and P_X^1. This is our measure of welfare loss. It is illustrated as the shaded area between P_X^0 and P_X^1 in Figure 5.9. For a fall in price below P_X^0, the welfare gain would be shown by a similar area below P_X^0.

To understand the origin of the term *consumer surplus* to describe the welfare changes we have been examining, consider the following question: How much would the person whose demand curve is illustrated in Figure 5.9 need to be paid to voluntarily give up the right to consume X_0 at a price of P_X^0? A price of P_X^2 would be sufficiently high to prompt this person to reduce purchases of X to zero. Hence, by our previous discussion, it would require extra expenditures given by area $P_X^2 A P_X^0$ to compensate this individual for doing without good X. Similarly, a person faced by the price P_X^0 chooses to consume X_0 and spends a total of $P_X^0 \cdot X_0$ on good X. In making these expenditures, he or she receives extra (or "surplus") welfare represented by the area $P_X^2 A P_X^0$ relative to a situation in which X is not available at all. In our study of monopoly and other market imperfections, we will see how these often result in a loss of this consumer surplus or, in some cases, a transfer of consumer surplus from consumers to other market participants.

Consumer Surplus

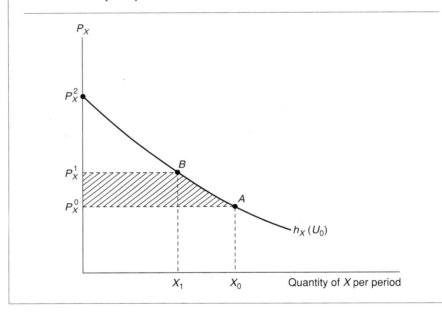

FIGURE 5.9

THE WELFARE LOSS OF A PRICE CHANGE

The shaded area to the left of the compensated demand curve, h_X, shows the amount that would have to be given to this individual to keep him or her as well-off at a price of P_X^1 as at a price of P_X^0. A consumer who buys X_0 at a price of P_X^0 receives a consumer surplus of $P_X^2 A P_X^0$ since this is the increase in expenditures that would have to be provided to make this person willing to do without X completely.

Welfare Changes and the Marshallian Demand Curve

So far, our graphic analysis of consumer surplus has made use of the compensated demand curve h_X. Because the location of this curve depends on the target level of utility assumed, there is some ambiguity about which curve to use. For example, in connection with Figure 5.9 we described the extra expenditures required to attain U_0 when good X costs P_X^1 rather than P_X^0. But in most actual applications this price rise will result in both substitution and income effects and a loss in utility to this individual (from, say, U_0 to U_1). That is, the actual market reaction to the rise in P_X would be to move from the point X_0, P_X^0 on the Marshallian demand curve (d_X) in Figure 5.10 to the point X_1, P_X^1 on that curve. At this new point, the individual will receive utility U_1, and for this level of utility the compensated demand curve is represented by $h_X(U_1)$ rather than the original curve, $h_X(U_0)$. The

FIGURE 5.10

WELFARE EFFECTS OF PRICE CHANGES AND THE MARSHALLIAN DEMAND CURVE

d_X is the usual Marshallian (nominal income constant) demand curve for good X. $h_X(U_0)$ and $h_X(U_1)$ denote the compensated demand curves associated with the utility levels experienced when P_X^0 and P_X^1, respectively, prevail. The area to the left of d_X between P_X^0 and P_X^1 is bounded by the similar areas to the left of $h_X(U_0)$ and $h_X(U_1)$. Hence, for small changes in price, the area to the left of d_X is a good measure of welfare loss.

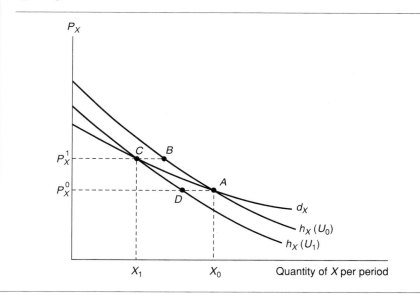

ambiguity then is whether the welfare loss is best described by the area $P_X^1 B A P_X^0$ (as in Figure 5.9) or by the area $P_X^1 C D P_X^0$ associated with the new curve, $h_X(U_1)$. Since the new area represents the reduction in expenditures that can be made in order to retain utility U_1 when the price of X falls from P_X^1 to P_X^0, it is unclear whether our original measure or this alternative measure more appropriately captures the change in welfare we seek to describe. It all depends on whether we assume that U_0 or U_1 is the appropriate utility target.

Fortunately, we have a compromise measure available. The size of the area to the left of the Marshallian demand curve between P_X^0 and P_X^1 (given by $P_X^1 C A P_X^0$) clearly falls between the size of the welfare losses defined by $h_X(U_0)$ and $h_X(U_1)$. Since information in the Marshallian curve is also more likely to be available from real-world data, this seems a very good compromise indeed.[9] Of course, if the price changes we were examining were quite small, there would be little distinction among these three measures, and it is common in many economic discussions of welfare gains or losses to be rather imprecise about exactly what type of demand curve is being used for the analysis.

EXAMPLE 5.5

LOSS OF CONSUMER SURPLUS FROM A RISE IN SOFT DRINK PRICE

These ideas can be illustrated with our well-worn soft drink example. From Example 5.2 we know that the compensated demand function for soft drinks is given by

$$X = h_X(P_X, P_Y, V) = \frac{VP_Y^{.5}}{P_X^{.5}} \tag{5.50}$$

so, by Equation 5.49, the welfare loss from a price increase from $P_X = .25$ to $P_X = 1$ is given by

$$\text{change in welfare} = \int_{.25}^{1} \frac{VP_Y^{.5} \, dP_X}{P_X^{.5}}$$

$$= 2VP_Y^{.5}P_X^{.5} \Big|_{P_X = .25}^{P_X = 1}. \tag{5.51}$$

If we assume $V = 2$ is the initial utility level, this loss (since $P_Y = 1$) is given by

$$\text{loss} = 4(1)^{.5} - 4(.25)^{.5} = 2, \tag{5.52}$$

which is exactly what we found in Example 5.3—when P_X rises to 1, expenditures must rise from 2 to 4 to keep this person from being made worse off. If the utility level experienced after the price rise is believed to be the more appropriate utility target for measuring the welfare loss, then $V = 1$ (see Example 5.3) and the loss would be given by

$$\text{loss} = 2(1)^{.5} - 2(.25)^{.5} = 1. \tag{5.53}$$

If the loss were evaluated using the uncompensated (Marshallian) demand function

---

[9] For a further discussion, see R. D. Willig, "Consumer's Surplus without Apology," *American Economic Review* (September 1976): 589–597.

$$X = d_X(P_X, P_Y, I) = \frac{I}{2P_X},\qquad(5.54)$$

the computation would be

$$loss = \int_{.25}^{1} \frac{I}{2P_X}\, dP_X$$

$$= I\frac{\ln P_X}{2}\Big|_{.25}^{1} = 0 - (-1.39) = 1.39,\qquad(5.55)$$

which does indeed represent a compromise between the two figures computed using the compensated functions.

QUERY: In this problem total consumer surplus cannot be computed since the demand curves are asymptotic to the price axis and the required integrals do not converge. How might you make an approximation to total consumer surplus in this case? Or, is our analysis only valid for relatively small changes in P_X?

SUMMARY

In this chapter we have used the utility-maximization model to study how the quantity of a good that an individual chooses responds to changes in income or to changes in that good's price. The final result of this examination is the derivation of the familiar downward-sloping demand curve. In arriving at that result, however, we have drawn a wide variety of insights from the general economic theory of choice:

- Proportional changes in all prices and income do not shift the individual's budget constraint and therefore do not change the quantities of goods chosen. In formal terms, demand functions are homogeneous of degree zero in all prices and income.

- When purchasing power changes (that is, when income increases with prices remaining unchanged), budget constraints shift and individuals will choose new commodity bundles. For normal

goods an increase in purchasing power causes more to be chosen. In the case of inferior goods, however, an increase in purchasing power causes less to be purchased. Hence, the sign of $\partial X_i/\partial I$ could be either positive or negative, although $\partial X_i/\partial I \geq 0$ is the most common case.

- A fall in the price of a good causes substitution and income effects that, for a normal good, cause more of the good to be purchased. For inferior goods, however, substitution and income effects work in opposite directions and no unambiguous prediction is possible.

- Similarly, a rise in price induces both substitution and income effects that, in the normal case, cause less to be demanded. For inferior goods the net result is again ambiguous.

- The Marshallian demand curve summarizes the total quantity of a good demanded at each possible price. Changes in price induce both substitution and income effects that prompt movements along the curve. For a normal good, $\partial X_i/\partial P_i \leq 0$ along this curve. If income, prices of other goods, or preferences change, the curve may shift to a new location.

■ Compensated demand curves illustrate movements along a given indifference curve for alternative prices. They are constructed by holding utility constant and exhibit only the substitution effects from a price change. Hence, their slope is unambiguously negative (or zero).

■ Income and substitution effects can be analyzed precisely by using the Slutsky equation. These effects can also be examined by using the revealed preference approach to theory of choice, thereby mitigating the need to assume the existence of utility functions.

■ The welfare changes that accompany price changes can sometimes be measured by the changing area under demand curves. These changes in consumer surplus are quite useful for evaluating the net effects on the allocation of resources of economic phenomena such as monopoly or taxation.

PROBLEMS

5.1

Thirsty Ed drinks only pure spring water, but he can purchase it in two different-sized containers—.75 liter and 2 liter. Because the water itself is identical, he regards these two "goods" as perfect substitutes.

a. Assuming Ed's utility depends only on the quantity of water consumed and that the containers themselves yield no utility, express this utility function in terms of quantities of .75L containers (X) and 2L containers (Y).

b. State Ed's demand function for X in terms of $P_X, P_Y,$ and I.

c. Graph the demand curve for X, holding I and P_Y constant.

d. How do changes in I and P_Y shift the demand curve for X?

e. What would the compensated demand curve for X look like in this situation?

5.2

David N. gets $3 per week as an allowance to spend any way he pleases. Since he only likes peanut butter and jelly sandwiches, he spends the entire amount on peanut butter (at $.05 per ounce) and jelly (at $.10 per ounce). Bread is provided free of charge by a concerned neighbor. David is a particular eater and makes his sandwiches with exactly 1 ounce of jelly and 2 ounces of peanut butter. He is set in his ways and will never change these proportions.

a. How much peanut butter and jelly will David buy with his $3 allowance in a week?

b. Suppose the price of jelly were to rise to $.15 an ounce. How much of each commodity would be bought?

c. By how much should David's allowance be increased to compensate for the rise in the price of jelly in part (b)?

d. Graph your results in parts (a) to (c).

e. In what sense does this problem only involve a single commodity, peanut butter and jelly sandwiches? Graph the demand curve for this single commodity.

f. Discuss the results of this problem in terms of the income and substitution effects involved in the demand for jelly.

5.3

Show that if Mr. Green is forced to spend a fixed amount of his income on a particular good, his utility level will be lower than if he could freely allocate his income.

5.4

Show that if there are only two goods (X and Y) to choose from, both cannot be inferior goods. If X is inferior, how do changes in income affect the demand for Y?

5.5

As defined in Chapter 3, an indifference map is homothetic if any straight line through the origin cuts all indifference curves at points of equal slope: The MRS depends on the ratio Y/X.

a. Prove that in this case $\partial X/\partial Z$ is a positive constant.

b. Prove that if an individual's tastes can be represented by a homothetic indifference map, price and quantity must move in opposite directions; that is, Giffen's paradox cannot occur.

5.6

Suppose that an individual's utility for X and Y is represented by the CES function (for $\delta = -1$):

$$\text{utility} = U(X, Y) = -\frac{1}{X} - \frac{1}{Y}.$$

a. Use the Lagrangian multiplier method to calculate the uncompensated demand functions for X and Y for this function.
b. Show that the demand functions calculated in part (a) are homogeneous of degree zero in P_X, P_Y, and I.
c. How do changes in I or in P_Y shift the demand curve for good X?

5.7

As in Example 5.1, assume that utility is given by

$$\text{utility} = U(X, Y) = X^{.3}Y^{.7}.$$

a. Use the uncompensated demand functions given in Example 5.1 to compute the indirect utility function and the expenditure function for this case.
b. Use the expenditure function calculated in part (a) together with Shephard's lemma (footnote 5) to compute the compensated demand function for good X.
c. Use the results from part (b) together with the uncompensated demand function for good X to show that the Slutsky equation holds for this case.

5.8

Suppose the utility function for goods X and Y is given by

$$\text{utility} = U(X, Y) = XY + Y.$$

a. Calculate the uncompensated (Marshallian) demand functions for X and Y and describe how the demand curves for X and Y are shifted by changes in I or in the price of the other good.
b. Calculate the expenditure function for X and Y.
c. Use the expenditure function calculated in part (b) to compute the compensated demand functions for goods X and Y. Describe how the compensated demand curves for X and Y are shifted by changes in income or by changes in the prices of the other good.

5.9

Over a three-year period, an individual exhibits the following consumption behavior:

	P_X	P_Y	X	Y
Year 1	3	3	7	4
Year 2	4	2	6	6
Year 3	5	1	7	3

Is this behavior consistent with the strong axiom of revealed preference?

5.10

Suppose the individual's utility function for three goods, X_1, X_2, and X_3, is "separable"; that is, assume that

$$U(X_1, X_2, X_3) = U_1(X_1) + U_2(X_2) + U_3(X_3)$$

$$\text{and } U_i' > 0 \quad U_i'' < 0 \quad \text{for } i = 1, 2, \text{ or } 3.$$

Show that
a. None of the goods can be inferior;
b. $\partial X_i / \partial P_i$ must be < 0.
In the Chapter 6 extensions we will return to examine this separable utility case in more detail.

SUGGESTED READINGS

Cook, P. J. "A 'One Line' Proof of the Slutsky Equation." *American Economic Review* 62 (March 1972): 139. *Clever use of duality to derive the Slutsky equation; uses the same method as in Chapter 5 but with rather complex notation.*

Fisher, F. M., and K. Shell. *The Economic Theory of Price Indices.* New York: Academic Press, 1972. *Complete, technical discussion of the economic properties of various price indexes; describes "ideal" indexes based on utility-maximizing models in detail.*

Mas-Colell, Andreu, Michael D. Whinston, and Jerry R. Green. *Microeconomic Theory.* New York: Oxford University Press, 1995.
Chapter 3 covers much of the material in this chapter at a somewhat higher level. Section I on measurement of the welfare effects of price changes is especially recommended.

Samuelson, Paul A. *Foundations of Economic Analysis.* Cambridge, Mass.: Harvard University Press, 1947. Chap. V.
Provides a complete analysis of substitution and income effects. Also develops the revealed preference notion.

Silberberg, E. *The Structure of Economics: A Mathematical Analysis.* 2d ed. New York: McGraw-Hill Book Company, 1990.

Good discussion of expenditure functions and the use of indirect utility functions.

Slutsky, E. E. "On the Theory of the Budget of the Consumer," reprinted in American Economic Review, *Readings in Price Theory.* Homewood, ILL.: Richard D. Irwin, 1952, pp. 27–56.
Original derivation of formal statement of income and substitution effects.

Varian, H. *Microeconomic Analysis.* 3d ed. New York: W. W. Norton and Co., 1992.
Formal development of preference notions. Extensive use of expenditure functions and their relationship to the Slutsky equation. Also contains a nice proof of Roy's identity.

EXTENSIONS

Shephard's Lemma, Roy's Identity, and Price Indices

In Chapters 4 and 5 we showed that there are a number of ways of exploring the individual's choice problem and a related variety of ways of deriving demand relationships. The purpose of this extension is to summarize these various relationships to illustrate how they all fit together. We also show how these relationships shed light on the interpretations of price indices.

Figure 5.11 offers a general guide. At the top of the figure are listed the two approaches to the individual's decision problem, utility maximization, and expenditure minimization. Each of these results in a solution in which the final goal achieved depends implicitly on the parameters of the problem—maximum indirect utility and minimal expentitures depend on prices of all goods and on the constraint in the problem (income or utility, respectively). In principle each approach also permits solving for demand functions—utility maximization (which holds nominal income constant) leads to Marshallian functions, and expenditure minimization (which holds utility constant) leads to compensated functions. Often that computation is burdensome, however, and can be accomplished more easily from the indirect utility and expenditure functions.

E5.1 Shephard's Lemma

As we described in footnote 5 of Chapter 5, applying the envelope theorem to the expenditure minimization problem yields

$$\frac{\partial E}{\partial P_X} = X = h_X(V, P_X, P_Y)$$

$$\frac{\partial E}{\partial P_Y} = Y = h_Y(V, P_X, P_Y). \tag{i}$$

That is, the compensated demand functions can be computed directly from the expenditure function by partial differentiation. This result is sometimes called *Shephard's lemma* after the ecomomist who discovered it in the context of input demand by firms (Shephard, 1953).

Expenditure Functions and Substitution in the CPI

The connection between expenditure functions and compensated demand curves illustrates some of the conceptual problems involved in computing price indices. For example, the U.S. Consumer Price Index

FIGURE 5.11

RELATIONSHIP AMONG DEMAND CONCEPTS

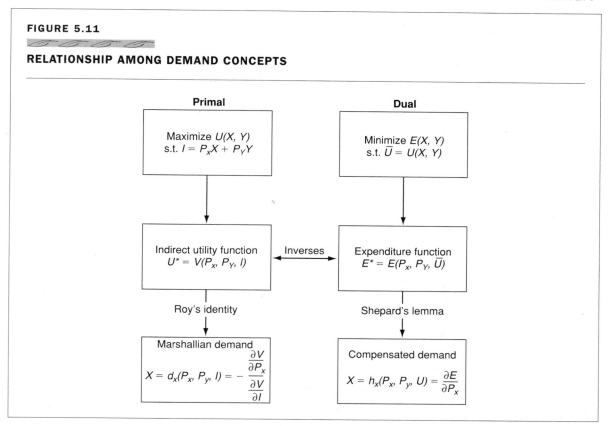

(CPI) is calculated by pricing a fixed market basket of goods each month. The resulting index is frequently used to adjust contracts such as those for Social Security or pension benefits for inflation. But Equation i makes clear that individuals will generally change the goods they buy when prices change, even if utility (V) is held constant. Stated another way, pricing a fixed market basket exaggerates the minimum expenditures required to achieve a given utility level. This exaggeration is illustrated in Figure 5.12. To achieve U_0 initially requires an expenditure of E_0, resulting in purchases of X_0, Y_0. If the price ratio P_X/P_Y falls, U_0 can now be achieved with expenditures E_1 by altering the consumption bundle to X_1, Y_1. Computing the expenditure level necessary to purchase the initial consumption bundle (X_0, Y_0) exaggerates the level of spending needed to reach

U_0. The extent of this "substitution bias" has been widely studied by economists. For example, Aizcorbe and Jackman (1993) conclude that such biases exaggerate the level of inflation shown in the CPI by about 0.2 percent per year.

E5.2 Roy's Identity

Marshallian demand functions can be derived from the indirect utility function, but in this case the computation is a bit more complex. Remember that the Lagrangian expression associated with individual utility maximization is

$$\mathcal{L} = U(X, Y) + \lambda(I - P_X X - P_Y Y). \qquad \text{(ii)}$$

Applying the envelope theorem to this expression yields

FIGURE 5.12

SUBSTITUTION BIAS IN THE CPI

Initially expenditures are given by E_0 and this individual buys X_0, Y_0. If P_X/P_Y falls, utility level U_0 can be reached most cheaply by consuming X_1, Y_1 and spending E_1. Purchasing X_0, Y_0 at the new prices would cost more than E_1. Hence, holding the consumption bundle constant imparts an upward bias to CPI-type computations.

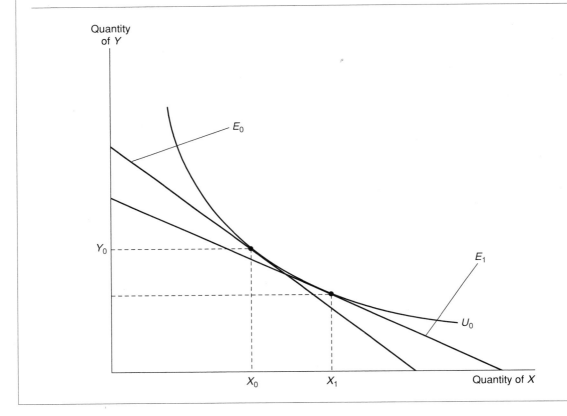

$$\frac{\partial U^*}{\partial P_X} = \frac{\partial \mathcal{L}}{\partial P_X} = -\lambda X \qquad \text{(iii)}$$

and

$$\frac{\partial U^*}{\partial I} = \lambda.$$

Consequently,

$$\frac{\dfrac{-\partial U^*}{\partial P_X}}{\dfrac{\partial U^*}{\partial I}} = \frac{\dfrac{-\partial V^*}{\partial P_X}}{\dfrac{\partial V^*}{\partial I}} = X = d_X(P_X, P_Y, I), \qquad \text{(iv)}$$

where the first equation follows from the definition of indirect utility, V, and the third is simply a reminder that the optimal X depends on the parameters P_X, P_Y, and I. This result is called Roy's identity, again after its discoverer (Roy, 1942).

E5.3 Cobb-Douglas Example

These results are easily demonstrated with our already overworked Cobb-Douglas utility function

$$U(X, Y) = X^{.5}Y^{.5}.$$

In Example 4.4 we calculated the indirect utility function for this case as

$$V(P_X, P_Y, I) = \frac{I}{2P_X^{.5}P_Y^{.5}}.$$

Roy's identity states that the Marshallian demand function can be computed as

$$X = \frac{\partial V^*/\partial P_X}{\partial V^*/\partial I} = \frac{\dfrac{.5I}{2P_X^{1.5}P_Y^{.5}}}{\dfrac{1}{2P_X^{.5}P_Y^{.5}}} = \frac{.5I}{P_X}, \qquad \textbf{(v)}$$

which is exactly the result derived in Example 4.2.

To derive compensated demand functions, we use the expenditure function first derived in Example 4.5:

$$E(P_X, P_Y, V) = 2VP_X^{.5}P_Y^{.5}$$

and apply Shephard's lemma:

$$h_X(P_X, P_Y, V) = \frac{\partial E}{\partial P_X} = \frac{VP_Y^{.5}}{P_X^{.5}}, \qquad \textbf{(vi)}$$

which is also precisely the function we calculated in Example 5.3. Notice that, even in this simple case, the compensated demand for X depends on the prices of both goods.

The CPI Again

Of course, the computations involved using Roy's identity or Shephard's lemma may not always be this simple. But these techniques often offer the most direct route to solving problems in the theory of demand. Some of the most severe of these problems arise in research on how actual consumer expenditure patterns should be taken into account in constructing price indices. Not only can the theory of demand shed light on the issue of substitution bias (see E5.1), but it also provides insights into such thorny questions as how new goods should enter such a index and how quality changes should be measured. More complete notions of demand can also be used to appraise the significance of the growth of "discount" retail outlets (such as Sam's Club or Price-Costco) and of how the lower prices consumers may obtain by shopping in these stores affect overall utility. The issue of how all such adjustments should be made to the CPI has sparked considerable political controversy, especially because biases in the existing CPI of more than one percent per year have been estimated by some analysts. Moulten (1996) provides a guide to the relationship between such estimates and the underlying theories of demand that are used to make them.

References

Aizcorbe, Ana M., and Patrick C. Jackman. "The Commodity Substitution Effect in CPI Data, 1982–91." *Monthly Labor Review* (December 1993): 25–33.

Deaton, A., and J. Muellbauer. *Economics and Consumer Behavior.* Cambridge: Cambridge University Press, 1980. Chap. 2.

Kreps, D. M. *A Course in Microeconomic Theory.* Princeton, NJ: Princeton University Press, 1990. Section 2.3.

Moulton, Brent R. "Bias in the Consumer Price Index: What Is the Evidence." *Journal of Economic Perspectives* (Fall 1996): 159–177.

Roy, R. *De l'utilité, contribution à la théorie des choix.* Paris: Hermann, 1942.

Shephard, R. W. *Cost and Production Functions.* Princeton, NJ: Princeton University Press, 1953.

CHAPTER 6

DEMAND RELATIONSHIPS AMONG GOODS

In Chapter 5 we examined how changes in the price of a particular good (say, good X) affected the quantity of that good chosen. Throughout the discussion we held the prices of all other goods constant. It should be clear, however, that a change in one of these other prices could also affect the quantity of X chosen. For example, if X were taken to represent the quantity of automobile miles that an individual drives, then this quantity might be expected to decline when the price of gasoline rises or to increase when air and bus fares rise. In this chapter we will use the utility-maximization model to study such relationships.

THE TWO-GOOD CASE

Figure 6.1 presents two examples of how the quantity of X chosen might be affected by a change in the price of good Y. In both panels of the figure, P_Y has fallen, thereby shifting the budget constraint outward from I_0 to I_1. In both cases also the quantity of good Y chosen has increased from Y_0 to Y_1 as a result of the decline in P_Y, as would be expected if Y is a normal good. For good X, however, the results shown in the two panels differ. In (a) the indifference curves are nearly L-shaped, implying a fairly small substitution effect. A decline in P_Y does not induce a very large move along U_0 as Y is substituted for X. That is, X drops relatively little as a result of the substitution effect. The income effect, however, reflects the greater purchasing power now available, and this causes the total quantity of X chosen to increase. Hence, $\partial X / \partial P_Y$ is negative (X and P_Y move in opposite directions).

In Figure 6.1b this situation is reversed—there $\partial X / \partial P_Y$ is positive. The relatively flat indifference curves in Figure 6.1b result in a large substitution effect from the fall in P_Y. The quantity of X declines sharply as Y is substituted for X along U_0. As in Figure 6.1a, the increased purchasing power from the decline in P_Y causes more X to be bought, but now the substitution effect dominates and the quantity of X declines to X_1. In this case, then, X and P_Y move in the same direction.

FIGURE 6.1

DIFFERING DIRECTIONS OF CROSS-PRICE EFFECTS

In both panels the price of Y has fallen. In (a) substitution effects are small so the quantity of X consumed increases along with Y. Since $\partial X/\partial P_Y < 0$, X and Y are gross complements. In (b) substitution effects are large so the quantity of X chosen falls. Since $\partial X/\partial P_Y > 0$, X and Y would be termed gross substitutes.

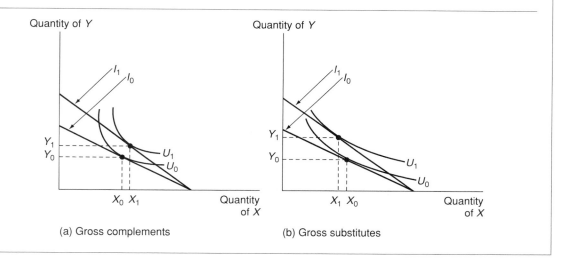

(a) Gross complements   (b) Gross substitutes

The ambiguity in the effect of changes in P_Y can be further illustrated by a Slutsky-type equation. By using procedures similar to those in Chapter 5, it is fairly simple to show that

A Mathematical Treatment

$$\frac{\partial X}{\partial P_Y} = \frac{\partial d_X}{\partial P_Y} = \left.\frac{\partial X}{\partial P_Y}\right|_{U = \text{constant}} - Y\frac{\partial X}{\partial I}, \qquad (6.1)$$

where the first term on the right, as before, represents the substitution effect and the second term is the income effect. Notice that in the income effect, the derivative $\partial X/\partial I$ is now multiplied by the amount of Y purchased since that quantity reflects the extent to which changes in P_Y affect purchasing power.

For the two-good case, the terms on the right side of Equation 6.1 have different signs. Assuming that indifference curves are convex, the substitution effect $\partial X/\partial P_Y \mid U = \text{constant}$ is positive. If we confine ourselves to moves along one indifference curve, increases in P_Y increase X and decreases in P_Y decrease the quantity of X chosen. But, assuming X is a normal good, the income effect $(-Y\,\partial X/\partial I)$ is clearly negative. Hence, the combined effect in Equation 6.1 is ambiguous; $\partial X/\partial P_Y$ could be either positive or negative. Even in the two-good case, the demand relationship between X and P_Y is rather complex.

EXAMPLE 6.1

ANOTHER SLUTSKY DECOMPOSITION FOR CROSS-PRICE EFFECTS

In Example 5.4 we examined the Slutsky decomposition for the effect of a change in the price of soft drinks (X) on soft drink purchases. Now let's look at the cross-price effect of a change in hamburger (Y) prices on soft drink purchases. Remember that the uncompensated and compensated demand functions for soft drinks are given by

$$d_X(P_X, P_Y, I) = \frac{I}{2P_X} \tag{6.2}$$

and

$$h_X(P_X, P_Y, V) = \frac{VP_Y^{.5}}{P_X^{.5}}, \tag{6.3}$$

respectively. As we have noted in several places, the fact that under the uncompensated function

$$\frac{\partial d_X}{\partial P_Y} = 0 \tag{6.4}$$

shows that changes in hamburger prices have no effect on soft drink purchases. To see why this is so, we can compute the substitution effect from the compensated demand function as

$$\frac{\partial X}{\partial P_Y}\bigg|_{U = \text{constant}} = \frac{\partial h_X}{\partial P_Y} = \frac{.5V}{P_X^{.5}P_Y^{.5}}. \tag{6.5}$$

But previously we found that indirect utility is given by

$$V = \frac{I}{2P_X^{.5}P_Y^{.5}} \tag{6.6}$$

so the substitution effect for this case is

$$\frac{\partial X}{\partial P_Y}\bigg|_{U = \text{constant}} = \frac{.25I}{P_XP_Y}. \tag{6.7}$$

Using the Marshallian demand function for $Y(Y = I/2P_Y)$, we can calculate the income effect in this problem (see Equation 6.1) as

$$-Y\frac{\partial X}{\partial I} = -\left(\frac{I}{2P_Y}\right)\left(\frac{1}{2P_X}\right) = -\frac{.25I}{P_XP_Y}. \tag{6.8}$$

Comparing Equations 6.7 and 6.8, it is clear that the income and substitution effects exactly cancel each other out here. Changes in hamburger prices have no effect on soft drink purchases because of this canceling of effects, not because the two goods are unrelated.

As a numerical illustration, suppose hamburger (Y) prices rose dramatically from 1 to 4. The compensated demand function shows that soft drink purchases should rise from 4 to 8 ($= 2 \cdot 2/.5$) if we are to hold indirect utility constant at $V = 2$. That is, the individual should substitute many soft drinks for the now more expensive hamburgers. But with a constant nominal income of 2, indirect utility cannot remain at $V = 2$—utility must fall because of the rise in hamburger prices to $V = [2/(2 \cdot .5 \cdot 2)] = 1$. With this reduced level of utility, the compensated demand function predicts that soft drink purchases will remain at 4 ($= 1 \cdot 2/.5$) rather than rising to reflect only the substitution effect. The two effects are therefore precisely offsetting. With other functional forms either of the effects could dominate, and $\partial d_X/\partial P_Y$ could have either sign.

QUERY: Why would it be incorrect to argue that if $\partial d_X/\partial P_Y = 0$, soft drinks and hamburgers must have no substitution possibilities—that is, they must be consumed in fixed proportions? Is there any case in which such a conclusion could be drawn?

For the case of many goods, it is a simple matter to generalize the Slutsky analysis (as represented by Equations 5.27 and 6.1) as

SUBSTITUTES AND COMPLEMENTS

$$\frac{\partial X_i}{\partial P_j} = \frac{\partial d_i}{\partial P_j} = \frac{\partial X_i}{\partial P_j}\bigg|_{U = \text{constant}} - X_j \frac{\partial X_i}{\partial I} \tag{6.9}$$

for any i and j (including $i = j$). This says that the change in the price of any good (here good j) induces income and substitution effects that may change the quantity of every good demanded. Equation 6.9 can be used to discuss the idea of substitutes and complements. Intuitively, these ideas are rather simple. Two goods are *substitutes* if one good may, as a result of changed conditions, replace the other in use. Some examples are tea and coffee, hamburgers and hot dogs, and butter and margarine. *Complements,* on the other hand, are goods that "go together," such as coffee and cream, fish and chips, or brandy and cigars. In some sense "substitutes" substitute for one another in the utility function, whereas "complements" complement each other.

There are two different ways to make these intuitive ideas precise. One of these focuses on the "gross" effects of price changes by including both income and substitution effects, while the other looks at substitution effects alone. Since both definitions are used, we will examine each in detail.

Gross Substitutes and Complements

Substitute and complementary relationships can be defined by referring to observed price reactions as:

DEFINITION

Gross Substitutes and Complements   Two goods, X_i and X_j, are said to be gross substitutes if

$$\frac{\partial X_i}{\partial P_j} > 0 \tag{6.10}$$

and gross complements if

$$\frac{\partial X_i}{\partial P_j} < 0. \tag{6.11}$$

That is, two goods are gross substitutes if a rise in the price of one good causes *more* of the other good to be bought. They are gross complements if a rise in the price of one good causes *less* of the other good to be purchased. For example, if the price of coffee rises, the demand for tea might be expected to increase (they are substitutes), whereas the demand for cream might decrease (coffee and cream are complements). Equation 6.9 makes it clear that this definition is a "gross" definition in that it includes both income and substitution effects that arise from price changes. Since these effects are in fact combined in any real-world observation we can make, it might be reasonable always to speak only of "gross" substitutes and "gross" complements.

Asymmetry of the Gross Definitions

There are, however, several things that are undesirable about the gross definitions of substitutes and complements. The most important of these is that the definitions are not symmetric. It is possible, by the definitions, for X_1 to be a substitute for X_2 and at the same time for X_2 to be a complement of X_1. The presence of income effects can produce paradoxical results. Let's look at a specific example:

EXAMPLE 6.2

ASYMMETRY IN CROSS-PRICE EFFECTS

Suppose the utility function for two goods (X and Y) is given by

$$U(X, Y) = \ln X + Y. \tag{6.12}$$

Setting up the Lagrangian expression

$$\mathcal{L} = ln\ X + Y + \lambda(I - P_X X - P_Y Y) \qquad (6.13)$$

yields the following first-order conditions:

$$\frac{\partial \mathcal{L}}{\partial X} = \frac{1}{X} - \lambda P_X = 0$$

$$\frac{\partial \mathcal{L}}{\partial Y} = 1 - \lambda P_Y = 0 \qquad (6.14)$$

$$\frac{\partial \mathcal{L}}{\partial \lambda} = I - P_X X - P_Y Y = 0.$$

Moving the terms in λ to the right and dividing the first equation by the second yields

$$\frac{1}{X} = \frac{P_X}{P_Y} \qquad (6.15)$$

$$P_X X = P_Y. \qquad (6.16)$$

Substitution into the budget constraint now permits us to solve for the Marshallian demand function for Y:

$$I = P_X X + P_Y Y = P_Y + P_Y Y. \qquad (6.17)$$

Hence,

$$P_Y Y = I - P_Y. \qquad (6.18)$$

This equation shows that an increase in P_Y must decrease spending on good Y (that is, $P_Y Y$). Therefore, since P_X and I are unchanged, spending on X must rise. So

$$\frac{\partial X}{\partial P_Y} > 0, \qquad (6.19)$$

and we would term X and Y gross substitutes. On the other hand, Equation 6.18 shows that spending on Y is independent of P_X. Consequently,

$$\frac{\partial Y}{\partial P_X} = 0 \qquad (6.20)$$

and, looked at in this way, X and Y would be said to be independent of each other—they are neither gross substitutes nor gross complements. Relying on gross market-based responses to define the relationship between X and Y would therefore run into ambiguity.

QUERY: In Example 3.4 we showed that a utility function of the form given by Equation 6.12 is nonhomothetic—the MRS does not depend only on the ratio of X to Y. Can asymmetry arise in the homothetic case?

NET SUBSTITUTES AND COMPLEMENTS

Because of the possible asymmetries involved in the definition of gross substitutes and complements, an alternative definition that focuses only on substitution effects is sometimes used:

DEFINITION

Net Substitutes and Complements[1] X_i and X_j are said to be net substitutes if

$$\left.\frac{\partial X_i}{\partial P_j}\right|_{U=\text{constant}} > 0 \qquad (6.21)$$

and net complements if

$$\left.\frac{\partial X_i}{\partial P_j}\right|_{U=\text{constant}} < 0. \qquad (6.22)$$

These definitions, then, look only at the substitution terms to determine whether two goods are substitutes or complements. This definition is both intuitively appealing (because it looks only at the shape of an indifference curve) and theoretically desirable (because it is unambiguous). Once X_i and X_j have been discovered to be substitutes, they stay substitutes, no matter in which direction the definition is applied. As a matter of fact, it can be shown that the definitions are perfectly symmetric in that

$$\left.\frac{\partial X_i}{\partial P_j}\right|_{U=\text{constant}} = \left.\frac{\partial X_j}{\partial P_i}\right|_{U=\text{constant}}. \qquad (6.23)$$

The substitution effect of a change in P_i on good X_j is identical to the substitution effect of a change in P_j on the quantity of X_i chosen. This symmetry is important in both theoretical and empirical work.[2]

The differences between the two definitions of substitutes and complements are easily demonstrated in Figure 6.1a. In this figure X and Y are gross complements, but they are net substitutes. The derivative $\partial X/\partial P_Y$ turns out

---

[1] Sometimes these are called "Hicksian" substitutes and complements, named after the British economist John Hicks, who originally developed the definitions.

[2] This symmetry is easily shown by using Shephard's lemma (see footnote 5, Chapter 5). Since $X_i = \partial E/\partial P_i$,

$$\left.\frac{\partial X_i}{\partial P_j}\right|_{U=\text{constant}} = \frac{\partial E^2}{\partial P_j \partial P_i},$$

but

$$\frac{\partial E^2}{\partial P_j \partial P_i} = \frac{\partial E^2}{\partial P_i \partial P_j} = \left.\frac{\partial X_j}{\partial P_i}\right|_{U=\text{constant}}$$

since, by Young's theorem (see Chapter 2), the order of partial differentiation is irrelevant.

to be negative (*X* and *Y* are gross complements) because the (positive) substitution effect is outweighed by the (negative) income effect (a fall in the price of *Y* causes real income to increase greatly and, consequently, actual purchases of *X* increase). However, as the figure makes clear, if there are only two goods from which to choose, they must be net substitutes, although they may be either gross substitutes or gross complements. Because we have assumed a diminishing *MRS*, the own-price substitution effect must be negative and, consequently, the cross-price substitution effect must be positive. Indeed, it can be shown that there can be only a "few" complementary relationships in the net sense.[3] Net substitution is the prevalent relationship among goods.

The symmetry of net cross-substitution effects (Equation 6.23) and the negativity of the own-substitution effect (discussed in Chapter 5) are the major results of the theory of individual choice. These results can, in principle, be tested using real-world data. However, because most actual market data involve the behavior of many demanders and because adding demand across individuals involves some difficult methodological problems (see Chapter 7), there are few convincing tests of the propositions. Instead, the results are used mainly in theoretical work and in the specification of useful demand functions that obey these properties.

COMPOSITE COMMODITIES

Our discussion in the previous section showed that the demand relationships among goods are quite complicated. In the most general case, an individual who consumes *n* goods will have demand functions that reflect $n(n + 1)/2$ different substitution effects.[4] When *n* is very large (as it surely is for all the specific goods that individuals actually consume), this general case can be unmanageable. It is often far more convenient to group goods into larger aggregates such as food, clothing, shelter, and so forth. At the most extreme level of aggregates, we might wish to examine one specific good (say, gasoline, which we might call *X*) and its relationship to "all other goods," which we might call *Y*. This is the procedure we have been using in many of our two-dimensional graphs, and we will continue to do so at many other places in this book. In this section we show the conditions under which this procedure can be defended. In the extension to this chapter, we explore more general issues involved in aggregating goods into larger groupings.

---

[3] See J. R. Hicks, *Value and Capital* (Oxford: Oxford University Press, 1939), p. 312 and problem 6.8.

[4] To see this, notice that all substitution effects, s_{ij}, could be recorded in an $n \times n$ matrix. However, symmetry of the effects ($s_{ij} = s_{ji}$) implies that only those terms on and below the principal diagonal of this matrix may be distinctly different from each other. This amounts to half the terms in the matrix ($\frac{1}{2}n^2$) plus the remaining half of the terms on the main diagonal of the matrix ($\frac{1}{2}n$).

Composite Commodity Theorem

Suppose consumers choose among n goods, but that we are only interested specifically in one of them, say, X_1. In general, the demand for X_1 will depend on the individual prices of the other $n-1$ commodities. But if all these prices move together, it may make sense to lump them into a single "composite commodity," Y. Formally, if we let $P_2^0 \ldots P_n^0$ represent the initial prices of these goods, then we assume that these prices can only vary together. They might all double, or all decline by 50 percent, but the relative prices of $X_2 \ldots X_n$ would not change. Now we define the composite commodity Y to be total expenditures on $X_2 \ldots X_n$, using the initial prices $P_2^0 \ldots P_n^0$:

$$Y = P_2^0 X_2 + P_3^0 X_3 + \cdots + P_n^0 X_n. \tag{6.24}$$

This person's initial budget constraint is given by

$$I = P_1 X_1 + P_2^0 X_2 + \cdots + P_n^0 X_n = P_1 X_1 + Y. \tag{6.25}$$

By assumption, all of the prices $P_2 \ldots P_n$ change in unison. Assume all of these prices change by a factor of t $(t > 0)$. Now the budget constraint is

$$I = P_1 X_1 + t P_2^0 Y_2 + \cdots + t P_n^0 X_n = P_1 X_1 + tY. \tag{6.26}$$

Consequently, the factor of proportionality, t, plays the same role in this person's budget constraint as did the price of Y (P_Y) in our earlier two-good analysis. Changes in P_1 or in t induce the same kinds of substitution effects we have been analyzing. So long as $P_2 \ldots P_n$ move together, we can therefore confine our examination of demand to choices between buying X_1 or buying "everything else."[5] Simplified graphs that show these two goods on their axes can therefore be defended rigorously so long as the conditions of this "composite commodity theorem" (that all other prices move together) are satisfied. Notice, however, that the theorem makes no predictions about how choices of $X_2 \ldots X_n$ behave—they need not move in unison. The theorem focuses only on total spending on $X_2 \ldots X_n$, not on how that spending is allocated among specific items (although this allocation is assumed to be done in a utility-maximizing way).

Generalizations and Limitations

The composite commodity theorem can be shown to apply to any group of commodities whose relative prices all move together. It is possible to have more than one such commodity if there are several groupings that obey the

[5] The idea of a "composite commodity" was introduced by J. R. Hicks in *Value and Capital*, 2d ed. (Oxford: Oxford University Press, 1946), pp. 312–313. Proof of the theorem relies on the notion that to achieve maximum utility, the ratio of the marginal utilities for $X_2 \ldots X_n$ must remain unchanged when $P_2 \ldots P_n$ all move together. Hence, the n-good problem can be reduced to the two-dimensional problem of equating the ratio of the marginal utility from X to that from Y to the "price ratio" P_1/t.

theorem (i.e., expenditures on "food," "clothing," and so forth). Hence, we have developed the following:

DEFINITION

Composite Commodity   A composite commodity is a group of goods for which all prices move together. These goods can be treated as a single "commodity" in that the individual behaves as if he or she were choosing between other goods and total spending on the entire composite group.

This definition and the related theorem are very powerful results. They help to simplify many problems that would otherwise be intractable. Still, one must be rather careful in applying the theorem to the real world because its conditions are quite stringent. Finding a set of commodities whose prices move together may be quite rare. Slight departures from strict proportionality may negate the composite commodity theorem if cross-substitution effects are large.

EXAMPLE 6.3

HOUSING COSTS AS A COMPOSITE COMMODITY

Suppose that an individual receives utility from three goods: food (X), housing services (Y) measured in hundreds of square feet, and household operations as measured by electricity use (Z).

   If the individual's utility is given by the three-good CES function:

$$\text{utility} = U(X, Y, Z) = -\frac{1}{X} - \frac{1}{Y} - \frac{1}{Z}, \qquad (6.27)$$

it is a relatively simple matter to use the Lagrangian technique to calculate demand functions for these goods as

$$X = \frac{I}{P_X + \sqrt{P_X P_Y} + \sqrt{P_X P_Z}}$$

$$Y = \frac{I}{P_Y + \sqrt{P_Y P_X} + \sqrt{P_Y P_Z}} \qquad (6.28)$$

$$Z = \frac{I}{P_Z + \sqrt{P_Z P_X} + \sqrt{P_Z P_Y}}.$$

If initially $I = 100$, $P_X = 1$, $P_Y = 4$, and $P_Z = 1$, then the demand functions predict

$$X^* = 25$$

$$Y^* = 12.5 \tag{6.29}$$

$$Z^* = 25.$$

Hence, 25 is spent on food and a total of 75 is spent on housing-related needs. If we assume that housing service prices (P_Y) and household operation prices (P_Z) always move together, we can use their initial prices to define the "composite commodity" housing (H):

$$H = 4Y + 1Z. \tag{6.30}$$

Here we also (arbitrarily) define the initial price of housing (P_H) to be 1. The initial quantity of housing is simply total dollars spent on H:

$$H = 4(12.5) + 1(25) = 75. \tag{6.31}$$

Furthermore, since P_Y and P_Z always move together, P_H will always be related to these prices by

$$P_H = P_Z = .25P_Y. \tag{6.32}$$

Using this information, we can recalculate the demand function for X as a function of I, P_X, and P_H:

$$X = \frac{I}{P_X + \sqrt{4P_XP_H} + \sqrt{P_XP_H}}$$

$$= \frac{I}{P_X + 3\sqrt{P_XP_H}}. \tag{6.33}$$

As before, initially $I = 100$, $P_X = 1$, and $P_H = 1$ so $X^* = 25$. Spending on housing can be most easily calculated from the budget constraint as $H^* = 75$, since here spending on housing represents "everything" other than food.

An Increase in Housing Costs. If the prices of Y and Z were to rise proportionally to $P_Y = 16$, $P_Z = 4$ (with P_X remaining at 1), P_H would also rise to $P_H = 4$. Equation 6.33 now predicts that the demand for X would fall to

$$X^* = \frac{100}{1 + 3\sqrt{4}} = \frac{100}{7} \tag{6.34}$$

and that housing purchases would be given by

$$P_HH^* = 100 - \frac{100}{7} = \frac{600}{7} \tag{6.35}$$

or, since $P_H = 4$,

$$H^* = 150/7. \tag{6.36}$$

Notice that this is precisely the level of housing purchases predicted by the original demand functions for three goods in Equations 6.28. With $I = 100$, $P_X = 1$, $P_Y = 16$, and $P_Z = 4$, these equations can be solved as

$$X^* = 100/7$$

$$Y^* = 100/28 \qquad (6.37)$$

$$Z^* = 100/14$$

so the total amount of the composite good "housing" consumed (according to Equation 6.30) is given by

$$H^* = 4Y^* + 1Z^* = 150/7. \qquad (6.38)$$

Hence, we obtained the same responses to price changes regardless of whether we chose to examine demands for the three goods X, Y, and Z or only to look at choices between X and the composite good H.

QUERY: How do we know that the demand function for X in Equation 6.33 continues to assure utility maximization? Why is the Lagrangian constrained maximization problem unchanged by making the substitutions represented by Equation 6.32?

So far in this chapter we have focused on what economists can learn about the relationships among goods by observing individuals' changing consumption of these goods in reaction to changes in market prices. In some ways this analysis skirts the central question of *why* coffee and cream go together or *why* fish and chicken may substitute for each other in a person's diet. To develop a deeper understanding of such questions, economists have begun to explore activities within individuals' households. That is, they have sought to model nonmarket types of activities such as parental child care, meal preparation, or do-it-yourself construction in order to understand how such activities ultimately result in demands for goods in the market.[6] In this section we briefly review some of these models. Our primary goal is to illustrate some of the implications of this approach for the traditional theory of choice that we have been examining.

HOME PRODUCTION ATTRIBUTES OF GOODS AND IMPLICIT PRICES

The starting point for most models of household production is to assume that individuals do not receive utility directly from goods they purchase in the market (as we have been assuming so far). Instead, it is only when market

Household Production Model

---

[6] For a more extensive look at some of the issues raised by this approach, see G. S. Becker, *A Treatise on the Family* (Cambridge, Mass.: Harvard University Press, 1981).

goods are combined with time inputs by the individual that utility-providing outputs are produced. In this view, then, raw beef and uncooked potatoes yield no utility until they are cooked together to produce stew. Similarly, market purchases of beef and potatoes can only be understood by examining the individual's preferences for stew and the underlying technology through which it is produced.

In formal terms, assume as before that there are three goods that a person might purchase in the market: X, Y, and Z. Purchasing these goods provides no direct utility, but the goods can be combined by the individual to produce either of two home-produced goods: a_1 or a_2. The technology of this household production can be represented by the production functions f_1 and f_2 (see Chapter 11 for a more complete discussion of the production function concept). Therefore,

$$a_1 = f_1(X, Y, Z)$$
$$a_2 = f_2(X, Y, Z)$$

(6.39)

and

$$\text{utility} = U(a_1, a_2).$$

(6.40)

The individual's goal is to choose X, Y, Z so as to maximize utility subject to the production constraints (Equations 6.39) and to a financial budget constraint:[7]

$$P_X X + P_Y Y + P_Z Z = I.$$

(6.41)

Although we will not examine in detail the results that can be derived from this general model, two insights that can be drawn from it might be mentioned. First, the model may help to clarify the nature of market relationships between goods. Because the production functions in Equations 6.39 are in principle measurable using detailed data on household operations, households can be treated as "multiproduct" firms and studied using many of the techniques economists use to study production.

A second insight provided by the household production approach is the notion of the "implicit" or "shadow" prices associated with the home-produced goods: a_1 and a_2. Since consuming more a_1, say, requires the use of more of the "ingredients" X, Y, and Z, this activity obviously has an opportunity cost in terms of the quantity of a_2 that can be produced. To produce more bread, say, the individual must not only divert some flour, milk, and eggs from using them to make cupcakes, but may also have to alter the relative quantities of these goods purchased because he or she is bound by the overall budget constraint given by Equation 6.41. Hence, bread will have an implicit price in terms of the number of cupcakes that must be

---

[7] Often household production theory also focuses on the individual's allocation of time to producing a_1 and a_2 or to working in the market. In Chapter 22 we look at a few simple models of this type.

foregone in order to be able to consume one more loaf. That implicit price will reflect not only the market prices of bread ingredients, but also the available household production technology and, in more complex models, the relative time inputs required to produce the two goods. As a starting point, however, the notion of implicit prices can be best illustrated with a very simple model.

A particularly simple form of the household production model was first developed by K. J. Lancaster to examine the underlying "attributes" of goods.[8] In this model it is the attributes of goods that provide utility to individuals, and each specific good contains a fixed set of attributes. If, for example, we focus only on the calories (a_1) and vitamins (a_2) that various foods provide, Lancaster's model assumes that utility is a function of these attributes and that individuals purchase various foods only for the purpose of obtaining the calories and vitamins they offer. In mathematical terms, the model assumes that the "production" equations (6.39) have the simple form

The Linear Attributes Model

$$a_1 = a_X^1 X + a_Y^1 Y + a_Z^1 Z$$
$$a_2 = a_X^2 X + a_Y^2 Y + a_Z^2 Z, \tag{6.42}$$

where a_X^1 represents the number of calories per unit of food X, a_X^2 represents the number of vitamins per unit of food X, and so forth. In this form of the model, then, there is no actual "production" in the home. Rather the decision problem is how to choose a diet that provides the optimal mix of calories and vitamins given the available food budget.

To begin our examination of the theory of choice under the attributes model, we first illustrate the budget constraint. In Figure 6.2 the ray $0X$ records the various combinations of a_1 and a_2 available from successively larger amounts of good X. Because of the linear production technology assumed in the attributes model (Equations 6.42), these combinations of a_1 and a_2 lie along such a straight line, though in more complex models of home production that might not be the case. Similarly, rays $0Y$ and $0Z$ show the quantities of the attributes a_1 and a_2 provided by various amounts of goods Y and Z that might be purchased.

Illustrating the Budget Constraints

If this person spends all of his or her income on good X, the budget constraint (Equation 6.41) allows the purchase of

$$X^* = \frac{I}{P_X}, \tag{6.43}$$

[8] See K. J. Lancaster, "A New Approach to Consumer Theory," *Journal of Political Economy* 74 (April 1966): 132–157.

FIGURE 6.2

UTILITY MAXIMIZATION IN THE ATTRIBUTES MODEL

The points X^*, Y^*, and Z^* show the amounts of attributes a_1 and a_2 that can be purchased by buying only X, Y, or Z, respectively. The shaded area shows all combinations that can be bought with mixed bundles. Some individuals may maximize utility at E, others at E'.

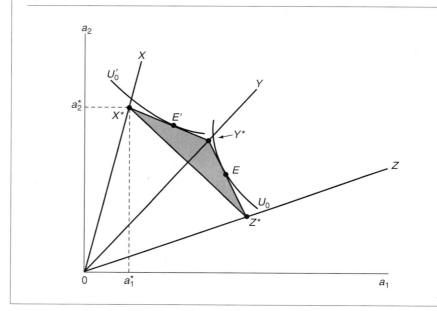

and that will yield

$$a_1^* = a_X^1 X^* = \frac{a_X^1 I}{P_X}$$

and

$$a_2^* = a_X^2 X^* = \frac{a_X^2 I}{P_X}. \tag{6.44}$$

This point is recorded as point X^* on the $0X$ ray in Figure 6.2. Similarly, the points Y^* and Z^* represent the combinations of a_1 and a_2 that would be obtained if all income were spent on good Y or good Z, respectively.

Bundles of a_1 and a_2 that are obtainable by purchasing both X and Y, respectively (with a fixed budget) are represented by the line joining X^* and

Y^* in Figure 6.2.[9] Similarly, the line X^*Z^* represents the combinations of a_1 and a_2 available from mixing X and Z, and the line Y^*Z^* shows combinations available from mixing Y and Z. All possible combinations from mixing the three market goods are represented by the shaded triangular area $X^*Y^*Z^*$.

Corner Solutions

One fact is immediately apparent from Figure 6.2—a utility-maximizing individual would never consume positive quantities of all three of these goods. Only the northeast perimeter of the $X^*Y^*Z^*$ triangle represents the maximal amounts of a_1 and a_2 available to this person given his or her income and the prices of the market goods. Individuals with a preference toward a_1 will have indifference curves similar to U_0 and will maximize utility by choosing a point such as E. The combination of a_1 and a_2 specified by that point can be obtained by consuming only goods Y and Z. Similarly, a person with preferences represented by the indifference curve U_0' will choose point E' and consume only goods X and Y. The attributes model therefore predicts that corner solutions at which individuals consume zero amounts of some commodities will be relatively common, especially in cases where individuals attach value to fewer attributes (here, two) than there are market goods to choose from (three). If income, prices, or preferences change, consumption patterns may also change abruptly. Goods that were previously consumed may cease to be bought and goods previously neglected may experience a significant increase in purchases. This is a direct result of the linear assumptions inherent in Equations 6.42. In household production models with greater substitutability assumptions, such discontinuous reactions are less likely.

SUMMARY

In this chapter we used the utility-maximizing model of choice to examine relationships among consumer goods. Although these relationships may be quite complex, the analysis presented here provided a number of ways of categorizing and simplifying them:

- When there are only two goods, the income and substitution effects from the change in the price of one good (say, P_Y) on the demand for another good (X) usually work in opposite directions. The sign of $\partial X/\partial P_Y$ is therefore ambiguous—its substitution

---

[9] Mathematically, suppose a fraction α of the budget is spent on X and $(1 - \alpha)$ on Y, then

$$a_1 = \alpha a_X^1 X^* + (1 - \alpha)a_Y^1 Y^*$$
$$a_2 = \alpha a_X^2 X^* + (1 - \alpha)a_Y^2 Y^*.$$

The line X^*Y^* is traced out by allowing α to vary between 0 and 1. The lines X^*Z^* and Y^*Z^* are traced out in a similar way as is the triangular area $X^*Y^*Z^*$.

effect is positive whereas its income effect is negative.

- In cases of more than two goods, demand relationships can be specified in two ways: Two goods (X_i and X_j) are "gross substitutes" if $\partial X_i/\partial P_j > 0$ and "gross complements" if $\partial X_i/\partial P_j < 0$. Unfortunately, since these price effects include income effects, they need not be symmetric. That is, $\partial X_i/\partial P_j$ does not necessarily equal $\partial X_j/\partial P_i$.

- Focusing only on the substitution effects of price changes does provide a symmetric definition. Two goods are "net substitutes" if $\partial X_i/\partial P_j \mid \overline{U} > 0$ and "net complements" if $\partial X_i/\partial P_j \mid \overline{U} < 0$. Since $\partial X_i/\partial P_j \mid \overline{U} = \partial X_j/\partial P_i \mid \overline{U}$, there is no ambiguity about these definitions.

- If a group of goods has prices that always move in unison, expenditures on these goods can be treated as a "composite commodity" whose "price" is given by the size of the proportional change in the composite goods' prices.

- An alternative way to develop the theory of choice among market goods is to focus on the ways in which market goods are used in household production to yield utility-providing attributes. This may provide additional insights into relationships among goods.

PROBLEMS

6.1

Heidi receives utility from two goods, goat's milk (M) and strudel (S), according to the utility function

$$U(M, S) = M \cdot S.$$

a. Show that increases in the price of goat's milk will not affect the quantity of strudel Heidi buys—that is, show that $\partial S/\partial P_M = 0$.

b. Develop an intuitive argument that explains why the substitution and income effects of a change in P_M are exactly offsetting in their effect on S in this problem.

6.2

Hard Times Burt buys only rotgut whiskey and jelly donuts to sustain him. For Burt, rotgut whiskey is an inferior good that exhibits Giffen's paradox, although rotgut whiskey and jelly donuts are Hicksian substitutes in the customary sense. Develop an intuitive explanation to suggest why a rise in the price of rotgut must cause fewer jelly donuts to be bought. That is, the goods must also be gross complements.

6.3

Donald, a frugal graduate student, consumes only coffee (C) and buttered toast (BT). He buys these items at the university cafeteria and always uses two pats of butter for each piece of toast. Donald spends exactly half of his meager stipend on coffee and the other half on buttered toast.

a. In this problem, buttered toast can be treated as a composite commodity. What is its price in terms of the prices of butter (P_B) and toast (P_T)?

b. Explain why $\partial C/\partial P_{BT} = 0$.

c. Is it also true here that $\partial C/\partial P_B$ and $\partial C/\partial P_T$ are equal to zero?

6.4

Ms. Sarah Traveler does not own a car and travels only by bus, train, or plane. Her utility function is given by

$$\text{utility} = B \cdot T \cdot P,$$

where each letter stands for miles traveled by a specific mode. Suppose that the ratio of the price of train travel to that of bus travel (P_T/P_B) never changes.

a. How might one define a composite commodity for ground transportation?

b. Phrase Sarah's optimization problem as one of choosing between ground (G) and air (P) transportation.

c. What are Sarah's demand functions for G and P?

d. Once Sarah decides on how much to spend on G, how will she allocate those expenditures between B and T?

6.5

Suppose that an individual consumes three goods, X_1, X_2, and X_3, and that X_2 and X_3 are similar commodities (i.e., cheap and expensive restaurant meals) with

$P_2 = KP_3$ where $K < 1$—that is, the goods' prices have a constant relationship to one another.

a. Show that X_2 and X_3 can be treated as a composite commodity.

b. Suppose both X_2 and X_3 are subject to a transaction cost of t per unit (for some examples, see Problem 6.6). How will this transaction cost affect the price of X_2 relative to that of X_3? How will this effect vary with the value of t?

c. Can you predict how an income-compensated increase in t will affect expenditures on the composite commodity X_2 and X_3? Does the composite commodity theorem strictly apply to this case?

d. How will an income-compensated increase in t affect how total spending on the composite commodity is allocated between X_2 and X_3?
(For a further discussion of the complications involved in this problem, see T. E. Borcherding and E. Silberberg, "Shipping the Good Apples Out: The Alchian-Allen Theorem Reconsidered," *Journal of Political Economy* (February 1978): 131–138.)

6.6

Apply the results of Problem 6.5 to explain the following observations:

a. It is difficult to find high-quality apples to buy in Washington state or good fresh oranges in Florida.

b. People with significant baby-sitting expenses are more likely to have those meals they eat out at expensive restaurants than are those without such expenses.

c. Those individuals with a high value of time are more likely to fly the Concorde than those with a lower value of time.

d. Individuals are more likely to search for bargains for expensive items than for cheap ones.
(*Note:* Observations (b) and (d) form the bases for perhaps the only two murder mysteries in which an economist solves the crime. See Marshall Jevons, *Murder at the Margin* and *The Fatal Equilibrium*.)

6.7

In general, uncompensated cross-price effects are not equal. That is,

$$\frac{\partial X_i}{\partial P_j} \neq \frac{\partial X_j}{\partial P_i}.$$

Use the generalized Slutsky equation to show that these effects are equal if the individual spends a constant fraction of income on each good regardless of relative prices.

6.8

Hicks's "second law" of demand states that the predominant relationship among goods is net substitutability (see footnote 3 of Chapter 6). To prove this result:

a. Show why compensated demand functions

$$X_i = h_i(P_1, \ldots, P_n, V)$$

are homogeneous of degree zero in $P_1 \ldots P_n$ for a given level of V.

b. Use Euler's theorem for homogeneous functions (for a statement of this theorem, see footnote 5 of Chapter 7) to show that

$$\sum_{j=1}^{n} P_j \frac{\partial X_i}{\partial P_j}\bigg|_{U = \text{constant}} = 0 \text{ (for all } i = 1, n).$$

c. Use the "first law of demand"

$$\left(\text{that } \frac{\partial X_i}{\partial P_i}\bigg|_{U = \text{constant}} \leq 0 \right)$$

to conclude that

$$\sum_{j \neq i} P_j \frac{\partial X_i}{\partial P_j}\bigg|_{U = \text{constant}} \geq 0,$$

that is, net substitution must prevail, on average.

6.9

A utility function is termed "separable" if it can be written as:

$$U(X, Y) = U_1(X) + U_2(Y)$$

where $U_i' > 0$, $U_i'' < 0$, and U_1, U_2 need not be the same function.

a. What does separability assume about the cross partial derivative U_{XY}? Give an intuitive discussion of what this condition means and in what situations it might be plausible.

b. Show that if utility is separable, neither good can be inferior.

c. Does the assumption of separability allow you to conclude definitively whether X and Y are gross substitutes or gross complements? Explain.

d. Use the Cobb-Douglas utility function to show that separability is not invariant with respect to monotonic transformations.

Note: Separable functions are examined in more detail in the Extensions to this chapter.

6.10

Example 6.3 computes the demand functions implied by the three-good CES utility function

$$U(X, Y, Z) = -\frac{1}{X} - \frac{1}{Y} - \frac{1}{Z}.$$

a. Use the demand function for X in Equation 6.28 to determine whether X and Y or X and Z are gross substitutes or gross complements.

b. How would you determine whether X and Y or X and Z are net substitutes or net complements?

SUGGESTED READINGS

Borcherding, T. E., and E. Silberberg. "Shipping the Good Apples Out—The Alchian-Allen Theorem Reconsidered." *Journal of Political Economy* (February 1978): 131–138.
Good discussion of the relationships among three goods in demand theory. See also Problems 6.5 and 6.6.

Hicks, J. R. *Value and Capital.* 2d ed. Oxford: Oxford University Press, 1946. Chaps. I–III and related appendices.
Proof of the composite commodity theorem. Also has one of the first treatments of net substitutes and complements.

Rosen, S. "Hedonic Prices and Implicit Markets." *Journal of Political Economy* (January/February 1974): 34–55.
Nice graphical and mathematical treatment of the attribute

approach to consumer theory and of the concept of "markets" for attributes.

Samuelson, P. A. "Complementarity—An Essay on the 40th Anniversary of the Hicks-Allen Revolution in Demand Theory." *Journal of Economic Literature* (December 1977): 1255–1289.
Reviews a number of definitions of complementarity and shows the connections among them. Contains an intuitive, graphical discussion and a detailed mathematical appendix.

Silberberg, E. *The Structure of Economics: A Mathematical Analysis.* 2d ed. New York: McGraw-Hill Book Company, 1990.
Good discussion of expenditure functions and the use of indirect utility functions to illustrate the composite commodity theorem and other results.

EXTENSIONS

Separable Utility and the Grouping of Goods

In Chapter 6 we saw that general utility theory implies rather little about demand relationships among goods. Other than the fact that net cross-substitution effects are symmetric, practically any type of relationship is possible. In this extension we examine a particular type of utility function for which it is

possible to make somewhat more definitive statements. These utility functions are called "separable" in the sense (to be made more precise later) that consumption decisions about one good or group of goods do not affect the utility received from some other good or group of goods. If this assumption is tenable, a number of useful results can be obtained. We also look at some empirical evidence on the ways in which goods might be categorized.

E6.1

Suppose an individual consumes only three goods X_1, X_2, and X_3 and that his or her utility function is of the separable form

$$U(X_1, X_2, X_3) = U_1(X_1) + U_2(X_2) + U_3(X_3),$$

where (i)

$$U_i' > 0 \quad U_i'' < 0 \quad \text{for } i = 1, 2, 3.$$

It is easy to show that $\partial X_2/\partial P_1$ and $\partial X_3/\partial P_1$ must both have the same sign—X_2 and X_3 must both be either gross substitutes for X_1 or gross complements for X_1. Since MU_i/P is the same for all goods, a rise in P_1 must cause X_2 and X_3 to move in the same direction. This result holds generally if utility is a separable function of n goods since an identical argument holds for the other $n - 1$ goods.

E6.2 Separability into Groups and Two-Stage Budgeting

A more general statement of separability is

$$U(X_1, X_2, \ldots, X_n) = U[U_1(X_{g1}), U_2(X_{g2}), \ldots, U_k(X_{gk})]$$

(ii)

where the set of goods $X_1, X_2, \ldots, X_n$ is partitioned into k mutually exclusive groups, $X_{g1} \ldots X_{gk}$ (i.e., food, clothing, shelter, and so forth). This functional representation assumes that changes in the consumption of a good from one group (food) do not affect the marginal utility of goods in another group (clothing).

An individual whose utility function is characterized by this type of separability will engage in "two-stage budgeting." That is, he or she will allocate total income among the groups of goods and then seek to maximize U_i ($i = 1, k$) given the expenditure to be devoted to that commodity group. A proof of this follows from an analog to the composite commodity theorem. Indeed, one result of the separability assumption is to allow spending on grouped items to be treated as a single good in empirical applications. With a suitable redefinition of terms, the ideas in Equations (i) and (ii) might also be applied to such issues as utility maximization for a family of k members or intertemporal income allocation over k time periods into the future.

Separability and Empirical Studies

Individuals consume literally millions of different goods. Some aggregation of these goods is essential. Unfortunately, neither of the two available theoretical approaches to aggregation are completely satisfying. The composite commodity theorem described in Chapter 6 requires that the relative prices for goods within one group remain constant over time—an assumption that has been rejected during many different historical periods. On the other hand, the kind of separability and two-stage budgeting indicated by the utility function in Equation (ii) also requires very strong assumptions about how changes in prices for a good in one group affect spending on goods in any other group. These assumptions appear to be rejected by the data (see Diewert and Wales, 1995).

Economists have tried to devise even more elaborate, hybrid methods of aggregation among goods. For example, Lewbel (1996) shows how the composite commodity theorem might be generalized to cases where within-group relative prices exhibit considerable variability. He uses this generalization for aggregating U.S. consumer expenditures into six large groups (food, clothing, household operation, medical care, transportation, and recreation). Using these aggregates, he concludes that his procedure is much more accurate than assuming separability among these expenditure categories.

References

Deaton, A., and J. Muellbauer. *Economics and Consumer Behavior.* Cambridge: Cambridge University Press, 1980, pp. 127–141.

Diewert, W. Erwin, and Terence J. Wales. "Flexible Functional Forms and Tests of Homogeneous Separability." *Journal of Econometrics* (June 1995): 259–302.

Lewbel, Arthur. "Aggregation without Separability: A Standardized Composite Commodity Theorem." *American Economic Review* (June 1996): 524–543.

Stoker, T. M. "Empirical Approaches to the Problem of Aggregation over Individuals." *Journal of Economic Literature* (December 1993): 1827–1845.

CHAPTER 7

MARKET DEMAND AND ELASTICITY

In Chapter 5 we showed how to construct the individual's demand curve for a good by examining changes in the utility-maximizing choices for the good in response to changing prices. In this chapter we will be concerned with "adding up" these individual demand curves to create a market demand curve, a concept that plays a crucial role in all of microeconomic theory. Considerable attention is devoted to examining how the position of the market demand curve might change in response to changing conditions. We also will be concerned with defining various "elasticity" measures since those measures are widely used in empirical work.

MARKET DEMAND CURVES

For ease of exposition, assume that there are only two goods (X and Y) and only two individuals (numbered 1 and 2) in an economy. The first person's demand function for good X is given by

$$X_1 = d_X^1(P_X, P_Y, I_1) \tag{7.1}$$

and the second person's demand for X by

$$X_2 = d_X^2(P_X, P_Y, I_2). \tag{7.2}$$

Two features of these demand functions should be noted. First, both individuals are assumed to face the same prices (P_X and P_Y). Each person is also assumed to be a *price taker,* who must accept the prices prevailing in the market. Second, each person's demand depends on his or her own income, since each is bound by a budget constraint that determines how much he or she can buy with income I_1 or I_2, respectively.

The total demand for X is simply the sum of the amounts demanded by the two individuals. Obviously, this market demand will depend on the parameters P_X, P_Y, I_1, and I_2. Mathematically,

$$\text{total } X = X_1 + X_2 = d_X^1(P_X, P_Y, I_1) + d_X^2(P_X, P_Y, I_2) \qquad (7.3)$$

or

$$\text{total } X = D_X (P_X, P_Y, I_1, I_2),$$

where the function D_X represents the market demand function for good X. Notice that in this case, market demand depends on the prices of both good X and good Y and on the incomes of each individual. To construct the market demand curve, P_X is allowed to vary while P_Y, I_1, and I_2 are held constant. If we assume that each individual's demand for good X is downward sloping, the market demand curve will also be. That is, a decrease in P_X will cause the quantity of X demanded in the market to increase because each individual will demand more.

A Graphical Construction

Figure 7.1 shows the construction of the market demand curve for X. For each price, the point on the market demand curve is found by summing the quantities demanded by each individual. For example, at a price of P_X^* individual 1 demands X_1^* and individual 2 demands X_2^*. The total quantity demanded in the market at P_X^* is therefore the sum of these two amounts: $X^* = X_1^* + X_2^*$. Consequently, the point X^*, P_X^* is one point on the market demand curve D_X. The other points on the curve are derived in a similar way.

FIGURE 7.1

CONSTRUCTION OF A MARKET DEMAND CURVE FROM INDIVIDUAL DEMAND CURVES

A market demand curve is the "horizontal sum" of each individual's demand curve. At each price the quantity demanded in the market is the sum of the amounts each individual demands. For example, at P_X^* the demand in the market is $X_1^* + X_2^* = X^*$.

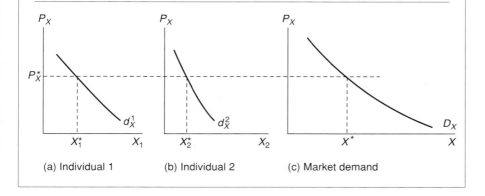

(a) Individual 1   (b) Individual 2   (c) Market demand

The market curve is simply the "horizontal sum" of each individual's demand curve.[1]

Shifts in the Market Demand Curve

The market demand curve, then, summarizes the *ceteris paribus* relationship between X and P_X. It is important to keep in mind that the curve is in reality a two-dimensional representation of a many-variable function. Changes in P_X result in movements along this curve. But changes in any of the other determinants of the demand for X cause the curve to shift to a new position. A general rise in incomes would, for example, cause the demand curve to shift outward (assuming X is a normal good) because each individual would choose to buy more X at every price. Similarly, a rise in P_Y would shift the demand curve for X outward if individuals regarded X and Y as substitutes, but shift the demand curve for X inward if the goods were regarded as complements. Accounting for all such shifts may sometimes require returning to examine the individual demand functions that comprise the market relationship, especially when examining situations in which the distribution of income changes thereby raising some incomes and reducing others. To keep matters straight, economists usually reserve the term "change in quantity demanded" for a movement along a fixed demand curve in response to a change in P_X. Alternatively, any shift in the position of the demand curve is referred to as a "change in demand."

EXAMPLE 7.1

SHIFTS IN MARKET DEMAND

These ideas can be illustrated with a simple set of linear demand functions. Suppose individual 1's demand for oranges (X—measured in dozens per year) is given by

$$X_1 = 10 - 2P_X + .1I_1 + .5P_Y, \tag{7.4}$$

where

P_X = **price of oranges (dollars per dozen)**

I_1 = **individual 1's income (in thousands of dollars)**

P_Y = **price of grapefruit (a gross substitute for oranges—dollars per dozen).**

---

[1] Although the construction here applies to uncompensated demand curves (that is, nominal income is being held constant), an identical procedure could be used to construct compensated market demand curves from compensated (constant utility) individual demand curves.

Individual 2's demand for oranges is given by

$$X_2 = 17 - P_X + .05I_2 + .5P_Y. \tag{7.5}$$

Hence, the market demand function is

$$D_X (P_X, P_Y, I_1, I_2) = X_1 + X_2 = 27 - 3P_X + .1I_1 + .05I_2 + P_Y. \tag{7.6}$$

Here the coefficient for the price of oranges represents the sum of the two individuals' coefficients as does the coefficient for grapefruit prices. This reflects the assumption that orange and grapefruit markets are characterized by the law of one price. Since the individuals have differing coefficients for income, however, the demand function depends on the distribution of income between them.

To graph Equation 7.6 as a market demand curve, we must assume values for I_1, I_2, and P_Y (since the demand curve only reflects the two-dimensional relationship between X and P_X). If $I_1 = 40$, $I_2 = 20$, and $P_Y = 4$, the market demand curve is given by

$$X = 27 - 3P_X + 4 + 1 + 4 = 36 - 3P_X, \tag{7.7}$$

which is a simple linear demand curve. If the price of grapefruit were to rise to $P_Y = 6$, the curve would, assuming incomes remain unchanged, shift outward to

$$X = 27 - 3P_X + 4 + 1 + 6 = 38 - 3P_X \tag{7.8}$$

whereas an income tax that took 10 (thousand dollars) from individual 1 and transferred it to individual 2 would shift the demand curve inward to

$$X = 27 - 3P_X + 3 + 1.5 + 4 = 35.5 - 3P_X \tag{7.9}$$

because individual 1 has a larger marginal effect of income changes on orange purchases. All of these changes shift the demand curve in a parallel way since, in this linear case, none of them affects either individual's coefficient for P_X. In all cases, a rise in P_X of .10 (ten cents) would cause X to fall by .30 (dozen per year).

QUERY: For this linear case when would it be possible to express market demand as a linear function of total income $(I_1 + I_2)$? Alternatively, suppose the individuals had differing coefficients for P_Y. Would that change the analysis in any fundamental way?

Although the construction illustrated previously concerned only two goods and two individuals, it is easily generalized. Suppose there are n goods (denoted by X_i, $i = 1, n$) with prices P_i, $i = 1, n$. Assume also there are m individuals in society. Then the jth individual's demand for the ith good will   **Generalizations** depend on all prices and on I_j, the income of this person. This can be denoted by

$$X_{ij} = d_{ij}(P_1, \ldots, P_n, I_j), \qquad (7.10)$$

where $i = 1, n$ and $j = 1, m$.

Using these individual demand functions, market demand concepts are provided by the following definitions.

DEFINITION

Market Demand The *market demand function* for a particular good (X_i) is the sum of each individual's demand for that good:

$$X_i = \sum_{j=1}^{m} X_{ij} = D_i(P_1, \ldots, P_n, I_1, \ldots, I_m). \qquad (7.11)$$

The *market demand curve* for X_i is constructed from the demand function by varying P_i while holding all other determinants of X_i constant. Assuming each individual's demand curve is downward sloping, this market demand curve also will be downward sloping.

Of course, this definition is just a generalization of our prior discussion, but three features warrant repetition. First, the functional representation of Equation 7.11 makes clear that the demand for X_i depends not only on P_i but also on the prices of all other goods. A change in one of those other prices would therefore be expected to shift the demand curve to a new position. Second, the functional notation indicates that the demand for X_i depends on the entire distribution of individuals' incomes. Although in many economic discussions it is customary to refer to the effect of changes in aggregate total purchasing power on the demand for a good, this approach may be a misleading simplification, since the actual effect of such a change on total demand will depend on precisely how the income changes are distributed among individuals. Finally, although they are obscured somewhat by the notation we have been using, the role of changes in preferences should be mentioned. We have constructed individuals' demand functions with the assumption that preferences (as represented by indifference curve maps) remain fixed. If preferences were to change, so would individual and market demand functions. Hence, market demand curves can clearly be shifted by changes in preferences. In many economic analyses, however, it is assumed that these changes occur so slowly that they may be implicitly held constant without misrepresenting the situation.

A Word on Notation Often in this book we shall be looking at only one market. In order to simplify the notation, in these cases we shall use the letter Q to refer to the quantity of the particular good demanded in this market and P to denote its price. As always, when we draw a demand curve in the Q–P plane, the *ceteris paribus* assumption is in effect. If any of the factors mentioned in the previous section (other prices, individuals' incomes, or preferences) should change, the Q–P demand curve will shift, and we should keep that possibility in mind. When we turn to consider relationships among two or more goods, however, we will return to the notation we have been using up until now (that is, denoting goods by X and Y or by X_i).

ELASTICITY

Economists frequently wish to summarize the way in which changes in one variable, say, A, affect some other variable, say, B. For example, an economist might be interested in measuring how the change in the price of a good affects the quantity demanded or how a change in income affects total expenditures. One problem that arises in attempting to develop such summary measures is that quite often A and B are not measured in the same units. The quantity of steak purchased is measured in pounds and ounces per year, and the price of steak is measured in dollars. We might then speak of an increase of 10 cents in the price of steak, leading to a fall of 2 pounds per year of steak purchases. Similarly, we could speak of a fall in the price of oranges by 10 cents per dozen, leading to an increase in orange purchases of .30 dozen per year (as was the case in Example 7.1). However, there now would be no easy way to answer the question of whether steak is more or less responsive to price changes than are oranges. The problem exists because the commodities are measured in different units. As a solution economists have developed the concept of *elasticity*, which will be introduced in this section.

A General Definition

Suppose that a particular variable B depends on another variable A and that this dependence is denoted by

$$B = f(A \ldots), \tag{7.12}$$

where the dots in the equation indicate that B may depend on other variables as well. We define the elasticity of B with respect to A (denoted by $e_{B,A}$) as

$$e_{B,A} = \frac{\text{percentage change in } B}{\text{percentage change in } A} = \frac{\Delta B/B}{\Delta A/A} = \frac{\partial B}{\partial A} \cdot \frac{A}{B}. \tag{7.13}$$

This expression shows how the variable B responds, *ceteris paribus*, to a 1 percent change in variable A. Although the partial derivative $\partial B/\partial A$ also shows how B changes when A changes, it is not as useful as the elasticity because it is measured in units of B per unit change in A. In the elasticity, multiplication of that partial derivative by A/B causes the units to "drop out," and the remaining expression is purely in terms of percentages. In our orange-steak example, we might know that a 1 percent change in the price of steak leads to a 2 percent change in the quantity bought, whereas a 1 percent change in the price of oranges leads to a 1 percent change in the quantity bought. Consequently, we could conclude that steak purchases were more responsive to price. The fact that steak and oranges are measured in different units no longer presents a problem because we are dealing only in relative percentage changes.

Price Elasticity of Demand

Although we shall come across many different applications of the concept of elasticity in this book, probably the most important is that of the price elasticity of demand. Changes in the price of a good (P) will lead to changes in the quantity purchased (Q), and the price elasticity of demand is intended to measure this response. Applying Equation 7.13, the price elasticity of demand would be defined as follows:

DEFINITION

Price Elasticity of Demand ($e_{Q,P}$)

$$e_{Q,P} = \frac{\text{percentage change in } Q}{\text{percentage change in } P} = \frac{\partial Q}{\partial P} \cdot \frac{P}{Q}. \tag{7.14}$$

This elasticity, then, records how Q changes (in percentage terms) in response to a percentage change in P. Since $\partial Q/\partial P$ is usually negative (that is, P and Q move in opposite directions, except in the case of Giffen's paradox), $e_{Q,P}$ usually will be negative.[2] For example, a value of $e_{Q,P}$ of -1 would mean that a 1 percent rise in price leads to a 1 percent decline in quantity, whereas a value of $e_{Q,P}$ of -2 would record the fact that a 1 percent rise in price causes quantity to decline by 2 percent.

A distinction is often made among values of $e_{Q,P}$ that are less than, equal to, or greater than -1. Specifically, the terminology used is as shown in Table 7.1. For an elastic curve, a price increase is met by a more than proportionate quantity decrease. For a unit elastic curve, the price increase and the quantity decrease are of identical proportional magnitudes. For an inelastic curve, price increases proportionally more than quantity decreases. If a curve is elastic, price affects quantity "a lot"; if a curve is inelastic, price does not have as much of an effect on quantity demanded. One way to classify goods is by

---

[2] Sometimes the elasticity of demand is defined as the absolute value of the definition in Equation 7.14. Consequently, under this alternative definition, elasticity is never negative; curves are classified as elastic, unit elastic, or inelastic, depending on whether $|e_{Q,P}|$ is greater than, equal to, or less than 1. The reader should recognize this distinction in examining empirical work, since there is no consistent usage in economic literature.

TABLE 7.1

TERMINOLOGY FOR A DEMAND CURVE TO DISTINGUISH VALUES OF $e_{Q,P}$

VALUE OF $e_{Q,P}$ AT A POINT	TERMINOLOGY OF CURVE AT THIS POINT
$e_{Q,P} < -1$	Elastic
$e_{Q,P} = -1$	Unit elastic
$e_{Q,P} > -1$	Inelastic

their price elasticities of demand. For example, the quantity of medical services demanded is undoubtedly very inelastic. The market demand curve may be almost vertical in this case, indicating that the quantity demanded is not responsive to price. On the other hand, it is likely that price changes will have a great effect on the quantity of candy bought (the demand is elastic). Here the market demand curve would be relatively flat. If market price were to change even slightly, the quantity demanded would change significantly.

Price Elasticity and Total Expenditure

The total expenditure on any good is the product of the price of the good (P) times the quantity chosen (Q). By using the concept of price elasticity of demand, it is possible to examine how total expenditure changes when the price of a good changes. Since Q is itself a function of P, differentiating PQ with respect to P yields

$$\frac{\partial PQ(P)}{\partial P} = Q + P \cdot \frac{\partial Q}{\partial P}. \tag{7.15}$$

Dividing both sides by Q, we have

$$\frac{\partial PQ/\partial P}{Q} = 1 + \frac{\partial Q}{\partial P} \cdot \frac{P}{Q} = 1 + e_{Q,P}. \tag{7.16}$$

Since Q is positive, the sign of $\partial PQ/\partial P$ will depend on whether $e_{Q,P}$ is greater than or less than -1. If $e_{Q,P} > -1$, demand is inelastic and the derivative is positive: Price and total expenditures move in the same direction. For example, an increase in price would raise total expenditures, since P would rise proportionally more than Q would fall. That situation has been observed in the demand for agricultural products. Since the demand for food is price inelastic, an increase in its price, perhaps due to bad weather, actually increases total expenditures on food.

TABLE 7.2

RESPONSES OF TOTAL EXPENDITURE TO PRICE CHANGES

	RESPONSES OF *PQ*	
DEMAND	PRICE INCREASE	PRICE DECREASE
Elastic	Falls	Rises
Unit elastic	No change	No change
Inelastic	Rises	Falls

On the other hand, if $e_{Q,P} < -1$, price and total expenditures will move in opposite directions. For example, an increase in price will reduce total expenditures, since quantity purchased will fall proportionately more than price rises. Table 7.2 (which is constructed from Equation 7.16) summarizes these responses of total expenditure to a change in price. These results will be useful for our examination of the behavior of firms.

Income Elasticity of Demand

Another type of elasticity frequently encountered in economics is the income elasticity of demand ($e_{Q,I}$). This concept records the relationship between income changes and quantity changes and is another application of the general definition given in Equation 7.13.

DEFINITION

Income Elasticity of Demand ($e_{Q,I}$)

$$e_{Q,I} = \frac{\text{percentage change in quantity}}{\text{percentage change in income}} = \frac{\partial Q}{\partial I} \cdot \frac{I}{Q}. \qquad (7.17)$$

For a normal good, $e_{Q,I}$ is positive since $\partial Q / \partial I$ is positive. For an inferior good, on the other hand, $e_{Q,I}$ is negative.

Among normal goods there is considerable interest about whether $e_{Q,I}$ is greater than or less than 1. Goods for which $e_{Q,I} > 1$ might be called luxury goods in the sense that purchases of these goods increase more rapidly than income. For example, if the income elasticity of demand for automobiles is 2.0, then the implication is that a 10 percent rise in income will lead to a 20 percent increase in automobile purchases. On the other hand, a good such as food probably has an income elasticity of less than 1. If the income elasticity of demand for food were 0.5, then the implication is that a 10 percent rise in income would result in only a 5 percent increase in food purchases.[3]

The final concept of elasticity we introduce in this chapter measures the reaction of quantity purchased (Q) to changes in the price of some other good (P'). We define this cross-price elasticity of demand as follows:

Cross-Price Elasticity

DEFINITION

Cross-Price Elasticity of Demand ($e_{Q,P'}$)

$$e_{Q,P'} = \frac{\partial Q}{\partial P'} \cdot \frac{P'}{Q}.$$

(7.18)

If Q and the other good are gross substitutes, $\partial Q/\partial P'$ will be positive, as will be $e_{Q,P'}$. When the goods are gross complements, $\partial Q/\partial P'$ and $e_{Q,P'}$ will be negative.

We have developed elasticity concepts as they apply to the market demand for a product because these provide convenient, measurable summaries of the responsiveness of quantity demanded to changes in various factors. By treating market demand as being composed of the demands of many "typical" individuals, it is possible to derive some important relationships among these elasticities. For this purpose, suppose that there are only two goods (X and Y) for the typical individual to choose from in maximizing utility and that, as before, the budget constraint is given by[4]

RELATIONSHIPS AMONG ELASTICITIES

$$P_X X + P_Y Y = I.$$

(7.19)

The typical individual's demand functions for X and Y are given by

$$X = d_X(P_X, P_Y, I)$$
$$Y = d_Y(P_X, P_Y, I),$$

(7.20)

---

[3] In light of our previous discussion, these definitions of income elasticity might be generalized to include possible changes in the distribution of income as well. In practice, however, the distinction is often disregarded.

[4] For most of the results presented here, the generalization to n goods is straightforward. However, the treatment of market demand reflecting the behavior of a typical individual raises many complications, some of which are examined in the extensions to this chapter.

and these demand functions are homogeneous of degree zero in all prices and income. We shall now derive some relationships among the demand elasticities for this typical individual that can then be taken to hold for the market demand function as a whole.

Sum of Income Elasticities for All Goods

Differentiation of the budget constraint (Equation 7.19) with respect to I yields

$$P_X \frac{\partial X}{\partial I} + P_Y \frac{\partial Y}{\partial I} = 1 \tag{7.21}$$

or, multiplying each term by (a complex form of) 1,

$$\frac{P_X \cdot X}{I} \cdot \frac{\partial X}{\partial I} \cdot \frac{I}{X} + \frac{P_Y \cdot Y}{I} \cdot \frac{\partial Y}{\partial I} \cdot \frac{I}{Y} = 1. \tag{7.22}$$

Now $P_X \cdot X/I$ is simply the proportion of income spent on good X, and $P_Y \cdot Y/I$ is a similar expression for good Y. Using s_X to denote the proportion of income spent on X, s_Y for the proportion of income spent on Y, and the definition of income elasticity of demand (Equation 7.17), we have

$$s_X e_{X,I} + s_Y e_{Y,I} = 1. \tag{7.23}$$

The weighted sum of the income elasticities of demand for *all* goods must be unity; that is, when income increases by 10 percent, the budget constraint requires that purchases as a whole increase by 10 percent. Equation 7.23 is sometimes referred to as a "generalized" Engel's law. It shows that for "every" good (or group of goods) that has an income elasticity of demand less than 1, there must exist goods that have income elasticities greater than 1. In fact, if there are only two goods, Equation 7.23 implies that knowledge of one good's income elasticity and of the share of income devoted to that good permits calculation of the income elasticity for the other good.

Slutsky Equation in Elasticities

In Chapter 5 we derived the Slutsky equation to show how an individual's demand for a good (say, X) responds to a change in its price. That equation was written as

$$\frac{\partial X}{\partial P_X} = \left. \frac{\partial X}{\partial P_X} \right|_{U = \text{constant}} - X \frac{\partial X}{\partial I}. \tag{7.24}$$

Multiplication of Equation 7.24 by P_X/X yields

$$\frac{\partial X}{\partial P_X} \cdot \frac{P_X}{X} = \left. \frac{\partial X}{\partial P_X} \cdot \frac{P_X}{X} \right|_{U = \text{constant}} - P_X \cdot X \cdot \frac{\partial X}{\partial I} \cdot \frac{1}{X}. \tag{7.25}$$

Multiplying numerator and denominator of the final term in this expression by I, we have

$$\frac{\partial X}{\partial P_X} \cdot \frac{P_X}{X} = \frac{\partial X}{\partial P_X} \cdot \frac{P_X}{X}\bigg|_{U = \text{constant}} - \frac{P_X \cdot X}{I} \cdot \frac{\partial X}{\partial I} \cdot \frac{I}{X}. \qquad (7.26)$$

Now we introduce a definition of the "substitution elasticity":

$$e^S_{X,P_X} = \frac{\partial X}{\partial P_X} \cdot \frac{P_X}{X}\bigg|_{U = \text{constant}}, \qquad (7.27)$$

which shows how the compensated demand for X responds to proportional compensated price changes. In other words, this is the price elasticity of demand for movement along the compensated demand curve. Combining that definition with the others developed in this chapter, Equation 7.26 becomes

$$e_{X,P_X} = e^S_{X,P_X} - s_X e_{X,I}. \qquad (7.28)$$

This equation therefore incorporates the Slutsky relationship in elasticity form. It shows how the price elasticity of demand can be disaggregated into substitution and income components and that the relative size of the income component depends on the proportion of total expenditures devoted to the good in question (that is, on s_X). The equation also shows that if a good has no substitutes ($e^S_{X,P_X} = 0$), price elasticity of demand is proportional to income elasticity, the factor of proportionality being s_X. Similarly, the extent to which that proportionality does hold can be used to judge the extent to which individuals are willing to make substitutions in their consumption choices. Hence, empirical estimates of income and uncompensated price elasticities can be used with Equation 7.28 to estimate compensated demand elasticities. Notice that for a good whose expenditure share (s_X) is small, uncompensated and compensated price elasticities are approximately equal.

Homogeneity

As a final example of deriving relationships among elasticities, we make use of the fact that demand functions are homogeneous of degree zero in all prices and income. Focusing on the demand for good X, for example, Euler's theorem for homogeneous functions shows that[5]

$$\frac{\partial X}{\partial P_X} \cdot P_X + \frac{\partial X}{\partial P_Y} \cdot P_Y + \frac{\partial X}{\partial I} \cdot I = 0. \qquad (7.29)$$

---

[5] Euler's theorem states that if a function $f(X_1, X_2, \ldots, X_n)$ is homogeneous of degree m [that is, if $f(tX_1, tX_2, \ldots, tX_n) = t^m f(X_1, X_2, \ldots, X_n)$ for any $t > 0$], then $f_1 \cdot X_1 + f_2 \cdot X_2 + \cdots + f_n \cdot X_n = mf(X_1, X_2, \ldots, X_n)$. Here we apply the theorem for the case in which $m = 0$. In Chapter 22 we make use of the theorem when $m = 1$ to show that competitively determined factor prices will cause total factor costs to equal the total value of output. Proof of Euler's theorem is fairly straightforward—it proceeds by differentiating the equation defining homogeneity with respect to t, and then setting $t = 1$.

Dividing this expression by X gives

$$\frac{\partial X}{\partial P_X} \cdot \frac{P_X}{X} + \frac{\partial X}{\partial P_Y} \cdot \frac{P_Y}{X} + \frac{\partial X}{\partial I} \cdot \frac{I}{X} = 0 \qquad (7.30)$$

or, using our definitions,

$$e_{X,P_X} + e_{X,P_Y} + e_{X,I} = 0. \qquad (7.31)$$

The fact that the demand elasticities for X with respect to all prices and income sum to 0 is an alternative way of stating the homogeneity property of demand functions: An equal percentage change in all prices and income will leave the demand for X unaffected.

EXAMPLE 7.2

COBB-DOUGLAS ELASTICITIES

In Example 4.2 we showed that an individual whose utility function has the Cobb-Douglas form

$$U(X, Y) = X^\alpha Y^\beta \qquad (7.32)$$

will have demand functions for X and Y of the form

$$X = \frac{\alpha I}{P_X}$$

$$Y = \frac{\beta I}{P_Y}. \qquad (7.33)$$

The elasticities implied by these functions are very easy to calculate. For example,

$$e_{X,P_X} = \frac{\partial X}{\partial P_X} \cdot \frac{P_X}{X} = -\frac{\alpha I}{P_X^2} \cdot \frac{P_X}{X} = -\frac{\alpha I}{P_X} \cdot \frac{1}{\left(\dfrac{\alpha I}{P_X}\right)} = -1. \qquad (7.34)$$

Similar calculations show that

$$e_{X,I} = 1,$$
$$e_{X,P_Y} = 0,$$
$$e_{Y,P_Y} = -1, \qquad (7.35)$$
$$e_{Y,I} = 1,$$
$$e_{Y,P_X} = 0.$$

Hence, these demand functions have quite elementary elasticity values. Since

$$s_X = \frac{P_X X}{I} = \alpha,$$

and   (7.36)

$$s_Y = \frac{P_Y Y}{I} = \beta,$$

constancy of the income shares provides another way of showing the unitary price elasticity of demand exhibited by the functions. Homogeneity holds trivially for these elasticity values

$$e_{X,P_X} + e_{X,P_Y} + e_{X,I} = -1 + 0 + 1 = 0. \tag{7.37}$$

More insightful, perhaps, is the elasticity version of the Slutsky equation which shows

$$e_{X,P_X} = e^S_{X,P_X} - s_X e_{X,I},$$

or

$$-1 = e^S_{X,P_X} - \alpha(1),$$

or

$$e^S_{X,P_X} = -(1 - \alpha) = -\beta. \tag{7.38}$$

In words, the price elasticity of demand for a compensated demand curve generated by the Cobb-Douglas function is equal to (minus) the expenditure share of the other good. This perhaps counterintuitive finding is in fact a special case of the more general result that

$$e^S_{X,P_X} = -(1 - s_X)\sigma \tag{7.39}$$

where σ is the elasticity of substitution first described in Chapter 3. Equation 7.38 is a special case of Equation 7.39 that applies to the Cobb-Douglas function, for which $\sigma = 1$. Although we will not prove the more general result here, we do examine this useful finding in more detail in Problems 7.9 and 7.10.

QUERY: For the Cobb-Douglas case where $\alpha = \beta = 0.5$, what is the compensated price elasticity of demand for each good? How would your answer change for the case of $\alpha = .3$, $\beta = .7$? Explain the differences in these two cases.

A wide variety of specific mathematical functions have been used by economists to represent demand functions and their related demand curves. In this section we will examine only two such functional forms—linear functions and constant elasticity functions. Other forms are illustrated in various problems throughout the book.

TYPES OF DEMAND CURVES

Linear Demand

Probably the simplest way of recording the relationship between quantity demanded (Q), the price of the good (P), income (I), and the price of other goods (P') is by means of a linear function of the form:[6]

$$Q = a + bP + cI + dP', \tag{7.40}$$

where a, b, c, and d are various demand parameters and

- $\partial Q/\partial P = b \leq 0$ (assuming Giffen's paradox does not occur);
- $\partial Q/\partial I = c \geq 0$ (assuming the good is normal); and
- $\partial Q/\partial P' = d \gtreqless 0$ (depending on whether P' is the price of a gross substitute or a gross complement).

As we showed in Example 7.1, if I and P' are held constant at $\bar{I}$ and $\overline{P}'$, respectively, then the demand function in Equation 7.40 can be written as

$$Q = a' + bP, \tag{7.41}$$

where $a' = a + c\bar{I} + d\overline{P}'$. The linear form of Equation 7.41 makes clear that the demand curve implied by this demand function is a straight line. Changes in I or P' would shift this curve to alternative positions by altering its Q-intercept, a'.[7]

Linear Demand and Elasticity

Although the simple form for a linear demand curve is easy to graph, it may at times be inappropriate for economic applications. Along a linear demand curve, $\partial Q/\partial P$ is constant. This means that a change in price from \$1 to \$2 (a doubling of price) is assumed to have the same effect on quantity demanded as a change from \$20 to \$21 (a 5 percent increase). In many applications this assumed similarity of response to very different proportional changes in price may be untenable.

An alternative way of stating this objection is to observe that the price elasticity of demand is not constant along a linear demand curve. If demand is reflected by Equation 7.41, then applying the definition of the price elasticity of demand yields

$$e_{Q,P} = \frac{\partial Q}{\partial P} \cdot \frac{P}{Q} = b \cdot \frac{P}{Q}. \tag{7.42}$$

But the value for this elasticity obviously varies along the demand curve $Q = a' + bP$; as P rises, Q falls and $e_{Q,P}$ becomes a larger negative number

---

[6] Notice that this equation is not homogeneous of degree zero in all prices and income. To make it so would require that $a = 0$ and that P, I, and P' be measured relative to an overall index of prices (say, the CPI).

[7] Notice here that, following usual economic convention, the dependent variable, Q, is shown graphically on the horizontal axis. Hence, a' represents the intercept on that axis.

FIGURE 7.2

THE ELASTICITY OF DEMAND VARIES ALONG
A STRAIGHT-LINE DEMAND CURVE

A straight-line demand curve may be inappropriate for empirical work because
it implies that reaction to proportional price changes will be quite different
depending on whether prices are high or low.

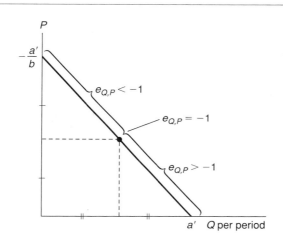

(remember, $b < 0$). In other words, demand becomes more elastic for higher
prices. Figure 7.2 illustrates this fact. When price, P, is halfway between 0 and
where the curve hits the vertical axis (where $P = -a'/b$), $e_{Q,P}$ has a value of -1.[8]
Above this midpoint, demand is elastic ($e_{Q,P} < -1$) and for a price below this
point, demand is inelastic ($e_{Q,P} > -1$). Hence, $e_{Q,P}$ can take on any nonpositive
value depending on which point on the curve happens to be observed.

EXAMPLE 7.3

PRICE ELASTICITY IN THE LINEAR DEMAND CASE

In Example 7.1 we calculated a hypothetical linear market demand curve for
oranges of form (now using the Q, P notation)

---

[8] Proof: If $P = -a'/2b$ (i.e., halfway between 0 and $-a'/b$), then $Q = a' + b(-a'/2b) = a'/2$. Hence,
$e_{Q,P} = bP/Q = b(-a'/2b) \div (a'/2) = -1$.

$$Q = 36 - 3P. \tag{7.43}$$

By definition, the price elasticity of demand is given by

$$e_{Q,P} = \frac{\partial Q}{\partial P} \cdot \frac{P}{Q} = -3\left(\frac{P}{Q}\right) = -3\left(\frac{P}{36 - 3P}\right), \tag{7.44}$$

which obviously depends on the value of P. Since $Q = 0$ if $P = 12$, we know demand is unit elastic when $P = 6$ and Equation 7.44 confirms that fact. For $P > 6$, demand is elastic. If, for example, $P = 8$, $Q = 12$ and $P \cdot Q = 96$. With $P = 7$, $Q = 15$ and $P \cdot Q = 105$. A fall in price increases total expenditures— a clear indication that demand is elastic in this range.

For $P < 6$, however, demand is inelastic. If $P = 5$, $Q = 21$ and $P \cdot Q = 105$ whereas at $P = 4$, $Q = 24$ and $P \cdot Q = 96$. Now a fall in price has reduced total expenditures—demand is inelastic.

Because elasticity varies along a linear demand curve (and along many other types of demand curves as well), one must be careful to specify the point at which elasticity is being measured. At $P = 8$, for example, Equation 7.44 shows that $e_{Q,P} = -3(8/12) = -2$ (demand is elastic) whereas at $P = 5$, $e_{Q,P} = -3(5/21) = -5/7$ (demand is inelastic). In empirical work using a series of observed P–Q points, a common practice is to report the elasticity at the average price prevailing over the sample period.

QUERY: For what value of P are total expenditures as large as possible? What is the general relationship between the price that yields maximum expenditures and the price elasticity of demand?

Constant Elasticity Functions
If one wished to assume that elasticities were constant over a range of price changes, an exponential demand function should be used:

$$Q = aP^b I^c P'^d, \tag{7.45}$$

where now $a > 0, b \leq 0, c \geq 0, d \gtrless 0$. For particular values of the shift variables (say, $\bar{I}$ and $\bar{P}'$) this could be written as

$$Q = a'P^b, \tag{7.46}$$

where $a' = aI^c P'^d$. An alternative way of writing Equation 7.46 is

$$ln\ Q = ln\ a' + b\ ln\ P, \tag{7.47}$$

which shows that the equation is linear in the natural logarithms (denoted by "ln") of Q and P.

Applying the definition of price elasticity to this case yields

$$e_{Q,P} = \frac{\partial Q}{\partial P} \cdot \frac{P}{Q} = \frac{ba'\ P^{b-1} \cdot P}{a'\ P^b} = b. \tag{7.48}$$

Consequently, the price elasticity of demand is constant (and equal to b) for this demand curve. Notice that the elasticity can be read directly from the mathematical form of the curve—it is given by the exponent of P and does not have to be calculated. This result is quite general as Example 7.4 shows.

EXAMPLE 7.4

ELASTICITIES, EXPONENTS, AND LOGARITHMS

Exponential demand curves (such as that shown in Equation 7.45) not only exhibit constant price elasticities of demand, but also have constant income and cross-price elasticities as well. In this case,

$$e_{Q,I} = c \qquad (7.49)$$

and

$$e_{Q,P'} = d. \qquad (7.50)$$

One can therefore read the elasticities directly from the exponents of function without having to make any mathematical computations.
   If

$$Q = 100P^{-1.5}I^{.5}P', \qquad (7.51)$$

we therefore know immediately that $e_{Q,P} = -1.5$, $e_{Q,I} = .5$, and $e_{Q,P'} = 1$. At $P = 1$, $I = 100$, and $P' = 4$, for example, this function predicts $Q = 4000$. If P were to rise by 1 percent (to 1.01), Equation 7.51 shows that Q would fall to $4000(1.01)^{-1.5} = 3940$—a 1.5 percent decline, just as would be predicted by the price elasticity exponent. Similarly, a 1 percent increase in income to 101 (with P remaining at 1 and P' at 4) would increase demand to $400(101)^{.5} = 4020$— a 0.5 percent increase as suggested by the exponent of the income term.
   Although the general form for the constant elasticity demand function in Equation 7.45 is nonlinear, it also can be simplified by taking natural logarithms:

$$ln(Q) = ln(a) + bln(P) + cln(I) + dln(P') \qquad (7.52)$$

or, for the example in Equation 7.51,

$$ln(Q) = 4.61 - 1.5ln(P) + 0.5ln(I) + ln(P'). \qquad (7.53)$$

The fact that this equation is linear in the logarithms of the variables Q, P, I, and P' makes it especially easy to use in econometric applications, some of which are discussed in the Extensions to this chapter.

QUERY: Is the demand function in Equation 7.51 homogeneous of degree zero in P, P', and I? How do the elasticity exponents indicate whether this is the case?

SUMMARY

In this chapter we used the theory of individual demand to construct the market demand function and related market demand curves. The market demand curve shows the *ceteris paribus* relationship between the price of a good and the total quantity demanded by all potential buyers. This concept, which is a fundamental tool for practically all economic analysis, will be used repeatedly in later chapters. Hence, some conclusions about the market demand curve bear repeating here:

- The market demand curve is negatively sloped on the assumption that most individuals will buy more when the price of a good falls. That is, most individuals are assumed to view most goods as normal goods, or, if the good is inferior, it is assumed that Giffen's paradox does not occur.

- For the usual Marshallian market demand curve, the utility level of the individual demander varies along the curve. Because nominal income is held constant, lower prices raise utility and higher prices lower utility.

- It is also possible to construct income-compensated market demand curves by horizontally summing each individual's compensated demand curve. Although we will use these at some places in the text, for the most part we will develop our analysis using the more familiar Marshallian curve.

- Movements along a given demand curve are measured by the price elasticity of demand, $e_{Q,P}$. This shows the percentage change in quantity from a 1 percent increase in price, when all other influences on demand are held constant.

- Changes in total expenditures on a good induced by changes in price can be predicted from the price elasticity of demand. If demand is inelastic $(0 > e_{Q,P} > -1)$, price and total expenditures move in the same direction. If demand is elastic $(e_{Q,P} < -1)$, price and total expenditures move in opposite directions.

- If other factors that enter the demand function (other prices, income, and preferences) change, the market demand curve will shift to a new position. Effects of changes in these other factors on quantity demanded (at a given price) can be measured by the income elasticity of demand $(e_{Q,I})$ or the cross-price elasticity of demand $(e_{Q,P'})$.

- There are a number of relationships among the various demand elasticities. For example, the Slutsky equation shows the relationship between uncompensated and compensated price elasticities. Homogeneity is reflected in the fact that the sum of the elasticities of demand for all of the arguments of a demand function is zero.

PROBLEMS

7.1

Imagine a market for X composed of four individuals: Mr. Pauper (P), Ms. Broke (B), Mr. Average (A), and Ms. Rich (R). All four have the same demand function for X: It is a function of income (I), P_X, and the price of an important substitute (Y), for X:

$$X = \frac{\sqrt{IP_Y}}{2P_X}.$$

a. What is the market demand function for X? If $P_X = P_Y = 1$, $I_P = I_B = 16$, $I_A = 25$, and $I_R = 100$, what is the total market demand for X? What is e_{X,P_X}? e_{X,P_Y}? $e_{X,I}$?

b. If P_X doubled, what would be the new level of X demanded? If Mr. Pauper lost his job and his income fell 50 percent, how would that affect the market demand for X? What if Ms. Rich's income were to drop 50 percent? If the government imposed a 100 percent tax on Y, how would the demand for X be affected?

c. If $I_P = I_B = I_A = I_R = 25$, what would be the total demand for X? How does that figure compare with your answer to (a)? Answer (b) for these new income levels and $P_X = P_Y = 1$.

d. If Ms. Rich found Z a necessary complement to X, her demand function for X might be described by the function

$$X = \frac{IP_Y}{2P_XP_Z}.$$

What is the new market demand function for X? If $P_X = P_Y = P_Z = 1$ and income levels are those described by (a), what is the demand for X? What is e_{X,P_X}? e_{X,P_Y}? $e_{X,I}$? e_{X,P_Z}? What is the new level of demand for X if the price of Z rises to 2? Notice that Ms. Rich is the only one whose demand for X drops.

7.2

Suppose there are n individuals, each with a linear demand curve for Q of the form

$$Q_i = a_i + b_iP + c_iI + d_iP' \qquad i = 1, n,$$

where the parameters a_i, b_i, c_i, and d_i differ among individuals. Show that at any point, the price elasticity of the market demand curve is independent of P' and the distribution of income. Would this be true if each individual's demand for Q were instead linear in logarithms? Explain.

7.3

Tom, Dick, and Harry constitute the entire market for scrod. Tom's demand curve is given by

$$Q_1 = 100 - 2P$$

for $P \le 50$. For $P > 50$, $Q_1 = 0$. Dick's demand curve is given by

$$Q_2 = 160 - 4P$$

for $P \le 40$. For $P > 40$, $Q_2 = 0$. Harry's demand curve is given by

$$Q_3 = 150 - 5P$$

for $P \le 30$. For $P > 30$, $Q_3 = 0$. Using this information, answer the following:

a. How much scrod is demanded by each person at $P = 50$? At $P = 35$? At $P = 25$? At $P = 10$? At $P = 0$?

b. What is the total market demand for scrod at each of the prices specified in part (a)?

c. Graph each individual's demand curve.

d. Use the individual demand curves and the results of part (b) to construct the total market demand curve for scrod.

7.4

Suppose that ham and cheese are pure complements—they will always be used in the ratio of one slice of ham to one slice of cheese to make a sandwich. Suppose also that ham and cheese sandwiches are the only goods that a consumer can buy and that bread is free. Show that if the price of a slice of ham equals the price of a slice of cheese,

a. The own-price elasticity of demand for ham is $-\frac{1}{2}$; and

b. The cross-price elasticity of a change in the price of cheese on ham consumption is also $-\frac{1}{2}$.

c. How would your answers to (a) and (b) change if a slice of ham cost twice as much as a slice of cheese?

d. (*Hint:* Use the Slutsky equation—what is the substitution elasticity here?)

7.5

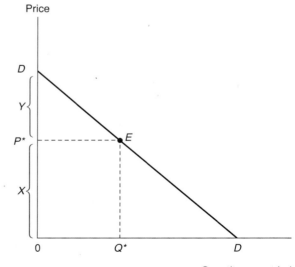

Price

D

Y

P^* ---------- E

X

0   Q^* D

Quantity per period

For the linear demand curve illustrated on page 222, show that the price elasticity of demand at any given point (say, point E) is given by minus the ratio of distance X to distance Y in the figure. How might you apply this result to a nonlinear demand curve?

7.6

A *luxury* is defined as a good for which the income elasticity of demand is greater than 1. Show that for a two-good economy, both goods cannot be luxuries. (*Hint:* What happens if both goods are luxuries and income is increased by 10 percent?)

7.7

The "expenditure elasticity" for a good is defined as the proportional change in total expenditures on the good in response to a 1 percent change in income. That is,

$$e_{P_X \cdot X, I} = \frac{\partial P_X X}{\partial I} \cdot \frac{I}{P_X X}.$$

Prove that $e_{P_X \cdot X, I} = e_{X, I}$. Show also that $e_{P_X \cdot X, P_X} = 1 + e_{\dot{X}, P_X}$. Both of these results are useful for empirical work in cases where quantity measures are not available, since income and price elasticities can be derived from expenditure elasticities.

7.8

Show that for a two-good world,

$$s_X e_{X, P_X} + s_Y e_{Y, P_X} = -s_X.$$

If the own-price elasticity of demand for X is known, what do we know about the cross-price elasticity for Y? (*Hint:* Begin by taking the total differential of the budget constraint and setting $dI = 0 = dP_Y$.)

7.9

In Example 7.2 we showed that with two goods the price elasticity of demand of a compensated demand curve is given by

$$e^S_{X, P_X} = -(1 - s_X)\sigma$$

where s_X is the share of income spent on good X and σ is the substitution elasticity. Use this result together with the elasticity interpretation of the Slutsky equation to show

a. that if $\sigma = 1$ (the Cobb-Douglas case)

$$e_{X, P_X} + e_{Y, P_Y} = -2.$$

b. that $\sigma > 1$ implies $e_{X, P_X} + e_{Y, P_Y} < -2$ and $\sigma < 1$ implies $e_{X, P_X} + e_{Y, P_Y} > -2$.

c. Explain your results intuitively and discuss how they might generalize to cases of more than two goods.

7.10

A formal definition of what we have been calling the substitution elasticity is

$$\sigma = \frac{d\ln Y/X}{d(\ln MRS)} = \left(\frac{d\ln MRS}{d\ln Y/X} \right)^{-1}.$$

a. Interpret this as an elasticity—what variables are being changed and how do these changes (in proportional terms) reflect the curvature of indifference curves. (See also the discussion in Chapter 11 of the elasticity of substitution in the context of a production function.)

b. Apply the definition of σ given above to the CES utility function

$$U(X, Y) = \frac{X^\delta}{\delta} + \frac{Y^\delta}{\delta}.$$

Show that $\sigma = \dfrac{1}{1 - \delta}$ and that this value is constant for all values of X and Y, thereby justifying the CES function's name.

SUGGESTED READINGS

Barten, A. P. "The Systems of Demand Function Approach: A Review." *Econometrica* (January 1977): 23–51.
A good survey of the statistical questions involved in trying to estimate a complete set of demand functions for consumer expenditures. Stresses theoretical restrictions that must hold across the equations.

Deaton, A. J. "Demand Analysis." In Z. Griliches and M. D. Intriligator, eds. *Handbook of Econometrics.* Amsterdam: North-Holland Publishing Co., 1984.
Good survey of the technical econometric issues that arise in demand analysis. Limited references to the empirical literature.

Ferber, R. "Consumer Economics: A Survey." *Journal of Economic Literature* 11 (December 1973): 1303–1342.
Good summary of the older empirical literature on consumer behavior.

Goldberger, Arthur S. *Functional Form and Utility: A Review of Consumer Demand Theory.* Boulder, Colo.: Westview Press, 1981.
Complete summary of elasticity relationships implied by utility maximization.

Houthakker, H. S., and L. D. Taylor. *Consumer Demand in the United States.* 2d ed. Cambridge, Mass.: Harvard University Press, 1970.
Complete analysis of all the categories of expenditures in the GNP consumption series; has several empirical anomalies but generally plausible elasticity estimates for most items.

Theil, H. *Theory and Measurement of Consumer Demand,* Vol. 1. Amsterdam: North-Holland Publishing Co., 1975. Chaps. 5 and 6.
Complete development of the "linear expenditure" system of demand equations; includes substantial theoretical background material.

Wold, H., and I. Jureen. *Demand Analysis.* New York: John Wiley & Sons, 1953.
Classic work on the empirical analysis of demand. Outdated but provides insights on many important issues of empirical specification.

EXTENSIONS

Aggregation and Estimation

In Chapters 4 through 6 we showed that the assumption of utility maximization implies several properties for individual demand functions:

- The functions are continuous;
- The functions are homogeneous of degree zero in all prices and income;
- Income-compensated substitution effects are negative; and
- Cross-price substitution effects are symmetric.

In this extension we will examine the extent to which these properties would be expected to hold for aggregated market demand functions and what, if any, restrictions should be placed on such functions. In addition, we illustrate some other issues that arise in estimating these aggregate functions and at some results from such estimates.

E7.1 Continuity

The continuity of individual demand functions clearly implies the continuity of market demand functions. But there are situations in which market demand functions may be continuous whereas individual functions are not. Consider the case where goods—such as an automobile—must be bought in large, discrete units. Here individual demand may be discontinuous, but the aggregated demands of many people may be (nearly) continuous.

E7.2 Homogeneity and Income Aggregation

Since each individual's demand function is homogeneous of degree zero in all prices and income, market demand functions are also homogeneous of degree zero in all prices and *individual* incomes. However, market demand functions are not necessarily homogeneous of degree zero in all prices and *total* income.

To see when demand might depend on total income, suppose individual i's demand for X is given by

$$X_i = a_i(P) + b(P)y_i \qquad i = 1, n \qquad \text{(i)}$$

where P is the vector of all market prices, $a_i(P)$ is a set of individual-specific price effects, and $b(P)$ is a marginal propensity to spend function that is the same across all individuals (although the value of this parameter may depend on market prices). In this case the market demand functions will depend on P and on total income

$$Y = \sum_{i=1}^{n} y_i. \qquad \text{(ii)}$$

This shows that market demand reflects the behavior of a single "typical" consumer. Gorman (1959) shows that this is the most general form of demand function that can represent such a typical consumer.

E7.3 Cross-Equation Constraints

Suppose a typical individual buys k items and that expenditures on each are given by

$$P_j X_j = \sum_{i=1}^{k} a_{ij} P_i + b_j Y \qquad j = 1, k. \qquad \text{(iii)}$$

If expenditures on these k items exhaust total income, that is,

$$\sum_{j=1}^{k} P_j X_j = Y, \qquad \text{(iv)}$$

summing over all goods shows that

$$\sum_{j=1}^{k} a_{ij} = 0 \quad \text{(for all } i\text{)} \qquad \text{(v)}$$

and that

$$\sum_{j=1}^{k} b_j = 1 \qquad \text{(vi)}$$

for each person. This implies that researchers are generally not able to estimate j expenditure functions for k goods independently. Rather, some account must be taken of relationships between the expenditure functions for different goods.

E7.4 Economic Practice

The degree to which these theoretical concerns are reflected in the actual practices of econometricians varies widely. At the least sophisticated level, an equation similar to (iii) might be estimated directly using ordinary least squares (OLS) with little attention to the ways in which the assumptions might be violated. Various elasticities could be calculated directly from this equation, though because of the linear form used these would not be constant for changes in P_i or Y. A constant elasticity formulation of Equation iii would be

$$ln(P_j X_j) = \sum_{i=1}^{k} a_{ij} ln(P_i) + b_j lnY \quad j = l, k \qquad \text{(vii)}$$

and here price and income elasticities would be given directly by

$$\begin{aligned}
e_{x_j, p_j} &= 1 + a_{ij} \\
e_{x_j, p_i} &= a_{ij} \quad (i \neq j) \qquad \text{(viii)} \\
e_{x_j, y} &= b_j
\end{aligned}$$

respectively (see also Problem 7.7). Notice here, however, that no specific attention is paid to biases introduced by use of aggregate income nor by the disregard of possible cross-equation restrictions such as those in Equations v and vi. Further restrictions are also implied by the homogeneity of each of the demand functions ($\sum_{i=1}^{k} a_{ij} + b_j = -1$), though this restriction too is often disregarded in the development of simple econometric estimates.

More sophisticated studies of aggregated demand equations seek to remedy these problems by explicit consideration of potential income distribution effects and by the estimation of entire systems of demand equation. Theil (1971, 1975) provides a good introduction to some of the procedures used.

TABLE 7.3

REPRESENTATIVE PRICE AND INCOME ELASTICITIES OF DEMAND

	PRICE ELASTICITY	INCOME ELASTICITY
Food	−0.21	+0.28
Medical services	−0.22	+0.22
Housing		
Rental	−0.18	+1.00
Owner occupied	−1.20	+1.20
Electricity	−1.14	+0.61
Automobiles	−1.20	+3.00
Beer	−0.26	+0.38
Wine	−0.88	+0.97
Marijuana	−1.50	0.00
Cigarettes	−0.35	+0.50
Abortions	−0.81	+0.79
Transatlantic air travel	−1.30	+1.40
Imports	−0.58	+2.73
Money	−0.40	+1.00

SOURCES: Food: H. Wold and L. Jureen, *Demand Analysis* (New York: John Wiley & Sons, Inc., 1953): 203. Medical services: income elasticity from R. Andersen and L. Benham, "Factors Affecting the Relationship between Family Income and Medical Care Consumption"; price elasticity from G. Rosenthal, "Price Elasticity of Demand for Short-Term General Hospital Services"; both in *Empirical Studies in Health Economics*, Herbert Klarman, ed. (Baltimore: Johns Hopkins Press, 1970). Housing: income elasticities from F. de Leeuw, "The Demand for Housing," *Review for Economics and Statistics* (February 1971); price elasticities from H. S. Houthakker and L. D. Taylor, *Consumer Demand in the United States* (Cambridge, Mass.: Harvard University Press, 1970): 166–67. Electricity: R. F. Halvorsen, "Residential Demand for Electricity," unpublished Ph.D. dissertation, Harvard University, December 1972. Automobiles: Gregory C. Chow, *Demand for Automobiles in the United States* (Amsterdam: North Holland Publishing Co., 1957). Beer and wine: J. A. Johnson, E. H. Oksanen, M. R. Veall, D. Fritz, "Short-Run and Long-Run Elasticities for Canadian Consumption of Alcoholic Beverages," *Review of Economics and Statistics* (February 1992): 64–74. Marijuana: T. C. Misket and F. Vakil, "Some Estimates of Price and Expenditure Elasticities among UCLA Students," *Review of Economics and Statistics* (November 1972): 474–75. Cigarettes: F. Chalemaker, "Rational Addictive Behavior and Cigarette Smoking," *Journal of Political Economy* (August 1991): 722–42. Abortions: M. H. Medoff, "An Economic Analysis of the Demand for Abortions," *Economic Inquiry* (April 1988): 253–59. Transatlantic air travel: J. M. Cigliano, "Price and Income Elasticities for Airline Travel," *Business Economics* (September 1980): 17–21. Imports: M. D. Chinn, "Beware of Econometricians Bearing Estimates," *Journal of Policy Analysis and Management* (Fall 1991): 546–67. Money: "Long-Run Income and Interest Elasticities of Money Demand in the United States," *Review of Economics and Statistics* (November 1991): 665–74. Price elasticity refers to interest rate elasticity.

Econometric Results

Table 7.3 reports a number of econometric estimates of representative price and income elasticities drawn from a variety of sources. The original sources for these estimates should be consulted to determine the extent to which the authors have been attentive to the theoretical restrictions outlined previously. Overall, these estimates accord fairly well with intuition—the demand for transatlantic air travel is more price elastic than is the demand for medical care, for example. Perhaps somewhat surprising are the high price and income elasticities for owner-occupied housing, since "shelter" is often regarded in everyday discussion as a necessity. The very high estimated income elasticity of demand for automobiles probably conflates the measurement of both quantity and quality demanded. But it does suggest why the automobile industry is so sensitive to the business cycle.

References

Gorman, W. M. "Separable Utility and Aggregation." *Econometrica* (November 1959): 469–481.

Shafer, W., and H. Sonnenschein. "Market Demand and Excess Demand Functions." In K. J. Arrow and M. D. Intriligator, eds. *Handbook of Mathematical Economics*, Vol. II. Amsterdam: North-Holland Publishing Co., 1982, pp. 671–693.

Stoker, T. M. "Empirical Approaches to the Problem of Aggregation over Individuals." *Journal of Economic Literature* (December 1993): 1827–1874.

Theil, H. *Principles of Econometrics*. New York: John Wiley & Sons, 1971, pp. 326–346.

———. *Theory and Measurement of Consumer Demand*, Vol. 1. Amsterdam: North-Holland Publishing Co., 1975. Chaps. 5 and 6.

CHOICE UNDER UNCERTAINTY

The three chapters of this part are concerned with individual behavior under conditions of uncertainty. In previous chapters our model of choice did not involve any such uncertainty—once an individual decided there was no uncertainty about the utility that would be received from his or her budgetary allocation. Here we show how these earlier models can be generalized to consider situations where the utility received from a chosen action is to some extent unpredictable. We begin in Chapter 8 with an analysis of "risk aversion." The purpose of the chapter is to show why individuals usually dislike the risks that uncertainty poses and are willing to pay something to reduce them. That discussion leads naturally to the study of markets for such risk-reducing products as insurance and mutual funds.

Chapter 9 continues the study of behavior under uncertainty by examining the topic of information. We show that in many ways decision making in uncertain situations is characterized by imperfect information. Hence we need to analyze how individuals obtain and use new information. The chapter illustrates a few of the difficult questions that arise in attempting to model such situations.

Finally, Chapter 10 concerns the uncertainty that arises in strategic interactions among people. It provides a basic introduction to the tools that have been developed in modern game theory to address such situations. Especially important is the introduction of concepts of "strategic equilibrium" that show how the outcomes of some games can be predicted through careful analysis of the choices available to the participants. We will encounter the equilibrium concepts defined in this chapter at several places later in the book.

CHAPTER 8

CHOICE IN UNCERTAIN SITUATIONS: EXPECTED UTILITY AND RISK AVERSION

In this chapter we look at some of the basic elements that characterize individuals' motivation when making choices in uncertain situations. We show how the notion of utility can be generalized to apply to cases in which outcomes are subject to some degree of randomness. We then use this expanded concept of utility to examine the phenomenon of "risk aversion." That is, we show why individuals generally dislike uncertain situations and may be willing to pay something to reduce the uncertainty they face. This finding leads directly to the study of insurance and other risk reduction strategies.

PROBABILITY AND EXPECTED VALUE

The study of individual behavior under uncertainty and the mathematical study of probability and statistics have a common historical origin in attempts to understand (and presumably to win) games of chance. The study of simple coin-flipping games, for example, has been unusually productive both in mathematics and in illuminating certain characteristics of human behavior that the games exhibit. Two statistical concepts that originated in such games, and will be quite useful in the remainder of this chapter, are *probability* and *expected value*.

The *probability* of a repetitive event happening is, roughly speaking, the relative frequency with which it will occur. For example, to say that the probability of obtaining a head on the flip of a fair coin is one-half means that one would expect that if a fair coin were flipped a large number of times, a head would appear in approximately one-half of the trials. Similarly, the probability of rolling a 2 on a single die is one-sixth. In approximately one out of every six rolls, a 2 will come up.

Suppose that a lottery offers n prizes (some of which may be 0 or even negative), $X_1, X_2, \ldots, X_n$, and that the probabilities of winning these prizes are $\pi_1, \pi_2, \ldots, \pi_n$. If we assume that one and only one prize will be awarded to a player, it must be the case that

$$\sum_{i=1}^{n} \pi_i = 1. \tag{8.1}$$

Equation 8.1 simply says that our list includes all possible outcomes of the lottery and that one of these has to occur. To provide a measure of the average payoff in this lottery, we define expected value as follows:

DEFINITION

Expected Value   For a lottery (X) with prizes $X_1, X_2, \ldots, X_n$ and probabilities of winning $\pi_1, \pi_2, \ldots, \pi_n$, the *expected value* of the lottery is[1]

$$\text{expected value} = E(X) = \pi_1 X_1 + \pi_2 X_2 + \cdots + \pi_n X_n$$

$$= \sum_{i=1}^{n} \pi_i X_i. \tag{8.2}$$

The expected value of the lottery is a weighted sum of the prizes, where the weights are the respective probabilities. It is simply the size of the prize that the player will win on the average. For example, suppose that Jones and Smith agree to flip a coin once. If a head comes up, Jones will pay Smith \$1; if a tail, Smith will pay Jones \$1. From Smith's point of view, there are two prizes in this game: For a head, $X_1 = +\$1$; for a tail, $X_2 = -\$1$, where the minus sign indicates that Smith must pay. From Jones's point of view, the game is exactly the same except the signs of the outcomes are reversed. Thus, the expected value of the game is

$$\frac{1}{2} X_1 + \frac{1}{2} X_2 = \frac{1}{2} (\$1) + \frac{1}{2} (-\$1) = 0. \tag{8.3}$$

---

[1] If the situation being examined has continuous outcomes (for example, the change in the price of a stock measured very precisely), then we need to modify this definition a bit. If the probability that an outcome of such a random event (X) is in a small interval (dx) is given by $f(x)\,dx$, then Equation 8.1 can be modified as

$$\int_{-\infty}^{\infty} f(x)\,dx = 1.$$

In this case the expected value of X is given by

$$E(X) = \int_{-\infty}^{\infty} x f(x)\,dx.$$

In many situations (for example, when X has a normal distribution), manipulation of such expected values can be much simpler than for the discrete case represented in Equation 8.2. See the extensions to this chapter for some illustrations.

The game has an expected value of 0. If the game were to be played a large number of times, it is not likely that either player would come out very far ahead.

Now suppose that the prizes of the game were changed so that (again from Smith's point of view) $X_1 = \$10$, $X_2 = -\$1$. Smith will win \$10 if a head comes up but will lose only \$1 if a tail appears. The expected value of this game is

$$\frac{1}{2} X_1 + \frac{1}{2} X_2 = \frac{1}{2} (\$10) + \frac{1}{2} (-\$1) = \$5 - \$.50 = \$4.50. \qquad (8.4)$$

If this game is played many times, Smith will certainly end up the big winner. In fact, Smith might be willing to pay Jones something for the privilege of playing the game. He might even be willing to pay as much as \$4.50 for a chance to play. Games such as those in Equation 8.3, which have an expected value of 0, or those in Equation 8.4, which cost their expected values (here \$4.50) for the right to play, are called (actuarially) *fair games*. A common observation is that, in many situations, people refuse to play actuarially fair games. This point is central to understanding developments in the theory of uncertainty and is taken up in the next section.

FAIR GAMES AND THE EXPECTED UTILITY HYPOTHESIS

People are generally unwilling to play fair games.[2] I may at times agree to flip a coin for small amounts of money, but if I were offered the chance to wager \$1000 on one coin flip, I would undoubtedly refuse. Similarly, people may sometimes pay a small amount of money to play an actuarially unfair game such as a state lottery, but they will avoid paying a great deal to play risky, but fair games.

St. Petersburg Paradox

A convincing example is the "St. Petersburg paradox," which was first investigated rigorously by the mathematician Daniel Bernoulli in the eighteenth century.[3] In the St. Petersburg paradox the following game is proposed: A coin is flipped until a head appears. If a head first appears on the nth flip, the player is paid $\$2^n$. This game has an infinite number of

---

[2] The games discussed here are assumed to yield no utility in their play other than the prizes; hence, the observation that many individuals gamble at "unfair" odds (for instance, in the game of roulette, where there are 38 possible outcomes but the house pays only 36 to 1 for a winning number) is not necessarily a refutation of this statement. Rather, such individuals can reasonably be assumed to be deriving some utility from the circumstances associated with the play of the game. It is therefore conceptually possible to differentiate the consumption aspect of gambling from the pure risk aspect.

[3] The original Bernoulli has been reprinted as D. Bernoulli, "Exposition of a New Theory on the Measurement of Risk," *Econometrica* 22 (January 1954): 23–36.

outcomes (a coin might be flipped from now until doomsday and never come up a head, although the likelihood of this is small), but the first few can easily be written down. If X_i represents the prize awarded when the first head appears on the ith trial, then

$$X_1 = \$2, \ X_2 = \$4, \ X_3 = \$8, \ldots, \ X_n = \$2^n. \tag{8.5}$$

The probability of getting a head for the first time on the ith trial is $\left(\frac{1}{2}\right)^i$; it is the probability of getting $(i - 1)$ tails and then a head. Hence, the probabilities of the prizes given in Equation 9.5 are

$$\pi_1 = \frac{1}{2}, \ \pi_2 = \frac{1}{4}, \ \pi_3 = \frac{1}{8}, \ \cdots, \ \pi_n = \frac{1}{2^n}. \tag{8.6}$$

The expected value of the St. Petersburg paradox game is infinite:

$$\text{expected value} = \sum_{i=1}^{\infty} \pi_i \, X_i = \sum_{i=1}^{\infty} 2^i \frac{1}{2^i}$$

$$= 1 + 1 + 1 + \cdots + 1 + \cdots = \infty. \tag{8.7}$$

Some introspection, however, should convince anyone that no player would pay very much (much less than infinity) to play this game. If I charged $1 billion to play the game, I would surely have no takers, despite the fact that $1 billion is still considerably less than the expected value of the game. This, then, is the paradox: Bernoulli's game is in some sense not worth its (infinite) expected dollar value.

Expected Utility Bernoulli's solution to this paradox was to argue that individuals do not care directly about the dollar prizes of a game; rather they respond to the utility these dollars provide. If it is assumed that the marginal utility of income declines as income increases, the St. Petersburg game may converge to a finite *expected utility* value that players would be willing to pay for the right to play. Bernoulli termed this expected utility value the "moral value" of the game because it represents how much the game is worth to the individual. Because utility may rise less rapidly than the dollar value of the prizes, it is possible that a game's moral value will fall short of its monetary expected value.

EXAMPLE 8.1

BERNOULLI'S SOLUTION TO THE PARADOX

Suppose, as did Bernoulli, that the utility of each prize in the St. Petersburg paradox is given by

$$U(X_i) = \ln (X_i). \qquad (8.8)$$

This natural logarithmic utility function exhibits diminishing marginal utility (that is, $U' > 0$, but $U'' < 0$), and the expected utility value of this game converges to a finite number:

$$\text{expected utility} = \sum_{i=1}^{\infty} \pi_i U(X)_i$$

$$= \sum_{i=1}^{\infty} \frac{1}{2^i} \ln (2^i). \qquad (8.9)$$

Some manipulation of this expression yields the result that the expected utility value of this game is 1.39.[4] An individual with this type of utility function might therefore be willing to invest resources that otherwise yield up to 1.39 units of utility (a certain wealth of about $4 provides this utility) in purchasing the right to play this game. Assuming that the very large prizes promised by the St. Petersburg paradox encounter diminishing marginal utility therefore permitted Bernoulli to offer a solution to the paradox.

Although Bernoulli's basic observation is extremely important to any discussion of individual behavior under uncertainty, this does not really solve the St. Petersburg paradox. So long as there is no upper bound on the utility function, the prizes in the game can be suitably redefined so as to regenerate the paradox. This problem and several others have prompted many investigators to adopt the assumption of a bounded utility function. It is assumed that there is some income level above which utility no longer increases with further increases in income. For example, suppose that the level of bliss is taken to be 2^{43} (which is about the total value of all physical assets in the United States). Then prizes greater than this are worth no more than 2^{43}. Under this assumption the *expected value* of the St. Petersburg game is a "reasonable" $44. This level of "bliss" is so far above any observable level of income as to be irrelevant to real-world problems. In this case the assumption of boundedness is merely a convenient assumption without any stringent empirical content.

QUERY: How would you define the prizes in this game so that the game would have an infinite expected utility value using the logarithmic utility function?

---

[4] Proof: Expected utility $= \sum_{i=1}^{\infty} 1/2^i \cdot \ln 2 = \ln 2 \sum_{i=1}^{\infty} i/2^i$. But the value of this final infinite series can be shown to be 2.0. Hence, expected utility $= 2 \ln 2 = 1.39$.

THE VON NEUMANN–MORGENSTERN THEOREM

In their book *The Theory of Games and Economic Behavior,* John von Neumann and Oscar Morgenstern developed mathematical models for examining the economic behavior of individuals under conditions of uncertainty.[5] To understand these interactions, it was necessary first to investigate the motives of the participants in such "games." Since the hypothesis that individuals make choices in uncertain situations based on expected utility seemed intuitively reasonable, the authors set out to show that this hypothesis could be derived from more basic axioms of "rational" behavior. The axioms represent an attempt by the authors to generalize some of the foundations of the theory of individual choice to cover uncertain situations. Although most of these axioms seem eminently reasonable at first glance, many important questions about their tenability have been raised. We will not pursue these questions here, however. Instead, we will show why von Neumann and Morgenstern concluded that maximizing expected utility seemed to be a reasonable goal to pursue in uncertain situations.[6]

The von Neumann–Morgenstern Utility Index

To begin, suppose that there are n possible prizes that an individual might win by participating in a game. Let these prizes be denoted by $X_1, X_2, \ldots, X_n$ and assume that these have been arranged in order of ascending desirability. X_1 is therefore the least preferred prize for the individual, and X_n is the most preferred prize. Now assign arbitrary utility numbers to these two extreme prizes. For example, it might be convenient to assign

$$U(X_1) = 0$$
$$U(X_n) = 1,$$

(8.10)

but any other pair of numbers would do equally well.[7] Using these two values of utility, the point of the von Neumann–Morgenstern theorem is to show that a reasonable way exists to assign specific utility numbers to the other prizes available. Suppose that we choose any other prize, say, X_i. Consider the following experiment. Ask the individual to state the probability, say, π_i, at which he or she would be indifferent between X_i with

---

[5] J. von Neumann and O. Morgenstern, *The Theory of Games and Economic Behavior* (Princeton, NJ: Princeton University Press, 1944). The axioms of rationality in uncertain situations are discussed in the appendix.

[6] For a discussion of some of the issues raised in the debate over the von Neumann–Morgenstern axioms, see Mark J. Machina, "Choice under Uncertainty: Problems Solved and Unsolved," *Journal of Economic Perspectives* (Summer 1987): 121–154.

[7] Technically, a von Neumann–Morgenstern utility index is unique only up to a choice of scale and origin—that is, only up to a "linear transformation." This requirment is more stringent than the requirement that a utility function be unique up to a monotonic transformation.

certainty, and a *gamble* offering prizes of X_n with probability π_i and X_1 with probability $(1 - \pi_i)$. It seems reasonable (although this is one of the problematic assumptions in the von Neumann–Morgenstern approach) that such a probability will exist: The individual will always be indifferent between a gamble and a sure thing, provided that in the gamble a high enough probability of winning the best prize is offered. It also seems likely that π_i will be higher the more desirable X_i is; the better X_i is, the better a chance of winning X_n must be offered to get the individual to gamble. The probability π_i therefore represents how desirable the prize X_i is. In fact, the von Neumann–Morgenstern technique is to define the utility of X_i as the expected utility of the gamble that the individual considers equally desirable to X_i:

$$U(X_i) = \pi_i \cdot U(X_n) + (1 - \pi_i) \cdot U(X_1). \tag{8.11}$$

Because of our choice of scale in Equation 8.10 we have

$$U(X_i) = \pi_i \cdot 1 + (1 - \pi_i) \cdot 0 = \pi_i. \tag{8.12}$$

By judiciously choosing the utility numbers to be assigned to the best and worst prizes, we have been able to show that the utility number attached to any other prize is simply the probability of winning the top prize in a gamble the individual regards as equivalent to the prize in question. This choice of utility numbers is arbitrary. Any other two numbers could have been used to construct this utility scale, but our initial choice (Equation 8.10) is a particularly convenient one.

Expected Utility Maximization

In line with the choice of scale and origin represented by Equation 8.10, suppose that probability π_i has been assigned to represent the utility of every prize X_i. Notice in particular that $\pi_1 = 0$, $\pi_n = 1$, and that the other utility values range between these extremes. Using these utility numbers, we can show that a "rational" individual will choose among gambles based on their expected "utilities" (that is, based on the expected value of these von Neumann–Morgenstern utility index numbers).

As an example, consider two gambles. One gamble offers X_2, with probability q, and X_3, with probability $(1 - q)$. The other offers X_5, with probability t, and X_6, with probability $(1 - t)$. We want to show that the individual will choose gamble 1 if and only if the expected utility of gamble 1 exceeds that of gamble 2. Now for the gambles:

$$\text{expected utility (1)} = q \cdot U(X_2) + (1 - q) \cdot U(X_3)$$
$$\text{expected utility (2)} = t \cdot U(X_5) + (1 - t) \cdot U(X_6). \tag{8.13}$$

Substituting the utility index numbers (that is, π_2 is the "utility" of X_2, and so forth) gives

$$\text{expected utility (1)} = q \cdot \pi_2 + (1 - q) \cdot \pi_3$$

$$\text{expected utility (2)} = t \cdot \pi_5 + (1 - t) \cdot \pi_6. \tag{8.14}$$

We wish to show that the individual will prefer gamble 1 to gamble 2 if and only if

$$q \cdot \pi_2 + (1 - q) \cdot \pi_3 > t \cdot \pi_5 + (1 - t) \cdot \pi_6. \tag{8.15}$$

To show this, recall the definitions of the utility index. The individual is indifferent between X_2 and a gamble promising X_1 with probability $(1 - \pi_2)$ and X_n with probability π_2. We can use this fact to substitute gambles involving only X_1 and X_n for all utilities in Equation 8.14 (even though the individual is indifferent between these, the assumption that this substitution can be made is another of the most problematic of the von Neumann–Morgenstern axioms). After a bit of messy algebra, we can conclude that gamble 1 is equivalent to a gamble promising X_n with probability $q\pi_2 + (1 - q)\pi_3$, and gamble 2 is equivalent to a gamble promising X_n with probability $t\pi_5 + (1 - t)\pi_6$. The individual will presumably prefer the gamble with the higher probability of winning the best prize. Consequently, he or she will choose gamble 1 if and only if

$$q\pi_2 + (1 - q)\pi_3 > t\pi_5 + (1 - t)\pi_6. \tag{8.16}$$

But this is precisely what we wanted to show in Equation 8.15. Consequently, we have proved that an individual will choose the gamble that provides the highest level of expected (von Neumann–Morgenstern) utility. We now make considerable use of this result, which can be summarized as follows:

OPTIMIZATION PRINCIPLE

Expected Utility Maximization If individuals obey the von Neumann–Morgenstern axioms of behavior in uncertain situations, they will act as if they choose that option which maximizes the expected value of their von Neumann–Morgenstern utility index.

RISK AVERSION

Two lotteries may have the same expected monetary value but may differ in their riskiness. For example, flipping a coin for $1 and flipping a coin for $1000 are both fair games, and both have the same expected value (0). However, the latter is in some sense more "risky" than the former, and fewer people would participate in the game where the prize was winning or losing $1000. The purpose of this section is to discuss the meaning of the term "risky" and to explain the widespread aversion to risk.

The term *risk* refers to the variability of the outcomes of some uncertain activity.[8] If variability is low, the activity may be approximately a sure thing. With no more precise notion of variability than this, it is possible to show why individuals, when faced with a choice between two gambles with the same expected value, usually will choose the one with a smaller variability of return. Intuitively, the reason behind this is that we usually assume that the marginal utility from extra dollars of prize money (that is, wealth) declines as the prizes get larger. A flip of a coin for $1000 promises a relatively small gain of utility if you win but a large loss of utility if you lose. A bet of only $1 is "inconsequential," and the gain in utility from a win approximately counterbalances the decline in utility from a loss.[9]

This argument is illustrated in Figure 8.1. Here W^* represents the individual's current wealth and $U(W)$ is a von Neumann–Morgenstern utility index that reflects how the individual feels about various levels of wealth. $U(W)$ is drawn as a concave function of W to reflect the assumption of a diminishing marginal utility. It is assumed that obtaining an extra dollar adds less to enjoyment as total wealth increases. Now suppose that the individual is offered two fair gambles: a 50–50 chance of winning or losing h or a 50–50 chance of winning or losing $2h$. The utility of present wealth is $U(W^*)$. The expected utility if he or she participates in gamble 1 is given by $U^h(W^*)$:

Risk Aversion and Fair Bets

$$U^h(W^*) = \frac{1}{2}U(W^* + h) + \frac{1}{2}U(W^* - h), \tag{8.17}$$

and the expected utility of gamble 2 is given by $U^{2h}(W^*)$:

$$U^{2h}(W^*) = \frac{1}{2}U(W^* + 2h) + \frac{1}{2}U(W^* - 2h). \tag{8.18}$$

It is geometrically clear from the figure that[10]

$$U(W^*) > U^h(W^*) > U^{2h}(W^*). \tag{8.19}$$

---

[8] Often the statistical concept of "variance" is used as a proxy for risk. Although we will not discuss this statistical notion in the body of this chapter, it is defined in the chapter's extensions and used in a few problems.

[9] An alternative, more general definition of risk aversion is that $E[U(W)] < U[E(W)]$ for any risky wealth, W. As we show, diminishing marginal utility assures this condition, but it does place conditions, perhaps unwarranted, on the nature of the utility function. Hence, the alternative definition may be preferred.

[10] To see why the expected utilities for bet h and bet $2h$ are those shown, notice that these expected utilities are simply the average of the utilities from a favorable and an unfavorable outcome. Since W^* is halfway between $W^* + h$ and $W^* - h$, U^h is also halfway between $U(W^* + h)$ and $U(W^* - h)$.

FIGURE 8.1

UTILITY OF WEALTH FROM TWO FAIR BETS OF DIFFERING VARIABILITY

If the individual's utility-of-wealth function is concave (that is, exhibits a diminishing marginal utility of wealth), he or she will refuse fair bets. A 50–50 bet of winning or losing h dollars, for example, yields less utility $[U^h(W^*)]$ than does refusing the bet. The reason for this is that winning h dollars means less to such an individual than does losing h dollars.

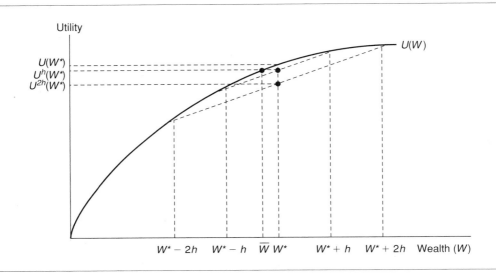

The individual therefore will prefer current wealth to that wealth combined with a fair gamble and will prefer a small gamble to a large one. The reason for this is that winning a fair bet adds to the individual's enjoyment less than losing hurts. Although the prizes are equal in expected value terms, in utility terms the loss is more serious.

Risk Aversion and Insurance

As a matter of fact, the individual might be willing to pay some amount to avoid participating in any gamble at all. Notice that a certain wealth of $\overline{W}$ provides the same utility as does participating in gamble 1. The individual will be willing to pay anything up to $W^* - \overline{W}$ to avoid participating in the gamble. This undoubtedly explains why people buy insurance. They are giving up a small, certain amount (the premium) to avoid the risky outcome that they are insured against. The premium a person pays for automobile collision insurance, for example, provides a policy that agrees to repair his or her car should an accident occur. The widespread use of such insurance would seem to imply that aversion to risk is quite common. Hence, we introduce the following definition:

DEFINITION

Risk Aversion   An individual who always refuses fair bets is said to be *risk averse*. If individuals exhibit a diminishing marginal utility of wealth, they will be risk averse. As a consequence, they will be willing to pay something to avoid taking fair bets.

EXAMPLE 8.2

WILLINGNESS TO PAY FOR INSURANCE

To illustrate the connection between risk aversion and insurance, consider an individual with a current wealth of $100,000 who faces the prospect of a 25 percent chance of losing his or her $20,000 automobile through theft during the next year. Suppose also that this person's von Neumann–Morgenstern utility index is logarithmic—that is, $U(W) = ln\ (W)$.

If this person faces next year without insurance, expected utility will be

$$\text{expected utility} = .75U\ (100{,}000) + .25\ U(80{,}000)$$

$$= .75\ ln\ 100{,}000 + .25\ ln\ 80{,}000 \qquad (8.20)$$

$$= 11.45714.$$

In this situation a fair insurance premium would be $5000 (25 percent of $20,000, assuming that the insurance company has only claim costs and that administrative costs are 0). Consequently, if this person completely insures the car, his or her wealth will be $95,000 regardless of whether the car is stolen. In this case, then,

$$\text{expected utility} = U(95{,}000)$$

$$= ln\ (95{,}000) \qquad (8.21)$$

$$= 11.46163.$$

This person is clearly better off when he or she purchases fair insurance. Indeed, we can determine the maximum amount that might be paid for this insurance protection (x) by setting

$$\text{expected utility} = U(100{,}000 - x)$$

$$= ln\ (100{,}000 - x) \qquad (8.22)$$

$$= 11.45714.$$

Solving this equation for x yields

$$100{,}000 - x = e^{11.45714}. \tag{8.23}$$

Therefore, the maximum premium is

$$x = 5426. \tag{8.24}$$

This person would be willing to pay up to $426 in administrative costs to an insurance company (in addition to the $5000 premium to cover the expected value of the loss). Even when such costs are paid, this person is as well off as he or she would be if forced to face the world uninsured.

QUERY: Suppose utility had been linear in wealth. Would this person be willing to pay anything more than the actuarially fair amount for insurance? How about the case where utility is a convex function of wealth?

MEASURING RISK AVERSION

In the study of economic choices in risky situations, it is sometimes convenient to have a quantitative measure of how averse to risk a person is. The most commonly used measure of risk aversion was initially developed by J. W. Pratt in the 1960s.[11] This risk aversion measure, $r(W)$, is defined as

$$r(W) = -\frac{U''(W)}{U'(W)}. \tag{8.25}$$

Since the distinguishing feature of risk-averse individuals is a diminishing marginal utility of wealth [$U''(W) < 0$], Pratt's measure is positive in such cases. It is easy to show that the measure is invariant with respect to linear transformations of the utility function; hence, it is not affected by which particular von Neumann–Morgenstern ordering is used.

Risk Aversion and Insurance Premiums

Perhaps the most useful feature of the Pratt measure of risk aversion is that it can be shown to be proportional to the amount an individual will pay for insurance against taking a fair bet. Suppose the winnings from such a fair bet are denoted by the random variable h (this variable may be either positive or negative). Since the bet is fair, $E(h) = 0$ (where E means "expected value"). Now let p be the size of the insurance premium that would make the individual exactly indifferent between taking the fair bet h and paying p with certainty to avoid the gamble:

---

[11] J. W. Pratt, "Risk Aversion in the Small and in the Large," *Econometrica* (January/April 1964): 122–136.

$$E[U(W + h)] = U(W - p), \qquad (8.26)$$

where W is the individual's current wealth. We now expand both sides of Equation 8.26 using Taylor's series.[12] Since p is a fixed amount, a simple linear approximation to the right-hand side of the equation will suffice:

$$U(W - p) = U(W) - pU'(W) + \text{higher order terms.} \qquad (8.27)$$

For the left-hand side, we need a quadratic approximation to allow for the variability in the gamble, h:

$$E[U(W + h)] = E\left[U(W) + hU'(W) + \frac{h^2}{2}U''(W)\right. \qquad (8.28)$$

$$\left. + \text{higher order terms}\right]$$

$$= U(W) + E(h)U'(W) + \frac{E(h^2)}{2}U''(W) \qquad (8.29)$$

$$+ \text{higher order terms.}$$

Now, remembering $E(h) = 0$, dropping the higher order terms, and using the constant k to represent $E(h^2)/2$, we can equate Equations 8.27 and 8.29 as

$$U(W) - pU'(W) \simeq U(W) + kU''(W) \qquad (8.30)$$

or

$$p \simeq -\frac{kU''(W)}{U'(W)} = kr(W) \qquad (8.31)$$

as was to be shown. That is, the amount that a risk-averse individual is willing to pay to avoid a fair bet is approximately proportional to Pratt's risk aversion measure. Since insurance premiums paid are observable in the real world, these are often used to estimate individuals' risk aversion coefficients or to compare such coefficients among groups of individuals. It is therefore possible to use market information to learn quite a bit about attitudes toward risky situations.

Risk Aversion and Wealth

An important question is whether an individual's degree of risk aversion increases or decreases for higher levels of wealth. Intuitively, one might assume that the willingness to pay to avoid a given fair bet would decline

---

[12] Taylor's series provides a way of approximating any differentiable function around some point. If $f(x)$ has derivatives of all orders, it can be shown that

$$f(x + h) = f(x) + hf'(x) + h^2/2f''(x) + \text{higher order terms.}$$

The point-slope formula in algebra is a simple example of Taylor's series.

as wealth increases, since diminishing marginal utility would make potential losses less serious for high-wealth individuals. Such an intuitive answer is not necessarily correct, however, because diminishing marginal utility also makes the gains from winning gambles less attractive. So the net result is indeterminate, depending on the precise shape of the utility function. Indeed, if utility is quadratic in wealth,

$$U(W) = a + bW + cW^2, \tag{8.32}$$

where $b > 0$, $c < 0$, Pratt's risk aversion measure is

$$r(W) = -\frac{U''(W)}{U'(W)} = \frac{-2c}{b + 2cW}, \tag{8.33}$$

which, contrary to intuition, increases as wealth increases.

On the other hand, if utility is logarithmic in wealth,

$$U(W) = \ln(W) \qquad (W > 0), \tag{8.34}$$

we have

$$r(W) = -\frac{U''(W)}{U'(W)} = \frac{1}{W}, \tag{8.35}$$

which does indeed decrease as wealth increases.

The utility function

$$U(W) = -e^{-AW} = -exp(-AW) \tag{8.36}$$

(where A is a positive constant) exhibits constant risk aversion over all ranges of wealth since now

$$r(W) = -\frac{U''(W)}{U'(W)} = \frac{A^2 e^{-AW}}{Ae^{-AW}} = A. \tag{8.37}$$

This feature of the exponential utility function can be used to provide some numerical estimates of the willingness to pay to avoid gambles, as the next example shows.

EXAMPLE 8.3

CONSTANT RISK AVERSION

Suppose an individual whose initial wealth is W_0 and whose utility is given by the function in Equation 8.36 is facing a 50–50 chance of winning or losing $1,000. How much ($F$) would he or she pay to avoid the risk? To find this value, we set the utility of $W_0 - F$ equal to the expected utility from the gamble:

$$-exp[-A(W_0 - F)] = -.5exp[-A(W_0 + 1000)] - .5exp[-A(W_0 - 1000)]. \tag{8.38}$$

Since the factor $-exp(-AW_0)$ is contained in all of the terms in Equation 8.38, this may be divided out, thereby showing that (for the exponential utility function) the willingness to pay to avoid uncertainty is independent of wealth. The remaining terms

$$exp(AF) = .5exp(-1000A) + .5exp(1000A) \qquad (8.39)$$

can now be used to solve for F for various values of A. If $A = .0001$, $F = 49.9$— a person with this degree of risk aversion would pay about $50 to avoid a fair bet of $1000. Alternatively, if $A = .0003$, this more risk-averse person would pay $F = 147.8$ to avoid the gamble. Since intuition suggests that these values are not unreasonable, values of the risk aversion parameter A in these ranges are sometimes used for empirical investigations.

QUERY: The calculations in this example suggest that willingness to pay to avoid a fair gamble is directly proportional to the size of the gamble and to the risk-aversion parameter A. Why does this particular utility function have these properties?

Relative Risk Aversion

It seems unlikely that the willingness to pay to avoid a given gamble is independent of the individual's level of wealth. A more appealing assumption may be that such willingness to pay is inversely proportional to wealth and that the expression

$$rr(W) = Wr(W) = -W\frac{U''(W)}{U'(W)} \qquad (8.40)$$

might then be expected to be approximately constant. Following the terminology proposed by J. W. Pratt,[13] the $rr(W)$ function defined in Equation 8.40 has come to be called "relative risk aversion." The power utility function

$$U(W) = \frac{W^R}{R} \text{ (for } R < 1, \neq 0)$$

and $\qquad\qquad\qquad\qquad\qquad\qquad\qquad\qquad\qquad\qquad\qquad (8.41)$

$$U(W) = ln \ W \text{ (for } R = 0)$$

exhibits diminishing absolute risk aversion:

$$r(W) = -\frac{U''(W)}{U'(W)} = -\frac{(R-1) \ W^{R-2}}{W^{R-1}} = -\frac{(R-1)}{W} \qquad (8.42)$$

but constant relative risk aversion:

---

[13] Pratt, "Risk Aversion."

$$rr(W) = Wr(W) = -(R - 1) = 1 - R. \tag{8.43}$$

Empirical evidence is generally consistent with values of R in the range of -3 to -1. Hence, individuals seem to be somewhat more risk averse than is implied by the logarithmic utility function, though in many applications that function provides a reasonable approximation. It is useful to note that the constant relative risk aversion utility function in Equation 8.41 has the same form as the general CES utility function we first described in Chapter 3 (see Equation 3.34). This provides some geometric intuition about the nature of risk aversion that we will explore later in this chapter.

EXAMPLE 8.4

CONSTANT RELATIVE RISK AVERSION

An individual whose behavior is characterized by a constant relative risk aversion utility function will be concerned about proportional gains or loss of wealth. We can therefore ask what fraction of initial wealth (F) such a person would be willing to give up to avoid a fair gamble of, say, 10 percent of initial wealth. First, we assume $R = 0$ so that the logarithmic utility function is appropriate. Setting the utility of this individual's certain remaining wealth equal to the expected utility of the 10 percent gamble yields

$$ln[(1 - F)W_0] = .5\ ln(1.1\ W_0) + .5\ ln(.9W_0). \tag{8.44}$$

Since each term contains $ln\ W_0$, initial wealth can be eliminated from this expression:

$$ln(1 - F) = .5[ln(1.1) + ln(.9)] = ln(.99)^{.5} \tag{8.45}$$

so

$$(1 - F) = (.99)^{.5} = .995$$

and

$$F = .005. \tag{8.46}$$

Hence, this person will sacrifice up to half of 1 percent of wealth to avoid the 10 percent gamble. A similar calculation can be used for the case $R = -2$ to yield

$$F = .015. \tag{8.47}$$

Hence, this more risk-averse person would be willing to give up 1.5 percent of his or her initial wealth to avoid a 10 percent gamble.

QUERY: With the constant relative risk aversion function, how does this person's willingness to pay to avoid a given absolute gamble (say, of 1000) depend on his or her initial wealth?

Although our analysis thus far in this chapter has offered insights on a number of issues, it seems rather different from the approach we took in other chapters. The basic model of utility maximization subject to a budget constraint seems to have been lost. In order to make further progress in our examination of behavior under uncertainty, we must therefore develop some new techniques that will permit us to bring the discussion of such behavior back into our standard choice-theoretic framework.

THE STATE-PREFERENCE APPROACH TO CHOICE UNDER UNCERTAINTY

States of the World and Contingent Commodities

To accomplish this goal, we start by assuming that outcomes of any random event can be categorized into a certain number of *states of the world*. We cannot predict exactly what will happen, say, tomorrow, but we assume that it is possible to categorize all of the possible things that might happen into a number of well-defined *states*. For example, we might make the very crude approximation of saying that the world will be in only one of two possible states tomorrow: It will be either "good times" or "bad times." One could make a much finer gradation of states of the world (involving even millions of possible states), but most of the essentials of the theory can be developed using only two states; therefore, no more complex definition will be used here.

A conceptual idea that can be developed concurrently with the notion of states of the world is that of *contingent commodities*. These are goods delivered only if a particular state of the world occurs. "$1 in good times" is an example of a contingent commodity that promises the individual $1 in good times but nothing should tomorrow turn out to be bad times. It is even possible, by stretching one's intuitive ability somewhat, to conceive of being able to purchase this commodity—I might be able to buy from someone the promise of $1 if tomorrow turns out to be good times. Since tomorrow could be bad, this good will probably sell for less than $1. If someone were also willing to sell me the contingent commodity "$1 in bad times," then I could assure myself of having $1 tomorrow by buying the two contingent commodities "$1 in good times" and "$1 in bad times."

Utility Analysis

Examining utility-maximizing choices among contingent commodities proceeds formally in much the same way we analyzed choices previously. The principal difference is that, after the fact, the individual will have obtained only one contingent good (depending on whether it turns out to be good or bad times). Before the existing uncertainty is resolved, however, the individual has two contingent goods from which to choose. We will denote these by W_g (wealth in good times) and W_b (wealth in bad times). Assuming that utility is independent of which state occurs[14] and that this individual believes that good times will occur with probability π, the expected utility associated with these two contingent goods is

$$V(W_g, W_b) = \pi U(W_g) + (1 - \pi)U(W_b). \tag{8.48}$$

This is the magnitude that this individual seeks to maximize given his or her initial wealth, W.

Prices of Contingent Commodities

Assuming that this individual can purchase a dollar of wealth in good times for P_g and a dollar of wealth in bad times for P_b, his or her budget constraint is

$$W = P_g W_g + P_b W_b. \tag{8.49}$$

The price ratio P_g/P_b shows how this person can trade dollars of wealth in good times for dollars in bad times. If, for example, $P_g = .80$ and $P_b = .20$, the sacrifice of \$1 of wealth in good times would permit this person to buy contingent claims yielding \$4 of wealth should times turn out to be bad. Whether such a trade would improve utility will, of course, depend on the specifics of the situation. But looking at problems involving uncertainty as situations in which various contingent claims are traded is the key insight offered by the state-preference model.

Fair Markets for Contingent Goods

If markets for contingent wealth claims are well developed and there is general agreement about the likelihood of good times (π), prices for these claims will be actuarially fair—that is, they will equal the underlying probabilities:

$$P_g = \pi$$
$$P_b = (1 - \pi). \tag{8.50}$$

Hence, the price ratio P_g/P_b will simply reflect the odds in favor of good times:

$$\frac{P_g}{P_b} = \frac{\pi}{1 - \pi}. \tag{8.51}$$

In our previous example, if $P_g = \pi = .8$ and $P_b = (1 - \pi) = .2$, then $\pi/(1 - \pi) = 4$. In this case the odds in favor of good times would be stated as

---

[14] This assumption is untenable in circumstances where utility of wealth depends on the state of the world. For example, the utility provided by a given level of wealth may differ depending on whether an individual is "sick" or "healthy." We will not pursue such complications here, however. For more of our analysis, utility will be assumed to be concave in wealth: $U'(W) > 0$, $U''(W) < 0$.

"4-to-1." Fair markets for contingent claims (such as insurance markets) will also reflect these odds. An analogy is provided by the "odds" quoted in horse races. These odds are "fair" when they reflect the true probabilities that various horses will win.

Risk Aversion

We are now in a position to show how risk aversion is manifested in the state-preference model. Specifically, we can show that, if contingent claims markets are fair, a utility-maximizing individual will opt for a situation in which $W_g = W_b$—that is, he or she will arrange matters so that the wealth ultimately obtained is the same no matter what state occurs.

As in previous chapters, maximization of utility (Equation 8.48) subject to a budget constraint (Equation 8.49) requires that this individual set the MRS of W_g for W_b equal to the ratio of these "goods" prices:

$$MRS = \frac{\partial V/\partial W_g}{\partial V/\partial W_b} = \frac{\pi U'(W_g)}{(1 - \pi)U'(W_b)} = \frac{P_g}{P_b}. \tag{8.52}$$

In view of the assumption that markets for contingent claims are fair (Equation 8.51) this first-order condition reduces to

$$\frac{U'(W_g)}{U'(W_b)} = 1$$

or[15]

$$W_g = W_b. \tag{8.53}$$

Hence, this individual, faced with fair markets in contingent claims on wealth, will be risk averse, choosing to insure the same level of wealth regardless of circumstances.

A Graphic Analysis

Figure 8.2 illustrates risk aversion with a graph. This individual's budget constraint (I) is shown to be tangent to the U_1 indifference curve where $W_g = W_b$—a point on the "certainty line" where wealth (W^*) is independent of which state of the world occurs. At W^* the slope of the indifference curve $[\pi/(1 - \pi)]$ is precisely equal to the price ratio P_g/P_b.

If the market for contingent wealth claims were not fair, utility maximization might not occur on the certainty line. Suppose, for example, that $\pi/(1 - \pi) = 4$ but that $P_g/P_b = 2$ because insuring wealth in bad times proves quite costly. In this case the budget constraint would resemble line I' in Figure 8.2 and utility maximization would occur below the certainty line.[16]

---

[15] Notice this step requires that utility be state independent and that $U'(W) > 0$.

[16] Since the MRS on the certainty line is always $\pi/(1 - \pi)$, tangencies with a flatter slope than this must occur below the line.

FIGURE 8.2

RISK AVERSIONS IN THE STATE-PREFERENCE MODEL

The line I represents the individual's budget constraint for contingent wealth claims: $W = P_g W_g + P_b W_b$. If the market for contingent claims is actuarially fair, $[P_g/P_b = \pi/(1 - \pi)]$, utility maximization will occur on the certainty line where $W_g = W_b = W^*$. If prices are not actuarially fair, the budget constraint may resemble I' and utility maximization will occur at a point where $W_g > W_b$.

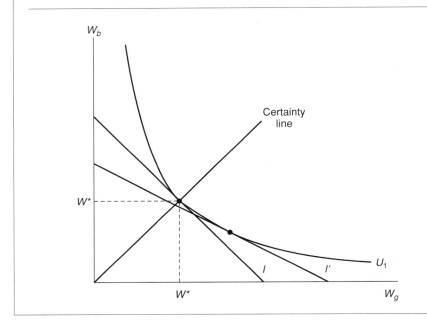

In this case this individual would gamble a bit by opting for $W_g > W_b$, since claims on W_b are relatively costly. Example 8.5 shows the usefulness of this approach in evaluating some of the alternatives that might be available.

EXAMPLE 8.5

INSURANCE IN THE STATE-PREFERENCE MODEL

We can illustrate the state-preference approach by recasting the auto insurance illustration from Example 8.2 as a problem involving the two contingent commodities "wealth with no theft" (W_g) and "wealth with a theft" (W_b). If, as before, we assume logarithmic utility and that the probability of a theft (that is, $1 - \pi$) is 0.25, we have

$$\text{expected utility} = .75U(W_g) + .25U(W_b)$$
$$= .75 \ln W_g + .25 \ln W_b. \tag{8.54}$$

If the individual takes no action, utility is determined by the initial wealth endowment, $W_g^* = 100,000$, $W_b^* = 80,000$, and so,

$$\text{expected utility} = .75 \ln 100,000 + .25 \ln 80,000$$
$$= 11.45714. \tag{8.55}$$

To study trades away from these initial endowments, we write the budget constraint in terms of the prices of the contingent commodities, P_g and P_b:

$$P_g W_g^* + P_b W_b^* = P_g W_g + P_b W_b. \tag{8.56}$$

Assuming these prices equal the probabilities of the two states ($P_g = .75$, $P_b = .25$), this constraint can be written

$$.75(100,000) + .25(80,000) = 95,000 = .75W_g + .25W_b, \tag{8.57}$$

that is, the expected value of wealth is \$95,000, and this individual can allocate this amount between W_g and W_b. Now maximization of utility with respect to this budget constraint yields $W_g = W_b = 95,000$. Consequently, the individual will move to the certainty line and receive an expected utility of

$$\text{expected utility} = \ln 95,000 = 11.46163, \tag{8.58}$$

a clear improvement over doing nothing. To obtain this improvement, the individual must be able to transfer \$5000 of wealth in good times (no theft) into \$15,000 of extra wealth in bad times (theft). A fair insurance contract would allow this since it would cost \$5000 but return \$20,000 to the individual should a theft occur (but nothing should no theft occur). Notice here that the wealth changes promised by insurance—$dW_b/dW_g = 15,000/-5,000 = -3$—exactly equal the negative of the odds ratio $-\pi/(1 - \pi) = -.75/.25 = -3$.

A Policy with a Deductible Provision. A number of other insurance contracts might be utility improving in this situation, though not all of them would lead to choices that lie on the certainty line. For example, a policy that cost \$5200 and returned \$20,000 in case of a theft would permit this person to reach the certainty line with $W_g = W_b = 94,800$ and

$$\text{expected utility} = \ln 94,800 = 11.45953, \tag{8.59}$$

which also exceeds the utility obtainable from the initial endowment. A policy that cost \$4900 and required the individual to incur the first \$1000 of a loss from theft would yield

$$W_g = 100,000 - 4900 = 95,100$$

$$W_b = 80,000 - 4900 + 19,000 = 94,100 \tag{8.60}$$

and

$$\text{expected utility} = .75 \; ln \; 95,100 + .25 \; ln \; 94,100$$

$$= 11.46004. \tag{8.61}$$

Even though this policy does not permit the individual to reach the certainty line, it is utility improving. Insurance need not be complete to offer the promise of higher utility.

QUERY: What is the maximum amount an individual would be willing to pay for an insurance policy under which he or she had to absorb the first $1000 of loss?

Risk Aversion and Risk Premiums

The state-preference model illustrated in Figure 8.2 is also especially useful for analyzing the relationship between risk aversion and individuals' willingness to accept risk. Consider two individuals, each of whom starts with a certain wealth, W^*. Each person seeks to maximize an expected utility function of the form

$$V(W_g, W_b) = \pi \frac{W_g^R}{R} + (1 - \pi) \frac{W_b^R}{R}. \tag{8.62}$$

Here the utility function exhibits constant relative risk aversion (see Example 8.4). Notice also that the function closely resembles the CES utility function we examined in Chapter 3 and elsewhere. Hence, the parameter R here determines both the degree of risk aversion and the degree of curvature of indifference curves implied by the function. A very risk-averse individual will have a large negative value for R and have sharply curved indifference curves such as the curve U_1 shown in Figure 8.3. An individual with more tolerance for risk will have a higher value of R and flatter indifference curves (such as U_2).[17]

Suppose now these individuals are faced with the prospect of losing h dollars of wealth in bad times. Such a risk would be acceptable to individual 2 if wealth in good times were to increase from W^* to W_2. For the very risk-averse individual 1, however, wealth would have to increase to W_1 to make the risk acceptable. The difference between W_1 and W_2 therefore indicates the effect of risk aversion on willingness to assume risk. Some of the problems in this chapter make use of this graphic device for showing the connection

---

[17] Tangency of U_1 and U_2 at W^* is assured since the MRS along the certainty line is given by $\pi/(1 - \pi)$ regardless of the value of R.

FIGURE 8.3

RISK AVERSION AND RISK PREMIUMS

Indifference curve U_1 represents the preferences of a very risk-averse individual, whereas the individual with preferences represented by U_2 is willing to assume more risk. When faced with the risk of losing h in bad times, person 2 will require compensation of $W_2 - W^*$ in good times, whereas person 1 will require a larger amount given by $W_1 - W^*$.

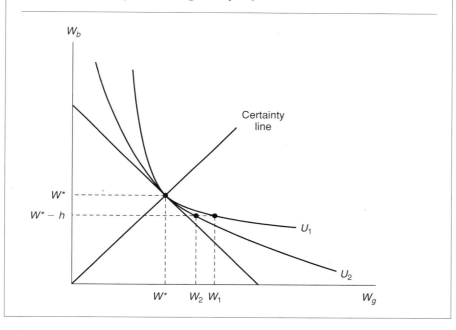

between preferences (as reflected by the utility function in Equation 8.62) and behavior in risky situations.

SUMMARY

In this chapter we provided some introductory material that will permit us to study individual behavior in uncertain situations. The basic results we surveyed included:

- In uncertain situations, individuals are concerned with the expected utility associated with various outcomes. If they obey the von Neumann–Morgenstern axioms, they will make choices in a way that maximizes expected utility.

- If we assume individuals exhibit a diminishing marginal utility of wealth, they will also be risk averse. That is, they will refuse to take bets that are actuarially fair.

- Risk-averse individuals will wish to insure themselves completely against uncertain events if insurance premiums are actuarially fair. They may be willing to pay actuarially unfair premiums to avoid taking risks.

- Decisions under uncertainty can be analyzed in a choice-theoretic framework by using the state-preference approach among contingent commodities. In such a model, if an individual's preferences are state independent and if prices are actuarially fair, individuals will prefer allocations along the "certainty line" that assure the same level of wealth regardless of which state occurs.

PROBLEMS

8.1

George is seen to place an even-money $100,000 bet on the Bulls to win the NBA Championship. If George has a logarithmic utility-of-wealth function and if his current wealth is $1,000,000, what must he believe the minimum probability that the Bulls will win is?

8.2

Show that if an individual's utility-of-wealth function is convex (rather than concave, as shown in Figure 8.1), he or she will prefer fair gambles to income certainty and may even be willing to accept somewhat unfair gambles. Do you believe this sort of risk-taking behavior is common? What factors might tend to limit its occurrence?

8.3

An individual purchases a dozen eggs and must take them home. Although making trips home is costless, there is a 50 percent chance that all of the eggs carried on any one trip will be broken during the trip. The individual considers two strategies:

Strategy 1: Take all 12 eggs in one trip.
Strategy 2: Take two trips with 6 in each trip.

a. List the possible outcomes of each strategy and the probabilities of these outcomes. Show that on the average, 6 eggs will remain unbroken after the trip home under either strategy.
b. Develop a graph to show the utility obtainable under each strategy. Which strategy will be preferable?
c. Could utility be improved further by taking more than two trips? How would this possibility be affected if additional trips were costly?

8.4

Suppose there is a 50–50 chance that a risk-averse individual with a current wealth of $20,000 will contract a debilitating disease and suffer a loss of $10,000.
a. Calculate the cost of actuarially fair insurance in this situation and use a utility-of-wealth graph (such as shown in Figure 8.1) to show that the individual will prefer fair insurance against this loss to accepting the gamble uninsured.
b. Suppose two types of insurance policies were available:
   (1) A fair policy covering the complete loss.
   (2) A fair policy covering only half of any loss incurred.
   Calculate the cost of the second type of policy and show that the individual will generally regard it as inferior to the first.

8.5

Ms. Fogg is planning an around-the-world trip on which she plans to spend $10,000. The utility from the trip is a function of how much she actually spends on it (Y), given by

$$U(Y) = \ln Y.$$

a. If there is a 25 percent probability that Ms. Fogg will lose $1000 of her cash on the trip, what is the trip's expected utility?
b. Suppose that Ms. Fogg can buy insurance against losing the $1000 (say, by purchasing traveler's checks) at an "actuarially fair" premium of $250. Show that her expected utility is higher if she purchases this insurance than if she faces the chance of losing the $1000 without insurance.

c. What is the maximum amount that Ms. Fogg would be willing to pay to insure her $1000?

8.6

In deciding to park in an illegal place, any individual knows that the probability of getting a ticket is p and that the fine for receiving the ticket is f. Suppose that all individuals are risk averse (that is, $U''(W) < 0$, where W is the individual's wealth).

Will a proportional increase in the probability of being caught or a proportional increase in the fine be a more effective deterrent to illegal parking? [*Hint:* Use the Taylor series approximation $U(W - f) = U(W) - fU'(W) + \frac{f^2}{2}U''(W)$.]

8.7

A farmer believes there is a 50–50 chance that the next growing season will be abnormally rainy. His expected utility function has the form

$$\text{expected utility} = \frac{1}{2} \ln Y_{NR} + \frac{1}{2} \ln Y_R,$$

where Y_{NR} and Y_R represent the farmer's income in the states of "normal rain" and "rainy," respectively.

a. Suppose the farmer must choose between two crops that promise the following income prospects:

CROP	Y_{NR}	Y_R
Wheat	$28,000	$10,000
Corn	19,000	15,000

Which of the crops will he plant?

b. Suppose the farmer can plant half his field with each crop. Would he choose to do so? Explain your result.

c. What mix of wheat and corn would provide maximum expected utility to this farmer?

d. Would wheat crop insurance, available to farmers who grow only wheat, which costs $4000 and pays off $8000 in the event of a rainy growing season, cause this farmer to change what he plants?

8.8

For the constant relative risk aversion utility function (Equation 8.62) we showed that the degree of risk aversion is measured by $(1 - R)$. In Chapter 3 we

showed that the elasticity of substitution for the same function is given by $1/(1 - R)$. Hence, the measures are reciprocals of each other. Using this result, discuss the following questions:

a. Why is risk aversion related to an individual's willingness to substitute wealth between states of the world? What phenomenon is being captured by both concepts?

b. How would you interpret the polar cases $R = 1$ and $R = -\infty$ in both the risk-aversion and substitution frameworks?

c. A rise in the price of contingent claims in "bad" times (P_b) will induce both substitution and income effects into the demands for W_g and W_b. If the individual has a fixed budget to devote to these two goods, how will choices among them be affected? Why might W_g rise or fall depending on the degree of risk aversion exhibited by the individual?

d. How would your analysis to part (c) change if the individual had an initial endowment of W_g^*, W_b^* and could trade from this endowment at prevailing market prices for contingent claims?

8.9

Investment in risk assets can be examined in the state-preference framework by assuming that W^* dollars invested in an asset with a certain return, r, will yield $W^*(1 + r)$ in both states of the world whereas investment in a risky asset will yield $W^*(1 + r_g)$ in good times and $W^*(1 + r_b)$ in bad times (where $r_g > r > r_b$).

a. Graph the outcomes from the two investments.

b. Show how a "mixed portfolio" containing both risk-free and risky assets could be illustrated in your graph. How would you show the fraction of wealth invested in the risky asset?

c. Show how individuals' attitudes toward risk will determine the mix of risk-free and risky assets they will hold. In what case would a person hold no risky assets?

d. If an individual's utility takes the constant relative risk aversion form (Equation 8.62), explain why this person will not change the fraction of risky assets held as his or her wealth increases.[18]

---

[18] This problem and the next are taken from J. E. Stiglitz, "The Effects of Income, Wealth, and Capital Gains Taxation in Risk Taking," *The Quarterly Journal of Economics* (May 1969), pp. 263–283.

8.10

Suppose the asset returns in Problem 8.9 are subject to taxation.

a. Show under the conditions of Problem 8.9 why a proportional tax on wealth will not affect the fraction of wealth allocated to risky assets.

b. Suppose only the returns from the safe asset were subject to a proportional income tax. How would this affect the fraction of wealth held in risky assets? Which investors would be most affected by such a tax?

c. How would your answer to part (b) change if all asset returns were subject to a proportional income tax?

(*Note:* This problem asks you to compute the *pre-tax* allocation of wealth that will result in *post-tax* utility maximization.)

SUGGESTED READINGS

Alchian, A. A. "The Meaning of Utility Measurement." *American Economic Review* 42 (1953): 26–50.
Concise, readable discussion of the meaning and implications of the von Neumann–Morgenstern axioms.

Arrow, K. J. "The Role of Securities in the Optimal Allocation of Risk Bearing." *Review of Economic Studies* 31 (1963): 91–96.
Introduces the state-preference concept and interprets securities as claims on contingent commodities.

———. "Uncertainty and the Welfare Economics of Medical Care." *American Economic Review* 53 (1963): 941–973.
Excellent discussion of the welfare implications of insurance. Has a clear, concise, mathematical appendix. Should be read in conjunction with Pauly's article on moral hazard (see Chapter 10).

Bernoulli, D. "Exposition of a New Theory on the Measurement of Risk." *Econometrica* 22 (1954): 23–36.
Reprint of the classic analysis of the St. Petersburg paradox.

Friedman, M., and L. J. Savage. "The Utility Analysis of Choice." *Journal of Political Economy* 56 (1948): 279–304.
Analyzes why individuals may both gamble and buy insurance. Very readable.

Huang, Chi-fu, and R. H. Litzenberger. *Foundations for Financial Analysis.* Amsterdam: North-Holland Publishing Co., 1988.
Presents a good discussion of measures of "stochastic dominance" and their relationship to risk aversion.

Machina, M. J. "Choice under Uncertainty: Problems Solved and Unsolved." *Journal of Economic Perspectives* (Summer 1987): 121–154.
Thorough and readable survey of the expected utility-maximization hypothesis. Nice discussion of the normative implications of various theories.

Mas-Colell, Andreu, Michael D. Whinston, and Jerry R. Green. *Microeconomic Theory.* New York: Oxford University Press, 1995, Chapter 6.
Provides a good summary of the foundations of expected utility theory. Also examines the "state independence" assumption in detail and shows that some notions of risk aversion carry over into cases of state dependence.

Pratt, J. W. "Risk Aversion in the Small and in the Large." *Econometrica* 32 (1964): 122–136.
Theoretical development of risk-aversion measures. Fairly technical treatment but readable.

Rothschild, M., and J. E. Stiglitz. "Increasing Risk: 1. A Definition." *Journal of Economic Theory* 2 (1970): 225–243.
Develops an economic definition of what it means for one gamble to be "riskier" than another. A sequel article in the Journal of Economic Theory *provides economic illustrations.*

EXTENSIONS

Portfolio Theory and the Pricing of Risk

In Chapter 8 we saw that individuals will pay something to avoid uncertainty and that the extent of the sacrifice will depend on their attitudes toward risk. This suggests that the interactions of many individuals will establish a market for "risk" in which uncertainty can be reduced for a "price." The problem, then, is to devise a way of quantifying risk that is amendable to analyzing its pricing. Perhaps the most well-developed models of this process can be found in the study of capital asset pricing, where economists have extensively examined the relationship between the expected return an asset offers and the risks associated with that return. Here we will briefly summarize some basic insights from this vast topic. First, a few statistical preliminaries are required.

Statistical Background

A variable X is termed a "random variable" if it takes on various values with specific probabilities. The "probability density function" for X [denoted by $f(x)$] indicates the probability that X will take on values within a narrow band, dx. Any function will serve as a probability density function provided

$$f(x) \geq 0$$

and

$$\int_{-\infty}^{\infty} f(x)dx = 1. \qquad (i)$$

Statisticians have employed a large variety of such functions to explain empirical observations. Perhaps the most useful of these is the Normal (or Gaussian) function

$$f(z) = \frac{1}{\sqrt{2\pi}} e^{-z^2/2}, \qquad (ii)$$

which has the familiar bell shape, being symmetric about zero. This particular function has played a major role in the development of the theory of the pricing of risk and in many other areas of statistics.

For any random variable, X, the *mean* (or expected value) is defined as

$$\mu_X = E(x) = \int_{-\infty}^{\infty} x f(x)\, dx, \qquad (iii)$$

and the variance of X is defined as

$$\sigma_X^2 = E[(x - \mu_x)^2] = \int_{-\infty}^{\infty} (x - \mu_x)^2 f(x)dx. \qquad (iv)$$

The square root of this variance (denoted by σ_x) is termed the standard deviation of X.

For the normal distribution in Equation ii it is a relatively simple matter to show that $\mu_z = 0$, $\sigma_z^2 = \sigma_z = 1$. This function can be generalized by noting that if

$$z = \frac{x - \mu_x}{\sigma_x} \qquad (v)$$

has the distribution function in Equation ii, the variable X is said to be normally distributed with mean μ_x and standard deviation σ_x. The distribution of X is therefore completely determined by the two parameters μ_x and σ_x.

If X_i and X_j are two random variables, the *covariance* between them is defined as

$$\sigma_{ij} = E(x_i - \mu_i)(x_j - \mu_j) = \int_{-\infty}^{\infty} \int_{-\infty}^{\infty} (x_i - \mu_x)(x_j - \mu_x)f(x_i, x_j)dx_i\, dx_j. \qquad (vi)$$

If X_i and X_j tend to rise and fall together, σ_{ij} will be positive. If these variables tend to move in opposite directions, σ_{ij} will be negative.

If Z represents a weighted average of two random variables, X_i and X_j,

$$Z = \alpha x_i + (1 - \alpha)x_j \qquad (vii)$$

where $0 \leq \alpha \leq 1$, then application of the various definitions shows that

$$\mu_Z = \alpha\mu_i + (1 - \alpha)\mu_j \qquad (viii)$$

and

$$\sigma_Z^2 = \alpha^2\sigma_i^2 + (1 - \alpha)^2\sigma_j^2 + 2\alpha(1 - \alpha)\sigma_{ij}. \qquad (ix)$$

For a further development of these concepts see Freund and Walpole (1980) or Hoel (1971) or any other introductory text on mathematical statistics. Here we make use of these concepts by assuming that the returns to financial assets (X_i) have a normal distribution. The mean of X_i (μ_i) indicates the expected return on asset i, whereas, as we shall see, the standard deviation of X_i (σ_i) is a starting place for discussing the risk associated with that asset. It is this variability of return that risk-averse investors seek to avoid.

E8.1 Portfolio Diversification

Equation ix provides the rationale for portfolio diversification. Even if two assets have identical distributions of returns $(\mu_i = \mu_j, \sigma_i = \sigma_j)$, mixing them in a portfolio can provide a more favorable risk-reward combination. In the case where the asset returns are independent $(\sigma_{ij} = 0)$, for example, an equal weighting would yield

$$\mu_Z = .5\mu_1 + .5\mu_2 = \mu_1 = \mu_2 \qquad \text{(x)}$$

$$\sigma_Z^2 = .25\sigma_1^2 + .25\sigma_2^2 = .5\sigma_1^2 = .5\sigma_2^2 \qquad \text{(xi)}$$

$$\sigma_Z = .707\sigma_1 = .707\sigma_2, \qquad \text{(xii)}$$

which provides the same return as holding either asset individually with reduced risk. If the assets had a negative covariance $(\sigma_{ij} < 0)$, holding both would provide even greater risk-reduction benefits.

E8.2 Efficient Portfolios

With many assets the portfolio allocation problem is to choose weights for these assets so as to minimize the standard deviation of the portfolio for each potential expected return. A solution to this optimization problem yields an efficiency frontier such as that represented by EE in Figure 8.4. Portfolios that lie below this frontier are inferior to those on the frontier, since they offer lower expected returns for any degree of risk. Portfolio returns above the frontier are unattainable. Sharpe (1970) discusses the mathematics associated with constructing the EE frontier.

Mutual Funds

The notion of portfolio efficiency has been widely applied to the study of mutual funds. In general, mutual funds are a good answer to small investors' diversification needs. Because such funds pool the funds of many individuals, they are able to achieve economies of scale in transactions and management costs. This permits fund owners to share in the fortunes of a much wider variety of equities than would be possible if each acted alone. But mutual fund managers have incentives of their own, so the portfolios they hold may not always be perfect representations of the risk attitudes of their clients. For example, Scharfstein and Stein (1990) develop a model that shows why mutual fund managers have incentives to "follow the herd" in their investment picks. Other studies, such as the classic investigation by Jensen (1968), find that mutual fund managers are seldom able to attain extra returns large enough to offset the expenses they charge investors. In recent years this has led many mutual fund buyers to favor "index" funds that seek simply to duplicate the market average (as represented, say, by the Standard and Poor's 500 stock index). Such funds have very low expenses and therefore permit investors to achieve diversification at minimal cost.

E8.3 Portfolio Separation

If there exists a risk-free asset with expected return μ_f and $\sigma_f = 0$, optimal portfolios will consist of mixtures of this asset with risky ones. All such portfolios will lie along the line PP in Figure 8.4 since this shows the maximum return attainable for each value of σ for various portfolio allocations. These allocations will contain only one specific set of risky assets—the set represented by point M. In equilibrium this will be the "market portfolio" consisting of all capital assets held in proportion to their market valuations. This market portfolio will provide an expected return of μ_M and a standard deviation of that return of σ_M. The equation for the line PP that represents any mixed portfolio is given by the linear equation

$$\mu_P = \mu_f + \frac{\mu_M - \mu_f}{\sigma_M} \cdot \sigma_P. \qquad \text{(xiii)}$$

This shows that the market line PP permits individual investors to "purchase" returns in excess of the risk-free return $(\mu_M - \mu_f)$ by taking on proportionally more risk (σ_P/σ_M). For choices on PP to the left of the market point, M, $\sigma_P/\sigma_M < 1$ and $\mu_f < \mu_P < \mu_M$. High-risk points to the right of M—which can be obtained by borrowing to produce a leveraged portfolio—will

FIGURE 8.4

EFFICIENT PORTFOLIOS

The frontier *EE* represents optimal mixtures of risky assets that minimize the standard deviation of the portfolio, σ, for each expected return, μ. A risk-free asset with return μ_f offers investors the opportunity to hold mixed portfolios along *PP* that mix this risk-free asset with the market portfolio, *M*.

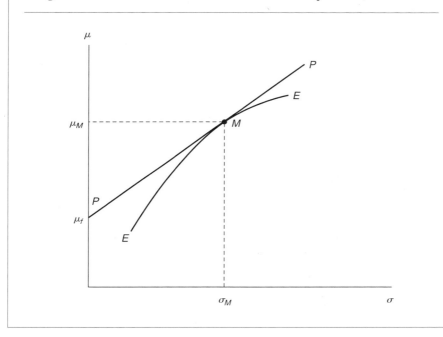

have $\sigma_P/\sigma_M > 1$ and will promise an expected return in excess of what is provided by the market portfolio ($\mu_P > \mu_M$). Tobin (1958) was one of the first economists to recognize the role that risk-free assets play in identifying the market portfolio and in setting the terms on which investors can obtain returns above risk-free levels.

E8.4 Individual Choices

Figure 8.5 illustrates the portfolio choices of various investors facing the options offered by the line *PP*. Individuals with low tolerance for risk *(I)* will opt for portfolios that are heavily weighted toward the risk-free asset. Investors willing to assume a modest degree of risk *(II)* will opt for portfolios close to the

market portfolio. High-risk investors *(III)* may opt for leveraged portfolios. Notice that all investors face the same "price" of risk ($\mu_M - \mu_f$) with their expected returns being determined by how much relative risk (σ_P/σ_M) they are willing to incur. Notice also that the risk associated with an investor's portfolio depends only on the fraction of the portfolio invested in the market portfolio (α) since $\sigma_P^2 = \alpha^2\sigma_M^2 + (1 - \alpha)^2 \cdot 0$. Hence, $\sigma_P/\sigma_M = \alpha$, so the investor's choice of portfolio is equivalent to his or her choice of risk.

E8.5 Capital Asset Pricing Model

Although the analysis of E8.4 shows how a portfolio that mixes a risk-free asset with the market portfolio will be priced, it does not describe the risk-return

FIGURE 8.5

INVESTOR BEHAVIOR AND RISK AVERSION

Given the market options PP, investors can choose how much risk they wish to assume. Very risk-averse investors (U_I) will hold mainly risk-free assets whereas risk takers (U_{III}) will opt for leveraged portfolios.

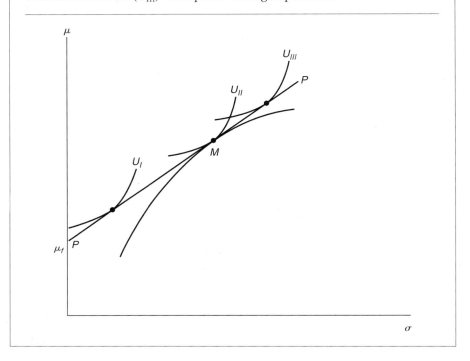

trade-off for a single asset. Since, assuming transactions are costless, an investor can always avoid risk unrelated to the overall market by choosing to diversify with a "market portfolio," such "unsystematic" risk will not warrant any excess return. An asset will, however, earn an excess return to the extent that it contributes to overall market risk. An asset that does not yield such extra returns would not be held in the market portfolio, so it would not be held at all. This is the fundamental insight of the capital asset pricing model (CAPM).

To examine these results formally, consider a portfolio that combines a small amount (α) of asset X with the market portfolio. The return on this portfolio (Z) would be given by

$$Z = \alpha X + (1 - \alpha)M. \tag{xiv}$$

Hence, the expected return would be

$$\mu_Z = \alpha\mu_X + (1 - \alpha)\mu_M \tag{xv}$$

with variance

$$\sigma_Z^2 = \alpha^2\sigma_X^2 + (1 - \alpha)^2\sigma_M^2 + 2\alpha(1 - \alpha)\sigma_{X,M}. \tag{xvi}$$

But our previous analysis shows

$$\mu_Z = \mu_f + (\mu_M - \mu_f) \cdot \frac{\sigma_Z}{\sigma_M}. \tag{xvii}$$

Setting Equation xv equal to xvii and differentiation with respect to α yields

$$\frac{\partial \mu_Z}{\partial \alpha} = \mu_X - \mu_M = \frac{(\mu_M - \mu_f)}{\sigma_M} \frac{\partial \sigma_Z}{\partial \alpha}; \quad \text{(xviii)}$$

by calculating $\dfrac{\partial \sigma_Z}{\partial \alpha}$ from Equation xvi and taking the limit as α approaches zero, we get

$$\mu_X - \mu_M = \frac{(\mu_M - \mu_f)}{\sigma_M}\left(\frac{\sigma_{X,M} - \sigma_M^2}{\sigma_M}\right), \quad \text{(xix)}$$

or, rearranging terms,

$$\mu_X = \mu_f + (\mu_M - \mu_f) \cdot \frac{\sigma_{X,M}}{\sigma_M^2}. \quad \text{(xx)}$$

Again, risk has a reward of $\mu_M - \mu_f$, but now the quantity of risk is measured by $\sigma_{X,M}/\sigma_M^2$—this ratio of the covariance between asset X and the market to the variance of the market return is referred to as the "beta" coefficient for the asset. Estimated beta coefficients for financial assets are reported in many publications.

Studies of the CAPM

This version of the capital asset pricing model carries very strong implications about the determinants of any asset's expected rate of return. Because of this simplicity, the model has been subject to a large number of empirical tests. In general these find that the model's measure of systematic risk ("beta") is indeed correlated with expected returns, while simpler measures of risk (for example, the standard deviation of past returns) are not. Perhaps the most influential early empirical test that reached such a conclusion was Fama and MacBeth (1973). But the

CAPM itself explains only a small fraction of differences in the returns of various assets. And, contrary to the CAPM, a number of authors have found that many other economic factors significantly affect expected returns. Indeed, a prominent recent challenge to the CAPM comes from one of its original founders—see Fama and French (1992).

References

Fama, E. F., and K. R. French. "The Cross Section of Expected Stock Returns." *Journal of Finance* 47 (1992): 427–466.

Fama, E. F., and J. MacBeth. "Risk, Return, and Equilibrium." *Journal of Political Economy* 8 (1973): 607–636.

Freund, J. E., and R. E. Walpole. *Mathematical Statistics.* 5th ed. Englewood Cliffs, NJ: Prentice-Hall, 1992.

Hoel, Paul G. *Introduction to Mathematical Statistics.* 5th ed. New York: John Wiley and Sons, 1984.

Jensen, M. "The Performance of Mutual Funds in the Period 1945–1964." *Journal of Finance* (May 1968): 386–416.

Lintner, J. "The Valuation of Risk Assets and the Selection of Risky Investments in Stock Portfolios and Capital Budgets." *Review of Economics and Statistics* (February 1965): 13–37.

Scharfstein, D. S., and J. Stein. "Herd Behavior and Investment." *American Economic Review* (June 1990): 465–489.

Sharpe, W. F. *Portfolio Theory and Capital Markets.* New York: McGraw Hill, 1970.

Tobin, J. "Liquidity Preference as Behavior Towards Risk." *Review of Economic Studies* (February 1958): 65–86.

CHAPTER 9

THE ECONOMICS OF INFORMATION

Information is a valuable economic resource. People who know where to buy high-quality goods cheaply can make their budgets stretch further than those who don't; farmers with access to better weather forecasting may be able to avoid costly mistakes; and government environmental regulation can be more efficient if it is based on good scientific knowledge. Although these observations about the value of information have long been recognized, formal economic modeling of information acquisition and its implications for resource allocation is fairly recent.[1] But, despite its late start, the study of information economics has become one of the major areas in current research. In this chapter we briefly survey some of the principal issues raised by this research. We will return to the observations made here at several places later in this book.

PROPERTIES OF INFORMATION

One difficulty encountered by economists who wish to study the economics of information is that "information" itself is not easy to define.[2] Unlike the economic goods we have been studying so far, the "quantity" of information obtainable from various actions is not well defined, and what information is obtained is not homogeneous among its users. The forms of economically useful information are simply too varied to permit the kinds of price-quantity characterizations we have been using for hamburgers and soft drinks. Instead, economists who wish to study information must take some care to specify what the informational

---

[1] The formal modeling of information is sometimes dated from the path-breaking article by G. J. Stigler, "The Economics of Information," *Journal of Political Economy* (June 1961): 213–225.

[2] Scientists have developed a very general definition of information based on communications theory. See C. E. Shannon and W. Weaver, *The Mathematical Theory of Communication* (Urbana, Ill.: University of Illinois Press, 1963).

environment is in a particular decision problem (this is sometimes called the *information set*) and how that environment might be changed through individual actions. As might be expected, this approach has resulted in a vast number of models of specific situations with little overall commonality among them.

A second complication involved in the study of information concerns some technical properties of information itself. Most information is durable and retains value after it has been used. Unlike a hot dog, which is consumed only once, knowledge of a special sale can be used not only by the person who discovers it, but also by any friends with whom the information is shared. The friends then may gain from this information even though they don't have to spend anything to obtain it. Indeed, in a special case of this situation, information has the characteristic of a pure *public good* (see Chapter 24). That is, the information is both *nonrival* in that others may use it at zero cost and *nonexclusive* in that no individual can prevent others from using the information. The classic example of these properties is a new scientific discovery. When some prehistoric people invented the wheel, others could use it without detracting from the value of the discovery, and everyone who saw the wheel could copy it freely. Because this situation significantly reduces incentives for making scientific discoveries, many countries have adopted patent laws as a way of privatizing information that would normally be public in nature.

These technical properties of information imply that market mechanisms may often operate imperfectly in allocating resources to information provision and acquisition. Standard models of supply and demand may therefore be of relatively limited use in understanding such activities. At a minimum, models have to be developed that accurately reflect the properties being assumed about the informational environment. Throughout the latter portions of this book, we will describe some of the situations in which such models are called for. Here, however, we will pay relatively little attention to supply-demand equilibria and will instead focus primarily on information issues that arise in the theory of individual choice.

THE VALUE OF INFORMATION

Developing models of information acquisition utilizes many of the same concepts that we introduced in connection with our study of uncertainty in the previous chapter. In many respects lack of information does represent a problem involving uncertainty for a decision maker. In the absence of perfect information, he or she may not be able to know exactly what the consequences of a particular action will be. Better information can reduce that uncertainty and therefore lead to better decisions that provide increased levels of utility.

Information and Subjective Possibilities

This relationship between uncertainty and information acquisition can be illustrated using the state-preference approach that we introduced in the previous chapter. There we assumed that an individual forms subjective opinions about the probabilities of the two states of the world, "good times" and "bad times." In this model, information is valuable because it allows the individual to revise his or her estimates of these probabilities and to take advantage of these revisions. For example, information that foretold that tomorrow would definitely be "good times" would cause the individual to revise his or her probabilities to $\pi_g = 1$, $\pi_b = 0$ and to change his or her purchases accordingly. When the information received is less definitive, the individual may only revise the probabilities slightly, but even small revisions may be quite valuable. If you ask some friends about their experiences with a few brands of cassette players you are thinking of buying, you may not want their opinions to dictate your choice. The prices of the players and other types of information (say, obtained from consulting *Consumer Reports*) will also affect your views. Ultimately, however, you must process all of these factors into a decision that reflects your assessment of the probabilities of various "states of the world" (in this case, the quality obtained from buying various brands). To the extent that information alters *a priori* probabilities and allows individuals to make better decisions, it is a resource that has economic value.

A Formal Model

To illustrate how the quest for information might be integrated with our model of individual choice, suppose that information can be measured by the number of "messages" (m) received. Suppose also the individual decision maker adjusts his or her subjective probabilities in response to these messages. Hence, π_g and π_b will be functions of m. The individual's goal now is to maximize

$$\text{expected utility} = \pi_g U(W_g) + \pi_b U(W_b) \tag{9.1}$$

subject to

$$I = P_g W_g + P_b W_b + P_m m, \tag{9.2}$$

where P_m is the per-unit cost of information messages (that is, the cost of a mechanic's time, of a phone call to gather price information, and so forth). Setting up the Lagrangian for this problem

$$\mathcal{L} = \pi_g U(W_g) + \pi_b U(W_b) + \lambda (I - P_g W_g - P b W_b - P_m m) \tag{9.3}$$

yields the following first-order conditions for a constrained maximum:

$$\frac{\partial \mathcal{L}}{\partial W_g} = \pi_g U'(W_g) - \lambda P_g = 0$$

$$\frac{\partial \mathcal{L}}{\partial W_b} = \pi_b U'(W_b) - \lambda P_b = 0$$

$$\frac{\partial \mathcal{L}}{\partial m} = \pi_g U'(W_g)\frac{dW_g}{dm} + \pi_b U'(W_b)\frac{dW_b}{dm} + U(W_g)\frac{d\pi_g}{dm} \qquad (9.4)$$

$$+ U(W_b)\frac{d\pi_b}{dm} - \lambda P_g\frac{dW_g}{dm} - \lambda P_b\frac{dW_b}{dm} - \lambda P_m = 0$$

$$\frac{\partial \mathcal{L}}{\partial \lambda} = I - P_g W_g - P_b W_b - P_m m = 0.$$

The first two of these equations simply restate the optimality result derived earlier. At a maximum the (subjective) ratio of expected marginal utilities should equal the price ratio P_g/P_b. The third equation states the basic marginal principle that this individual should purchase additional information messages up to the point at which the expected marginal gain from another message is equal to the cost of the message and the budgetary reallocations it prompts. Notice that additional information increases utility in two ways: (1) it permits the individual to revise his or her choices of W_g and W_b so as to achieve a higher expected utility using the revised probability estimates; and (2) it may raise the expected utility associated with a particular choice of W_g and W_b by revising the probabilities attached to the two states. In general, it might be expected that the first of these reasons would be the most important motive for a risk-averse individual to acquire information.[3]

EXAMPLE 9.1

THE VALUE OF INFORMATION ON PRICES

In our previous, well-worn hamburger/soft drink examples, we have been assuming that the consumer knows the prices of each of these items with certainty. We can illustrate the economic value of information now by assuming instead that the $1 price for hamburgers is an average for two burger joints, one of which charges $.75 and the other $1.25. The consumer would obviously prefer to shop at the less expensive stand (assuming the hamburgers being sold are identical), but doesn't know which stand offers the lower price. The consumer could just choose one of the stands randomly, or he or she could invest in a phone call to find out the prices. How much would he or she be willing to pay for this information?

---

[3] In the case of state independence and fair markets for contingent commodities, we have shown that $W_g = W_b$. Since $\pi_g + \pi_b = 1$, $d\pi_g/dm = -d\pi_b/dm$. Hence, the second part of the expression for optimal information choice is equal to zero, and only the first motive for acquiring information is operative.

To approach this problem, we use the indirect utility function for hamburgers and soft drinks that (in Example 4.4) we computed as

$$V = .5IP_X^{-.5}P_Y^{-.5}, \tag{9.5}$$

where, as before, I represents income (assumed to be \$2 here), P_X represents the price of soft drinks (assumed to be \$.25), and P_Y represents the price of hamburgers (which may be either \$.75 or \$1.25). If the consumer chooses where to shop randomly—say, by flipping a coin—expected utility will be

$$\text{expected utility} = .5V(P_Y = .75) + .5V(P_Y = 1.25)$$
$$= .5(2.309) + .5(1.789) = 2.049. \tag{9.6}$$

If the consumer knew which stand offers a lower price, he or she would obviously shop there, and utility would be

$$\text{expected utility} = V(P_Y = .75) = 2.309. \tag{9.7}$$

Price information about hamburgers, therefore, raises utility both by changing the probabilities of the events (shopping at the cheap stand now becomes a certainty) and by allowing the consumer to make a utility-maximizing decision that takes advantage of the low price. A consumer with an income of \$1.77 (= \$2.00 · 2.049/2.309) who knew which stand was cheaper would have the same utility as a consumer with \$2.00 who had to choose stands randomly. Such a consumer would therefore be willing to pay up to \$.23 for the information. The information is clearly worth the price of a phone call. In the extensions to this chapter we pursue further the issue of searching for lower prices.

QUERY: Why does the expected utility for an uninformed consumer here ($V = 2.049$) exceed the expected utility for a consumer who can buy hamburgers at their average price (\$1) with certainty ($V = 2.00$)? Does this violate the assumption of risk aversion?

Asymmetry of Information

One implication of our study of information acqusition is that the level of information that an individual buys will depend on the per-unit price of information messages. Unlike the market price for most goods (which are assumed to be the same for everyone), there are many reasons to believe that these information costs may differ significantly among individuals. Some individuals may possess specific skills relevant to information acquisition (they may be trained mechanics, for example) whereas others may not possess such skills. Some individuals may have other types of experiences that yield valuable information, whereas others may lack that experience. For example, the seller of a product will usually know more about its limitations than will a buyer, since the seller will know precisely how the good was made and where possible problems might arise. Similarly, large-scale repeat buyers of a good may have greater access to information about it than would first-time buyers. Finally, some individuals may have invested in some types of information services (for example, by having a computer link to a brokerage firm or by subscribing to *Consumer Reports*) that make the marginal cost of obtaining additional information lower than for someone without such an investment.

All of these factors suggest that the level of information may differ among the participants in market transactions. Of course, in many instances, information costs may be low and such differences may be minor. Most people can appraise the quality of fresh vegetables fairly well just by looking at them, for example. But when information costs are high and variable across individuals, we would expect them to find it advantageous to acquire different amounts of information.

INFORMATION AND INSURANCE

The market for insurance is characterized by a number of informational asymmetries. Most of these arise from differences between buyers and sellers of insurance in their information about the uncertain event being insured against. Because buyers of insurance directly face these uncertainties, they are often in a better position to know the true likelihood of their occurrence and are frequently able to take actions that may affect that likelihood. A car owner in an urban area, for example, knows whether he or she is parking in an area where cars are likely to be stolen and could, possibly at some cost, choose to park in a safer place. Automobile insurance firms, on the other hand, find it prohibitively costly to discover how each policy holder parks and must instead base rates on an assumed average behavior. Because this type of situation is not unique to insurance markets, but characterizes a large number of transactions involving informational asymmetries, we will examine it in some detail. The concepts of "moral hazard" and "adverse selection" that we will describe are perhaps the most important discoveries of modern information theory.

MORAL HAZARD

Individuals can take a variety of actions that may influence the probability that a risky event will occur. Homeowners contemplating possible losses from fire, for example, can install sprinkler systems or keep fire extinguishers at convenient locations. Similarly, people may buy antitheft devices for cars or keep physically fit in an attempt to reduce the likelihood of illness. In these activities, utility-maximizing individuals will pursue the risk reduction up to the point at which marginal gains from additional precautions are equal to the marginal cost of these precautions.

In the presence of insurance coverage, however, this calculation may change. If a person is fully insured against losses, he or she will have a reduced incentive to undertake costly precautions and may therefore increase the likelihood of a loss occurring. In the automobile insurance case, for example, a person who has a policy that covers theft may park in less safe areas or refrain from installing antitheft devices. This behavioral response to insurance coverage is termed "moral hazard."

DEFINITION

Moral Hazard The effect of insurance coverage on individuals' decisions to undertake activities that may change the likelihood of incurring losses.

The use of the term "moral" to describe this response is perhaps unfortunate. There is nothing particularly "immoral" about the behavior being described—individuals are simply responding to the incentives they face. In some applications, this response might even be desirable.[4] But, because insurance providers may find it very costly to measure and evaluate such responses, moral hazard may have important implications for the allocation of resources. To examine these, we need a simple utility-maximizing model.

A Mathematical Model

Suppose a risk-averse individual faces the possibility of incurring a loss (L) that will reduce his or her initial wealth (W_0). The probability of loss is given by π, and this probability can be reduced by the amount (A) that an individual spends on preventative measures. If we assume state independence, we can let $U(W)$ represent the individual's utility in both state 1 (no loss) and state 2 (loss). In the absence of insurance coverage, wealth in the two states is given by

$$W_1 = W_0 - A$$
$$W_2 = W_0 - A - L,$$

(9.8)

and the individual chooses A to maximize

$$\text{expected utility} = E = (1 - \pi)U(W_1) + \pi U(W_2).$$

(9.9)

---

[4] For example, people with medical insurance may be encouraged to seek early treatment because the insurance reduces the out-of-pocket cost of medical care.

Remembering that π is a function of A, the first-order condition for a maximum is therefore

$$\frac{\partial E}{\partial A} = -U(W_1)\frac{\partial \pi}{\partial A} - (1 - \pi)U'(W_1)$$

$$+ U(W_2)\frac{\partial \pi}{\partial A} - \pi U'(W_2) = 0$$

(9.10)

or

$$\pi U'(W_2) + (1 - \pi)U'(W_1) = [U(W_2) - U(W_1)]\frac{\partial \pi}{\partial A}.$$

(9.11)

This result has the commonsense interpretation that the individual should undertake precautionary activities up to the point at which the expected marginal utility cost of spending one more dollar on such activities (the left side of Equation 9.11) is equal to the reduction ($\partial \pi / \partial A$ is negative) in the expected value of the utility loss that might be encountered in bad times.

With insurance coverage the story is a bit more complex. Now the individual may purchase insurance coverage that pays X if a loss incurs, and the premium for this coverage is given by P (which will obviously depend on X). Wealth in the two possible states is now given by

Behavior with Insurance and Perfect Monitoring

$$W_1 = W_0 - A - P$$
$$W_2 = W_0 - A - P - L + X,$$

(9.12)

and the individual chooses A and X to maximize expected utility. If the insurance provider could monitor precautionary activities and therefore know the probability of loss, it could charge a fair insurance premium of

$$P = \pi X.$$

(9.13)

With such a policy

$$W_1 = W_0 - A - \pi X,$$
$$W_2 = W_0 - A - L + (1 - \pi)X.$$

(9.14)

Assuming state independence, this person can maximize expected utility by choosing X so that $W_1 = W_2$, which, as in our previous models, requires full insurance coverage (that is, $X = L$). With full coverage, the first-order condition for a utility-maximizing choice of A is

$$\frac{\partial E}{\partial A} = -(1 - \pi)U'(W_1)\left(1 + L\frac{\partial \pi}{\partial A}\right) - U(W_1)\frac{\partial \pi}{\partial A}$$

$$- \pi U'(W_2)\left(1 + L\frac{\partial \pi}{\partial A}\right) + U(W_2)\frac{\partial \pi}{\partial A} = 0$$

(9.15)

or, using the fact that $W_1 = W_2$,

$$1 = -L\frac{\partial \pi}{\partial A}.\qquad(9.16)$$

This condition is directly analogous to the one derived earlier for the uninsured case, although now with the availability of full insurance, it can be stated more simply. At the utility-maximizing choice, the marginal cost of an extra unit of prevention (which here is just 1) should equal the marginal reduction in the expected loss provided by that extra spending. Hence, with full insurance and the actuarially fair premiums made possible by perfect monitoring, precautionary purchases are still made at the optimal levels.

The Information Problem and Imperfect Monitoring

Our analysis so far has been based on the unreasonable assumption that insurance providers know the probability that an individual will incur a loss and can therefore charge the actuarially fair premium for coverage. When individuals can undertake precautionary activities, this assumption seems particularly doubtful. It would seem to require that the provider constantly monitor people's activities to determine what the true probability of loss is. In addition, it would require the provider to quote a different premium to each buyer to reflect his or her own precautionary activities. Obtaining such information may be prohibitively costly in most circumstances, and insurers will have to adopt less fully informed methods of premium setting.

In the simplest case, the insurer might set a premium based on the average probability of loss experienced by some group of people, with no variation allowed for specific individual precautionary activities.[5] With such a policy, however, each individual has an incentive to reduce his or her precautionary activities since these are costly and, in the presence of full insurance, yield no benefits in terms of utility. This result can be shown directly for the full insurance case. If $X = L$ in Equations 9.12, $W_1 = W_2$ regardless of the premium charged or the precautions undertaken. Since premiums now do not depend on A, however, it is clear that utility is maximized when $A = 0$. Even when premiums do depend partly on A, the resulting utility maximum will be characterized by too little precautionary spending and, perhaps, too much insurance. In essence then, the distorting effect of moral hazard on the

---

[5] Another possibility is that the insurer may be able to categorize individuals into various risk categories (for example, "smokers" versus "nonsmokers," "urban" versus "rural" residents, and so forth). In the next section we examine some of the issues that arise in markets characterized by such risk clauses.

allocation of resources arises from the informational asymmetry between individuals and insurance providers with respect to the ability to monitor precautions taken.[6]

EXAMPLE 9.2

MORAL HAZARD AND MONITORING

In several of the examples in Chapter 8, we examined an individual's decision about buying insurance against theft of a car worth $20,000. Here we look at his or her decision about whether to install an antitheft device that costs $1950 and promises to reduce the probability of auto theft from .25 to .15. In terms of expected values, the installation clearly makes sense since the expected gain of $2000 ($.10 \cdot 20{,}000$) exceeds the cost of the device. Expected utility from installing the device

$$\textbf{expected utility} = .85 \; ln \; (100{,}000 - 1950)$$
$$+ .15 \; ln \; (100{,}000 - 20{,}000 - 1950) \qquad \textbf{(9.17)}$$
$$= 11.4590$$

also exceeds expected utility without the device (11.4571—see Equation 8.55) so an uninsured individual will take this precaution.

Insurance and Moral Hazard. With insurance available, however, this may not be the case. Specifically, assume that the individual can purchase full insurance coverage for $5200—this premium represents $5000 for the expected loss and a $200 charge associated with administrative costs. Assume also that the insurance company makes no effort to monitor installation of antitheft devices. In this case expected utility with the insurance policy (11.4595—see Equation 8.59) exceeds expected utility with the device, so the individual will opt for buying insurance instead.

Monitoring of Antitheft Devices. If insurance providers can monitor installation of antitheft devices, the calculation might change again. Suppose

---

[6] If insurance providers can partly monitor precautionary spending (perhaps by observing individual insurance purchases), the analysis becomes more complex though the possibility for inefficient resource allocation remains if this monitoring is incomplete. For a discussion, see S. Shavell, "On Moral Hazard and Insurance," *Quarterly Journal of Economics* (November 1979): 541–562.

that it would cost $10 to determine whether an owner had installed such a device. In this case the insurance premium for a person with an antitheft device would be $3210—$3000 expected loss ($.15 \cdot 20{,}000$), $200 for administrative costs, and the $10 monitoring cost. If an individual purchases such a policy (and an antitheft device), his or her wealth will be $94,840 ($= 100{,}000 - 3210 - 1950$) with certainty since, if a theft occurs, insurance will completely cover the loss. Expected utility now is given by

$$\text{expected utility} = ln\,(94{,}840) = 11.4600, \tag{9.18}$$

which exceeds that available either from buying the antitheft device without insurance or from buying an unmonitored policy. Hence, whether the insurance availability deters all precautionary spending depends crucially on the costs of monitoring the spending.

QUERY: Suppose monitoring of antitheft devices costs $100 per policy that must be paid whether or not an individual actually installs a device. What decision would he or she make now?

ADVERSE SELECTION

A second, related way in which informational asymmetries may affect market transactions arises when different individuals may have different probabilities of experiencing unfavorable outcomes. If (as in the moral hazard case) individuals know the probabilities of loss more accurately than do insurance providers, insurance markets may not function properly since providers may not be able to set premiums based on accurate measures of expected loss. The resulting equilibria may be undesirable for many market participants.

A Graphical Illustration

Figure 9.1 pictures the situation of two individuals who each start with an initial wealth of W_0 and face the possibility of a loss, L. Point E represents the initial position of these individuals—they receive W_0 in state 1 (no loss) and $W_0 - L$ in state 2 (loss). Suppose that the individuals face different probabilities of loss—the high-risk individual has a probability of loss of π_H whereas the low-risk individual faces a probability of π_L (which is lower than π_H). With fair insurance and state independence (as we saw in Chapter 8), both individuals would prefer to move to the certainty line. The lines EF and EG are drawn with slopes $-(1 - \pi_L)/\pi_L$ and $-(1 - \pi_H)/\pi_H$, respectively, and show the market opportunities for each person to trade W_1 for W_2 by buying

FIGURE 9.1

EQUILIBRIA WITH DIFFERENTIAL RISKS

With perfect information, low-risk individuals move along the market insurance line *EF*, choosing point *F*. High-risk individuals move along *EG*, choosing point *G*. With imperfect information, both types of individuals will choose *F*, which is not viable.

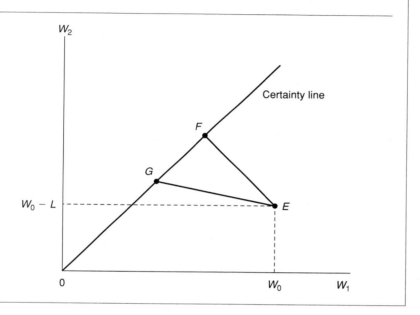

fair insurance.[7] The low-risk individual then maximizes utility at point *F* whereas the high-risk individual chooses point *G*.

If insurance providers have imperfect information about which individuals fall into the low- and high-risk categories, however, the solution in Figure 9.1 will be unstable. The difficulty is, of course, that point *F* provides more wealth in both states than does point *G* and will therefore be preferred by high-risk individuals. They will have an incentive to purchase insurance intended for low-risk buyers, and, in the absence of information about risk categories, the insurer will have no basis for declining to offer coverage to them. With a mixed group of clients, however,

---

[7] These slopes can be derived from Equation 9.14, which shows that a $1 increase in insurance (X) reduces W_1 by π and increases W_2 by $(1 - \pi)$.

the insurer will face a higher average probability of loss than π_L and will, on average, lose money on each policy sold. Point F is not a viable equilibrium for a mixed client group.

Pooling   One conceivable solution would be for the insurer to offer a policy whose premium is based on the average probability of loss, $\bar{\pi} = (\pi_H + \pi_L)/2$. This pooled possibility is indicated by the line EH in Figure 9.2. Although both types of individuals will not necessarily opt for complete coverage at point H (since EH no longer accurately reflects the true probabilities each person knows he or she faces), they may settle for a policy such as M that provides

FIGURE 9.2

IMPOSSIBILITY OF A POOLED EQUILIBRIUM

A pooled insurance policy offers opportunities given by EH. A point such as M on this line cannot be an equilibrium, since insurance options (N) exist that are profitable to insurers and to low-risk individuals, but not to high-risk individuals.

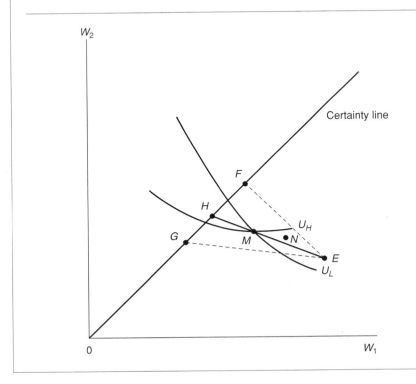

partial coverage. But M cannot be a final equilibrium since at M further trading opportunities exist for low-risk individuals. This can be shown as follows. At M the low-risk individuals' indifference curve (U_L) is steeper than the high-risk individuals' (U_H).[8] Consequently, insurance policies exist (say, N) that are unattractive to high-risk individuals but are both attractive to low-risk individuals and profitable to insurers (since they lie below EF).

Assuming no barriers prevent the selling of fairly priced insurance, policies such as N will be offered and will attract low-risk individuals. Point M will therefore no longer be an equilibrium since the pooled probability of loss will rise above $\bar{\pi}$. In this situation, therefore, the pooled equilibrium M will not be viable.

If this market with asymmetric information is to have a viable equilibrium, it must be separated in some way—that is, high-risk individuals must have an incentive to purchase one type of insurance policy and low-risk individuals to purchase another. One such solution is illustrated in Figure 9.3. Here insurers offer policy G, and high-risk individuals respond by opting for complete insurance. If we let U_H represent the indifference curve for high-risk individuals that passes through G, any policy for low-risk persons that lies above U_H will not be viable since insurers cannot prevent those with high risks from taking advantage of it. In this situation, the best policy that low-risk individuals can obtain is one such as J. This policy lies slightly below U_H, but is economically viable (since it lies on EF) and promises more utility to low-risk individuals than does facing the world uninsured. The policies G and J, therefore, represent a separating equilibrium in this case.

Economists who have studied the adverse selection problem in detail have made a number of observations about the nature of the separating equilibrium in Figure 9.3. Most obviously, this equilibrium is clearly inferior to the full information equilibrium illustrated in Figure 9.1. If insurers could determine the true risks associated with selling to specific individuals,

Separating Equilibria

---

[8] Since expected utility is given by $(1 - \pi)U(W_1) + \pi U(W_2)$, the MRS is given by

$$\frac{-dW_2}{dW_1} = \frac{(1 - \pi)U'(W_1)}{(\pi)U'(W_2)}.$$

Assuming both individuals have the same utility function and noting that each has the same wealth at M, the MRS's differ only because the underlying probabilities of loss differ. Since

$$(1 - \pi_L)/\pi_L > (1 - \pi_H)/\pi_H,$$

the low-risk individual's indifference curve will be steeper. This proof follows the analysis presented in M. Rothschild and J. Stiglitz, "Equilibrium in Competitive Insurance Markets: An Essay on the Economics of Imperfect Information," *Quarterly Journal of Economics* (November 1976): 629–650.

low-risk individuals would be better off and high-risk individuals would be no worse off. Although informational asymmetries will prevent this "first best" equilibrium from being obtained, a variety of other possibilities (such as government regulations or cross-subsidization between high- and low-risk policies by insurers themselves) may yield improvements for both individuals over the equilibrium illustrated in Figure 9.3.

Market Signaling   One route to such improvements involves possible attempts by low-risk individuals to inform insurers of their true status. We have seen that such individuals could clearly benefit from sharing what they know with insurers. The primary difficulty is whether the "signals" they seek to send to insurers will be believable since high-risk individuals would also benefit if they could convince insurers that they too were low risk.

FIGURE 9.3

A SEPARATING EQUILIBRIUM

With imperfect information, G and J represent a possible separating equilibrium. Here high-risk individuals opt for complete coverage (G), and low-risk individuals receive partial coverage (J) that is attractive to them but not to high-risk individuals.

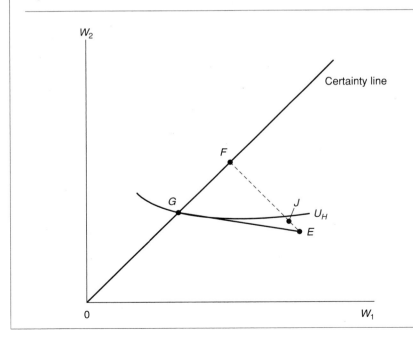

It is the possibility that signals may be inaccurate that makes the study of the subject interesting. If insurers could simply ask each client which risk category he or she represented and get accurate replies, the informational asymmetry described in the previous section would be inconsequential. Economists have, therefore, been more interested in the possibility that insurers may be able to infer accurate probabilities by observing clients' market behavior. The proper setting may give each individual the incentive to reveal his or her true situation, and insurers may then be able to take advantage of these *market signals.* An obvious illustration is provided by the situation shown in Figure 9.3. In this equilibrium, high-risk individuals purchase type *G* policies and obtain full coverage, whereas low-risk individuals purchase type *J* policies and receive only partial coverage. The separating equilibrium, therefore, identifies an individual's risk category. Possibly, insurers could use this information to offer better policies to low-risk individuals (at least until high-risk individuals learn what is happening).

More generally, market signals may be drawn from a number of sources provided that the economic behavior being observed by insurers accurately reflects risk categories. One necessary condition for this to occur is that the costs to individuals of taking the signaling action must be related to the probability of loss. If costs were the same regardless of risk class, individuals would face similar incentives to "send" signals, and the informational value of signals would be lost. For example, it is common for insurance companies to charge higher auto insurance premiums for high-performance sports cars than for similarly priced sedans. A possible explanation is that individuals' auto purchases may indicate their driving habits—perhaps sports car owners always drive as if they were in a road race. The separating equilibrium attained from auto purchase information will be sustainable, however, only if high-risk individuals have an aversion to driving sedans. Otherwise, they may switch car purchases as a way to obtain lower cost insurance. In formal terms, auto selections are a good signal only if it is sufficiently costly (perhaps in psychological terms) for high-risk individuals to adopt the market behavior of low-risk individuals. Some of these possibilities are examined in the next example.

EXAMPLE 9.3

ADVERSE SELECTION IN INSURANCE

Our analysis of installation of automobile antitheft devices in Example 9.2 can also be framed as an adverse selection problem. If insurers knew which owners had installed such devices, they could price policies accordingly. Owners without the devices would face a probability of loss of 0.25 and would pay a $5000 premium for insurance coverage (for simplicity here we assume there are no administrative costs of writing insurance). In this case the owner will fully insure and receive an expected utility of

$$\text{expected utility} = ln\,(100{,}000 - 5000)$$
$$= ln\,(95{,}000) = 11.4616. \qquad (9.19)$$

Since we wish to focus on differing probabilities of loss and not on the cost of antitheft devices, assume that another set of owners have installed such devices at some time in the past. The cost of the device is therefore a sunk cost that will not affect the current decision. Owners with such devices have a probability of loss of 0.15 and face an actuarially fair premium of $3000. With complete insurance, expected utility will be

$$\text{expected utility} = ln\,(97{,}000) = 11.4825. \qquad (9.20)$$

If insurers cannot discern whether an owner has installed a device, both types of owners will purchase low-risk policies. Assuming 50 percent of all cars have the devices, the insurer will experience a 0.20 loss rate and lose an average of $1000 per policy with a $3000 premium. A pooled premium rate of $4000 would clearly be attractive to high-risk owners, but low-risk owners would refuse to buy the policy since they would be better off without insurance:

$$ln(96{,}000) < .85\,ln(100{,}000) + .15\,ln(80{,}000)$$
$$11.4721 < 11.4795. \qquad (9.21)$$

The pooled equilibrium is therefore not viable, since low-risk individuals would refuse to participate in it.

Separating Equilibria. A situation in which high-risk individuals opt for full insurance (at a $5000 premium) and low-risk individuals buy no insurance is a possible separating equilibrium here, but this offers opportunities for insurers to offer partial policies that would be attractive to low-risk owners. To discover the best of these, we must find a fair policy for low-risk buyers that is not attractive to high-risk buyers. Since the premium from such a policy will be $0.15X$ (where X is the amount of the loss covered), we need to solve the following inequality:

$$.75\,ln(100{,}000 - .15X) + .25\,ln(80{,}000 + .85X) < ln(95{,}000), \qquad (9.22)$$

which has an approximate solution of

$$X < 3000. \qquad (9.23)$$

Hence, a low-risk policy can only cover $3000 of a low-risk owner's loss if it is not to be too attractive to high-risk owners. The expected utility of a low-risk owner who buys such a policy (which costs $450 = .15 \cdot 3000$) is

$$.85 \, ln(99,550) + .15 ln(82,550) = 11.4803. \qquad (9.24)$$

Although this figure exceeds the expected utility of a low-risk individual who declines to buy insurance (Equation 9.21), it falls well short of what such an individual might achieve in a full information equilibrium. Low-risk individuals might therefore invest in signaling in order to improve their situation from what it would be under this separating equilibrium. You are now asked to investigate such signaling.

QUERY: If only low-risk owners could buy a certificate indicating installation of an antitheft device, how much would they pay for it? How much would forged certificates have to cost to prevent high-risk owners from using them?

SUMMARY

In this chapter we have provided a survey of some issues that arise in modeling markets in which information is imperfect. Here these issues have been approached mainly from the point of view of an individual decision maker. Issues that arise in studying the consequences of imperfect information for the behavior of firms or for overall market performance will be taken up in later chapters. Several of the conclusions from this chapter will have relevance to these later analyses as well.

- Information is valuable because it permits individuals to increase the expected utility of their decisions. They might, therefore, be willing to pay something to acquire additional information.

- Information has a number of special properties (such as differing costs of acquisition and some aspects of a public good) that suggest that inefficiencies associated with imperfect and asymmetric information may be quite prevalent.

- The presence of asymmetric information may affect a variety of market outcomes, many of which are illustrated in the context of insurance theory. In this case, insurers may have less information about potential risks than do insurance purchasers.

- If insurers are unable to monitor the behavior of insured individuals accurately, moral hazard may arise—being insured will affect individuals' willingness to make precautionary expenditures. Such behavioral effects can arise in any contractual situation in which monitoring costs are high.

- Informational asymmetries can also lead to adverse selection in insurance markets. The resulting equilibria (if they exist) may often be Pareto inefficient. In some cases market signaling can reduce these inefficiencies.

PROBLEMS

9.1

A farmer's tomato crop is wilting, and he must decide whether to water it. If he waters the tomatoes, or if it rains, the crop will yield $1,000 in profits; but if the tomatoes get no water, they will yield only $500. Operation of the farmer's irrigation system costs $100. The farmer seeks to maximize expected profits from tomato sales.

a. If the farmer believes there is a 50 percent chance of rain, should he water?
b. What is the maximum amount the farmer would pay to get information from an itinerant weather forecaster who can predict rain with 100 percent accuracy?
c. How would your answer to part (b) change if the forecaster were only 75 percent accurate?

9.2

In Problem 8.5 Ms. Fogg was quite willing to buy insurance against a 25 percent chance of losing $1,000 of her cash on her around-the-world trip. Suppose that people who buy such insurance tend to become more careless with their cash and that their probability of losing $1,000 rises to 30 percent. What is the actuarially fair insurance premium in this situation? Will Ms. Fogg buy insurance now? (*Note:* This problem and Problem 9.3 illustrate moral hazard.)

9.3

Problem 8.4 examined a cost-sharing health insurance policy and showed that risk-averse individuals would prefer full coverage. Suppose, however, that people who buy cost-sharing policies take better care of their own health so that the loss suffered when they are ill is reduced from $10,000 to $7,000. Now what would be the actuarially fair price of a cost-sharing policy? Is it possible that some individuals might prefer the cost-sharing policy to complete coverage? What would determine whether an individual had such preferences? (A graphical approach to this problem should suffice.)

9.4

Blue-eyed people are more likely to lose their expensive watches than are brown-eyed people. Specifically, there is an 80 percent probability that a blue-eyed individual will lose a $1,000 watch during a year, but only a 20 percent probability that a brown-eyed person will. Blue-eyed and brown-eyed people are equally represented in the population.
a. If an insurance company assumes blue-eyed and brown-eyed people are equally likely to buy watch-loss insurance, what will the actuarially fair insurance premium be?
b. If blue-eyed and brown-eyed people have logarithmic utility-of-wealth functions and current wealths of $10,000 each, will these individuals buy watch insurance at the premium calculated in part (a)?

c. Given your results from part (b), will the insurance premiums be correctly computed? What should the premium be? What will the utility for each type of person be?
d. Suppose that an insurance company charged different premiums for blue-eyed and brown-eyed people. How would these individuals' maximum utilities compare to those computed in parts (b) and (c)? (This problem is an example of adverse selection in insurance.)

9.5

Suppose there are two types of workers, high-ability workers and low-ability workers. Workers' wages are determined by their ability—high-ability workers earn $50,000, low-ability workers earn $30,000. Firms cannot measure workers' abilities but they can observe whether a worker has a high school diploma. Workers' utility depends on the difference between their wages and the costs they incur in obtaining a diploma.
a. If the cost of obtaining a high school diploma is the same for high-ability and low-ability workers, can there be a separating equilibrium in this situation in which high-ability workers get high-wage jobs and low-ability workers get low wages?
b. What is the maximum amount that a high-ability worker would pay to obtain a high school diploma? Why must a diploma cost more than this for a low-ability person if having a diploma is to permit employers to identify high-ability workers?

9.6

Suppose Molly Jock wishes to purchase a high-definition television to watch the Olympic Greco-Roman wrestling competition. Her current income is $20,000, and she knows where she can buy the television she wants for $2,000. She has heard the rumor that the same set can be bought at Crazy Eddie's (recently out of bankruptcy) for $1,700, but is unsure if the rumor is true. Suppose this individual's utility is given by

$$\text{utility} = ln(Y),$$

where Y is her income after buying the television.
a. What is Molly's utility if she buys from the location she knows?
b. What is Molly's utility if Crazy Eddie's really does offer the lower price?

c. Suppose Molly believes there is a 50–50 chance that Crazy Eddie does offer the lower-priced television, but it will cost her $100 to drive to the discount store to find out for sure (the store is far away and has had its phone disconnected). Is it worth it to her to invest the money in the trip?

9.7

Suppose an individual knows that the prices of a particular color TV have a uniform distribution between $300 and $400. The individual sets out to obtain price quotes by phone.

a. Calculate the expected minimum price paid if this individual calls n stores for price quotes.
b. Show that the expected price paid declines with n but at a diminishing rate.
c. Suppose phone calls cost $2 in terms of time and effort. How many calls should this individual make in order to maximize his or her gain from search?[9]

9.8

Suppose the individual in Problem 9.7 adopts a "reservation price strategy"—that is, he or she will buy from the first retailer who meets this reservation price maximum. Under the conditions of Problem 9.7, what price should be set in order to maximize the gain from search?

9.9

Use a graph similar to Figure 9.3 to describe how the degree of risk aversion exhibited by high-risk individuals will affect the existence of viable separating equilibria. Would low-risk individuals be better or worse off if high-risk individuals were very risk averse?

---

[9] Problems 9.7 and 9.8 are based on material found in the extensions to Chapter 9.

9.10

In some cases individuals may care about the date at which the uncertainty they face is resolved. Suppose, for example, that an individual knows that his or her consumption will be 10 units today (C_1) but that tomorrow's consumption (C_2) will be either 10 or 2.5 depending on whether a coin comes up heads or tails. Suppose also that the individual's utility function has the simple Cobb-Douglas form

$$U(C_1, C_2) = \sqrt{C_1 C_2}.$$

a. If an individual cares only about the expected value of utility, will it matter whether the coin is flipped just before day 1 or just before day 2? Explain.
b. More generally, suppose that the individual's expected utility depends on the timing of the coin flip. Specifically, assume that

$$\text{expected utility} = E_1[(E_2\{U(C_1, C_2)\})^\alpha]$$

where E_1 represents expectations taken at the start of day 1, E_2 represents expectations at the start of day 2, and α represents a parameter that indicates timing preferences. Show that if $\alpha = 1$, the individual is indifferent about when the coin is flipped.
c. Show that if $\alpha = 2$, the individual will prefer early resolution of the uncertainty—that is, flipping the coin at the start of day 1.
d. Show that if $\alpha = .5$, the individual will prefer later resolution of the uncertainty (flipping at the start of day 2).
e. Explain your results intuitively and indicate their relevance for information theory. (*Note:* This problem is an illustration of "resolution seeking" and "resolution-averse" behavior. See D. M. Kreps and E. L. Porteus, "Temporal Resolution of Uncertainty and Dynamic Choice Theory," *Econometrica* [January 1978]: 185–200.)

SUGGESTED READINGS

Deaton, A., and J. Muellbauer. *Economics and Consumer Behavior.* Cambridge: Cambridge University Press, 1980.
Chapter 10 discusses consumer behavior under uncertainty and includes good discussions of intertemporal decision making and search theory.

Diamond, P., and M. Rothschild. *Uncertainty in Economics: Readings and Exercises,* revised ed. San Diego, CA: Academic Press, 1989.
Contains reprints of many of the articles mentioned in this chapter. Also includes brief summaries of related literature and a variety of problems and exercises.

Ehrlich, I., and G. S. Becker. "Market Insurance, Self-Insurance and Self-Protection." *Journal of Political Economy* (July/August 1972): 623–658.
Focuses on the relationship between market insurance and self-insurance (a substitute) or self-protection (a complement). Uses a state-preference approach similar to the one in Chapter 8.

Pauly, M. "The Economics of Moral Hazard: Comment." *American Economic Review* (June 1968): 531–537.
A comment on Arrow's article on medical insurance (see Chapter 8), which uses a simple graphic argument to show how reactions to the reduced out-of-pocket costs of medical care from being insured may make complete coverage non-Pareto optimal.

Phlips, L. *The Economics of Imperfect Information.* Cambridge: Cambridge University Press, 1988.
Covers many of the topics in this chapter. Particularly nice discussions of auctions and signaling equilibria.

Rothschild, M. "Searching for the Lowest Price When the Distribution of Prices Is Unknown." *Journal of Political Economy* (July/August 1974): 689–711.
Mathematically difficult paper that examines models where consumers learn about the distribution of prices as they search. Finds that, in many instances, adoption of a "reservation price" (that is, a price that represents the maximum price a searcher will accept) constitutes an optimal search rule.

Rothschild, M., and J. Stiglitz. "Equilibrium in Competitive Insurance Markets: An Essay on the Economics of Imperfect Information." *Quarterly Journal of Economics* (November 1976): 629–650.
Presents a nice graphic treatment of the self-selection problem. Contains ingenious illustrations of various possibilities for separating equilibria.

Stigler, G. "The Economics of Information." *Journal of Political Economy* (June 1961): 213–225.
Classic examination of the role of search in obtaining price information.

Stiglitz, J. "Information and Economic Analysis: A Perspective." *Economic Journal,* Supplement to Volume 95 (1985): 21–41.
Offers a broad overview of the ways in which considerations of imperfect information may affect traditional economic analysis.

EXTENSIONS

The Economics of Search

Example 9.1 illustrates how information about unknown prices is valuable to individuals. One way in which such information can be gathered is through systematic search. Calling a few discount stores when buying a big-ticket item obviously makes sense, though it seems that one could push matters too far. Checking every store in the country or adopting elaborate search schemes when purchasing toothpaste would seem nonoptimal. In this extension we look at some models of these commonsense observations.

Statistical Background

As before, we need a bit of statistical background to develop a model of search behavior. If X is a random variable with a probability density function $f(x)$ (see

the extensions to Chapter 8 for a discussion of random variables), then the "cumulative distribution function" $F(z)$ is defined as

$$F(z) = \int_{-\infty}^{z} f(x)dx. \qquad \textbf{(i)}$$

That is, $F(z)$ gives the probability that X is less than or equal to Z for any given value of Z. The cumulative distribution function gives an alternative way of describing the distribution of a random variable. Notice that the cumulative distribution function and the probability density function are closely related to each other since $F' = f$.

For our examination of the search issue, we assume that an individual is seeking to buy a good at the lowest possible price, but that he or she only knows the distribution of prices (p, which can only be nonnegative) being offered by various stores. That is, he or she knows $f(p)$ and $F(p)$ but not which store offers which price.

E9.1 The Diminishing Marginal Benefit of Search

Suppose this individual decides to sample (by a phone call or an actual visit) n stores, compare their prices, and buy from the cheapest one. The probability that a paticular store will offer a given price (say, p_0) and that this will be lower than that offered by the $n - 1$ other stores is given by

$$[1 - F(p_0)]^{n-1} f(p_0). \qquad \text{(ii)}$$

That is, this probability is given by the probability that $P > P_0$ for $n - 1$ stores times the probability that one store offers P_0. Taking the expected value of all such prices gives the expected minimum price the searcher will pay after checking at n stores:

$$P_{min}^{n} = \int_0^{\infty} [1 - F(p)]^{n-1} f(p) p \, dp. \qquad \text{(iii)}$$

Since $(1 - F)$ is less than one, this minimum price decreases as the number of stores sampled increases. It is also straightforward to show that the expected gain from adding one more store to the sample (that is, $P_{min}^{n-1} - P_{min}^{n}$) also diminishes as n increases.[10]

---

[10] Since

$$\mu_p = \int_0^{\infty} p \, f(p) dp = \int_0^{\infty} [1 - F(p)] dp,$$

Equation iii can be written as

$$P_{min}^{n} = \int_0^{\infty} [1 - F(p)]^n dp = \int_0^{\infty} [1 - F(p)]^{n-1} [1 - F(p)] \, dp$$

$$= P_{min}^{n-1} - \int_0^{\infty} [1 - F(p)]^{n-1} F(p) dp.$$

Hence, $P_{min}^{n-1} - P_{min}^{n}$ diminishes with n.

E9.2 Costs of Search

If gathering price information is costly, not all potential information will be collected. Instead, a utility-maximizing searcher will choose n so that the expected reduction in price from the nth search is exactly equal to the cost of the search, c. Because search encounters diminishing returns, increases in c will reduce the utility-maximizing value of n. Similarly, individuals who face higher search costs will pay higher expected prices. These results were first highlighted by Stigler (1960) in a famous study of used car prices.

Price Dispersion

The existence of high search costs implies that markets need not necessarily obey the "law of one price." In the absence of such costs, individuals would always seek out the lowest price, ensuring that this is the only price that can prevail in equilibrium. Search costs, however, tend to separate markets, even for homogeneous goods. For example, Gaynor and Polachek (1994) find that incomplete information about physicians' prices causes patients to pay an average 30 percent more than they would with more complete price information. Additional costs from imperfect information were found to be highest for important but infrequently purchased services such as hospital follow-up visits. On the other hand, general office and pediatric visits, services that are used repeatedly, exhibited much smaller costs from imperfect price information.

There are several ways in which consumers' information costs can be reduced and price dispersions reduced. Many states require "price posting" for products such as gasoline or prescription drugs, thereby providing a low-cost route to comparison shopping. Price advertising in the media is another low cost way to inform consumers. The U.S. Federal Trade Commission has prodded many professions, such as attorneys or real estate agents, to remove bans on price advertising. The commission argues that the primary effect of such bans on price advertising is to increase price dispersion and provide supercompetitive returns to some suppliers. Finally, consumers can reduce price dispersions themselves by purchasing price information. A number of automobile-purchase and apartment-rental services have been developed for that purpose in recent years.

E9.3 Reservation Price Strategy

Choosing a price search strategy on *a priori* grounds may not be optimal. If one were to encounter a surprisingly low price at, say, the fifth store sampled, it would make little sense to visit remaining $n - 5$ ones. One sequential search strategy that is optimal in a variety of circumstances is for the individual to choose a *reservation price* (p_R) and accept the first price found that is equal to or lower than p_R. The reservation price should be chosen so that the expected gain from one more search once p_R has been achieved is equal to the cost of that search, c. That is, we wish to know the expected value of $p_R - p$ for values of $p \leq p_R$. Setting this value equal to c permits the solution of an optimal p_R.

$$c = \int_0^{p_R} (p_R - p)f(p)dp \qquad \text{(iv)}$$

Now an increase in c will cause this person to opt for a higher reservaton price and he or she will visit fewer stores.[11] In this sequential strategy, just as in the fixed sample size strategy, increases in search costs reduce the amount of search individuals do.

Reservation Wages

This approach to search theory has been most extensively applied to the problem of unemployed workers looking for jobs. In that application, the optimal strategy consists of choosing a minimum acceptable wage that must be met before a job is accepted. The theoretical and empirical literature on the relationship between reservation wages and the job search prices is very large (see, for example, Kiefer and Neumann, 1989). Perhaps the most important finding from such studies is that reservation wages tend to decline over time as unemployment spells lengthen. There also appears to be evidence that generous unemployment benefits raise reservation wages. In most of these cases, however, reservation wages are not measured directly but are instead inferred from the behavior of individual workers. Some economists (for example, Cox and Oaxaca, 1992) have tried to measure reservation wages (or prices) directly in controlled experiments. Although creating these experiments poses a variety of conceptual problems, evidence from them seems generally supportive of the conclusions implied by the observed search behavior of workers in the labor market.

E9.4 Distribution of Prices

Optimal search strategy will also depend on the characteristics of the distribution of prices. The greater the μ_p, the greater the search intensity that will be warranted, *ceteris paribus*. Individuals will be more likely to search for expensive goods than for cheap ones. Similarly, the greater the dispersion of prices, the more search will be optimal. Obviously, if $\sigma_P = 0$ (as is implied by the "law of one price" under perfect competition), any search would be superfluous. All such results depend on an individual's knowledge of the distribution of prices before search begins, though Rothschild (1974) shows that qualitatively similar results can be derived when individuals have no *a priori* information about prices and must infer the distribution from information gathered in their search.

References

Cox, J. C., and R. L. Oaxaca. "Direct Tests of the Reservation Wage Property," *Economic Journal* (November 1992): 1423–1432.

Gaynor, M., and S. W. Polachek. "Measuring Information in the Market: An Application to Physician Services." *Southern Economic Journal* (April 1994): 815–831.

Kiefer, N. M., and G. R. Neumann. *Search Models and Applied Labor Economics.* Cambridge: Cambridge University Press, 1989.

Rothschild, M. "Searching for the Lowest Price When the Distribution of Prices Is Unknown." *Journal of Political Economy* (July–August 1974): 689–711.

Stigler, G. J. "The Economics of Information." *Journal of Political Economy* (June 1961): 213–225.

---

[11] Integration by parts shows that

$$c = \int_0^{p_R} (p_R - p)f(p)dp = p_R F(p_R) - \int_0^{p_R} pf(p)dp$$

$$= \int_0^{p_R} F(p)dp,$$

which makes it clear that p_R and c are positively related.

GAME THEORY AND STRATEGIC EQUILIBRIUM

Uncertainty also affects individual decision-making in situations that require dealing with other people. When the utility that an individual receives depends on the actions that others take, he or she must make some sort of conjecture about what those actions will be. Such conjectures, by their very nature, involve uncertainty. But, by studying the options open to all of the individuals in a particular situation, it may be possible to make some progress in analyzing utility-maximizing behavior. The formal tools for doing this come from "game theory." As the name implies, the subject of game theory involves the study of strategic, gamelike situations, ranging from the trivial (tic-tac-toe, blackjack) to the awesomely complex (antimissile defense). In this chapter we provide an introduction to this topic together with some illustrations of the kinds of strategic equilibria that can arise in relatively simple games. These tools will be useful at several places later in the book, especially in Chapter 20, which uses game theory to study strategic interactions among the firms in an industry.

BASIC CONCEPTS

Game theory models seek to portray complex strategic situations in a highly simplified and stylized setting. Much like the previous models in this book, game theory models abstract from most of the personal and institutional details of a problem in order to arrive at a representation of the situation that is mathematically tractable. This ability to get to the "heart" of the problem is the greatest strength of this type of modeling.

Any situation in which individuals must make strategic choices and in which the final outcome will depend on what each person chooses to do can be viewed as a *game*. All games have three basic elements: (1) players; (2) strategies; and (3) payoffs. Games may be *cooperative*, in which players can make binding agreements, or *noncooperative*, where such agreements are not possible. Here we will be concerned primarily with noncooperative games. The basic elements listed below are included in such games.

Players Each decision-maker in a game is called a "player." These players may be individuals (as in poker games), firms (as in oligopoly markets), or entire nations (as in military conflicts). All players are characterized as having the ability to choose from among a set of possible actions they might take.[1] Usually, the number of players is fixed throughout the "play" of a game, and games are often characterized by the number of players (that is, two-player, three-player, or n-player games). In this chapter we will primarily study two-player games and will denote these players by A and B. One of the important assumptions usually made in game theory (as in most of economics) is that the specific identity of the players is irrelevant. There are no "good guys" or "bad guys" in a game, and players are not assumed to have any special abilities or shortcomings. Each player is simply assumed to choose the course of action that yields the most favorable outcome, after taking the actions of his or her opponent into account.

Strategies Each course of action open to a player in a game is called a "strategy." Depending on the game being examined, a strategy may be a very simple action (take another card in blackjack) or a very complex one (build a laser-based antimissile defense), but each strategy is assumed to be a well-defined, specific course of action.[2] Usually, the number of strategies available to each player will be finite; many aspects of game theory can be illustrated for situations in which each player has only two strategies available. In noncooperative games, players cannot reach binding agreements with each other about what strategies they will play—each player is uncertain about what the other will do.

Payoffs The final returns to the players of a game at its conclusion are called "payoffs." Payoffs are usually measured in levels of utility obtained by the players, although frequently monetary payoffs (say, profits for firms) are used

---

[1] Sometimes one of the players in a game is taken to be "nature." For this player, actions are not "chosen" but rather occur with certain probabilities. For example, the weather may affect the outcomes of a game, but it is not "chosen" by nature. Rather, particular weather outcomes are assumed to occur with various probabilities. Games against nature can be analyzed using the methods developed in Chapter 9.

[2] In games involving a sequence of actions (for example, most board games, such as chess), a specification of strategies may involve several decision points (each move in chess). Assuming perfect knowledge of how the game is played, such complex patterns can often be expressed by choices among a large but finite set of pure strategies, each of which specifies a complete course of action until the game is completed. See our discussion of "extensive" and "normal" forms and D. M. Kreps, *Game Theory and Economic Modeling*, Oxford University Press (1990), Chapter 3.

instead. In general, it is assumed that players can rank the payoffs of a game ordinally from most preferred to least preferred and will seek the highest ranked payoff attainable. Payoffs incorporate all aspects associated with outcomes of a game; these include both explicit monetary payoffs and implicit feelings by the players about the outcomes, such as whether they are embarrassed or gain self-esteem. Players prefer payoffs that offer more utility to those that offer less.

Notation

Usually it is not necessary to write down a game in formal notation—a literary description of the situation will do. But, for stating results in a compact way, some notation can help to clarify matters. Following standard custom we will denote a particular game G between two players (A and B) by:

$$G[S_A, S_B, U_A (a,b), U_B (a,b)] \tag{10.1}$$

where S_A and S_B represent the set of strategies that are available for players A and B respectively and U_A and U_B represent the utility obtained by the players when A and B choose particular strategies ($a \subset S_A$, $b \subset S_B$).

NASH EQUILIBRIUM IN GAMES

In the economic theory of markets, the concept of equilibrium is developed to indicate a situation in which both suppliers and demanders are content with the market outcome. Given the equilibrium price and quantity, no market participant has an incentive to change his or her behavior. The question therefore arises whether there are similar equilibrium concepts in game theory models. Are there strategic choices that, once made, provide no incentives for the players to alter their behavior further? Do these equilibria then offer believable explanations of the outcome of games?

Although there are several ways to formalize equilibrium concepts in game theory, the most frequently used approach was originally proposed by Cournot (see Chapter 19) in the nineteenth century and generalized in the early 1950s by J. Nash.[3] Under Nash's procedure a pair of strategies, say, (a^*, b^*), is defined to be an equilibrium if a^* represents player A's best strategy when B plays b^* and b^* represents B's best strategy when A plays a^*. Formally, a pair of strategies is a Nash equilibrium if

$$U_A(a^*, b^*) \geq U_A(a', b^*) \text{ for all } a' \subset S_A$$

and

$$U_B(a^*, b^*) \geq U_B(a^*, b') \text{ for all } b' \subset S_B \tag{10.2}$$

---

[3] John Nash, "Equilibrium Points in n-person games," *Proceedings of the National Academy of Sciences* 36 (1950): 48–49.

Even if one of the players reveals the (equilibrium) strategy he or she will use, the other player cannot benefit from knowing this. For nonequilibrium strategies, this is not the case. As we shall see, if one player knows what the other's strategy will be, he or she can often benefit from that knowledge and choose another strategy. This may, in turn, reduce the payoff received by the player who has revealed his or her strategy, providing an incentive to do something else.

Not every game has a Nash equilibrium pair of strategies. And, in some cases, a game may have multiple equilibria, some of which are more plausible than others. Some Nash equilibria may not be especially desirable for the players in a game. And, in some cases, other equilibrium concepts may be more reasonable than those proposed by Nash. Still, we now have an initial working definition of equilibrium with which to start our study of game theory:

DEFINITION

Nash Equilibrium Strategies   A pair of strategies (a^*, b^*) represents an equilibrium solution to a two-player game if a^* is an optimal strategy (in the sense of Equation 10.2) for A against b^* and b^* is an optimal strategy for B against a^*.[4]

AN ILLUSTRATIVE DORMITORY GAME

As a way of illustrating the game-theoretic approach to strategic modeling, let's examine a simple example in which two students (A and B) must decide how loudly to play their stereos in a dorm. Each person may choose to play his or her equipment either loudly (L) or softly (S). We wish to examine possible equilibrium choices in this situation. It should be stressed at the outset that this game is not especially realistic—it is intended for pedagogic purposes only.

The Game in Extensive Form

Figure 10.1 illustrates the specific details of the dorm game. In this game "tree," the action proceeds from left to right, and each "node" represents a decision point for the person indicated there. The first move in this game belongs to A: he or she must choose a decibel level, L or S. Because B's decisions occur to the right of A's, the tree indicates that B makes the decision after A. At this stage, two versions of the game are possible depending on whether B knows what choice A made. First we will look at the case where

---

[4] Although this definition is stated only for two-player games, the generalization to n-persons is straightforward, though notationally cumbersome.

FIGURE 10.1

THE DORMITORY GAME IN EXTENSIVE FORM

In this game A chooses a loud (L) or a soft (S) stereo volume, then B makes a similar choice. The oval surrounding B's nodes indicates that they share the same (lack of) information—B does not know what strategy A has chosen. Payoffs (with A's first) are listed at the right.

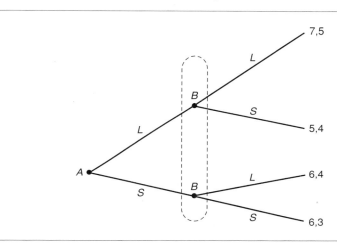

B does not have this information. The larger oval surrounding B's two decision nodes indicates that both nodes share the same (lack of) information. B must choose L or S without knowing what A has done. Later we will examine the case where B does have this information.

The numbers at the end of each tree branch indicate payoffs, here measured in utility to these two dorm mates. Each pair of payoffs lists A's utility first. For example, the payoffs in Figure 10.1 show that if A chooses S and B chooses L, utility will be 6 for A and 4 for B. Other payoffs are interpreted similarly.

The Game in Normal Form

Although the game tree in Figure 10.1 offers a useful visual presentation of the complete structure of a game, sometimes it is more convenient to describe games in tabular (or "normal") form. Table 10.1 provides such a presentation for the dormitory game. In the table, A's strategies (S or L) are shown at the left, and B's strategies are shown across the top. Payoffs (again with A's coming first) corresponding to the various strategic choices are shown in the body of the table. Figure 10.1 and Table 10.1 convey exactly the same

TABLE 10.1

THE DORMITORY GAME IN NORMAL FORM

		B's STRATEGIES	
		L	S
A's STRATEGIES L		7, 5	5, 4
S		6, 4	6, 3

information about this game, though usually it is more convenient to work with the tabular, normal form.

Dominant Strategies and Nash Equilibria

Table 10.1 makes clear that adoption of a loud-play strategy is a dominant strategy for person B. No matter what strategy A chooses, the L strategy provides greater utility to B than does the S strategy. Of course, since the structure of the game is known to both players, A will recognize that B has such a dominant strategy. Hence, A will opt for the strategy that does the best against B's choice of L. As can be seen from Table 10.1, A will consequently also choose to play his or her music loudly (L). Considerations of strategy dominance, therefore, suggest that the A:L, B:L strategy choice will be made and that the resulting utility payoffs will be 7 (to A) and 5 (to B).

The A:L, B:L strategy choice also obeys the Nash criterion for equilibrium. If A knows that B will play L, his or her best choice is L. Similarly, if B knows A will play L his or her best choice is also L (indeed, since L is a dominant strategy for B this is the best choice no matter what A does). The A:L, B:L choice, therefore, meets the symmetry required by the Nash criterion.

To see why the other strategy pairs in Table 10.1 do not meet the Nash criterion, let us consider them one at a time. If the players announce A:S, B:L, this provides A with a chance to better his or her position—if A knows B will opt for L, he or she can obtain greater utility by choosing L. The choice A:S, B:L is therefore not a Nash equilibrium. Neither of the two outcomes in which B chooses S meets the Nash criterion either. As we have already pointed out, no matter what A does, B can improve its utility by choosing L instead. Since L strictly dominates S for B, no outcome in which B plays S can be a Nash equilibrium.

EXISTENCE OF NASH EQUILIBRIA

Although the dorm game illustrated in Figure 10.1 contains a unique Nash equilibrium, that is not a general property of all two-person games. Example 10.1 illustrates a simple game (Rock, Scissors, Paper) in which no Nash equilibrium exists and another game (Battle of the Sexes) that contains two

Nash equilibria. These examples make clear, therefore, that the Nash approach may not always identify a unique equilibrium solution to a two-person game. Rather, one must explore the details of each game situation to determine whether there exist believable Nash equilibria.

EXAMPLE 10.1

SAMPLE NASH EQUILIBRIA

Table 10.2 illustrates two familiar games that reflect differing possibilities for Nash equilibria. Part (a) of the table depicts the children's finger game Rock, Scissors, Paper. The zero payoffs along the diagonal show that if players adopt the same strategy, no payments are made. In other cases the payoffs indicate a $1 payment from loser to winner under the usual hierarchy (Rock breaks Scissors, Scissors cut Paper, Paper covers Rock). As anyone who has played this game knows, there is no equilibrium. Any strategy pair is unstable because it offers at least one of the players an incentive to adopt another strategy. For example, (*A:* Scissors, *B:* Scissors) provides an incentive for either *A* or *B* to choose Rock. Similarly (*A:* Paper, *B:* Rock) obviously encourages *B* to choose Scissors. The irregular cycling behavior exhibited in the play of this game clearly indicates the absence of a Nash equilibrium.

Battle of the Sexes.   In the Battle of the Sexes game, a husband (*A*) and wife (*B*) are planning a vacation. *A* prefers mountain locations; *B* prefers the

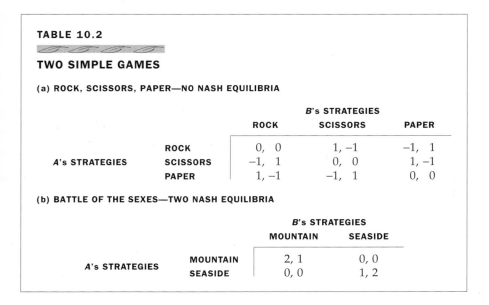

TABLE 10.2

TWO SIMPLE GAMES

(a) ROCK, SCISSORS, PAPER—NO NASH EQUILIBRIA

		B's STRATEGIES		
		ROCK	SCISSORS	PAPER
	ROCK	0, 0	1, −1	−1, 1
A's STRATEGIES	SCISSORS	−1, 1	0, 0	1, −1
	PAPER	1, −1	−1, 1	0, 0

(b) BATTLE OF THE SEXES—TWO NASH EQUILIBRIA

		B's STRATEGIES	
		MOUNTAIN	SEASIDE
A's STRATEGIES	MOUNTAIN	2, 1	0, 0
	SEASIDE	0, 0	1, 2

seaside. Both players prefer a vacation spent together to one spent apart. The payoffs in part (b) of Table 10.2 reflect these preferences. Here both of the joint vacations represent Nash equilibria. With (*A:* Mountain, *B:* Mountain) neither player can gain by taking advantage of knowing the other's strategy. Similar comments apply to (*A:* Seaside, *B:* Seaside). Hence, this is a game with two Nash equilibria.

QUERY: Are any of the strategies in either of these games dominant? Why aren't separate vacations Nash equilibria in the Battle of the Sexes?

There are, however, certain types of two-person games in which a Nash equilibrium must exist. Intuitively, games in which the participants have a large number of strategies will often offer sufficient flexibility to ensure that at least one Nash equilibrium must exist. Such games arise in two contexts. First, games in which the strategies chosen by *A* and *B* are alternative levels of a single continuous variable include an "infinite" number of potential strategies and such games are guaranteed to have a Nash equilibrium. The most important class of such games involves games where players are two firms that must choose the price they will charge for a single product. Some games of this type together with illustrations of the types of Nash equilibria they exhibit are discussed in Chapter 20.

Another way in which games may contain a sufficiently "large" number of strategies is to permit players to use "mixed" strategies. In such games there may be relatively few "pure" strategies like the ones we have been examining—perhaps only two. But each player is permitted to play these pure strategies with certain, pre-selected probabilities. In the dorm game, for example, *A* might flip a coin to determine whether to play music loudly or softly—that is, he or she would play each strategy with probability ½. If each player can choose to play the available pure strategies with any probabilities he or she might choose, the game will be converted into one with an infinite number of (mixed) strategies and, again, the existence of a Nash equilibrium is assured. Example 10.2 provides an illustration of how the consideration of mixed strategies can add to the Nash equilibrium outcomes in the Battle of the Sexes game that we have already examined.

EXAMPLE 10.2

BATTLE OF THE SEXES WITH MIXED STRATEGIES

To show how the introduction of mixed strategies may add Nash equilibria to a given game, let's return to the Battle of the Sexes game in Example 10.1.

Suppose that the spouses in the problem tire of constant bickering about vacations and decide to let "chance" decide. Specifically, suppose A decides to choose his mountain strategy with probability r and seaside with probability $1 - r$. Similarly, suppose B chooses her mountain strategy with probability s and seaside probability with $1 - s$. Given these probabilities, the outcomes of the game occur with the following probabilities: mountain-mountain, rs; mountain-seaside, $r(1 - s)$; seaside-mountain, $(1 - r)(s)$; and seaside-seaside $(1 - r)(1 - s)$. A's expected utility is then given by

$$E(U_A) = rs(2) + r(1 - s)(0) + (1 - r)(s)(0) + (1 - r)(1 - s)(1)$$
$$= 1 - r - s + 3rs = 1 - s + r(3s - (1)).$$

(10.3)

Obviously, A's optimal choice of r depends on B's probability, s. If $s < \frac{1}{3}$, utility is maximized by choosing $r = 0$. If $s > \frac{1}{3}$, A should opt for $r = 1$. And when $s = \frac{1}{3}$, A's expected utility is $\frac{2}{3}$ no matter what value of r is chosen. Figure 10.2 illustrates A's optimal choices of r given these various values of s.

For spouse B, expected utility is given by

$$E(U_B) = rs(1) + r(1 - s)(0) + (1 - s)(r)(0) + (1 - r)(1 - s)(2)$$
$$= 2 - 2r - 2s + 3rs = 2 - 2r + s(3r - 2).$$

(10.4)

Now when $r < \frac{2}{3}$, B's expected utility is maximized by choosing $s = 0$. When $r > \frac{2}{3}$, utility is maximized by choosing $s = 1$. And when $r = \frac{2}{3}$, B's expected utility is independent of what s she chooses. These optimal choices are also shown in Figure 10.2.

Nash equilibria are shown in Figure 10.2 by the intersections of the optimal response curves for A and B. That is, the intersections obey the conditions summarized in Equations 10.2. Notice that there are three such intersections. Two of these we have seen previously: $r = 0, s = 0$ and $r = 1, s = 1$ represent the joint vacation strategies we discussed in Example 10.1. But $r = \frac{2}{3}, s = \frac{1}{3}$ is a new Nash equilibrium that was unavailable before the introduction of mixed strategies. More generally, Figure 10.2 provides a hint of why games with a continuum of strategies must have Nash equilibria—in general, continuous optimal response functions will intersect somewhere and those intersections will be Nash equilibria.

QUERY: Is the mixed strategy equilibrium illustrated in this problem particularly desirable to the players? If the spouses could cooperate in reaching a decision, would they opt for such a mixed strategy solution?

Unfortunately, the proof of the existence of a Nash equilibrium in two-person games with a continuum of strategies is difficult and requires

FIGURE 10.2

NASH EQUILIBRIA IN MIXED STRATEGIES IN THE BATTLE OF THE SEXES GAME

With mixed strategies, A plays "mountains" with probability r, and B plays mountains with probability s. The figure shows each player's optimal choice given the other player's choice. This game has three Nash equilibria (denoted by E): (1) $r = 0$, $s = 0$; (2) $r = 1$, $s = 1$; and (3) $r = \frac{2}{3}$, $s = \frac{1}{3}$.

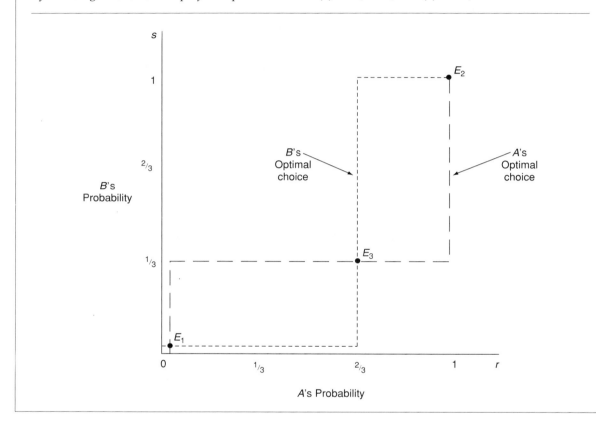

a number of technical assumptions. Hence, we will not attempt to present it here. Rather, most of our analysis of two-person games will involve explicitly solving for any Nash equilibria that may exist. Interested readers may wish to explore mathematically sophisticated existence proofs on their own.[5]

[5] See, for example, D. Fudenberg and J. Tirole, *Game Theory* (Cambridge, Mass.: M17 Press, 1992), section 1.3.

Nash equilibria arise because of the strategic uncertainties inherent in a situation. Nothing guarantees that these equilibria will be especially desirable from the players' perspectives. Probably the most famous example of a two-person game with an undesirable Nash equilibrium outcome is the Prisoner's Dilemma game, first discussed by A. W. Tucker in the 1940s. The title stems from the following game situation. Two people are arrested for a crime. The district attorney has little evidence in the case and is eager to extract a confession. She separates the suspects and tells each, "If you confess and your companion doesn't, I can promise you a reduced (six-month) sentence, whereas on the basis of your confession, your companion will get 10 years. If you both confess, you will each get a three-year sentence." Each suspect also knows that if neither of them confesses, the lack of evidence will cause them to be tried for a lesser crime for which they will receive two-year sentences. The normal form payoff matrix for this situation is illustrated in Table 10.3. The "confess" strategy dominates for both A and B. Hence, these strategies constitute a Nash equilibrium and the district attorney's ploy looks successful. However, notice that an ironclad agreement by both prisoners not to confess would reduce their prison terms from three to two years. This "rational" solution is not stable, and each prisoner has an incentive to squeal on his or her colleague. This then is the "dilemma": Outcomes that appear to be optimal are not stable when subjected to the Nash criterion. Example 10.3 demonstrates another game, this time with an environmental twist, in which the Nash equilibrium is not especially desirable from the players' perspectives.

THE PRISONER'S DILEMMA

EXAMPLE 10.3
THE TRAGEDY OF THE COMMON

The term "Tragedy of the Common" has come to signify environmental problems of overuse that arise when scarce resources are treated as "common

---

TABLE 10.3

THE PRISONER'S DILEMMA

		B	
		CONFESS	**NOT CONFESS**
A	**CONFESS**	A: 3 years B: 3 years	A: 6 months B: 10 years
	NOT CONFESS	A: 10 years B: 6 months	A: 2 years B: 2 years

property."[6] A game-theoretic illustration of this issue can be developed by assuming that two herders (the familiar A and B) are deciding how many of the yaks in their herds to graze on the village common. The problem is that the common is quite small and can rapidly succumb to overgrazing.

In order to add some mathematical structure to this problem, let Y_A, Y_B represent the number of yaks that are brought to the common and suppose that the per yak value of grazing on the common (in terms say of increased yak milk) is given by

$$V(Y_A, Y_B) = 200 - (Y_A + Y_B)^2. \tag{10.5}$$

Notice that this function implies both that an extra yak reduces V ($V_i < 0$) and that this marginal effect increases with additional grazing ($V_{ii} < 0$).

To find the Nash equilibrium grazing strategies, we solve herder A's value maximization problem

$$\underset{Y_A}{\text{Max }} Y_A V = \underset{Y_A}{\text{Max }} [200Y_A - Y_A(Y_A + Y_B)^2]. \tag{10.6}$$

The first order condition for a maximum is

$$200 - 2Y_A^2 - 2Y_AY_B - Y_A^2 - 2Y_AY_B - Y_B^2 = 200 - 3Y_A^2 - 4Y_AY_B - Y_B^2 \tag{10.7}$$
$$= 0.$$

Similarly, for B the optimal strategy choice solves

$$200 - 3Y_B^2 - 4Y_BY_A - Y_A^2 = 0. \tag{10.8}$$

For a Nash equilibrium, the values for Y_A and Y_B must solve both Equations 10.7 and 10.8. Using the symmetry condition $Y_A = Y_B$, these can be solved as

$$200 = 8Y_A^2 = 8Y_B^2 \tag{10.9}$$

or

$$Y_A = Y_B = 5. \tag{10.10}$$

Hence, each herder will bring 5 yaks to the common and will obtain $500[= 5 \cdot (200 - 10^2)]$ in return. Given this choice, neither herder has an incentive to change his or her behavior.

That the Nash equilibrium is not the best use of the common can be shown by noting that $Y_A = Y_B = 4$ provides greater total revenue [$544 = 4(200 - 64)$] to each herder.[7] But $Y_A = Y_B = 4$ is not a stable equilibrium. If, say, A announces $Y_A = 4$, herder B can solve equation 10.8 as

$$3Y_B^2 + 16Y_B - 184 = 0 \tag{10.11}$$

---

[6] This term was popularized by G. Hardin in "The Tragedy of the Common," *Science* 162: 1243–1248 (1968).

[7] Actually, the total value of the common [$Y(200 - Y^2)$] is maximized when $Y = \sqrt{66} = 8.1$, though bringing 0.1 yak to the common may require more skill than the herders have.

which has a solution of 5.6 yaks. Rounding this to 6 shows that A's value would now be 400, whereas B's would be 600. As in the Prisoner's Dilemma game, $Y_A = Y_B = 4$ provides an incentive for each herder to cheat.

QUERY: If this game were played repetitively (say, each day), would you expect the Nash equilibrium to persist?

Cooperation and Repetition

Games such as the Prisoner's Dilemma or the Tragedy of the Common suggest that cooperation among players may yield outcomes that are preferred by both players. Providing a model of cooperation in the games we have been looking at, however, is difficult because the logic of the Nash equilibrium concept suggests that any other solution will be unstable. We could, of course, look at institutions that exist beyond a particular game (for example, the laws of contracts) to investigate how cooperative outcomes might be fostered, but that approach would divert us from the purpose of this chapter.[8] Instead, here we look at ways in which certain types of cooperative behavior might be facilitated in games that are played repeatedly. Because repetition may bring home directly to players the inefficiencies inherent in a single-period Nash equilibrium, it seems plausible that repeated play might foster cooperation. In the Prisoner's Dilemma, for example, it seems doubtful that the district attorney's ploy could succeed if used repeatedly, especially if the same suspects were always involved. Surely, even the most dim-witted criminal would eventually catch on. Similarly, it seems unlikely that the yak herders in Example 10.3 would persist in overgrazing on the common every day without eventually trying something else. To examine such possibilities we need to develop some ways of describing games that are played over time. We begin, in the next section, by showing how the Nash equilibrium concept needs to be modified in such games. Then we will return to the issue of how repetition may foster cooperation.

A TWO-PERIOD DORMITORY GAME

In order to illustrate Nash equilibria in dynamic (multiperiod) games, we will return to a reformulated version of the dormitory game presented at the beginning of this chapter. We present this new game in extensive form in order to understand its temporal aspects. Figure 10.3 repeats our prior game, but now we assume that A sets his or her decibel level first and that B can hear this before turning the stereo on. In graphical terms, the oval around B's nodes has been eliminated in Figure 10.3 to indicate this additional

[8] But see our discussion of property and contracts in Chapter 24.

CHOICE UNDER UNCERTAINTY

FIGURE 10.3

THE DORMITORY GAME IN SEQUENTIAL FORM

In this form of the dormitory game, B knows A's stereo choice. Strategies for B must be phrased taking this information into account. (See Table 10.4.)

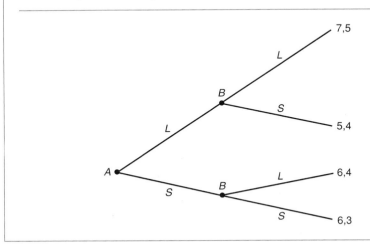

---

information. In effect, this game has now been converted into a two-period game. With this change, B's strategic choices must be phrased in a way that takes the information available at the start of period two into account. Although B will make his or her choice at the start of the game, we need to state a complete set of strategies for all the possible actions B might propose taking.

In Table 10.4 we indicate such an extended set of strategies. In all, there are four such strategies covering the possible informational contingencies. Each strategy is stated as a pair of actions indicating what B will do depending on its information. The strategy (L, L) indicates that B chooses L if A chooses L (his or her first strategy) and L also if A chooses S (the second strategy). Similarly (S, L) indicates that B chooses S if A chooses L and B chooses L if A chooses S. Although this table conveys little more than did the previous normal form for the dormitory game (Table 10.1), explicit consideration of contingent strategy choices does enable us to explore equilibrium notions for this two-period game.

Somewhat surprisingly, there are three Nash equilibria in this game: (1) A:L, B:(L, L); (2) A:L, B:(L, S); and (3) A:S, B:(S, L). Each of these strategy meets the criterion of being optimal for each player given the strategy of the other. Pairs (2) and (3) are implausible, however. Each of these pairs

TABLE 10.4

CONTINGENT STRATEGIES IN THE DORMITORY GAME

		B's STRATEGIES			
		L, L	*L, S*	*S, L*	*S, S*
A's STRATEGIES	*L*	7, 5	7, 5	5, 4	5, 4
	S	6, 4	6, 3	6, 4	6, 3

incorporates a noncredible threat on the part of player *B* that he or she would not carry out if it were in a position to do so. Consider, for example, the pair *A:L, B:(L, S)*. Under this Nash equilibrium, *B* promises to play *S* if *A* plays *S*. A glance at Figure 10.3 shows that this threat is not credible. If *B* were presented with the fact of *A* having chosen *S*, he or she will obtain utility of 3 if *S* is chosen, but 4 if *L* is chosen. The threat implicit in the *(L, S)* strategy is therefore not believable. Even though *B*'s strategy *(L, S)* is one component of a Nash equilibrium, person *A* should be able to infer the noncredibility of the threat implicit in it.

By eliminating strategies that involve noncredible threats, *A* can conclude that *B* would never play *(L, S)* or *(S, L)*. Proceeding in this way, the dormitory game is reduced to the payoff matrix originally shown in Table 10.1 and, as we discussed, in that case *L, L* (always playing *L*) is a dominant strategy for *B*. *A* can recognize this and will opt for strategy *L*. The Nash equilibrium *A:L, B:L, L* is therefore the only one of the three in Table 10.4 that does not involve noncredible threats. Such an equilibrium is termed a "subgame perfect," which we define more formally as follows:

DEFINITION

Subgame Perfect   A Nash equilibrium in which the strategy choices of each player do not involve noncredible threats. That is, no strategy in such an equilibrium requires a player to carry out an action that would not be in its interest at the time the choice must be made.

To understand this terminology, we note that a "subgame" is simply that portion of a larger game that begins at one decision node and includes all future actions stemming from that node. For a Nash equilibrium to qualify for subgame perfection, it must also be a Nash equilibrium in each subgame of a larger game. A Nash equilibrium that did not meet this criteria would incorporate at least one strategy that contains the threat to make a choice that the player would not actually make (according to the Nash criterion) when the game reached that point. Hence the key aspect of such subgame perfection is that this equilibrium cannot incorporate a noncredible threat.

For example, in Figure 10.3 the Nash equilibrium $A:L$, $B:(L, L)$ is subgame perfect because once the game reaches either of B's decision nodes, the choice $B:L$ is optimal. However, the Nash equilibrium $A:L$, $B:(L, S)$ is not a subgame perfect equilibrium. B would not actually choose S in the subgame stemming from his or her decision node once A has opted for his or her second strategy, S. That is, $B:S$ is not a Nash equilibrium for the subgame starting at this node. Hence, what appears to be an equilibrium for this extended game by the Nash criterion does not meet the criterion for subgame perfection.

Given this refined concept of equilibrium in multiperson games, we can now proceed to explore how cooperation might be fostered in games that are played repeatedly.

REPEATED GAMES

Many economic situations can be modeled as games that are played repeatedly. Consumers' regular purchases from a particular retailer, firms' day-to-day competition for customers, or workers' attempts to outwit their supervisors all have elements of strategic interaction that occur repetitively. In this section we study some of the formal properties of such situations.

As in the illustrative dormitory game, an important aspect of a repeated game is the expanded strategy sets that become available to the players. Not only can players select specific strategies at each stage of the game, but they also can specify strategies that indicate how outcomes from prior stages of the game will be incorporated into future play. This in turn opens the way for the consideration of credible threats and subgame perfection.

One of the most important distinctions among repeated games is the number of repetitions incorporated in a game. In games with a fixed, finite number of repetitions, there is relatively little room for the development of innovative strategies. On the other hand, games that are to be repeated infinitely many times, or, what amounts to the same thing, repeated games in which players cannot identify a clear ending point, offer a much wider array of options.

A Prisoner's Dilemma Finite Game Illustration

Consider, for example, the game shown in Table 10.5. Here A has two strategies (U, D) as does B (L, R). Clearly if the game is to be played only once, the Nash equilibrium $A:U$, $B:L$ might be expected as an outcome. Any other strategy choice is unstable, giving at least one of the players an incentive to alter his or her behavior. Notice, however, that the payoffs under the Nash equilibrium $(1, 1)$, are universally inferior to those available from the unstable strategy choice $A:D$, $B:R$, which promises payoffs $(2, 2)$.

TABLE 10.5

A PRISONER'S DILEMMA GAME TO BE PLAYED REPEATEDLY

		B's STRATEGIES	
		L	R
A's STRATEGIES	U	1, 1	3, 0
	D	0, 3	2, 2

Suppose now that this game is to be played repeatedly for a finite number of periods, T. Any expanded strategy in which player A asserts that he or she will play D in the game's final period (say, as a result of prior plays in the game) is not credible. When period T arrives, the logic of the Nash equilibrium will assert itself and A will ultimately choose strategy U or risk seeing his or her payoff during period T become 0. Similarly, any of player B's extended set of strategies that promises to play R in the final period will contain a noncredible threat.

Hence, any subgame perfect equilibrium outcome for this game can consist only of strategies that promise to play the Nash equilibrium strategies $A:U, B:L$ in the final round. But the logic that applies in period T also applies in period $T - 1$. Any threat by A or B to play other than their Nash equilibrium strategies in period $T - 1$ is not credible. Subgame perfection requires that strategies $A:U, B:L$ be played in period $T - 1$ as well. Continuing this backward induction proof suggests that the only subgame perfect equilibrium in this finite game is to require the Nash equilibrium to occur in every period. The potential gains from $A:D, B:R$ will remain elusive throughout the game.

This backward induction logic does not work, however, if the players in this game believe it will be repeated an infinite number of times. In this case, each player can announce a "trigger strategy" promising to play his or her optimal cooperative strategy ($A:D$ or $B:R$) so long as the other player does. When one player deviates from this pattern, however, the game reverts to the repeating single-period Nash equilibrium.

Whether the twin trigger strategy choice represents a subgame perfect equilibrium depends on whether the threat (promise) to play comparatively is credible. To examine the question we have to look at the subgame proceeding inward from any specific period, say K. Supposing A announces that he or she will continue to play the trigger strategy by playing cooperatively in period K, what is B's optimal response? If he or she continues to play cooperatively, payoffs of 2 can be expected to persist

A Game with Infinite Repetitions

indefinitely. If he or she decides to "cheat" (by playing R in period K), the payoff in period K will be 3 but then fall to 1 in all future periods because cooperation has broken down. Assuming B discounts the future with a discount factor δ, the present value[9] of continued cooperation is

$$2 + \delta 2 + \delta^2 2 + \ldots = \frac{2}{1 - \delta}, \tag{10.12}$$

whereas the payoff from cheating is

$$3 + \delta 1 + \delta^2 1 + \ldots = 3 + \frac{\delta}{1 - \delta}. \tag{10.13}$$

Continued cooperation will be credible, therefore, if

$$2/(1 - \delta) > 3 + \delta/(1 - \delta), \tag{10.14}$$

which will occur for

$$\delta > \frac{1}{2}. \tag{10.15}$$

In other words, B will find continued cooperative play desirable providing he or she does not discount the future gains from such cooperation too highly. Example 10.4 shows that even yak herders may cooperate in some circumstances.

EXAMPLE 10.4

THE TRAGEDY OF THE COMMON REVISITED

The overgrazing of yaks on the village common encountered in Example 10.3 may not persist in an infinitely repeated game. To simplify, assume that each herder has only two strategies available—to bring either 4 or 5 yaks to the common. Payoffs for this game can be computed from equation 10.5 and are illustrated in Table 10.6. Here the Nash equilibrium, (A:5, B:5) is inferior to the cooperative outcome (A:4, B:4), but this latter choice is unstable when the game is played for any finite number of repetitions.

With an infinite number of repetitions, however, both players would find it attractive to adopt cooperative trigger strategies providing

$$544/(1 - \delta) > 595 + 476\delta/(1 - \delta), \tag{10.16}$$

which holds for

$$\delta > 51/119 = .43. \tag{10.17}$$

---

[9] The factor δ is similar to the term $1/(1 + r)$ used in the present value formula. See Chapter 23 Appendix for details.

TABLE 10.6

PAYOFFS IN THE REPEATED YAK GRAZING GAME

		B's STRATEGIES	
		4	**5**
A's STRATEGIES	**4**	544, 544	476, 595
	5	595, 476	500, 500

Providing the herders are reasonably farsighted (that is, have a high enough δ), cooperation is a subgame perfect equilibrium in this infinitely repeated game.

QUERY: How do you interpret the discount rates (δ) required here for cooperation? Do the conditions for cooperation seem likely to be fulfilled?

Folk Theorems

These numerical illustrations suggest that cooperation may represent a subgame perfect equilibrium in games where both players can gain unambiguously from such cooperation. That is, potential losses, such as those that occur in the Prisoner's Dilemma, may not occur if games are played repetitively. The formal statement of these general results are sometimes called *Folk Theorems* because they were widely believed by economists to be true before they were actually proven. Although there are many versions of these theorems, perhaps the most widely referenced was developed by J. Friedman in 1971.[10] He showed that any infinitely repeated game in which there exist payoffs that are preferred by both players to the payoffs attainable under a Nash equilibrium will have a subgame perfect equilibrium that achieves these payoffs providing the players are "patient enough." Such patient players (that is, those with suitably high δ's) will always find it attractive to stick to trigger strategies that promise returns long into the future. The prospect of infinite repetition succeeds in counteracting the nonoptimal outcomes guaranteed by the Nash logic in games played only a few times. Cooperative-type outcomes therefore become more believable.

---

[10] J. Friedman, "A Non-Cooperative Equilibrium for Supergames," *Review of Economic Studies* (March 1971): 1–12.

GAMES OF INCOMPLETE INFORMATION

The games that we examined in this chapter were games of complete information. That is, the entire structure of the game is known to both players. It is possible to relax these stringent informational assumptions in several ways. Even in single-stage games, considerable uncertainty may arise when players do not know each other's payoffs. Obviously, player A cannot make reasonable conjectures about what B will do if he or she does not know with any certainty what B's payoffs are. Additional aspects of imperfect information can arise is multistage games when players' strategies in previous stages are only partly observable. In the repeated Prisoner's Dilemma, for example, the logic of trigger strategies would be undermined if player A could not accurately detect whether B had cheated in previous periods. To examine all these informational possibilities would be to take us too far afield here. In Chapter 20, however, we will illustrate how imperfect information may play an important role in determining the outcomes of game-type interactions in markets served by relatively few firms.

SUMMARY

This chapter has provided a brief introduction to the tools of game theory with particular attention to the ways in which concepts of strategic equilibria can aid in explaining outcomes in uncertain situations. The primary results of the chapter are:

- All games are characterized by similar structures involving players, strategies available, and payoffs obtained through their play.

- The Nash equilibrium concept provides an intriguing attractive solution concept to a game under which each player's strategy choice is optional given the choices made by the other players. Not all games have unique Nash equilibria, however.

- Two-person noncooperative games with continuous strategy sets will usually possess Nash equi-

libria. Games with only a finite set of strategies will also have Nash equilibria in mixed strategies in which the pure strategies are played with certain probabilities.

- Multistage and repeated games may have many Nash equilibria, some of which are not believable because they involve noncredible threats. Nash equilibria that do not involve such threats are termed subgame perfect equilibria.

- Outcomes that are unambiguously superior to a Nash equilibrium may be attainable in infinitely repeated games through the use of trigger strategies. Existence of such cooperative outcomes will generally require that players not discount future payoffs too heavily.

PROBLEMS

10.1

Players A and B are engaged in a coin-matching game. Each shows a coin as either heads or tails. If the coins match, B pays A \$1. If they differ, A pays B \$1.

a. Write down the payoff matrix for this game, and show that it does not contain a Nash equilibrium.
b. How might the players choose their strategies in this case?

10.2

Smith and Jones are playing a number-matching game. Each chooses either 1, 2, or 3. If the numbers match, Jones pays Smith $3. If they differ, Smith pays Jones $1.

a. Describe the payoff matrix for this game and show that it does not possess a Nash equilibrium strategy pair.

b. Show that with mixed strategies this game does have a Nash equilibrium if each player plays each number with probability ⅓. What is the value of this game?

10.3

Fudenberg and Tirole (1992) developed a game of stag-hunting based on an observation originally made by Rousseau. The two players in the game may either cooperate in catching a stag or each may set out on his own to catch a hare. The payoff matrix for this game is given by

		Player **B**	
		STAG	HARE
Player **A**	STAG	2, 2	0, 1
	HARE	1, 0	1, 1

a. Describe the Nash equilibria in this game.

b. Suppose B believes that A will use a mixed strategy in choosing how to hunt. How will B's optimal strategy choice depend on the probability A will play stag?

c. Suppose this game is expanded to n players (the game Rousseau had in mind) and that all n must cooperate in order for a stag to be caught. Assuming that the payoffs for one specific player, say B, remain the same and that all the other $n-1$ players will opt for mixed strategies, how will B's optimal strategy depend on the probabilities with which each of the other players plays stag? Explain why cooperation seems less likely in this larger game.

10.4

Players A and B have found $100 on the sidewalk and are arguing about how it should be split. A passerby suggests the following game: "Each of you state the number of dollars that you wish (d_A, d_B). If $d_A + d_B \leq 100$ you can keep the figure you name and I'll take the remainder. If $d_A + d_B > 100$, I'll keep the $100." Is there a unique Nash equilibrium in this game of continuous strategies?

10.5

The mixed strategy Nash equilibrium for the Battle of the Sexes game described in Example 10.4 may depend on the numerical values of the payoffs. To generalize this solution, assume that the payoff matrix for the game is given by

		B's STRATEGIES	
		MOUNTAIN	SEASIDE
A's STRATEGIES	MOUNTAIN	K, 1	0, 0
	SEASIDE	0, 0	1, K

where $K \geq 1$. Show how the Nash equilibrium in mixed strategies for this game depends on the value of K.

10.6

Consider the following dynamic game. Player B announces, "I have a bomb strapped to my body. If you (A) do not give me $1, I will set it off, killing each of us." Illustrate this game in extensive form and assess whether B's announced strategy for the game meets the criterion of subgame perfection.

10.7

In *A Treatise on the Family* (Cambridge: Harvard University Press, 1981), G. Becker proposes his famous Rotten Kid theorem as a game between a (potentially rotten) child, A, and his or her parent, B. A moves first and chooses an action, r, that affects both his or her own income $Y_A(r)$ $(Y_A' > 0)$ and the income of the parent $Y_B(r)$ $(Y_B' < 0)$. In the second stage of the game, the parent leaves a monetary bequest of L to the child. The child cares only for his or her own utility, $U_A(Y_A + L)$, but the parent maximizes $U_B(Y_B - L) + \lambda U_A$ where $\lambda > 0$ reflects the parent's altruism toward the child. Prove that the child will opt for that value of r that maximizes $Y_A + Y_B$ even though he or she has no altruistic intentions. (*Hint:* You must first find the parent's optimal bequest, then solve for the child's optimal strategy, given this subsequent parental behavior.)

10.8

The game of "chicken" is played by two macho teens who speed toward each other on a single-lane road. The first to veer off is branded the chicken, whereas the one who doesn't turn gains peer group esteem. Of course, if neither veers, both die in the resulting crash.

Payoffs to the chicken game are provided in the following table.

		B's STRATEGIES	
		CHICKEN	NOT CHICKEN
A's	CHICKEN	2, 2	1, 3
STRATEGIES	NOT CHICKEN	3, 1	0, 0

a. Does this game have a Nash equilibrium?
b. Is a threat by either not to chicken-out a credible one?
c. Would the ability of one player to firmly commit to a not-chicken strategy (by, for example, throwing away the steering wheel) be desirable for that player?

10.9

Consider the following game in which players A and B have 3 pure strategies

		B's STRATEGIES		
		L	M	R
	U	5, 5	2, 6	0, 7
A's STRATEGIES	M	6, 2	3, 3	0, 0
	D	7, 0	0, 0	1, 1

a. Suppose the game is played only once, what are the Nash equilibria in pure strategies?
b. Suppose this game is played exactly twice, what are the subgame perfect equilibria in pure strategies?
c. If this game were played repeatedly, under what conditions would the repeated A:U, B:L strategy be sustainable? How does your answer depend on your answers to parts a and b?

10.10

Consider the following sealed-bid auction for a rare baseball card. Player A values the card being auctioned at $600, player B values the card at $500, and these valuations are known to each player who will submit a sealed bid for the card. Whoever bids the most will win the card. If equal bids are submitted, the auctioneer will flip a coin to decide the winner. Each player must now decide how much to bid.

a. How would you categorize the strategies in this game? Do some strategies dominate others?
b. Does this game have a Nash equilibrium? Is it unique?
c. How would this game change if each player did not know the other's valuation for the card?

SUGGESTED READINGS

Fudenberg, D., and J. Tirole. *Game Theory.* Cambridge, Mass: MIT Press, 1991.
A complete text. Provides sketches of the proofs of several existence theorems for Nash equilibria. Also offers extensive coverage of recent topics involving games with incomplete information.

Gibbons, R. *Game Theory for Applied Economists.* Princeton: Princeton University Press, 1992.
A good introduction to many topics in game theory together with a large set of fully worked applications. Gibbons does a fine job of recasting many standard economic models in game-theoretic terms.

Kreps, D. M. *Game Theory and Economic Modeling.* Oxford: Clarendon Press, 1990.
An expanded version of a series of lectures. Hence, it lacks the completeness of a text. But this is a fine book for getting a feel for the purposes of game theory in its economic context.

Luce, R. D., and H. Raiffa. *Games and Decisions.* New York: John Wiley & Sons, 1957.
A classic text on game theory. Does not cover many later topics, especially those on repeated games. But the book does provide a number of useful links between game theory and statistical decision theory.

Von Neumann, J., and O. Morganstern. *Theory of Games and Economic Behavior.* Princeton: Princeton University Press, 1944.
The pioneering work in game theory. Some of the mathematics here is very difficult and has been superseded by more recent advances. But the book's development of the basic principles of the subject—especially expected utility maximization—remains one of the best sources available.

PRODUCTION AND SUPPLY

In this part we examine the production and supply of economic goods. Institutions that coordinate the transformation of inputs into outputs are called *firms*. They may be large institutions (such as General Motors, IBM, or the U.S. Department of Defense) or small ones (such as "Mom and Pop" stores or self-employed individuals). Although they may pursue different goals (IBM may seek maximum profits, whereas an Israeli kibbutz may try to make members of the kibbutz as well off as possible), all firms must make certain basic choices in the production process. The purpose of Part IV is to develop some methods of analyzing those choices.

In Chapter 11 we examine ways of modeling the physical relationship between inputs and outputs. We introduce the concept of a production function, a useful abstraction from the complexities of real-world production processes. Two measurable aspects of the production function are stressed: its returns to scale (that is, how output expands when all inputs are increased) and its elasticity of substitution (that is, how easily one input may be replaced by another while maintaining the same level of output). We also briefly describe how technical improvements are reflected in production functions.

The production function concept is then used in Chapter 12 to discuss costs of production. It is assumed that all firms seek to produce their output at the lowest possible cost, an assumption that permits the development of cost functions for the firm. Chapter 12 also focuses on how costs may differ depending on the amount of time a firm has to respond to changing circumstances. Both short-run and long-run cost functions are important components of our analysis of the supply decision.

In Chapter 13 we investigate the firm's supply decision; that is, we examine the factors that determine how much output a firm will produce. To do so we generally assume that the firm's manager will make output choices so as to achieve the maximum possible profit. In Chapter 13 we study the implications of this profit-maximization hypothesis in some detail. The chapter concludes with the fundamental model of supply behavior by profit-maximizing firms that we will use in many subsequent chapters.

CHAPTER 11

PRODUCTION FUNCTIONS

The principal activity of any firm is to turn inputs into outputs. Because economists are interested in the choices that the firm makes in accomplishing this goal, but wish to avoid discussing many of the engineering intricacies involved, they have chosen to construct an abstract model of production. In this model the relationship between inputs and outputs is formalized by a *production function* of the form

$$q = f(K, L, M, \ldots),\qquad\qquad (11.1)$$

where q represents the firm's output of a particular good during a period,[1] K represents the machine (that is, capital) usage during the period, L represents hours of labor input, M represents raw materials used,[2] and the notation indicates the possibility of other variables affecting the production process. Equation 11.1 is assumed to provide, for any conceivable set of inputs, the engineer's solution to the problem of how best to combine those inputs to get output.

In this section we shall study the change in output that is brought about by a change in one of the productive inputs. For the purposes of this examination (and indeed for most of the purposes of this book), it will be more convenient to use a simplified production function defined as follows:

VARIATIONS IN ONE INPUT

---

[1] Here we use a lowercase q to represent one firm's output. We reserve the uppercase Q to represent total output in a market.

[2] All inputs are assumed to be homogeneous—an obvious oversimplification. Sometimes raw material inputs are disregarded and output, q, is measured in terms of "value added."

DEFINITION

Production Function   The firm's *production function* for a particular good, q,

$$q = f(K, L) \tag{11.2}$$

shows the maximum amount of the good that can be produced using alternative combinations of capital (K) and labor (L).

Of course, most of our analysis will hold for any two inputs to the production process we might wish to examine. The terms "capital" and "labor" are used only for convenience. Similarly, it would be a simple matter to generalize our discussion to cases involving more than two inputs; and, occasionally, we will do so. For the most part, however, limiting our discussion to two inputs will be quite helpful because we can show these inputs on two-dimensional graphs.

Marginal Physical Product   To study variation in a single input, we define marginal physical product as follows:

DEFINITION

Marginal Physical Product   The *marginal physical product* of an input is the additional output that can be produced by employing one more unit of that input while holding all other inputs constant. Mathematically,

$$\text{marginal physical product of capital} = MP_K = \frac{\partial q}{\partial K} = f_K$$

$$\text{marginal physical product of labor} = MP_L = \frac{\partial q}{\partial L} = f_L. \tag{11.3}$$

Notice that the mathematical definitions of marginal product use partial derivatives, thereby properly reflecting the fact that all other input usage is held constant while the input of interest is being varied. For an example, consider a farmer hiring one more laborer to harvest the crop but holding all other inputs constant. The extra output this laborer produces is that farmhand's marginal physical product, measured in physical quantities, such as bushels of wheat, crates of oranges, or heads of lettuce. We might observe, for example, that 50 workers on a farm are able to produce 100 bushels of wheat per year, whereas 51 workers, with the same land and equipment, can produce 102 bushels. The marginal physical product of the fifty-first worker is then 2 bushels per year.

We might expect that the marginal physical product of an input depends on how much of that input is used. Labor, for example, cannot be added indefinitely to a given field (while keeping the amount of equipment, fertilizer, and so forth fixed) without eventually exhibiting some deterioration in its productivity. Mathematically, the assumption of diminishing marginal physical productivity is an assumption about the second-order partial derivatives of the production function:

Diminishing Marginal Productivity

$$\frac{\partial MP_K}{\partial K} = \frac{\partial^2 q}{\partial K^2} = f_{KK} < 0$$

$$\frac{\partial MP_L}{\partial L} = \frac{\partial^2 q}{\partial L^2} = f_{LL} < 0. \tag{11.4}$$

This assumption has a long history in economic analysis. In the nineteenth century, for example, Thomas Malthus argued that since the quantity of land is fixed but population is growing, the principle of a diminishing marginal productivity of labor implied serious problems for the future of humanity. In fact, Malthus's prediction was the primary reason that economics came to be called the "dismal science." Most modern economists would agree that Malthus did not adequately recognize the possibility that increases in capital equipment and technical advances (which, although held constant in our definition, in fact change over time) would prevent the decline of labor's productivity in agriculture. Nevertheless, the observation that the marginal productivity of labor (or any other input) declines when *all other inputs* are held constant is still recognized by economists as an empirically valid proposition.

In common usage the term "labor productivity" often means *average productivity*. When it is said that a certain industry has experienced productivity increases, this is taken to mean that output per unit of labor input has increased. Although the concept of average productivity is not nearly as important in theoretical economic discussions as marginal productivity is, it receives a great deal of attention in empirical discussions. Because average productivity is easily measured (say, as so many bushels of wheat per labor-hour input), it is often used as a measure of efficiency. We define the average product of labor (AP_L) to be

Average Physical Productivity

$$AP_L = \frac{\text{output}}{\text{labor input}} = \frac{q}{L} = \frac{f(K, L)}{L}. \tag{11.5}$$

Notice that AP_L depends on the level of capital employed. This observation will prove to be quite important when we examine the measurement of technical progress at the end of this chapter.

EXAMPLE 11.1

A TWO-INPUT PRODUCTION FUNCTION

Suppose the production function for flyswatters during a particular period can be represented by

$$q = f(K, L) = 600K^2L^2 - K^3L^3. \tag{11.6}$$

To construct the marginal and average productivity relations of labor (L) for this function, we must assume a particular value for the other input, capital (K). Suppose $K = 10$. Then the production function is given by

$$q = 60{,}000L^2 - 1000L^3. \tag{11.7}$$

Marginal Product.   The marginal productivity function is given by

$$MP_L = \frac{\partial q}{\partial L} = 120{,}000L - 3000L^2, \tag{11.8}$$

which diminishes as L increases, eventually becoming negative. This implies that q reaches a maximum value. Setting MP_L equal to 0,

$$120{,}000L - 3000L^2 = 0 \tag{11.9}$$

yields

$$40L = L^2 \tag{11.10}$$

or

$$L = 40 \tag{11.11}$$

as the point at which q reaches its maximum value. Labor input beyond 40 units per period actually reduces total output. For example, when $L = 40$, Equation 11.7 shows that $q = 32$ million flyswatters, whereas when $L = 50$, production of flyswatters amounts to only 25 million.

Average Product.   To find the average productivity of labor in flyswatter production, we divide q by L, still holding $K = 10$:

$$AP_L = \frac{q}{L} = 60{,}000L - 1000L^2. \tag{11.12}$$

Again, this is an inverted parabola that reaches its maximum value when

$$\frac{\partial AP_L}{\partial L} = 60{,}000 - 2000L = 0, \tag{11.13}$$

which occurs when $L = 30$. At this value for labor input, Equation 11.12 shows that $AP_L = 900{,}000$, and Equation 11.8 shows that MP_L is also 900,000. When

AP_L is at a maximum, average and marginal productivities of labor are equal.[3]

Notice the relationship between total output and average productivity that is illustrated by this example. Even though total production of flyswatters is greater with 40 workers (32 million) than with 30 workers (27 million), output per worker is higher in the second case. With 40 workers, each worker produces 800,000 flyswatters per period, whereas with 30 workers each worker produces 900,000. Because capital input (flyswatter presses) is held constant, in this example the diminishing marginal productivity of labor eventually results in a declining level of output per worker.

QUERY: How would an increase in K from 10 to 11 affect the MP_L and AP_L functions here? Explain your results intuitively.

ISOQUANT MAPS AND THE RATE OF TECHNICAL SUBSTITUTION

To illustrate possible substitution of one input for another in a production function, we use its *isoquant map*. Again we study a production function of the form $q = f(K, L)$, with the understanding that "capital" and "labor" are simply convenient examples of any two inputs that might happen to be of interest. An isoquant (from *iso*, meaning "equal") records those combinations of K and L that are able to produce a given level of output. For example, all those combinations of K and L that fall on the curve labeled "$q = 10$" in Figure 11.1 are capable of producing ten units of output per period. This isoquant then records the fact that there are many alternative ways of producing ten units of output. One way might be represented by point A: We would use L_A and K_A to produce ten units of output. Alternatively, we might prefer to use relatively less capital and more labor and therefore would choose a point such as B. Hence, we may define an isoquant as follows:

DEFINITION

Isoquant An *isoquant* shows those combinations of K and L that can produce a given level of output (say, q_0). Mathematically, an isoquant records the set of K and L that satisfies

$$f(K, L) = q_0. \tag{11.14}$$

---

[3] This result is quite general. Since

$$\frac{\partial AP_L}{\partial L} = \frac{L \cdot MP_L - q}{L^2},$$

at a maximum $L \cdot MP_L = q$ or $MP_L = AP_L$.

FIGURE 11.1

AN ISOQUANT MAP

Isoquants record the alternative combinations of inputs that can be used to produce a given level of output. The slope of these curves shows the rate at which L can be substituted for K while keeping output constant. The negative of this slope is called the (marginal) rate of technical substitution (RTS). In the figure the RTS is positive and diminishing for increasing inputs of labor.

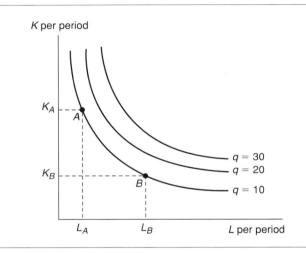

There are many isoquants in the $K - L$ plane. Each isoquant represents a different level of output. Isoquants record successively higher levels of output as we move in a northeasterly direction. Presumably, using more of each of the inputs will permit output to increase. Two other isoquants (for $q = 20$ and $q = 30$) are shown in Figure 11.1. You will notice the similarity between an isoquant map and the individual's indifference curve map discussed in Parts II and III. They are indeed similar concepts, since both represent "contour" maps of a particular function. For isoquants, however, the labeling of the curves is measurable—an output of ten units per period has a quantifiable meaning. Economists are therefore more interested in studying the shape of production functions than in examining the exact shape of utility functions.

The Marginal Rate of Technical Substitution (RTS) The slope of an isoquant shows how one input can be traded for another while holding output constant. Examining the slope provides information about the technical possibility of substituting labor for capital. A formal definition is provided by:

DEFINITION

Marginal Rate of Technical Substitution The *marginal rate of technical substitution (RTS)* shows the rate at which labor can be substituted for capital while holding output constant along an isoquant. In mathematical terms,

$$RTS \ (L \ for \ K) = \frac{-dK}{dL}\bigg|_{q \ = \ q_0}.$$ (11.15)

In this definition the notation is intended as a reminder that output is to be held constant as L is substituted for K. The particular value of this trade-off rate will depend not only on the level of output but also on the quantities of capital and labor being used. Its value depends on the point on the isoquant map at which the slope is to be measured.

In order to examine the shape of production function isoquants, it is useful to prove the following result: the RTS (of L for K) is equal to the ratio of the marginal physical productivity of labor (MP_L) to the marginal physical productivity of capital (MP_K). The proof of this assertion proceeds by setting up the total differential of the production function:

RTS and Marginal Productivities

$$dq = \frac{\partial f}{\partial L} \cdot dL + \frac{\partial f}{\partial K} \cdot dK = MP_L \cdot dL + MP_K \cdot dK,$$ (11.16)

which records how small changes in L and K affect output. Along an isoquant, $dq = 0$ (output is constant) so

$$MP_L \cdot dL = -MP_K \cdot dK.$$ (11.17)

This says that along an isoquant, the gain in output from increasing L slightly is exactly balanced by the loss in output from suitably decreasing K. Rearranging terms a bit gives

$$-\frac{dK}{dL}\bigg|_{q \ = \ q_0} = RTS \ (L \ for \ K) = \frac{MP_L}{MP_K}$$ (11.18)

as was to be shown.

We can use the result of Equation 11.18 to see that those isoquants that we observe must be negatively sloped. Since both MP_L and MP_K will be nonnegative (no firm would choose to use a costly input that reduced output), the RTS also will be positive (or perhaps zero). Because the slope of an isoquant is the negative of the RTS, any firm we observe will not be operating on the positively sloped portion of an isoquant. Although it is mathematically possible to devise production functions whose isoquants have positive slopes at some points, it would not make economic sense for a firm to operate at those input choices.

Reasons for a Diminishing *RTS*   The isoquants in Figure 11.1 are drawn not only with a negative slope (as they should be) but also as convex curves. Along any one of the curves, the *RTS* is *diminishing*. For high ratios of K to L, the *RTS* is a large positive number, indicating that a great deal of capital can be given up if one more unit of labor becomes available. On the other hand, when a lot of labor is already being used, the *RTS* is low, signifying that only a small amount of capital can be traded for an additional unit of labor if output is to be held constant. This assumption would seem to have some relationship to the assumption of diminishing marginal productivity. A hasty use of Equation 11.18 might lead one to conclude that a rise in L accompanied by a fall in K would result in a rise in MP_K, a fall in MP_L, and, therefore, a fall in the *RTS*. The problem with this quick "proof" is that the marginal productivity of an input depends on the level of *both* inputs—changes in L affect MP_K and vice versa. It is generally not possible to derive a diminishing *RTS* from the assumption of diminishing marginal productivity alone.

To see why this is so mathematically, assume that $q = f(K, L)$ and that f_K and f_L are positive (that is, the marginal productivities are positive). Assume also that $f_{KK} < 0$ and $f_{LL} < 0$ (that the marginal productivities are diminishing). In order to show that isoquants are convex, we would like to show that $d(RTS)/dL < 0$. Since $RTS = f_L/f_K$, we have

$$\frac{dRTS}{dL} = \frac{d(f_L/f_K)}{dL}. \tag{11.19}$$

Because f_L and f_K are functions of both K and L, we must be careful in taking the derivative of this expression:

$$\frac{dRTS}{dL} = \frac{[f_K(f_{LL} + f_{LK} \cdot dK/dL) - f_L(f_{KL} + f_{KK} \cdot dK/dL)]}{(f_K)^2}. \tag{11.20}$$

Using the fact that $dK/dL = -f_L/f_K$ along an isoquant and Young's theorem ($f_{KL} = f_{LK}$), we have

$$\frac{dRTS}{dL} = \frac{(f_K^2 f_{LL} - 2f_K f_L f_{KL} + f_L^2 f_{KK})}{(f_K)^3}. \tag{11.21}$$

Since we have assumed $f_K > 0$, the denominator of this function is positive.

Hence, the whole fraction will be negative if the numerator is negative. Because f_{LL} and f_{KK} are both assumed to be negative, the numerator definitely will be negative if f_{KL} is positive. If we can assume this, we have shown that $dRTS/dL < 0$ (that the isoquants are convex).[4]

Intuitively, it seems reasonable that the cross-partial derivative $f_{KL} = f_{LK}$ should be positive. Since $f_{LK} = \partial MP_L / \partial K$, we are interested in how an increase in capital affects the marginal physical productivity of labor (or vice versa), and it seems plausible that if workers had more capital, they would have higher marginal productivities. But, although this is probably the most prevalent case, it does not necessarily have to be so. Many plausible production functions have $f_{KL} < 0$, at least for some input values. When we assume a diminishing RTS (as we will throughout most of our discussion), we are therefore making a somewhat stronger assumption than simply diminishing marginal productivities for each input—specifically, we are assuming that marginal productivities diminish "rapidly enough" to compensate for any possible negative cross-productivity effects.

Importance of Cross-Productivity Effects

EXAMPLE 11.2

A DIMINISHING *RTS*

In Example 11.1 the production function for flyswatters was given by

$$q = f(K, L) = 600K^2L^2 - K^3L^3. \qquad (11.22)$$

General marginal productivity functions for this production function are

$$MP_L = f_L = \frac{\partial q}{\partial L} = 1200K^2L - 3K^3L^2$$

$$\qquad (11.23)$$

$$MP_K = f_K = \frac{\partial q}{\partial K} = 1200KL^2 - 3K^2L^3.$$

Notice that each of these depends on the values of both inputs. Simple factoring shows that these marginal productivities will be positive for values of K and L for which $KL < 400$.

Since

$$f_{LL} = 1200K^2 - 6K^3L$$

---

[4] As we pointed out in Chapter 2, functions for which the numerator in Equation 11.21 is negative are called (strictly) quasi-concave functions.

and

$$f_{KK} = 1200L^2 - 6KL^3,$$ (11.24)

it is clear that this function exhibits diminishing marginal productivities for sufficiently large values of K and L. Indeed, again by factoring each expression, it is easy to show that $f_{LL}, f_{KK} < 0$ if $KL > 200$. Even within the range $200 < KL < 400$ where the marginal productivity relations for this function behave "normally," however, this production function may not necessarily have a diminishing RTS. Cross-differentiation of either of the marginal productivity functions (Equation 11.23) yields

$$f_{KL} = f_{LK} = 2400KL - 9K^2L^2,$$ (11.25)

which is positive only for $KL < 266$.

The numerator of Equation 11.21 will therefore definitely be negative for $200 < KL < 266$, but for larger scale flyswatter factories, the case is not so clear since f_{KL} is negative. When f_{KL} is negative, increases in labor input reduce the marginal productivity of capital. Hence, the intuitive argument that the assumption of diminishing marginal productivities yields an unambiguous prediction about what will happen to the RTS ($= f_L/f_K$) as L increases and K falls is incorrect. It all depends on the relative effects on marginal productivities of diminishing marginal productivities (which tend to reduce f_L and increase f_K) and the contrary effects on cross-marginal productivities (which tend to increase f_L and reduce f_K). Still, for this flyswatter case, it is true that the RTS is diminishing throughout the range of K and L, where marginal productivities are positive. For higher values of K and L, the diminishing marginal productivities exhibited by the function are sufficient to overcome the influence of a negative value for f_{KL} on the convexity of isoquants.

QUERY: For cases where $K = L$, what can be said about the marginal productivities of this production function? How would this simplify the numerator for Equation 11.21? How does this permit you to more easily evaluate this expression for some larger values of K and L?

RETURNS TO SCALE

We now proceed to characterize production functions. The first important question that might be asked about them is how output responds to increases in all inputs together. For example, suppose that all inputs were doubled: Would output double or would the relationship not be quite so simple? This is a question of the *returns to scale* exhibited by the production function that has been of interest to economists ever since Adam Smith intensively studied the production of pins. Smith identified two forces that came into operation when the conceptual experiment of doubling all inputs was performed. First, a doubling of scale permits a greater division of labor and specialization of function. Hence, there is some presumption that efficiency might increase— production might more than double. Second, doubling of the inputs also entails some loss in efficiency because managerial overseeing may become more difficult given the larger scale of the firm. Which of these two tendencies will have a greater effect is an important empirical question.

Presenting a technical definition of these concepts is misleadingly simple:

DEFINITION

Returns to Scale If the production function is given by $q = f(K, L)$ and all inputs are multiplied by the same positive constant, m (where $m > 1$), we classify the *returns to scale* of the production function by

EFFECT ON OUTPUT	RETURNS TO SCALE
I. $f(mK, mL) = mf(K, L) = mq$	Constant
II. $f(mK, mL) < mf(K, L) = mq$	Decreasing
III. $f(mK, mL) > mf(K, L) = mq$	Increasing

In intuitive terms, if a proportionate increase in inputs increases output by the same proportion, the production function exhibits constant returns to scale.[5] If output increases less than proportionately, the function exhibits diminishing returns to scale. And if output increases more than proportionately, there are increasing returns to scale. It is theoretically possible for a function to exhibit constant returns to scale for some levels of input usage and increasing or decreasing returns for other levels. Often, however, economists refer to *the* degree of returns to scale of a production function with the implicit notion that only a fairly narrow range of variation in input usage and the related level of output is being considered.

Constant Returns to Scale and the *RTS*

Constant returns-to-scale production functions occupy an important place in economic theory. This is primarily because there are economic reasons for expecting an industry's production function to exhibit constant returns. If all production in an industry is carried on in plants of an "efficient" size, then doubling all inputs could most reasonably be accomplished by doubling the number of these plants. But presumably this would double output since there are now exactly twice as many plants. Hence, the *industry* would behave as if it had a constant returns-to-scale production function. As long as doubling

---

[5] Mathematically, such constant returns-to-scale functions are said to be "homogeneous of degree 1" or, sometimes, "linear homogeneous." The general notion of homogeneous functions was discussed briefly in Chapter 5 (see especially footnote 1).

of inputs is brought about by doubling the number of optimally sized plants, this will be the case.

Constant returns-to-scale production functions have the useful theoretical property that the *RTS* between two factors, say, K and L, depends only on the *ratio* of K to L, not on the scale of production. This can be shown with an intuitive argument. Suppose that we have a constant returns-to-scale production function such that when $K = 10$ and $L = 10$, $q = 20$. Suppose also that at this point the *RTS* of L for K is equal to 2. Therefore, 8 units of K and 11 units of L also will yield $q = 20$. Now consider doubling all inputs. What we want to show is that the *RTS* at the new input configuration ($K = 20$, $L = 20$) is also equal to 2. We know, because of the assumption of constant returns to scale, that the input combination ($K = 20$, $L = 20$) will produce 40 units of output and so will the input combination ($K = 16$, $L = 22$). Therefore, the *RTS* at ($K = 20$, $L = 20$) is given by $-(-4)/2 = 2$. That was the result to be shown: The *RTS* does not depend on the scale of production, but only on the ratio of K to L.[6]

Geometrically, all the isoquants of a constant returns-to-scale production function are "radial blowups" of the unit isoquant. Along any ray through the origin (a line along which K/L is constant), the slope of the isoquants is the same. This is illustrated in Figure 11.2, which also shows that the isoquants are equally spaced as output expands; thus, they exhibit the constant proportional relationship between increases in all inputs and increases in output.[7]

The *n*-Input Case

The definition of returns to scale can be easily generalized to a production function with n inputs. If that production function is given by

$$q = f(X_1, X_2, \ldots, X_n),$$ (11.26)

and all inputs are multiplied by a positive constant m, we have

$$f(mX_1, mX_2, \ldots, mX_n) = m^k f(X_1, X_2, \ldots, X_n) = m^k q$$ (11.27)

for some constant k. If $k = 1$, the production function exhibits constant returns

---

[6] For a formal proof, see Problem 11.10.

[7] As we discussed in Part II, functions for which all level curves are radial expansions are called *homothetic*. Any monotonic transformation of a homogeneous function will be homothetic (see Problem 11.10). Hence, even functions that do not necessarily exhibit constant returns to scale may have homothetic isoquant maps. Two important cases are the Cobb-Douglas and CES functions discussed later in this chapter.

FIGURE 11.2

**ISOQUANT MAP FOR A CONSTANT
RETURNS-TO-SCALE PRODUCTION FUNCTION**

For a constant returns-to-scale production function, the *RTS* depends only on
the ratio of *K* to *L*, not on the scale of production. Consequently, each isoquant
will be a radial blowup of the unit isoquant. Along any ray through the origin
(a ray of constant *K/L*), the *RTS* will be the same on all isoquants.

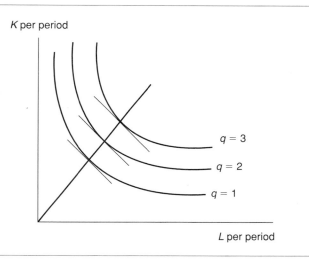

to scale. Diminishing and increasing returns to scale correspond to the cases
$k < 1$ and $k > 1$, respectively.

The crucial part of this mathematical definition is the requirement that all
inputs be increased by the same proportion, *m*. In many real-world
production processes, this provision may make little economic sense. For
example, a firm may have only one "boss" and that number would not
necessarily be doubled even if all other inputs were. Or the output of a farm
may depend on the fertility of the soil. It may not be literally possible to
double the acres planted while maintaining fertility, since the new land may
not be as good as that already under cultivation. Hence, some inputs may
have to be fixed (or at least imperfectly variable) for most practical purposes.
In such cases some degree of diminishing productivity (a result of increasing
employment of variable inputs) seems likely, although this cannot properly
be called "diminishing returns to scale" because of the presence of inputs that
are held fixed.

**THE ELASTICITY
OF SUBSTITUTION**

Another important characteristic of the production function is how "easy" it is to substitute one input for another. Is it, for example, relatively simple to substitute capital for labor while keeping output constant? This is essentially a question of the shape of a single isoquant rather than a question about the whole isoquant map. Along one isoquant it has been assumed that the rate of technical substitution will decrease as the capital-labor ratio decreases (that is, as K/L decreases); now we wish to define some parameter that measures this degree of responsiveness. If the RTS does not change at all for changes in K/L, we might say that substitution is easy, since the ratio of the marginal productivities of the two inputs does not change as the input mix changes. Alternatively, if the RTS changes rapidly for small changes in K/L, we would say that substitution is difficult, since minor variations in the input

FIGURE 11.3

GRAPHIC DESCRIPTION OF THE ELASTICITY OF SUBSTITUTION

In moving from point A to point B on the $q = q_0$ isoquant, both the capital-labor ratio (K/L) and the RTS will change. The elasticity of substitution (σ) is defined to be the ratio of these proportional changes. It is a measure of how curved the isoquant is.

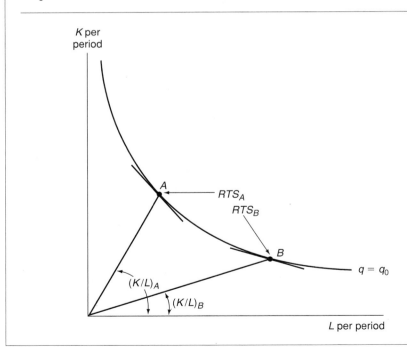

mix will have a substantial effect on the inputs' relative productivities. A scale-free measure of this responsiveness is provided by the *elasticity of substitution,* a concept we briefly encountered in Part II. Now we can provide a formal definition:

DEFINITION

Elasticity of Substitution   For the production function $q = f(K, L)$, the *elasticity of substitution* (σ) measures the proportionate change in K/L relative to the proportionate change in the *RTS* along an isoquant. That is,

$$\sigma = \frac{\text{percent } \Delta(K/L)}{\text{percent } \Delta RTS} = \frac{dK/L}{dRTS} \cdot \frac{RTS}{K/L} = \frac{\partial ln\, K/L}{\partial ln\, RTS} . \qquad (11.28)$$

Since, along an isoquant, K/L and *RTS* are assumed to move in the same direction, the value of σ is always positive. Graphically, this concept is illustrated in Figure 11.3 as a movement from point A to point B on an isoquant. In this movement both the *RTS* and the ratio K/L will change, and we are interested in the relative magnitude of these changes. If σ is high, the *RTS* will not change much relative to K/L, and the isoquant will be relatively flat. On the other hand, a low value of σ implies a rather sharply curved isoquant: The *RTS* will change by a substantial amount as K/L changes. In general, it is possible that the elasticity of substitution will vary as one moves along an isoquant and as the scale of production changes. Frequently, however, it is convenient to assume that σ is constant along an isoquant. If constant returns to scale are also assumed, then, since all the isoquants are merely radial blowups of each other, σ will be the same along all isoquants. Many investigations of real-world production functions have centered on this *constant returns-to-scale, constant elasticity of substitution* type.[8] Some of the most important of these functions are discussed in detail later in this chapter.

Generalizing the elasticity of substitution to the many-input case raises several complications. One possible approach is to adopt a definition analogous to Equation 11.28; that is, to define the elasticity of substitution

The *n*-Input Case

---

[8] The elasticity of substitution can be phrased directly in terms of the production function and its derivatives in the constant returns-to-scale case as

$$\sigma = \frac{(\partial q/\partial L) \cdot (\partial q/\partial K)}{q \cdot (\partial^2 q/\partial L \partial K)}.$$

But this form is quite cumbersome. Hence usually the logarithmic definition in Equation 11.28 is easiest to apply. For a compact summary, see P. Berck and K. Sydsaeter, *Economist's Mathematical Manual* (Berlin: Springer-Verlag, 1991), Chapter 4.

between two inputs to be the proportionate change in the ratio of the two inputs to the proportionate change in the *RTS* between them while holding output constant. To make this definition complete, it would also be necessary to require that all inputs other than the two being examined be held constant. However, this latter requirement (which is not relevant when there are only two inputs) restricts the value of this potential definition. In real-world production processes, it is likely that any change in the ratio of two inputs will also be accompanied by changes in the levels of other inputs. Some of these other inputs may be complementary with the ones being changed, whereas others may be substitutes, and to hold them constant creates a rather artificial restriction. For this reason an alternative definition of the elasticity of substitution that permits such complementarity and substitutability is generally used in the *n*-good case. We will briefly describe this alternative concept in the next chapter and make more extensive use of it when we examine input demands in Chapter 21.

SOME COMMON PRODUCTION FUNCTIONS

In this section we illustrate four simple production functions, each characterized by a different elasticity of substitution. These are illustrated only for the case of two inputs, but generalization to many inputs is easily accomplished as shown by the extensions for this chapter. Again, these functions closely resemble the utility functions described in Chapter 3.

Case 1: Linear Function ($\sigma = \infty$)

Suppose that the production function is given by

$$q = f(K, L) = aK + bL. \tag{11.29}$$

It is easy to show that this production function exhibits constant returns to scale: For any $m > 0$,

$$f(mK, mL) = amK + bmL = m(aK + bL) = mf(K, L). \tag{11.30}$$

All isoquants for this production function are parallel straight lines with slope $-b/a$. Such an isoquant map is pictured in panel (a) of Figure 11.4. Since along any straight-line isoquant, the *RTS* is constant, the denominator in the definition of σ (Equation 11.28) is equal to 0, and hence σ is equal to infinity. Although this linear production function is a useful example, it is rarely encountered in practice because few production processes are characterized by such ease of substitution. Indeed, in this case capital and labor can be thought of as perfect substitutes for each other. An industry characterized by such a production function could use *only* capital or *only* labor depending on these inputs' prices. It is hard to envision such a production process: Every machine needs someone to press its buttons, and every laborer requires some capital equipment, however modest.

The production function characterized by $\sigma = 0$ is the important case of a *fixed-proportions production function*. Capital and labor must always be used in a fixed ratio. The isoquants for this production function are L-shaped and are pictured in panel (b) of Figure 11.4. A firm characterized by this production function will always operate along the ray where the ratio K/L is constant. To operate at some point other than at the vertex of the isoquants would be inefficient, since the same output could be produced with fewer inputs by moving along the isoquant toward the vertex. Because K/L is a constant, it is easy to see from the definition of the elasticity of substitution that σ must equal 0.

Case 2: Fixed Proportions ($\sigma = 0$)

The mathematical form of the fixed-proportions production function is given by

$$q = \min (aK, bL) \quad a, b > 0, \tag{11.31}$$

where the operator "min" means that q is given by the smaller of the two values in parentheses. For example, suppose that $aK < bL$; then $q = aK$ and we would say that capital is the binding constraint in this production process. The employment of more labor would not raise output, and hence the marginal product of labor is zero; additional labor is superfluous in this case. Similarly, if $aK > bL$, labor is the binding constraint on output and additional capital is superfluous. When $aK = bL$, both inputs are fully utilized. When this happens, $K/L = b/a$ and production takes place at a vertex on the isoquant map. If both inputs are costly, this is the only cost-minimizing place to operate. The locus of all such vertices is a straight line through the origin with a slope given by b/a.

The fixed-proportions production function has a wide range of applications.[9] Many machines, for example, require a certain number of people to run them, but any excess labor is superfluous. Consider combining capital (a lawn mower) and labor to mow a lawn. It will always take one person to run the mower, and either input without the other is not able to produce any output at all. It may be that many machines are of this type and require a fixed complement of workers per machine.[10]

---

[9] With the form reflected by Equation 11.31, the fixed-proportions production function exhibits constant returns to scale since

$$f(mK, mL) = \min (amK, bmL) = m \cdot \min (aK, bL) = mf(K, L)$$

for any $m > 0$. Increasing or decreasing returns can be easily incorporated into the functions by using a nonlinear transformation of this functional form, such as $[f(K, L)]^\gamma$ where γ may be greater than or less than unity.

[10] The lawn mower example points up another possibility, however. Presumably there is some leeway in choosing what size of lawn mower to buy. Hence, prior to the actual purchase, the capital-labor ratio in lawn mowing can be considered variable: Any device, from a pair of clippers to a gang mower, might be chosen. Once the mower is purchased, however, the capital-labor ratio becomes fixed.

FIGURE 11.4

ISOQUANT MAPS FOR PRODUCTION FUNCTIONS WITH VARIOUS VALUES FOR σ

Three possible values for the elasticity of substitution are illustrated in these figures. In (a) capital and labor are perfect substitutes. In this case the *RTS* will not change as the capital-labor ratio changes. In (b), the fixed-proportions case, no substitution is possible. The capital-labor ratio is fixed at b/a. A case of limited substitutability is illustrated in (c).

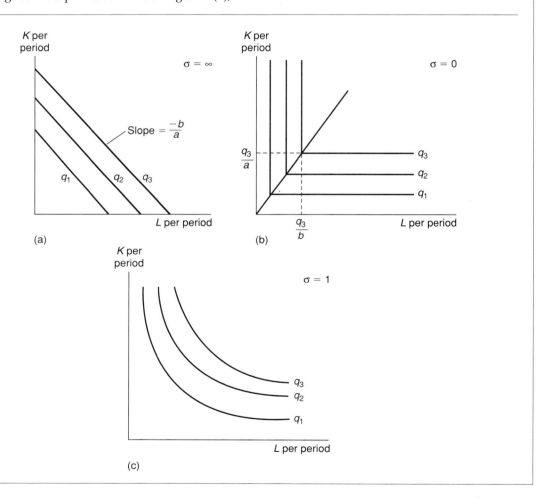

The production function for which $\sigma = 1$ is called a *Cobb-Douglas production function*[11] and provides a middle ground between the two polar cases previously discussed. Isoquants for the Cobb-Douglas case have the "normal" convex shape and are shown in panel (c) of Figure 11.4. The mathematical form of the Cobb-Douglas production function is given by

Case 3: Cobb-Douglas ($\sigma = 1$)

$$q = f(K, L) = AK^a L^b, \qquad (11.32)$$

where A, a, and b are all positive constants.

The Cobb-Douglas function can exhibit any degree of returns to scale depending on the values of a and b. Suppose all inputs were increased by a factor of m. Then

$$f(mK, mL) = A(mK)^a(mL)^b = Am^{a+b}K^a L^b$$
$$= m^{a+b}f(K, L). \qquad (11.33)$$

Hence, if $a + b = 1$, the Cobb-Douglas function exhibits constant returns to scale since output also increases by a factor of m. If $a + b > 1$, the function exhibits increasing returns to scale, whereas $a + b < 1$ corresponds to the decreasing returns-to-scale case. For the constant returns-to-scale case, it is a simple matter to show that the elasticity of substitution is 1 for the Cobb-Douglas function.[12] This fact has led researchers to use the function for a general description of aggregate production relationships in many countries.

The Cobb-Douglas function has also proved to be quite useful in many applications because it is linear in logarithms:

$$\ln q = \ln A + a \ln K + b \ln L. \qquad (11.34)$$

The constant a is then the elasticity of output with respect to capital input,

---

[11] Named after C. W. Cobb and P. H. Douglas. See P. H. Douglas, *The Theory of Wages* (New York: Macmillan Co., 1934), pp. 132–135.

[12] For the Cobb-Douglas,

$$RTS = \frac{f_L}{f_K} = \frac{bAK^a L^{b-1}}{aAK^{a-1}L^b} = \frac{b}{a}\frac{K}{L}.$$

or

$$\ln RTS = \ln\left(\frac{b}{a}\right) + \ln\left(\frac{K}{L}\right).$$

Hence:

$$\sigma = \frac{\partial \ln K/L}{\partial \ln RTS} = 1.$$

and b is the elasticity of output with respect to labor input.[13] These constants can sometimes be estimated from actual data, and such estimates may be used to measure returns to scale (by examining the sum $a + b$) and for other purposes.

Case 4: CES Production Function

A functional form that incorporates all of the three previous cases and allows σ to take on other values as well is the Constant Elasticity of Substitution (CES) production function first introduced by Arrow et al. in 1961.[14] This function is given by

$$q = f(K, L) = [K^\rho + L^\rho]^{\epsilon/\rho} \tag{11.35}$$

for $\rho \leq 1$, $\rho \neq 0$, and $\epsilon > 0$. This function closely resembles the CES utility function discussed in Chapter 3, though now we have added the exponent ϵ/ρ to permit explicit introduction of scale factors. For $\epsilon > 1$ the function exhibits increasing returns to scale, whereas for $\epsilon < 1$ it exhibits diminishing returns.

Direct application of the definition of σ to this function[15] gives the important result that

$$\sigma = \frac{1}{1 - \rho}. \tag{11.36}$$

Hence, the linear, fixed proportions and Cobb-Douglas cases correspond to $\rho = 1$, $\rho = -\infty$, and $\rho = 0$, respectively. Proof of this result for the fixed proportions and Cobb-Douglas cases requires a limit argument.

Often the CES function is used with a distributional weight, β $(0 \leq \beta \leq 1)$, to indicate the relative significance of the inputs:

$$q = f(K, L) = [\beta K^\rho + (1 - \beta)L^\rho]^{\epsilon/\rho}. \tag{11.37}$$

With constant returns to scale and $\rho = 0$, this function converges to the Cobb-Douglas form

---

[13] The proof follows those used in Chapter 7. Define the output elasticity for capital, say, as

$$e_{q,K} = \frac{\partial q}{\partial K} \cdot \frac{K}{q} = \frac{\partial \ln q}{\partial \ln K}.$$

Hence, by Equation 11.34, $e_{q,K} = a$. Similarly, $e_{q,L} = b$.

[14] K. J. Arrow, H. B. Chenery, B. S. Minhas, and R. M. Solow, "Capital-Labor Substitution and Economic Efficiency," *Review of Economics and Statistics* (August 1961): 225–250.

[15] Since $RTS = f_L/f_K = \dfrac{\epsilon/\rho q^{1-\rho/\epsilon}\rho L^{\rho-1}}{\epsilon/\rho q^{1-\rho/\epsilon}\rho K^{\rho-1}} = \left(\dfrac{L}{K}\right)^{\rho-1} = \left(\dfrac{K}{L}\right)^{1-\rho}$, the definition shows $\sigma = \dfrac{\partial \ln K/L}{\partial \ln RTS} = \dfrac{1}{1-\rho}$.

Notice that the presence of ρ in the scale effect, ϵ/ρ, assures that f_L, f_K are positive even when $\rho < 0$.

$$q = f(K, L) = K^\beta L^{1-\beta}, \tag{11.38}$$

which (as we discuss in Chapter 21) suggests a close connection between the parameter β and the income shares accruing to capital and labor.

EXAMPLE 11.3

A COBB-DOUGLAS PRODUCTION FUNCTION

The Cobb-Douglas production function offers a particularly simple example for illustrating the returns to scale and elasticity of substitution concepts. It also provides a chance to return once again to hamburgers (q), which are produced according to the Cobb-Douglas function

$$q = 10K^{1/2}L^{1/2}. \tag{11.39}$$

Because the exponents in this function sum to 1.0, it exhibits constant returns to scale—with $K = 10$, $L = 10$, $q = 100$ hamburgers per hour, whereas with $K = 20$, $L = 20$, production is 200 hamburgers per hour. The isoquant map for hamburger production can be derived by setting output equal to various values. For example, the 50-hamburger isoquant is given by

$$q = 50 = 10K^{1/2}L^{1/2} \tag{11.40}$$

or

$$KL = 25. \tag{11.41}$$

Similarly, 100 hamburgers can be produced using combinations of K and L that satisfy

$$KL = 100. \tag{11.42}$$

The isoquants in this Cobb-Douglas function are therefore rectangular hyperbolas as shown in Figure 11.5. As is the case for all constant returns-to-scale production functions, these isoquants are simply radial expansions of the unit isoquant.

The RTS in hamburger production can easily be calculated:

$$RTS\ (L\ \text{for}\ K) = f_L/f_K = \frac{5L^{-1/2}K^{1/2}}{5L^{1/2}K^{-1/2}} = \frac{K}{L}. \tag{11.43}$$

This result illustrates three facts about the curvature of hamburger isoquants. First, the RTS clearly diminishes as L increases and K decreases. Second, RTS depends only on the ratio of K to L, not on the absolute level of these inputs. In this case a doubling of K and L does not change the RTS. Finally, Equation 11.43 makes clear that the elasticity of substitution

FIGURE 11.5

**GRAPH OF THE $q = 50$ AND $q = 100$ ISOQUANTS
FOR THE PRODUCTION FUNCTION $q = 10K^{1/2}L^{1/2}$**

These isoquants are taken directly from Equations 11.41 and 11.42. They show
the combinations of K and L that can produce 50 and 100 hamburgers per hour,
respectively. The isoquants clearly display a diminishing RTS.

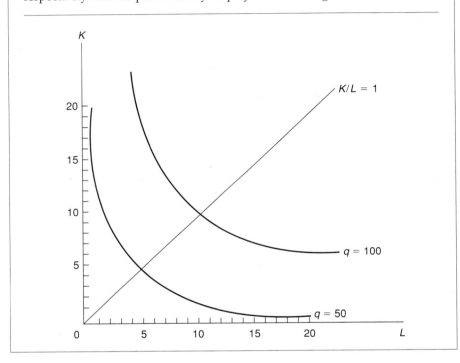

is 1 here—the RTS changes exactly in proportion to changes in the
K/L ratio (indeed, they are equal) for movements along the isoquant.
In later chapters we will return to our examination of hamburger production as we pursue the nature of supply-demand equilibrium in this
market.

QUERY: In what ways would the isoquant map for hamburger production be
changed if the production function exhibited increasing returns to scale
($q = 10K^{2/3}L^{2/3}$) or decreasing returns to scale ($q = 10K^{1/3}L^{1/3}$)?

Methods of production improve over time, and it is important to be able to capture these improvements in the production function concept. A simplified view of such progress is provided by Figure 11.6. Initially, isoquant q_0 records those combinations of capital and labor that can be used to produce an output level of q_0. Following the development of superior production techniques, this isoquant shifts to q_0'. Now the same level of output can be produced with fewer inputs. One way to measure this improvement is by noting that with a level of capital input of, say, K_1, it previously took L_2 units of labor to produce q_0, whereas now it takes only L_1. Output per worker has risen from q_0/L_2 to q_0/L_1. But one must be careful in this type of calculation. An increase in capital input to K_2 would also have permitted a reduction in labor input

TECHNICAL PROGRESS

FIGURE 11.6

TECHNICAL PROGRESS

Technical progress shifts the q_0 isoquant toward the origin. The new q_0 isoquant, q_0', shows that a given level of output can now be produced with less input. For example, with K_1 units of capital, it now only takes L_1 units of labor to produce q_0, whereas before the technical advance, it took L_2 units of labor.

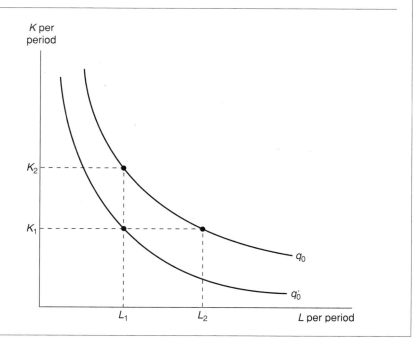

to L_1 along the original q_0 isoquant. In this case output for workers would also rise, although there would have been no true technical progress. Use of the production function concept can help to differentiate between these two concepts and therefore allow economists to obtain an accurate estimate of the rate of technical change.

Measuring Technical Progress

The first observation to be made about technical progress is that historically the rate of growth of output over time has exceeded the growth rate that can be attributed to the growth in conventionally defined inputs. Suppose that we let

$$q = A(t)f(K, L) \tag{11.44}$$

be the production function for some good (or perhaps for society's output as a whole). The term $A(t)$ in the function represents all the influences that go into determining q besides K (machine-hours) and L (labor-hours). Changes in A over time represent technical progress. For this reason A is shown as a function of time. Presumably $dA/dt > 0$: Particular levels of input of labor and capital become more productive over time.

Differentiating Equation 11.44 with respect to time gives

$$\frac{dq}{dt} = \frac{dA}{dt} \cdot f(K, L) + A \cdot \frac{df(K, L)}{dt}$$

$$= \frac{dA}{dt} \cdot \frac{q}{A} + \frac{q}{f(K, L)} \left[\frac{\partial f}{\partial K} \cdot \frac{dK}{dt} + \frac{\partial f}{\partial L} \cdot \frac{dL}{dt} \right]. \tag{11.45}$$

Dividing by q gives

$$\frac{dq/dt}{q} = \frac{dA/dt}{A} + \frac{\partial f/\partial K}{f(K, L)} \cdot \frac{dK}{dt} + \frac{\partial f/\partial L}{f(K, L)} \cdot \frac{dL}{dt} \tag{11.46}$$

or

$$\frac{dq/dt}{q} = \frac{dA/dt}{A} + \frac{\partial f}{\partial K} \cdot \frac{K}{f(K, L)} \cdot \frac{dK/dt}{K} + \frac{\partial f}{\partial L} \cdot \frac{L}{f(K, L)} \cdot \frac{dL/dt}{L}.$$

Now, for any variable x, $(dx/dt)/x$ is the rate of growth of x per unit of time. We shall denote this by G_x.[16] Hence, Equation 11.46 can be written in terms of growth rates as

$$G_q = G_A + \frac{\partial f}{\partial K} \cdot \frac{K}{f(K, L)} \cdot G_K + \frac{\partial f}{\partial L} \cdot \frac{L}{f(K, L)} \cdot G_L, \tag{11.47}$$

but

---

[16] Two useful features of this definition are: (1) $G_{x \cdot y} = G_x + G_y$—that is, the growth rate of a product of two variables is the sum of each one's growth rate; and (2) $G_{x/y} = G_x - G_y$.

$$\frac{\partial f}{\partial K} \cdot \frac{K}{f(K, L)} = \frac{\partial q}{\partial K} \cdot \frac{K}{q} = \text{elasticity of output with respect to capital input}$$

$$= e_{q,K}$$

and

$$\frac{\partial f}{\partial L} \cdot \frac{L}{f(K, L)} = \frac{\partial q}{\partial L} \cdot \frac{L}{q} = \text{elasticity of output with respect to labor input}$$

$$= e_{q,L}.$$

Therefore, our growth equation finally becomes

Growth Accounting

$$G_q = G_A + e_{q,K}G_K + e_{q,L}G_L. \tag{11.48}$$

This shows that the rate of growth in output can be broken down into the sum of two components: growth attributed to changes in inputs (K and L) and other "residual" growth (that is, changes in A) that represents technical progress.

Equation 11.48 provides a way of estimating the relative importance of technical progress (G_A) in determining the growth of output. For example, in a pioneering study of the entire U.S. economy between the years 1909 and 1949, R. M. Solow recorded the following values for the terms in the equation:[17]

$$G_q = 2.75 \text{ percent per year}$$

$$G_L = 1.00 \text{ percent per year}$$

$$G_K = 1.75 \text{ percent per year}$$

$$e_{q,L} = 0.65$$

$$e_{q,K} = 0.35.$$

Consequently,

$$G_A = G_q - e_{q,L}G_L - e_{q,K}G_K$$

$$= 2.75 - 0.65(1.00) - 0.35(1.75)$$

$$= 2.75 - 0.65 - 0.60 \tag{11.49}$$

$$= 1.50.$$

The conclusion Solow reached, then, was that technology advanced at a rate of 1.5 percent per year from 1909 to 1949. More than one-half of the growth

---

[17] R. M. Solow, "Technical Progress and the Aggregate Production Function," *Review of Economics and Statistics* 39 (August 1957): 312–320.

in real output could be attributed to technical change rather than to growth in the physical quantities of the factors of production.

More recent evidence has tended to confirm Solow's conclusions about the relative importance of technical change. Two puzzles have been presented by this evidence, however. First is the question of the origin of technical change. Since the definition in Equation 11.49 computes technical advance as the "residual" growth in output that is not explained by growth in inputs, the concept itself remains unexplained. Perhaps progress comes about through the use of better machinery or more skilled workers. Or perhaps it arises from the adoption of better means of organizing production or of providing the proper incentives to managers and workers. It is even possible that technical advance just happens, thereby improving all production techniques (this is consistent with the way technical change is modeled in Equation 11.44).

Whatever the source of technical progress, the second puzzle shown by the data is that the rate of advance seems to have slowed on a worldwide basis after the mid-1970s. Why this might be a major cause of concern is suggested by the Solow findings. Using Equation 11.48 to compute the growth in output per worker yields

$$G_{q/L} = G_q - G_L = G_A + e_{q,K}G_K - (1 - e_{q,L})G_L$$
$$= G_A + e_{q,K}(G_K - G_L), \tag{11.50}$$

and applying the Solow figures gives

$$G_{q/L} = 2.75 - 1.00 = 1.75 \cong 1.50 + .35(.75). \tag{11.51}$$

Hence, six-sevenths $(1.50 \div 1.75)$ of the growth in output per worker is explained by technical advance with only one-seventh being explained by increases in the conventional capital-labor ratio. Any slowdown in technical change, therefore, has serious negative consequences for the growth of wages in the economy. Despite a vast literature on this topic, however, there is no general agreement on the causes of the decline.

EXAMPLE 11.4

TECHNICAL PROGRESS IN THE COBB-DOUGLAS FUNCTION

Since fast-food restaurants are constantly innovating, we might not want to assume the production function in Example 11.3 represents the function that will be used for all time. Instead, hamburger production may change over time according to

$$q = 10e^{.05t}K^{1/2}L^{1/2}. \tag{11.52}$$

For $t = 0$ this is the same function we studied previously, but for later times hamburger production experiences technical improvements. Specifically, a given input combination will produce 5 percent more hamburgers each period as time proceeds. Taking logarithms of Equation 11.52 yields

$$ln \, q = ln \, 10 + .05t + \frac{1}{2} ln \, K + \frac{1}{2} ln \, L, \qquad (11.53)$$

and differentiation with respect to t gives the growth equation

$$\frac{dq/dt}{q} = .05 + \frac{1}{2}\frac{dK/dt}{K} + \frac{1}{2}\frac{dL/dt}{L}$$

or

$$G_q = .05 + \frac{1}{2}G_K + \frac{1}{2}G_L. \qquad (11.54)$$

With a constant K and L ($G_K = G_L = 0$), therefore, $G_q = .05$—that is, output grows at 5 percent per period. At $t = 10$, for example,

$$q = 10e^{.5}K^{1/2}L^{1/2}$$
$$= 16.5K^{1/2}L^{1/2}, \qquad (11.55)$$

and the $q = 100$ isoquant is given by

$$100/16.5 = K^{1/2}L^{1/2}$$

or

$$KL = 36.7, \qquad (11.56)$$

which is much closer to the origin than the $q = 100$ isoquant calculated in Example 11.3. Alternatively, at $t = 10$ an input combination of $K = 10$, $L = 10$ will yield an output of 165 hamburgers per period rather than the 100 obtained previously. In the absence of technical change, hamburger producers would have had to use additional physical quantities of inputs (such as $K = L = 16.5$ or $K = 27.2$, $L = 10$) to obtain this level of output.

QUERY: At $t = 10$ what is hamburger output per worker when $K = 10$? What K would be needed to yield the same level of output per worker in the absence of technical change?

SUMMARY

In this chapter we illustrated the ways in which economists conceptualize the production process of turning inputs into outputs. The fundamental tool is the production function, which, in its simplest form, assumes that output per period (q) is a simple function of capital and labor inputs during that period, $q = f(K, L)$. Using this starting point, we developed several basic results for the theory of production:

- If all but one of the inputs are held constant, a relationship between the single variable input and output can be derived. From this relationship one can derive the marginal physical productivity (*MP*) of the input as the change in output resulting from a one-unit increase in the use of the input. The marginal physical productivity of an input is assumed to decline as use of the input increases.

- The entire production function can be illustrated by its isoquant map. The (negative of the) slope of an isoquant is termed the marginal rate of technical substitution (*RTS*) since it shows how one input can be substituted for another while holding output constant. The *RTS* is the ratio of the marginal physical productivities of the two inputs.

- Isoquants are usually assumed to be convex—they obey the assumption of a diminishing *RTS*. This assumption cannot be derived exclusively from the assumption of diminishing marginal physical productivities. One must also be concerned with the effect of changes in one input on the marginal productivity of other inputs.

- The returns to scale exhibited by a production function record how output responds to proportionate increases in all inputs. If output increases proportionately with input use, there are constant returns to scale. If there are greater than proportionate increases in output, there are increasing returns to scale, whereas if there are less than proportionate increases in output, there are decreasing returns to scale.

- The elasticity of substitution (σ) provides a measure of how easy it is to substitute one input for another in production. A high σ implies nearly straight isoquants, whereas a low σ implies that isoquants are nearly L-shaped.

- Technical progress shifts the entire production function and its related isoquant map. Technical improvements may arise from the use of improved, more productive inputs, or from better methods of economic organization.

PROBLEMS

11.1

Digging clams by hand in Sunset Bay requires only labor input. The total number of clams obtained per hour (*q*) is given by

$$q = 100\sqrt{L}$$

where *L* is labor input per hour.
a. Graph the relationship between *q* and *L*.
b. What is the average productivity of labor in Sunset Bay? Graph this relationship and show that AP_L diminishes for increases in labor input.
c. Show that the marginal productivity of labor in Sunset Bay is given by

$$MP_L = 50/\sqrt{L}.$$

Graph this relationship and show that $MP_L < AP_L$ for all values of *L*. Explain why this is so.

11.2

Suppose the production function for widgets is given by

$$q = KL - .8K^2 - .2L^2$$

where *q* represents the annual quantity of widgets produced, *K* represents annual capital input, and *L* represents annual labor input.
a. Suppose $K = 10$; graph the total and average productivity of labor curves. At what level of labor input does this average productivity reach a maximum? How many widgets are produced at that point?
b. Again assuming that $K = 10$, graph the MP_L curve. At what level of labor input does $MP_L = 0$?
c. Suppose capital inputs were increased to $K = 20$. How would your answers to parts (a) and (b) change?
d. Does the widget production function exhibit constant, increasing, or decreasing returns to scale?

11.3

Power Goat Lawn Company uses two sizes of mowers to cut lawns. The smaller mowers have a 24-inch blade and are used on lawns with many trees and obstacles. The larger mowers are exactly twice as big as the smaller mowers and are used on open lawns where maneuverability is not so difficult. The two production functions available to Power Goat are:

	OUTPUT PER HOUR (SQUARE FEET)	CAPITAL INPUT (# OF 24" MOWERS)	LABOR INPUT
Large mowers	8000	2	1
Small mowers	5000	1	1

a. Graph the $q = 40{,}000$ square feet isoquant for the first production function. How much K and L would be used if these factors were combined without waste?

b. Answer part (a) for the second function.

c. How much K and L would be used without waste if half of the 40,000-square-foot lawn were cut by the method of the first production function and half by the method of the second? How much K and L would be used if three-fourths of the lawn were cut by the first method and one-fourth by the second? What does it mean to speak of fractions of K and L?

d. On the basis of your observations in part (c), draw a $q = 40{,}000$ isoquant for the combined production functions.

11.4

The production of barstools (q) is characterized by a production function of the form

$$q = K^{1/2} \cdot L^{1/2} = \sqrt{K \cdot L}.$$

a. What is the average productivity of labor and capital for barstool production (AP_L will depend on K, and AP_K will depend on L)?

b. Graph the AP_L curve for $K = 100$.

c. For this particular function show that $MP_L = \frac{1}{2}AP_L$, and $MP_K = \frac{1}{2}AP_K$. Using that information, add a graph of the MP_L function to the graph calculated in part (b) (again for $K = 100$). What is unusual about this curve?

d. Sketch the $q = 10$ isoquant for this production function.

e. Using the results from part (c), what is the RTS on the $q = 10$ isoquant at the points: $K = L = 10$; $K = 25$, $L = 4$; and $K = 4$, $L = 25$? Does this function exhibit a diminishing RTS?

11.5

Suppose that

$$q = L^{\alpha}K^{\beta} \quad 0 < \alpha < 1, 0 < \beta < 1, \alpha + \beta = 1.$$

a. Show that $e_{q,L} = \alpha$, $e_{q,K} = \beta$.

b. Show that $MP_L > 0$, $MP_K > 0$; $\partial^2 q/\partial L^2 < 0$, $\partial^2 q/\partial K^2 < 0$.

c. Show that the RTS depends only on K/L, but not on the scale of production, and that the RTS (L for K) diminishes as L/K increases.

11.6

Show that for the constant returns-to-scale CES production function

$$q = [K^{\rho} + L^{\rho}]^{1/\rho}$$

a. $MP_K = \left(\dfrac{q}{K}\right)^{1-\rho}$ and $MP_L = \left(\dfrac{q}{L}\right)^{1-\rho}$

b. $RTS = \left(\dfrac{L}{K}\right)^{1-\rho}$. Use this to show that $\sigma = 1/(1 - \rho)$.

c. Determine the output elasticities for K and L. Show that their sum equals 1.

d. Prove that

$$\frac{q}{L} = \left(\frac{\partial q}{\partial L}\right)^{\sigma}.$$

Hence, show

$$ln\left(\frac{q}{L}\right) = \sigma \, ln\left(\frac{\partial q}{\partial L}\right).$$

Note: The latter equality is useful in empirical work, since in some cases we may approximate $\partial q/\partial L$ by the competitively determined wage rate. Hence, σ can be estimated from a regression of $ln(q/L)$ on $ln\,w$.

11.7

Consider a production function of the form

$$q = \beta_0 + \beta_1\sqrt{KL} + \beta_2 K + \beta_3 L$$

where

$$0 \le \beta_i \le 1 \quad i = 0 \ldots 3$$

a. If this function is to exhibit constant returns to scale, what restrictions should be placed on the parameters $\beta_0 \ldots \beta_3$?

b. Show that in the constant returns-to-scale case this

function exhibits diminishing marginal productivities and that the marginal productivity functions are homogeneous of degree zero.

c. Calculate σ in this case. Is σ constant?

11.8

Show that Euler's theorem (see footnote 5 of Chapter 7) implies that for a constant returns-to-scale production function $[q = f(K, L)]$,

$$q = f_K \cdot K + f_L \cdot L.$$

Use this result to show that for such a production function, if $MP_L > AP_L$, MP_K must be negative. What does this imply about where production must take place? Can a firm ever produce at a point where AP_L is increasing?

11.9

As in Problem 11.8, again use Euler's theorem to prove that for a constant returns-to-scale production function with only two inputs (K and L), f_{KL} must be positive. Interpret this result.

11.10

Constant returns-to-scale production functions are

sometimes called homogeneous of degree 1. More generally, as we showed in footnote 1 of Chapter 5, a production function would be said to be homogeneous of degree k if

$$f(tK, tL) = t^k f(K, L).$$

a. Show that if a production function is homogeneous of degree k, its marginal productivity functions are homogeneous of degree $k - 1$.

b. Use the result from part (a) to show that marginal productivities for any constant returns-to-scale production function depend only on the ratio K/L.

c. Use the result from part (b) to show that the RTS for a constant returns-to-scale production function depends only on the ratio K/L.

d. More generally, show that the RTS for any homogeneous function is independent of the scale of operation—all isoquants are radial expansions of the unit isoquant. Hence, such a function is homothetic.

e. Show that the results from part (d) apply to any monotonic transformation of a homogeneous function. That is, show that any such transformation of a homogeneous function is homothetic.

SUGGESTED READINGS

Berck, P., and K. Sydsaeter. *Economist's Mathematical Manual*. Berlin: Spinger-Verlag, 1991.
Provides a succinct review of production function concepts and functional forms. See especially Chapter 25.

Clark, J. M. "Diminishing Returns." *Encyclopaedia of the Social Sciences*, Vol. 5. New York: Crowell-Collier and Macmillan, 1931, pp. 144–146.
Lucid discussion of the historical development of the diminishing returns concept.

Douglas, P. H. "Are There Laws of Production?" *American Economic Review* 38 (March 1948): 1–41.
Basic methodological analysis of the uses and misuses of production functions.

———. "The Cobb-Douglas Production Function Once Again: Its History, Its Testing, and Some Empirical Values." *Journal of Political Economy* 84 (October 1976): 903–916.

Comprehensive review of the literature on Cobb-Douglas production functions.

Ferguson, C. E. *The Neoclassical Theory of Production and Distribution*. New York: Cambridge University Press, 1969.
Fairly complete discussion of production function theory. Good use of three-dimensional graphs.

Fuss, M., and D. McFadden. *Production Economics: A Dual Approach to Theory and Application*. Amsterdam: North-Holland Publishing Co., 1980.
Modern approach with heavy emphasis on the use of duality.

Machlup, F. "On the Meaning of Marginal Product." Reprinted in American Economic Association, *Readings in the Theory of Income Distribution*. Philadelphia: Blakiston Co., 1951, pp. 158–174.

Nice methodological development of the proper use of the marginal product notion.

Mas-Collell, A., M. D. Whinston, and J. R. Green, *Microeconomic Theory:* New York: Oxford University Press, 1995.
Chapter 5 provides a sophisticated, if somewhat spare, reivew of production theory. The use of the profit function (see the Extensions to Chapter 13) is quite sophisticated and illuminating.

Shephard, R. W. *Theory of Cost and Production Functions.* Princeton, N.J.: Princeton University Press, 1978.
Extended analysis of the dual relationship between production and cost functions.

Stigler, G. J. "The Division of Labor Is Limited by the Extent of the Market." *Journal of Political Economy* 59 (June 1951): 185–193.
Careful tracing of the evolution of Smith's ideas about economies of scale.

EXTENSIONS

Many-Input Production Functions

Most of the production functions illustrated in Chapter 11 can be easily generalized to many-input cases. Here we show this for the Cobb-Douglas and CES cases and then examine two quite flexible forms that such production functions might take. In all of these examples, the β's are nonnegative parameters, and the n inputs are represented by $X_1 \ldots X_n$.

E11.1 Cobb-Douglas

The many-input Cobb-Douglas production function is given by

$$q = \prod_{i=1}^{n} X_i^{\beta_i}. \tag{i}$$

a. It is easy to show that this function exhibits constant returns to scale if

$$\sum_{i=1}^{n} \beta_i = 1. \tag{ii}$$

b. In the constant-returns-to-scale Cobb-Dougles function, β_i is the elasticity of q with respect to input X_i. Since $0 \le \beta_i < 1$, each input exhibits diminishing marginal productivity.

c. Any degree of increasing returns to scale can be incorporated into this function depending on

$$\epsilon = \sum_{i=1}^{n} \beta_i. $$

E11.2 The Solow Growth Model

The many-input Cobb-Douglas production function is a primary feature of many models of economic growth. For example, Solow's (1956) pioneering model of equilibrium growth can be most easily derived using a two-input, constant-returns-to-scale Cobb-Douglas function of the form

$$Y = AK^{\alpha}L^{1-\alpha} \tag{iii}$$

where A is a technical change factor that can be represented by exponential growth of the firm

$$A = e^{at}. \tag{iv}$$

Dividing both sides of equation iii by L yields

$$y = e^{at}k^{\alpha} \tag{v}$$

where

$$y = Y/L, k = K/L.$$

Solow shows that economies will evolve toward an equilibrium value of k (the capital-labor ratio). Hence cross-crounty differences in growth rates can be accounted for only by differences in the technical change factor, a.

Two features of Equation v argue for including more inputs in the Solow model. First, the equation as it stands is incapable of explaining the large differences in per capita output (y) that are observed around the world. Assuming $\alpha = .3$, say, (a figure consistent with many empirical studies), it would take cross-country differences in K/L of as much as 4,000,000-to-1 to explain the 100-to-1 differences in per capita income observed—a clearly unreasonable magnitude. By introducing additional inputs, such as human capital, these differences become more explainable.

A second shortcoming of the simple Cobb-Douglas formulation of the Solow model is that it offers no explanation of the technical change parameter, a—its value is determined "exogenously." By adding additional factors it becomes easier to understand how the parameter a may respond to economic incentives. This is the key insight of recent literature on "endogenous" growth theory (for a summary, see Romer, 1996).

E11.3 CES

The many-input constant elasticity of substitution (CES) production function is given by

$$q = \left[\sum \beta_i X_i^\rho \right]^{\epsilon/\rho}, \rho \le 1. \qquad \text{(vi)}$$

a. By substituting mX_i for each input, it is easy to show that this function exhibits constant returns to scale for $\epsilon = 1$. For $\epsilon > 1$, the function exhibits increasing returns to scale.
b. The production function exhibits diminishing marginal productivities for each input since $\rho \le 1$.
c. As in the two-input case, the elasticity of substitution here is given by

$$\sigma = \frac{1}{1 - \rho} \qquad \text{(vii)}$$

and this elasticity applies to substitution between any two of the inputs.

Checking the Cobb-Douglas in the Soviet Union

One way in which the multi-input CES function is used to determine whether the estimated substitution parameter (ρ) is consistent with the value implied by the Cobb-Douglas ($\rho = 0$, $\sigma = 1$). For example, in a study of five major industries in the former Soviet Union, E. Bairam (1991) finds that the Cobb-Douglas provides a relatively good explanation of changes in output in most major manufacturing sectors. Only for food processing does a lower value for σ seem appropriate.

The next two examples illustrate flexible form production functions that may approximate any general function of n imputs. In the Chapter 12 extensions, we examine the cost function analogues to some of these functions, which are more widely used than the production functions themselves.

E11.4 Generalized Leontief

$$q = \sum_{i=1}^{n} \sum_{j=1}^{n} \beta_{ij} \sqrt{X_i X_j}, \ \beta_{ij} = \beta_{ji}$$

a. The function considered in Problem 11.7 is a simple generalization of this function for the case $n = 2$. For $n = 3$, the function would have linear terms in the three inputs together with three radical terms representing all possible cross-products of the inputs.
b. The function exhibits constant returns to scale as can be shown by using mX_i. Increasing returns to scale can be incorporated into the function by using the transformation

$$q' = q^\epsilon, \ \epsilon > 1.$$

c. Because each input appears both linearly and under the radical, the function exhibits diminishing marginal productivities to all inputs.
d. The restriction $\beta_{ij} = \beta_{ji}$ is used to ensure symmetry of the second-order partial derivatives.

E11.5 Translog

$$\ln q = \beta_0 + \sum_{i-1}^{n} \beta_i \ln X_i$$

$$+ 0.5 \sum_{i=1}^{n} \sum_{j=1}^{n} \beta_{ij} \ln X_i \ln X_j,$$

$$\beta_{ij} = \beta_{ji}$$

a. Note that the Cobb-Douglas function is a special case of this function where $\beta_0 = \beta_{ij} = 0$ for all i, j.
b. As for the Cobb-Douglas, this function may assume any degree of returns to scale. If

$$\sum_{i=1}^{n} \beta_i = 1$$

and

$$\sum_{j=1}^{n} \beta_{ij} = 0$$

for all i, this function exhibits constant returns to scale. The proof requires some care in dealing with the double summation sign.

c. Again, the condition $\beta_{ij} = \beta_{ji}$ is required to assure equality of the cross-partial derivatives.

Immigration

Because the translog production function incorporates a large number of substitution possibilities among various inputs, it has been widely used to study the ways in which newly arrived workers may substitute for existing workers. Of particular interest is the way in which the skill level of immigrants may lead to differing reactions in the demand for skilled and unskilled workers in the domestic economy. Studies of both the United States and many other countries (Canada, Germany, France, and so forth) have suggested that the overall size of such effects is modest, especially given relatively small immigration flows. But there is some evidence that unskilled immigrant workers may act as substitutes for unskilled domestic workers but complements to skilled domestic workers. Hence increased immigration flows may exacerbate trends toward rising wage differentials. For a summary, see Borjas (1994).

References

Bairam, Erkin. "Elasticity of Substitution, Technical Progress and Returns to Scale in Branches of Soviet Industry: A New CES Production Function Approach." *Journal of Applied Economics* (January–March 1991): 91–96.

Borjas, G. J. "The Economics of Immigration." *Journal of Economic Literature* (December 1994): 1667–1717.

Christenson, L. R., D. W. Jorgenson, and L. J. Lau. "Transcendental Logarithmic Production Frontiers." *Review of Economics and Statistics* (February 1973): 28–45.

Diewert, W. E. "Functional Forms for Profit and Transformation Functions." *Journal of Economic Theory* (June 1973): 284–315.

Fuss, M., and D. McFadden, eds. *Production Economics: A Dual Approach to Theory and Applications.* Amsterdam: North-Holland Publishing Co., 1978. See especially Chap. I.1, "Cost Revenue and Profit Functions," and Chap. II.1, "A Survey of Functional Forms in the Economic Analysis of Production."

Romer, David. *Advanced Macroeconomics.* New York: McGraw Hill Book Company, 1996.

Solow, R. M. "A Contribution to the Theory of Economic Growth." *Quarterly Journal of Economics* (1956): 65–94.

CHAPTER 12

COSTS

In Chapter 11 we discussed ways of conceptualizing the relationship between inputs and outputs in the production process. Now we wish to show how this production function can be used to illustrate the costs that a firm incurs in its productive activities. Ultimately, we will be able to use such information together with information about the firm's revenues to show how much it will choose to produce. But we will delay that topic until Chapter 13. Here we will only be concerned with questions about the costs associated with hiring the inputs that the firm chooses to employ.

DEFINITIONS OF COSTS

Before we can discuss the theory of costs, some difficulties about the proper definition of "costs" must be cleared up. At least three different notions can be distinguished: opportunity cost, accounting cost, and "economic" cost. For economists the most important of these is *social*, or *opportunity*, *cost*. Because resources are limited, any decision in an economy to produce some good necessitates doing without some other good. When an automobile is produced, for example, an implicit decision has been made to do without, say, 15 bicycles that could have been produced using the labor, metal, chrome, and glass that went into making the automobile. The opportunity cost of one automobile is then 15 bicycles. Since expressing opportunity costs in terms of physical goods is often inconvenient, monetary units are sometimes chosen instead. Indeed, the price of a car may adequately reflect the goods that were given up by its being produced. If this were true, we would say that the opportunity cost of an automobile is $20,000 worth of other goods. This may not always be the case, however. If, for example, the car were produced with resources that could not be usefully employed elsewhere, the opportunity cost of its production might have been zero.

Although the opportunity cost notion is primarily conceptual, the two other concepts of cost are both directly related to the firm's theory of choice:

(1) accounting cost and (2) economic cost. The accountant's view of cost stresses out-of-pocket expenses, historical costs, depreciation, and other bookkeeping entries. The economist's definition of cost (which in obvious ways draws on the idea of opportunity cost) is that the cost of any input is given by the size of the payment necessary to keep the resource in its present employment. Alternatively, the economic cost of using an input is what that input would be paid in its next best use. One way to distinguish between these two views is to consider how the costs of various resources (labor, capital, and entrepreneurial services) are defined under each system.

Labor Costs

Economists and accountants regard labor costs in much the same way. To accountants, expenditures on labor are current expenses and hence are costs of production. For economists, labor is an *explicit* cost. Labor services (labor-hours) are contracted at some hourly wage rate (w), and it is usually assumed that this is the amount the labor services would earn in their best alternative employment.

Capital Costs

In the case of capital services (machine-hours), the two concepts of cost differ greatly. In calculating capital costs, accountants use the historical price of the particular machine under investigation and apply some more-or-less arbitrary depreciation rule to determine how much of that machine's original price to charge to current costs. Economists regard the historical price of a machine as a "sunk cost," which is irrelevant to the productive process. They instead regard the *implicit* cost of the machine to be what someone else would be willing to pay for its use. Thus, the cost of one machine-hour is the *rental rate* for that machine in its best alternative use. By continuing to use the machine itself, the firm is implicitly foregoing the rental rate someone else would be willing to pay to use it. This rental rate for one machine-hour will be denoted by v.[1]

Costs of Entrepreneurial Services

The owner of a business is a residual claimant who is entitled to whatever extra revenues or losses are left after paying all input costs. To an accountant these would be called "profits" (which might be either positive or negative). Economists, however, ask whether owners (or "entrepreneurs") also encounter opportunity costs by working at a particular firm or devoting some of

---

[1] Sometimes the symbol r is chosen to represent the rental rate on capital. Since this variable is often confused with the related though distinct concept of the market interest rate, an alternative symbol was chosen here. The exact relationship between v and the interest rate is examined in Chapter 23.

their funds to its operation. If so, these services should be considered an input to the firm, and some cost should be imputed to them. For example, suppose a highly skilled computer programmer starts a software firm with the idea of keeping any (accounting) profits that might be generated. Then the programmer's time is clearly an input to the firm, and a cost should be inputed for it. Perhaps the wage that the programmer might command if he or she worked for someone else could be used for that purpose. Hence, some part of the accounting profits generated by the firm would be categorized as entrepreneurial costs by economists. Residual economic profits would be smaller than accounting profits and might be negative if the programmer's opportunity costs exceeded the accounting profits being earned by the business.

Economic Costs   In this book, not surprisingly, we shall use economists' definition of cost:

DEFINITION

Economic Cost   The *economic cost* of any input is the payment required to keep that input in its present employment. Equivalently, the economic cost of an input is the remuneration the input would receive in its best alternative employment.

Use of this definition is not meant to imply that accountants' concepts are irrelevant to economic behavior. Indeed, accounting procedures are integrally important to any manager's decision-making process because they can greatly affect the rate of taxation to be applied against profits. Accounting data are also readily available, whereas data on economic costs must often be developed separately. Economists' definitions, however, do have the desirable features of being broadly applicable to all firms and of forming a conceptually consistent system. They therefore are best suited for a general theoretical analysis.

Two Simplifying Assumptions   As a start, we will make two simplifications about the inputs a firm uses. First, it generally will be assumed, as before, that there are only two inputs: homogeneous labor (L, measured in labor-hours) and homogeneous capital (K, measured in machine-hours). Entrepreneurial costs will be assumed to be included in capital costs. That is, it will be assumed that the primary opportunity costs faced by a firm's owner are those associated with the capital that the owner provides.

A second simplification will be that the inputs to the firm are hired in perfectly competitive markets. Firms can buy (or sell) all the labor or capital services they want at the prevailing rental rates (w and v). In graphic terms the supply curve for these resources that the firm faces is horizontal at the prevailing factor prices. Both w and v are treated as "parameters" in the firm's decisions; there is nothing the firm can do to affect them. These conditions will be relaxed in later chapters (notably Chapter 21), but for the moment the perfectly competitive assumption is a convenient and useful one to make.

Economic Profits and Cost Minimization

Given these simplifying assumptions, total costs for the firm during a period are given by

$$\text{total costs} = TC = wL + vK, \tag{12.1}$$

where, as before, L and K represent input usage during the period. Assuming the firm produces only one output, its total revenues are given by the price of its product (P) times its total output [$q = f(K, L)$ where $f(K, L)$ is the firm's production function]. Economic profits (π) are then the difference between total revenues and total economic costs:

DEFINITION

Economic Profits *Economic profits* (π) are the difference between a firm's total revenues and its total costs:

$$\pi = \text{total revenue} - \text{total cost} = Pq - wL - vK$$
$$= Pf(K, L) - wL - vK \tag{12.2}$$

Equation 12.2 shows that the economic profits obtained by a firm are a function of the amount of capital and labor employed. If, as we will assume in many places in this book, the firm seeks maximum profits, we might study its behavior by examining how K and L are chosen so as to maximize Equation 12.2. This would, in turn, lead to a theory of the "derived demand" for capital and labor inputs—a topic we take up explicitly in Chapter 21.

Here, however, we wish to develop a theory of costs that is somewhat more general and might apply to firms that are not necessarily profit maximizers. Hence, we begin our study of costs by finessing a discussion of output choice for the moment. That is, we assume that for some reason the firm has decided to produce a particular output level (say, q_0). The firm's revenues are therefore fixed at Pq_0. Now we wish to examine how the firm might choose to produce q_0 at minimal costs.

COST-MINIMIZING INPUT CHOICES

Mathematically, this is a constrained minimization problem. But before proceeding with a rigorous solution, it might be useful to state the result to be derived with an intuitive argument. In order to minimize the cost of producing a given level of output, a firm should choose that point on the q_0 isoquant at which the rate of technical substitution of L for K is equal to the ratio w/v: It should equate the rate at which K can be traded for L in the productive process to the rate at which they can be traded in the marketplace. Suppose that this were not true. In particular, suppose that the firm were producing output level q_0 using $K = 10$, $L = 10$, and assume that the RTS was 2 at this point. Assume also that $w = \$1$, $v = \$1$, and hence that $w/v = 1$ (which is unequal to 2). At this input combination, the cost of producing q_0 is \$20. It is easy to show this is not the minimal input cost. q_0 can also be produced using $K = 8$ and $L = 11$; we can give up two units of K and keep output constant at q_0 by adding one unit of L. But at this input combination the cost of producing q_0 is \$19, and hence the initial input combination was not optimal. A proof similar to this one can be demonstrated whenever the RTS and the ratio of the input costs differ.

Mathematical Analysis

Mathematically, we seek to minimize total costs, given $q = f(K, L) = q_0$. Setting up the Lagrangian expression

$$\mathscr{L} = wL + vK + \lambda[q_0 - f(K, L)], \tag{12.3}$$

the first-order conditions for a constrained minimum are

$$\frac{\partial \mathscr{L}}{\partial L} = w - \lambda \frac{\partial f}{\partial L} = 0$$

$$\frac{\partial \mathscr{L}}{\partial K} = v - \lambda \frac{\partial f}{\partial K} = 0 \tag{12.4}$$

$$\frac{\partial \mathscr{L}}{\partial \lambda} = q_0 - f(K, L) = 0$$

or, dividing the first two equations,

$$\frac{w}{v} = \frac{\partial f/\partial L}{\partial f/\partial K} = RTS(L \text{ for } K). \tag{12.5}$$

This says that the cost-minimizing firm should equate the RTS for the two inputs to the ratio of their prices.[2]

---

[2] Equation 12.4 also shows that

$$\frac{1}{\lambda} = \frac{\partial f/\partial L}{w} = \frac{\partial f/\partial K}{v}.$$

This means that the marginal productivity per dollar spent should be the same for all inputs used. In other words, the ratio of marginal benefit (that is, increased output) to marginal cost should be the same for all inputs actually employed. If an input did not meet this benefit-cost test, it would not be used. Similarly, λ here represents marginal cost—that is, the extra cost involved in producing one more unit of output.

Graphical Analysis

The result is shown graphically in Figure 12.1. Given the output isoquant q_0, we wish to find the least costly point on the isoquant. From Equation 12.1, all lines of equal cost are parallel straight lines with slopes $-w/v$. Three lines of equal total cost are shown in Figure 12.1: $TC_1 < TC_2 < TC_3$. It is clear from the figure that the minimum total cost for producing q_0 is given by TC_1, where the total cost curve is just tangent to the isoquant. The cost-minimizing input combination is L^*, K^*. This combination will be a true minimum if the isoquant is convex (if the RTS diminishes for decreases in K/L). Our mathematical and graphic analyses arrive at the same conclusion:

OPTIMIZATION PRINCIPLE

Cost Minimization In order to minimize the cost of any given level of input (q_0), the firm should produce at that point on the q_0 isoquant for which the RTS (of L for K) is equal to the ratio of the inputs' rental prices (w/v).

FIGURE 12.1

MINIMIZATION OF COSTS GIVEN $q = q_0$

A firm is assumed to choose K and L to minimize total costs. The condition for this minimization is that the rate at which K and L can be traded technically (while keeping $q = q_0$) should be equal to the rate at which these inputs can be traded in the market. In other words, the RTS (of L for K) should be set equal to the price ratio w/v. This tangency is shown in the figure; costs are minimized at TC_1 by choosing inputs K^* and L^*.

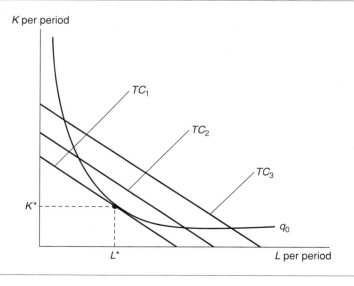

Dual Problem: Output Maximization

A result identical to that just derived can be obtained by considering the dual formulation of the firm's primal cost-minimization problem: For a given total cost of inputs (say, TC_1), maximize the level of output. Mathematically, the Lagrangian expression for this problem is

$$\mathcal{L}^D = f(K, L) + \lambda^D(TC_1 - wL - vK), \tag{12.6}$$

and it is a simple matter to show that the first-order conditions for this problem are identical to those already derived in Equation 12.4. A graphic demonstration is provided in Figure 12.2. There the maximum output attainable with total cost TC_1 is q_0, which results when the input combination L^*, K^* is utilized. All other combinations of inputs that lie along TC_1 are below the q_0 isoquant and hence yield less output than does this optimal combination. Therefore, the solution derived in Figure 12.2 is identical to that in Figure 12.1. For most of our subsequent analysis we will make use of the primal cost-minimization approach, but at times we will rely on the dual

---

FIGURE 12.2

DUAL OUTPUT-MAXIMIZATION PROBLEM

The dual approach to cost minimization is for the firm to maximize output for a given expenditure of total cost (TC_1). Under this approach too, the firm chooses the input combination L^*, K^* for which the RTS is equal to the ratio of the input's rental rates, w/v.

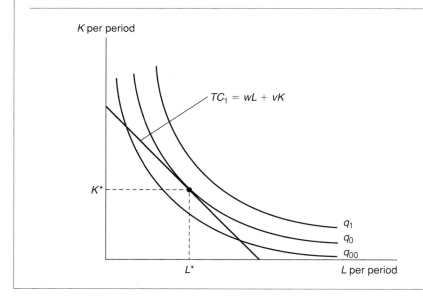

formulation of the problem to provide insights into the economic consequences of cost minimization.

Figure 12.2 exhibits the formal similarity between the firm's cost-minimization problem and the individual's utility-maximization problem. In both cases we took prices as fixed parameters and derived the tangency conditions. In Chapter 5 we then asked the comparative statics question of how the utility-maximizing choice of goods would change if a price were to change. The analysis of this change permitted the construction of the familiar downward-sloping demand curve. An interesting question is whether the firm's demand for an input could be developed analogously here. Could we change some input price (change the slope of the TC curves) and then trace out the effects of this price change on the quantity of the factor demanded? The analogy to the individual's utility-maximization process can be misleading at this point. In order to analyze what happens to K^*, say, as v changes, we also have to know what happens to the output level chosen by the firm. The demand for K is a *derived demand*, based on the demand for the firm's output. We cannot answer questions about K^* without looking at the interaction of supply and demand in the goods market. Although the analogy to the theory of individual behavior is useful in pointing out basic similarities, it is not an exact analogy—the derivation of a firm's demand for an input involves additional issues about the firm's desired output level that do not arise in the consumer's problem. These are taken up in Chapter 21.

A firm can perform an analysis such as that presented above for each level of output: For each q it finds the input choice that minimizes the cost of producing q. If input costs (w and v) remain constant for all amounts the firm may demand, we can easily trace out this locus of cost-minimizing choices. This procedure is shown in Figure 12.3. The line $0E$ records the cost-minimizing tangencies for successively higher levels of output. For example, the minimum cost for producing output level q_1 is given by TC_1 and inputs K_1 and L_1 are used. Other tangencies in the figure can be interpreted in a similar way. The locus of these tangencies is called the firm's *expansion path*, because it records how input usage expands as output expands while holding the prices of the inputs constant.

As Figure 12.3 shows, the expansion path need not be a straight line. The use of some inputs may increase faster than others as output expands. Which inputs expand more rapidly will depend on the shape of the production isoquants. Since cost minimization requires that the RTS always be set equal to the ratio w/v, and since the w/v ratio is assumed to be constant, the shape of the expansion path will be determined by where a particular RTS occurs

FIGURE 12.3

THE FIRM'S EXPANSION PATH

The firm's expansion path is the locus of cost-minimizing tangencies. Assuming fixed input prices, the curve shows how inputs increase as output increases.

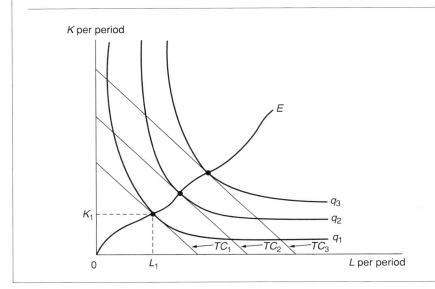

on successively higher isoquants. If the production function exhibits constant returns to scale (or, more generally, if it is homothetic), the expansion path will be a straight line since the RTS depends only on the ratio of K to L.

It would seem reasonable to assume that the expansion path will be positively sloped; that is, successively higher output levels will require more of both inputs. This need not be the case, however, as Figure 12.4 illustrates. Increases of output beyond q_2 actually cause the quantity of labor used to decrease. In this range, labor would be said to be an *inferior input.* The occurrence of inferior inputs is then a theoretical possibility that may happen, even when isoquants have their usual convex shape.

Much theoretical discussion has centered on the analysis of factor inferiority. Whether inferiority is likely to occur in real-world production functions is a difficult empirical question to answer. It seems unlikely that such comprehensive magnitudes as "capital" and "labor" could be inferior, but a finer classification of inputs may bring inferiority to light. For example, the use of shovels may decline as production of building foundations (and the use of backhoes) increases. In this book we shall not be particularly concerned with the analytical issues raised by this pos-

FIGURE 12.4

FACTOR INFERIORITY

With this particular set of isoquants, labor is an inferior input, since less L is chosen as output expands beyond q_2.

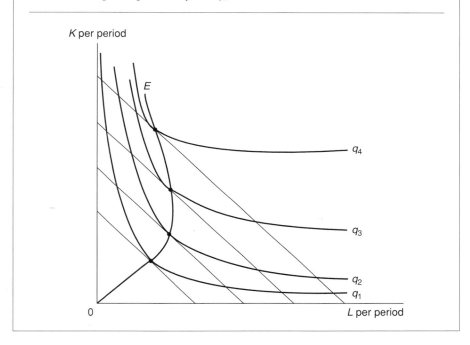

sibility, although complications raised by inferior inputs will be mentioned in a few places.

EXAMPLE 12.1

MINIMIZING COSTS FOR A COBB-DOUGLAS PRODUCTION FUNCTION

Suppose again that the hourly production of hamburgers at Hamburger Heaven (q) depends on the number of grills (K) and workers (L) hired each hour according to the Cobb-Douglas production function

$$q = 10K^{1/2}L^{1/2}. \tag{12.7}$$

If grills can be rented for v per hour and workers can be hired at w per hour, total costs of hamburger production are given by

$$TC = vK + wL. \tag{12.8}$$

Suppose this burger emporium wished to produce, say, 40 hamburgers per hour. Then the relevant Lagrangian expression for the firm's cost-minimization problem would be

$$\mathcal{L} = vK + wL + \lambda(40 - 10K^{1/2}L^{1/2}). \tag{12.9}$$

First-order conditions for a minimum are

$$\frac{\partial \mathcal{L}}{\partial K} = v - \lambda 5(L/K)^{1/2} = 0$$

$$\frac{\partial \mathcal{L}}{\partial L} = w - \lambda 5(K/L)^{1/2} = 0 \tag{12.10}$$

$$\frac{\partial \mathcal{L}}{\partial \lambda} = 40 - 10K^{1/2}L^{1/2} = 0.$$

The third of these simply says that production must take place on the $q = 40$ isoquant. Dividing the second equation by the first yields

$$\frac{w}{v} = \frac{K}{L} = RTS. \tag{12.11}$$

If, for example, w and v were each $4 per hour, Equation 12.11 indicates that the firm should use equal amounts of K and L. In this case $K = 4$, $L = 4$ would be sufficient to produce 40 hamburgers. Total costs of the 40 hamburgers would be $32. Any other input combination that can also produce 40 hamburgers has a greater total cost. For example, $K = 8$, $L = 2$ will also yield an output of 40, but in this case total cost is $40.

Cost minimization is also indicated by considering marginal productivities. With $K = L = 4$, $MP_L = MP_K = 5$ hamburgers per hour. An extra $1 spent on either labor or grills would yield 1.25 extra hamburgers (0.25 units of the input times a marginal productivity of 5). Alternatively, an extra hamburger costs $.80 (=1/1.25) since it can be produced by hiring either 1/5 of a labor-hour or 1/5 of a grill-hour.

The Expansion Path. Notice that in this problem the production function exhibits constant returns to scale so that the expansion path is a straight line. Equation 12.11 shows the equation for this straight line. If $w = v$, the firm will also choose $K = L$ for cost minimization. Of course, if $w \neq v$, input combinations where $K = L$ would not be cost minimizing although the expansion path would still be linear. If, for example, grills rented for $12 per hour and wages were $4, Equation 12.11 indicates that the expansion path would be those combinations of grills and workers for which $K/L = 1/3$. The firm would produce hamburgers using relatively more of the cheaper input (labor) and less of the expensive input (capital).

QUERY: If $v = 12$, $w = 4$, what should be true about MP_K and MP_L at the cost-minimizing input combination? Is this in fact the case when $q = 40$?

With the construction of the cost-minimizing expansion path, we are in a position to examine the firm's overall cost structure. To do so it will be convenient to use the expansion path solutions to derive the total cost function:

COST FUNCTIONS

DEFINITION

Total Cost Function   The *total cost function* shows that for any set of input costs and for any output level, the minimum total cost incurred by the firm is

$$TC = TC(v, w, q). \qquad (12.12)$$

Figure 12.3 makes clear that total costs increase as output, q, increases. We will begin by analyzing this relationship between total cost and output while holding input prices fixed. Then we will consider how a change in an input price shifts the expansion path and its related cost functions.

Although the total cost function provides complete information about the output-cost relationship, it is often convenient to analyze costs on a per unit of output basis, since that approach corresponds more closely to our analysis of demand, which focused on the price per unit of a commodity. Two different unit cost measures are widely used in economics: (1) average cost, which is the cost per unit of output; and (2) marginal cost, which is the cost of one more unit of output. The relationship of these concepts to the total cost function is described in the following definitions:

Average and Marginal Cost Functions

DEFINITION

Average and Marginal Cost Functions   The *average cost function* (AC) is found by computing total costs per unit of output:

$$\text{average cost} = AC(v, w, q) = \frac{TC(v, w, q)}{q}. \qquad (12.13)$$

The *marginal cost function* (MC) is found by computing the change in total costs for a change in output produced:

$$\text{marginal cost} = MC(v, w, q) = \frac{\partial TC(v, w, q)}{\partial q}. \tag{12.14}$$

Notice that in these definitions, average and marginal costs depend both on the level of output being produced and on the prices of inputs. In many places throughout this book we will graph simple two-dimensional relationships between costs and output. As Equations 12.12, 12.13, and 12.14 make clear, all such graphs are drawn on the assumption that the prices of inputs remain constant and that technology does not change. If input prices change or if technology advances, cost curves generally will shift to new positions. Later in this chapter we will explore the likely direction and size of such shifts.

Graphical Analysis of Total Costs

Figures 12.5a and 12.6a illustrate two possible shapes for the relationship between total cost and the level of the firm's output. In Figure 12.5a total cost is simply proportional to output. Such a situation would arise if the underlying production function exhibits constant returns to scale. In that case, suppose K_1 units of capital input and L_1 units of labor input are required to produce one unit of output. Then

$$TC(q = 1) = vK_1 + wL_1. \tag{12.15}$$

To produce m units of output then requires mK_1 units of capital and mL_1 units of labor because of the constant returns-to-scale assumption.[3] Hence,

$$TC(q = m) = vmK_1 + wmL_1 = m(vK_1 + wL_1)$$
$$= m \cdot TC(q = 1), \tag{12.16}$$

and the proportionality between output and cost is established.

The situation in Figure 12.6a is somewhat more complicated. There it is assumed that initially the TC curve is concave; although initially costs rise rapidly for increases in output, that rate of increase slows as output expands into the midrange of output. Beyond this middle range, however, the TC curve becomes convex, and costs begin to rise progressively more rapidly. One possible reason for such a shape for the total cost curve is that there is some third factor of production (say, the services of an entrepreneur) that is fixed as capital and labor usage expands. In this case the initial concave

---

[3] The input combination mL_1, mK_1 minimizes the cost of producing m units of output, since the ratio of the inputs is still K_1/L_1 and the RTS for a constant returns-to-scale production function depends only on that ratio. Hence, the RTS for the new input combination will equal the ratio w/v (as required for cost minimization), since the original input combination was assumed to minimize cost also.

FIGURE 12.5

**TOTAL, AVERAGE, AND MARGINAL COST CURVES
FOR THE CONSTANT RETURNS-TO-SCALE CASE**

In (a) total costs are proportional to output level. Average and marginal costs,
as shown in (b), are equal and constant for all output levels.

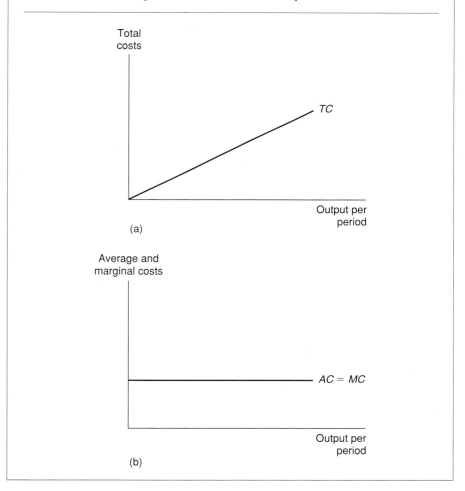

section of the TC curve might be explained by the increasingly optimal usage
of the entrepreneur's services—he or she needs a moderate level of
production to utilize his or her skills fully. Beyond the point of inflection,
however, the entrepreneur becomes overworked in attempting to coordinate

FIGURE 12.6

TOTAL, AVERAGE, AND MARGINAL COST CURVES FOR THE CUBIC TOTAL COST CURVE CASE

If the total cost curve has the cubic shape shown in (a), average and marginal cost curves will be U-shaped. In (b) the marginal cost curve passes through the low point of the average cost curve at output level q^*.

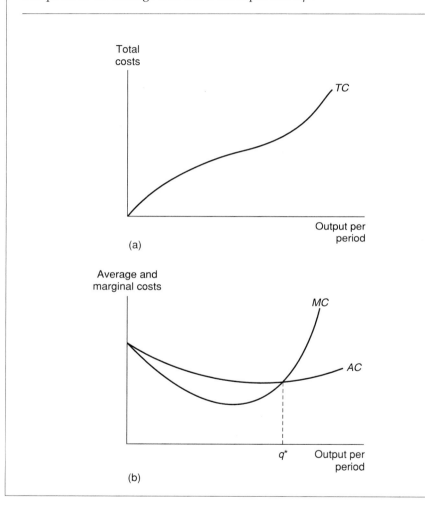

production, and diminishing returns set in. Hence, total costs rise rapidly.

A variety of other explanations have been offered for the cubic-type total cost curve in Figure 12.6, but we will not examine them here. Ultimately, the shape of the *TC* curve is an empirical question that can only be determined by examining real-world data. Instead, our purpose here is to investigate the theoretical consequences of such a shape.

Graphical Analysis of Average and Marginal Costs

Information from the total cost curves can be used to construct the average and marginal cost curves shown in Figures 12.5b and 12.6b. For the constant returns-to-scale case (Figure 12.5), this is quite simple. Since total costs are proportional to output, average and marginal costs are constant and equal for all levels of output.[4] These costs are shown by the horizontal line $AC = MC$ in Figure 12.5b.

For the cubic total cost curve case (Figure 12.6), computation of the average and marginal cost curves requires some geometric intuition. As the definition in Equation 12.14 makes clear, marginal cost is simply the slope of the *TC* curve. Hence, because of the assumed shape of the curve, the *MC* curve is U-shaped, with *MC* falling over the concave portion of the *TC* curve and rising beyond the point of inflection. Since the slope is always positive, however, *MC* is always greater than zero. Average costs (*AC*) start out being equal to marginal cost for the "first" unit of output.[5] As output expands, *AC* exceeds *MC*, however, since *AC* reflects both the marginal cost of the last unit produced and the somewhat higher marginal costs of the previously produced units. So long as $AC > MC$, average costs must be falling. Because the lower costs of the newly produced units are below average cost, they

---

[4] Mathematically, since $TC = aq$ (where a is the cost of 1 unit of output),

$$AC = \frac{TC}{q} = a = \frac{\partial TC}{\partial q} = MC.$$

[5] Technically, $AC = MC$ at $q = 0$. This can be shown by L'Hopital's rule, which states that if $f(a) = g(a) = 0$,

$$\lim_{x \to a} \frac{f(x)}{g(x)} = \lim_{x \to a} \frac{f'(x)}{g'(x)}.$$

In this case $TC = 0$ at $q = 0$, so that

$$\lim_{q \to 0} AC = \lim_{q \to 0} \frac{TC}{q} = \lim_{q \to 0} \frac{\partial TC/\partial q}{1} = \lim_{q \to 0} MC$$

or

$$AC = MC \text{ at } q = 0,$$

which was to be shown.

continue to pull average costs downward. Eventually, however, marginal costs start to rise and eventually (at q^*), they equal average cost. Beyond this point $MC > AC$, and average costs must be rising because they are being pulled upward by increasingly higher marginal costs. Consequently, we have shown that the AC curve also has a U-shape and that it reaches a low point at q^*, where AC and MC intersect.[6] In empirical studies of cost functions, there is considerable interest in this point of minimum average cost, since it reflects the "minimum efficient scale" (MES) for the particular production process being examined. The point also is theoretically important because of the role it plays in perfectly competitive price determination in the long run (see Chapter 14).

CHANGES IN INPUT PRICES

Thus far in our analysis of costs, we have held input prices constant so that we could study the two-dimensional relationship between costs and quantity produced. When input prices change, the firm's cost-minimizing expansion path will change, and the cost curves that are based on that path will shift. In this section we will examine such shifts. For simplicity we will primarily study only increases in input prices, although analogous results would hold for declines in such prices.

Homogeneity

A first obvious result we can demonstrate is that the total cost function is homogeneous of degree 1 in input prices. That is, if all input prices were to increase in the same proportion, t, the total costs for producing any given output level would also be multiplied by t. The reason for this result is that such a simultaneous increase in input prices does not change the ratio of the inputs' prices. The cost-minimizing input choice is not affected by such an increase, and the firm's expansion path remains unaffected. If, prior to the increase in input prices, the firm employed the combination L_1, K_1 to produce q_1, total costs would have been

$$TC_1 = vK_1 + wL_1. \tag{12.17}$$

---

[6] Mathematically, we can find the minimum AC by setting its derivative equal to 0:

$$\frac{\partial AC}{\partial q} = \frac{\partial \frac{TC}{q}}{\partial q} = \frac{q \cdot \frac{\partial TC}{\partial q} - TC \cdot 1}{q^2} = \frac{q \cdot MC - TC}{q^2} = 0$$

or

$$q \cdot MC - TC = 0 \quad \text{or} \quad MC = TC/q = AC.$$

If both v and w rise by the same proportion, t, the firm will continue to use L_1, K_1 to produce q_1, but now total costs (TC_1') will be

$$TC_1' = tvK_1 + twL_1 = t(vK_1 + wL_1) = tTC_1, \qquad (12.18)$$

which is what we wished to show.

Because the total cost function is homogeneous of degree 1 in all input prices, the average and marginal cost functions based on that total cost function also will be homogeneous of degree 1 for such price changes. If, as in Equation 12.18, we let costs following the input price change be represented by primes and assume all input prices increase by t, we have

$$TC' = tTC,$$

$$AC' = \frac{TC'}{q} = t\frac{TC}{q} = tAC, \qquad (12.19)$$

and

$$MC' = \frac{\partial TC'}{\partial q} = t\frac{\partial TC}{\partial q} = tMC. \qquad (12.20)$$

One consequence of these results is that in a "pure" inflationary situation (one in which all prices rise at the same rate), firms' input costs will all rise at the same rate, and there will be no incentives for the firms to alter their input choices (or, as we will see, to alter their output choice).

CHANGE IN THE PRICE OF ONE INPUT

If only one input price changes, the story is more complicated. Because such a price change alters the ratios of the inputs' prices, the firm's cost-minimizing choice of inputs will be affected and a new expansion path must be derived. Here we will examine three questions about this kind of change: (1) the qualitative direction of the effect on total, average, and marginal costs; (2) the degree of substitution among inputs introduced by such a change; and (3) the quantitative effect on total, average, and marginal costs.

Direction of Effect

An increase in the price of an input must increase the total cost for any output level (or, at least, leave TC unaffected). If the input substitutions induced by the rise in the cost of one input actually caused total costs to fall, then the firm would not have been minimizing costs in the first place, since the new input combination chosen would have been even less expensive prior to the price rise. One implication of the cost-minimization assumption therefore is that a rise in an input cost increases total cost.[7] A similar argument holds for average costs. Since a rise in the price of an input causes total cost to rise, average costs for any output level (which are simply given by TC/q) must also rise. Again, the assumption of cost minimization provides an unambiguous result.

The situation for marginal costs is made somewhat complicated by the possibility that the input being examined may be inferior. In this (admittedly rare) case, an increase in the inferior input's price will cause firms to use relatively less of that input and, surprisingly, that will reduce marginal costs. The precise reason for this perverse result need not detain us here, although the persistent reader may wish to pursue the matter independently. When the input being examined is not inferior, it is a simple matter to show that an increase in its price will raise marginal cost as well.[8]

---

[7] This can be shown formally by the envelope theorem. Remember that the firm's problem is to minimize $TC = vK + wL$, subject to $f(K, L) = q_0$. The Lagrangian expression for this problem is

$$\mathcal{L} = vK + wL + \lambda[q_0 - f(K, L)].$$

Now the envelope theorem states that at the minimum expenditure level,

$$\frac{\partial TC}{\partial v} = \frac{\partial \mathcal{L}}{\partial v} = K > 0,$$

and

$$\frac{\partial TC}{\partial w} = \frac{\partial \mathcal{L}}{\partial w} = L > 0.$$

These results not only show that an increase in input prices will increase total cost but also introduce again Shephard's lemma (see footnote 5 of Chapter 5), which in this case states that the input demand function can be found from the total cost function by partial differentiation. Since output is held constant in this derivation, these input demand functions also are constant output demand functions. We will examine these in detail in Chapter 21. The extensions to this chapter also make use of this result to study input substitution.

[8] Again, the envelope theorem can be employed. Making use of the Lagrangian expression in footnote 7 (or Equation 12.3), we have the important result that

$$MC = \frac{\partial TC}{\partial q} = \frac{\partial \mathcal{L}}{\partial q} = \lambda.$$

As in all constrained optimization problems, the Lagrangian multiplier shows the change in the objective function (here TC) with respect to the constraint (q). For any input (say, capital),

$$\frac{\partial MC}{\partial v} = \frac{\partial^2 \mathcal{L}}{\partial v \partial q} = \frac{\partial^2 \mathcal{L}}{\partial q \partial v} = \frac{\partial K}{\partial q},$$

which is positive or negative, depending on whether K is a normal or an inferior input (see Figures 12.3 and 12.4). For a more detailed discussion, see C. E. Ferguson, *The Neoclassical Theory of Production and Distribution* (Cambridge: Cambridge University Press, 1969), pp. 136–153.

As we remarked previously, a change in the price of an input will cause a cost-minimizing firm to alter its input choices. One way to measure this change is to examine how the ratio of input usage (K/L) changes in response to a change in w/v, while holding q constant. That is, we wish to examine the derivative

$$\frac{\partial\left(\dfrac{K}{L}\right)}{\partial\left(\dfrac{w}{v}\right)} \qquad (12.21)$$

along an isoquant.

Putting this in proportional terms as

$$s = \frac{\partial\ K/L}{\partial\ w/v} \cdot \frac{w/v}{K/L} = \frac{\partial\ \ln K/L}{\partial\ \ln w/v} \qquad (12.22)$$

gives an alternative and more intuitive definition of the elasticity of substitution.[9] In the two-input case, s must be nonnegative: An increase in w/v will be met by an increase in K/L (or, in the limiting fixed-proportions case, K/L will stay constant). Large values of s indicate that firms change their input proportions significantly in response to changes in input prices, whereas low values indicate that changes in input prices have relatively little effect.

When there are only two inputs, the substitution elasticity defined in Equation 12.22 is identical to that defined in Chapter 11 (see Equation 11.28). This can be easily demonstrated by remembering that a cost-minimizing firm will equate its RTS (of L for K) to the input price ratio w/v. The great advantage of the definition given in Equation 12.22 is that it can be more easily generalized to the many-input case than can the definition of the previous chapter. Specifically, we have the following definition:

DEFINITION

Partial Elasticity of Substitution (s_{ij})   The *partial elasticity of substitution* between two inputs (X_i and X_j) with prices w_i and w_j is given by

---

[9] This definition is usually attributed to R. G. D. Allen, who developed it in an alternative form in his *Mathematical Analysis for Economists* (New York: St. Martin's Press, 1938), pp. 504–509.

$$s_{ij} = \frac{\partial\, X_i/X_j}{\partial\, w_j/w_i} \cdot \frac{w_j/w_i}{X_i/X_j} = \frac{\partial\, \ln\,(x_i/x_j)}{\partial\, \ln\,(w_i/w_j)} \qquad (12.23)$$

where output and all other input prices are held constant.

The word *partial* is used in this definition to differentiate the concept from the production function–based definition developed in Chapter 11. In fact, s_{ij} is a very flexible concept because it permits the firm to alter the usage of inputs other than X_i or X_j when input prices change, whereas other input usage was held constant in our prior definition. Suppose that energy prices rise and we wish to know how this affects the ratio of energy to capital input while holding output constant. Although we would expect energy input to fall, it is possible that the firm will substitute a third input, say, labor, for *both* energy and capital so that capital input may fall too. Hence, depending on the specific sizes of these changes, it is possible that the energy-capital ratio may in fact rise. In such a case we might call energy and capital "complements," because of the way their joint usage relates to labor input. Although we will not examine the implications of these possibilities for production and cost theory here, the extensions in this chapter show how s_{ij} can be calculated if the cost function is known. The concept is also quite useful for studying the derived demand for inputs, as we will show in Chapter 21.

Quantitative Size of Shifts in Cost Curves

We have already shown that increases in an input price will raise total, average, and (except in the inferior input case) marginal costs. We are now in a position to judge the extent of such increases. First, and most obviously, the increase in costs will be influenced importantly by the relative significance of the input in the production process. If an input constitutes a large fraction of total costs, an increase in its price will raise costs significantly. A rise in the wage rate would sharply increase home-builders' costs because labor is a major input in construction. On the other hand, a price rise for a relatively minor input will have a small cost impact. An increase in nail prices will not raise home costs very much.

A less obvious determinant of the extent of cost increases is input substitutability. If firms can easily substitute another input for the one that has risen in price, there may be little increase in costs. Increases in copper prices in the late 1960s, for example, had little impact on electric utilities' costs of distributing electricity because they found they could easily substitute aluminum for copper cables. Alternatively, if the firm finds it difficult or impossible to substitute for the input that has become more costly, costs may rise rapidly. The cost of gold jewelry, along with the price of gold, rose rapidly during the early 1970s because there was simply no substitute for the raw input.

Although it is possible to give a precise mathematical statement of the quantitative sizes of all of these effects, to do so would risk further cluttering the book with symbols.[10] For our purposes it is sufficient to rely on the previous intuitive discussion. This should serve as a reminder that changes in the price of an input will have the effect of shifting firms' cost curves, with the size of the shift depending on the relative importance of the input and the substitution possibilities that are available.

Technical Progress

Improvements in technology will also shift cost curves. Since such improvements permit a given level of output to be produced with fewer inputs, it seems clear that total costs will fall. With constant returns to scale this is easy to demonstrate. In this case costs at time zero are given by

$$TC_0 = TC_0(q, v, w) = C_0(v, w)q \qquad (12.24)$$

where $C_0(v, w)$ is the initial cost of producing one unit of output. If the production function is that given in Equation 11.44 [that is, $q = A(t)f(K, L)$], then unit costs at any time, t, are given by

$$C_t(v, w) = C_0(v, w)/A(t), \qquad (12.25)$$

and total costs are given by

$$TC_t(q, v, w) = C_t(v, w)q = TC_0/A(t). \qquad (12.26)$$

Hence, total costs fall over time at the rate of technical change. Average and marginal costs also fall at the rate $A(t)$. Note that, in this case, technical progress is "neutral" in that it does not affect firms' relative input choices. These choices depend only on the input prices v and w, not on the firm's scale of operations nor on the amount of technical change that has occurred. In cases where technical progress takes a more complex form or in cases of increasing or decreasing returns to scale, the analysis is more complex, and we shall not pursue it here. Even in these more complex cases, however, technical change will usually cause all costs to fall.

EXAMPLE 12.2

A COBB-DOUGLAS COST FUNCTION

Returning to our hamburger-grilling example, remember that cost minimization requires

---

[10] For a relatively complete statement, see Ferguson, *Neoclassical Theory of Production and Distribution*, pp. 154–160.

$$\frac{w}{v} = \frac{K}{L}. \qquad (12.27)$$

To compute the total cost function implied by this condition requires that we use Equation 12.27 together with the production function to express total costs as a function of q, v, and w. Sometimes that can involve quite a lot of tedious algebra, but in this case it is a relatively simple manipulation. Given the hamburger production function,

$$q = 10K^{1/2}L^{1/2}, \qquad (12.28)$$

division by K yields

$$\frac{q}{K} = 10\left(\frac{L}{K}\right)^{1/2}, \qquad (12.29)$$

and using the cost-minimization requirement yields

$$\frac{q}{K} = 10\left(\frac{v}{w}\right)^{1/2}. \qquad (12.30)$$

Hence,

$$K = \frac{q}{10} w^{1/2}v^{-1/2} \qquad (12.31)$$

so

$$vK = \frac{q}{10} w^{1/2}v^{1/2}. \qquad (12.32)$$

A similar chain of substitutions yields

$$wL = \frac{q}{10} w^{1/2}v^{1/2} \qquad (12.33)$$

and, since

$$TC = vK + wL, \qquad (12.34)$$

we have

$$TC = .2qw^{1/2}v^{1/2}. \qquad (12.35)$$

This is the total cost function for hamburger production. For specific input prices, the function implies a simple relationship between hamburger output and total costs. If $w = v = \$4$, for example,

$$TC = 0.8q. \qquad (12.36)$$

As before, it costs $32 to produce 40 hamburgers if costs are minimized. Total costs of any other level of production can also be quickly calculated from Equation 12.36.

Per-Unit Costs. Because of the constant returns-to-scale nature of the hamburger production function, average and marginal costs are constant (and equal) for all possible output levels:

$$AC = \frac{TC}{q} = 0.8 \tag{12.37}$$

$$MC = \frac{\partial TC}{\partial q} = 0.8. \tag{12.38}$$

The average and marginal cost of producing a hamburger is always $.80.

Change in Input Prices. If an input price should change, the firm would use K and L in different proportions, and this changed expansion path would be reflected by a shifting cost function. When $v = \$9$ and $w = \$4$, for example,

$$TC = 0.2qw^{1/2}v^{1/2} = 1.2q. \tag{12.39}$$

Hence, the average and marginal cost of each hamburger has increased to $1.20. By knowing the total cost function, it is unnecessary to recalculate cost-minimizing input choices—that is done "automatically," since the total cost function was derived from the cost-minimization assumption. When input prices change, the new relationship between TC and q can be found by substituting the new input prices into the cost function.

Technical Progress. If, as in Example 11.4, we assume hamburger production experiences technical progress that can be represented by

$$q = A(t)f(K, L) = e^{.05t}f(K, L), \tag{12.40}$$

then total costs at any time are given by

$$TC_t = TC_0/A(t) = e^{-.05t}TC_0 = e^{-.05t}[.2qw^{1/2}v^{1/2}]. \tag{12.41}$$

After ten years of cooking progress, costs are given by

$$TC_{10} = .607TC_0 = .121qw^{1/2}v^{1/2}. \tag{12.42}$$

With $w = v = 4$,

$$TC_{10} = .48q, \tag{12.43}$$

so total, average, and marginal costs have fallen by 40 percent from their previous level of .80. Even if capital costs had risen to $v = \$9$ in year 10, total costs would have been given by

$$TC_{10} = .73q, \tag{12.44}$$

so costs would have fallen about 10 percent despite the rise in capital costs.

QUERY: What is the elasticity of hamburger costs with respect to changes in w or v? Why are these elasticities less than 1.0? Are they affected by technical progress?

SHORT-RUN, LONG-RUN DISTINCTION

It is customary in economics to make a distinction between the "short run" and the "long run." Although no very precise temporal definition can be provided for these terms, the general purpose of the distinction is to differentiate between a short period during which economic actors have only limited flexibility in their actions and a longer period that provides greater freedom. One area of study in which this distinction is quite important is in the theory of the firm and its costs, since economists are interested in examining supply reactions during different potential time intervals. In the remainder of this chapter, we will examine the implications of such differential response periods.

To illustrate this distinction we assume that capital input is held constant at a level of K_1, and that (in the short run) the firm is only free to vary its labor input. Implicitly, we are assuming that alterations in the level of capital input are infinitely costly in the short run. As a result of this assumption, we may write the short-run production function as

$$q = f(K_1, L), \tag{12.45}$$

where this notation explicitly shows that capital inputs may not vary. Of course, the level of output still may be changed by the firm altering its use of labor.

A Note on Flexibility

Before turning to look at this process, we should comment on this method of analysis. It is obvious that any firm uses far more than two inputs in its production process. The level of usage of some of these inputs may be changed on rather short notice. Firms may ask workers to work overtime hours, hire part-time replacements from an employment agency, or rent equipment (such as power tools or automobiles) from some other firm. It may take a somewhat longer time for the level of usage of other inputs to be adjusted; for example, to hire new full-time workers is a relatively time-consuming (and costly) process. Similarly, ordering new machines designed according to unique specifications may involve a considerable time lag. At the most lengthy extreme, new factories can be built, new managers can be recruited and trained, and raw material supplies can be discovered and extracted. To cover all such variations of input types in any detail is an impossibility. Consequently, we will proceed by using only the two-input model we have been analyzing and by holding the level of capital input fixed.

Such a treatment should not be taken to imply that in some way labor is a more flexible input than capital. As we have just pointed out, this need not be the case. Rather, all we wish to do is to make a distinction between fixed and variable inputs, and this approach will enable us to do so. We could substitute any other appropriate input names for "capital" and "labor" in the discussion that follows.

Total cost for the firm continues to be defined as

$$TC = vK + wL \qquad (12.46)$$

Short-Run Total Costs

for our short-run analysis, but now capital input is fixed at K_1. To denote this fact, we will write

$$STC(K_1) = vK_1 + wL, \qquad (12.47)$$

where the S indicates that we are analyzing short-run costs with the level of capital input fixed (at K_1). Throughout our analysis we will use this method to indicate short-run costs, while the long-run costs derived previously will be denoted by TC, AC, and MC.

The two types of input costs in Equation 12.47 are given special names. The term vK_1 is referred to as (short-run) *fixed costs*; since K_1 is constant, these costs will not change in the short run. The term wL is referred to as (short-run) *variable costs,* since labor input can indeed be varied in the short run. Using the symbols $SFC(K_1)$ for short-run fixed costs and $SVC(K_1)$ for short-run variable costs, we have

Fixed and Variable Costs

$$SFC(K_1) = vK_1$$

$$SVC(K_1) = wL$$

and therefore

$$STC(K_1) = SFC(K_1) + SVC(K_1). \qquad (12.48)$$

More generally, we have the following definitions:

DEFINITION

Short-Run Fixed and Variable Costs *Short-run fixed costs* (SFC) are costs associated with inputs that cannot be varied in the short run. *Short-run variable costs* (SVC) are costs of those inputs that can be varied in order to change the firm's output level.

The importance of this distinction is to differentiate between those variable costs that the firm can avoid by producing nothing in the short run and those costs that are fixed and must be paid regardless of the output level chosen (even zero).

Nonoptionality of Short-Run Costs

It is important to understand that short-run costs are not the minimal costs for producing the various output levels. Because we are holding capital fixed in the short run, the firm does not have the flexibility of input choice that we assumed when we discussed cost minimization earlier in this chapter. Rather, to vary its output level in the short run, the firm will be forced to use "nonoptimal" input combinations: The RTS will not be equal to the ratio of the input prices. This is shown in Figure 12.7. In the short run, the firm is constrained to use K_1 units of capital. To produce output level q_0, it therefore will use L_0 units of labor. Similarly, it will use L_1 units of labor to produce q_1, and L_2 units to produce q_2. The total costs of these input combinations are given by STC_0, STC_1, and STC_2, respectively. Only for the input combination K_1, L_1 is output being produced at minimal cost. Only at that point is the RTS equal to the ratio of the input prices. From Figure 12.7 it is clear that q_0 is being produced with "too much" capital in this short-run situation. Cost minimization should suggest a southeasterly movement along the q_0 isoquant, indicating a substitution of labor for capital in production. Similarly, q_2 is being produced with "too little" capital, and costs could be reduced by substituting capital for labor. Neither of these substitutions is possible in the short run. Over a longer period, however, the firm will be able to change its level of capital input and will adjust its input usage to the cost-minimizing combinations. We have already discussed this flexible case earlier in this chapter and shall return to it to illustrate the connection between long-run and short-run cost curves.

Short-Run Marginal and Average Costs

Frequently, it is more useful to analyze short-run costs on a per-unit of output basis rather than on a total basis. The two most important per-unit concepts that can be derived from the short-run total cost function are the *short-run average total cost function* ($SATC$) and the *short-run marginal cost function* (SMC). These concepts are defined as

$$SATC(K_1) = \frac{\text{total costs}}{\text{total output}} = \frac{STC(K_1)}{q}$$

$$SMC(K_1) = \frac{\text{change in total costs}}{\text{change in output}} = \frac{\partial STC(K_1)}{\partial q},$$

(12.49)

where we have continued to record the level of capital input usage (K_1) that is fixed in the short run. These definitions for average and marginal costs are

FIGURE 12.7

"NONOPTIMAL" INPUT CHOICES MUST BE MADE IN THE SHORT RUN

Because capital input is fixed at K_1 in the short run, the firm cannot bring its RTS into equality with the ratio of input prices. Given the input prices, q_0 should be produced with more labor and less capital than it will be in the short run, whereas q_2 should be produced with more capital and less labor than it will be.

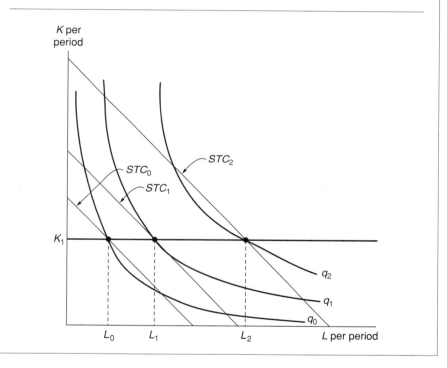

identical to those developed previously for the long-run, fully flexible case, and the derivation of cost curves from the total cost function proceeds in exactly the same way. Because the short-run total cost curve has the same general type of cubic shape as did the total cost curve in Figure 12.6a, these short-run average and marginal cost curves will also be U-shaped.

Occasionally, it is helpful to use Equation 12.48 to divide short-run average total costs into two components: *short-run average fixed costs* (SAFC) and *short-run average variable costs* (SAVC). These are defined as

Short-Run Average Fixed and Variable Costs

$$SAFC(K_1) = \frac{\text{total fixed costs}}{\text{output}} = \frac{SFC(K_1)}{q}$$

$$SAVC(K_1) = \frac{\text{total variable costs}}{\text{output}} = \frac{SVC(K_1)}{q},$$

(12.50)

where it is obvious that

$$SAFC(K_1) + SAVC(K_1) = \frac{SFC(K_1)}{q} + \frac{SVC(K_1)}{q}$$

$$= \frac{STC(K_1)}{q} = SATC(K_1).$$

(12.51)

This differentiation between short-run average fixed and variable costs will be useful for explaining firms' short-run supply decisions in the next chapter.

Relationship between Short-Run and Long-Run Cost Curves

By considering all possible variations in capital input, we can establish the relationship between the short-run costs and the fully flexible long-run costs that were derived previously in this chapter. Figure 12.8 shows this relationship for both the constant returns-to-scale and cubic total cost curve cases. Short-run total costs for three levels of capital input are shown, although of course it would be possible to show many more such short-run curves. The figures show that long-run total costs (TC) are always less than short-run total costs, except at that output level for which the assumed fixed capital input is appropriate to long-run cost minimization. For example, as in Figure 12.7, with capital input of K_1, the firm can obtain full cost minimization when q_1 is produced. Hence, short-run and long-run total costs are equal at this point. For output levels other than q_1, however, $STC(K_1) > TC$, as was the case in Figure 12.7.

Technically, the long-run total cost curves in Figure 12.8 are said to be an "envelope" of their respective short-run curves. These short-run total cost curves can be represented parametrically by

$$STC(q, K) = \text{total cost,} \tag{12.52}$$

where the family of short-run curves is generated by allowing capital input to vary. The long-run envelope curve (TC) must obey both Equation 12.52 and the further stipulation that for any q, capital input should be chosen to minimize total cost; that is, capital input should be chosen so that for any specific output level, q,

$$\frac{\partial STC(q, K)}{\partial K} = 0. \tag{12.53}$$

By solving Equations 12.52 and 12.53 together to eliminate K, it is possible to

FIGURE 12.8

TWO POSSIBLE SHAPES FOR LONG-RUN TOTAL COST CURVES

By considering all possible levels of capital input, the long-run total cost curve (TC) can be traced out. In (a) the underlying production function exhibits constant returns to scale—in the long run, though not in the short run, total costs are proportional to output. In (b) the long-run total cost curve has a cubic shape, as do the short-run curves. Diminishing returns set in more sharply for the short-run curves, however, because of the assumed fixed level of capital input.

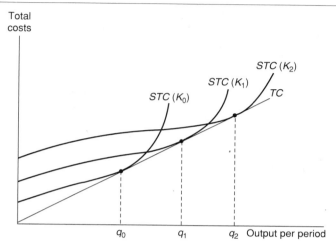

(a) Constant Returns to Scale

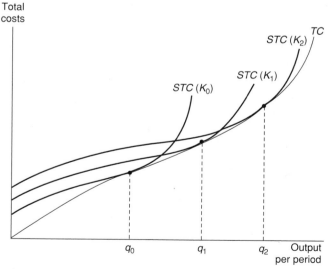

(b) Cubic Total Cost Curve Case

derive the long-run total cost curve. This solution will be identical to the one found by minimizing total cost directly as we did earlier in this chapter. In Example 12.3, we show this result numerically.

Per-Unit Cost Curves

The envelope total cost curve relationships exhibited in Figure 12.8 can be used to show geometric connections between short-run and long-run average and marginal cost curves. These are presented in Figure 12.9 for the constant returns-to-scale case and in Figure 12.10 for the cubic total cost curve case. In both cases, short-run and long-run average costs are equal at that output for which the (fixed) capital input is appropriate. At q_1, for example, $SATC(K_1) = AC$ since K_1 is used in producing q_1 at minimal costs. For movements away from q_1, short-run average costs exceed long-run average costs, thus reflecting the cost-minimizing nature of the long-run total cost curve. In the constant returns-to-scale case in Figure 12.9, for example, an increase in output from q_1 to q_1^* raises average cost slightly from AC to C_1, whereas long-run average cost continues to be AC for such a movement. This reflects the diminishing returns that occur in the short run (because of a fixed capital input), but not in the long run.

FIGURE 12.9

LONG-RUN AVERAGE AND MARGINAL COST CURVES FOR THE CONSTANT RETURNS-TO-SCALE CASE

This figure is derived from the cost curves shown in Figure 12.8a. Because the underlying production function exhibits constant returns to scale, long-run average and marginal costs will be constant (and equal) over all output ranges. In this figure, three sets of short-run curves are also shown for three different levels of capital input.

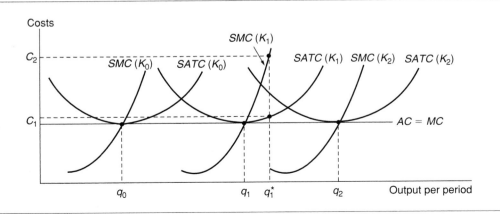

FIGURE 12.10

AVERAGE AND MARGINAL COST CURVES FOR THE CUBIC COST CURVE CASE

This set of curves is derived from the total cost curves shown in Figure 12.11b. The AC and MC curves have the usual U-shapes, as do the short-run curves. At q_1, long-run average costs are minimized. The configuration of curves at this minimum point is quite important.

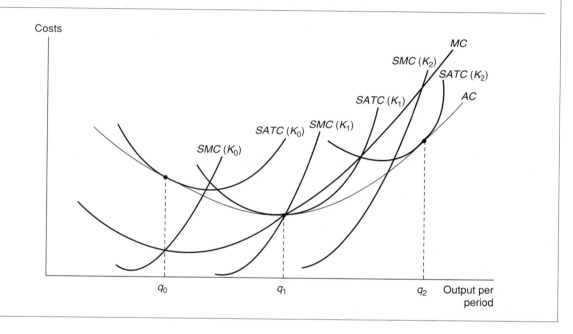

For marginal costs, similar conclusions occur. Short-run and long-run marginal costs are equal for output levels where the short-run fixed capital stock is appropriate. But for increases in output beyond these levels, short-run marginal costs rise rapidly. At q_1^* in Figure 12.9, for example, short-run marginal costs of C_2 greatly exceed the constant long-run marginal cost, MC.

Because the minimum point of the long-run average cost curve (AC) plays a major role in the theory of long-run price determination, it is important to note the various curves that pass through this point in Figure 12.10. First, as is always true for average and marginal cost curves, the MC curve passes through the low point of the AC curve. At q_1 long-run average and marginal costs are equal. Associated with q_1 is a certain level of capital input (say, K_1), and the short-run average cost curve for this level of capital input [$SATC(K_1)$] is tangent to the AC curve at its minimum point. The $SATC(K_1)$ curve also reaches its minimum at output level q_1. For movements away from q_1, the AC curve is much flatter than the $SATC(K_1)$ curve, and this reflects the greater flexibility open to firms in the long run. Short-run costs rise rapidly because capital inputs are fixed. In the long run, such inputs are not fixed, and diminishing marginal productivities do not occur so abruptly. Finally, because the $SATC(K_1)$ curve reaches its minimum at q_1, the short-run marginal cost curve [$SMC(K_1)$] also passes through this point. The minimum point of the AC curve therefore brings together the four most important per-unit costs. At this point

$$AC = MC = SATC(K_1) = SMC(K_1). \tag{12.54}$$

For this reason, as we shall show in Chapter 14, the output level q_1 is an important equilibrium point for a competitive firm in the long run.

EXAMPLE 12.3

SHORT-RUN COBB-DOUGLAS COSTS

Previously, we calculated total costs of hamburger production on the assumption that both inputs could be varied. Suppose now that the number of grills is fixed at K_1 in the short run. Now the short-run Cobb-Douglas production function is

$$q = 10K_1^{1/2}L^{1/2} \tag{12.55}$$

and

$$STC = vK_1 + wL = vK_1 + \frac{wq^2}{100K_1}. \tag{12.56}$$

If, for example, the firm has four grills to operate, $K_1 = 4$ and

$$STC = 4v + \frac{wq^2}{400}. \tag{12.57}$$

Again, in order to calculate total costs we need to know w and v. Table 12.1 shows the relationship between short-run total costs and output for the case where $w = v = \$4$ for three fixed levels of capital input: 1, 4, and 9 grills. Notice that short-run total costs are positive even when $q = 0$ (since fixed capital costs must be paid).

In the final column of Table 12.1, we have used Equation 12.36 from Example 12.2 to calculate long-run total costs. For each output level but one, short-run total costs exceed long-run total costs. This is also illustrated in Figure 12.11. Notice also that for $q = 0$, long-run total costs are zero. The capital costs that are unavoidable in the short run can be avoided in the long run if the hamburger firm cancels the leases on its grills.

TABLE 12.1

SHORT-RUN AND LONG-RUN TOTAL COSTS
FOR $q = 10K^{1/2}L^{1/2}$ **WHEN** $w = v = \$4$

(1)	(2)	(3)	(4)	(5)
(q)	STC(K = 1)	STC(K = 4)	STC(K = 9)	TC
0	$ 4.00	$ 16.00	$36.00	$ 0.00
10	8.00	17.00	36.44	8.00
20	20.00	20.00	37.78	16.00
30	40.00	25.00	40.00	24.00
40	68.00	32.00	43.11	32.00
50	104.00	41.00	47.11	40.00
60	148.00	52.00	52.00	48.00
70	200.00	65.00	57.78	56.00
80	260.00	80.00	64.44	64.00
90	328.00	97.00	72.00	72.00
100	404.00	116.00	80.44	80.00

An Envelope Derivation.   An alternative way of deriving this firm's long-run total cost curve is to use the envelope procedure described in the previous section. If we continue to assume $w = v = \$4$, we can use Equation 12.56 to write

$$STC = 4K + \frac{4q^2}{100K} \qquad (12.58)$$

and then differentiate this expression with respect to (the now variable) K:

$$\frac{\partial STC}{\partial K} = 4 - \frac{4q^2}{100K^2}. \qquad (12.59)$$

Setting this derivative equal to zero (since we wish to minimize STC with respect to K, for each level of output) we have

$$4 = \frac{4q^2}{100K^2} \qquad (12.60)$$

or

$$K = \frac{q}{10}. \qquad (12.61)$$

Substituting this optimal solution for K back into the short-run total cost function (Equation 12.58) yields

FIGURE 12.11

SHORT-RUN AND LONG-RUN TOTAL COST CURVES FOR $q = 10K^{1/2}L^{1/2}$

Since this production function possesses constant returns to scale, the TC curve is a straight line. The short-run curves for $K = 1$, $K = 4$, and $K = 9$ lie above this line, except at output levels $q = 10$, $q = 40$, and $q = 90$, respectively. At these output levels, the constant short-run level of K is also appropriate for long-run cost minimization. Hence, at these output levels, the short-run and long-run total cost curves are tangent.

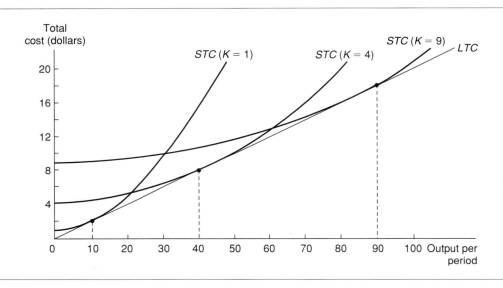

$$TC = .4q + .4q = .8q, \tag{12.62}$$

which is a rather long-winded way to show what we already know from Example 12.2 (see Equation 12.36).

Per-Unit Cost Function. Average and marginal cost relationships can be derived from the short-run and long-run total cost curves we have already calculated. These are illustrated in Figure 12.12. As before, long-run average and marginal costs are constant at $.80, and the short-run average cost curves have a general U-shape. Other relationships between long-run and short-run cost curves discussed in the previous section are also apparent in the figure.

QUERY: Why would an increase in w to $5 increase both short-run average and marginal costs, whereas an increase in v to $5 would increase only short-run average costs? How would the cost curves shift in these two cases?

FIGURE 12.12

SHORT-RUN AND LONG-RUN AVERAGE AND MARGINAL COST CURVES FOR $q = 10K^{1/2}L^{1/2}$

For this production function, AC and MC are constant over all ranges of output. Since $w = v = \$4$, this constant average cost is \$.80 per unit. The short-run average cost curves, however, do have a general U-shape, since K is held constant in the short run. The $SATC$ curves are tangent to the AC curve at output levels $q = 10$, $q = 40$, and $q = 90$.

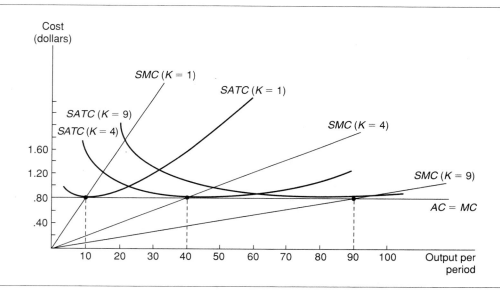

SUMMARY

In this chapter we have examined the relationship between the level of output that a firm produces and the input costs that level of production requires. The resulting cost curves should generally be familiar to you since they are widely used in most courses in introductory economics. Here we have shown how such curves reflect the firm's underlying production function together with the firm's desire to minimize costs. By developing cost curves from these basic foundations, we were able to illustrate a number of important findings:

- A firm that wishes to minimize the economic costs of producing a particular level of output should choose that input combination for which the rate of technical substitution (RTS) is equal to the ratio of the inputs' rental prices.

- Repeated application of this minimization procedure yields the firm's expansion path. Since the expansion path shows how input usage expands with the level of output, it also shows the relationship between output level and total cost. That relationship is summarized by the total cost function—$TC(q, v, w)$—which shows production costs as a function of output levels and input prices.

- The firm's average cost ($AC = TC/q$) and marginal cost ($MC = \partial TC/\partial q$) functions can be derived directly from the total cost function. If the total cost curve has a general cubic shape, the AC and MC curves will be U-shaped.

- All cost curves are drawn on the assumption that the input prices are held constant. When input prices change, cost curves will shift to new positions. The extent of the shifts will be determined by the overall importance of the input whose price has changed and by the ease with which the firm may substitute one input for another. Technical progress will also shift cost curves.

- In the short run, the firm may not be able to vary some inputs. It can then alter its level of production only by changing its employment of variable inputs. In so doing, it may have to use nonoptimal, higher cost input combinations than it would choose to use if it were possible to vary all inputs.

PROBLEMS

12.1

In a famous article [J. Viner, "Cost Curves and Supply Curves," *Zeitschrift fur Nationalokonomie* 3 (September 1931): 23–46], Viner criticized his draftsman who could not draw a family of *SATC* curves whose points of tangency with the U-shaped *AC* curve were also the minimum points on each *SATC* curve. The draftsman protested that such a drawing was impossible to construct. Whom would you support in this debate?

12.2

Show that for a production function with $\sigma = \infty$, the cost-minimizing input ratio, if it is unique, will generally require the use of only capital or only labor. In such a situation, what will be the firm's expansion path? On what will the shape of its marginal and average cost curves depend? How will these cost curves shift as the price of the input that is utilized rises?

12.3

Professor Smith and Professor Jones are going to produce a new introductory textbook. As true scientists they have laid out the production function for the book as

$$q = S^{1/2}J^{1/2},$$

where q = the number of pages in the finished book, S = the number of working hours spent by Smith, and J = the number of hours spent working by Jones.

Smith values his labor as $3 per working hour. He has spent 900 hours preparing the first draft. Jones, whose labor is valued at $12 per working hour, will revise Smith's draft to complete the book.

a. How many hours will Jones have to spend to produce a finished book of 150 pages? Of 300 pages? Of 450 pages?

b. What is the marginal cost of the 150th page of the finished book? Of the 300th page? Of the 450th page?

12.4

Suppose that a firm's fixed proportion production function is given by

$$q = \min(5K, 10L),$$

and that the rental rates for capital and labor are given by $v = 1$, $w = 3$.

a. Calculate the firm's long-run total, average, and marginal cost curves.

b. Suppose that K is fixed at 10 in the short run. Calculate the firm's short-run total, average, and marginal cost curves. What is the marginal cost of the 10th unit? The 50th unit? The 100th unit?

12.5

Suppose that a firm's production function is given by the Cobb-Douglas function

$$q = K^{\alpha}L^{\beta}$$

(where $\alpha, \beta > 0$) and that the firm can purchase all the K and L it wants in competitive input markets at rental rates of v and w, respectively.

a. Show that cost minimization requires

$$\frac{vK}{\alpha} = \frac{wL}{\beta}.$$

What is the shape of the expansion path for this firm?

b. Assuming cost minimization, show that total costs can be expressed as a function of q, v, and w of the form

$$TC = Bq^{1/\alpha + \beta} w^{\beta/\alpha} + B_v v^{\alpha/\alpha + \beta},$$

where B is a constant depending on α and β. *Hint:* This part may be most easily worked by using the results from part (a) to solve successively for TC as a function of L and TC as a function of K and then substituting into the production function.

c. Show that if $\alpha + \beta = 1$, TC is proportional to q.

d. Calculate the firm's marginal cost curve. Show that

$$e_{MC,w} = \frac{\beta}{\alpha + \beta}.$$

$$e_{MC,v} = \frac{\alpha}{\alpha + \beta}.$$

12.6

For the total cost curve calculated in Problem 12.5, use Shephard's lemma (see footnote 7) to compute the (constant output) demand function for L as a function of w, v, and q_0.

12.7

A firm producing hockey sticks has a production function given by

$$q = 2\sqrt{K \cdot L}.$$

In the short run, the firm's amount of capital equipment is fixed at $K = 100$. The rental rate for K is $v = \$1$, and the wage rate for L is $w = \$4$.

a. Calculate the firm's short-run total cost curve. Calculate the short-run average cost curve.

b. What is the firm's short-run marginal cost function? What are the STC, $SATC$, and SMC for the firm if it produces 25 hockey sticks? Fifty hockey sticks? One hundred hockey sticks? Two hundred hockey sticks?

c. Graph the $SATC$ and the SMC curves for the firm. Indicate the points found in part (b).

d. Where does the SMC curve intersect the $SATC$ curve? Explain why the SMC curve will always intersect the $SATC$ curve at its lowest point.

12.8

Suppose, as in Problem 12.7, a firm produces hockey sticks with a production function of $q = 2\sqrt{KL}$. Capital stock is fixed at $\overline{K}$ in the short run.

a. Calculate the firm's total costs as a function of q, w, v, and $\overline{K}$.

b. Given q, w, and v, how should the capital stock be chosen to minimize total cost?

c. Use your results from part (b) to calculate the long-run total cost of hockey stick production.

d. For $w = \$4$, $v = \$1$, graph the long-run total cost curve for hockey stick production. Show that this is an envelope for the short-run curves computed in part (a) by examining values of $\overline{K}$ of 100, 200, and 400.

12.9

An enterprising entrepreneur purchases two firms to produce widgets. Each firm produces identical products, and each has a production function given by

$$q = \sqrt{K_i L_i} \qquad i = 1, 2.$$

The firms differ, however, in the amount of capital equipment each has. In particular, firm 1 has $K_1 = 25$, whereas firm 2 has $K_2 = 100$. Rental rates for K and L are given by $w = v = \$1$.

a. If the entrepreneur wishes to minimize short-run total costs of widget production, how should output be allocated between the two firms?

b. Given that output is optimally allocated between the two firms, calculate the short-run total, average, and marginal cost curves. What is the marginal cost of the 100th widget? The 125th widget? The 200th widget?

c. How should the entrepreneur allocate widget production between the two firms in the long run? Calculate the long-run total, average, and marginal cost curves for widget production.

d. How would your answer to part (c) change if both firms exhibited diminishing returns to scale?

12.10

Suppose the total cost function for a firm is given by

$$TC = qw^{2/3}v^{1/3}.$$

a. Use Shephard's lemma (footnote 7) to compute the constant output demand functions for inputs L and K.

b. Use your results from part (a) to calculate the underlying production function for q.

12.11

Suppose the total cost function for a firm is given by

$$TC = (.5v + \sqrt{vw} + .5w)q.$$

a. Use Shephard's lemma to compute the constant output demand function for each input, K and L.

b. Use the results from part (a) to compute the underlying production function for q.

c. You can check the result by using results from Extension E12.2 to show that the CES cost function with $\sigma = \beta = .5$ generates this total cost function.

SUGGESTED READINGS

Allen, R. G. D. *Mathematical Analysis for Economists.* New York: St. Martin's Press, 1938. Various pages—see index.
Complete mathematical analysis of substitution possibilities and cost functions. Notation somewhat difficult.

Ferguson, C. E. *The Neoclassical Theory of Production and Distribution.* Cambridge: Cambridge University Press, 1969. Chap. 6.
Nice development of cost curves, especially strong on graphic analysis.

Fuss, M., and D. McFadden. *Production Economics: A Dual Approach to Theory and Applications.* Amsterdam: North-Holland Publishing Co., 1978.
Difficult and quite complete treatment of the dual relationship between production and cost functions. Some discussion of empirical issues.

Knight, F. H. "Cost of Production and Price over Long and Short Periods." *Journal of Political Economy* 29 (April 1921): 304–335.

Classic treatment of the short-run, long-run distinction.

Marshall, A. *Principles of Economics.* 8th ed. New York: Crowell-Collier and Macmillan, 1970. Book 5. Chaps. 8–11.
Good literary analysis of early cost theory. See also Marshall's mathematical appendix.

Nadiri, M. I. "Producers Theory." In K. J. Arrow and M. D. Intriligater, eds. *Handbook of Mathematical Economics.* Vol. 2. Amsterdam: North-Holland Publishing Company, 1982, pp. 431–490.
Complete description of mathematical production theory. A nice survey of the properties of production and cost functions and relationships among these properties. Also a brief discussion of multiproduct firms.

Viner, J. "Cost Curves and Supply Curves." Reprinted in American Economic Association, *Readings in Price Theory.* Homewood, Ill.: Richard D. Irwin, 1952.
Classic article on the envelope relationship between short-run and long-run cost curves. Famous for Viner's criticism of his draftsman (see Problem 12.1).

EXTENSIONS

Input Substitutability

Throughout Chapter 12 we stressed that a change in input prices may affect all the inputs that a firm uses by changing the cost-minimizing mix. Here we examine the nature of these substitutions implied by various types of cost (and production) functions. We show that some common forms for cost functions offer very limited possibilities for input substitution and that a more general form (the translog) might be considered for greater flexibility. Throughout we use only constant returns-to-scale cost functions (the exponent of output, q, is always 1), but these are readily generalizable to cases of nonconstant (but homothetic) returns-to-scale cost functions.

E12.1 Cobb-Douglas Cost Function

The Cobb-Douglas cost function for two inputs (K and L) is given by (see Example 12.2)

$$TC = q(v^{\alpha} w^{\beta}) \text{ where } \alpha + \beta = 1.$$

a. Application of Shephard's lemma shows that the constant output demand functions for K and L are

$$K = \frac{\partial TC}{\partial v} = \alpha \left(\frac{w}{v}\right)^{\beta} q$$

$$L = \frac{\partial TC}{\partial w} = \beta \left(\frac{v}{w}\right)^{\alpha} q$$

b. By the definition given in this chapter, the elasticity of substitution between K and L can be measured by

$$s = \frac{\partial(K/L)}{\partial(w/v)} \cdot \frac{(w/v)}{(K/L)} = \frac{\partial \ln (K/L)}{\partial \ln (w/v)}.$$

Dividing the two equations in part (a) provides an easy proof that $s = 1$ for this case.

E12.2 CES Cost Function

The CES cost function for two inputs is given by

$$TC = q[\beta^{\sigma} v^{1 - \sigma} + (1 - \beta)^{\sigma} w^{1 - \sigma}]^{1/1 - \sigma}.$$

a. For this function Shephard's lemma can be used to calculate the constant output demand functions for K and L as

$$K = \alpha_1 v^{-\sigma} q$$

$$L = \alpha_2 w^{-\sigma} q,$$

where α_1 and α_2 are constants.

b. The results from part (a) together with the definition of s in E12.1 show that

$$s = \sigma.$$

That is, the elasticity of substitution is the same and constant for all values of K and L whether calculated from the production or the cost function.

c. The results of this problem can be used to prove Problem 12.11, part (c).

E12.3 Translog Cost Function

One commonly used approximation to any arbitrary cost function is the translog function:

$$\ln TC = \ln q + \beta_0 + \beta_1 \ln w + (1 - \beta_1) \ln v$$
$$+ \beta_2 (\ln w)^2 + \beta_3 (\ln v)^2 + \beta_4 \ln w \ln v.$$

a. If this function is to be homogeneous of degree 1 in w and v, $\beta_2 + \beta_3 + \beta_4 = 0$.

b. This function clearly reduces to the Cobb-Douglas cost function if $\beta_2 = \beta_3 = \beta_4 = 0$.

c. Differentiation of the total cost function and application of Shephard's lemma show that the shares of total costs accounted for by K and L are given by

$$s_K = \frac{vK}{TC} = (1 - \beta_1) + 2\beta_3 \ln v + \beta_4 \ln w$$

$$s_L = \frac{wL}{TC} = \beta_1 + 2\beta_2 \ln w + \beta_4 \ln v.$$

Hence, the cost shares depend on both input prices.

E12.4 Multi-Input Cost Functions

The three cost functions given in E12.1–E12.3 can be readily generalized to many inputs ($X_1 \ldots X_n$) with prices $w_1 \ldots w_n$ as

- Cobb-Douglas

$$TC = q \prod_{i=1}^{n} w_i^{\beta_i} \quad \text{where } \sum_{i=1}^{n} \beta_i = 1$$

- CES

$$TC = q \left[\sum_{i=1}^{n} \beta_i w_i^{1 - \sigma} \right]^{1/1 - \sigma}$$

- Translog

$$\ln TC = \ln q + \beta_0 + \sum_{i=1}^{n} \beta_i \ln w_i$$
$$+ 0.5 \sum_i \sum_j \beta_{ij} \ln w_i \ln w_j$$

where $\sum \beta_i = 1, \beta_{ij} = \beta_{ji}.$

It can be shown that the partial elasticity of subtitution (s_{ij}) can be computed from these cost funcions as

$$s_{ij} = \frac{TC \cdot TC_{ij}}{TC_i \cdot TC_j}.$$

a. If you do not wish to take this result on faith, prove it for the two-input case or see Sato and Koizumi (1973).
b. This definition of s_{ij} can be used to show that $s_{ij} = 1$ for the Cobb-Douglas case and that s_{ij} is a constant for the CES case.
c. Generalizing the results of E12.3 shows that cost shares for the multi-input translog cost function are given by[1]

$$s_i = \frac{w_i X_i}{TC} = \beta_i + \sum_{j=1}^{n} \beta_{ij} \, ln \, w_j.$$

d. For the translog case, the partial elasticity of substitution is given by

$$s_{ij} = (\beta_{ij} + s_i s_j)/s_i s_j \text{ (for } i \neq j).$$

This latter result is useful in empirical work because it shows how the partial elasticities of substitution can be computed directly from information obtained in the cost share equations in part (c).

Competition between Truck and Rail Transport

The translog cost function has become widely used to examine input substitutability in a variety of contexts. Some of the most interesting of these

---

[1] Often in empirical work this equation is augmented with a term in $ln \, q$ to allow for scale effects in input shares.

applications are in the area of transportation economics. Recent years have seen a significant deregulation of the trucking and railroad industries, both in the United States and throughout the world. Success of these actions, especially in the case of railroads for which only one firm may serve a market, depends importantly on a high degree of substitutability by shippers among transportation modes. Most econometric studies have found these conditions to be reasonably well satisfied.

For example, in a study of the transportation of fruits and vegetables from the western United States, Westbrook and Buckley (1990) use a modification of the translog cost function to estimate substitution elasticities between truck and rail transportation. For the period following deregulation, the authors find that quite high elasticities characterize both the Chicago and New York markets. They interpret these results as favoring continued deregulation of the transportation industry.

References

Ferguson, C. E. *The Neoclassical Theory of Production and Distribution.* Cambridge: Cambridge University Press, 1969.

Fuss, M., and D. McFadden, eds. *Production Economics: A Dual Approach to Theory and Applications.* Amsterdam: North-Holland Publishing Co., 1978.

Sato, R., and T. Koizumi. "On Elasticities of Substitution and Complementarity." *Oxford Economic Papers* (March 1973): 44–50.

Westbrook, M. D., and P. A. Buckley. "Flexible Functional Firms and Regularity: Assessing the Competitive Relationship between Truck and Rail Transportation." *Review of Economics and Statistics* (November 1990): 623–630.

CHAPTER 13

PROFIT MAXIMIZATION AND SUPPLY

In Chapter 12 we examined the way in which firms minimize costs for any level of output they may choose. In this chapter we will focus on how the level of output is chosen by profit-maximizing firms. Before investigating that decision, however, it is appropriate to discuss briefly the nature of firms and the ways in which firms' choices may be analyzed.

As we pointed out at the beginning of our analysis of production, a firm is an association of individuals who have organized themselves for the purpose of turning inputs into outputs. Different individuals will provide different types of inputs, such as workers' skills and varieties of capital equipment, with the expectation of receiving some sort of reward for doing so.

THE NATURE AND BEHAVIOR OF FIRMS

Contractual Relationships within Firms

The nature of the contractual relationship between the providers of inputs to a firm may be quite complicated. Each provider agrees to devote his or her input to production activities under a set of understandings about how it is to be used and what benefit is to be expected from that use. In some cases these contracts are explicit. Workers often negotiate contracts that specify in considerable detail what hours are to be worked, what rules of work are to be followed, and what rate of pay is to be expected. Similarly, capital owners invest in a firm under a set of explicit legal principles about the ways in which that capital may be used, the compensation the owner can expect to receive, and whether the owner retains any profits or losses after all economic costs have been paid. Despite these formal arrangements, it is clear that many of the understandings between the providers of inputs to a firm are implicit: Relationships between managers and workers follow certain procedures about who has the authority to do what in making production decisions. Among workers numerous implicit understandings exist about how work tasks are to be shared; and capital owners may delegate much of their authority to managers and workers to make decisions on their behalf (General Motors' shareholders, for example, are never involved in how assembly-line equipment will be used, though technically they own it). All of these explicit and implicit relationships change in response to experiences and events external to the firm. Much as a basketball team will try out new plays and defensive strategies, so too firms will alter the nature of their internal organizations in order to achieve better long-run results.[1]

Modeling Firms' Behavior

These complicated relationships among the providers of inputs to a firm pose some problems for economists who wish to develop theoretical generalizations about how firms behave. In our study of demand theory, it made some sense to talk about choices by a rational consumer because we were examining decisions by only a single person. But for firms, many individuals may be involved in decisions, and any detailed study of such decisions may quickly become deeply mired in the subjects of psychology, sociology, and group dynamics.

Although some economists have adopted such a "behavioral" approach to studying firms' decisions, most have found that approach too cumbersome for general purposes. Rather, they have adopted a "holistic" approach that treats the firm as a single decision-making unit and sweeps away all the complicated behavioral issues about relationships among input providers. Under this approach it is often convenient to assume that a firm's decisions are made by a single dictatorial manager who rationally pursues some goal. At times issues raised by the complexities of actual decision-making procedures within the firm can be introduced to show how they influence the dictatorial manager's ability to achieve the desired goals, but for the most part, it is assumed that the manager can exercise a relatively free hand.

PROFIT MAXIMIZATION

Most models of supply assume that the firm and its manager pursue the goal of achieving the largest economic profits possible. Hence, we will use the following definition:

DEFINITION

Profit-Maximizing Firm   A *profit-maximizing firm* chooses both its inputs and its outputs with the sole goal of achieving maximum economic profits. That is, the firm seeks to make the difference between its total revenues and its total economic costs as large as possible.

---

[1] The initial development of the theory of the firm from the notion of the contractual relationships involved can be found in R. H. Coase, "The Nature of the Firm," *Economica* (November 1937): 386–405.

This assumption—that firms seek maximum economic profits—has a long history in economic literature. It has much to recommend it. It is plausible because firm owners may indeed seek to make their asset as valuable as possible. And competitive markets may punish firms that do not maximize profits. The assumption also yields interesting theoretical results that can explain actual firms' decisions.

If firms are strict profit maximizers, they will make decisions in a "marginal" way. The entrepreneur will perform the conceptual experiment of adjusting those variables that can be controlled until it is impossible to increase profits further. This involves, say, looking at the incremental, or "marginal," profit obtainable from producing one more unit of output or at the additional profit available from hiring one more laborer. As long as this incremental profit is positive, the extra output will be produced or the extra laborer will be hired. When the incremental profit of an activity becomes zero, the entrepreneur has pushed that activity far enough, and it would not be profitable to go further.

Profit Maximization and Marginalism

This relationship between profit maximization and marginalism can be most clearly demonstrated if we examine the output level that a firm will choose to produce in attempting to obtain maximum profits. First, we must define "profits." In its activities a firm sells some level of output, q, at a market price of P per unit. Total revenues (TR) are therefore given by

Output Choice

$$TR(q) = P(q) \cdot q, \tag{13.1}$$

where we have allowed for the possibility that the selling price the firm receives might be affected by how much it sells. In the production of q, certain *economic* costs are incurred and, as in Chapter 12, we will denote these by $TC(q)$.

The difference between revenues and costs is called economic profits (π). Because both revenues and costs depend on the quantity produced, economic profits will also. That is,

$$\pi(q) = P(q) \cdot q - TC(q) = TR(q) - TC(q). \tag{13.2}$$

The necessary condition for choosing the value of q that maximizes profits is found by setting the derivative of Equation 13.2 with respect to q equal to 0:[2]

$$\frac{d\pi}{dq} = \pi'(q) = \frac{dTR}{dq} - \frac{dTC}{dq} = 0, \tag{13.3}$$

---

[2] Notice that this is an unconstrained maximization problem: The constraints in the problem are implicit in the revenue and cost functions. Specifically, the demand curve facing the firm determines the revenue function, and the firm's production function (together with input prices) determines its costs. We will explore these "built-in" constraints further later in this chapter.

so the first-order condition for a maximum is that

$$\frac{dTR}{dq} = \frac{dTC}{dq}.$$ (13.4)

This is simply a mathematical statement of the marginal revenue equals marginal cost rule usually studied in introductory economics courses. Hence, we have the following:

OPTIMIZATION PRINCIPLE

Profit Maximization   In order to maximize economic profits, the firm should choose that output for which marginal revenue is equal to marginal cost. That is,

$$MR = \frac{dTR}{dq} = \frac{dTC}{dq} = MC.$$ (13.5)

We have already discussed the concept of marginal cost in Chapter 12. Here we simply note that the marginal cost notion implied by Equation 13.5 may be either a short-run or a long-run concept depending on the nature of the problem being examined. "Marginal revenue" refers to the revenue provided by the last unit sold. Although we shall investigate this concept in detail in the next section, it may be worthwhile here to indicate the intuitive logic behind the first-order condition in Equation 13.5. If a firm decided to produce at an output level for which marginal revenue exceeded marginal cost, it could not be maximizing profits, since the production of one more unit of output would yield more in additional revenue than it would cost to produce. Similarly, if marginal revenue were less than marginal costs, reducing output by one unit would lower costs by a greater amount than it would lower revenue, and this action would increase profits. Assuming that it is in fact possible for the firm to make "small" adjustments, marginalism and profit maximization are synonymous.

Second-Order Conditions   Equation 13.4 or 13.5 is only a necessary condition for a profit maximum. For sufficiency it is also required that

$$\left.\frac{d^2\pi}{dq^2}\right|_{q\,=\,q^*} = \left.\frac{d\pi'(q)}{dq}\right|_{q\,=\,q^*} < 0$$ (13.6)

or that "marginal" profit must be decreasing at the optimal level of q. For q less than q^* (the optimal level of output), profit must be increasing [$\pi'(q) > 0$]; and for q greater than q^*, profit must be decreasing [$\pi'(q) < 0$]. Only if this condition holds has a true maximum of profits been achieved.

These relationships are illustrated in Figure 13.1, where the top panel depicts **Graphical Analysis** typical cost and revenue functions. For low levels of output, costs exceed revenues and therefore economic profits are negative. In the middle ranges of output, revenues exceed costs; this means that profits are positive. Finally, at high levels of output, costs rise sharply and again exceed revenues. The vertical distance between the revenue and cost curves (that is, profits) is shown in Figure 13.1b. Here profits reach a maximum at q^*. At this level of output it is also true that the slope of the revenue curve (marginal revenue) is equal to the slope of the cost curve (marginal cost). It is clear from the figure that the sufficient conditions for a maximum are also satisfied at this point, since profits are increasing to the left of q^* and decreasing to the right of q^*. Output level q^* is therefore a true profit maximum. This is not so for output level q^{**}. Even though marginal revenue is equal to marginal cost at this output, profits are in fact a minimum there.

MARGINAL REVENUE

It is the revenue obtained from selling one more unit of output that is relevant to the profit-maximizing firm's output decision. If the firm can sell all it wishes without having any effect on market price, the market price will indeed be the extra revenue obtained from selling one more unit. Phrased in another way, if a firm's output decisions will not affect market price, marginal revenue is equal to the price at which a unit sells.

A firm may not always be able to sell all it wants at the prevailing market price, however. If it faces a downward-sloping demand curve for its good, more output can be sold only by reducing the good's price. In this case the revenue obtained from selling one more unit will be less than the price of that unit because, in order to get consumers to take the extra unit, the price of all other units must be lowered. This result can be easily demonstrated. As before, total revenue (TR) is simply the product of the quantity sold (q) times the price at which it is sold (P), which may depend on q also. Marginal revenue (MR) is then defined to be the change in TR resulting from a change in q:

DEFINITION

Marginal Revenue

$$\text{marginal revenue} = MR(q) = \frac{dTR}{dq} = \frac{d[P(q) \cdot q]}{dq} = P + q \cdot \frac{dP}{dq} \qquad (13.7)$$

Notice that the marginal revenue is a function of output. In general, MR will be different for different levels of q. From Equation 13.7 it is easy to see that if price does not change as quantity increases ($dP/dq = 0$), then marginal

FIGURE 13.1

MARGINAL REVENUE MUST EQUAL MARGINAL COST FOR PROFIT MAXIMIZATION

Since profits are defined to be revenues (TR) minus costs (TC), it is clear that profits reach a maximum when the slope of the revenue function (marginal revenue) is equal to the slope of the cost function (marginal cost). This equality is only a necessary condition for a maximum, as may be seen by comparing points q^* (a true *maximum*) and q^{**} (a true *minimum*) for both of which marginal revenue equals marginal cost.

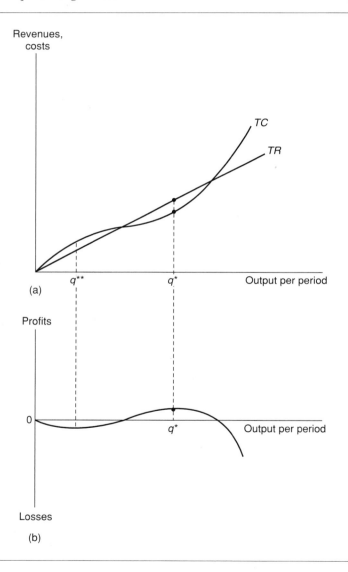

revenue will be equal to price. In this case we say that the firm is a *price taker* since its decisions do not influence the price it receives. On the other hand, if price falls as quantity increases ($dP/dq < 0$), then marginal revenue will be less than price. A profit-maximizing entrepreneur must know how increases in output will affect the price received before making an optimal output decision. If increases in q cause market price to fall, this must be taken into account.

EXAMPLE 13.1

MARGINAL REVENUE FROM A LINEAR DEMAND FUNCTION

Suppose a sub sandwich (also called grinders, torpedoes, or, in Philadelphia, hoagies) shop faces a simple linear demand curve for its daily output over period (q) of the form

$$q = 100 - 10P. \tag{13.8}$$

Solving for price, we have

$$P = -q/10 + 10, \tag{13.9}$$

and total sub revenues (as a function of q) are given by

$$TR = Pq = -q^2/10 + 10q. \tag{13.10}$$

The sub firm's marginal revenue function is

$$MR = \frac{dTR}{dq} = \frac{-q}{5} + 10, \tag{13.11}$$

and, in this case, $MR < P$ for all values of q. If, for example, the firm produces 40 subs per day, Equation 13.9 shows that it will receive a price of $6 per sandwich. But at this level of output Equation 13.11 shows that MR is only $2. If the firm produces 40 subs per day, total revenue will be $240 (= $6 × 40), whereas, if it produced 39 subs, total revenue would be $238 (= $6.1 × 39) since price will rise slightly when less is produced. Hence, the marginal revenue from the fortieth unit sold is considerably less than its price. Indeed, for $q = 50$, marginal revenue is zero (total revenues are a maximum at $250 = $5 × 50), and any further expansion in daily sub output will actually result in a reduction in total revenue to the firm.

To determine the profit-maximizing level of sub output, we must know the firm's costs. If subs can be produced at a constant average and marginal cost of $4, Equation 13.11 shows that $MR = MC$ at a daily output of 30 subs. With this level of output, each sub will sell for $7 and profits are $90 [= ($7 − $4) · 30]. Even though price exceeds average and marginal cost here by a substantial margin, it would not be in the firm's interest to expand output. With $q = 35$, for example, price will fall to $6.50 and profits will fall to \$87.50 [= (\$6.50 − \$4.00) · 35]. Marginal revenue, not price, is the primary determinant of profit-maximizing behavior.

QUERY: How would an increase in the marginal cost of sub production to \$5 affect the output decision of this firm? How would it affect the firm's profits?

Marginal Revenue and Elasticity

The concept of marginal revenue is directly related to the concept of demand elasticity developed in Chapter 7. Remember that the elasticity of market demand ($e_{Q,P}$) was defined as the percentage change in quantity that results from a 1 percent change in price:

$$e_{Q,P} = \frac{dQ/Q}{dP/P} = \frac{dQ}{dP} \cdot \frac{P}{Q}.$$

If we use $e_{q,P}$ to denote the price elasticity of the demand curve facing a single firm, this definition can be combined with Equation 13.7 to give

$$MR = P + \frac{q\,dP}{dq} = P\left(1 + \frac{q}{P} \cdot \frac{dP}{dq}\right) = P\left(1 + \frac{1}{e_{q,P}}\right). \qquad (13.12)$$

If the demand curve facing the firm is negatively sloped, $e_{q,P} < 0$ and marginal revenue will be less than price as we have already shown. If demand is elastic ($e_{q,P} < -1$), marginal revenue will be positive. If demand is elastic, the sale of one more unit will not affect price "very much," and hence more revenue will be yielded by the sale. In fact, if demand facing the firm is infinitely elastic ($e_{q,P} = -\infty$), marginal revenue will equal price. The firm is, in this case, a price taker. However, if demand is inelastic ($e_{q,P} > -1$), marginal revenue will be negative. Increases in q can be obtained only through "large" declines in market price, and these declines will actually cause total revenue to decrease.

The relationship between marginal revenue and elasticity is summarized by Table 13.1.

TABLE 13.1

RELATIONSHIP BETWEEN ELASTICITY AND MARGINAL REVENUE

$e_{q,P} < -1$	$MR > 0$
$e_{q,P} = -1$	$MR = 0$
$e_{q,P} > -1$	$MR < 0$

If we assume the firm wishes to maximize profits, Equation 13.12 can be extended to illustrate the connection between price and marginal cost. Setting $MR = MC$ yields

The Inverse Elasticity Rule

$$MC = P\left(1 + \frac{1}{e_{q,P}}\right)$$

or

$$\frac{P - MC}{P} = -\frac{1}{e_{q,P}}. \tag{13.13}$$

That is, the gap between price and marginal cost will decrease as the demand curve facing the firm becomes more elastic. Indeed, in the case of a price-taking firm, $e_{q,P} = -\infty$ so $P = MR = MC$ and there is no gap. Since, as we shall see in later chapters, the gap between price and marginal cost is an important measure of inefficient resource allocation, Equation 13.13 is widely used in empirical studies of market organization. Notice also that Equation 13.13 only makes sense if the demand curve facing the firm is elastic ($e_{q,P} < -1$). If $e_{q,P}$ were greater than -1, Equation 13.13 would imply a negative marginal cost—an obvious impossibility. Hence, profit-maximizing firms will choose to operate only at points on the demand curves they face where demand is elastic. Of course, when there are many firms producing a single good, the demand curve facing one firm may be quite elastic even though the overall market demand curve is not.

Any demand curve has a marginal revenue curve associated with it. If, as we often assume, the firm must sell all its output at one price, it is convenient to think of the demand curve facing the firm as an *average revenue curve*. That is, the demand curve shows the revenue per unit (in other words, the price) yielded by alternative output choices. The marginal revenue curve, on the other hand, shows the extra revenue provided by the last unit sold. In the usual case of a downward-sloping demand curve, the marginal revenue curve will lie below the demand curve since, according to Equation 13.7, $MR < P$. In Figure 13.2 we have drawn such a curve, together with the demand curve from which it was derived. Notice that for output levels greater than q_1, marginal revenue is negative. As output increases from 0 to q_1, total revenues ($P \cdot q$) increase. However, at q_1 total revenues ($P_1 \cdot q_1$) are as large as possible; beyond this output level, price falls proportionately faster than output rises.

Marginal Revenue Curve

In Chapter 7 we talked in detail about the possibility of a demand curve's shifting because of changes in income, prices of other goods, or preferences. Whenever a demand curve does shift, its associated marginal revenue curve also shifts. This should be obvious, since a marginal revenue curve cannot be calculated without referring to a specific demand curve.

FIGURE 13.2

MARKET DEMAND CURVE AND ASSOCIATED MARGINAL REVENUE CURVE

Since the demand curve is negatively sloped, the marginal revenue curve will fall below the demand ("average revenue") curve. For output levels beyond q_1, MR is negative. At q_1, total revenues ($P_1 \times q_1$) are a maximum; beyond this point additional increases in q actually cause total revenues to fall because of the concomitant declines in price.

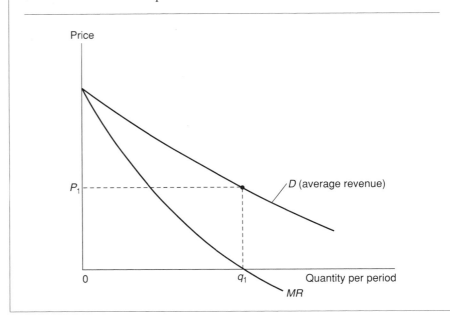

SHORT-RUN SUPPLY BY A PRICE-TAKING FIRM

We are now ready to study the supply decision of a profit-maximizing firm. In this chapter we will only examine the case in which the firm is a price taker, since we will be looking at other cases in considerably more detail later on. Also, we will only focus on supply decisions in the short run here, since long-run questions are the primary focus of Chapter 14. The firm's set of short-run cost curves are therefore the appropriate model for our analysis.

Profit-Maximizing Decision

Figure 13.3 shows the firm's short-run decision. The market price is given by P^*. The demand curve facing the firm is therefore a horizontal line through P^*. This line is labeled $P^* = MR$ as a reminder that an extra unit always can

FIGURE 13.3

SHORT-RUN SUPPLY CURVE FOR A PRICE-TAKING FIRM

In the short run a price-taking firm will produce the level of output for which $SMC = P$. At P^*, for example, the firm will produce q^*. The SMC curve also shows what will be produced at other prices. For prices below $SAVC$, however, the firm will choose to produce no output. The heavy lines in the figure represent the firm's short-run supply curve.

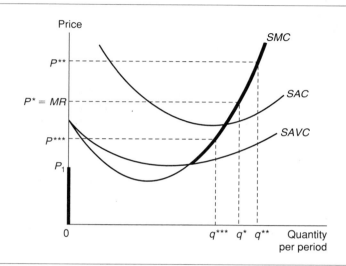

be sold by this price-taking firm without affecting the price. Output level q^* provides maximum profits, since at q^* price is equal to short-run marginal cost. The fact that profits are positive can be seen by noting that at q^* price exceeds average costs. The firm earns a profit on each unit sold. If price were below average cost (as is the case for P^{***}), the firm would have a loss on each unit sold. If price and average cost were equal, profits would be zero.

A geometric proof that profits are a maximum at q^* would proceed as follows. For output levels slightly less than q^*, price (P^*) exceeds short-run marginal cost. Reducing output below q^* would cut back on revenues more than on costs, and profits would fall. For output levels greater than q^*, marginal costs exceed P^*. Producing more than q^* would now cause costs to rise more rapidly than revenues, and again profits would fall. This means that if a firm produces either more or less than q^*, its profits will be lowered. Only at q^* are profits at a maximum. Notice that at q^* the marginal cost curve has a positive slope. This is required if profits are to be a true maximum. If $P = MC$ on a negatively sloped section of the marginal cost curve, this would not be a point of maximum profits, since increasing output would yield more in revenues (price times the amount produced) than this production would cost (marginal cost would decline if the MC curve has a negative slope). Consequently, profit maximization requires both that $P = MC$ and that marginal cost be increasing at this point.[3]

The Firm's Short-Run Supply Curve

The positively sloped portion of the short-run marginal cost curve is the short-run supply curve for this price-taking firm, since the curve shows how much the firm will produce for every possible market price. For example, as Figure 13.3 shows, at a higher price of P^{**}, the firm will produce q^{**} since it will find it in its interest to incur the higher marginal costs q^{**} entails. With a price of P^{***}, on the other hand, the firm opts to produce less (q^{***}) since only a lower output level will result in lower marginal costs to meet this lower price. By considering all possible prices that the firm might face, we can see by the marginal cost curve how much output the firm should supply at each price.

For very low prices we have to be careful about this conclusion. Should market price fall below P_1, the profit-maximizing decision would be to produce nothing. As Figure 13.3 shows, prices less than P_1 do not cover average variable costs. There will be a loss on each unit produced in addition to the loss of all fixed costs. By shutting down production, the firm still must pay fixed costs, but it avoids the losses incurred on each unit produced. Since, in the short run, the firm cannot close down and avoid all costs, its best decision is to produce no output. On the other hand, a price only slightly above P_1 means the firm should produce some output. Even though profits may be negative (which they will be if price falls below short-run average total costs, the case at P^{***}), as long as variable costs are covered, the profit-maximizing decision is to continue production. Fixed costs must be paid in any case, and any price that covers variable costs will provide revenue

---

[3] Mathematically, since

$$\pi(q) = Pq - TC(q),$$

profit maximization requires

$$\pi'(q) = P - MC(q) = 0$$

and

$$\pi''(q) = -MC'(q) < 0.$$

Hence, it is required that $MC'(q) > 0$; marginal cost must be increasing.

as an offset to the fixed costs.[4] Hence, we have a complete description of this firm's supply decisions in response to alternative prices for its output. These are summarized in the following definition:

DEFINITION

Short-Run Supply Curve   The firm's *short-run supply curve* shows how much it will produce at various possible output prices. For a profit-maximizing firm that takes the price of its output as given, this curve consists of the positively sloped segment of the firm's short-run marginal cost above the point of minimum average variable cost. For prices below this level, the firm's profit-maximizing decision is to shut down and produce no output.

Of course, any factor that shifts the firm's short-run marginal cost curve (such as changes in input prices or changes in the level of fixed inputs employed) will also shift the short-run supply curve. In Chapter 14 we will make extensive use of this type of analysis to study the operations of perfectly competitive markets.

EXAMPLE 13.2

SHORT-RUN SUPPLY

In our hamburger joint example from Chapter 12, we found that the firm's short-run total cost curve when it uses four grills was

$$STC = 4v + \frac{wq^2}{400},$$ (13.14)

---

[4] Some algebra may clarify matters. Since we know total costs equal the sum of fixed and variable costs:

$$STC = SFC + SVC,$$

profits are given by

$$\pi = TR - STC = P \cdot q - SFC - SVC.$$

If $q = 0$, variable costs and revenues are 0, so

$$\pi = -SFC.$$

The firm will only produce something if $\pi > -SFC$. But that means that

$$P \cdot q > SVC \quad \text{or} \quad P > SVC/q = SAVC.$$

where v and w are the per-unit costs of capital and labor, respectively. If $w = v = \$4$, this can be written as

$$STC = 16 + \frac{q^2}{100}. \tag{13.15}$$

Short-run marginal cost is now given by

$$SMC = \frac{\partial STC}{\partial q} = \frac{2q}{100} = \frac{q}{50}. \tag{13.16}$$

Profit maximization requires setting price equal to marginal cost:

$$P = SMC = \frac{q}{50}, \tag{13.17}$$

and the short-run supply curve (with q as a function of P) is given by

$$q = 50P. \tag{13.18}$$

To find this firm's shut-down price, we can use Equation 13.15, which shows that

$$SVC = q^2/100 \tag{13.19}$$

and

$$SAVC = \frac{SVC}{q} = \frac{q}{100}. \tag{13.20}$$

Consequently, minimum value for $SAVC$ occurs when q and $SMC = 0$. Equation 13.18 therefore reflects the firm's supply curve for any positive price—the firm will only shut down when $P = 0$. Notice, however, that short-run average total costs are given by

$$SAC = \frac{STC}{q} = \frac{16}{q} + \frac{q}{100} \tag{13.21}$$

and minimum short-run average cost occurs when

$$\frac{dSAC}{dq} = \frac{-16}{q^2} + \frac{1}{100} = 0 \tag{13.22}$$

or when $q = 40$ (and $SAC = SMC = .80$). For any price less than $.80, the firm will incur a loss. If, for example, $P = \$.60$, Equation 13.18 shows that the firm should produce $q = 30$ hamburgers per hour. Total revenues are $18 ($= \$.60 \cdot 30$), but total costs are given by

$$STC = 16 + \frac{q^2}{100} = 16 + 9 = 25 \tag{13.23}$$

and the firm will lose $7 per hour. Of course, this is far better than producing nothing, since then the firm would lose the $16 per hour it must pay for its fixed number of grills.

If price exceeds $.80, the firm will make positive economic profits. At a price of $1 per hamburger, for example, the firm produces 50 hamburgers per hour and earns positive profits of $9 per hour ($TR = \$50$, $STC = \$41$). When price is $.80, profits are exactly zero ($TR = \$32$, $TC = \$32$).

QUERY: Would an increase in the grill rent to $v = \$5$ change the firm's short-run supply decisions? How about an increase in the wage to $w = \$5$?

Thus far, we have treated the firm's decision problem as one of choosing a profit-maximizing level of output. But our discussion in Chapter 11 made clear that the firm's output is, in fact, determined by the inputs it chooses to employ, a relationship that is summarized by the production function $q = f(K, L)$. Consequently, the firm's economic profits can also be expressed as a function of the inputs it employs:

PROFIT MAXIMIZATION AND INPUT DEMAND

$$\pi(K, L) = Pq - TC(q) = Pf(K, L) - (vK + wL). \qquad (13.24)$$

Viewed in this way, the profit-maximizing firm's decision problem becomes one of choosing the appropriate levels of capital and labor input.[5] The first-order conditions for a maximum are

$$\frac{\partial \pi}{\partial K} = P \frac{\partial f}{\partial K} - v = 0$$

$$\frac{\partial \pi}{\partial L} = P \frac{\partial f}{\partial L} - w = 0. \qquad (13.25)$$

These conditions make the intuitively appealing point that a profit-maximizing firm should hire any input up to the point at which its marginal contribution to revenues is equal to the marginal cost of hiring the input. That is, the firm should implicitly perform a benefit-cost calculation for each unit of an input hired and cease hiring when the input's marginal contribution to profits reaches zero. In Chapter 21 we will examine the consequences of this observation in considerable detail since they provide the foundation of the theory of input demand. For the moment, however, we wish only to observe

---

[5] Throughout our discussion in this section, we will assume that the firm is a price taker so the prices of its output and its inputs can be treated as fixed parameters. Results can be generalized fairly easily in the case where prices depend on quantity.

that the first-order conditions given in Equation 13.25 also imply cost minimization (since they imply that the $RTS = w/v$) and that these can generally be solved for the profit-maximizing levels of capital and labor input that the firm should hire.

Second-Order Conditions

Because the profit function in Equation 13.24 depends on two variables, K and L, the second-order conditions for a profit maximum are somewhat more complex than in the single-variable case we examined earlier. In Chapter 2, we showed that in order to ensure a true maximum it is required that

$$\pi_{KK} < 0 \quad \pi_{LL} < 0$$

and

$$\pi_{KK}\pi_{LL} - \pi_{KL}^2 > 0. \tag{13.26}$$

These conditions amount to requiring that the inputs capital and labor exhibit sufficiently diminishing marginal productivities so that marginal costs increase as output expands. They therefore reflect the type of second-order conditions we have examined earlier in this chapter. To see why, notice from Equation 13.25 that $\pi_{KK} = Pf_{KK}$ and $\pi_{LL} = Pf_{LL}$. Hence, diminishing marginal productivities ($f_{KK}, f_{LL} < 0$) will ensure that π_{KK} and π_{LL} will be negative. But, diminishing marginal productivity for each input is not sufficient to ensure increasing marginal costs. Since expanding output usually requires the firm to use both more capital *and* more labor, we must also ensure that increases in capital input do not raise the marginal productivity of labor (and thereby reduce marginal cost) by a large enough amount to reverse the effect of diminishing marginal productivity of labor itself. The second part of Equation 13.26 therefore requires that such cross-productivity effects be relatively small—that they be dominated by diminishing marginal productivities of the inputs. If these conditions are satisfied, marginal costs will be increasing at the profit-maximizing choices for K and L, and the first-order conditions will represent a local maximum.

The Supply Function

To develop the connection between supply behavior in this input-oriented view of the firm's choices and our prior discussion of output decisions, we can recognize that the first-order conditions for profit maximization (Equation 13.25) can generally be solved for the optimal input combination of capital (K^*) and labor (L^*) as functions of the parameters P, v, and w:

$$K^* = K^*(P, v, w)$$

$$L^* = L^*(P, v, w). \tag{13.27}$$

These input choices can then be substituted into the production function to yield the profit-maximizing output choice (q^*):

$$q^* = f(K^*, L^*) = f[K^*(P, v, w), L^*(P, v, w)]$$
$$= q^*(P, v, w). \tag{13.28}$$

Because this function shows how much the firm will produce at various prices for its product and various input costs, it is called a supply function:

DEFINITION

Supply Function The *supply function* for a profit-maximizing firm that takes both output price (P) and input prices (v, w) as fixed is written as

$$\text{quantity supplied} = q^*(P, v, w) \tag{13.29}$$

to indicate the dependence of output choices on both product price and input cost considerations.

We will not make extensive use of this supply function here. It will be much easier for our purposes to rely on a graphical treatment of supply based on the firm's marginal cost curve. Usually no information will be lost by utilizing this simplification. But the supply function does provide a convenient reminder of two points that are not apparent from the marginal cost curve approach to supply: (1) The firm's output decision is fundamentally a decision about hiring inputs; and (2) changes in input costs will alter the hiring of inputs and hence affect output choices as well. Consequently, when it seems especially important to highlight this connection between input and output choices, we will want to return to this approach to supply. In the extensions to this chapter we explore another way of analyzing firms' choices through the use of profit functions.

EXAMPLE 13.3

COMPUTATION OF A SUPPLY FUNCTION

Our previous burger emporium example is not quite appropriate for the development of a supply function because the assumed production function is characterized by constant returns to scale. In situations where both K (grills) and L (workers) are variable, marginal costs will be constant and unaffected by how much the firm chooses to produce. If market price equals this marginal cost, the quantity supplied is not unique since $P = MC$ is satisfied everywhere. Similarly, if $P > MC$, there is no profit-maximizing solution. To introduce increasing marginal costs, we must assume that a third, fixed input (say, seating capacity [F] measured in square meters) enters the burger production function, which is now given by

$$q = 10K^{.25}L^{.25}F^{.5}. \tag{13.30}$$

We assume that, in the short run, eating space is limited to an area four meters square. Hence, $F = 16$ and the short-run production function is given by

$$q = 40K^{.25}L^{.25}. \tag{13.31}$$

Notice that the firm's production function now exhibits diminishing returns to scale for increases in the variable inputs, K and L. The firm's profits are given by

$$\pi = Pq - TC$$
$$= P40K^{.25}L^{.25} - vK - wL - R, \tag{13.32}$$

where R is the (fixed) rent the firm must pay for eating space.

First-order conditions for a profit maximum are

$$\frac{\partial \pi}{\partial K} = 10PK^{-.75}L^{.25} - v = 0$$

$$\frac{\partial \pi}{\partial L} = 10PK^{.25}L^{-.75} - w = 0. \tag{13.33}$$

Consequently,

$$10PK^{-.75}L^{.25} = v \tag{13.34}$$

$$10PK^{.25}L^{-.75} = w. \tag{13.35}$$

As before, in these examples, division of 13.35 by 13.34 yields the cost-minimization result that

$$\frac{K}{L} = \frac{w}{v}. \tag{13.36}$$

Solving this equation for L and substitution into Equation 13.34 yields (after some manipulation) the capital demand equation

$$K = \frac{(10P)^2}{v^{1.5}w^{.5}}, \tag{13.37}$$

and a similar substitution for K in Equation 13.35 yields the labor demand equation

$$L = \frac{(10P)^2}{v^{.5}w^{1.5}}. \tag{13.38}$$

Finally, substitution of these back into the short-run production function (Equation 13.31) yields

$$q = \frac{40(10P)}{(vw)^{.5}}, \tag{13.39}$$

which is the short-run supply function we seek. Notice that this function is homogeneous of degree zero in P, v, and w. That is, if P, w, and v were all to double, quantity supplied would not change. If $w = v = \$4$, the function becomes

$$q = 100P. \tag{13.40}$$

So if $P = \$1$, the firm will supply 100 hamburgers per hour. Equations 13.37 and 13.38 show that these will be produced using 6.25 $(= \frac{100}{16})$ grills and 6.25 workers per hour. Substitution of these input values into the short-run production function (Equation 13.31) shows that they are indeed sufficient to produce 100 hamburgers per hour. With these inputs, short-run variable costs will be $50 (6.25 \cdot \$4 + 6.25 \cdot \$4)$ and revenues will be $100. Since revenues cover variable costs, the firm will choose to produce in the short run even if its fixed rent results in a loss in overall terms.

If the price of hamburgers were to rise, this profit-maximizing firm would produce more. If $P = \$1.50$, for example, the firm would produce 150 burgers per hour using $K = L = \frac{225}{16} = 14.1$. The higher price has also led to a substantial increase in the hiring of inputs.

A Shift in Supply. The supply function in Equation 13.39 also permits an examination of how the firm's supply decisions would be affected by a change in input prices. Suppose, for example, a benevolent government dictated a minimum wage for workers of $9 per hour. Then the supply function would become

$$q = \frac{400P}{(36)^{.5}} = \frac{400P}{6}. \tag{13.41}$$

At a price of $1 the firm would now only produce $\frac{400}{6}$ $(= 66.7)$ hamburgers per hour. To do so it would utilize $\frac{100}{24} = 4.2$ grills and $\frac{100}{54} = 1.9$ workers. Notice that the higher wage has reduced the hiring of workers both because the firm chooses to produce fewer hamburgers per hour and because it substitutes capital for labor in production (now $K/L = \frac{9}{4}$). In Chapter 21 we will examine this relationship between input costs and hiring in considerably more detail.

QUERY: How would a change in F affect the hamburger supply function? What factors would enter into the firm's long-run decision about what size seating capacity to install?

A profit-maximizing firm that decides to produce a positive output in the short run must find that decision to be more favorable than a decision to produce nothing. This improvement in welfare is termed (short-run) *producer surplus*. It reflects what the firm gains by being able to participate in market transactions. Specifically, if the firm were prevented from making such

PRODUCER SURPLUS IN THE SHORT RUN

transactions, output would be zero and profits would equal $-FC$, since short-run analysis assumes that fixed costs are unavoidable. Production of the profit-maximizing output, q^*, would yield profits of π^* (which might still be negative). Hence, the firm gains $\pi^* + FC$ relative to a situation with no transactions. Economists call this figure short-run producer surplus.

A Graphic Analysis   Figure 13.4 illustrates a firm's short-run supply (marginal cost) curve together with the prevailing market price (P^*). At that price, the firm opts to produce q^*. In this situation, short-run producer's surplus can be shown to be given by the shaded area below P^* and above MC (or S) in the figure. In mathematical terms this area is given by the integral

$$\textbf{producer surplus} = \int_0^{q^*} [P^* - MC(q)]dq = (P^*q - TC)\Big|_{q=0}^{q=q^*}$$

$$= P^*q^* - TC(q^*) - [P^* \cdot 0 - TC(0)] \qquad (13.42)$$

$$= \pi^* + FC.$$

FIGURE 13.4

SHORT-RUN PRODUCER SURPLUS

The shaded area between market price (P^*) and the short-run supply curve ($S = MC$) represents the sum of short-run profits and fixed costs. This represents the gain to the firm of being able to produce q^* rather than producing nothing.

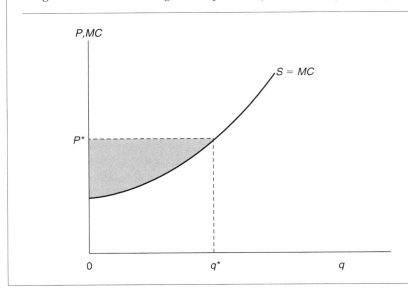

Since *FC* is constant, changes in producer surplus as a result of changes in market price are reflected as changes in short-run profits. Again, such changes can be measured by the changes in the area below market price above the short-run supply curve. This analysis is pursued a bit further in the extensions to this chapter by introducing the firm's profit function.

Although the short-run concept of producer surplus is sometimes used to illustrate the value of market transactions to firms, the more usual practice is to focus on producer surplus in the long run as an overall measure of producer's welfare under various possible allocations of resources. Since fixed costs do not exist in the usual long-run analysis and equilibrium profits under perfect competition with free entry are also zero, short-run producer surplus is, by definition, zero. In long-run analysis, rather, attention focuses on the prices of the firm's inputs and how these prices relate to what they would be in the absence of transactions in the market in question. Somewhat surprisingly, however, this different notion of surplus can still be represented as the area below market price and above the market supply curve, as we shall see in Chapter 14.

**Long-Run
Producer Surplus**

EXAMPLE 13.4

SHORT-RUN PRODUCER SURPLUS

In Example 13.2 we calculated the short-run cost function for hamburger production as

$$STC = 16 + .01q^2 \qquad (13.43)$$

and the supply curve as

$$q = 50P. \qquad (13.44)$$

With a price of, say, $1 the firm will produce 50 burgers per day, have total costs of $41, and earn short-term profits of $9. Hence, producer surplus is $25. This is composed of $9 in profits plus $16 in fixed costs from paying rent on the firm's four grills.

Since the firm's supply function is simply a straight line through the origin, a geometric computation of producer surplus is especially simple here. The producer surplus area is a triangle with base $q = 50$ and height $P = \$1$. Hence, its area is given by ½ (1)(50) = $25. As expected, the geometric and numerical computations agree.

QUERY: How would you make a similar producer surplus computation for the more complex supply situation in Example 13.3?

REVENUE MAXIMIZATION

One simple alternative to assuming profit maximization is provided by the assumption of revenue maximization. In addition to the fact that this is a very simple hypothesis to model, several other observations suggest it may accurately capture some aspects of firms' behavior. Most important, when firms are uncertain about the demand curve they actually face or when they have no very reliable notion of the marginal costs of their output (as may be especially true in multiproduct firms), the decision to try to maximize sales may be a reasonable rule of thumb for assuring their long-term survival. Indeed, a number of management consulting firms stress to their clients the importance of maximizing their "market share" as a way of protecting themselves against the vagaries of the market.

Graphical Analysis

A strictly revenue-maximizing firm would choose to produce that level of output for which marginal revenue is zero. That is, it should proceed to the point at which selling further units actually causes total revenues to fall. This choice is illustrated in Figure 13.5. For the firm that faces the demand curve[6] d, maximum revenues are obtainable by producing output level q^*. For $q < q^*$, mr is positive so selling more increases total revenues (though possibly not profits). For $q > q^*$, however, mr is negative so further sales actually reduce total revenues because of the price reductions that are required to get demanders to buy the good. Since we know that

$$mr = P\left(1 + \frac{1}{e_{q,P}}\right),\tag{13.45}$$

$mr = 0$ implies that $e_{q,P} = -1$: Demand will be unit elastic at q^*.

This revenue-maximizing choice might be contrasted to the output level that a profit-maximizing firm would choose, q^{**}. At q^{**} marginal revenue equals short-run marginal cost (given by SMC in Figure 13.5). Increasing output beyond q^{**} would reduce profits since $mr < SMC$. Even though revenues continue to increase up to q^*, units of output beyond q^{**} bring in less than they cost to produce. Since mr is positive at q^{**}, Equation 13.45 shows that demand must be elastic ($e_{q,P} < -1$) at this point.

Constrained Revenue Maximization

A firm that chooses to maximize revenues is giving no attention to its costs nor to the profitability of the sales it is making. Indeed, it is quite possible that the output level q^* in Figure 13.5 may yield negative profits to the firm. Since no firm can survive forever with negative profits, it may be more realistic to assume that firms must meet some minimum level of profitability from their

---

[6] For our development here and in subsequent chapters, we use a lowercase d to represent the demand curve facing the firm. We will use an uppercase D to represent the market demand curve. The marginal revenue curves associated with d and D are denoted by mr and MR, respectively.

FIGURE 13.5

REVENUE MAXIMIZATION

A firm that seeks to maximize total revenues will produce where marginal revenue is equal to zero (q^*). If the firm faces a minimum profit constraint, it may choose an output level between the profit-maximizing level (q^{**}) and q^*.

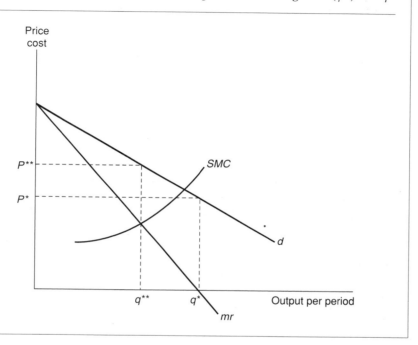

activities. Hence, although they may be prompted to produce more than q^{**} because of a variety of motives for maximizing revenues, they may stop short of q^* because of the need to assure an acceptable level of profitability. They will, therefore, behave as constrained revenue maximizers and will opt for some output level between q^{**} and q^*.

EXAMPLE 13.5

SALES MAXIMIZATION

A simple numerical example of these issues can be developed from the linear demand relationship we studied earlier. To give the example concrete meaning, assume that a firm produces sidewalk slabs at a constant average and marginal cost of $4 each. The weekly demand for slabs facing the firm is given by

$$q = 100 - 10P. \tag{13.46}$$

As before, we can solve for total revenues as a function of q:

$$TR = Pq = 10q - q^2/10 \tag{13.47}$$

and then find marginal revenue as

$$mr = \frac{dTR}{dq} = 10 - \frac{q}{5}. \tag{13.48}$$

Total revenues are maximized when $mr = 0$—that is, when $q = 50$. At an output of 50 slabs per week, Equation 13.47 shows that total revenue will be $250. Since slabs cost $4 each, the firm will have profits of $50 ($= \$250 - 50 \times \$4$) per week. If the firm wished to maximize profits, it should produce where marginal revenue equals marginal cost:

$$mr = 10 - q/5 = MC = 4 \tag{13.49}$$

or $q = 30$. Although this level of output yields less in total revenues ($210), total profits per week are nearly twice as large ($90 = \$210 - 30 \times \$4$) as for the revenue-maximizing choice.

Constrained Revenue Maximization. A minimum required profit goal of between $50 and $90 would yield an intermediate choice for this firm. Suppose, for example, that the firm's owners required at least $80 per week in profits from their investment in slab molds. Then the firm might seek to maximize total revenues subject to the constraint that

$$\pi = TR - TC = 10q - q^2/10 - 4q = 80. \tag{13.50}$$

Rearranging the terms of this constraint a bit yields

$$q^2 - 60q + 800 = 0 \tag{13.51}$$

or

$$(q - 40)(q - 20) = 0. \tag{13.52}$$

Clearly, the solution $q = 40$ yields maximum revenues ($240) from among the output options of between 20 and 40, all of which yield at least $80 in weekly profits.

QUERY: Suppose this firm's owners derived utility from profits and total revenue. How might a utility-maximizing combination of these two financial outcomes be chosen?

So far we have tended to treat the owner of a firm (that is, the owner of the firm's capital) and the manager of that firm as if they were the same person. This treatment makes the assumption of profit-maximizing behavior believable—a person who maximizes the profits in a firm that he or she owns will succeed in making as much income as possible from this ownership. Then the process of profit maximization is consistent with the process of utility maximization.

In many cases, however, managers do not actually own the firm for which they work. Rather, there is a separation between the ownership of the firm and the control of its behavior by hired managers. In this case, a manager acts as an *agent* for the owner.

MANAGERS AND THE PRINCIPAL-AGENT PROBLEM

DEFINITION

Agent An *agent* is a person who makes economic decisions for another party; for example, the manager of a firm who is hired to act for the owner is an agent.

Adam Smith understood the basic conflict between owners and managers. In *The Wealth of Nations,* he observed that "the directors of . . . companies, being the managers of other people's money than of their own, it cannot well be expected that they should watch over it with the same anxious vigilance with which [owners] watch over their own."[7] Using such famous British institutions as the Royal African Company, the Hudson's Bay Company, and the East India Company as examples, Smith went on to point out some of the consequences of management by nonowners. His observations provide an important starting point for the study of modern firms.

Conflicts in the Agent Relationship

The principal issue raised by the existence of manager-agents is illustrated in Figure 13.6, which shows the indifference curve map of a manager's preferences between the firm's profits (which are of primary interest to the owners) and various benefits (such as fancy offices or travel in the corporate jet or helicopter) that accrue mainly to the manager.[8] This indifference curve map has the same shape as those in Part II on the presumption that both profits and benefits provide utility to the manager.

To construct the budget constraint that the manager faces in seeking to maximize his or her utility, assume first that the manager is also the owner of this firm. If the manager chooses to have no special benefits from the job,

---

[7] Adam Smith, *The Wealth of Nations* (New York: Random House, Modern Library Edition, 1937), p. 700.

[8] Figure 13.6 is based on a figure presented in Michael C. Jensen and William H. Meckling, "Theory of the Firm: Managerial Behavior, Agency Costs and Ownership Structure," *Journal of Financial Economics* (October 1976): 305–360.

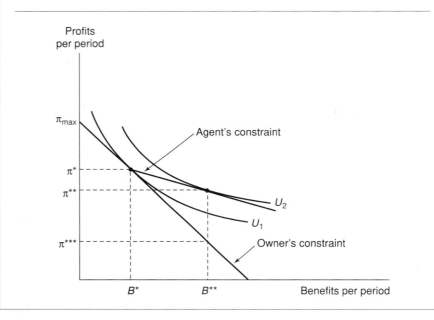

FIGURE 13.6

**INCENTIVES FOR A MANAGER ACTING
AS AN AGENT FOR A FIRM'S OWNERS**

If a manager were the sole owner of a firm, π^*, B^* would be chosen since this combination of profits and benefits provides maximum utility. If the manager owns only one-third of the firm, however, the perceived budget constraint will be flatter, and B^{**}, π^{**} will be chosen.

profits will be π_{max}. Each dollar of benefits received by the manager reduces these profits by one dollar. The budget constraint will have a slope of -1, and profits will reach zero when benefits total π_{max}.

Given this budget constraint, the owner-manager maximizes utility by opting for profits of π^* and benefits of B^*. Profits of π^*, while less than π_{max}, still represent maximum profits in this situation since any other owner-manager would also wish to receive B^* in benefits. That is, B^* represents a true cost of doing business so, given these costs, the firm's manager really does maximize profits.

Agents' Incentives   Now suppose that the manager is not the only owner of this firm. Instead, assume that, say, one-third of the capital of the firm is owned by the manager and the other two-thirds are owned by outside investors who play no role in operating the firm. In this case the manager will act as if he or she no longer faces a budget constraint that requires that one dollar of profits be sacrificed for each dollar of benefits. Now a dollar of benefits costs the manager only $.33 in profits since the other $.67 is effectively paid by the other owners in terms of reduced profits on their investment. Although the new budget constraint continues to include the point B^*, π^* (since the manager could still make the same decision a sole owner could), for benefits greater than B^* the slope of the budget constraint is only $-\frac{1}{3}$; profits from the manager's portion of the business decline by only $.33 for each dollar in benefits received. Given this new budget constraint, the manager would choose point B^{**}, π^{**} to maximize his or her utility. Being only a partial owner of the firm causes the manager to choose a lower level of profits and a higher level of benefits than would be chosen by a sole owner.

Point B^{**}, π^{**} is not attainable by this firm. Although the cost of one dollar of benefits appears to be only $.33 in profits for the manager, in reality, of course, the benefits cost one dollar. When the manager opts for B^{**} in benefits, the loss in profits (from π^* to π^{***}) is greater for the firm as a whole than for him or her personally. The firm's owners are harmed by having to rely on an agency relationship with the firm's manager. It appears that the smaller the fraction of the firm that is owned by the manager, the greater the distortions that will be induced by this relationship.

Implications for Owners

The situation illustrated in Figure 13.6 is representative of a variety of "principal-agent" problems that arise in economics. Whenever one person (the principal) hires another person (the agent) to make decisions, the motivation of this agent must be taken into account since the agent may make different decisions than the principal would. Examples of this relationship occur not only in the management of firms, but also in such diverse applications as hiring investment advisers (do they really put their clients' interests first?); relying on an automobile mechanic's assessment in ordering repairs; and following a physician's advice about the necessity of an operation.

The firm's owners would be unlikely to take the kind of behavior illustrated in Figure 13.6 lying down. They are being forced to accept lower profits than might be earned on their investments in exchange for manager-oriented benefits that provide no value to them personally. What can they do? Most obviously, they can refuse to invest in the firm if they know the manager will behave in this manner. In such a case the manager would have two options. First, he or she could go it alone and finance the company completely with his or her own funds. The firm would then simply return to the owner-manager situation in which B^*, π^* is the preferred choice of benefits and profits. Alternatively, the manager may obtain outside financing if the operation is too expensive to finance alone. In this case the manager must

Management Contracts

work out some sort of contractual arrangement with the would-be owners to induce them to invest.

One possible contract would be for the manager to agree to finance all of the benefits out of his or her share of the profits. This would make the would-be owners happy (since they would get the same level of profits no matter how many benefits the manager chose). But, when a dollar of benefits costs one dollar, any choice of benefits greater than $B*$ will result in lower utility for the manager. In this situation, a manager who succumbed to the desire for benefits seemingly created by the agency relationship would actually be made worse off.

Writing a contract under which managers pay for benefits entirely out of their share of the profits is probably impossible for owners to do, anyway. Enforcing the provisions of such a contract would require constant supervision of the managers' activities—something the owners would prefer not to do because that would force them into a managerial role. Instead, they may try to develop less strict contracts that give managers an incentive to economize on benefits and thereby pursue goals closer to pure profit maximization. By offering such contract options as profit-sharing bonuses, stock option plans, and company-financed pensions, the owners may be able to give managers an incentive to make profit-maximizing choices.

EXAMPLE 13.6

USING THE CORPORATE JET

United Biscuits, Inc., owns a fleet of corporate jets used mainly for business purposes. After firing the prior CEO for misusing the corporate fleet, the directors of UBI wish to structure a management contract that provides better incentives for cost control. All would-be applicants for the job have the same utility function for salary (s, measured in hundreds of thousands of dollars) and jet use (j, which can be only 0 or 1) of the form

$$U(s, j) = .1\sqrt{s} + j. \tag{13.53}$$

All applicants also have job offers from other firms promising them a utility level of at most 2.0. Since excessive jet use is very costly, the directors realize that UBI profits (exclusive of the CEO's salary) will be 800 (thousand) if $j = 0$, but only 162 if $j = 1$. Hence, the directors are willing to offer the CEO up to 638 providing they can be assured he or she will not use the corporate fleet for personal use. A salary of slightly more than 400 will just be sufficient to get a potential candidate to accept a position with no jet usage ($U > 2$). That would be a more profitable contract than hiring a CEO with a required salary of 100 together with unrestricted plane use. Although this contract also offers $U > 2$, under the former contract net profits are 400 whereas under the second they are only 62.

Contract Monitoring. Unfortunately, the directors of UBI find it difficult to monitor nonbusiness jet use. If they sign a contract for 400 (and $j = 0$), the new CEO still has an incentive to use the jet, thereby raising his or her utility from 2 to 3. Such a decision would prove disastrous for the owners—with personal plane use their net profits fall to −238.

A Profit-Sharing Contract. The owners might therefore be willing to pay something to monitor jet usage and to ensure that the terms of the high-salary contract are met. Alternatively, they could write a profit-sharing contract that might be self-enforcing. A salary promise of 50 percent of profits, for example, would be sufficient to attract a potential CEO ($U = 2.0$) provided he or she resolves not to use the jet. The candidate will realize that his or her utility will be lower with jet usage ($U = 1.9$) under such a profit-sharing contract and will presumably refrain from such behavior.

QUERY: How might the analysis of this contractual situation change if profits were not a "perfect signal" of jet use?

SUMMARY

In this chapter we studied the supply decision of a profit-maximizing firm. Our general goal was to show how such a firm responds to price signals from the marketplace, and in addressing that question, we developed a number of analytical results:

- In order to maximize profits, the firm should choose to produce that output level for which marginal revenue (the revenue from selling one more unit) is equal to marginal cost (the cost of producing one more unit).

- If a firm is a price taker, its output decisions do not affect the price of its output so marginal revenue is given by this price. If the firm faces a downward-sloping demand for its output, however, it can sell more only at a lower price. In this case marginal revenue will be less than price and may even be negative.

- Marginal revenue and the price elasticity of demand are related by the formula

$$MR = P\left(1 + \frac{1}{e_{q,P}}\right),$$

where P is the market price of the firm's output and $e_{q,P}$ is the price elasticity of demand for its product.

- The supply curve for a price-taking, profit-maximizing firm is given by the positively sloped portion of its marginal cost curve above the point of minimum average variable cost (AVC). If price falls below minimum AVC, the firm's profit-maximizing choice is to shut down and produce nothing.

- The firm's profit-maximization problem can also be approached as a problem in optimal input choice. Although this alternative approach yields the same results as does an approach based on output choices, it does help to clarify the relationship between input costs and supply decisions.

- In the short run firms obtain producer surplus in

the form of short-run profits and coverage of fixed costs that would not be earned if they produced zero output.

- In situations of imperfect information, firms may opt for output decision rules that require less knowledge than does profit maximization. A particularly simple alternative is that of sales maximization in which the firm expands output to the point at which marginal revenue is equal to zero. In

some cases, however, such decisions may be constrained by minimum profit requirements.

- Because managers act as agents for the firm's owners, they may not always make decisions that are consistent with profit maximization. Contractual provisions may therefore be structured so as to bring profit-maximizing behavior and the manager's utility-maximizing behavior more closely into line.

PROBLEMS

13.1

John's Lawn Mowing Service is a small business that acts as a price taker (i.e., $MR = P$). The prevailing market price of lawn mowing is $20 per acre. John's costs are given by

$$\text{total cost} = .1q^2 + 10q + 50,$$

where $q =$ the number of acres John chooses to cut a day.
a. How many acres should John choose to cut in order to maximize profit?
b. Calculate John's maximum daily profit.
c. Graph these results and label John's supply curve.

13.2

Would a lump-sum profits tax affect the profit-maximizing quantity of output? How about a proportional tax on profits? How about a tax assessed on each unit of output?

13.3

Suppose that a firm faces a constant elasticity demand curve of the form

$$q = 256P^{-2}$$

and has a *marginal cost* curve of the form

$$MC = 0.001q.$$

a. Graph these demand and marginal cost curves.
b. Calculate the marginal revenue curve associated with the demand curve. Graph this curve.
c. At what output level does marginal revenue equal marginal cost?

13.4

A firm faces a demand curve given by

$$q = 100 - 2P.$$

Marginal and average costs for the firm are constant at $10 per unit.
a. What output level should the firm produce to maximize profits? What are profits at that output level?
b. What output level should the firm produce to maximize revenues? What are profits at that output level?
c. Suppose the firm wishes to maximize revenues subject to the constraint that it earn $12 in profits for each of the 64 machines it employs. What level of output should it produce?
d. Graph your results.

13.5

This problem concerns the relationship between demand and marginal revenue curves for a few functional forms. Show that:
a. for a linear demand curve, the marginal revenue curve bisects the distance between the vertical axis and the demand curve for any price.
b. for any linear demand curve, the vertical distance between the demand and marginal revenue curves is $-1/b \cdot q$, where b (<0) is the slope of the demand curve.
c. for a constant elasticity demand curve of the form $q = aP^b$, the vertical distance between the demand and marginal revenue curves is a constant ratio of the height of the demand curve, with this constant depending on the price elasticity of demand.

d. for any downward-sloping demand curve, the vertical distance between the demand and marginal revenue curves at any point can be found by using a linear approximation to the demand curve at that point and applying the procedure described in part (b).

e. Graph the results of parts (a) through (d) of this problem.

13.6
Universal Widget produces high-quality widgets at its plant in Gulch, Nevada, for sale throughout the world. The cost function for total widget production (q) is given by

$$\text{total cost} = .25q^2.$$

Widgets are demanded only in Australia (where the demand curve is given by $q = 100 - 2P$) and Lapland (where the demand curve is given by $q = 100 - 4P$). If Universal Widget can control the quantities supplied to each market, how many should it sell in each location in order to maximize total profits? What price will be charged in each location?

13.7
The production function for a firm in the business of calculator assembly is given by

$$q = 2\sqrt{L},$$

where q is finished calculator output and L represents hours of labor input. The firm is a price taker for both calculators (which sell for P) and workers (which can be hired at a wage rate of w per hour).

a. What is the supply function for assembled calculators [$q = f(P, w)$]?

b. Explain both algebraically and graphically why this supply function is homogeneous of degree zero in P and w and why profits are homogeneous of degree one in these variables.

c. Show explicitly how changes in w shift the supply curve for this firm.

13.8
The market for high-quality caviar is dependent on the weather. If the weather is good, there are many fancy parties and caviar sells for $30 per pound. In bad weather it sells for only $20 per pound. Caviar produced one week will not keep until the next week. A small caviar producer has a cost function given by

$$TC = \tfrac{1}{2}q^2 + 5q + 100,$$

where q is weekly caviar production. Production decisions must be made before the weather (and the price of caviar) is known, but it is known that good weather and bad weather each occur with a probability of 0.5.

a. How much caviar should this firm produce if it wishes to maximize the expected value of its profits?

b. Suppose the owner of this firm has a utility function of the form

$$\text{utility} = \sqrt{\pi},$$

where π is weekly profits. What is the expected utility associated with the output strategy defined in part (a)?

c. Can this firm owner obtain a higher utility of profits by producing some output other than that specified in parts (a) and (b)? Explain.

d. Suppose this firm could predict next week's price, but could not influence that price. What strategy would maximize expected profits in this case? What would expected profits be?

13.9
Suppose that a firm engaged in the illegal copying of computer CDs has a daily short-run total cost function given by

$$STC = q^2 + 25.$$

a. If illegal computer CDs sell for $20, how many will the firm copy each day? What will its profits be?

b. What is the firm's short-run producer surplus at $P = \$20$?

c. Develop a general expression for this firm's producer surplus as a function of the price of illegal CDs.

13.10
In Example 13.2 we computed the general short-run total cost curve for Hamburger Heaven as

$$STC = 4v + \frac{wq^2}{400}.$$

a. Assuming that this establishment takes the price of hamburgers as given (P), calculate its profit function (see the extensions to Chapter 13), π^* (P, v, w).

b. Show that the supply function calculated in Example 13.2 can be calculated as $\partial\pi^*/\partial P = q$ (for $w = v = 4$).

c. Show that the firm's demand for workers, L, is given by $-\partial\pi^*/\partial w$.

d. Show that the producer surplus calculated in Example 13.4 can be computed as

$$\int_0^{P^*} \partial\pi^*/\partial P \, dp$$

for $w = v = 4.$

e. Show how the approach used in part (d) can be used to evaluate the increase in producer surplus (and in short-run profits) if P rises from \$1 to \$1.50.

SUGGESTED READINGS

Arrow, K. J. *The Limits of Organization.* New York: Norton, 1974.
A general inquiry into the internal operations of firms (and other organizations). Stresses how economic incentives affect these operations.

Coase, R. H. "The Nature of the Firm." *Economica* (November 1937): 386–405.
A classic analysis of the contractual nature of the firm.

Ferguson, C. E. "Static Models of Average-Cost Pricing." *Southern Economic Journal* 23 (1957): 272–284.
An exploration of the consequences of markup pricing behavior.

Friedman, M. "The Methodology of Positive Economics." In *Essays in Positive Economics.* Chicago: University of Chicago Press, 1953, pp. 3–43.
Basic statement of Friedman's positivist views about the role of assumptions in economics.

Griliches, Z. "Are Farmers Rational?" *Journal of Political Economy* 68 (1960): 68–71.
A fascinating methodological discussion of the best way to treat farmers' decision making in the economics of agriculture.

Kaplan, A. D. H., J. B. Dirlam, and R. F. Lanzillotti. *Pricing in Big Business: A Case Approach.* Washington, D.C.: The Brookings Institution, 1958.
Classic study of pricing decisions in a sample of large corporations.

Machlup, F. "Theories of the Firm: Marginal, Behavioral, Managerial." *American Economic Review* 47 (1957): 1–33.
Influential article on the "marginalist debate" over the proper approach to theories of the firm.

Silberberg, E. *The Structure of Economics: A Mathematical Analysis.* New York: McGraw-Hill Book Company, 1978, pp. 107–114.
Gives a detailed development of the supply function for a profit-maximizing firm.

Williamson, O. E. "The Modern Corporation: Origins, Evolution, Attributes." *Journal of Economic Literature* 19 (December 1981): 1537–1568.
A good literate survey of the nature of modern corporations.

EXTENSIONS

The Profit Function

For some applications, the analysis of profit maximization provided in Chapter 13 may be too indirect, and it is more expedient to focus explicitly on the firm's profits and their dependence on output price and input costs. Specifically, since by definition,

$$\textbf{profits} = \pi = P \cdot q - vK - wL$$

and variables q, K, and L are endogenous (they are

determined through profit-maximizing decisions), we can write

$$\text{maximum profits} = \pi^* = \pi^*(P, v, w).$$

This representation, which is analogous to the indirect utility function that we introduced in Chapter 4, is called a *profit function*—it shows how the firm's profits ultimately depend on the market parameters the firm faces (and, implicitly, on the firm's technology and on the demand for its product). Here we will examine some properties of this function and illustrate a few applications of the concept.

E13.1 Homogeneity

The profit function is homogeneous of degree one in P, v, and w. Since a doubling of P, v, and w will precisely double revenues and costs, the profit-maximizing output will not change. Hence, π^* will double also.

E13.2 Responses to Price Changes

Partial differentiation of the profit function shows

$$\frac{\partial \pi^*}{\partial P} = q \geq 0, \quad \frac{\partial \pi^*}{\partial v} = -K \leq 0, \quad \frac{\partial \pi^*}{\partial w} = -L \leq 0.$$

These qualitative results are exactly what would be predicted by using Figure 13.3.

E13.3 Envelope Results

Since the function π^* (P, v, w) is itself the result of a maximization process, the envelope theorem applies to the derivatives calculated in E13.2. The first of these $(\partial \pi^*/\partial P)$ provides an alternative way of computing the supply function for a profit-maximizing firm, whereas the derivatives $\partial \pi^*/\partial v$ and $\partial \pi^*/\partial w$ provide a way of computing the demands for K and L. These input demand functions differ from those computed from the total cost function in Chapter 12 because now they allow output to vary. Which of these different concepts of input demand should be used depends on whether q is allowed to change in response to changes in input prices. We will return to this distinction in Chapter 21.

E13.4 Convexity of the Profit Function

For any two output prices, P_1 and P_2, it is easy to show that

$$\pi^*(0.5P_1 + 0.5P_2, v, w)$$
$$\leq 0.5\pi^*(P_1, v, w) + 0.5\pi^*(P_2, v, w).$$

That is, the profit function is *convex* in output prices. This can be shown by letting $\overline{P} = 0.5P_1 + 0.5P_2$ and $\overline{q}$, $\overline{K}$, and $\overline{L}$ be profit-maximizing choices at $\overline{P}$. Obviously,

$$\pi^*(P_1, v, w) \geq P_1\overline{q} - v\overline{K} - w\overline{L}$$

and

$$\pi^*(P_2, v, w) \geq P_2\overline{q} - v\overline{K} - w\overline{L},$$

since π^* indicates the highest value of profits. Adding these two equations and dividing by 2 yields the required result.

Price Stabilization

Convexity of the profit function implies that a single firm will generally prefer a fluctuating output price to one that is stabilized (say, through government intervention) at its mean value. The result runs contrary to the direction of economic policy in many less developed countries, which tends to stress the desirability of stabilization of commodity prices. Several factors may account for this seeming paradox. First, many plans to "stabilize" commodity prices are in reality plans to raise the average level of these prices. Cartels of producers often have this as their primary goal, for example. Second, the convexity result applies for a single, price-taking firm. From the perspective of the entire market, total revenues from stabilized or fluctuating prices will depend on the nature of the demand for the product.[1] A third complication that must be addressed in assessing price stabilization schemes is firms' expectation of future prices. When commodities can be stored, optimal production decisions in the presence of price stabilization schemes can be quite complex. Finally, the purpose of price stabilization schemes may in some situations be more focused on reducing risks for the consumers of basic commodities such as food, rather than on the welfare of producers. Still, this fundamental property of the

---

[1] Specifically, for a constant elasticity demand function, total revenue will be a concave function of price if demand is inelastic, but convex if demand is elastic. Hence, in the elastic case, producers will obtain higher total revenues from a fluctuating price than from a price stabilized at its mean value.

profit function suggests caution in devising price stabilization schemes that have desirable long-run effects on producers. For an extended, theoretical analysis of these issues, see Newbury and Stiglitz (1981).

E13.5 Short-Run Producer Surplus

The profit function can also be used to define the short-run producer surplus as the change in profits as price rises from zero to its market value, P^*:

$$\text{producer surplus} = \int_0^{P^*} \partial \pi^*/\partial P \, dp$$
$$= \pi^*(P^*, v, w) - \pi^*(0, v, w),$$

which is the definition given in Chapter 13. The envelope result that the firm's supply function is given by

$$\frac{\partial \pi^*}{\partial P} = q^*(P, v, w)$$

can be used to show that this integral is identical to the one calculated in Equation 13.42.

The Short-Run Costs of Disease

Disease episodes can severely disrupt markets leading to short-run losses in producer and consumer surplus. For firms these losses can be computed as the short-run losses of profits from temporarily lower prices for their output or from the temporarily higher input prices they must pay. A particular extensive set

of such calculations is provided by Harrington, Krupnick, and Spofford (1991) in their detailed study of a giardiasis outbreak in Pennsylvania in 1983. Although consumers suffered most of the losses associated with this outbreak, the authors also calculate substantial losses for restaurants and bars in the immediate area. Such losses arose both from reduced business for these firms and from the need temporarily to use bottled water and other high-cost inputs in their operations. Quantitative calculations of these losses are usually based on profit functions described by the author.

References

Berck, P., and K. Sydsaeter. *Economists' Mathematical Manual.* Berlin: Springer-Verlag, 1991. Chap. 25.

Harrington, W. A., J. Krupnick, and W. O. Spofford. *Economics and Episodic Disease: The Benefits of Preventing a Giardiasis Outbreak.* Baltimore: Johns Hopkins University Press, 1991.

McFadden, D. "Cost, Revenue and Profit Functions." In M. Fuss and D. McFadden, eds., *Production Economics: A Dual Approach to Theory and Applications.* Amsterdam: North-Holland Publishing Company, 1978, pp. 60–110.

Newbury, D. M. G. and J. E. Stiglitz. *The Theory of Commodity Price Stabilization.* Oxford: Oxford University Press, 1981.

PERFECT COMPETITION

In Parts II–IV we used various optimization hypotheses to develop models to explain the demand for goods by utility-maximizing individuals and the supply of goods by profit-maximizing firms. In this part we will bring these two strands of analysis together to describe the process by which prices are determined. We will focus only on one specific model of price determination, the perfectly competitive model. That model assumes a large enough number of demanders and suppliers of each good so that each must be a price taker. In Part VI we will illustrate some of the models that result from relaxing the strict price-taking assumptions of the competitive case, but in this part we assume price-taking behavior throughout.

Chapter 14 develops the familiar partial equilibrium model of price determination in competitive markets. The principal result is the Marshallian "cross" diagram of supply and demand that we first discussed in Chapter 1. This model illustrates a "partial" equilibrium view of price determination because it focuses only on a single market. In Chapter 14 we show how this limited focus permits a relatively detailed analysis of how such a single market operates. Especially important are the demonstration of the way in which market equilibria may differ between the short run and the long run and the discussion of how possibilities for entry in the long run severely constrain the types of outcomes that are possible.

Chapter 15 continues the analysis of partial equilibrium competitive models by examining some of the ways such models are applied. A specific focus of the chapter is on showing how the competitive model can be used to judge the welfare consequences for market participants of various changes in market equilibria.

Although the partial equilibrium competitive model is quite useful for studying a single market in detail, it is inappropriate for examining relationships between markets because it cannot illustrate precisely how changes in the equilibrium price in one market affect prices in other markets. To capture such cross-market effects requires the development of "general" equilibrium models—a topic we take up in Chapter 16. There we show how an entire economy can be viewed as a system of interconnected competitive markets that determine all prices simultaneously. We develop such a model and then use it to study some of the features of a competitive price system.

Chapter 17 begins by describing what it means for an economy to allocate its available resources "efficiently" and then shows that, under certain circumstances, reliance on a perfectly competitive price system will achieve this result. Hence, the analysis offers some support for Adam Smith's conception of the price system as an "invisible hand," directing resources to where they are most valued. But the chapter also offers some warnings about situations that may invalidate the connection between perfect competition and economic efficiency and briefly examines equity questions associated with competitive allocations. A final section of the chapter focuses on problems of transactions and information costs. It shows how the existence of such costs may affect the equilibrium prices and quantities arrived at by competitive markets.

CHAPTER 14

THE PARTIAL EQUILIBRIUM
COMPETITIVE MODEL

In this chapter we describe the familiar model of price determination under perfect competition originally developed by Alfred Marshall in the late nineteenth century. That is, we provide a fairly complete analysis of the supply-demand mechanism as it applies to a single market. This is perhaps the most widely used model for studies of the pricing of particular products, and a thorough knowledge of it is an important starting place for many economic analyses.

In the analysis of competitive pricing, it is important to decide the length of time that is to be allowed for a *supply response* to changing demand conditions. The establishment of equilibrium prices will be different if we are talking about a very short period of time during which most inputs are fixed or if we are envisioning a very long-run process in which it is possible for new firms to enter an industry. For this reason it has been traditional in economics to discuss pricing in three different time periods: (1) very short run, (2) short run, and (3) long run. Although it is not possible to give these terms an exact chronological definition, the essential distinction being made concerns the nature of the supply response that is assumed to be possible. In the *very short run*, there is no supply response: Quantity supplied is fixed and does not respond to changes in demand. In the *short run*, existing firms may change the quantity they are supplying, but no new firms can enter the industry. In the *long run*, new firms may enter an industry, thereby producing a very flexible supply response. In this chapter we will discuss each of these possibilities.

TIMING OF THE SUPPLY RESPONSE

In the very short run, or the *market period*, there is no supply response. The goods are already "in" the marketplace and must be sold for whatever the market will bear. In this situation, price acts only as a device to ration

PRICING IN THE VERY SHORT RUN

demand. Price will adjust to clear the market of the quantity that must be sold during the period. Although the market price may act as a signal to producers in future periods, it does not perform such a function in the current period because current period output is fixed. Figure 14.1 depicts this situation. Market demand is represented by the curve D. Supply is fixed at Q^*, and the price that clears the market is P_1. At P_1 individuals are willing to take all that is offered in the market. Sellers want to dispose of Q^* without regard to price (suppose that the good in question is perishable and will be worthless if it is not sold in the very short run). Hence, P_1, Q^* is an equilibrium price-quantity combination. If demand should shift to D', the equilibrium price would increase to P_2, but Q^* would stay fixed since no supply response is possible. The *supply curve* in this situation, then, is a vertical straight line at output Q^*.

The analysis of the very short run is not particularly useful for many markets. Such a theory may adequately represent some situations in which goods are perishable or must be sold on a given day, as is the case in auctions.

FIGURE 14.1

PRICING IN THE VERY SHORT RUN

When quantity is fixed in the very short run, price acts only as a device to ration demand. With quantity fixed at Q^*, price P_1 will prevail in the marketplace if D is the market demand curve. At this price, individuals are willing to consume exactly that quantity available. If demand should shift upward to D', the equilibrium market price would rise to P_2.

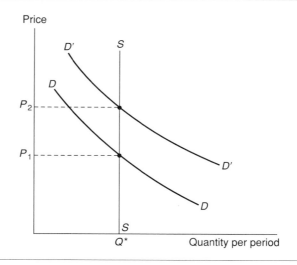

Indeed, the study of auctions provides a number of insights about the informational problems involved in arriving at equilibrium prices which we take up in Chapter 18. But auctions are unusual in that supply is fixed. The far more usual case involves some degree of supply response to changing demand. It is presumed that a rise in price will bring additional quantity into the market. In the remainder of this chapter, we shall examine this process.

Before beginning our analysis, we should note that increases in quantity supplied need not come only from increased production. In a world in which some goods are durable (that is, last longer than a single period), current owners of these goods may supply them in increasing amounts to the market as price rises. For example, even though the supply of Rembrandts is fixed, we would not want to draw the market supply curve for these paintings as a vertical line, such as that shown in Figure 14.1. As the price of Rembrandts rises, individuals and museums will become increasingly willing to part with them. From a market point of view, therefore, the supply curve for Rembrandts will have an upward slope, even though no new production takes place. A similar analysis would follow for many types of durable goods, such as antiques, used cars, back issues of the *National Geographic*, or corporate shares, all of which are in nominally "fixed" supply. Since we are more interested in examining how demand and production are related, we shall not analyze those cases (which may involve complex questions about supplier behavior over time) in detail.

In short-run analysis the number of firms in an industry is fixed. It is assumed that firms do not have sufficient flexibility either to enter or to leave a given industry. However, those firms in the industry are able to adjust the quantity they are producing in response to changing conditions. They will do this by altering levels of employment for those inputs that can be varied in the short run, and we shall investigate this supply decision here. Before beginning the analysis, we should perhaps state explicitly the assumptions of this perfectly competitive model.

SHORT-RUN PRICE DETERMINATION

DEFINITION

Perfect Competition   A *perfectly competitive industry* is one that obeys the following assumptions:
1. There are a large number of firms, each producing the same homogeneous product.
2. Each firm attempts to maximize profits.
3. Each firm is a price taker: It assumes that its actions have no effect on market price.
4. Prices are assumed to be known by all market participants—information is perfect.

5. Transactions are costless: Buyers and sellers incur no costs in making exchanges (for more on this and the previous assumption, see Chapter 17).

Now we will make use of these assumptions to study price determination in the short run.

Short-Run Market Supply Curve

In Chapter 13 we showed how to construct the short-run supply curve for a single profit-maximizing firm. To construct a market supply curve, we start by recognizing that the quantity of output supplied to the entire market in the short run is simply the sum of the quantities supplied by each firm. Since each firm uses the same market price to determine how much to produce, the total amount supplied to the market by all firms will obviously depend on price. This relationship between price and quantity supplied is called a *short-run market supply curve*. Figure 14.2 illustrates the construction of the curve. For simplicity assume there are only two firms, A and B. The short-run supply (that is, marginal cost) curves for firms A and B are shown in Figures 14.2a and 14.2b. The market supply curve shown in Figure 14.2c is the horizontal sum of these two curves. For example, at a price of P_1, firm A is willing to supply q_1^A, and firm B is willing to supply q_1^B. Therefore, at this price the total supply in the market is given by Q_1, which is equal to $q_1^A + q_1^B$. The other points on the curve are constructed in an identical way. Because each firm's supply curve has a positive slope, the market supply curve will also have a positive slope. The positive slope reflects the fact that short-run marginal costs increase as firms attempt to increase their outputs.

Short-Run Market Supply

More generally, if we let $q_i (P, v, w)$ represent the short-run supply function for each of the n firms in the industry, we can define the short-run market supply function as follows:

DEFINITION

Short-Run Market Supply Function The *short-run market supply function* shows total quantity supplied by each firm to a market:

$$Q_S(P, v, w) = \sum_{i=1}^{n} q_i (P, v, w). \qquad (14.1)$$

Notice that the firms in the industry are assumed to face the same market price and the same prices for inputs (though this latter assumption can easily

FIGURE 14.2

SHORT-RUN MARKET SUPPLY CURVE

The supply (marginal cost) curves of two firms are shown in (a) and (b). The market supply curve (c) is the horizontal sum of these curves. For example, at P_1 firm A supplies q_1^A, firm B supplies q_1^B, and total market supply is given by $Q_1 = q_1^A + q_1^B$.

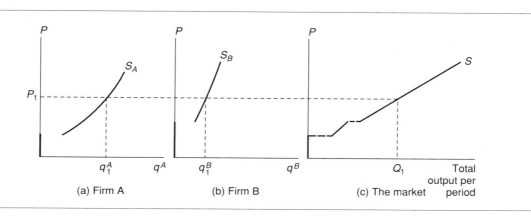

(a) Firm A   (b) Firm B   (c) The market   Total output per period

be relaxed). The *short-run market supply curve* shows the two-dimensional relationship between Q and P, holding v and w (and each firm's underlying technology) constant. The notation makes clear that if v, w, or technology were to change, the supply curve would shift to a new location.

Short-Run Supply Elasticity

One way of summarizing the responsiveness of the output of firms in an industry to higher prices is by the *short-run supply elasticity*. This measure shows how proportional changes in market price are met by changes in total output. Consistent with the elasticity concepts developed in Chapter 7, this is defined as follows:

DEFINITION

Short-Run Elasticity of Supply ($e_{S,P}$)

$$e_{S,P} = \frac{\text{percentage change in } Q \text{ supplied}}{\text{percentage change in } P} = \frac{\partial Q_S}{\partial P} \cdot \frac{P}{Q_S}. \qquad (14.2)$$

Since quantity supplied is an increasing function of price ($\partial Q_S/\partial P > 0$), the supply elasticity is positive. High values for $e_{S,P}$ imply that small increases in market price lead to a relatively large supply response by firms, since marginal costs do not rise steeply and input price interaction effects are small. Alternatively, a low value for $e_{S,P}$ implies that it takes relatively large changes in price to induce firms to change their output levels, since marginal costs rise rapidly. Notice that, as for all elasticity notions, computation of $e_{S,P}$ requires that input prices and technology be held constant.

EXAMPLE 14.1

A SHORT-RUN SUPPLY FUNCTION

In Chapter 12 we computed Hamburger Heaven's short-run total cost function as

$$STC = 4v + \frac{wq^2}{400},$$ (14.3)

and in Chapter 13 we used the short-run marginal cost function to construct the firm's short-run supply curve by equating price to SMC

$$P = SMC = \frac{2wq}{400}$$ (14.4)

and solving for q:

$$q = \frac{200P}{w}.$$ (14.5)

For the case $w = \$4$, this resulted in a simple linear supply function of the form

$$q = 50P.$$ (14.6)

Now, assume there are 100 identical hamburger emporia in a particular city and let each firm's hourly output be denoted as q_i $(i = 1, \ldots, 100)$. The supply function for each firm is now

$$q_i = 50P \quad (i = 1, \ldots, 100).$$ (14.7)

Here we have implicitly assumed that each firm sells its output at the same price. This reflects the "law of one price" in competitive markets. The market supply function is given by

$$Q_S = \sum_{i=1}^{100} q_i = 100 \cdot (50P) = 5{,}000P,$$ (14.8)

where Q_S is the total quantity supplied to the market (as a function of market price, P). Notice that if the wage were to rise to $w = \$5$, each firm's supply function would be given by

$$q_i = 40P, \tag{14.9}$$

and the market supply function would be given by

$$Q_S = \sum q_i = 4{,}000P. \tag{14.10}$$

At each price, fewer hamburgers would now be supplied—the rise in wages has shifted the supply curve upward.

Elasticity of Supply. Here it is a simple matter to compute the short-run elasticity of supply. Since (for $w = 4$)

$$e_{S,P} = \frac{\partial Q_S}{\partial P} \cdot \frac{P}{Q_S} = 5{,}000 \cdot \frac{P}{Q_S} = \frac{5{,}000P}{5{,}000P} = 1, \tag{14.11}$$

the short-run supply curve is unit elastic (as might also have been computed by noting the unitary exponent for price in the supply function). For $P = \$1$, $Q_S = 5{,}000$ whereas for $P = \$1.10$, $Q_S = 5{,}500$—a 10 percent increase in price therefore results in a 10 percent increase in quantity supplied.

QUERY: Why doesn't the elasticity of supply depend on the wage in this problem? Under what circumstances would there be such a dependence?

We are now ready to combine demand and supply curves to demonstrate the establishment of equilibrium prices in the market. Figure 14.3 shows this process. Looking first at Figure 14.3b, we see the market demand curve D (ignore D' for the moment) and the short-run supply curve S. The two curves intersect at a price of P_1 and a quantity of Q_1. This price-quantity combination represents an *equilibrium* between the demands of individuals and the costs of firms. The equilibrium price P_1 serves two important functions. First, this price acts as a signal to producers by providing them with information with which to decide how much should be produced. In order to maximize profits, firms will produce that output level for which marginal costs are equal to P_1. In the aggregate, then, production will be Q_1. A second function of the price is to ration demand. Given the market price P_1, utility-maximizing individuals will decide how much of their limited incomes to devote to buying the particular good. At a price of P_1, total quantity demanded will be Q_1, and this is precisely the amount that will be produced. Hence, we define equilibrium price as follows:

Equilibrium Price Determination

DEFINITION

Equilibrium Price An *equilibrium price* is one at which quantity demanded is equal to quantity supplied. At such a price, neither demanders nor suppliers have an incentive to alter their economic decisions. Mathematically, an equilibrium price, P^*, solves the equation:

$$Q_D(P^*, P', I) = Q_S(P^*, v, w) \qquad (14.12)$$

or, more compactly,

$$Q_D(P^*) = Q_S(P^*). \qquad (14.13)$$

The definition given in Equation 14.12 makes clear that an equilibrium price depends on the values of many exogenous factors such as incomes or prices of other goods and of firms' inputs. As we will see in the next section, changes in any of these factors will likely result in a change in the equilibrium price required to equate quantity supplied to quantity demanded.

The implications of the equilibrium price (P_1) for a typical firm and for a typical individual are shown in Figures 14.3a and 14.3c, respectively. For the

---

FIGURE 14.3

INTERACTIONS OF MANY INDIVIDUALS AND FIRMS DETERMINE MARKET PRICE IN THE SHORT RUN

Market demand curves and market supply curves are each the horizontal sum of numerous components. These market curves are shown in (b). Once price is determined in the market, each firm and each individual treat this price as a fixed parameter in their decisions. Although individual firms and persons are impotent in determining price, their interaction as a whole is the sole determinant of price. This is illustrated by a shift in an individual's demand curve to d'. If only one individual reacts in this way, market price will not be affected. However, if everyone exhibits an increased demand, market demand will shift to D'; in the short run, price will rise to P_2.

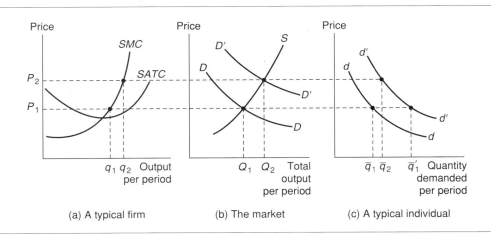

(a) A typical firm (b) The market (c) A typical individual

typical firm the price P_1 will cause an output level of q_1 to be produced. The firm earns a small profit at this particular price because short-run average total costs are covered. The demand curve d (ignore d' for the moment) for a typical individual is shown in Figure 14.3c. At a price of P_1, this individual demands $\bar{q}_1$. By adding up the quantities that each individual demands at P_1 and the quantities that each firm supplies, we can see that the market is in equilibrium. The market supply and demand curves provide a convenient way of making such a summation.

Market Reaction to a Shift in Demand

The three panels in Figure 14.3 can be used to show two important facts about short-run market equilibrium: the individual's "impotence" in the market and the nature of short-run supply response. First, suppose that a single individual's demand curve were to shift outward to d', as shown in Figure 14.3c. Since it was assumed that there are many demanders, this shift will have practically no effect on the market demand curve. Consequently, market price will be unaffected by the shift to d'; that is, price will remain at P_1. Of course, at this price, the person for whom the demand curve has shifted will consume slightly more $(\bar{q}_1')$, as is shown in Figure 14.3c. But this amount is an inconsequential part of the market.

If many individuals experience shifts outward in their demand curves, the entire market demand curve may shift. Figure 14.3b shows the new demand curve D'. The new equilibrium point will be at P_2, Q_2: At this point, supply-demand balance is reestablished. Price has increased from P_1 to P_2 in response to the demand shift. Notice also that the quantity traded in the market has increased from Q_1 to Q_2. The rise in price has served two functions. First, as in our previous analysis of the very short run, it has acted to ration demand. Whereas at P_1 a typical individual demanded $\bar{q}_1'$, now at P_2 only $\bar{q}_2$ is demanded. The rise in price has also acted as a signal to the typical firm to increase production. In Figure 14.3a the firm's profit-maximizing output level has increased from q_1 to q_2 in response to the price rise. That is what we mean by a *short-run supply response:* An increase in market price acts as an inducement to increase production. Firms are willing to increase production (and to incur higher marginal costs) because price has risen. If market price had not been permitted to rise (suppose that government price controls were in effect), firms would not have increased their outputs. At P_1 there would now be an excess (unfilled) demand for the good in question. If market price is allowed to rise, a supply-demand equilibrium can be reestablished so that what firms produce is again equal to what individuals demand at the prevailing market price. Notice also that at the new price P_2, the typical firm has increased its profits. This increasing profitability in the short run will be important to our discussion of long-run pricing later in this chapter.

TABLE 14.1

▱ ▱ ▱ ▱

REASONS FOR SHIFTS IN DEMAND OR SUPPLY CURVES

DEMAND CURVES SHIFT BECAUSE	SUPPLY CURVES SHIFT BECAUSE
• Incomes change • Prices of substitutes or complements change • Preferences change	• Input prices change • Technology changes • Number of producers changes

▱ ▱ ▱ ▱

SHIFTS IN SUPPLY AND DEMAND CURVES: A GRAPHICAL ANALYSIS

In previous chapters we established many reasons why either a demand curve or a supply curve might shift. These reasons are briefly summarized in Table 14.1. Although most of these merit little additional explanation, it is important to note that a change in the number of firms will shift the short-run market supply curve (since the sum in Equation 14.1 will be over a different number of firms). This observation allows us to tie together short-run and long-run analysis.

It seems likely that the types of changes described in Table 14.1 are constantly occurring in real-world markets. When either a supply curve or a demand curve does shift, equilibrium price and quantity will change. In this section we shall investigate graphically the relative magnitudes of such changes and show that the outcome depends on the shapes of the curves.

Shifts in Supply Curves: Importance of the Shape of the Demand Curve

Consider first a shift upward in the short-run supply curve for a good. Such a shift, for example, might have resulted from an increase in the prices of inputs used by firms to produce the good. Whatever the cause of the shift, it is important to recognize that the effect of the shift on the equilibrium level of P and Q will depend on the shape of the demand curve for the product. Figure 14.4 illustrates two possible situations. The demand curve in Figure 14.4a is relatively price elastic; that is, a change in price substantially affects quantity demanded. For this case, a shift in the supply curve from S to S' will cause equilibrium price to rise only moderately (from P to P'), whereas quantity declines sharply (from Q to Q'). Rather than being "passed on" in higher prices, the increase in the firms' input costs is met primarily by a decrease in quantity (a movement down each firm's marginal cost curve) and only a slight increase in price.

This situation is reversed when the market demand curve is inelastic. In Figure 14.4b a shift in the supply curve causes equilibrium price to rise substantially, whereas quantity is little changed. The reason for this is that individuals do not reduce their demands very much if prices rise.

FIGURE 14.4

EFFECT OF A SHIFT IN THE SHORT-RUN SUPPLY CURVE DEPENDS ON THE SHAPE OF THE DEMAND CURVE

In (a) the shift upward in the supply curve causes price to increase only slightly whereas quantity declines sharply. This results from the elastic shape of the demand curve. In (b) the demand curve is inelastic; price increases substantially, with only a slight decrease in quantity.

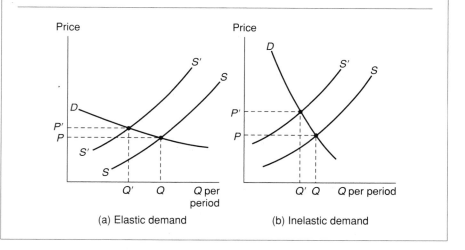

(a) Elastic demand   (b) Inelastic demand

Consequently, the shift upward in the supply curve is almost entirely passed on to demanders in the form of higher prices.

In a procedure identical to that we just used, we can show that a given shift in a market demand curve will have different implications for P and Q, depending on the shape of the short-run supply curve. Two illustrations are shown in Figure 14.5. In Figure 14.5a the supply curve for the good in question is inelastic. In this situation a shift outward in the market demand curve will cause price to increase substantially. On the other hand, the quantity traded increases only slightly. Intuitively, what has happened is that the increase in demand (and in Q) has caused firms to move up their steeply sloped marginal cost curves. The concomitant large increase in price serves to ration demand.

Figure 14.5b shows a relatively elastic short-run supply curve. Such a curve would occur for an industry in which marginal costs do not rise steeply in response to output increases. For this case an increase in demand produces a substantial increase in Q. However, because of the nature of the supply

Shifts in Demand Curves: Importance of the Shape of the Supply Curve

FIGURE 14.5

EFFECT OF A SHIFT IN THE DEMAND CURVE DEPENDS ON THE SHAPE OF THE SHORT-RUN SUPPLY CURVE

In (a) supply is inelastic; a shift in demand causes price to increase greatly, with only a small concomitant increase in quantity. In (b), on the other hand, supply is elastic; price rises only slightly in response to a demand shift.

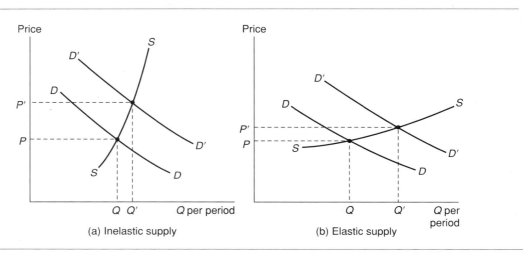

(a) Inelastic supply

(b) Elastic supply

curve, this increase is not met by great cost increases. Consequently, price rises only moderately.

These examples again demonstrate Marshall's observation that demand and supply simultaneously determine price and quantity. Recall his analogy from Chapter 1: Just as it is impossible to say which blade of a scissors does the cutting, so too is it impossible to attribute price solely to demand or to supply characteristics. Rather, the effect that shifts in either a demand curve or a supply curve will have depends on the shapes of both of the curves. Example 14.2 illustrates some of these points.

EXAMPLE 14.2

CHANGING SHORT-RUN EQUILIBRIA

Continuing our hamburger example (just after you thought it was safe), suppose the hourly market demand for hamburgers in the city we have been studying is given by

$$Q_D = 10{,}000 - 5{,}000P. \tag{14.14}$$

To find the equilibrium price, we set quantity demanded equal to quantity supplied:

$$Q_D = 10{,}000 - 5{,}000P = Q_S = 5{,}000P \tag{14.15}$$

and solve for the price (P^*) that equates these two magnitudes:

$$10{,}000 = 10{,}000P \tag{14.16}$$

so

$$P^* = 1 \tag{14.17}$$

and

$$Q_D = Q_S = 5{,}000.$$

If the wage of hamburger workers were to rise to $5, the supply curve would be

$$Q_S = 4{,}000P, \tag{14.18}$$

and the new market equilibrium would be

$$Q_D = 10{,}000 - 5{,}000P = Q_S = 4{,}000P$$

$$10{,}000 = 9{,}000P \tag{14.19}$$

$$P^* = 1.11$$

$$Q^* = 4{,}444. \tag{14.20}$$

At the old price of $1, $Q_D = 5{,}000$ and $Q_S = 4{,}000$, so the rise to $1.11 restores equilibrium in two ways: (1) by increasing the quantity supplied; and (2) by reducing the quantity demanded. In this example these two responses are of approximately equal magnitude, but that need not be so. If the demand curve were flatter, for example, price would rise less, and a relatively larger portion of the quantity adjustment would be reflected in a move along the demand curve. Alternatively, if demand were steeper, there would be a greater rise in price, and more of the quantity change would arise from movement along the supply curve.[1]

---

[1] The demand functions

$$Q_D = 15{,}000 - 10{,}000P \tag{i}$$

and

$$Q_D = 6{,}000 - 1{,}000P \tag{ii}$$

each have an equilibrium of $P^* = 1$, $Q^* = 5{,}000$ with the initial supply curve. The shift in supply results in a new equilibrium of $P^* = 1.071$, $Q^* = 4{,}286$ in case (i) but an equilibrium of $P^* = 1.20$, $Q^* = 4{,}800$ in case (ii).

A similar analysis would hold for an increase in demand. Suppose demand were to increase to

$$Q_D = 12,000 - 5,000P. \tag{14.21}$$

Assuming our original supply curve, the new market equilibrium would be

$$Q_D = 12,000 - 5,000P = Q_S = 5,000P \tag{14.22}$$

or

$$P^* = 1.20$$
$$Q^* = 6,000. \tag{14.23}$$

At the old price of \$1, now $Q_D = 7,000$ and $Q_S = 5,000$, so the rise in price restores equilibrium by prompting an increase in quantity supplied and a reduction in quantity demanded. Again the relative change in price and quantity is determined by the slopes of the curves, a point we next illustrate with a general mathematical development.

QUERY: Does the change in price and quantity from a shift in demand confirm that the short-run elasticity of supply in this case is 1.0 (as calculated in Example 14.1)? What do the calculations for a shift in supply indicate about the price elasticity of demand for hamburgers over the range observed? How does this compare to the elasticities implied by the demand curves in footnote 1?

MATHEMATICAL MODEL OF SUPPLY AND DEMAND

A general mathematical model of the supply-demand process can further illuminate the comparative statics of changing equilibrium prices and quantities. Suppose that the demand function can be represented by

$$Q_D = D(P, \alpha), \tag{14.24}$$

where α is a parameter that allows us to shift the demand curve. It might represent consumer income, prices of other goods (this would permit the tying together of supply and demand in several related markets), or changing preferences. In general we expect $\partial D / \partial P = D_P < 0$, but $\partial D / \partial \alpha = D_\alpha$ may have any sign, depending precisely on what the parameter α means. Using this same procedure, we can write the supply relationship as

$$Q_S = S(P, \beta), \tag{14.25}$$

where β is a parameter that shifts the supply curve and might include such factors as input prices, technical changes, or (for a multiproduct firm) prices of other potential outputs. Here $\partial S/\partial P = S_P > 0$, but $\partial S/\partial \beta = S_\beta$ may have any sign. The model is closed by requiring that in equilibrium,[2]

$$Q_D = Q_S. \qquad (14.26)$$

To analyze the comparative statics of this simple model, we write the total differentials of the demand and supply functions as

$$dQ_D = D_P dP + D_\alpha d\alpha \qquad (14.27)$$

and

$$dQ_S = S_P dP + S_\beta d\beta.$$

Since maintenance of equilibrium requires that

$$dQ_D = dQ_S, \qquad (14.28)$$

we can solve these equations for the change in equilibrium price for any combination of shifts in demand (α) or supply (β). For example, suppose the demand parameter α were to change while β remains constant. Then, using the equilibrium condition, we have

$$D_P dP + D_\alpha d\alpha = S_P dP \qquad (14.29)$$

or, manipulating terms a bit,

$$\frac{\partial P}{\partial \alpha} = \frac{D_\alpha}{S_P - D_P}. \qquad (14.30)$$

Since the denominator of this expression is positive, the sign of $\partial P/\partial \alpha$ will be the same as the sign of D_α. If α represents consumer income (and the good in question is normal), D_α would be positive, and a rise in income would shift demand outward. This, as Equation 14.30 also indicates, would cause equilibrium price to rise, a result already reflected graphically in Figure 14.5.

---

[2] The model could be further modified to show how the equilibrium quantity supplied is to be allocated among the firms in the industry. If, for example, the industry is composed of n identical firms, the output of any one of them would be given by

$$q = \frac{Q}{n}.$$

In the short run, with n fixed, this would add little to our analysis. In the long run, however, n must also be determined by the model, as we show later in this chapter.

An Elasticity Interpretation

Further algebraic manipulation of Equation 14.30 yields a more useful comparative statics result. Multiplying both sides of that equation by α/P gives

$$e_{P,\alpha} = \frac{\partial P}{\partial \alpha} \cdot \frac{\alpha}{P} = \frac{D_\alpha}{S_P - D_P} \cdot \frac{\alpha}{P}$$

$$= \frac{D_\alpha \dfrac{\alpha}{Q}}{(S_P - D_P) \cdot \dfrac{P}{Q}} = \frac{e_{Q,\alpha}}{e_{S,P} - e_{Q,P}}. \tag{14.31}$$

Since the elasticities in this equation are frequently available from empirical studies, this equation can be a convenient way to make rough estimates of the effects of various events on equilibrium prices. As an example, suppose again that α represents consumer income and that there is interest in predicting how an increase in income affects the equilibrium price of, say, automobiles. Suppose empirical data suggest that $e_{Q,I} = e_{Q,\alpha} = 3.0$, $e_{Q,P} = -1.2$ (these figures are from Table 7.3) and assume that $e_{S,P} = 1.0$. Substituting these figures into Equation 14.31 yields

$$e_{P,\alpha} = \frac{e_{Q,\alpha}}{e_{S,P} - e_{Q,P}} = \frac{3.0}{1.0 - (-1.2)}$$

$$= \frac{3.0}{2.2} = 1.36. \tag{14.32}$$

The empirical elasticity estimates therefore suggest that each 1 percent rise in consumer incomes results in a 1.36 percent rise in the equilibrium price of automobiles. Estimates of other kinds of shifts in supply or demand can be similarly modeled by manipulating Equations 14.27 and 14.28 and obtaining empirical estimates of the necessary parameters.

EXAMPLE 14.3

EQUILIBRIA WITH CONSTANT ELASTICITY FUNCTIONS

An even more complete analysis of supply-demand equilibrium can be provided if we use specific functional forms. Constant elasticity functions are especially useful for this purpose. Suppose the demand for automobiles is given by

$$Q_D \, (P,I) = 0.1 \, P^{-1.2} \, I^3 \tag{14.33}$$

where price (P) is measured in dollars as is real family income (I). The supply function for automobiles is

$$Q_S (P, w) = 6,400 \; Pw^{-.5} \qquad (14.34)$$

where w is the hourly wage of automobile workers. Notice that the elasticities assumed here are those used previously in the text ($e_{Q,P} = -1.2$, $e_{Q,I} = 3.0$, and $e_{S,P} = 1$). If the values for the "exogenous" variables I and w are $20,000 and $25 respectively, demand-supply equilibrium requires

$$Q_D = .1 \; P^{-1.2} \; I^3 = 8 \times 10^{11} \; P^{-1.2}$$
$$= Q_S = 6,400 \; Pw^{-.5} = 1,280 \; P \qquad (14.35)$$

or

$$P^{2.2} = 8 \times 10^{11}/1,280 = 6.25 \times 10^8$$

or

$$P^* = 9,957$$
$$Q^* = 1,280 \cdot P^* = 12,745,000. \qquad (14.36)$$

Hence, the initial equilibrium in the automobile market has a price of nearly $10,000 with nearly 13 million cars being sold.

A Shift in Demand. A 10 percent rise in real family income, all other factors remaining constant, would shift the demand function to

$$Q_D = 1.06 \times 10^{12} \; P^{-1.2} \qquad (14.37)$$

and proceeding as before:

$$P^{2.2} = 1.06 \times 10^{12}/1,280 = 8.32 \times 10^8 \qquad (14.38)$$

or

$$P^* = 11,339$$
$$Q^* = 14,514,000. \qquad (14.39)$$

As we predicted earlier, the 10 percent rise in real income raised car prices by nearly 14 percent. In the process, quantity sold increased by nearly 2 million automobiles.

A Shift in Supply. An exogenous shift in automobile supply as a result, say, of changing auto workers' wages would also affect market equilibrium. If wages were to rise to $30 per hour, the supply function (Equation 14.34) would shift to

$$Q_S(P, w) = 6,400 \; P(30)^{-.5} = 1,168 \; P \qquad (14.40)$$

and returning to our original demand function (with $I = $20,000$) would yield

$$P^{2.2} = 8 \times 10^{11}/1,168 = 6.85 \times 10^8 \qquad (14.41)$$

or

$$P^* = 10,381$$

$$Q^* = 12,125,000.$$

(14.42)

The 20 percent rise in wages, therefore, led to a 4.3 percent rise in auto prices and a decline in sales of more than 600,000 units. Changing equilibria in many types of markets can be approximated by using this general approach together with empirical estimates of the relevant elasticities.

QUERY: Do the results of changing auto workers' wages agree with what might have been predicted using an equation similar to Equation 14.31?

LONG-RUN ANALYSIS

We saw in Chapter 12 that in the long run, a firm may adapt all of its inputs to fit market conditions. For long-run analysis, therefore, we should use the firm's long-run cost curves, since these curves reflect flexibility in all inputs. A profit-maximizing firm that is a price taker will produce that output level for which price is equal to long-run marginal cost (MC). However, we must consider a second and ultimately more important influence on price in the long run: the possibility of the entry of entirely new firms into the industry or the exit of existing firms from the industry. In mathematical terms we must allow the number of firms, n, to vary in response to economic incentives. The perfectly competitive model assumes that there are no special costs of entering or exiting from an industry. Consequently, new firms will be lured into any market in which (economic) profits are positive. Similarly, firms will leave any industry in which profits are negative. The entry of new firms will cause the short-run industry supply curve to shift outward, since there are now more firms producing than there were previously. Such a shift will cause market price (and industry profits) to fall. The process will continue until no firm contemplating entering the industry is able to earn a profit.[3] At that point, entry will cease and an equilibrium number of firms will be in the industry. A similar argument can be made for the case in which some of the firms in an industry are suffering short-run losses. Some firms will choose to leave the industry, and this will cause the supply curve to shift to the left. Market price will rise, thus restoring profitability to those firms remaining in the industry.

---

[3] Remember that we are using the economists' definition of profits here. These profits represent a return to the owner of a business in excess of that which is strictly necessary to keep him or her in the business. Hence, when we talk about a firm earning "zero" profits, we mean that no entrepreneurial income is being earned in excess of that which could be earned from alternative investments.

For the purposes of this chapter, we shall assume that all the firms in an industry have identical cost curves; that is, no firm controls any special resources or technologies.[4] Because all firms are identical, the equilibrium long-run position requires that each firm earn exactly zero economic profits. In graphic terms the long-run equilibrium price must settle at the low point of each firm's long-run average total cost curve. Only at this point do the two equilibrium conditions $P = MC$ (which is required for profit maximization) and $P = AC$ (which is required for zero profit) hold. It is important to emphasize, however, that these two equilibrium conditions have rather different origins. Profit maximization is a goal of firms. The $P = MC$ rule therefore derives from the behavioral assumptions we have made about firms and is similar to the output decision rule used in the short run. The zero-profit condition is not a goal for firms. Firms obviously would prefer to have large, positive profits. The long-run operation of the market, however, forces all firms to accept a level of zero economic profits ($P = AC$) because of the willingness of firms to enter and to leave an industry in response to the possibility of making supranormal returns. Although the firms in a perfectly competitive industry may earn either positive or negative profits in the short run, in the long run only a level of zero profits will prevail. Hence, we can summarize this analysis by the following definition:

Equilibrium Conditions

DEFINITION

Long-Run Competitive Equilibrium   A *perfectly competitive industry* is in *long-run equilibrium* if there are no incentives for profit-maximizing firms to enter or to leave the industry. This will occur when the number of firms is such that $P = MC = AC$ and each firm operates at the low point of its long-run average cost curve.

In order to discuss long-run pricing in detail, we must make an assumption about how the entry of new firms into an industry affects the costs of firms' inputs. The simplest assumption we might make is that entry has no effect on the costs of those inputs—perhaps because the industry is a relatively small hirer in its various input markets. Under this assumption, no matter how many firms enter (or leave) an industry, each firm will retain the same set of cost curves with which it started. This assumption of constant input

LONG-RUN EQUILIBRIUM: CONSTANT-COST CASE

---

[4] If firms have different costs, very low-cost firms can earn positive long-run profits, and such extra profits will be reflected in the price of the resource that accounts for the firm's low costs. In this sense the assumption of identical costs is not very restrictive since an active market for the firm's inputs will ensure that average costs (which include opportunity costs) are the same for all firms. See also the discussion of Ricardian rent later in this chapter.

costs may not be tenable in many important cases, which we will look at in the next section. For the moment, however, we wish to examine the equilibrium conditions for a *constant-cost industry*.

Initial Equilibrium

Figure 14.6 demonstrates long-run equilibrium for an industry. For the market as a whole (Figure 14.6b), the demand curve is given by D and the short-run supply curve by SS. The short-run equilibrium price is therefore P_1. The typical firm (Figure 14.6a) will produce output level q_1, since at this level of output, price is equal to short-run marginal cost (SMC). In addition, with a market price of P_1, output level q_1 is also a long-run equilibrium position for the firm. The firm is maximizing profits, since price is equal to long-run marginal costs (MC). Figure 14.6a also implies our second long-run equilibrium property: Price is equal to long-run average costs (AC). Consequently, economic profits are zero, and there is no incentive for firms either to enter or to leave the industry. The market depicted in Figure 14.6 is therefore in both

FIGURE 14.6

LONG-RUN EQUILIBRIUM FOR A PERFECTLY COMPETITIVE INDUSTRY: CONSTANT-COST CASE

An increase in demand from D to D' will cause price to rise from P_1 to P_2 in the short run. This higher price will create profits in the industry, and new firms will be drawn into the market. If it is assumed that the entry of these new firms has no effect on the cost curves of the firms in the industry, new firms will continue to enter until price is pushed back down to P_1. At this price, economic profits are zero. The long-run supply curve (LS) will therefore be a horizontal line at P_1. Along LS, output is increased by increasing the number of firms, each producing q_1.

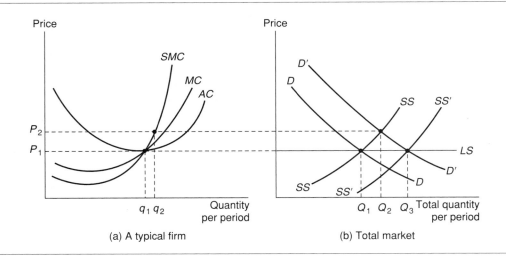

(a) A typical firm

(b) Total market

short-run and long-run equilibrium. Firms are in equilibrium because they are maximizing profits, and the number of firms is stable because economic profits are zero. This equilibrium will tend to persist until either supply or demand conditions change.

Responses to an Increase in Demand

Suppose now that the market demand curve in Figure 14.6b shifts outward to D'. If SS is the relevant short-run supply curve for the industry, then in the short run, price will rise to P_2. The typical firm, in the short run, will choose to produce q_2 and will earn profits on this level of output. In the long run, these profits will attract new firms into the market. Because of the constant-cost assumption, this entry of new firms will have no effect on input costs. New firms will continue to enter the market until price is forced down to the level at which there are again no pure economic profits. The entry of new firms therefore will shift the short-run supply curve to SS', where the equilibrium price (P_1) is reestablished. At this new long-run equilibrium, the price-quantity combination P_1, Q_3 will prevail in the market. The typical firm again will produce at output level q_1, although now there will be more firms than in the initial situation.

Infinitely Elastic Supply

We have shown that the *long-run supply curve* for the constant-cost industry will be a horizontal straight line at price P_1. This curve is labeled LS in Figure 14.6b. No matter what happens to demand, the twin equilibrium conditions of zero long-run profits (since free entry is assumed) and profit maximization will ensure that no price other than P_1 can prevail in the long run.[5] For this reason, P_1 might be regarded as the "normal" price for this commodity. If the constant-cost assumption is abandoned, however, the long-run supply curve need not have this infinitely elastic shape, as we show in the next section.

EXAMPLE 14.4

INFINITELY ELASTIC LONG-RUN SUPPLY

Handmade bicycle frames are produced by a number of identically sized firms. Total (long-run) monthly costs for a typical firm are given by

$$TC = q^3 - 20q^2 + 100q + 8,000, \qquad (14.43)$$

---

[5] These equilibrium conditions also point out what seems to be, somewhat imprecisely, an "efficient" aspect of the long-run equilibrium in perfectly competitive markets: The good under investigation will be produced at minimum average cost.

where q is the number of frames produced per month. Demand for handmade bicycle frames is given by

$$Q_D = 2{,}500 - 3P,\qquad(14.44)$$

where Q_D is the quantity demanded per month and P is the price per frame. To determine the long-run equilibrium in this market, we must find the low point of the typical firm's average cost curve. Since

$$AC = q^2 - 20q + 100 + \frac{8{,}000}{q}\qquad(14.45)$$

and

$$MC = 3q^2 - 40q + 100\qquad(14.46)$$

and we know this minimum occurs where $AC = MC$, we can solve for this output level:

$$q^2 - 20q + 100 + \frac{8{,}000}{q} = 3q^2 - 40q + 100$$

or

$$2q^2 - 20q = \frac{8{,}000}{q},\qquad(14.47)$$

which has a convenient solution of $q = 20$. With a monthly output of 20 frames, each producer has a long-run average and marginal cost of $500. This then is the long-run equilibrium price of bicycle frames (handmade frames cost a bundle as any cyclist can attest). With $P = \$500$, Equation 14.44 shows $Q_D = 1{,}000$. The equilibrium number of firms is therefore simply 50. When each of these 50 firms produces 20 frames per month, supply will precisely balance what is demanded at a price of $500.

If demand in this problem were to increase to

$$Q_D = 3{,}000 - 3P,\qquad(14.48)$$

we would expect long-run output and the number of frames to increase. Assuming that entry into the frame market is free and that such entry does not alter costs for the typical bicycle maker, the long-run equilibrium price will remain at $500 and a total of 1,500 frames per month will be demanded. That will require 75 frame makers, so 25 new firms will enter the market in response to the increase in demand.

QUERY: Presumably, the entry of frame makers in the long run is motivated by the short-run profitability of the industry in response to the increase in demand. Suppose each firm's short-run costs were given by $STC = 50q^2 - 1{,}500q + 20{,}000$. Show that short-run profits are zero when the industry is in long-term equilibrium. What are the industry's short-run profits as a result of the increase in demand?

Contrary to the short-run situation, long-run analysis has very little to do with the shape of the (long-run) marginal cost curve. Rather, the zero-profit condition centers attention on the low point of the long-run average cost curve as the factor most relevant to long-run price determination. In the constant-cost case, the position of this low point does not change as new firms enter the industry. Consequently, only one price can prevail in the long run regardless of how demand shifts—the long-run supply curve is horizontal at this price. Once the constant-cost assumption is abandoned, this need not be the case. If the entry of new firms causes average costs to rise, the long-run supply curve will have an upward slope. On the other hand, if entry causes average costs to decline, it is even possible for the long-run supply curve to be negatively sloped. We shall now discuss these possibilities.

SHAPE OF THE LONG-RUN SUPPLY CURVE

The entry of new firms into an industry may cause the average costs of all firms to rise for several reasons. New and existing firms may compete for scarce inputs, thus driving up their prices. New firms may impose "external costs" on existing firms (and on themselves) in the form of air or water pollution, and new firms may increase the demand for tax-financed services (police forces, sewage treatment plants, and so forth), and the required taxes may show up as increased costs for all firms. Figure 14.7 demonstrates two market equilibria in such an *increasing cost industry*. The initial equilibrium price is P_1. At this price the typical firm produces q_1, and total industry output is Q_1. Suppose now that the demand curve for the industry shifts outward to D'. In the short run, price will rise to P_2, since this is where D' and the industry's short-run supply curve (SS) intersect. At this price the typical firm will produce q_2 and will earn a substantial profit. This profit then attracts new entrants into the market and shifts the short-run supply curve outward.

Suppose that this entry of new firms causes the cost curves of all firms to rise. The new firms may compete for scarce inputs, thereby driving up the prices of these inputs. A typical firm's new (higher) set of cost curves is shown in Figure 14.7b. The new long-run equilibrium price for the industry is P_3 (here $P_3 = MC = AC$), and at this price Q_3 is demanded. We now have two points (P_1, Q_1 and P_3, Q_3) on the long-run supply curve. All other points on the curve can be found in an analogous way by considering all possible shifts in the demand curve. These shifts will trace out the long-run supply curve LS. Here LS has a positive slope because of the increasing cost nature of the industry. Notice that the LS curve is somewhat flatter than the short-run supply curves. This indicates the greater flexibility in supply response that is possible in the long run. Still, the curve is upward sloping, so price rises with increasing demand. This situation is probably quite common and we will have more to say about it in later sections.

Increasing Cost Industry

FIGURE 14.7

AN INCREASING COST INDUSTRY HAS A POSITIVELY SLOPED LONG-RUN SUPPLY CURVE

Initially, the market is in equilibrium at P_1, Q_1. An increase in demand (to D') causes price to rise to P_2 in the short run, and the typical firm produces q_2 at a profit. This profit attracts new firms into the industry. The entry of these new firms causes costs for a typical firm to rise to the levels shown in (b).

With this new set of curves, equilibrium is reestablished in the market at P_3, Q_3. By considering many possible demand shifts and connecting all the resulting equilibrium points, the long-run supply curve (LS) is traced out.

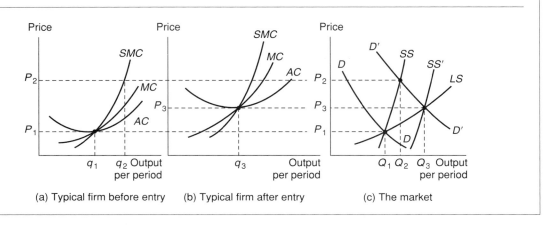

(a) Typical firm before entry   (b) Typical firm after entry   (c) The market

Decreasing Cost Industry

Not all industries exhibit constant or increasing costs. In some cases, the entry of new firms may reduce the costs of firms in an industry. For example, the entry of new firms may provide a larger pool of trained labor from which to draw than was previously available, thus reducing the costs associated with the hiring of new workers. Similarly, the entry of new firms may provide a "critical mass" of industrialization, which permits the development of more efficient transportation and communications networks. Whatever the exact reason for the cost reductions, the final result is illustrated in the three panels of Figure 14.8. The initial market equilibrium is shown by the price-quantity combination P_1, Q_1 in Figure 14.8c. At this price the typical firm produces q_1 and earns exactly zero in economic profits. Now suppose that market demand shifts outward to D'. In the short run, price will increase to P_2 and the typical firm will produce q_2. At this price level, positive profits are being earned. These profits cause new entrants to come into the market. If this entry causes costs to decline, a new set of cost curves for the typical firm might resemble those shown in Figure 14.8b. Now the new equilibrium price is P_3; at this price, Q_3 is demanded. By considering all possible shifts in demand, the long-run supply curve, LS, can be traced out. This curve has a negative slope because of the decreasing cost nature of the industry. Therefore, as

FIGURE 14.8

A DECREASING COST INDUSTRY HAS A NEGATIVELY SLOPED LONG-RUN SUPPLY CURVE

Initially, the market is in equilibrium at P_1, Q_1. An increase in demand to D' causes price to rise to P_2 in the short run, and the typical firm produces q_2 at a profit. This profit attracts new firms to the industry. If the entry of these new firms causes costs for the typical firm to fall, a set of new cost curves might look like those in (b). With this new set of curves, market equilibrium is reestablished at P_3, Q_3. By connecting such points of equilibrium, a negatively sloped long-run supply curve (LS) is traced out.

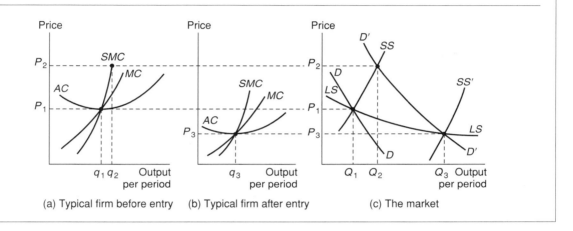

(a) Typical firm before entry   (b) Typical firm after entry   (c) The market

output expands, price falls. This possibility has been used as the justification for protective tariffs to shield new industries from foreign competition. It is assumed (only occasionally correctly) that the protection of the "infant industry" will permit it to grow and ultimately to compete at lower world prices.

Thus, we have shown that the long-run supply curve for a perfectly competitive industry may assume a variety of shapes. The principal determinant of the shape is the way in which the entry of firms into the industry affects costs. The following definitions cover the various possibilities:

Classification of Long-Run Supply Curves

DEFINITIONS

Constant, Increasing, and Decreasing Cost Industries An industry supply curve exhibits one of three shapes:

Constant cost: Entry does not affect input costs; the long-run supply curve is horizontal at the long-run equilibrium price.

Increasing cost: Entry increases input costs; the long-run supply curve is positively sloped.

Decreasing cost: Entry reduces input costs; the long-run supply curve is negatively sloped.

Now we show how the shape of the long-run supply curve can be further quantified.

LONG-RUN ELASTICITY OF SUPPLY

The long-run supply curve for an industry incorporates information on both internal firm adjustments to changing prices and changes in the number of firms and input costs in response to profit opportunities. All of these supply responses are summarized in the following elasticity concept:

DEFINITION

Long-Run Elasticity of Supply   The *long-run elasticity of supply* ($e_{LS,P}$) records the proportionate change in long-run industry output in response to a proportionate change in product price. Mathematically,

$$e_{LS,\,P} = \frac{\text{percentage change in } Q}{\text{percentage change in } P} = \frac{\partial Q_{LS}}{\partial P} \cdot \frac{P}{Q_{LS}}. \qquad (14.49)$$

The value of this elasticity may be positive or negative, depending on whether the industry exhibits increasing or decreasing costs. As we have seen, in the constant-cost case, $e_{LS,P}$ is infinite, since industry expansions or contractions can occur without having any effect on product prices.

Empirical Estimates

It is obviously important to have good empirical estimates of long-run supply elasticities. These indicate whether production can be expanded with only a slight increase in relative price (that is, supply is price elastic) or whether expansions in output can occur only if relative prices rise sharply (that is, supply is price inelastic). Such information can be used to assess the likely effect of shifts in demand on long-run prices and to evaluate alternative policy proposals intended to increase supply. Table 14.2 presents several long-run supply elasticity estimates. These relate primarily (though not exclusively) to natural resources because economists have devoted considerable attention to the implications of increasing demand for the prices of such resources.

TABLE 14.2

SELECTED ESTIMATES OF LONG-RUN SUPPLY ELASTICITIES

Agricultural acreage	
Corn	0.18
Cotton	0.67
Wheat	0.93
Aluminum	Nearly infinite
Chromium	0–3.0
Coal (eastern reserves)	15.0–30.0
Natural gas (U.S. reserves)	0.20
Oil (U.S. reserves)	0.76
Urban housing	
Density	5.3
Quality	3.8

SOURCES: Agricultural acreage—M. Nerlove, "Estimates of the Elasticities of Supply of Selected Agricultural Commodities," *Journal of Farm Economics* 38 (May 1956): 496–509. Aluminum and chromium—estimated from U.S. Department of Interior, *Critical Materials Commodity Action Analysis* (Washington, D.C.: U.S. Government Printing Office, 1975). Coal—estimated from M. B. Zimmerman,"The Supply of Coal in the Long Run: The Case of Eastern Deep Coal," MIT Energy Laboratory Report No. MITEL 75–021 (September 1975). Natural gas—based on estimate for oil (see text) and J. D. Khazzoom, "The FPC Staff's Econometric Model of Natural Gas Supply in the United States," *The Bell Journal of Economics and Management Science* (Spring 1971): 103–117. Oil—E. W. Erickson, S. W. Millsaps, and R. M. Spann, "Oil Supply and Tax Incentives," *Brookings Papers on Economic Activity* 2 (1974): 449–478. Urban housing—B. A. Smith, "The Supply of Urban Housing," *Journal of Political Economy* 40 (August 1976): 389–405.

The estimated elasticities for agricultural products are "acreage elasticities"; that is, they reflect how the number of acres planted in a particular crop responds to that crop's price. Assuming a constant yield per acre, these then can be translated directly into the supply elasticity concept defined in Equation 14.49. Although all of the reported elasticities are relatively low (less than 1), all are positive, indicating that increases in prices do lead to increases in output.

Two different types of supply elasticity are reported for natural resources in Table 14.2. For aluminum and chromium the figures refer to the relationship between annual production and market price. They show that the long-run supply of aluminum is nearly infinitely elastic at current market prices, since aluminum deposits are reasonably accessible given current technology. On the other hand, the supply elasticity for chromium is considerably lower, primarily because large price increases would be required to make existing deposits economically attractive.

For coal, natural gas, and oil, supply elasticities refer to the responsiveness of economically accessible reserves to price. In order to relate these elasticities directly to the notion of current production, one would also need a theory of firms' profit-maximizing output decisions from existing resource stocks.[6] The data show that coal reserves are far more price responsive than oil and natural gas reserves. That result derives primarily from the accessibility of the additional reserves and their geological features. Natural gas has a particularly low elasticity because it is usually found in conjunction with oil, but it has a much lower value per well than does its associated oil. For example, at present market prices, the oil produced from the typical oil-gas well is worth four times the value of the gas produced from such a well. Hence, the effect of an increase in the price of natural gas alone on drilling is only about one-fourth the effect of an increase in the price of oil.

The final estimates in Table 14.2 refer to two aspects of the supply of urban housing. They show that "more housing" can be produced in two ways: by increasing residential density while holding house quality constant and by increasing quality while holding density constant. Both of these output measures seem to be quite responsive to price.

COMPARATIVE STATICS ANALYSIS OF LONG-RUN EQUILIBRIUM

Earlier in this chapter we showed how to develop a simple comparative statics analysis of changing short-run equilibria in competitive markets. By using estimates of the long-run elasticities of demand and supply, exactly the same sort of analysis can be conducted for the long run as well.

For example, the hypothetical auto market model in Example 14.3 might serve equally well for long-run analysis, though some differences in interpretation might be required. Indeed, often in applied models of supply and demand, it is not clear whether the author intends his or her results to reflect the short run or the long run and some care must be taken to understand how the issue of entry is being handled.

Industry Structure

One aspect of the changing long-run equilibria in a perfectly competitive market that is obscured by using a simple supply-demand analysis is how the number of firms varies as market equilibria change. Because, as we will see in Part VI, the functioning of markets may in some cases be affected by the number of firms and because there may be direct public policy interest

---

[6]For a brief discussion of such a theory, see Chapter 23.

in entry and exit from an industry, some additional analysis is required. In this section we will examine in detail determinants of the number of firms in the constant-cost case. Brief reference will also be made to the increasing-cost case, and some of the problems for this chapter examine that case in more detail.

Shifts in Demand

Since the long-run supply curve for a constant-cost industry is infinitely elastic, analyzing shifts in market demand is particularly easy. If the initial equilibrium industry output is Q_0 and q^* represents the output level for which the typical firm's long-run average cost is minimized, then the initial equilibrium number of firms (n_0) is given by

$$n_0 = \frac{Q_0}{q^*}. \tag{14.50}$$

A shift in demand that changes equilibrium output to Q_1 will, in the long run, change the equilibrium number of firms to

$$n_1 = \frac{Q_1}{q^*}, \tag{14.51}$$

and the change in the number of firms is given by

$$n_1 - n_0 = \frac{Q_1 - Q_0}{q^*}. \tag{14.52}$$

That is, the change in the equilibrium number of firms is completely determined by the extent of the demand shift and by the optimal output level for the typical firm.

Changes in Input Costs

Even in the simple constant-cost industry case, analyzing the effect of an increase in an input price (and hence an upward shift in the infinitely elastic long-run supply curve) is relatively complicated. First, in order to calculate the fall in industry output, it is necessary to know both the extent to which minimum average cost is increased by the input price rise and how such an increase in the long-run equilibrium price affects total quantity demanded. Knowledge of the typical firm's average cost function and of the price elasticity of demand permits such a calculation to be made in a straightforward way. But an increase in an input price may also change the minimum average cost output level for the typical firm. Such a possibility is illustrated in Figure 14.9. Both the average and marginal costs have been shifted upward by the input price rise, but because average cost has shifted up by a relatively greater extent than the marginal cost, the typical firm's optimal output level has increased from q_0^* to q_1^*. If the relative sizes of the shifts in cost curves were

FIGURE 14.9

AN INCREASE IN AN INPUT PRICE MAY CHANGE LONG-RUN EQUILIBRIUM OUTPUT FOR THE TYPICAL FIRM

An increase in the price of an input will shift both average and marginal cost curves upward. The precise effect of these shifts on the typical firm's optimal output level (q^*) will depend on the relative magnitudes of the shifts.

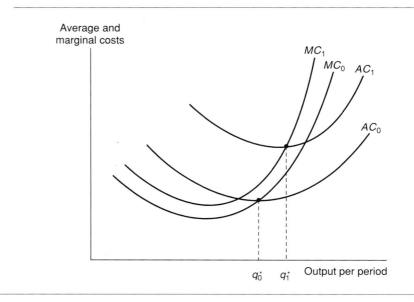

reversed, however, the typical firm's optimal output level would have fallen.[7] Taking account of this change in optimal scale, Equation 14.52 becomes

$$n_1 - n_0 = \frac{Q_1}{q_1^*} - \frac{Q_0}{q_0^*},$$ (14.53)

and a number of possibilities arise.

If $q_1^* \geq q_0^*$, the decline in quantity brought about by the rise in market price will definitely cause the number of firms to fall. However, if $q_1^* < q_0^*$, the result

---

[7]A simple mathematical proof would proceed as follows. Optimal output, q^*, is defined such that

$$AC(v, w, q^*) = MC(v, w, q^*).$$

Differentiating both sides of this expression, by, say, v, yields

$$\frac{\partial AC}{\partial v} + \frac{\partial AC}{\partial q^*} \cdot \frac{\partial q^*}{\partial v} = \frac{\partial MC}{\partial v} + \frac{\partial MC}{\partial q^*} \cdot \frac{\partial q^*}{\partial v};$$

will be indeterminate. Industry output will fall, but optimal firm size also will fall, so that the ultimate effect on the number of firms depends on the relative magnitude of these changes. A decline in the number of firms still seems the most likely outcome when an input price rise causes industry output to fall, but an increase in n is at least a theoretical possibility.

EXAMPLE 14.5

RISING INPUT COSTS AND INDUSTRY STRUCTURE

A rise in costs for bicycle frame makers will alter the equilibrium described in Example 14.4, but the precise effect on market structure will depend on how costs increase. The effects of an increase in fixed costs are fairly clear—the long-run equilibrium price will rise and the size of the typical firm will also increase. This latter effect occurs because a rise in fixed costs raises AC but not MC. In order to assure that the equilibrium condition for $AC = MC$ holds, output (and MC) must also rise. For example, if a rise in shop rents causes the typical frame maker's costs to increase to

$$TC = q^3 - 20q^2 + 100q + 11{,}616, \qquad (14.54)$$

then it is an easy matter to show that $MC = AC$ when $q = 22$. This rise in cost has therefore increased the efficient scale of bicycle frame operations by 2 bicycle frames per month. At $q = 22$, long-run average and marginal cost is 672, and that will be the long-run equilibrium price for frames. At this price

$$Q_D = 2{,}500 - 3P = 484 \qquad (14.55)$$

so there will be room in the market now for only 22 ($= 484 \div 22$) firms. The rise in fixed costs resulted not only in an increase in price but also in a major reduction in the number of frame makers (from 50 to 22).

Increases in other types of input costs may, however, have more complex effects. Although a complete analysis would require an examination of frame makers' production functions and their related input choices, we can provide

---

but $\partial AC / \partial q^* = 0$, since average costs are minimized. By manipulating terms, we have

$$\frac{\partial q^*}{\partial v} = \left\{ \frac{\partial MC}{\partial q^*} \right\}^{-1} \cdot \left[\frac{\partial AC}{\partial v} - \frac{\partial MC}{\partial v} \right]$$

Since $\partial MC / \partial q > 0$ at the minimum AC, $\partial q^* / \partial v$ will be positive or negative, depending on the relative shifts in the AC and MC curves. For a more complete analysis see E. Silberberg, *The Structure of Economics* (New York: McGraw-Hill Book Company, 1978), pp. 209–211.

a simple illustration by assuming that a rise in some variable input prices causes the typical firm's total cost function to become

$$TC = q^3 - 8q^2 + 100q + 4,950. \tag{14.56}$$

Now

$$MC = 3q^2 - 16q + 100$$

and

$$\tag{14.57}$$

$$AC = q^2 - 8q + 100 + \frac{4,950}{q}.$$

Hence, setting $MC = AC$ yields

$$2q^2 - 8q = \frac{4,950}{q}, \tag{14.58}$$

which has a solution of $q = 15$. This particular change in the TC curve has therefore significantly reduced the optimal size for frame shops. With $q = 15$, Equations 14.57 show $AC = MC = 535$, and with this new long-run equilibrium price,

$$Q_D = 2,500 - 3P = 895. \tag{14.59}$$

These 895 frames will, in equilibrium, be produced by about 60 firms ($895 \div 15 = 59.67$—problems don't always work out evenly!). Even though the increase in costs results in a higher price, the equilibrium number of frame makers expands from 50 to 60 because the optimal size of each shop is now much smaller.

QUERY: How do the total, marginal, and average functions derived from Equation 14.56 differ from those in Example 14.4? Are costs always greater (for all levels of q) for the former cost curve? Why is long-run equilibrium price higher with the former curves? (See footnote 7 for a formal discussion.)

PRODUCER SURPLUS IN THE LONG RUN

In Chapter 13 we described the concept of short-run producer surplus, which represents the return to a firm's owners that is in excess of what would be earned if output were zero. We showed that this consisted of the sum of short-run profits plus short-run fixed costs. Since in long-run equilibrium profits are zero and there are no fixed costs, all such short-run surplus is eliminated. Owners of firms are indifferent about whether they are in a particular market or not because they could earn identical returns on their investments elsewhere. Suppliers of firms' inputs may not be indifferent about the level of production in a particular industry, however. In the constant-cost case, of course, input prices are assumed to be independent of the level of production on the presumption that inputs can earn the same amount in alternative occupations. But in the increasing-cost case, entry will bid up some input prices and suppliers of these inputs will be made better off. Consideration of these price effects leads to the notion of long-run producer surplus:

DEFINITION

Long-Run Producer Surplus   *Long-run producer surplus* represents the additional returns to the inputs to an industry in excess of what these inputs would earn if industry output were zero.

It is perhaps surprising that long-run producer surplus can be shown graphically in much the same way as short-run producer surplus. It is given by the area above the *long-run* supply curve and below equilibrium market price. In the constant-cost case long-run supply is infinitely elastic and this area will equal zero, showing that there are no such excess returns. With increasing costs, however, long-run supply will be positively sloped and excess returns to inputs will be generated as industry output expands. Since this notion of long-run producer surplus is widely used in applied analysis (see Chapter 15), we will provide a formal development.

Long-run producer surplus can be most easily illustrated with a situation first described by David Ricardo in the early part of the nineteenth century.[8] Assume there are many parcels of land on which a particular crop might be grown. These range from very fertile land (low costs of production) to very poor, dry land (high costs). The long-run supply curve for the crop (Q) is constructed as follows. At low prices only the best land is used. As output increases, higher-cost plots of land are brought into production because higher prices make it profitable to use this land. The long-run supply curve is positively sloped because of the increasing costs associated with using less fertile land.

Market equilibrium in this situation is illustrated in Figure 14.10. At an equilibrium price of P^*, owners of both the low-cost and the medium-cost firms earn (long-run) profits. The "marginal firm" earns exactly zero economic profits. Firms with even higher costs stay out of the market because they would incur losses at a price of P^*. Profits earned by the intramarginal firms can persist in the long run, however, because they reflect

Ricardian Rent

---

[8]See David Ricardo, *The Principles of Political Economy and Taxation* (1817; reprinted London: J. M. Dent and Son, 1965), chapters 2 and 32.

FIGURE 14.10

RICARDIAN RENT

Owners of low-cost and medium-cost land can earn long-run profits. Long-run producers' surplus represents the sum of all these rents—area P^*EB in panel (d). Usually Ricardian rents will be capitalized into input prices.

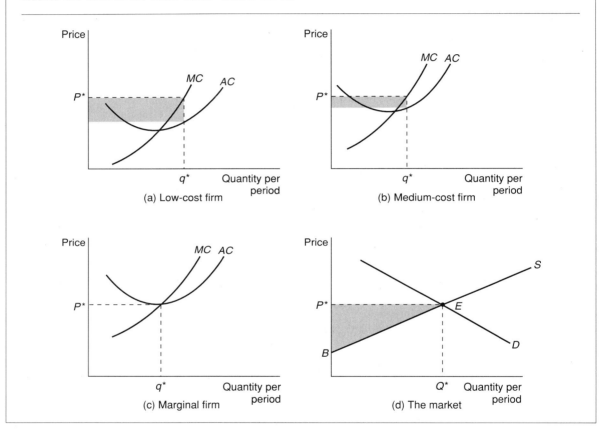

(a) Low-cost firm

(b) Medium-cost firm

(c) Marginal firm

(d) The market

a return to a unique resource—low-cost land. Free entry cannot erode these profits even over the long term. The sum of these long-run profits constitutes long-run producer surplus as given by area P^*EB in panel (d) of Figure 14.10. Equivalence of these areas can be shown by recognizing that each point in the supply curve in panel (d) represents minimum average cost for some firm. For each such firm, $P - AC$ represents profits per unit of output. Total long-run profits can then be computed by summing over all units of output.[9]

The long-run profits for the low-cost firms in Figure 14.10 will often be reflected in prices for the unique resources owned by those firms. In Ricardo's initial analysis, for example, one might expect fertile land to sell for more than an untillable rock pile. Since such prices will reflect the present value (see Chapter 23) of all future profits, these profits are said to be "capitalized" inputs' prices. Examples of capitalization include such disparate phenomena as the higher prices of nice houses with convenient access for commuters, the high value of rock and sport stars' contracts, and the lower value of land near toxic waste sites. Notice that in all of these cases it is market demand that determines rents—these rents are not traditional input costs that indicate foregone opportunities.

Capitalization of Rents

It is the scarcity of low-cost inputs that creates the possibility of Ricardian rent. If low-cost farmland were available at infinitely elastic supply, there would be no such rent. More generally, any input that is "scarce" (in the sense that it has a positively sloped supply curve to a particular industry) will obtain rents in the form of earning a higher return than would be obtained if industry output were zero. In such cases, increases in output not only raise firms' costs (and thereby the price for which the output will sell), but also

Input Supply and Long-Run Producer Surplus

---

[9]More formally, suppose each firm produces q^* and that in the long-run equilibrium, $Q^* = n^*q^*$ (where n^* is the equilibrium number of firms and Q^* is total industry output). Suppose also the inverse of the supply function (competitive price as a function of quantity supplied) is given by $P = P(Q) = P(iq^*)$ and $P^* = P(Q^*) = P(n^*q^*)$. Now, in long-run equilibrium, profits for firm i are given by

$$\pi_i = (P^* - AC_i)q^*,$$

and total profits are given by

$$\pi = \int_0^{n^*} \pi_i \, di = \int_0^{n^*} (P^* - AC_i)q^* \, di$$

$$= \int_0^{n^*} P^* q^* \, di - \int_0^{n^*} AC_i q^* \, di$$

$$= P^* n^* q^* - \int_0^{n^*} P(iq^*)q^* \, di$$

$$= P^* Q^* - \int_0^{Q^*} P(Q)dQ,$$

which is the shaded area in panel (d) of Figure 14.10.

generate factor rents for inputs. The sum of all such rents is again measured by the area above the long-run supply curve and below equilibrium price. Changes in the size of this area of long-run producer surplus indicate changing rents earned by inputs to the industry. Notice that although long-run producer surplus is measured using the market supply curve, it is inputs to the industry that actually receive this surplus. Empirical measurements of changes in long-run producer surplus are widely used in applied welfare analysis to indicate how suppliers of various inputs fare as conditions change. Problem 14.7 and several of the problems in Chapter 15 provide some numerical illustrations of the connection between input rents and long-run producer surplus.

SUMMARY

In this chapter we have developed a detailed model of competitive price determination in a single market. This model of supply and demand, which was first articulated by Alfred Marshall in the latter part of the nineteenth century, is at the heart of much of microeconomic analysis. Its principal properties include the following:

- In the short run, equilibrium prices are established by the interaction of what demanders are willing to pay (as reflected by the demand curve) and what firms are willing to produce (as reflected by the short-run supply curve). These prices are treated as fixed in both demanders' and suppliers' decision-making processes.

- A shift in either demand or supply will cause the equilibrium price to change. The extent of such a change will depend on the slopes of the various curves and can be modeled using fairly simple comparative statics techniques.

- Firms may earn positive profits in the short run. Since fixed costs must always be paid, firms will choose a positive output providing revenues exceed variable costs.

- In the long run the number of firms is variable in response to profit opportunities. The assump-

tion of free entry and exit implies that the firms in a competitive industry will earn zero economic profits in the long run ($P = AC$). Since firms also seek maximum profits, the equality $P = MC = AC$ implies that firms will operate at the low points of their long-run average cost curves.

- The shape of the long-run supply curve depends on how entry and exit affect firms' input costs. In the constant-cost case, input prices do not change and the long-run supply curve is horizontal. If entry raises input costs, the long-run supply curve will have a positive slope.

- Changes in long-run market equilibrium will also change the number of firms. Precise predictions about the extent of these changes is made difficult by the possibility that the minimum average cost level of output may be affected by changes in input costs or by technical progress.

- If changes in the long-run equilibrium in a market change the prices of inputs to that market, this will affect the welfare of suppliers of those inputs. Such changes can be measured by changes in the value of long-run producer surplus.

PROBLEMS

14.1

Suppose that there are 100 identical firms in a perfectly competitive industry. Each firm has a short-run total cost curve of the form

$$C = \frac{1}{300} q^3 + 0.2q^2 + 4q + 10.$$

a. Calculate the firm's short-run supply curve with q as a function of market price (P).
b. On the assumption that there are no interaction effects among costs of the firms in the industry, calculate the short-run industry supply curve.
c. Suppose that market demand is given by $Q = -200P + 8,000$. What will be the short-run equilibrium price-quantity combination?

14.2

Suppose that there are 1,000 identical firms producing diamonds and that the total cost curve for each firm is given by

$$C = q^2 + wq,$$

where q is the firm's output level and w is the wage rate of diamond cutters.

a. If $w = 10$, what will be the firm's (short-run) supply curve? What is the industry's supply curve? How many diamonds will be produced at a price of 20 each? How many more diamonds would be produced at a price of 21?
b. Suppose that the wages of diamond cutters depend on the total quantity of diamonds produced and that the form of this relationship is given by

$$w = 0.002Q,$$

where Q represents total industry output, which is 1,000 times the output of the typical firm.
   In this situation, show that the firm's marginal cost (and short-run supply) curve depends on Q. What is the industry supply curve? How much will be produced at a price of 20? How much more will be produced at a price of 21? What do you conclude about the shape of the short-run supply curve?

14.3

A perfectly competitive market has 1,000 firms. In the very short run, each of the firms has a fixed supply of 100 units. The market demand is given by

$$Q = 160,000 - 10,000P.$$

a. Calculate the equilibrium price in the very short run.
b. Calculate the demand schedule facing any one firm in this industry.
c. Calculate what the equilibrium price would be if one of the sellers decided to sell nothing or if one seller decided to sell 200 units.
d. At the original equilibrium point, calculate the elasticity of the industry demand curve and the elasticity of the demand curve facing any one seller.
Suppose now that in the short run, each firm has a supply curve that shows the quantity the firm will supply (q_i) as a function of market price. The specific form of this supply curve is given by

$$q_i = -200 + 50P.$$

Using this short-run supply response, answer questions (a) through (d) above.

14.4

Suppose the demand for frisbees is given by

$$Q = 100 - 2P$$

and the supply by

$$Q = 20 + 6P.$$

a. What will be the equilibrium price and quantities for frisbees?
b. Suppose the government levies a tax of $4 per frisbee. Now what will be the equilibrium quantity, the price consumers will pay, and the price firms will receive? How is the burden of the tax shared by buyers and sellers?
c. How would your answers to parts (a) and (b) change if the supply curve were instead

$$Q = 70 + P?$$

What do you conclude by comparing these two cases?

14.5

Wheat is produced under perfectly competitive conditions. Individual wheat farmers have U-shaped, long-run average cost curves that reach a minimum average cost of $3 per bushel when 1,000 bushels are produced.

a. If the market demand curve for wheat is given by

$$Q_D = 2,600,000 - 200,000P,$$

where Q_D is the number of bushels demanded per year and P is the price per bushel, in long-run equilibrium what will be the price of wheat, how much total wheat will be demanded, and how many wheat farms will there be?

b. Suppose demand shifts outward to

$$Q_D = 3,200,000 - 200,000P.$$

If farmers cannot adjust their output in the short run, what will market price be with this new demand curve? What will the profits of the typical farm be?

c. Given the new demand curve described in part (b), what will be the new long-run equilibrium? (That is, calculate market price, quantity of wheat produced, and the new equilibrium number of farms in this new situation.)

d. Graph your results.

14.6

A perfectly competitive industry has a large number of potential entrants. Each firm has an identical cost structure such that long-run average cost is minimized at an output of 20 units ($q_i = 20$). The minimum average cost is $10 per unit. Total market demand is given by

$$Q = 1,500 - 50P.$$

a. What is the industry's long-run supply schedule?

b. What is the long-run equilibrium price (P^*)? The total industry output (Q^*)? The output of each firm (q^*)? The number of firms? And the profits of each firm?

c. The short-run total cost curve associated with each firm's long-run equilibrium output is given by

$$C = 0.5q^2 - 10q + 200.$$

Calculate the short-run average and marginal cost curves. At what output level does short-run average cost reach a minimum?

d. Calculate the short-run supply curve for each firm and the industry short-run supply curve.

e. Suppose now that the market demand function shifts upward to $Q = 2,000 - 50P$. Using this new demand curve, answer part (b) for the very short run when firms cannot change their outputs.

f. In the short run, use the industry short-run supply curve to recalculate the answers to (b).

g. What is the new long-run equilibrium for the industry?

14.7

Suppose that the demand for stilts is given by

$$Q = 1,500 - 50P$$

and that the long-run total operating costs of each stilt-making firm in a competitive industry are given by

$$TC = 0.5q^2 - 10q.$$

Entrepreneurial talent for stilt making is scarce. The supply curve for entrepreneurs is given by

$$Q_S = 0.25w,$$

where w is the annual wage paid.

Suppose also that each stilt-making firm requires one (and only one) entrepreneur (hence, the quantity of entrepreneurs hired is equal to the number of firms). Long-run total costs for each firm are hence given by

$$TC = 0.5q^2 - 10q + w.$$

a. What is the long-run equilibrium quantity of stilts produced? How many stilts are produced by each firm? What is the long-run equilibrium price of stilts? How many firms will there be? How many entrepreneurs will be hired, and what is their wage?

b. Suppose that the demand for stilts shifts outward to

$$Q = 2,428 - 50P.$$

Answer the questions posed in part (a).

c. Since stilt-making entrepreneurs are the cause of the upward sloping long-run supply curve in this problem, they will receive all rents generated as industry output expands. Calculate the increase in rents between parts (a) and (b). Show that this value is identical to the change in long-run producer surplus as measured along the stilt supply curve.

14.8

Suppose that the long-run total cost function for the typical mushroom producer is given by

$$TC = wq^2 - 10q + 100,$$

where q is the output of the typical firm and w represents the hourly wage rate of mushroom pickers. Suppose also that the demand for mushrooms is given by

$$Q = -1,000P + 40,000$$

where Q is total quantity demanded and P is the market price of mushrooms.

a. If the wage rate for mushroom pickers is \$1, what will be the long-run equilibrium output for the typical mushroom picker?

b. Assuming that the mushroom industry exhibits constant costs and that all firms are identical, what will be the long-run equilibrium price of mushrooms, and how many mushroom firms will there be?

c. Suppose the government imposed a tax of \$3 for each mushroom picker hired (raising total wage costs, w, to \$4). Assuming that the typical firm continues to have costs given by

$$TC = wq^2 - 10q + 100,$$

how will your answers to parts (a) and (b) change with this new, higher wage rate?

d. How would your answers to (a), (b), and (c) change if market demand were instead given by

$$Q = -1,000P + 60,000?$$

SUGGESTED READINGS

Henderson, J. M., and R. E. Quandt. *Microeconomic Theory: A Mathematical Approach.* 3d ed. New York: McGraw-Hill Book Company, 1980. Chap. 6.
Covers much the same material as this chapter, with some useful algebraic examples. Also a nice discussion of futures markets.

Knight, F. H. *Risk, Uncertainty and Profit.* Boston: Houghton Mifflin Co., 1921. Chaps. 5 and 6.
Classic treatment of the role of economic events in motivating industry behavior in the long run.

Marshall, A. *Principles of Economics.* 8th ed. New York: Crowell-Collier and Macmillan Co., 1920. Book 5, chaps. 1, 2, and 3.
Classic development of the supply-demand mechanism.

Meade, J. E. "External Economies and Diseconomies in a Competitive Situation." *Economic Journal* 62 (March 1952): 54–67.
Early discussion of the notion of externalities in competitive markets in the long run.

Reynolds, L. G. "Cut-Throat Competition." *American Economic Review* 30 (December 1940): 736–747.
Critique of the notion that there can be "too much" competition in an industry.

Robinson, J. "What Is Perfect Competition?" *Quarterly Journal of Economics* 49 (1934): 104–120.
Critical discussion of the perfectly competitive assumptions.

Stigler, G. J. "Perfect Competition, Historically Contemplated." *Journal of Political Economy* 65 (1957): 1–17.
Fascinating discussion of the historical development of the competitive model.

CHAPTER 15

APPLIED COMPETITIVE ANALYSIS

The model of a perfectly competitive market that we developed in the previous chapter provides the basis for much applied microeconomic analysis. Using these principles of supply and demand has proven to be a good way to get started in an investigation of many real-world markets. In this chapter we provide a brief description of some of these uses. Before beginning, two warnings may be appropriate. First, our analysis here will look only at a single market; that is, we will employ a partial equilibrium approach. In Chapter 16 we explore a series of general equilibrium models that permit an investigation of repercussions in many markets simultaneously. In such models some of the simple results of supply and demand analysis may not hold. Similarly, a warning about the strict assumptions that underlie the competitive model should also be kept in mind. The most important such assumption is that of price-taking behavior on the part of both suppliers and demanders. When economic actors have some influence on market price, alternative models are required. Several such models are examined in Part V of this book.

ECONOMIC EFFICIENCY AND WELFARE ANALYSIS

Long-run competitive equilibria may have the desirable property of allocating resources "efficiently." Although we will have far more to say about this concept in a general equilibrium context in Chapter 17, here we can offer a partial equilibrium description of why the result might hold. Remember from Chapter 5 that the area below a demand curve and above market price represents consumer surplus—the extra utility consumers receive from choosing to purchase a good voluntarily rather than being forced to do without it. Similarly, as we saw in Chapter 14, producer surplus is measured as the area below market price and above the long-run supply curve, which represents the extra return that productive inputs receive rather than having no transactions in the good. Overall then, the area between the demand curve and the supply curve represents the sum of consumer and producer surplus, and therefore reflects the total additional value obtained by market participants by being able to make market transactions. It seems clear that this total area is maximized at the competitive market equilibrium.

Figure 15.1 shows a simplified proof. Given the demand curve *(D)* and the long-run supply curve *(S)*, the sum of consumer and producer surplus is given by distance *AB* for the first unit produced. Total surplus continues to increase as additional output is produced up to the competitive equilibrium level, *Q**. This level of production will be achieved when price is at the competitive level, *P**. Total consumer surplus is represented by the light shaded area in the figure, total producer surplus by the darker shaded area. Clearly, for output levels less than *Q**, (say, Q_1), total surplus would be

A Graphic Proof

FIGURE 15.1

COMPETITIVE EQUILIBRIUM AND CONSUMER/PRODUCER SURPLUS

At the competitive equilibrium *(Q*)* the sum of consumer surplus (shaded lighter gray) and producer surplus (shaded darker) is maximized. For an output level less than *Q**, say, Q_1, there is a deadweight loss of consumer and producer surplus given by area *FEG*.

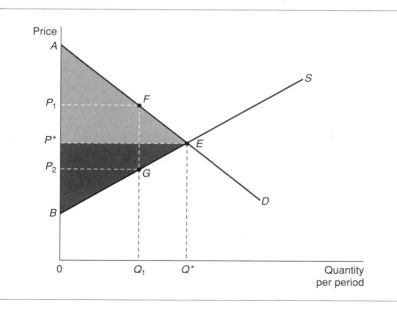

reduced. One sign of this misallocation is that at Q_1, demanders would value an additional unit of output at P_1, whereas marginal costs would be given by P_2. Since $P_1 > P_2$, total welfare would clearly increase by producing one more unit of output. A transaction that involved trading this extra unit at any price between P_1 and P_2 would be mutually beneficial—both parties would gain.

The total welfare loss that occurs at output level Q_1 is given by area *FEG*. The distribution of surplus at output level Q_1 will depend on the precise (nonequilibrium) price that prevails in the market. At a price of P_1 consumer surplus would be reduced substantially to area AFP_1, whereas producers might actually gain since producer surplus is now P_1FGB. At a low price such as P_2 the situation would be reversed, with producers being much worse off than they were initially. Hence, the distribution of the welfare losses from producing less than Q^* will depend on the price at which transactions are conducted. The size of the total loss, however, is given by *FEG*, regardless of the price settled upon.[1]

A Mathematical Proof

Mathematically, we wish to maximize

consumer surplus + producer surplus =

$$[U(Q) - PQ] + [PQ - \int_0^Q P(Q)\, dQ] = U(Q) - \int_0^Q P(Q)\, dQ, \quad (15.1)$$

where $U(Q)$ is the utility function of the representative consumer and $P(Q)$ is the long-run supply relation. In long-run equilibria along the long-run supply curve, $P(Q) = AC = MC$. Maximization of Equation 15.1 with respect to Q yields

$$U'(Q) = P(Q) = AC = MC, \quad (15.2)$$

so maximization occurs where the marginal value of Q to the representative consumer is equal to market price. But this is precisely the competitive supply-demand equilibrium since the demand curve represents consumers' marginal valuations, whereas the supply curve reflects marginal (and, in long-term equilibrium, average) cost.

Applied Welfare Analysis

The conclusion that the competitive equilibrium maximizes the sum of consumer and producer surplus mirrors a series of more general economic efficiency "theorems" we will examine in Chapter 17. Describing the major caveats that attach to these theorems is best delayed until that more extended discussion. Here we are more interested in showing how the competitive model is used to examine the consequences of changing economic conditions on the welfare of market participants. Usually such

---

[1] Increases in output beyond Q^* also clearly reduce welfare. See Problem 15.1.

welfare changes are measured by looking at changes in consumer and producer surplus.

EXAMPLE 15.1
WELFARE LOSS COMPUTATIONS

Use of consumer and producer surplus notions makes possible the explicit calculation of welfare losses from restrictions on voluntary transactions. In the case of linear demand and supply curves, this computation is especially simple since the areas of loss are frequently triangular. For example, if demand is given by

$$Q_D = 10 - P \tag{15.3}$$

and supply by

$$Q_S = P - 2, \tag{15.4}$$

market equilibrium occurs at the point $P^* = 6$, $Q^* = 4$. Restriction of output to $\overline{Q} = 3$ would create a gap between what demanders are willing to pay ($P_D = 10 - \overline{Q} = 7$) and what suppliers require ($P_S = 2 + \overline{Q} = 5$). The welfare loss from restricting transactions is therefore given by a triangle with a base of 2 ($= P_D - P_S = 7 - 5$) and a height of 1 (the difference between Q^* and $\overline{Q}$). Hence, the welfare loss is one dollar if P is measured in dollars per unit and Q is measured in units. More generally, the loss will be measured in the units in which $P \cdot Q$ is measured.

Computations with Constant Elasticity Curves. More realistic results can usually be obtained by using constant elasticity demand and supply curves based on econometric studies. In Example 14.3, we examined such a model of the U.S. automobile market. We can simplify that example a bit by assuming P is measured in thousands of dollars, Q in millions of automobiles, and that demand is given by

$$Q_D = 200 \, P^{-1.2} \tag{15.5}$$

and supply by

$$Q_S = 1.3 \, P. \tag{15.6}$$

Equilibrium in the market is given by $P^* = 9.87$, $Q^* = 12.8$. Suppose now that government policy restricts automobile sales to 11 (million) in order to control emissions of pollutants. An approximation to the direct welfare loss from such a policy can be found by the triangular method used earlier. With $\overline{Q} = 11$, $P_D = (11/200)^{-.83} = 11.1$, $P_S = 11/1.3 = 8.46$. Hence, the welfare loss "triangle" is given by $.5(P_D - P_S)(Q^* - \overline{Q}) = .5(11.1 - 8.46)$ $(12.8 - 11) = 2.38$. Here the units are those of P times Q: billions of dollars. The approximate[2] value of the welfare loss is therefore $2.4 billion, which might be weighed against the expected gain from emissions control.

Distribution of Loss. In the automobile case, the welfare loss is shared about equally by consumers and producers. An approximation for consumers' losses is given by $.5(P_D - P^*)(Q^* - \overline{Q}) = .5(11.1 - 9.87)(12.8 - 11) = 1.11$ and for producers by $.5(9.87 - 8.46)(12.8 - 11) = 1.27$. Because the price elasticity of demand is somewhat greater (in absolute value) than the price elasticity of supply, consumers incur somewhat less than half the loss and producers somewhat more than half. With an even more price elastic demand curve, consumers would incur an even smaller share of the loss.

QUERY: How does the size of the total welfare loss from a quantity restriction depend on the elasticities of supply and demand? What determines how the loss will be shared?

PRICE CONTROLS AND SHORTAGES

Sometimes governments may seek to control prices at below equilibrium levels. Although adoption of such policies may be based on noble motives, the controls deter long-run supply responses and create welfare losses for both consumers and producers. A simple analysis of this possibility is provided by Figure 15.2. Initially the market is in long-run equilibrium at P_1, Q_1 (point E). An increase in demand from D to D' would cause the price to rise to P_2 in the short run and encourage entry by new firms. Assuming this market is characterized by increasing costs (as reflected by the positively sloped, long-run supply curve, LS), price would fall somewhat as a result of this entry, ultimately settling at P_3. If these price changes were regarded as undesirable, the government could, in principle, prevent them by imposing a legally enforceable ceiling price of P_1. This would cause firms to continue to supply their previous output (Q_1) and, because at P_1 demanders now want to purchase Q_4, there will be a shortage, given by $Q_4 - Q_1$.

Welfare Evaluation

The welfare consequences of this price-control policy can be evaluated by comparing consumer and producer surplus measures prevailing under this policy to those that would have prevailed in the absence of controls.

---

[2] A more precise estimate of the loss can be obtained by integrating $P_D - P_S$ over the range $Q = 11$ to $Q = 12.8$. With exponential demand and supply curves this integration is often quite simple. In the present case, the technique yields an estimated welfare loss of 2.28, thereby indicating that the triangular approximation is not too bad, even for relatively large price changes. In later analysis, therefore, we will use such approximations.

FIGURE 15.2

PRICE CONTROLS AND SHORTAGES

A shift in demand from D to D' would raise price to P_2 in the short run. Entry over the long run would yield a final equilibrium of P_3, Q_3. Controlling the price at P_1 would prevent these actions and yield a shortage of $Q_4 - Q_1$. Relative to the uncontrolled situation, the price control yields a transfer from producers to consumers (area P_3CEP_1) and a deadweight loss of foregone transactions given by the two areas $AE'C$ and $CE'E$.

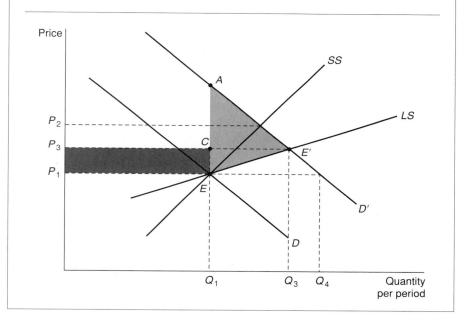

First, the buyers of Q_1 gain consumer surplus given by area P_3CEP_1 because they can buy this good at a lower price than would exist in an uncontrolled market. This gain reflects a pure transfer from producers out of the amount of producer surplus that would exist without controls. What current consumers have gained from the lower price, producers have lost. Though this transfer does not represent a loss of overall welfare, it does clearly affect the relative well-being of the market participants.

Second, the area $AE'C$ represents the value of additional consumer surplus that would have been attained without controls. Similarly, the area $CE'E$ reflects additional producer surplus available in the uncontrolled situation. Together, these two areas (that is, area $AE'E$) represent the total value of mutually beneficial transactions that are prevented by the government policy of controlling price. This is, therefore, a measure of the pure welfare costs of that policy.

Disequilibrium Behavior

The welfare analysis depicted in Figure 15.2 also suggests some of the types of behavior that might be expected as a result of the price-control policy. Assuming that observed market outcomes are generated by

$$Q(P_1) = \min \, [Q_D(P_1), \, Q_S(P_1)], \tag{15.7}$$

suppliers will be content with this outcome, but demanders will not be since they will be forced to accept a situation of excess demand. They have an incentive to signal their dissatisfaction to suppliers through increasing price offers. Such offers may not only tempt existing suppliers to make illegal transactions at higher than allowed prices, but may encourage new entrants to make such transactions. It is this kind of activity that leads to the prevalence of black markets in most instances of price control. Modeling the resulting transactions is difficult for two reasons. First, these may involve nonprice-taking behavior since the price of each transaction must be individually negotiated rather than being set by "the market." Second, nonequilibrium transactions will often involve imperfect information since any pair of market participants will not generally know what other transactors are doing, though such actions may affect their welfare by changing the options available. Some progress has been made modeling such disequilibrium behavior using game theory techniques (see Chapters 10 and 20). However, other than the obvious prediction that transactions will occur at prices above the price ceiling, no very general results have been obtained.[3] The types of black market transactions undertaken will depend on the specific institutional details of the situation.

TAX INCIDENCE ANALYSIS

The partial equilibrium model of competitive markets has also been widely used to study the impact of taxes. Although, as we will point out, these applications are necessarily limited by their inability to analyze tax effects that spread through many markets, they do provide important insights on a number of issues.

A Mathematical Model

The effects of taxes can be most easily studied using the mathematical model of supply and demand that was introduced in Chapter 14. Now, however, we need to make a distinction between the price paid by demanders (P_D) and

---

[3] See J. Bénassy, "Nonclearing Markets: Microeconomic Concepts and Macroeconomic Applications," *Journal of Economic Literature* (June 1993): 732–761.

the price received by suppliers (P_S) since a per-unit tax (t) introduces a "wedge" between these two magnitudes of the form:

$$P_D - P_S = t \qquad (15.8)$$

or, in terms of the small price changes we wish to examine,

$$dP_D - dP_S = dt. \qquad (15.9)$$

Maintenance of equilibrium in the market requires

$$dQ_D = dQ_S,$$

or

$$D_P dP_D = S_P dP_S, \qquad (15.10)$$

where D_P, S_P are the price derivatives of the demand and supply functions, respectively. We can use Equations 15.9 and 15.10 to solve for the effect of the tax on P_D:

$$D_P dP_D = S_P dP_S = S_P(dP_D - dt). \qquad (15.11)$$

Hence,

$$\frac{dP_D}{dt} = \frac{S_P}{S_P - D_P} = \frac{e_S}{e_S - e_D}, \qquad (15.12)$$

where e_S and e_D represent the price elasticities of supply and demand, respectively, and the final equation is derived by multiplication of numerator and denominator by P/Q. A similar set of manipulations for the change in supply price gives:

$$\frac{dP_S}{dt} = \frac{e_D}{e_S - e_D}. \qquad (15.13)$$

Because $e_D \leq 0$, $e_S \geq 0$, these calculations provide the obvious results

$$\frac{dP_D}{dt} \geq 0$$

$$\frac{dP_S}{dt} \leq 0. \qquad (15.14)$$

If $e_D = 0$ (demand is perfectly inelastic), $dP_D/dt = 1$ and the per-unit tax is completely paid by demanders. Alternatively, if $e_D = -\infty$, $dP_S/dt = -1$ and the tax is wholly paid by producers. More generally, division of Equation 15.13 by Equation 15.12 yields

$$-\frac{dP_S/dt}{dP_D/dt} = -\frac{e_D}{e_S}, \qquad (15.15)$$

which shows that the actor with the less elastic responses (in absolute value) will experience most of the price change occasioned by the tax.

A Welfare Analysis
Figure 15.3 permits a simplified welfare analysis of the tax incidence issue. Imposition of the unit tax, t, creates a vertical wedge between the supply and demand curves and quantity traded declines to Q^{**}. Demanders incur a loss of consumer surplus given by area $P_D FEP^*$, of which $P_D FHP^*$ is transferred to the government as a portion of total tax revenues. The balance of total tax revenues ($P^* HGP_S$) is paid by producers, who incur a total loss of producer surplus given by area $P^* EGP_S$. Notice that the reduction in combined consumer and producer surplus exceeds total tax revenues collected by area FEG. This area represents a "deadweight" loss that arises because some mutually beneficial transactions are discouraged by the tax. In general, the sizes of all of the various areas illustrated in Figure 15.3 will be affected by the price elasticities involved. To determine the final incidence of the producers' share of the tax would require an explicit analysis of input markets—the burden of the tax would be reflected in reduced rents for those inputs characterized by relatively inelastic supply.

FIGURE 15.3

TAX INCIDENCE ANALYSIS

Imposition of a specific tax of amount t per unit creates a "wedge" between the price consumers pay (P_D) and what suppliers receive (P_S). The extent to which consumers or producers pay the tax depends on the price elasticities of demand and supply.

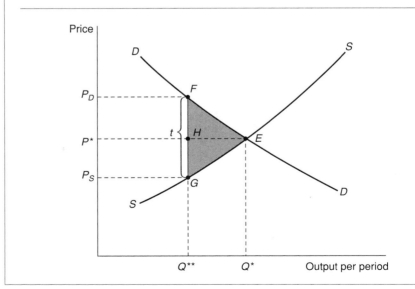

All nonlump-sum taxes involve deadweight losses because they alter the behavior of economic actors. The size of such losses will depend in a rather complex way on the elasticities of demand and supply in the market. A linear approximation to the deadweight loss accompanying a small tax, dt, is given by

Deadweight Loss and Elasticity

$$DW = -.5(dt)\,(dQ). \tag{15.16}$$

But from the definition of elasticity, we know

$$dQ = e_D dP_D \cdot Q_0/P_0, \tag{15.17}$$

where Q_0 and P_0 are the pretax values for quantity and price, respectively. Combining Equations 15.17 and 15.12 yields

$$dQ = e_D[e_S/(e_S - e_D)]dt\, Q_0/P_0, \tag{15.18}$$

and substitution into Equation 15.16 provides a final expression for the loss:

$$DW = -.5 \left(\frac{dt}{P_0}\right)^2 [e_D e_S/(e_S - e_D)]\, P_0 Q_0. \tag{15.19}$$

Clearly, deadweight losses are zero in cases in which either e_D or e_S is zero since then the tax does not alter the quantity of the good traded. More generally, deadweight losses are smaller in situations where e_D or e_S is small. In principle, Equation 15.19 can be used to evaluate the deadweight losses accompanying any complex tax system. This information might provide some insights on how a tax system could be designed to minimize the overall "excess burden" involved in collecting a needed amount of tax revenues.

EXAMPLE 15.2

THE DEADWEIGHT LOSS FROM TAXES

In Example 15.1 we examined the loss of consumer and producer surplus that would occur if automobile sales were cut from their equilibrium level of 12.8 (million) to 11 (million). An auto tax of $2,640 (i.e., 2.64 thousand dollars) would accomplish this reduction since it would introduce exactly the wedge between demand and supply price that was calculated previously. Since $e_D = -1.2$ and $e_S = 1.0$ in Example 15.1, and initial spending on automobiles is approximately $126 (billion), Equation 15.19 predicts that the deadweight loss from the auto tax would be

$$DW = .5 \left(\frac{2.64}{9.87}\right)^2 (1.2/2.2)(126) = 2.46. \tag{15.20}$$

This loss of 2.46 billion dollars is approximately the same as the loss from emissions control calculated in Example 15.1. It might be contrasted to total tax collections, which in this case amount to $29 billion ($2,640 per automobile times 11 million automobiles in the post-tax equilibrium). Here, the deadweight loss equals approximately 8 percent of total tax revenues collected.

Marginal Burden. An incremental increase in the auto tax would be relatively more costly in terms of deadweight losses. Suppose the government decided to round the auto tax upward to a flat $3,000 per car. In this case, car sales would drop to approximately 10.7 (million). Tax collections would amount to $32.1 billion, an increase of $3.1 billion over what was computed previously. Equation 15.20 can be used to show that deadweight losses now amount to $3.17 billion—an increase of $0.71 billion above the losses experienced with the lower tax. At the margin then, additional deadweight losses amount to about 23 percent ($= .72/3.1$) of additional revenues collected. Hence, marginal and average excess burden computations may differ significantly.

QUERY: Can you explain intuitively why the marginal burden of a tax exceeds its average burden? Under what conditions would the marginal excess burden of a tax exceed additional tax revenues collected?

Transactions Costs   Although we have developed this discussion in terms of tax incidence theory, models incorporating a wedge between buyers' and sellers' prices have a number of other applications in economics. Perhaps the most important of these concern costs associated with making market transactions. In some cases these costs may be explicit. Most real estate transactions, for example, take place through a third-party broker, who charges a fee for the service of bringing buyer and seller together. Similar explicit transactions fees occur in the trading of stocks and bonds, boats and airplanes, and practically everything that is sold at auction. In all of these instances, buyers and sellers are willing to pay an explicit fee to an agent or broker who facilitates the transaction. In other cases transactions costs may be largely implicit. Individuals trying to purchase a used car, for example, will spend considerable time and effort reading classified advertisements and examining vehicles, and these activities amount to an implicit cost of making the transaction.

To the extent that transactions costs are on a per-unit basis (as they are in the real estate, securities, and auction examples), our previous taxation example applies exactly. From the point of view of the buyers and sellers, it makes little difference whether t represents a per-unit tax or a per-unit transactions fee, since the analysis of the fee's effect on the market will be the same. That is, the fee will be shared between buyers and sellers, depending on the specific elasticities involved. Trading volume will be lower than in the absence of such fees.[4] A somewhat different analysis would hold, however, if transactions costs were a lump-sum amount per transaction. In that case individuals would seek to reduce the number of transactions made, but the existence of the charge would not affect the supply-demand equilibrium itself. For example, the cost of driving to the supermarket is mainly a lump-sum transaction cost on shopping for groceries. The existence of such a charge may not significantly affect the price of food items or the amount of food consumed (unless it tempts people to grow their own), but the charge will cause individuals to shop less frequently, to buy larger quantities on each trip, and to hold larger inventories of food in their homes than would be the case in the absence of such a cost.

More generally, taxes or transactions costs may affect some attributes of transactions more than others. In our formal model, we assumed that such costs were based only on the physical quantity of goods sold. The desire to minimize costs on the part of both suppliers and demanders therefore led them to reduce quantity traded. When transactions involve several dimensions (such as quality, risk, or timing), taxes or transactions costs may affect some or all of these dimensions depending on the precise basis on which the costs are assessed. For example, a tax on quantity may cause firms to upgrade product quality, or information-based transactions costs may encourage firms to produce less risky, standardized commodities. Similarly, a per-transaction cost (travel costs of getting to the store) may cause individuals to make fewer but larger transactions (and hold larger inventories). The possibilities for these various substitutions will obviously depend on the particular circumstances of the transaction. We will examine several examples of cost-induced changes in attributes of transactions in later chapters.[5]

Effects on the Attributes of Transactions

---

[4] This analysis does not consider possible benefits obtained from brokers. To the extent that these services are valuable to the parties in the transaction, demand and supply curves will shift outward to reflect this value. Hence, trading volume may actually expand with the availability of services that facilitate transactions, although the costs of such services will continue to create a wedge between sellers' and buyers' prices.

[5] For a general treatment of this topic, see Y. Barzel, "An Alternative Approach to the Analysis of Taxation," *Journal of Political Economy* (December 1976): 1177–1197.

Restrictions on the flow of goods in international commerce have effects similar to those we just examined for taxes. Impediments to free trade may reduce mutually beneficial transactions and cause a variety of transfers among the various parties involved. Once again the competitive model of supply and demand is frequently used to study these effects.

Gains from International Trade

Figure 15.4 illustrates the domestic demand and supply curves for a particular good, say, shoes. In the absence of international trade, the domestic equilibrium price of shoes would be P^* and quantity would be Q^*. Although this equilibrium would exhaust all mutually beneficial transactions between domestic shoe producers and domestic demanders, opening of international trade presents a number of additional options. If world shoe prices, P_W, are less than the prevailing domestic price P^*, the opening of trade will cause

---

FIGURE 15.4

OPENING OF INTERNATIONAL TRADE INCREASES TOTAL WELFARE

Opening of international trade lowers price from P^* to P_W. At P_W domestic producers supply Q_2 and demanders buy Q_1. Imports amount to $Q_1 - Q_2$. The lower price results in a transfer from domestic producers to consumers (shaded lighter gray) and a net gain of consumer surplus (shaded darker gray).

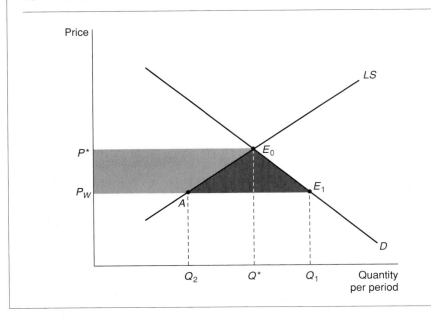

prices to fall to this world level.[6] This drop in price will cause quantity demanded to increase to Q_1, whereas quantity supplied by domestic producers will fall to Q_2. Imported shoes will amount to $Q_1 - Q_2$. In short, what shoes domestic producers do not supply at the world price are instead provided by foreign sources.

The shift in the market equilibrium from E_0 to E_1 causes a large increase in consumer surplus given by area $P^*E_0E_1P_W$. Part of this gain reflects a transfer from domestic shoe producers (area $P^*E_0A\,P_W$), and part represents an unambiguous welfare gain (area E_0E_1A). The source of consumer gains here is obvious—buyers get shoes at a lower price than was previously available in the domestic market. As in our analysis of taxation, losses of producer surplus are experienced by those inputs that give the long-run supply curve its upward slope. If, for example, the domestic shoe industry experiences increasing costs because shoemaker wages are driven up as industry output expands, then the decline in output from Q^* to Q_2 as a result of trade will reverse this process, causing shoemaker wages to fall.

Tariff Protection and the Politics of Trade

Shoemakers are unlikely to take wage losses arising from shoe imports lying down. Instead, they will press the government for protection from the flood of imported footwear. Since the loss of producer surplus is experienced by relatively few individuals, whereas consumer gains from trade are spread across many shoe buyers, shoemakers may have considerably greater incentives to organize opposition to imports than consumers would have to organize to keep trade open. The result may be the adoption of protectionist measures.

Historically, the most important type of protection employed has been a tariff: a tax on the imported good. The effects of such a tax are shown in Figure 15.5. Now comparisons begin from the free trade equilibrium, E_1. Imposition of a per-unit tariff on shoes for domestic buyers of amount t raises the effective price to $P_W + t = P_R$. This price rise causes quantity demanded to fall from Q_1 to Q_3, whereas domestic production expands from Q_2 to Q_4. The total quantity of shoe imports falls from $Q_1 - Q_2$ to $Q_3 - Q_4$. Since each imported pair of shoes is now subject to a tariff, total tariff revenues are given by the area BE_2DC, measured by $t(Q_3 - Q_4)$.

Imposition of the tariff on imported shoes creates a variety of welfare effects. Total consumer surplus is reduced by area $P_RE_2E_1P_W$. Part of this, as we have seen, is transferred into tariff revenues and part is transferred into increased domestic producer's surplus (area P_RBAP_W). The two triangles

---

[6] Throughout our analysis we will assume that this country is a price taker in the world market and can purchase all of the imports it wishes without affecting the price, P_W. For an analysis of an upward sloping supply curve for imports, see Problem 15.10.

FIGURE 15.5

EFFECTS OF A TARIFF

Imposition of a tariff of amount t raises price to $P_R = P_W + t$. This results in collection of tariff revenue (area BE_2DC), a transfer from consumers to producers (area P_RBAP_W), and two triangles measuring deadweight loss (shaded). A quota has similar effects, though in this case no revenues are collected.

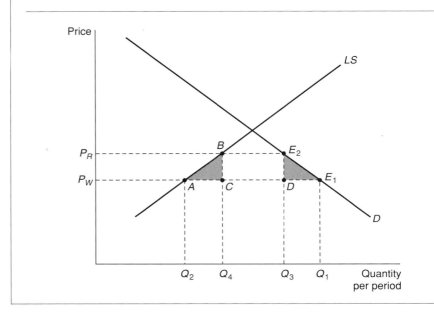

BCA and E_2E_1D represent losses of consumer surplus that are not transferred to anyone; these are a deadweight loss from the tariff and are similar to the excess burden imposed by any tax. All of these areas can be measured if good empirical estimates of the domestic supply and demand elasticities for imported goods are available, as we now show.

Quantitative Estimates of Deadweight Losses

Estimates of the sizes of the welfare loss triangle in Figure 15.5 can be readily calculated. Since $P_R = (1 + t)P_W$, the proportional change in quantity demanded brought about by this price rise is given by

$$\frac{Q_3 - Q_1}{Q_1} = \frac{P_R - P_W}{P_W} \cdot e_D = te_D \qquad (15.21)$$

and the area of triangle E_2E_1D is given by

$$DW_1 = .5(P_R - P_W)(Q_1 - Q_3) = -.5t^2 e_D P_W Q_1. \qquad (15.22)$$

Similarly, the loss in consumer surplus represented by area BCA is given by

$$DW_2 = .5(P_R - P_W)(Q_4 - Q_2) = .5t^2 e_S P_W Q_2. \qquad (15.23)$$

Notice that the values of both DW_1 and DW_2 are convex functions of the tariff rate (t) and each depends on the initial value of total revenues. When imports initially represent a large share of the domestic market and e_D and e_S are of similar sizes (in absolute value) this suggests that DW_1 will generally be the larger of the two deadweight losses. These also may sometimes be large relative to total transfers to producers (area $P_R BAP_W$), thereby leading to rather large estimates for the "costs" of some tariffs relative to the value of production benefits generated.

In recent years, tariffs have come to play a much reduced role in international trade. They have been gradually negotiated downward under the General Agreement of Tariffs and Trade (GATT). The decline in tariffs has not necessarily meant a decline in protectionism, however. In their place are a number of restrictive measures including quotas, "voluntary" export restraints, and a series of nonquantitative restrictions such as those incorporated into seemingly beneficial health, safety, and environmental regulation. Many of these new types of restrictions can be illustrated by adapting the tariff model we have already developed in Figure 15.5.

Other Types of Trade Protection

A quota that limits imports to $Q_3 - Q_4$ would have effects that are very similar to those shown in the figure: market price would rise to P_R; a substantial transfer from consumers to domestic producers would occur (area $P_R BAP_W$); and there would be deadweight losses represented by the triangles BCA and E_2E_1D. With a quota, however, no revenues are collected by the government, so the loss of consumer surplus represented by area BE_2DC must go elsewhere. It might be captured by owners of import licenses or by foreign producers, depending on how quota rights are assigned.

Nonquantitative restrictions such as inspection or testing requirements also impose cost and time delays that can be treated as an "implicit" tariff on imports. For example, at one time all imported aluminum baseball bats had to be tested by officials of the Japanese Little League, thereby raising their price relative to domestically produced bats. Figure 15.5 can easily be adapted to illustrate the effects of these prevalent and costly impediments to trade.

EXAMPLE 15.3

TRADE AND TARIFFS

These various aspects of trade policy can be illustrated with our simplified model of the automobile market. As we have shown previously, with a demand function given by

$$Q_D = 200P^{-1.2} \qquad (15.24)$$

and supply by

$$Q_S = 1.3P, \qquad (15.25)$$

the domestic market has a long-run equilibrium of

$$P^* = 9.87$$

$$Q^* = 12.8. \qquad (15.26)$$

If automobiles were available at a world price of 9 (thousand dollars), demand would expand to $Q_D = 14.3$, whereas domestic supply would shrink to $Q_S = 11.7$. Imports would then amount to 2.6 (million) cars. As shown in Figure 15.4, consumers would gain significantly by the availability of imports (consumer surplus would expand by approximately 11.8 billion dollars) though a significant portion of this gain (10.7 billion) would represent a transfer from domestic producers to consumers.

Effects of a Tariff. If pressure from domestic producers leads the government to adopt, say, a $500 tariff, the world price of cars will rise to 9.5 (thousand dollars), quantity demanded will contract (to 13.4), and domestic supply will expand (to 12.4). Imports would contract to 1.0 (million) cars. The welfare effects of these changes can be calculated directly, or can be approximated by the expressions in Equations 16.22 and 16.23. A direct calculation of DW_1 yields[7]

$$DW_1 = .5 \,(.5) \,(14.3 - 13.4) = 0.225 \qquad (15.27)$$

and for DW_2, we have

$$DW_2 = .5 \,(.5) \,(12.4 - 11.7) = 0.175. \qquad (15.28)$$

Hence, the total deadweight loss from the tariff (0.4 billion) is approximately equal to total tariff revenue (0.5 billion).

---

[7] Since the tariff here is approximately $t = .055$, Equation 15.22 yields an approximate value of DW_1 of 0.234, whereas Equation 15.23 shows $DW_2 = 0.159$. The estimated total deadweight loss is approximately 0.4 billion.

Effects of a Quota. An automobile import quota of 1 million cars would have identical effects to that of a $500 tariff. Equilibrium price would rise by $500 and there would be a large transfer from domestic consumers to domestic producers. Deadweight losses of $0.4 billion would also be the same as before. Now, however, there would be no tariff revenues. The $0.5 billion loss in consumer surplus will instead be transferred to whomever can appropriate the rights to import cars. Since the right to import a car is worth $500, it seems likely there will be active interest in acquiring such rights.

QUERY: What is the total transfer from consumers to producers as a result of the auto tariff or quota in this problem? Who would ultimately receive this transfer?

SUMMARY

In this chapter we have shown how the competitive model can be used to investigate a wide range of economic activities and policies. Some of the general lessons from these applications include:

- The concepts of consumer and producer surplus provide useful ways of analyzing the effects of economic changes on the welfare of market participants. Changes in consumer surplus represent changes in the overall utility consumers receive from consuming a particular good. Changes in long-run producer surplus represent changes in the returns product inputs receive.

- Price controls involve both transfers between producers and consumers and losses of transactions that could benefit both consumers and producers.

- Tax incidence analysis concerns the determination of which economic actor ultimately bears the

burden of a tax. In general, this incidence will fall mainly on the actors who exhibit inelastic responses to price changes. Taxes also involve deadweight losses that constitute an "excess" burden in addition to the burden imposed by the actual tax revenues collected.

- Transactions costs can sometimes be modeled as taxes. Both taxes and transactions costs may affect the attributes of transactions depending on the basis on which the costs are incurred.

- Trade restrictions such as tariffs or quotas create both transfers between consumers and producers and deadweight losses of economic welfare. The effects of many types of trade restrictions can be modeled as being equivalent to a per-unit tariff.

PROBLEMS

15.1
Suppose that the demand for broccoli is given by

$$Q = 1,000 - 5P$$

where Q is quantity per year measured in hundreds of bushels and P is price in dollars per hundred bushels. The long-run supply curve for broccoli is given by

$$Q = 4P - 80.$$

a. Show that the equilibrium quantity here is $Q = 400$. At this output what is the equilibrium price? How much in total is spent on broccoli? What is consumer surplus at this equilibrium? What is producer surplus at this equilibrium?
b. How much in total consumer and producer surplus would be lost if $Q = 300$ instead of $Q = 400$?
c. Show how the allocation between suppliers and demanders of the loss of total consumer and producer surplus described in part (b) depends on the price at which broccoli is sold. How would the loss be shared if $P = 140$? How about if $P = 95$?
d. What would the total loss of consumer and producer surplus be if $Q = 450$ rather than $Q = 400$? Show that the size of this total loss also is independent of the price at which the broccoli is sold.

15.2

The handmade snuffbox industry is composed of 100 identical firms, each having short-run total costs given by

$$STC = 0.5q^2 + 10q + 5$$

and short-run marginal costs by

$$SMC = q + 10,$$

where q is the output of snuffboxes per day.
a. What is the short-run supply curve for each snuffbox maker? What is the short-run supply curve for the market as a whole?
b. Suppose the demand for total snuffbox production is given by

$$Q = 1,100 - 50P.$$

What will be the equilibrium in this marketplace? What will each firm's total short-run profits be?
c. Graph the market equilibrium and compute total short-run producer surplus in this case.
d. Show that the total producer surplus you calculated in part (c) is equal to total industry profits plus industry short-run fixed costs.

15.3

The perfectly competitive videotape copying industry is composed of many firms that can copy five tapes per day at an average cost of $10 per tape. Each firm must also pay a royalty to film studios and the per-film royalty rate (r) is an increasing function of total industry output (Q) given by

$$r = .002Q.$$

Demand is given by

$$Q = 1,050 - 50P.$$

a. Assuming the industry is in long-run equilibrium, what will be the equilibrium price and quantity of copied tapes? How many tape firms will there be? What will the per-film royalty rate be?
b. Suppose that the demand for copied tapes increases to

$$Q = 1,600 - 50P.$$

Now, what is the long-run equilibrium price and quantity for copied tapes? How many tape firms are there? What is the per-film royalty rate?
c. Graph these long-run equilibria in the tape market and calculate the increase in producer surplus between the situations described in parts (a) and (b).
d. Show that the increase in producer surplus is precisely equal to the increase in royalties paid as Q expands incrementally from its level in part (b) to its level in part (c).

15.4

Consider again the market for broccoli described in Problem 15.1.
a. Suppose demand for broccoli shifted outward to

$$Q = 1,270 - 5P.$$

What would be the new equilibrium price and quantity in this market?
b. What would be the new levels of consumer and producer surplus in this market?
c. Suppose the government had prevented the price of broccoli from rising from its equilibrium level of Problem 15.1. Describe how the consumer and producer surplus measures described in part (b) would be reallocated or lost entirely.

15.5

Returning once more to the broccoli market described in Problem 15.1, suppose that the government instituted a $45 per-hundred-bushel tax on broccoli.

a. How would this tax affect equilibrium in the broccoli market?
b. How would this tax burden be shared between buyers and sellers of broccoli?
c. What is the excess burden of this tax?
d. Suppose now the demand for broccoli shifted to

$$Q = 2,200 - 15P.$$

Answer parts (a) and (b) for this alternative demand curve.
e. Suppose now that the broccoli market is characterized by the original demand curve described in Problem 15.1 but that the supply curve is

$$Q = 10P - 800.$$

Answer parts (a) and (b) for this case.
f. What do you conclude by comparing these three cases of tax incidence we have examined for the broccoli market?

15.6
Suppose the government imposed a $3 tax on snuffboxes in the industry described in Problem 15.2.
a. How would this tax change the market equilibrium?
b. How would the burden of this tax be shared between snuffbox buyers and sellers?
c. Calculate the total loss of producer surplus as a result of the taxation of snuffboxes. Show that this loss equals the change in total short-run profits in the snuffbox industry. Why don't fixed costs enter into this computation of the change in short-run producer surplus?

15.7
Suppose that the government institutes a $5.50 per-film tax on the film copying industry described in Problem 15.3.
a. Assuming that the demand for copied films is that given in part (a) of Problem 15.3, how will this tax affect the market equilibrium?
b. How will the burden of this tax be allocated between consumers and producers? What will be the loss of consumer and producer surplus?
c. Show that the loss of producer surplus as a result of this tax is borne completely by the film studios. Explain your result intuitively.

15.8
The domestic demand for portable radios is given by

$$Q = 5,000 - 100P$$

where price (P) is measured in dollars and quantity (Q) is measured in thousands of radios per year. The domestic supply curve for radios is given by

$$Q = 150P.$$

a. What is the domestic equilibrium in the portable radio market?
b. Suppose portable radios can be imported at a world price of $10 per radio. If trade were unencumbered, what would the new market equilibrium be? How many portable radios would be imported?
c. If domestic portable radio producers succeeded in getting a $5 tariff implemented, how would this change the market equilibrium? How much would be collected in tariff revenues? How much consumer surplus would be transferred to domestic producers? What would the deadweight loss from the tariff be?
d. How would your results from part (c) be changed if the government reached an agreement with foreign suppliers to limit "voluntarily" the portable radios they export to 1,250,000 per year? Explain how this differs from the case of a tariff.

15.9
In Example 15.3 we showed that the deadweight loss from a tariff of $500 on imported autos was approximately equal to the amount of tariff revenues collected. How would the marginal excess burden from increasing the tariff to $600 compare to the marginal tariff revenues collected? Explain your result intuitively.

15.10
In our analysis of tariffs we assumed that the country in question faced a perfectly elastic supply curve for imports. Now assume that this country faces a positively sloped supply curve for imported goods.
a. Show graphically how the level of imports will be determined.
b. Use your graph from part (a) to demonstrate the effects of a tariff in this market.

c. Carefully identify the sources of the various changes in consumer and producer surplus that are brought about by the tariff in part (b).

d. Show how the deadweight losses brought about by the tariff in this case will depend on the elasticity of demand and the elasticities of supply of domestic and imported goods.

SUGGESTED READINGS

Borenstein, S. "The Evolution of U.S. Airline Competition." *Journal of Economic Perspectives* (Spring 1992): 45–74.
Careful empirical analysis of the ways in which competition is (or is not) manifested in the U.S. airline industry.

Bosworth, B., and G. Burtless. "Effective Tax Reform in Labor Supply, Investments, and Saving." *Journal of Economic Perspectives* (Winter 1992): 3–75.
Illustrates how the impact of taxes can be modeled in a variety of markets.

Mokre, M. R., and D. G. Tarr. "Effects of Restrictions in United States Imports: Five Case Studies and Theory." *Federal Trade Commission Report* (June 1980). *Lays out the theory of trade distortions and applies the theory to U.S. trade in CB radios, color televisions, sugar, footwear, and textiles.*

deMelo, J., and D. G. Tarr. "The Welfare Costs of U.S. Quotas in Textiles, Steel, and Autos." *Review of Economics and Statistics* (August 1990): 489–497.
A nice study of the quota question in a general equilibrium context. Finds that the quotas studied have the same quantitative effects as a tariff rate of about 20 percent.

Winston, C. "Economic Deregulation: Days of Reckoning for Macroeconomists." *Journal of Economic Literature* (September 1993): 1283–1289.
Reviews the empirical evidence on a number of deregulation efforts during the 1980s.

CHAPTER 16

GENERAL COMPETITIVE EQUILIBRIUM

In Chapters 14 and 15 we examined how the forces of supply and demand interact to determine the price of a single commodity. Although that analysis is quite useful for illustrating the kinds of factors that influence market outcomes, it has one major limitation—it looks at only one market at a time. But we know from our prior analyses that in reality markets are highly interconnected. Pricing outcomes in one market will usually have effects in other markets, and these effects, in turn, will ripple throughout the economy, perhaps even to the extent of affecting the price-quantity equilibrium in the original market. For example, suppose individuals' preferences shift toward consuming poultry and away from consuming beef, perhaps because of health concerns. This will have the effect of shifting the demand curve for poultry outward and the demand curve for beef inward with the expected effects on the prices of these two goods. In our partial equilibrium analysis that would be the end of the story. But, in a general equilibrium view of the many markets that constitute an economy, the story has just begun. Rising poultry prices may lure more firms into the business, and this entry of firms may raise prices for such inputs as grain, poultry farms, and chicken pluckers. Such changes in input prices will feed back into the poultry market by shifting the poultry supply curve. Similarly, declining prices of beef, besides affecting the demand for cowhands and other beef inputs, will also feed back into the poultry market by convincing some people that eating beef wasn't so bad after all.

Partial equilibrium models are clearly inadequate to analyze all of these effects. Instead, we need an economic model that permits us to view many markets simultaneously. Although the construction of such general equilibrium (multimarket) models has been of interest to economists for some time (indeed, many of the tools we will present in this chapter were first

GENERAL EQUILIBRIUM MODELS

developed in the nineteenth century), it was not until the advent of modern computer technology that it became possible to apply such models to actual market situations. In this chapter we will only make a few comments about these important innovations in economic model building since we will be more interested in developing the theory of general equilibrium price determination. The extensions to this chapter describe a few recent attempts at computer-oriented model building.

PERFECTLY COMPETITIVE PRICE SYSTEM

The model we will develop in this chapter is primarily an elaboration of the supply-demand model that we presented in Chapter 14. Here we will assume that all markets are of the type described in that chapter and refer to such a set of markets as a *perfectly competitive price system.* The assumption is that there is some large number of homogeneous goods in this simple economy. Included in this list of goods are not only consumption items but also factors of production (whose pricing is described in Part VII). Each of these goods has an *equilibrium price,* established by the action of supply and demand.[1] At this set of prices, every market is cleared in the sense that suppliers are willing to supply that quantity which is demanded and consumers will demand that quantity which is supplied. We also assume that there are no transaction or transportation charges and that both individuals and firms have perfect knowledge of prevailing market prices.

The Law of One Price

Because of the zero transactions cost and perfect information assumptions, each good obeys the law of one price: A homogeneous good trades at the same price no matter who buys it or which firm sells it. If one good traded at two different prices, demanders would rush to buy the good where it was cheaper, and firms would try to sell all their output where the good was more expensive. These actions in themselves would tend to equalize the price of the good. In the perfectly competitive market, then, each good must have only one price. This is why we may speak unambiguously of *the* price of a good.

---

[1] One aspect of this market interaction should be made clear from the outset. The perfectly competitive market only determines relative (not absolute) prices. In this chapter, we speak primarily of relative prices. It makes no difference whether the prices of apples and oranges are $.10 and $.20, respectively, or $10 and $20. The important point in either case is that two apples can be exchanged for one orange in the market. In the final sections of the chapter, we will briefly examine the role of money and the determination of absolute prices.

The perfectly competitive model assumes that people and firms react to prices in specific ways:

Assumptions about Perfect Competition

1. There are assumed to be a large number of people buying any one good. Each person takes all prices as given and adjusts his or her behavior to *maximize utility*, given the prices and his or her budget constraint. People may also be suppliers of productive services (for example, labor), and in such decisions they also regard prices as given.[2]
2. There are assumed to be a large number of firms producing each good, and each firm produces only a small share of the output of any one good. In making input and output choices, firms are assumed to operate to *maximize profits*. The firms treat all prices as given when making these profit-maximizing decisions.

These various assumptions should be familiar since we have been making them throughout this book. Our purpose here is to show how an entire economic system operates when all markets work in this way.

As a simple illustration of why a general equilibrium approach is needed, Figure 16.1 shows the market for one good, say, wine, and three other markets related to it: (1) the market for grape pickers; (2) the market for a related product, cloth; and (3) the market for weavers. Suppose that initially all of these markets are in equilibrium as shown by the original sets of supply and demand curves in the four panels of Figure 16.1. That is, the equilibrium price of wine is given by P_1, wages of grape pickers by w_1, the price of cloth by P_2, and the wages of weavers by w_2. Since these prices act to equate the amount supplied and demanded in each of these markets, this general equilibrium will persist from period to period until something happens to change it.

THE NECESSITY OF GENERAL EQUILIBRIUM

Assume now that such a change does occur. Imagine a situation where the government announces that wine has been found to cure the common cold, so everyone decides to drink more of it. An initial consequence of this discovery is that the demand for wine will shift outward to D'. In our previous analysis this shift would cause the price of wine to rise and that

Transmission of Effects across All Markets

---

[2] Since one price represents the wage rate, the relevant budget constraint is in reality a time constraint. This is the way we treat individuals' labor-leisure choices in Chapter 22.

FIGURE 16.1

THE MARKET FOR WINE AND SEVERAL RELATED MARKETS

Initially, the market for wine is in equilibrium (at P_1) as are the markets for grape pickers, cloth, and weavers. An increase in demand for wine will disturb these equilibria. Virtually all of the supply and demand curves will shift in the process of establishing a new general equilibrium.

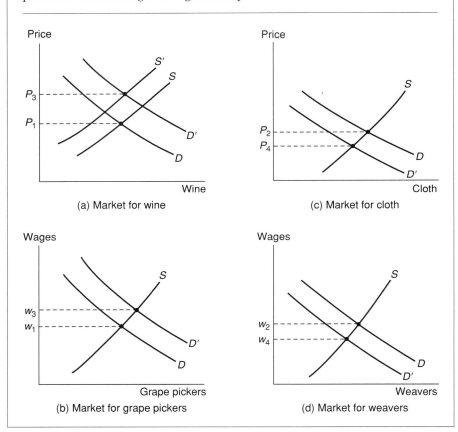

(a) Market for wine

(c) Market for cloth

(b) Market for grape pickers

(d) Market for weavers

would be, more or less, the end of the analysis. Now, however, we wish to follow the repercussions of what has happened in the wine market into the other markets shown in Figure 16.1. A first possible reaction would be in the market for grape pickers. Since wine prices have risen, the demand for labor used to harvest grapes will rise, so the demand curve for labor in Figure 16.1b will shift to D'. This will tend to raise wages of grape pickers, which will, in turn, raise the costs of wine makers. The supply curve for wine (which, under perfect competition, just reflects wine makers' marginal costs) will shift to S'.

What happens to the market for cloth? Since people have an increased desire for wine, they may reduce their demands for cloth since wine makes them feel equally warm with less on. The demand for cloth will shift inward to D' and cloth prices will fall. That will reduce the demand for weavers, and the wage associated with that occupation will fall.

We could continue this story indefinitely. We could ask how the lower price of cloth affects the wine market. Or we could ask whether weavers discouraged by their falling wages might consider picking grapes, thereby shifting the labor supply curve in Figure 16.1b outward. To follow this chain of events further would add little to our story. Eventually, we would expect all four markets to reach a new equilibrium such as that illustrated by the new supply-demand intersections in the figure. Once all the repercussions have been worked out, the final result would be a rise in wine prices (to P_3), a rise in the wages of grape pickers (to w_3), a fall in cloth prices (to P_4), and a fall in the wages of weavers (to w_4). This is what we mean then by a smoothly working system of perfectly competitive markets. Following any disturbance, all of the markets eventually reestablish a new set of equilibrium prices at which quantity demanded is equal to quantity supplied in each market.[3]

Unfortunately, the model illustrated in Figure 16.1 is not a very precise one, since we shifted the various curves more or less arbitrarily to arrive at the new equilibrium. To develop a precise mathematical statement of the model would be quite cumbersome, however, and would require at least eight equations (to represent the supply and demand functions in each market) to determine the four equilibrium prices and four equilibrium quantities in the figure. To avoid the burden of introducing all of this notation, we will instead describe a very simple graphical model of general equilibrium involving only two goods, which we will call X and Y. This model will prove to be very useful because it incorporates many of the features of far more complex general equilibrium representations of the economy. We will make extensive

A SIMPLE GRAPHICAL MODEL OF GENERAL EQUILIBRIUM

---

[3] Actually, the question of whether many markets can establish a set of prices that brings equilibrium to each of them is a major and difficult theoretical question that we take up later in this chapter.

use of the model in later chapters in cases where a multimarket analysis is needed.

General Equilibrium Demand

Ultimately, demand patterns in an economy are determined by individuals' preferences. For our simple model we will assume that all individuals have identical preferences, which can be represented by an indifference curve map[4] defined over quantities of the two goods, X and Y. The benefit of this approach for our purposes is that this indifference curve map (which is identical to the ones used in Chapters 3–6) shows how individuals rank consumption bundles containing both goods. These rankings are precisely what we mean by "demand" in a general equilibrium context. Of course, we cannot actually illustrate which bundles of commodities will be chosen until we know the budget constraints that demanders face. Since incomes are generated as individuals supply labor, capital, and other resources to the production process, we must delay this illustration until we have examined the forces of production and supply in our model.

General Equilibrium Supply

Developing a notion of general equilibrium supply in this two-good model is a somewhat more complex process than describing the demand side of the market since we have not thus far illustrated production and supply of two goods simultaneously. Our approach is to use the familiar production possibility curve (see Chapter 1) for this purpose. By detailing the way in which this curve is constructed, we can also use this construction to examine the ways in which markets for outputs and inputs are related.

Edgeworth Box Diagram

Construction of the production possibility curve for two outputs (X and Y) begins with the assumption that there are fixed amounts of capital and labor inputs that must be allocated to the production of the two goods. The possible allocations of these inputs can be illustrated with an Edgeworth box diagram with dimensions given by the total amounts of capital and labor available.

---

[4] There are some technical problems in using a single indifference curve map to represent the preferences of an entire community of individuals. In this case the marginal rate of substitution (that is, the slope of the community indifference curve) will depend on how the available goods are distributed among individuals: The increase in total Y required to compensate for a one-unit reduction in X will depend on which specific individual(s) the X is taken from. Although we will not discuss this issue in detail here, it has been widely examined in the international trade literature. For an early example, see Tibor de Scitovszky, "A Reconsideration of the Theory of Tariffs," *Review of Economic Studies* (Summer 1942): 89–110.

FIGURE 16.2

CONSTRUCTION OF AN EDGEWORTH BOX DIAGRAM FOR PRODUCTION

The dimensions of this diagram are given by the total quantities of labor and capital available. Quantities of these resources devoted to X production are measured from origin O_X; quantities devoted to Y are measured from O_Y. Any point in the box represents a fully employed allocation of the available resources to the two goods.

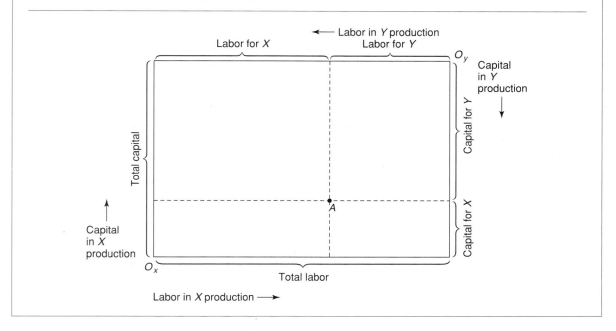

In Figure 16.2 the length of the box represents total labor-hours and the height of the box represents total capital-hours. The lower left-hand corner of the box represents the "origin" for measuring capital and labor devoted to production of good X. The upper right-hand corner of the box represents the origin for resources devoted to Y. Using these conventions, any point in the box can be regarded as a fully employed allocation of the available resources between goods X and Y. Point A, for example, represents an allocation in which the indicated number of labor-hours are devoted to X production together with a specified number of hours of capital. Production of good Y uses whatever labor and capital are "left over." Point A in Figure 16.2, for example, also shows the exact amount of labor and capital used in the production of good Y. Any other point in the box has a similar interpretation. Thus, the Edgeworth box shows every possible way the existing capital and labor might be used to produce X and Y.

Efficient Allocations   Many of the allocations shown in Figure 16.2 are technically inefficient in that it is possible to produce both more X and more Y by shifting capital and labor around a bit. In our model we assume that competitive markets will not exhibit such inefficient input choices (for reasons we will explore in more detail in the next chapter). Hence, we wish to discover the efficient allocations in Figure 16.2 since these illustrate the actual production outcomes in this model. To do so, we introduce isoquant maps for good X (using O_X as the origin) and good Y (using O_Y as the origin) as shown in Figure 16.3. In this figure it is clear that the arbitrarily chosen allocation A is inefficient.

With capital (K) and labor (L) allocated in this way, Y_2 is produced together with X_2. By moving along the Y_2 isoquant to P_3, we can hold Y output constant and increase X output to X_3. Thus, point A was not an efficient allocation since we were able to increase output of one good

FIGURE 16.3

EDGEWORTH BOX DIAGRAM OF EFFICIENCY IN PRODUCTION

This diagram adds production isoquants for X and Y to Figure 16.2. It then shows technically efficient ways to allocate the fixed amounts of K and L between the production of the two outputs. The line joining O_X and O_Y is the locus of these efficient points. Along this line the RTS (of L for K) in the production of good X is equal to the RTS in the production of Y.

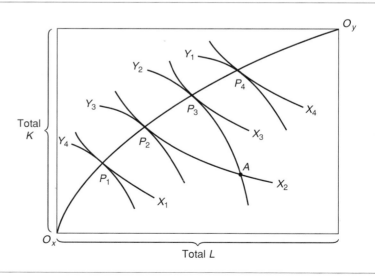

(X) without decreasing output of the other good (Y). Although both point A and point P_3 represent fully employed allocations of the available resources, the allocation at point P_3 results in good X using more capital and less labor whereas Y uses more labor and less capital than at point A.

The efficient allocations in Figure 16.3 are those such as P_1, P_2, P_3, and P_4, where the isoquants are tangent to one another. At any other points in the box diagram, the two goods' isoquants will intersect, and we can show inefficiency as we did for point A. At the points of tangency, however, this kind of unambiguous improvement cannot be made. In going from P_2 to P_3, for example, more X is being produced, but at the cost of less Y being produced, so P_3 is not "more efficient" than P_2—both of the points are efficient. Tangency of the isoquants for good X and good Y implies that their slopes are equal. That is, the *RTS* of capital for labor is equal in X and Y production. In the next chapter, we will show how competitive input markets will lead firms to make such efficient input choices.

The curve joining O_X and O_Y that includes all of these points of tangency therefore shows all of the efficient allocations of capital and labor. Points off this curve are inefficient in that unambiguous increases in output can be obtained by reshuffling inputs between the two goods. Points in $O_X O_Y$ are all efficient allocations, however, because more X can be produced only by cutting back on Y production and vice versa.

The efficiency locus in Figure 16.3 shows the maximum output of Y that can be produced for any preassigned output of X. We can use this information to construct a *production possibility frontier,* which shows the alternative outputs of X and Y that can be produced with the fixed capital and labor inputs. In Figure 16.4 the $O_X O_Y$ locus has been taken from Figure 16.3 and transferred onto a graph with X and Y outputs on the axes. At O_X, for example, no resources are devoted to X production; consequently, Y output is as large as is possible with the existing resources. Similarly, at O_Y, the output of X is as large as possible. The other points on the production possibility frontier (say, P_1, P_2, P_3, and P_4) are derived from the efficiency locus in an identical way. Hence, we have derived the following definition:

Production Possibility Frontier

DEFINITION

Production Possibility Frontier   The *production possibility frontier* shows those alternative combinations of two outputs that can be produced with fixed quantities of inputs if those inputs are employed efficiently.

FIGURE 16.4

PRODUCTION POSSIBILITY FRONTIER

The production possibility frontier shows the alternative combinations of X and Y that can be efficiently produced by a firm with fixed resources. The curve can be derived from Figure 16.3 by varying inputs between the production of X and Y while maintaining the conditions for efficiency. The negative of the slope of the production possibility curve is called the rate of product transformation (RPT).

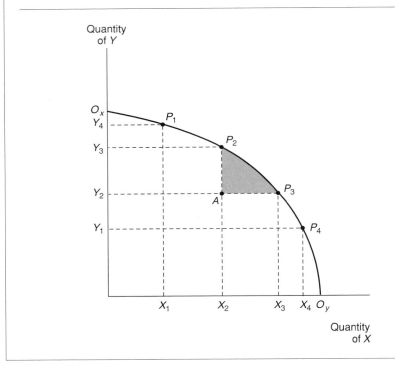

Rate of Product Transformation

The slope of the production possibility frontier shows how X output can be substituted for Y output when total resources are held constant. For example, for points near O_X on the production possibility frontier, the slope is a small negative number, say, $-\frac{1}{4}$, implying that by reducing Y output by 1 unit, X output could be increased by 4. Near O_Y, on the other hand, the slope is a large negative number, say, -5, implying that Y output must be reduced by 5 units to permit the production of one more X. The slope of the production possibility frontier, then, clearly shows the possibilities that exist for trading Y for X in production. The negative of this slope is called the *rate of product transformation* (*RPT*):

DEFINITION

Rate of Product Transformation The *rate of product transformation (RPT)* between two outputs is the negative of the slope of the production possibility frontier for those outputs. Mathematically,

$$RPT \text{ (of } X \text{ for } Y) = -\text{slope of production possibility frontier}$$

$$= -\frac{dY}{dX} \text{ (along } O_X O_Y). \tag{16.1}$$

The *RPT* records how X can be technically traded for Y while continuing to keep the available productive inputs efficiently employed.

Shape of the Production Possibility Frontier

The production possibility frontier illustrated in Figure 16.4 exhibits an increasing *RPT*. For output levels near O_X, relatively little Y must be sacrificed to obtain one more X ($-dY/dX$ is small). Near O_Y, on the other hand, additional X may be obtained only by substantial reductions in Y output ($-dY/dX$ is large). In this section we shall show why this concave shape might be expected to characterize most production situations.

A first step in that analysis is to recognize that *RPT* is equal to the ratio of the marginal cost of X (MC_X) to the marginal cost of Y (MC_Y). Intuitively, this result is obvious. Suppose, for example, that X and Y are produced only with labor. If it takes 2 labor-hours to produce one more X, we might say that MC_X is equal to 2. Similarly, if it takes only 1 labor-hour to produce an extra Y, MC_Y is equal to 1. But in this situation it is clear that the *RPT* is 2: Two Y must be foregone to provide enough labor so that X may be increased by 1 unit. Hence, the *RPT* is indeed equal to the ratio of the marginal costs of the two goods.

More formally, suppose that the costs (say, in terms of the "disutility" experienced by factor suppliers) of any output combination are denoted by $C(X, Y)$. Along the production possibility frontier, $C(X, Y)$ will be constant since the inputs are in fixed supply. Hence, we can write the total differential of the cost function as

$$dC = \frac{\partial C}{\partial X} \cdot dX + \frac{\partial C}{\partial Y} \cdot dY = 0 \tag{16.2}$$

for changes in X and Y along the production possibility frontier. Manipulating Equation 16.2 yields

$$RPT = -\frac{dY}{dX} \text{ (along } O_X O_Y) = \frac{\partial C/\partial X}{\partial C/\partial Y} = \frac{MC_X}{MC_Y}, \tag{16.3}$$

which was precisely what we wished to show: The *RPT* is a measure of the relative marginal costs of the two goods.

To demonstrate reasons why the *RPT* might be expected to rise for clockwise movements along the production possibility frontier, we can proceed by showing why the ratio of MC_X to MC_Y should rise as X output expands and Y output contracts. We first present two relatively simple arguments that apply only to special cases; then we turn to a more sophisticated general argument.

Diminishing Returns

The most common rationale offered for the concave shape of the production possibility frontier is the assumption that both goods are produced under conditions of diminishing returns. Hence, increasing the output of good X will raise its marginal cost, whereas decreasing the output of Y will reduce its marginal cost. Equation 16.3 then shows that the *RPT* will increase for movements along the production possibility frontier from O_X to O_Y. A problem with this explanation, of course, is that it applies only to cases in which both goods exhibit diminishing returns to scale, and that assumption is at variance with the theoretical reasons for preferring the assumption of constant or even increasing returns to scale we have mentioned elsewhere in this book.

Specialized Inputs

If some inputs were "more suited" for X production than for Y production (and vice versa), the concave shape of the production frontier also could be explained. In that case, increases in X output would require drawing progressively less suitable inputs into the production of that good. Marginal costs of X therefore would rise. Marginal costs for Y, on the other hand, would fall, as smaller output levels for Y would permit the use of only those inputs most suited for Y production. Such an argument might apply, for example, to a farmer with a variety of types of land under cultivation in different crops. In trying to increase the production of any one crop, the farmer would be forced to grow it on increasingly unsuitable parcels of land. Although this type of specialized input assumption has considerable importance in explaining a variety of real-world phenomena, it is nonetheless at variance with our general assumption of homogeneous factors of production. It cannot serve as a fundamental explanation for concavity.

Differing Factor Intensities

Even if inputs are homogeneous and production functions exhibit constant returns to scale, the production possibility frontier will be concave if goods

X and Y use inputs in different proportions.[5] In the production box diagram of Figure 16.3 , for example, good X is *capital intensive* relative to good Y. That is, at every point along the O_XO_Y contract curve, the ratio of K to L in X production exceeds the ratio of K to L in Y production: The bowed curve O_XO_Y is always above the main diagonal of the Edgeworth box. If, on the other hand, good Y had been relatively capital intensive, the O_XO_Y contract curve would have been bowed downward below the diagonal. Although a formal proof that unequal factor intensities result in a concave production possibility frontier will not be presented here, it is possible to suggest intuitively why that occurs. Consider any two points on the frontier O_XO_Y in Figure 16.4—say, P_1 (with coordinates X_1, Y_4) and P_3 (with coordinates X_3, Y_2). One way of producing an output combination "between" P_1 and P_3 would be to produce the combination

$$\frac{X_1 + X_3}{2}, \frac{Y_4 + Y_2}{2}.$$

Because of the constant returns-to-scale assumption, that combination would be feasible and would fully utilize both factors of production. The combination would lie at the midpoint of a straight-line chord joining points P_1 and P_3. Although such a point is feasible, it is not efficient, as can be seen by examining points P_1 and P_3 in the box diagram of Figure 16.3. Because of the bowed nature of the contract curve, production at a point midway between P_1 and P_3 would be off the contract curve: Producing at a point such as P_2 would provide more of both goods. The production possibility frontier in Figure 16.4 therefore must "bulge out" beyond the straight line P_1P_3. Since such a proof could be constructed for any two points on O_XO_Y, we have shown that the frontier is concave; that is, the *RPT* increases as the output of good X increases. When production is reallocated in a northeast direction along the O_XO_Y contract curve (in Figure 16.3), the capital-labor ratio decreases in the production of *both* X and Y. Since good X is capital intensive, this change raises MC_X. On the other hand, since good Y is labor intensive, MC_Y falls. Hence, the relative marginal cost of X (as represented by the *RPT*) rises.

The reason we have devoted so much of this chapter to the concept of the production possibility frontier is that it is the most important tool for studying issues that arise in analyzing the production of two goods simultaneously. The curve demonstrates that there are many possible

Opportunity Cost

---

[5] If, in addition to homogeneous factors and constant returns to scale, each good also used K and L in the same proportions under optimal allocations, then the production possibility frontier would be a straight line.

efficient combinations of the two goods and that producing more of one good necessitates cutting back on the production of some other good. This is precisely what economists mean by the term *opportunity cost*. The cost of producing more X can be most readily measured by the reduction in Y output that this entails. The cost of one more unit of X therefore is best measured as the *RPT* (of X for Y) at the prevailing point on the production possibility frontier. This then is our general formulation of the supply concept.

EXAMPLE 16.1

PRODUCTION POSSIBILITIES FOR GUNS AND BUTTER

As a simple example of concavity arising from diminishing returns to scale, suppose guns (X) and butter (Y) (for some reason, these are the traditional goods for production possibility frontiers) are produced using only labor according to the production functions

$$X = \sqrt{L_X}$$
$$Y = \frac{1}{2}\sqrt{L_Y},$$

(16.4)

where L_X and L_Y represent labor devoted to X and Y production, respectively. If labor supply is fixed at 100, we know

$$L_X + L_Y = 100,$$

(16.5)

and substituting from Equations 16.4 yields

$$X^2 + 4Y^2 = 100.$$

(16.6)

This production possibility frontier is therefore a quarter ellipse (since X and Y must be positive). Taking the total differential of Equation 16.6 shows

$$2X dX + 8Y dY = 0$$

(16.7)

or

$$-\frac{dY}{dX} = RPT = \frac{X}{4Y},$$

(16.8)

which clearly increases as X rises and Y falls. This increasing *RPT* of guns for butter stems directly from the diminishing returns[6] assumed in Equations 16.4. An alternative demonstration of concavity would note that the points $X = 10$, $Y = 0$ and $X = 0$, $Y = 5$ both lie on this production possibility frontier.

---

[6] For an example of concavity with production functions exhibiting constant returns to scale, see Problem 16.3.

But if $X = 5$, it is in fact possible to produce $Y = 4.33$, which is significantly greater than the level of butter output that lies at the midpoint of the straight line joining the end points of the production possibility frontier ($Y = 2.5$).

QUERY: Suppose the citizens of this simple economy were able to trade with the rest of the world at the rate of four guns for one unit of butter. What outputs should they produce in order to take maximum advantage of this trading opportunity?

Given these notions of demand and supply in our simple two-good economy, we can now illustrate how equilibrium prices are determined. Figure 16.5 shows the production possibility frontier for the economy (*PP*), and the set of indifference curves represents individuals' preferences for these goods. First, consider the price ratio P_X/P_Y. At this price ratio, firms will choose to produce the output combination X_1, Y_1. Profit-maximizing firms will choose the more profitable point on *PP*. At X_1, Y_1 the ratio of the two goods' prices (P_X/P_Y) is equal to the ratio of the goods' marginal costs (the *RPT*), so profits are maximized there. On the other hand, given this budget constraint (line C)[7] individuals will demand X_1', Y_1'. Consequently, with these prices, there is an excess demand for good X (individuals demand more than is being produced), whereas there is an excess supply of good Y. The workings of the marketplace therefore will cause P_X to rise and P_Y to fall. The price ratio P_X/P_Y will rise; the price line will take on a steeper slope. Firms will respond to these price changes by moving clockwise along the production possibility frontier; that is, they will increase their production of good X and decrease their production of good Y. Similarly, individuals will respond to the changing prices by substituting Y for X in their consumption choices. These actions of both firms and individuals, then, serve to eliminate the excess demand for X and the excess supply of Y as market prices change.

Equilibrium is reached at X^*, Y^* with a price ratio of P_X^*/P_Y^*. With this price ratio,[8] supply and demand are equilibrated for both good X and good Y. Given P_X and P_Y, firms will produce X^* and Y^* in maximizing their profits. Similarly, with a budget constraint given by C^*, individuals will demand X^* and Y^*. The operation of the price system has cleared the markets for both

Determination of Equilibrium Prices

---

[7] It is important to recognize why the budget constraint has this location. Since P_X and P_Y are given, the value of total production is $P_X \cdot X_1 + P_Y \cdot Y_1$. This is the value of "GDP" in the simple economy pictured in Figure 16.5. It is also, therefore, the total income accruing to people in society. Individuals' budget constraint therefore passes through X_1, Y_1 and has a slope of $-P_X/P_Y$. This is precisely the budget constraint labeled C in the figure.

[8] Notice again that competitive markets only determine equilibrium relative prices. Determination of the absolute price level requires the introduction of money into this barter model.

FIGURE 16.5

DETERMINATION OF EQUILIBRIUM PRICES

With a price ratio given by P_X/P_Y, firms will produce X_1, Y_1; society's budget constraint will be given by line C. With this budget constraint, individuals demand X_1' and Y_1'; that is, there is an excess demand for good X ($X_1' - X_1$), and an excess supply of good Y ($Y_1 - Y_1'$). The workings of the market will move these prices toward their equilibrium levels P_X^*, P_Y^*. At those prices, society's budget constraint will be given by line C^*, and supply and demand will be in equilibrium. The combination X^*, Y^* of goods will be chosen.

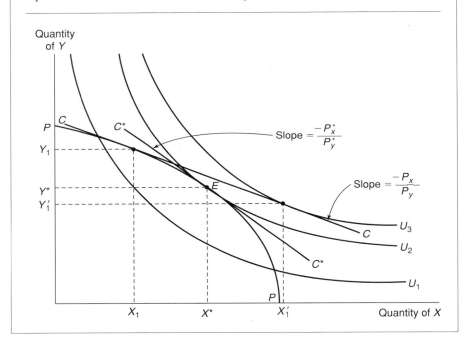

X and Y simultaneously. This figure therefore provides a "general equilibrium" view of the supply-demand process for two markets working together. For this reason we will make considerable use of this figure in our subsequent analysis.

EXAMPLE 16.2

GENERAL EQUILIBRIUM PRICING

In Example 16.1 we saw that the production possibility frontier for guns (X) and butter (Y) can be represented by the quarter ellipse

$$X^2 + 4Y^2 = 100. \tag{16.9}$$

Suppose that this community's preferences can be represented by

$$\text{utility} = U(X,Y) = \sqrt{XY}. \tag{16.10}$$

Under perfect competition, profit-maximizing firms will equate the RPT calculated in Equation 16.8 (which is also the ratio of the two goods' marginal costs) to the price ratio P_X/P_Y:

$$RPT = \frac{X}{4Y} = \frac{P_X}{P_Y}. \tag{16.11}$$

For consumers, utility maximization requires that

$$MRS = \frac{Y}{X} = \frac{P_X}{P_Y}, \tag{16.12}$$

as we have shown in many previous numerical examples based on Cobb-Douglas utility functions. Equilibrium requires that firms and individuals face the same price ratio. Hence,

$$RPT = \frac{X}{4Y} = \frac{P_X}{P_Y} = \frac{Y}{X} = MRS \tag{16.13}$$

or

$$X^2 = 4Y^2.$$

This equilibrium should also be on the production possibility frontier. Therefore,

$$X^2 + 4Y^2 = 2X^2 = 100,$$

and

$$X^* = \sqrt{50} = 7.07$$

$$Y^* = \sqrt{12.5} = 3.54 \tag{16.14}$$

are the equilibrium outputs of guns and butter. With these outputs we can use Equation 16.12 to calculate

$$\frac{P_X^*}{P_Y^*} = \frac{\sqrt{12.5}}{\sqrt{50}} = \frac{1}{2}. \tag{16.15}$$

In equilibrium, the relative price of good X is $\frac{1}{2}$ (alternatively, the relative price of Y is 2). If we choose arbitrarily to let $P_X^* = 1$, then $P_Y^* = 2$ and the total value of output is

$$P_X^* X^* + P_Y^* Y^* = 1 \cdot \sqrt{50} + 2 \cdot \sqrt{12.5} = 2\sqrt{50}. \tag{16.16}$$

In this problem the community's utility is 5, which also happens to be the largest value attainable given the constraints imposed by the existing production possibilities—an observation we will explore more fully in the next chapter.

QUERY: Why do the other allocations on the guns-butter production possibility frontier calculated in Example 16.1 yield lower utility than the allocation calculated here? At each of these other points, is X in excess supply or in excess demand?

COMPARATIVE STATICS ANALYSIS

As in our partial equilibrium analysis, the equilibrium price ratio P_X^*/P_Y^* illustrated in Figure 16.5 will tend to persist until either preferences or production technologies change. This competitively determined price ratio reflects these two basic economic forces. If preferences were to shift, say, toward good X, P_X/P_Y would rise, and a new equilibrium would be established by a clockwise move along the production possibility curve. More X and less Y would be produced to meet these changed preferences. Similarly, technical progress in the production of good X would shift the production possibility curve outward as illustrated in Figure 16.6. This would tend to lower the relative price of X and increase the quantity of X consumed (assuming X is a normal good). In the figure the quantity of Y consumed also increases as a result of the income effect arising from the technical advance; but a slightly different drawing of the figure could have reversed that result if the substitution effect had been dominant.

EXAMPLE 16.3

CHANGES IN GENERAL EQUILIBRIUM PRICES

The comparative statics properties of our simple guns-butter economy can be illustrated by assuming that the outbreak of war causes a shift in preferences toward guns as reflected by a new utility function of the form

$$U(X, Y) = X^{3/4}Y^{1/4}. \tag{16.17}$$

With this function the marginal rate of substitution is given by

$$MRS = \frac{\partial U/\partial X}{\partial U/\partial Y} = \frac{3Y}{X}. \tag{16.18}$$

Market equilibrium therefore requires

$$MRS = \frac{3Y}{X} = \frac{P_X}{P_Y} = RPT = \frac{X}{4Y} \tag{16.19}$$

FIGURE 16.6

EFFECTS OF TECHNICAL PROGRESS IN X PRODUCTION

Technical advances that lower marginal costs of X production will shift the production possibility frontier. This will generally create income and substitution effects that cause the quantity of X produced to increase (assuming X is a normal good). Effects on the production of Y are ambiguous since income and substitution effects work in opposite directions.

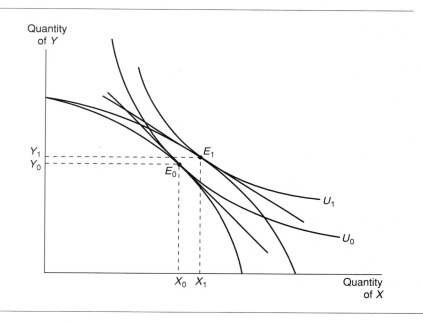

or

$$X^2 = 12Y^2.$$

Substituting this equilibrium condition into the equation for the possibility frontier yields

$$X^2 + 4Y^2 = 12Y^2 + 4Y^2 = 16Y^2 = 100$$

or

$$Y^* = 2.5$$

$$X^* = 8.66.$$ **(16.20)**

Wartime preferences for guns have therefore caused a major movement along the production possibility frontier—butter production is reduced by about 30 percent (from 3.54 to 2.5), and gun production is increased by more than 20 percent (from 7.07 to 8.66). Because of the diminishing returns inherent in these goods' production functions, such a reallocation causes a rather sharp rise in the relative price of guns:

$$\frac{P_X^*}{P_Y^*} = \frac{X}{4Y} = \frac{8.66}{10} = .866. \tag{16.21}$$

Whereas previously (in Example 16.2) each gun sold for $\frac{1}{2}$ unit of butter, now its price is nearly $\frac{7}{8}$ that of a unit of butter. This price rise both provides a signal to producers to increase gun production and information to utility-maximizing consumers about the increasing opportunity costs this entails.

QUERY: Suppose all possibilities for war cease and utility shifts to $U = X^{1/4}Y^{3/4}$. What would the relative prices of guns and butter become? How does the allocation of labor between these two goods change from wartime to peacetime?

GENERAL EQUILIBRIUM MODELING

Our simple general equilibrium model therefore reinforces Marshall's observations about the importance of both supply and demand forces in the price determination process. By providing an explicit connection between the markets for all goods, the general equilibrium model makes it possible to examine more complex questions about market relationships than is possible by looking only at one market at a time. General equilibrium modeling also permits an examination of the connections between goods and factor markets, and we can illustrate that with an important historical case.

The Corn Laws Debate

High tariffs on grain imports were imposed by the British government following the Napoleonic wars. Debate over the effects of these "corn laws" dominated the analytical efforts of economists between the years 1829 and 1845. A principal focus of the debate concerned the effect that elimination of the tariffs would have on factor prices, a question that continues to have relevance today, as we will see.

The production possibility frontier in Figure 16.7 shows those combinations of grain (X) and manufactured goods (Y) that could be produced by British factors of production. Assuming (somewhat contrary to actuality) that the corn laws completely prevented trade, market equilibrium would be at E with the domestic price ratio given by P_X^*/P_Y^*. Removal of the tariffs would reduce this price ratio to P_X'/P_Y'. Given that new ratio, Britain would produce combination A and consume combination B. Grain imports would amount to $X_B - X_A$, and these would be financed by export of manufactured goods

FIGURE 16.7

ANALYSIS OF THE CORN LAWS DEBATE

Reduction of tariff barriers on grain would cause production to be reallocated from point E to point A. Consumption would be reallocated from E to B. If grain production is relatively capital intensive, the relative price of capital would fall as a result of these reallocations.

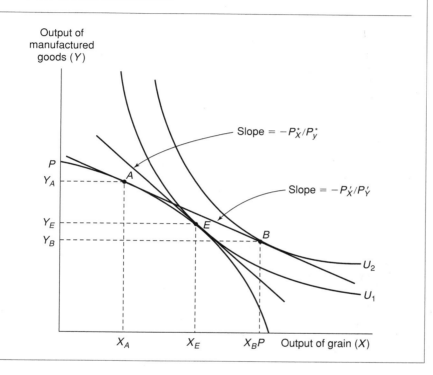

equal to $Y_A - Y_B$. Overall utility for the typical British consumer would be increased by the opening of trade. Use of the production possibility diagram therefore demonstrates the implications relaxing the tariffs would have for the production of both goods.

By referring back to the Edgeworth production box diagram that lies behind the production possibility frontier (Figure 16.3), it is also possible to analyze the effect of tariff reductions on factor prices. The movement from point E to point A in Figure 16.7 is similar to a movement from P_3 to P_1 in Figure 16.3 where production of X is decreased and production of Y is increased.

Trade and Input Prices

This figure also records the reallocation of capital and labor made necessary by such a move. If we assume that grain production is relatively capital intensive, the movement from P_3 to P_1 causes the ratio of K to L to rise in both industries.[9] This in turn will cause the relative price of capital to fall (and the relative price of labor to rise). Hence, we conclude that repeal of the corn laws would be harmful to capital owners (that is, landlords) and helpful to laborers. It is not surprising that landed interests fought repeal of the laws.

Political Support for Trade Policies

The possibility that trade policies may affect the relative incomes of various factors of production continues to exert a major influence on political debates about such policies. In the United States, for example, exports tend to be intensive in their use of skilled labor, whereas imports tend to be intensive in unskilled labor input. By analogy to our discussion of the corn laws, therefore, it might be expected that further movements toward free trade policies would result in rising relative wages for skilled workers and in falling relative wages for unskilled workers. It is not surprising therefore that unions representing skilled workers (the machinists or aircraft workers) tend to favor free trade, whereas unions of unskilled workers (those in textiles, shoes, and related businesses) tend to oppose it.

EXISTENCE OF GENERAL EQUILIBRIUM PRICES

In prior sections we have more or less assumed that competitive markets can reach an equilibrium in which the forces of supply and demand are balanced in all markets simultaneously. But, given the assumptions we have made, such a simultaneous solution is by no means assured. Beginning with the nineteenth-century investigations by Leon Walras, economists have used increasingly sophisticated tools to examine whether a set of prices that equilibrates all markets exists and, if so, how this set of prices can be found. In this section we will explore some aspects of this question.

A Simple Mathematical Model

The essential aspects of the modern solution to the Walrasian problem can be demonstrated for the case where no production takes place. Suppose that there are n goods, in absolutely fixed supply, in this economy and that they are distributed in some way among the individuals in society. Let S_i $(i = 1, \ldots, n)$ be the total supply of good i available, and let the price of good i be represented by P_i $(i = 1, \ldots, n)$. The total demand for

---

[9] In the corn laws debate, attention centered on the factors land and labor. For convenience, here we shall identify "land" as being synonymous with capital.

good i depends on all the prices, and this function represents the sum of the individuals' demand functions for good i. This total demand function is denoted by

$$D_i(P_1, \ldots, P_n)$$

for $i = 1, \ldots, n$.

Since we are interested in the whole set of prices $P_1, \ldots, P_n$, it will be convenient to denote this whole set by P. Hence, the demand functions can be written as

$$D_i(P).$$

Walras' problem then can be stated formally as: Does there exist an *equilibrium set of prices* (P^*) such that

$$D_i(P^*) = S_i \tag{16.22}$$

for all values of i? The question posed by Walras is whether a set of prices exists for which supply is equal to demand *in all markets simultaneously*.

Excess Demand Functions

In what follows it will be more convenient to work with excess demand functions for good i at any set of prices (P), which are defined to be[10]

$$ED_i(P) = D_i(P) - S_i. \tag{16.23}$$

Using this notation, the equilibrium conditions can be rewritten as

$$ED_i(P^*) = D_i(P^*) - S_i = 0. \tag{16.24}$$

This condition states that at the equilibrium prices, excess demand is to be equal to zero in all markets.[11]

Walras himself noted several interesting features about the system of Equations 16.24. First, it can be assumed that demand functions (and hence the excess demand functions) are *homogeneous of degree zero*. If all prices were to double (including the wages of labor), the quantity demanded of every good would remain unchanged. Hence, we can only hope to establish equilibrium relative prices in a Walrasian-type model. A second assumption made by Walras was that the demand functions (and therefore the excess demand functions) are *continuous:* If prices were to change by only a small

---

[10] Although we will not do so, supply behavior can be introduced here by making S_i depend on P also.

[11] This equilibrium condition will be amended slightly later to allow for goods whose equilibrium price is zero.

amount, quantities demanded would change by only a small amount. The assumptions of homogeneity and continuity are both direct results of the theory of consumer behavior that was presented in Part II.

Walras' Law

A final observation that Walras made is that the n excess demand functions are not independent of one another. The equations are related by the formula

$$\sum_{i=1}^{n} P_i \cdot ED_i(P) = 0. \tag{16.25}$$

Equation 16.25 is usually called *Walras' law*. The equation states that the "total value" of excess demand is zero at *any* set of prices. There can be neither excess demand for all goods together nor excess supply. Proving Walras' law is a simple matter, although it is necessary to introduce some cumbersome notation. The proof rests on the fact that each individual in the economy is bound by a budget constraint. A simple example of the proof is given in the footnote;[12] the generalization of this proof is left to the reader.

Walras' law, it should be stressed, holds for any set of prices, not just for equilibrium prices. The law can be seen to apply trivially to an equilibrium set of prices, since each of the excess demand functions will be equal to zero at this set of prices. Walras' law shows that the equilibrium conditions in n markets are not independent. We do not have n independent equations in n unknowns (the P's). Rather, Equation 16.24 represents only $(n-1)$ independent equations, and hence we can hope to determine only $(n-1)$ of the prices.

---

[12] Suppose that there are two goods (A and B) and two individuals (Smith and Jones) in society. Let $D_A^S, D_B^S, S_A^S, S_B^S$ be Smith's demands and supplies of A and B and use a similar notation for Jones' demands and supplies. Smith's budget constraint may be written as

$$P_A D_A^S + P_B D_B^S = P_A S_A^S + P_B S_B^S$$

or

$$P_A(D_A^S - S_A^S) + P_B(D_B^S - S_B^S) = 0$$

or

$$P_A ED_A^S + P_B ED_B^S = 0,$$

where ED_A^S and ED_B^S represent the excess demand of Smith for A and B, respectively.

A similar budget constraint holds for Jones:

$$P_A ED_A^J + P_B ED_B^J = 0,$$

and therefore letting ED_A and ED_B represent total excess demands for A and B, it must be the case that

$$P_A \cdot (ED_A^S + ED_A^J) + P_B \cdot (ED_B^S + ED_B^J) = P_A \cdot ED_A + P_B \cdot ED_B = 0.$$

This is Walras' law exactly as it appears in Equation 16.25.

But this is what would have been expected in view of the homogeneity property of the demand functions. We can hope to determine only equilibrium *relative prices*; nothing in this model permits the derivation of absolute prices.

Walras' Proof of the Existence of Equilibrium Prices

Having recognized these technical features of the system of excess demand equations, Walras turned to the question of the existence of a set of equilibrium (relative) prices. He tried to establish that the n equilibrium conditions of Equation 16.24 were sufficient, in this situation, to ensure that such a set of prices would in fact exist, and therefore that the exchange model had a consistent theoretical framework. A first indication that this existence of equilibrium prices might be assured is provided by a simple counting of equations and unknowns. The market equilibrium conditions provide $(n-1)$ *independent* equations in $(n-1)$ unknown relative prices. Hence, the elementary algebra of solving simultaneous linear equations suggests that an equilibrium solution might exist.

Unfortunately, as Walras recognized, the act of solving for equilibrium prices is not nearly as simple a matter as counting equations and unknowns. First, the equations are not necessarily linear. Hence, the well-known conditions for the existence of solutions to simultaneous linear equations do not apply in this case. Second, from consideration of the economics of the problem, it is clear that all the equilibrium prices must be nonnegative. A negative price has no meaning in the context of this problem. To attack these two difficulties, Walras developed a very tedious proof, which involved solving for equilibrium prices in a series of successive approximations. Without presenting Walras' proof in detail, it is instructive to see how he approached the problem.

Start with some initial, arbitrary set of prices. Holding the other $(n-1)$ prices constant, find the equilibrium price in the market for good 1. Call this "provisional" equilibrium price P'_1. Now, holding P'_1 and the other $(n-2)$ prices constant, solve for the equilibrium price in the market for good 2. Call this price P'_2. Notice that in changing P_2 from its initial position to P'_2, the price initially calculated for market 1 need no longer be an equilibrium price, since good 1 may be a substitute or a complement to good 2. This is a reflection of the fact that the system of equations is indeed simultaneous. Using the provisional prices P'_1 and P'_2, solve for a provisional P'_3. The proof proceeds in this way until a complete set of provisional relative prices has been calculated.

In the second iteration of Walras' proof, $P'_2, \ldots, P'_n$ are held constant while a new equilibrium price is calculated for the first good. Call this new provisional price P''_1. Proceeding as outlined above, an entire new set of provisional relative prices $(P''_1, \ldots, P''_n)$ can be calculated. The proof continues to iterate in this way until a reasonable approximation to a set of equilibrium prices is achieved.

The importance of Walras' proof is its ability to demonstrate the simultaneous nature of the problem of finding equilibrium prices. It is, however, a cumbersome proof and is generally not used today. More recent work has utilized some relatively simple tools of advanced mathematics to demonstrate the existence of equilibrium prices in a formal and elegant way. In order to demonstrate such a proof, one advanced mathematical theorem must be described.

Brouwer's Fixed-Point Theorem

Since this section is purely mathematical, it is perhaps best to plunge right in by stating Brouwer's theorem:

Any continuous mapping [$F(X)$] of a closed, bounded, convex set into itself has at least one fixed point (X^*) such that $F(X^*) = X^*$.

Before analyzing this theorem on a word-by-word basis, perhaps an example will aid in understanding the terminology. Suppose that $f(x)$ is a continuous function defined on the interval [0, 1] and that $f(x)$ takes on values also on the interval [0, 1]. This function then obeys the conditions of Brouwer's theorem; it must be the case that there exists some x^* such that $f(x^*) = x^*$. This fact is demonstrated in Figure 16.8. It is clear from this figure that any function, as long as it is continuous (as long as it has no "gaps"), must cross the 45° line somewhere. This point of crossing is a *fixed point*, since f maps this point (x^*) into itself.

To study the more general meaning of the theorem, it is first necessary to define the terms "mapping," "closed," "bounded," and "convex." Definitions of these concepts will be presented in an extremely intuitive, nonrigorous way, because the costs of mathematical rigor greatly outweigh its possible benefits for the purposes of this book.

A *mapping* is simply a rule that associates the points in one set with points in another (possibly the same) set. The most commonly encountered mappings are those that associate one point in n-dimensional space with some other point in n-dimensional space. Suppose that F is the mapping we wish to study. Then let X be a point for which the mapping is defined: The mapping associates X with some other point $Y = F(X)$. If a mapping is defined over a subset of an n-dimensional space (S), and if every point in S is associated (by the rule F) with some other point in S, the mapping is said to map S *into* itself. In Figure 16.8 the function f maps the unit interval into itself. A mapping is *continuous* if points that are "close" to each other are mapped into other points that are "close" to each other.

The *Brouwer fixed-point theorem* considers mappings defined on certain kinds of sets. These sets are required to be closed, bounded, and convex. Perhaps the simplest way to describe such sets is to say that they look like

FIGURE 16.8

A GRAPHICAL ILLUSTRATION OF BROUWER'S FIXED-POINT THEOREM

Since any continuous function must cross the 45° line somewhere in the unit square, this function must have a point for which $f(x^*) = x^*$. This point is called a "fixed point."

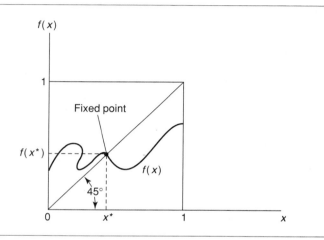

(n-dimensional analogies of) soap bubbles. They are *closed* in the sense that they contain their boundaries; the sets are *bounded* because none of their dimensions is infinitely large; and they are *convex* because they have no "holes" in them. A technical description of the properties of such sets can be found in any elementary topology book.[13] For our purposes, however, it is only necessary to recognize that Brouwer's theorem is intended to apply to certain types of conveniently shaped sets. In order to use the theorem to prove the existence of equilibrium prices, therefore, we must first describe the set of points that has these desirable properties.

Proof of the Existence of Equilibrium Prices

The key to applying Brouwer's theorem to the exchange model just developed is to choose a suitable way for "normalizing" prices. Since only relative prices matter in the exchange model, it is convenient to assume that prices have been defined so that the sum of all prices is 1. Mathematically,

---

[3] For a development of the mathematics used in general equilibrium theory, see G. Debreu, *Theory of Value* (New York: John Wiley & Sons, 1959), chap. 1.

for any arbitrary set of prices $(P_1, \ldots, P_n)$, we instead can deal with *normalized* prices of the form[14]

$$P_i' = \frac{P_i}{\sum\limits_{i=1}^{n} P_i}.$$

(16.26)

These new prices will retain their original relative values $(P_i'/P_j' = P_i/P_j)$ and will sum to 1:

$$\sum_{i=1}^{n} P_i' = 1.$$

(16.27)

Because of the homogeneity of degree zero of all the excess demand functions, this kind of normalization always can be made. Hence, for the remainder of this proof, it will be assumed that the feasible set of prices (call this set S) is composed of all possible combinations of n nonnegative numbers that sum to 1. To avoid complex notation, we shall drop the special symbols we have been using for such prices.

This set, S, is the one to which we can apply Brouwer's theorem. The set S is closed, bounded, and convex.[15] To apply Brouwer's theorem, it is necessary to define a continuous mapping of S into itself. By a judicious choice of this mapping, it is possible to show that the fixed point dictated by the theorem is in fact a set of equilibrium relative prices.

Free Goods

Before demonstrating the details of the proof, it is necessary to redefine what is meant by an "equilibrium set of prices." We do not really require that excess demand be equal to zero in every market for an equilibrium. Rather, goods may exist for which the markets are in equilibrium but for which the available supply exceeds demand; there is negative excess demand. For this to be the case, however, it is necessary that the price of this particular good be zero. Hence, the equilibrium conditions of Equation 16.24 may be rewritten to take account of such *free goods:*

$$ED_i(P^*) = 0 \text{ for } P_i^* > 0$$

$$ED_i(P^*) \leq 0 \text{ for } P_i^* = 0.$$

(16.28)

Notice that such a set of equilibrium prices continues to obey Walras' law.

---

[14] One additional assumption must be made here; that is, at least one of the prices is nonzero. In economic terms this means that at least one good is scarce. Without this assumption a normalization of prices would not be possible—but, then again, studying economics in such a case would be unnecessary, since there would be no economic problem of scarcity.

[15] In two dimensions the set simply would be a straight line joining the coordinates (0, 1) and (1, 0). In three dimensions the set would be a triangular-shaped plane with vertices at (0, 0, 1), (0, 1, 0), and (1, 0, 0). It is easy to see that each of these sets is closed, bounded, and convex.

Mapping the Set of Prices into Itself

Using this definition of equilibrium and remembering that prices have been normalized to sum to 1, it is now possible to construct a continuous function that transforms one set of prices into another. The function to be defined builds on the Walrasian idea that in order to achieve equilibrium, prices of goods that are in excess demand should be raised, whereas those in excess supply should have their prices lowered. Hence, define the mapping $F(P)$ for any (normalized) set of prices, P, such that the ith component of $F(P)$, denoted by $F^i(P)$, is given by

$$F^i(P) = P_i + ED_i(P) \qquad (16.29)$$

for all i. The mapping then performs the necessary task of appropriately raising and lowering prices. If, at P_i, good i is in excess demand $[ED_i(P) > 0]$, the price P_i is raised, whereas if excess demand is negative, P_i is reduced. Because the excess demand functions are assumed to be continuous, this mapping also will be continuous. Two problems with the mapping of Equation 16.29 remain. First, nothing ensures that the new prices will be nonnegative. Hence, the mapping must be redefined to be

$$F^i(P) = \text{Max} \, [P_i + ED_i(P), \, 0] \qquad (16.30)$$

for all i. The term "Max" here simply means that the new prices defined by the mapping F must be either positive or zero; prices are not allowed to go negative. The mapping of Equation 16.30 is also continuous.

A second problem with the mapping of Equation 16.30 is that the recalculated prices are not necessarily normalized; they will not sum to 1. It would be a simple matter, however, to normalize these new prices so that they do sum to 1.[16] To avoid introducing additional notation, assume that this normalization has been done and therefore that

$$\sum_{i=1}^{n} F^i(P) = 1. \qquad (16.31)$$

---

[16] In order to accomplish this normalization, it is first necessary to show that not all of the transformed prices will be zero; it is necessary to show that $P_i + ED_i(P) > 0$ for some i. This can be proved by contradiction. Assume that $P_i + ED_i(P) \leq 0$ for all i. Multiply this expression by P_i and sum over all values of i, giving

$$\sum_{i=1}^{n} P_i^2 + \sum_{i=1}^{n} P_i ED_i(P) \leq 0.$$

But

$$\sum_{i=1}^{n} P_i ED_i = 0$$

by Walras' law. Hence,

$$\sum_{i=1}^{n} P_i^2 \leq 0$$

and this implies that $P_i = 0$ for all i. However, we have already ruled out this situation (see footnote 14), and therefore we have proved that at least one of the transformed prices must be positive.

Application of Brouwer's Theorem

With this normalization, then, F satisfies the conditions of the Brouwer fixed-point theorem. It is a continuous mapping of the set S into itself. Hence, there exists a point (P^*) that is mapped into itself. For this point,

$$P_i^* = \text{Max}\ [P_i^* + ED_i(P^*), 0] \tag{16.32}$$

for all i.

But this says that P^* is an equilibrium set of prices: for $P_i^* > 0$,

$$P_i^* = P_i^* + ED_i(P^*)$$

or

$$ED_i(P^*) = 0; \tag{16.33}$$

and for $P_i^* = 0$,

$$P_i^* + ED_i(P^*) \le 0$$

or

$$ED_i(P^*) \le 0. \tag{16.34}$$

Therefore, it has been shown that the set of excess demand functions does in fact possess an equilibrium solution consisting of nonnegative prices. The simple exchange model developed here is consistent in that the market supply and demand functions necessarily have a solution. The homogeneity and continuity properties of the demand functions and the ability of Walras' law to tie together supply and demand are jointly responsible for this result.[17]

Generalizations

Although this proof is a relatively old one in the field of general equilibrium analysis, it does exhibit features of much of the more recent literature in this field. In particular, practically all modern proofs use Walras' law and rely on some type of fixed-point theorem. More recent work has tended to focus on ways in which the proof of the existence of general equilibrium prices can be generalized to situations involving more complex supply assumptions and on how equilibrium prices can actually be computed. In later chapters of this book, we will examine some of these alternative supply assumptions such as cases of imperfect competition and problems caused by "public goods" (which we define in the next chapter). The extensions to this chapter show some of the ways in which general equilibrium models have been applied using computers.

---

[17] The proof used in this section represents a simplified (and considerably vulgarized) version of a proof first presented by J. Kemeny and J. L. Snell, *Mathematical Models in the Social Sciences* (New York: Blaisdell Publishing Co., 1962), pp. 35–41.

EXAMPLE 16.4

A GENERAL EQUILIBRIUM WITH THREE GOODS

The economy of Oz is composed only of three precious metals: (1) silver, (2) gold, and (3) platinum. There are 10 (thousand) ounces of each metal available. The demand for gold is given by

$$D_2 = -2\frac{P_2}{P_1} + \frac{P_3}{P_1} + 11 \qquad (16.35)$$

and for platinum by

$$D_3 = -\frac{P_2}{P_1} - 2\frac{P_3}{P_1} + 18.$$

Notice that the demands for gold and platinum depend on the relative prices of the two goods and that these demand functions are homogeneous of degree zero in all three prices. Notice also that we have not written out the demand function for silver but, as we will show, it can be derived from Walras' law.

Equilibrium in the gold and platinum markets requires that demand equal supply in both markets simultaneously:

$$-2\frac{P_2}{P_1} + \frac{P_3}{P_1} + 11 = 10 \qquad (16.36)$$

$$-\frac{P_2}{P_1} - 2\frac{P_3}{P_1} + 18 = 10.$$

This system of simultaneous equations can be solved rather easily as

$$\frac{P_2}{P_1} = 2 \qquad \frac{P_3}{P_1} = 3. \qquad (16.37)$$

In equilibrium, therefore, gold will have a price twice that of silver and platinum a price three times that of silver. The price of platinum will be 1.5 times that of gold.

Walras' Law and the Demand for Silver. Since Walras' law must hold in this economy, we know

$$P_1 ED_1 = -P_2 ED_2 - P_3 ED_3. \qquad (16.38)$$

Solving Equations 16.36 for the excess demands (by moving the fixed supplies to the left-hand side) and substituting into Walras' law yields

$$P_1 ED_1 = 2\frac{P_2^2}{P_1} - \frac{P_2 P_3}{P_1} - P_2 + \frac{P_2 P_3}{P_1} + 2\frac{P_3^2}{P_1} - 8P_3 \qquad (16.39)$$

or

$$ED_1 = 2\frac{P_2^2}{P_1^2} + 2\frac{P_3^2}{P_1^2} - \frac{P_2}{P_1} - 8\frac{P_3}{P_1}.$$ (16.40)

As expected, this function is homogeneous of degree zero in the relative prices, and the market for silver is also in equilibrium ($ED_1 = 0$) at the relative prices computed previously. (Check this yourself!)

A Change in Supply. If gold supply decreases to 7 and platinum supply increases to 11, we would expect relative prices to change. It seems likely that the relative price of gold will rise. Similarly, since the rise in gold price will reduce the demand for platinum and platinum supply has increased, the relative price of platinum should fall. But that will reduce the demand for gold, so the end result is unclear—clearly, a simultaneous solution is called for. In fact, the solution to

$$-2\frac{P_2}{P_1} + \frac{P_3}{P_1} + 11 = 7$$ (16.41)

and

$$-\frac{P_2}{P_1} - 2\frac{P_3}{P_1} + 18 = 11$$

is

$$\frac{P_2}{P_1} = 3 \qquad \frac{P_3}{P_1} = 2.$$ (16.42)

So the price of gold rises relative to both silver and platinum. The price of platinum falls relative to that of silver. All of these effects can only be captured in a simultaneous model.

QUERY: Is the silver market still in equilibrium given the new supplies of gold and platinum?

MONEY IN GENERAL EQUILIBRIUM MODELS

Thus far in this chapter, we showed how competitive markets can establish a set of relative prices at which all markets are in equilibrium simultaneously. At several places we stressed that such competitive market forces determine only relative, not absolute, prices and that to examine how the absolute price level is determined we must introduce money into our models. Although a complete examination of this topic is more properly studied as part of macroeconomics, here we can briefly explore some questions of the role of money in a competitive economy that relate directly to microeconomics.

Money serves two primary functions in any economy: (1) It facilitates transactions by providing an accepted medium of exchange; and (2) it acts as a store of value so that economic actors can better allocate their spending decisions over time. Any commodity can serve as "money" provided it is generally accepted for exchange purposes and is durable from period to period. Today most economies tend to use government-created (fiat) money because the costs associated with its production (e.g., printing paper with portraits of past or present rulers or keeping records on magnetic tape) are very low. In earlier times, however, commodity money was common with the particular good chosen ranging from the familiar (gold and silver) to the obscure and even bizarre (sharks' teeth or, on the island of Yap, large stone wheels). Societies probably choose the particular form that their money will take as the result of a wide variety of economic, historical, and political forces.

Nature and Function of Money

One of the most important functions usually played by money is to act as an accounting standard or *numéraire*. In the previous section we showed that a competitive market system for n goods can generally arrive at an equilibrium set of prices $(P_1, \ldots, P_n)$ at which all markets are in equilibrium. But these prices are unique only up to a common multiple since market forces of demand and supply can only determine relative, not absolute, prices. In principle any good (say, good k) could be chosen as an accounting standard, and we could always refer to the prices of the other $n-1$ goods in terms of this good:

Money as the Accounting Standard

$$P'_1 = \frac{P_1}{P_k}$$

$$P'_2 = \frac{P_2}{P_k} \qquad (16.43)$$

$$\vdots$$

$$P'_n = \frac{P_n}{P_k}.$$

Since it is always true that

$$\frac{P_i}{P_j} = \frac{P_i/P_k}{P_j/P_k} = \frac{P'_i}{P'_j} \qquad (16.44)$$

for any pair of goods i and j, relative prices will be unaffected by which good (or possibly basket of goods) is chosen as the accounting standard. For example, if 1 apple (good i) exchanges for 2 plums (good j),

$$\frac{P_i}{P_j} = \frac{2}{1}, \qquad (16.45)$$

and it makes little difference how those prices are quoted. If, for example, a society chooses clams as a unit of account, an apple might exchange for 4 clams and a plum for 2 clams. Then, if we let clams be the *numéraire* good k,

$$\frac{P'_i}{P'_j} = \frac{P_i/P_k}{P_j/P_k} = \frac{4}{2} = \frac{2}{1} = \frac{P_i}{P_j}. \tag{16.46}$$

We could change from counting in clams to counting in sharks' teeth (good 1) by knowing that 10 sharks' teeth exchange for 1 clam. Then the price of our goods in sharks' teeth would be

$$P''_i = \frac{P_i}{P_k} \cdot \frac{P_k}{P_1} = 4 \cdot 10 = 40$$

and   (16.47)

$$P''_j = \frac{P_j}{P_k} \cdot \frac{P_k}{P_1} = 2 \cdot 10 = 20,$$

and 1 apple (which costs 40 teeth) would still exchange for 2 plums, which cost 20 teeth each.

Of course, using clams or sharks' teeth is not very common. Instead, societies usually adopt fiat money as their accounting standard. An apple might exchange for half a piece of paper picturing George Washington (i.e., $.50) and a plum for one-fourth of such a piece of paper ($.25). Thus, with this monetary standard, the relative price remains two for one. Choice of an accounting standard does not, however, necessarily dictate any particular absolute price level. An apple might exchange for 4 clams or 400, but as long as a plum exchanges for half as many clams, relative prices will be unaffected by the absolute level that prevails. But absolute price levels are obviously important, especially to individuals who wish to use money as a store of value. A person with a large investment in clams obviously cares about how many apples they will buy. Although a complete theoretical treatment of the price level issue is beyond the scope of this book, we do offer some brief comments on it here.

Commodity Money   In an economy where money is produced in a way similar to any other good (gold is mined, clams are dug, or sharks are caught), the relative price of money is determined like any other relative price—by the forces of demand and supply. Economic forces that affect either the demand or supply of money will also affect these relative prices. For example, Spanish importation of gold from the New World during the fifteenth and sixteenth centuries greatly expanded gold supplies and caused the relative price of gold to fall. That is, the prices of all other goods rose relative to that of gold—there was general inflation in the prices of practically everything in terms of gold.

Similar effects would arise from changes in any factor that affected the equilibrium price for the good chosen as money.

For the case of fiat money produced by the government, the analysis can be extended a bit. In this situation the government is the sole supplier of money and can generally choose how much it wishes to produce.[18] What effects will the level of money production have on the real economy? In general, the situation would seem to be identical to that for commodity money. A change in money supply will disturb the general equilibrium of all relative prices, and although it seems likely that an expansion in supply will lower the relative price of money (that is, result in an inflation in the money prices of other goods), any more precise prediction would seem to depend on the results of a detailed general equilibrium model.

Fiat Money and the Classical Dichotomy

Beginning with David Hume, however, classical economists argued that money (especially fiat money) differs from other economic goods and should be considered to be outside the real economic system of demand, supply, and relative price determination. In this view the economy can be dichotomized into a real sector in which relative prices are determined and a monetary sector where the absolute price level (that is, the value of fiat money) is set. Money, therefore, acts only as a "veil" for real economic activity—the quantity of money available has no effect on the real sector.

Unfortunately, developing general equilibrium models that exhibit the classical dichotomy between monetary and real sectors presents some conceptual difficulties. If preferences for money are treated like those for any other good (since money makes transactions easier, it also yields utility), then only special types of preferences result in the classical dichotomy. Specifically, if individuals' marginal rates of substitution (MRS) between any two real commodities are assumed to be independent of the quantity of money they have (and a similar assumption is made about firms' rates of product transformation between these goods), then relative prices determined by the forces of supply and demand will be independent of the quantity of money in circulation. In the absence of such assumptions, however, individuals' relative preferences and firms' relative productive abilities will be affected by the quantity of money, and the classical dichotomy will not exist. Some of the problems at the end of this chapter explore these various possibilities.

Money, Utility, and Production

---

[18] By being a monopoly supplier of money (which is produced at low cost), the government may make long-run profits from its seigniorage activities.

**Transactions
Demand**

A limiting case of these special assumptions about preferences and technology is that the quantity of money has no effect on real forces—that is, the quantity of money in circulation does not enter either individuals' utility functions or firms' production functions. So why do individuals and firms use money? One possible assumption is that these actors "need" money to make transactions even though money *per se* yields no utility or productivity. If, for example, there are two nonmonetary goods (X and Y) in the economy, total transactions per period are given by $P_X^* X^* + P_Y^* Y^*$ (where P_X^* and P_Y^* are equilibrium prices associated with the equilibrium quantities X^* and Y^*). Conducting these transactions requires that a certain fraction (say, α) of their total value be available as circulating money. The demand for money is therefore

$$D_M = \alpha(P_X^* X^* + P_Y^* Y^*), \tag{16.48}$$

and monetary equilibrium requires that

$$D_M = S_M, \tag{16.49}$$

where S_M is the quantity of money supplied by the government.

A doubling of the money supply would throw this system into disequilibrium; at the prior equilibrium level of transactions for X and Y, there would now be an excess supply of money, and according to Walras' law (Equation 16.25), this would be balanced by a net excess demand for goods.

Equilibrium could be restored in this economy by a precise doubling of equilibrium nominal prices. This would double the transactions demand for money, but, because relative prices would be unchanged, it would not alter equilibrium quantities of X and Y:

$$\begin{aligned} D_M' &= \alpha(2P_X^* X^* + 2P_Y^* Y^*) \\ &= 2\alpha(P_X^* X^* + P_Y^* Y^*) \\ &= 2D_M. \end{aligned} \tag{16.50}$$

In this system, therefore, nominal equilibrium prices are proportional to the money supply, and the classical dichotomy is complete.[19] Money is truly a veil—it has no effect on the real economy.

---

[19] This leads directly to the Quantity Theory of the Demand for Money, first suggested by Hume:

$$D_M = \frac{1}{V} \cdot P \cdot Q,$$

where D_M is the demand for money, V is the velocity of monetary circulation ($= 1/\alpha$ in our model), P is the overall price level, and Q is a measure of the quantity of transactions (often approximated by real GDP).

SUMMARY

In this chapter we have showed how the partial equilibrium model of competitive price determination that we developed in Chapter 14 can be generalized to represent multiple markets. The principal complication encountered in making this generalization is the need to take into account relationships among many markets for different goods and factors of production. Our examination of such issues reached the following conclusions:

- Simple Marshallian models of supply and demand in several markets may not in themselves be adequate for addressing general equilibrium questions because they do not provide a direct way of tying the markets together and illustrating the feedback effects that occur when market equilibria change.

- A simple general equilibrium model of relative price determination for two goods can be developed using an indifference curve map to represent demands for the goods and the production possibility frontier to represent supply. This model is useful for examining comparative statics questions in a general equilibrium context.

- Construction of the production possibility frontier from the Edgeworth box diagram also permits an

integration of factor markets into a simple general equilibrium model. The shape of the production possibility frontier illustrates how reallocating factors of production among outputs affects the marginal costs associated with producing those outputs. Specifically, the slope of the production possibility frontier—the rate of product transformation—measures the ratio of the two goods' marginal costs.

- Whether a set of competitive prices exists that will equilibrate many markets simultaneously is a complex theoretical question. Such a set of prices will generally exist if demand and supply functions are suitably continuous and if Walras' law (which requires that net excess demand be zero at any set of prices) holds.

- Incorporating money into a general equilibrium model is a major focus of macroeconomic research. In some cases such monetary models will exhibit the classical dichotomy in that monetary forces will have no effect on relative prices observed in the "real" economy. These cases are rather restrictive, however, so the extent to which the classical dichotomy holds in the real world remains an unresolved issue.

PROBLEMS

16.1

Suppose the production possibility frontier for cheeseburgers (C) and milkshakes (M) is given by

$$C + 2M = 600.$$

a. Graph this function.
b. Assuming that people prefer to eat two cheeseburgers with every milkshake, how much of each product will be produced? Indicate this point on your graph.
c. Given that this fast-food economy is operating efficiently, what price ratio (P_C/P_M) must prevail?

16.2

Suppose the production possibility frontier for guns (X) and butter (Y) is given by

$$X^2 + 2Y^2 = 900.$$

a. Graph this frontier.
b. If individuals always prefer consumption bundles in which $Y = 2X$, how much X and Y will be produced?
c. At the point described in part (b), what will be the RPT and hence what price ratio will cause production to take place at that point? (This slope should

be approximated by considering small changes in X and Y around the optimal point.)

d. Show your solution on the figure from part (a).

16.3

Suppose an economy produces only two goods, X and Y. Production of good X is given by

$$X = K_X^{1/2} L_X^{1/2},$$

where K_X and L_X are the inputs of capital and labor devoted to X production. The production function for good Y is given by

$$Y = K_Y^{1/3} L_Y^{2/3},$$

where K_Y and L_Y are the inputs of capital and labor devoted to Y production. The supply of capital is fixed at 100 units and the supply of labor is fixed at 200 units. Hence, if both units are fully employed,

$$K_X + K_Y = K_T = 100$$

$$L_X + L_Y = L_T = 200.$$

Using this information, complete the following questions.

a. Show how the capital-labor ratio in X production $(K_X/L_X = k_X)$ must be related to the capital-labor ratio in Y production $(K_Y/L_Y = k_Y)$ if production is to be efficient.

b. Show that the capital-labor ratios for the two goods are constrained by

$$\alpha_X k_X + (1 - \alpha_X)k_Y = \frac{K_T}{L_T} = \frac{100}{200} = \frac{1}{2},$$

where α_X is the share of total labor devoted to X production [that is, $\alpha_X = L_X/L_T = L_X/(L_X + L_Y)$].

c. Use the information from parts (a) and (b) to compute the efficient capital-labor ratio for good X for any value of α_X between 0 and 1.

d. Graph the Edgeworth production box for this economy and use the information from part (c) to develop a rough sketch of the production contract curve.

e. Which good, X or Y, is capital intensive in this economy? Explain why the production possibility curve for the economy is concave.

f. Calculate the mathematical form of the production possibility frontier for this economy (this calcula-

tion may be rather tedious!). Show that, as expected, this is a concave function.

16.4

The purpose of this problem is to examine the relationship among returns to scale, factor intensity, and the shape of the production possibility frontier.

Suppose there are fixed supplies of capital and labor to be allocated between the production of good X and good Y. The production function for X is given by

$$X = K^\alpha L^\beta$$

and for Y by

$$Y = K^\gamma L^\delta,$$

where the parameters α, β, γ, δ will take on different values throughout this problem.

Using either intuition, a computer, or a formal mathematical approach, derive the production possibility frontier for X and Y in the following cases:

a. $\alpha = \beta = \gamma = \delta = \frac{1}{2}$.

b. $\alpha = \beta = \frac{1}{2}$, $\gamma = \frac{1}{3}$, $\delta = \frac{2}{3}$.

c. $\alpha = \beta = \frac{1}{2}$, $\gamma = \delta = \frac{2}{3}$.

d. $\alpha = \beta = \gamma = \delta = \frac{2}{3}$.

e. $\alpha = \beta = .6$, $\gamma = .2$, $\delta = 1.0$.

f. $\alpha = \beta = .7$, $\gamma = .6$, $\delta = .8$.

Do increasing returns to scale always lead to a convex production possibility frontier? Explain.

16.5

The country of Podunk produces only wheat and cloth, using as inputs land and labor. Both are produced by constant returns-to-scale production functions. Wheat is the relatively land-intensive commodity.

a. Explain in words, or with diagrams, how the price of wheat relative to cloth (p) determines the land-labor ratio in each of the two industries.

b. Suppose that p is given by external forces (this would be the case if Podunk were a "small" country trading freely with a "large" world). Show, using the Edgeworth box, that if the supply of labor increases in Podunk, the output of cloth will rise and the output of wheat will fall.

16.6

Suppose two individuals (Smith and Jones) each have 10 hours of labor to devote to producing either ice cream (X) or chicken soup (Y). Smith's utility function is given by

$$U_S = X^{.3}Y^{.7}$$

whereas Jones' is given by

$$U_J = X^{.5}Y^{.5}.$$

The individuals do not care whether they produce X or Y, and the production function for each good is given by

$$X = 2L$$

$$Y = 3L,$$

where L is the total labor devoted to production of each good. Using this information,
a. What must the price ratio, P_X/P_Y, be?
b. Given this price ratio, how much X and Y will Smith and Jones demand? (*Hint:* Set the wage equal to 1 here.)
c. How should labor be allocated between X and Y to satisfy the demand calculated in part (b)?

16.7

Suppose there are only three goods (X_1, X_2, and X_3) in an economy and that the excess demand functions for X_2 and X_3 are given by

$$ED_2 = -3P_2/P_1 + 2P_3/P_1 - 1$$

$$ED_3 = 4P_2/P_1 - 2P_3/P_1 - 2.$$

a. Show that these functions are homogeneous of degree zero in P_1, P_2, and P_3.

b. Use Walras' law to show that if $ED_2 = ED_3 = 0$, ED_1 also must be 0. Can you also use Walras' law to calculate ED_1?
c. Solve this system of equations for the equilibrium relative prices P_2/P_1 and P_3/P_1. What is the equilibrium value for P_3/P_2?

16.8

Use the simple two-good model of general equilibrium pricing developed in this chapter to illustrate a situation in which there will be two equilibrium price ratios by relaxing the assumption that the production possibility frontier is concave. Explain your result intuitively.

16.9

Return to Problem 16.6 and now assume that Smith and Jones conduct their exchanges in paper money. The total supply of such money is $60, and each individual wishes to hold a stock of money equal to $\frac{1}{4}$ of the value of transactions made per period.
a. What will the money wage rate be in this model? What will the nominal prices of X and Y be?
b. Suppose the money supply increases to $90. How will your answers to part (a) change? Does this economy exhibit the classical dichotomy between its real and monetary sectors?

16.10

Suppose silver is used as the medium of exchange in the economy described in Example 16.4. Does this economy exhibit the classical dichotomy?

SUGGESTED READINGS

Arrow, K. J., and F. H. Hahn. *General Competitive Analysis.* Amsterdam: North-Holland Publishing Co., 1978. Chaps. 1, 2, and 4.
Sophisticated mathematical treatment of general equilibrium analysis. Each chapter has a good literary introduction.

Debreu, G. "Existence of Competitive Equilibrium." In K. J. Arrow and M. D. Intriligator, eds. *Handbook of Mathematical Economics.* Vol. 2. Amsterdam: North-Holland Publishing Co., 1982, pp. 697–743.
Fairly difficult survey of existence proofs based on fixed-point theorems. Contains a comprehensive set of references.

Debreu, G. *Theory of Value.* New York: John Wiley & Sons, 1959.
Basic reference, difficult mathematics. Does have a good introductory chapter on the mathematical tools used.

Harberger, A. "The Incidence of the Corporate Income Tax." *Journal of Political Economy* (January/February 1962): 215–240.
Nice use of a two-sector general equilibrium model to examine the final burden of a tax on capital.

Mas-Colell, A., M. D. Whinston, and J. R. Green. *Microeconomic Theory.* Oxford: Oxford University Press, 1995.

Part Four is devoted to general equilibrium analysis. Chapters 17 (existence) and 18 (connections to game theory) are especially useful. Chapters 19 and 20 pursue several of the topics in the Extensions to this chapter.

Scarf, H. E. "The Computation of Equilibrium Prices: An Exposition." In K. J. Arrow and M. D. Intriligator, eds. *Handbook of Mathematical Economics*. Vol. 2. Amsterdam: North-Holland Publishing Co., 1982, pp. 1007–1061.

Illustrates Scarf's algorithm for computing equilibrium prices. This method is widely used in computer modeling.

Shoven, J. B., and J. Whalley. "Applied General Equilibrium Models of Taxation and International Trade." *Journal of Economic Literature* (September 1984): 1007–1051.

Good survey of applications of large-scale general equilibrium models. Nice discussion of the theoretical foundations of the models and how these affect the results obtained.

EXTENSIONS

Computable General Equilibrium Models

Recent improvements in computer technology have made it feasible to develop computable general equilibrium (CGE) models of considerable detail. These may involve literally hundreds of industries and individuals, each with somewhat different technologies or preferences. The general methodology employed with these models is to assume various forms for production and utility functions, then choose particular parameters of those functions based on empirical evidence. Numerical general equilibrium solutions are then generated by the models and compared to real-world data. After "calibrating" the models to reflect reality, various policy elements in the models are varied as a way of providing general equilibrium estimates of the overall impact of those policy changes. In this extension we briefly review a few of these types of applications.

E16.1 Trade Models

One of the first uses for applied general equilibrium models was to the study of the impact of trade barriers. Because much of the debate over the effects of such barriers (or of their reduction) focuses on impacts on real wages, such general equilibrium models are especially appropriate for the task.

Two unusual features tend to characterize such models. First, because the models often have an explicit focus on domestic versus foreign production of specific goods, it is necessary to introduce a large degree of product differentiation into individuals' utility functions. That is, "U.S. textiles" are treated as being different from "Mexican textiles" even though in most trade theories, textiles might be treated as homogeneous goods. Modelers have found that they must allow for only limited substitutability among such goods if their models are to replicate actual trade patterns.

A second feature of CGE models of trade is the interest in incorporating increasing returns-to-scale technologies into their production sectors. This permits the models to capture one of the primary advantages of trade to smaller economies. Unfortunately, introduction of the increasing returns-to-scale assumption also requires that the models depart from perfectly competitive, price-taking assumptions. Often some type of markup pricing, together with Cournot-type imperfect competition (see Chapter 19), is used for this purpose.

North American Free Trade

Some of the most extensive CGE modeling efforts have been devoted to analyzing the impact of the North American Free Trade Agreement (NAFTA). Virtually all of these models find that the agreement offered welfare gains to all of the countries involved. Gains for Mexico accrued primarily because of reduced U.S. trade barriers on Mexican textiles and steel. Gains to Canada came primarily from an increase ability to benefit from economies of scale in certain key industries. Brown (1992) surveys a number of CGE models of North American free trade and concludes that gains on the order of 2–3 percent of GDP might be experienced by both of these countries. For the United States, gains from NAFTA might be considerably smaller, but even in this case, significant welfare gains were found to be associated with the increased competitiveness of domestic markets.

E16.2 Tax and Transfer Models

A second major use of CGE models is to evaluate potential changes in a nation's tax and transfer policies. For these applications, considerable care must be taken in modeling the factor supply side of the models. For example, at the margin, the effects of rates of income taxation (either positive or negative) can have important labor supply effects that only a general equilibrium approach can model properly. Similarly, tax/transfer policy can also affect savings and investment decisions, and for these two it may be necessary to adopt more detailed modeling procedures (for example, differentiating individuals by age so as to examine effects of retirement programs).

The Dutch MIMIC Model

Probably the most elaborate tax/transfer CGE model is that developed by the Dutch Central Planning Bureau—the Micro Macro Model to Analyze the Institutional Context (MIMIC). This model puts emphasis on social welfare programs and on some of the problems they seek to ameliorate (most notably unemployment, which is missing from many other CGE models). Gelauff and Graaflund (1994) summarize the main features of the MIMIC model. They also use it to analyze such policy proposals as the 1990s tax reform in the Netherlands and potential changes to the generous unemployment and disability benefits in that country.

E16.3 Environmental Models

CGE models are also appropriate for understanding the ways in which environmental policies may affect the economy. In such applications the production of pollutants is considered as a major side effect of the other economic activities in the model. By specifying environmental goals in terms of a given reduction in these pollutants, it is possible to use these models to study the economic costs of various strategies for achieving these goals. One advantage of the CGE approach is to provide some evidence on the impact of environmental policies on income distribution—a topic largely omitted from more narrow, industry-based modeling efforts.

Assessing CO_2 Reduction Strategies

Concern over the possibility that CO_2 emissions in various energy-using activities may be contributing to global warming has led to a number of plans for reducing these emissions. Because the repercussions of such reductions may be quite widespread and varied, CGE modeling is one of the preferred assessment methods. Perhaps the most elaborate such model is that developed by the OECD—the General Equilibrium Environmental Model (GREEN) model. The basic structure of this model is described by Burniaux, Nicoletti, and Oliviera-Martins (1992). The model has been used to simulate various policy options that might be adopted by European nations to reduce CO_2 emissions, such as institution of a carbon tax or increasingly stringent emissions regulations for automobiles and power plants. In general, these simulations suggest that economic costs of these policies would be relatively modest given the level of restrictions currently anticipated. But most of the policies would have adverse distributional effects that may require further attention through government transfer policy.

E16.4 Regional and Urban Models

A final way in which CGE models can be used is to examine economic issues that have important spatial dimensions. Construction of such models requires careful attention to issues of transportation costs and moving costs associated with labor mobility, since particular interest is focused on where transactions occur. Incorporation of these costs into CGE models is in many ways equivalent to adding extra levels of product differentiation because these affect the relative prices of otherwise homogeneous goods. Calculation of equilibria in regional markets can be especially sensitive to how transport costs are specified.

Changing Government Procurement

CGE regional models have been widely used to examine the local impact of major changes in government spending policies. For example, Holtman, Robinson, and Subramanian (1996) use a CGE model to evaluate the regional impact of reduced defense expenditures on the California economy. They find that the size of the effects depends importantly on the assumed costs of migration for skilled workers. A similar finding is reported by Bernat and Hanson (1995), who examine possible reductions in U.S. farm-price-support payments. Though such reductions would offer overall efficiency gains to the economy, they could have significant negative impacts on rural areas.

References

Bernat, G. A., and K. Hanson. "Regional Impacts of Farm Programs: A Top-Down CGE Analysis." *Review of Regional Studies* (Winter 1995): 331–350.

Brown, D. K. "The Impact of North American Free Trade Area: Applied General Equilibrium Models," in N. Lustig, B. P. Bosworth, and R. Z. Lawrence, eds. *North American Free Trade: Assessing the Impact.* Washington, DC: The Brookings Institution, 1992, pp. 26–68.

Burniaux, J. M., G. Nicoletti, and J. Oliviera-Martins. "Green: A Global Model for Quantifying the Costs of Policies to Curb CO_2 Emissions." *OECD Economic Studies* (Winter 1992): 49–92.

Gelauff, G. M. M, and J. J. Graaflund. *Modeling Welfare State Reform.* Amsterdam: North Holland Publishing Co., 1994.

Hoffman, S., S. Robinson, and S. Subramanian. "The Role of Defense Cuts in the California Recession: Computable General Equilibrium Models and Interstate Fair Mobility." *Journal of Regional Science* (November 1996): 571–595.

CHAPTER 17

THE EFFICIENCY OF
PERFECT COMPETITION

Although most people recognize the equilibrium properties of the competitive price system (after all, prices usually do not fluctuate widely from day to day), they see little overall pattern to the resulting allocation of resources. The relationships described by the competitive model presented in the previous chapter are so complex that it is hard to believe that any desirable outcome will emerge from the chaos. This view provides an open-ended rationale to tinker with the system—since the results of market forces are chaotic, surely human societies can do better through careful planning.

It took the genius of Adam Smith to challenge this view, which was probably the prevalent one in the eighteenth century. To Smith, the competitive market system represented the polar opposite from chaos. Rather, it provided a powerful "invisible hand" that ensured that resources would find their way to where they were most valued, thereby enhancing the "wealth" of the nation. In Smith's view, reliance on the economic self-interest of individuals and firms would result in a (perhaps surprisingly) desirable social outcome.

SMITH'S INVISIBLE HAND HYPOTHESIS

Smith's initial insights gave rise to modern welfare economics. Specifically, his widely quoted "invisible hand" image provided the impetus for what is now called the "fundamental theorem" of welfare economics—that there is a close correspondence between the efficient allocation of resources and the competitive pricing of these resources. In this chapter we will investigate this correspondence in some detail. We begin by defining economic efficiency in a variety of contexts. These definitions, all of which draw on the work of the nineteenth-century economist Vilfred Pareto, have already been described briefly in earlier chapters; our goal here is to draw these discussions together and illustrate their underlying relationship to the competitive allocation of resources.

PARETO EFFICIENCY

We begin with Pareto's definition of economic efficiency.

DEFINITION

Pareto Efficient Allocation   An allocation of resources is *Pareto efficient* if it is not possible (through further reallocations) to make one person better off without making someone else worse off.

The Pareto definition then identifies particular allocations as being "inefficient" if unambiguous improvements are possible. Notice that the definition does not require interperson comparisons of utility. "Improvements" are defined by individuals themselves.

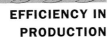

EFFICIENCY IN PRODUCTION

In simple terms, an economy is efficient in production if it is on its production possibility frontier. Formally, we can use Pareto's terminology to define productive efficiency as follows:

DEFINITION

Productive Efficiency   An allocation of resources is *efficient in production* (or "technically efficient") if no further reallocation would permit more of one good to be produced without necessarily reducing the output of some other good.

As for Pareto efficiency itself, it is perhaps easiest to grasp this definition by studying its converse—an allocation would be inefficient if it were possible to move existing resources around a bit and get additional amounts of one good and no less of anything else. With technically efficient allocations, no such unambiguous improvements are possible. The trade-offs among outputs necessitated by movements along the production possibility frontier reflect the technically efficient nature of all of the allocations on the frontier.

Technical efficiency is an obvious precondition for overall Pareto efficiency. Suppose resources were allocated so that production was inefficient; that is, production was occurring at a point inside the production possibility frontier. It would then be possible to produce more of at least one good and no less of anything else. This increased output could be given to some lucky person making him or her better off (and no one else worse off). Hence, inefficiency in production is also Pareto inefficiency. As we shall see in the next section, however, technical efficiency does not guarantee Pareto efficiency. An economy can be efficient at producing the wrong goods—

devoting all available resources to producing left shoes would be a technically efficient use of those resources, but surely some Pareto improvement could be found in which everyone would be better off. Before discussing this issue, however, we must examine the conditions required for productive efficiency more thoroughly.

A discussion of efficiency in production and its relationship to the production possibility frontier is somewhat more complex than our simple presentation in Chapter 16 might imply. Because production is divided among many firms, we must be concerned not only with the ways in which a single firm uses its resources (as we essentially were in the previous chapter), but also with how resources are allocated among firms. To facilitate this examination, we will break the question down into three separate issues: (1) resource allocation within a single firm; (2) allocation of productive resources among firms; and (3) coordination of firms' output choices. Results for each of these issues will be summarized by a general "Allocation Rule." All of these rules must hold to ensure productive efficiency.

Efficient Choice of Inputs for a Single Firm

In Chapter 16 we examined the situation of a firm having fixed inputs of capital and labor. There we showed that the firm will have allocated these inputs efficiently if they are fully employed and if the rate of technical substitution *(RTS)* between capital and labor is the same for every output the firm produces. Previously, we developed a detailed graphical proof of this assertion; here we will use a mathematical approach. Assume the firm produces two goods, X and Y, and that the total available inputs of capital and labor are given by $\bar{K}$ and $\bar{L}$. The production function for good X is given by

$$X = f(K_X, L_X), \qquad (17.1)$$

where K_X and L_X are capital and labor devoted to X production. If we assume full employment, $K_Y = \bar{K} - K_X$, $L_Y = \bar{L} - L_X$, and the production function for good Y is

$$Y = g(K_Y, L_Y) = g(\bar{K} - K_X, \bar{L} - L_X). \qquad (17.2)$$

Technical efficiency requires that X output be as large as possible for any predetermined value of Y output (say, $\bar{Y}$). Setting up the Lagrangian expression for this constrained maximum problem yields

$$\mathcal{L} = f(K_X, L_X) + \lambda[\bar{Y} - g(\bar{K} - K_X, \bar{L} - L_X)]. \qquad (17.3)$$

Differentiation with respect to K_X, L_X, and λ gives the following first-order conditions for a constrained maximum:

$$\frac{\partial \mathcal{L}}{\partial K_X} = f_K + \lambda g_K = 0$$

$$\frac{\partial \mathcal{L}}{\partial L_X} = f_L + \lambda g_L = 0 \tag{17.4}$$

$$\frac{\partial \mathcal{L}}{\partial \lambda} = \bar{Y} - g(\bar{K} - K_X, \bar{L} - L_X) = 0.$$

Moving the terms in λ to the right-hand side of the first two of these equations, we have

$$\frac{f_K}{f_L} = \frac{g_K}{g_L}, \tag{17.5}$$

and, using the result (from Chapter 11) that the *RTS* is the ratio of the inputs' marginal productivities, that implies[1]

$$RTS_X \ (K \ \text{for} \ L) = RTS_Y \ (K \ \text{for} \ L). \tag{17.6}$$

This is precisely the result we showed graphically in Figure 16.3.

Efficient Allocation of Resources among Firms   Resources must also be allocated in some efficient way among firms in order to ensure overall productive efficiency. Intuitively, resources should be allocated to those firms where they can be most efficiently used. More precisely, the condition for efficient allocation is that the marginal physical product of any resource in the production of a particular good is the same no matter which firm produces that good.

A mathematical proof of this rule is straightforward. Suppose that there are two firms producing the same good *(X)* and that their production functions are given by $f_1(K_1, L_1)$ and $f_2(K_2, L_2)$. Assume also that total supplies of capital and labor are given by $\bar{K}$ and $\bar{L}$. The allocational problem is then to maximize

$$X = f_1(K_1, L_1) + f_2(K_2, L_2), \tag{17.7}$$

subject to the constraints

$$K_1 + K_2 = \bar{K}$$
$$L_1 + L_2 = \bar{L}. \tag{17.8}$$

Upon substituting the constraints into Equation 17.7, the maximization problem becomes

---

[1] All of these results hold only for an interior maximum in which both inputs are actually used to produce both goods. If that were not the case, these first-order conditions would have to be amended.

$$X = f_1(K_1, L_1) + f_2(\bar{K} - K_1, \bar{L} - L_1). \qquad (17.9)$$

First-order conditions for a maximum are

$$\frac{\partial X}{\partial K_1} = \frac{\partial f_1}{\partial K_1} + \frac{\partial f_2}{\partial K_1} = \frac{\partial f_1}{\partial K_1} - \frac{\partial f_2}{\partial K_2} = 0$$

$$\frac{\partial X}{\partial L_1} = \frac{\partial f_1}{\partial L_1} + \frac{\partial f_2}{\partial L_1} = \frac{\partial f_1}{\partial L_1} - \frac{\partial f_2}{\partial L_2} = 0$$

$$(17.10)$$

or

$$\frac{\partial f_1}{\partial K_1} = \frac{\partial f_2}{\partial K_2}$$

and

$$(17.11)$$

$$\frac{\partial f_1}{\partial L_1} = \frac{\partial f_2}{\partial L_2},$$

as was to be shown.

EXAMPLE 17.1

GAINS FROM EFFICIENTLY ALLOCATING LABOR

To examine the quantitative gains in output from allocating resources efficiently, suppose that two rice farms have production functions of the simple form

$$q = K^{1/4} L^{3/4}, \qquad (17.12)$$

but that one rice farm is more mechanized than the other. If capital for the first farm is given by $K_1 = 16$ and for the second farm by $K_2 = 625$, we have

$$q_1 = 2L_1^{3/4}$$
$$q_2 = 5L_2^{3/4}. \qquad (17.13)$$

If the total labor supply is 100, an equal allocation of labor to these two farms will provide total rice output of

$$Q = q_1 + q_2 = 2(50)^{3/4} + 5(50)^{3/4} = 131.6. \qquad (17.14)$$

An efficient allocation is found by setting the marginal productivities equal:

$$\frac{\partial q_1}{\partial L_1} = \left(\frac{3}{2}\right) L_1^{-1/4} = \frac{\partial q_2}{\partial L_2} = \frac{15}{4} L_2^{-1/4}. \qquad (17.15)$$

Hence, for efficiency labor should be allocated so that

$$L_1 = \left(\frac{5}{2}\right)^{-4} L_2 = .0256 L_2. \tag{17.16}$$

Given the greater capitalization of farm 2, practically all of the available labor should be devoted to it. With 100 units of labor, 97.4 units should be allocated to farm 2 with only 2.6 units to farm 1. In this case total output will be

$$Q = q_1 + q_2 = 2(2.6)^{3/4} + 5(97.4)^{3/4} = 159.1. \tag{17.17}$$

This represents a gain of more than 20 percent over the rice output obtained under the equal allocation.

QUERY: Suppose capital were not fixed in this problem. How should capital *and* labor be allocated between the two farms?

Efficient Choice of Output by Firms

Even though resources may be efficiently allocated both within a firm and among all firms, there is still one other condition of efficient production that must be obeyed: Firms must produce efficient combinations of outputs. Roughly speaking, firms that are good at producing hamburgers should produce hamburgers and those good at producing cars should produce cars.

Consider two firms (A and B) that each produce both cars and trucks. Let their production possibility curves be given by those in Figure 17.1. Suppose that firm A chooses to produce at a point, P_1^A (100 cars and 50 trucks), where its *RPT* (of trucks for cars) is $\frac{2}{1}$. At this point, firm A must give up 2 cars if it is to produce one more truck. Suppose also that firm B chooses to produce 100 cars and 50 trucks but that at this point its *RPT* (of trucks for cars) is $\frac{1}{1}$. In this case productive efficiency can be improved by having firm A produce more cars (since it is relatively efficient in this) and firm B produce more trucks. For example, firm A could produce 102 cars and 49 trucks, whereas B could move to producing 99 cars and 51 trucks. By this reordering of production, the total output of cars has been increased without decreasing the total output of trucks. Hence, the initial choices of firms A and B were inefficient. Only if this conclusion holds is it impossible to make such a beneficial reallocation. This result is particularly interesting in that it shows that output may be increased, even if the inputs to each firm are fixed, by having firms produce the "correct" output combinations.

Theory of Comparative Advantage

One of the most important applications of this conclusion is in the study of international trade, where it is used as the basis for the *theory of comparative advantage*. This theory was first proposed by Ricardo, who argued that countries should specialize in producing those goods of which they are

FIGURE 17.1

GRAPHICAL DEMONSTRATION OF EFFICIENT OUTPUT CHOICE

If two firms' rates of product transformation differ, total output can be increased by moving these firms toward equalization of those rates. In the figure, firm A is relatively efficient at producing cars, and firm B is relatively efficient at producing trucks. If each firm were to specialize in its efficient product, total output could be increased.

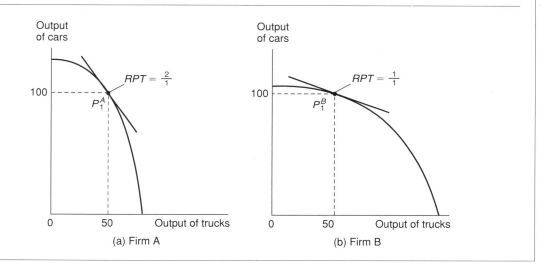

(a) Firm A

(b) Firm B

relatively more efficient producers.[2] The countries then should trade with the rest of the world to obtain needed commodities. If countries do specialize in this way, total world production will be greater than if each country tried to produce a balanced bundle of goods. To demonstrate this fact, let us look again at Figure 17.1. Now we can take the two production possibility curves to represent those of two different countries with fixed resources. Points P_1^A and P_1^B may represent the countries' pretrade production choices. Since the RPT differs between the two countries, world output could be increased by having country A produce more cars and country B produce more trucks. The countries should proceed to specialize in this way until their RPT's are equilibrated. With country A specializing in car production, it can trade with country B to get the trucks it needs; similarly, B can trade with A for cars. Because total world output has been increased as a result of specialization,

[2] See D. Ricardo, *The Principles of Political Economy and Taxation* (1817; reprint ed., London: J. M. Dent and Son, 1965), pp. 81–93.

both countries now may be better off. This is the logic that provides intellectual support for the belief that "free trade is the best policy." It is important to note that the analysis uses only information about the product transformation rates between the two goods in each country, not about marginal productivity differences between countries. It is possible that a country could have an "absolute" advantage in the production of every good (in the sense that its marginal productivity of labor in the production of *every* good exceeded that of its trading partner), but such a country would still benefit from specialization and trade.

EXAMPLE 17.2

COMPARATIVE ADVANTAGE IN RICARDO'S WORLD

In his original discussion of the comparative advantage concept, Ricardo assumed that production possibility frontiers were linear. Consider the following hypothetical marginal cost data (expressed in a common currency) for England and Portugal for the two goods wine and cloth:

	MARGINAL COSTS	
	ENGLAND	PORTUGAL
Wine	8	2
Cloth	4	2

In Ricardo's analysis, marginal costs were assumed to be constant (and equal to average costs). Consequently, if we let total resource costs be fixed for each country at 100, the production probability frontier for England is

$$8W + 4C = 100,$$

and for Portugal it is   (17.18)

$$2W + 2C = 100.$$

Clearly, the *RPT*'s differ between these countries:

$$RPT \text{ (England)} = -\frac{dC}{dW} = 2$$

(17.19)

$$RPT \text{ (Portugal)} = -\frac{dC}{dW} = 1.$$

In this situation Ricardo argued that even though Portugal has an absolute cost advantage in producing both goods, both countries could benefit from trade, since wine is relatively less costly in Portugal and cloth is relatively less costly in England. That is, England has a "comparative advantage" in cloth, Portugal in wine.

The Gains from Recognizing Comparative Advantage. Suppose prior to trade, each country devotes half of its resources to each good. Then for England

$$W = \frac{50}{8} = 6.25$$

$$C = \frac{50}{4} = 12.5,$$

and for Portugal $\qquad\qquad$ (17.20)

$$W = \frac{50}{2} = 25$$

$$C = \frac{50}{2} = 25.$$

World output can be unambiguously increased if England were to produce less wine (and more cloth) with the opposite change occurring in Portugal. If, for example, England were to devote all of its resources to cloth, output there would be $C = 25$. Now if Portugal were to shift its production to allocating 70 percent of total inputs to wine, it would produce

$$W = \frac{70}{2} = 35$$

$$C = \frac{30}{2} = 15.$$

Hence, world wine output has risen from 31.25 to 35, and cloth output has risen from 37.5 to 40. Even though the supply of inputs in each country has not changed, world output has been unambiguously increased through recognition of comparative advantage.

QUERY: In this example (as in most cases involving linear production possibility frontiers), England's resource allocation has been "completely specialized" in cloth production. Would any output pattern short of complete specialization promise an unambiguous improvement over this allocation? If production possibility curves were concave rather than linear, is complete specialization likely to be efficient?

Technical efficiency is not a sufficient condition for Pareto efficiency. The right mix of goods must also be produced. It does little good for an economy to be an efficient producer of yo-yos and xylophones if no one wants these

EFFICIENCY IN PRODUCT MIX

goods. In order to assure Pareto efficiency, we need some way to tie individuals' preferences and production possibilities together. The condition necessary to ensure that the right goods are produced is that the *marginal rate of substitution* for any two goods must be *equal* to the *rate of product transformation* of the two goods. Simply phrased, the psychological rate of trade-off between the two goods in people's preferences must be equal to the rate at which they can be traded off in production.

A Graphical Proof   Figure 17.2 illustrates the requirement for efficiency in product mix for a very simple case. It assumes that in this society there are only two goods (*X*

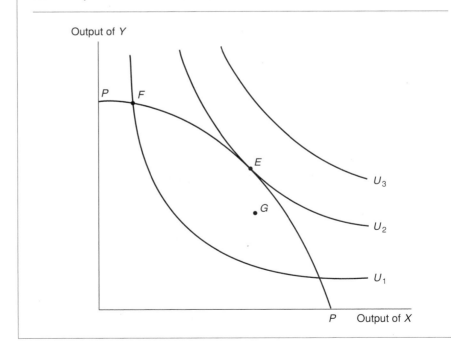

FIGURE 17.2

EFFICIENCY IN PRODUCT MIX IN A ROBINSON CRUSOE ECONOMY

In a single-person economy, the curve *PP* represents those combinations of *X* and *Y* that can be produced. Every point on *PP* is efficient in a production sense. However, only the output combination at point *E* is a true utility maximum for the individual. At *E* the individual's *MRS* is equal to the rate at which *X* can technically be traded for *Y* (*RPT*).

and Y) being produced and that there is only one individual (Robinson Crusoe?) or perhaps many individuals with identical preferences. Those combinations of X and Y that can be produced are given by the production possibility frontier PP. Any point on PP represents a point of technical efficiency. By superimposing the individual's indifference map on Figure 17.2, however, we see that only one point on PP provides maximum utility. This point of maximum utility is at E, where the curve PP is tangent to the individual's highest indifference curve, U_2. At this point of tangency, the individual's MRS (of X for Y) is equal to the technical RPT (of X for Y); hence, this is the required condition for overall efficiency. Notice that point E is preferred to every other point that is efficient in a productive sense. In fact, for any point (other than point E) such as F on the curve PP, there exist points that are inefficient but that are preferred to F. In Figure 17.2 the "inefficient" point G is preferred to the "efficient" point F. It would be preferable from the individual's point of view to produce inefficiently rather than be forced to produce the "wrong" combination of goods in an efficient way. Point E (which is efficiently produced) is superior to any such "second-best" solutions.

To demonstrate this result mathematically, assume there are only two goods (X and Y) and one individual in society (again Robinson Crusoe) whose utility function is given by $U(X, Y)$. Assume also that this society's production possibility frontier can be written in implicit form as $T(X, Y) = 0$. Robinson's problem is to maximize utility subject to this production constraint. Setting up the Lagrangian expression for this problem yields

A Mathematical Proof

$$\mathcal{L} = U(X, Y) + \lambda[T(X, Y)], \qquad (17.22)$$

and the first-order conditions for an interior maximum are

$$\frac{\partial \mathcal{L}}{\partial X} = \frac{\partial U}{\partial X} + \lambda \frac{\partial T}{\partial X} = 0$$

$$\frac{\partial \mathcal{L}}{\partial Y} = \frac{\partial U}{\partial Y} + \lambda \frac{\partial T}{\partial Y} = 0 \qquad (17.23)$$

$$\frac{\partial \mathcal{L}}{\partial \lambda} = T(X, Y) = 0.$$

Combining the first two of these equations yields

$$\frac{\partial U/\partial X}{\partial U/\partial Y} = \frac{\partial T/\partial X}{\partial T/\partial Y} \qquad (17.24)$$

or

$$MRS \ (X \text{ for } Y) = -\frac{dY}{dX} \ (\text{along } T) = RPT \ (X \text{ for } Y), \qquad (17.25)$$

as Figure 17.2 illustrated. We have shown that only if individuals' preferences are taken into account will resources be allocated in a Pareto efficient way. Without such an explicit reference to preferences, it would be possible, by reallocating production, to raise at least one person's utility without reducing anyone else's.

EXAMPLE 17.3

UTILITY-MAXIMIZING PRODUCT MIX

Several examples in Chapter 16 utilized a production possibility frontier for guns (X) and butter (Y) of the form

$$X^2 + 4Y^2 = 100 \tag{17.26}$$

together with a utility function of the form

$$\text{utility} = U(X,Y) = \sqrt{XY} \tag{17.27}$$

to describe a general equilibrium model of price determination for the two goods. This situation could also be looked at as a problem in the efficient allocation of resources, independent of pricing notions—the goal is simply to maximize utility, given the constraint imposed by the production possibility frontier. Setting up the Lagrangian for this problem

$$\mathcal{L} = \sqrt{XY} + \lambda(100 - X^2 - 4Y^2) \tag{17.28}$$

yields first-order conditions of

$$\frac{\partial \mathcal{L}}{\partial X} = \frac{1}{2}\left(\frac{Y}{X}\right)^{1/2} - 2\lambda X = 0$$

$$\frac{\partial \mathcal{L}}{\partial Y} = \frac{1}{2}\left(\frac{X}{Y}\right)^{1/2} - 8\lambda Y = 0 \tag{17.29}$$

$$\frac{\partial \mathcal{L}}{\partial \lambda} = 100 - X^2 - 4Y^2 = 0.$$

Dividing the first two equations produces the familiar result

$$\frac{Y}{X} = \frac{1}{4}\frac{X}{Y}$$

or

$$X^2 = 4Y^2, \tag{17.30}$$

and, as before, substitution into the production possibility frontier provides an optimal solution of

$$X^* = \sqrt{50} = 7.07$$

$$Y^* = \sqrt{12.5} = 3.54 \tag{17.31}$$

and

$$\text{utility} = \sqrt{X^*Y^*} = 5. \qquad (17.32)$$

Any other point on the production possibility frontier provides a lower utility than this optimal level. Such a welfare loss would be similar to the losses in consumer surplus illustrated in Chapter 15.

It is, of course, no accident that the optimal solution calculated for this purely allocational problem is identical to the general equilibrium solution computed in Example 16.2. That the invisible hand of the price mechanism leads to an equilibrium that is efficient provides a proof of the efficiency of competitive markets in this simple context.

QUERY: Allocations such as $X = 8$, $Y = 3$ or $X = 5$, $Y = 4.33$ are clearly inefficient. How would you measure the degree of inefficiency involved in such alternative allocations?

COMPETITIVE PRICES AND EFFICIENCY

The essence of the relationship between perfect competition and the efficient allocation of resources can easily be summarized. Attaining a Pareto efficient allocation of resources requires that (except when corner solutions occur) the rate of trade-off between any two goods, say, X and Y, should be the same for all economic agents. In a perfectly competitive economy the ratio of the price of X to the price of Y provides this common rate of trade-off to which all agents will adjust. Because prices are treated as fixed parameters in both individuals' utility-maximizing decisions and firms' profit-maximizing decisions, all trade-off rates between X and Y will be equalized to the rate at which X and Y can be traded in the market (P_X/P_Y). Since all agents face the same prices, all trade-off rates will be equalized and an efficient allocation will be achieved.

Efficiency in Production

To show that competitive pricing can lead to efficiency in production, consider first the requirement that a firm have identical rates at which it can trade one input for another (the rate of technical substitution, RTS) in all those outputs that it produces. This is ensured by the existence of perfectly competitive markets for inputs. In minimizing costs the firm will equate the RTS between any two inputs, say, labor and capital, to the ratio of their competitive rental prices (w/v). This will be true for any output that the firm happens to produce; hence, the firm will be equating all its RTS's to the common price ratio w/v. In this way, without any external direction, the firm will be led to adopt efficient input proportions in a decentralized way.

This requires that every firm that produces a particular good, say, X, has identical marginal productivities of labor in the production of X. In Chapter 13 we showed that a profit-maximizing firm will hire additional units of any input (say, labor) up to the point at which its marginal contribution to revenues is equal to the marginal cost of hiring the input (see Equation 13.25). If we let P_X represent the price of the good being sold and f^1 and f^2 represent the production functions for two firms that produce X, then profit maximization requires that

$$P_X f_L^1 = w$$

and (17.33)

$$P_X f_L^2 = w.$$

Since both firms face both the same price for X and the same competitive wage rate, these equations imply

$$f_L^1 = f_L^2.$$ (17.34)

Consequently, every firm will have the same marginal productivity of labor in the production of X. The market has succeeded in bringing about an efficient allocation of each input among firms.

Finally, the requirement is that the rate of product transformation (RPT— this is the rate at which one output can be traded for another in production) between any two goods, say, X and Y, be the same for all firms. That a perfectly competitive price system will ensure this can be most easily shown by recalling that the RPT (of X for Y) is equal to the ratio of the marginal cost of X (MC_X) to that of Y (MC_Y). But each profit-maximizing firm will produce that output level for which marginal cost is equal to the market price. Therefore, for every firm, $P_X = MC_X$ and $P_Y = MC_Y$, and hence $MC_X/MC_Y = P_X/P_Y$ for all firms.

This discussion demonstrates that the profit-maximizing, decentralized decisions of many firms can achieve technical efficiency in production without any central direction. Competitive market prices act as signals to unify the multitude of decisions that firms make into one coherent, efficient pattern. Relying on the self-interest of entrepreneurs is a theoretically plausible way of prompting the production sector to act efficiently.

Efficiency in Product Mix Proving that perfectly competitive markets lead to efficiency in the relationship between production and preferences is also straightforward. Since the price ratios quoted to consumers are the same ratios that the market presents to firms, the MRS shared by all individuals will be identical to the RPT that is shared by all firms. This will be true for any pair of goods. Consequently, an efficient mix of goods will be produced. Again, notice the two important functions that market prices perform. First, they ensure that supply and demand will be equalized for all goods. If a good were produced in too great amounts, a market reaction would set in (its price would fall) that would cut back on the production of the good and shift resources into other employment. The equilibrating of supply and demand in the market therefore assures that there will be neither excess demand nor excess supply. Second, equilibrium prices provide market trade-off rates for both firms and individuals to use as parameters in their decisions. Because these trade-off rates are identical for both firms and individuals, efficiency is assured.

Our discussion of general equilibrium modeling in Chapter 16 provides **A Graphical Proof** precisely the tools required to show this result graphically. Figure 17.3 repeats Figure 16.5, but now we are more interested in the efficiency properties of the general equilibrium solution illustrated. Given the production possibility frontier PP and preferences represented by the indifference curves, it is clear that X^*, Y^* represents the efficient output mix (compare this figure to Figure 17.2). Possibly X^*, Y^* could be decided upon in a centrally planned economy

FIGURE 17.3

COMPETITIVE EQUILIBRIUM AND EFFICIENCY IN OUTPUT MIX

Although all of the output combinations on PP are technically efficient, only combination X^*, Y^* is Pareto optimal. A competitive equilibrium price ratio of P_X^*/P_Y^* will lead this economy to this Pareto efficient solution (see also Figure 16.5).

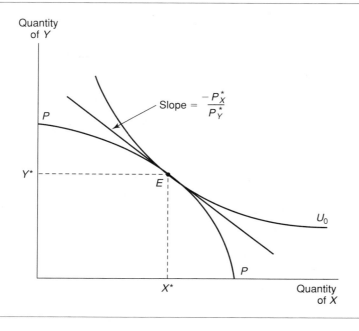

if the planning board had adequate information about production possibilities and individuals' preferences. Alternatively, as we showed in Chapter 16, reliance on competitive markets and the self-interest of firms and individuals will also lead to this allocation. Only with a price ratio of P_X^*/P_Y^* will supply and demand be in equilibrium in this model, and that equilibrium will occur at the efficient product mix, E. Smith's invisible hand ensures not only that production is technically efficient (that output combinations lie on the production possibility frontier), but also that the forces of supply and demand lead to the Pareto efficient output combination. More complex models of competitive equilibrium price determination reach essentially the same conclusion.[3] Similarly, reversing all the arguments we have made would show that any Pareto efficient allocation can be attained through suitably chosen competitive equilibrium prices for both inputs and outputs. These results constitute the "fundamental theorem of welfare economics."

Laissez-Faire Policies   In its most dogmatic expression, the correspondence between competitive equilibrium and Pareto efficiency provides "scientific" support for the laissez-faire position taken by many economists. For example, Smith's assertion that

> . . . the natural effort of every individual to better his own condition, when suffered to exert itself with freedom and security, is so powerful a principle that it is alone, and without any assistance, not only capable of carrying on the society to wealth and prosperity, but of surmounting a hundred impertinent obstructions with which the folly of human laws too often encumbers its operations. . . .[4]

has been shown to have considerable theoretical validity. Again, as Smith noted, it is not the "public spirit" of the baker that provides bread for individuals' consumption. Rather, bakers (and other producers) operate in their own self-interest in responding to market signals. Individuals also respond to these signals in deciding how to allocate their incomes. Government intervention in this smoothly functioning process may only result in a loss of Pareto efficiency.

Such a sweeping conclusion, of course, vastly overstates the general applicability of the simple model we have been using. No one should attempt to draw policy recommendations from a theoretical structure that pays so little attention to institutional details in the real world. Still, the efficiency properties of the competitive system do provide a benchmark, a place to start to examine reasons why competitive markets may fail.

---

[3] See, for example, K. J. Arrow and F. H. Hahn, *General Competitive Analysis* (San Francisco: Holden-Day, 1971), chapters 4 and 5.

[4] A. Smith, *The Wealth of Nations* (New York: Random House, Modern Library Edition, 1937), p. 508.

Factors that may distort the ability of competitive markets to achieve efficiency can be classed into three general groupings that include most of the interesting cases: (1) imperfect competition, (2) externalities, (3) public goods. Here we provide a brief summary of these and will return to them in later chapters. In the next sections we provide more extended discussions of problems related to information and distribution.

EFFECTS OF DEPARTURES FROM THE COMPETITIVE ASSUMPTIONS

Imperfect Competition

"Imperfect competition" includes all those situations in which economic agents exert some market power in determining price. In this case, as the analysis of Chapter 13 illustrated, these agents will take such effects into account in their decisions. A firm that faces a downward-sloping demand curve for its product, for example, will recognize that the marginal revenue from selling one more unit is less than the market price of that unit. Since it is the marginal return to its decisions that motivates the profit-maximizing firm, marginal revenue rather than market price becomes the important magnitude. Market prices no longer carry the informational content required to achieve Pareto efficiency. Other cases of market power result in similar informational shortcomings.

As an example, consider the efficiency conditions diagrammed in Figure 17.4. Point E represents an efficient allocation in that, at this point, the MRS (of X for Y) is equal to the RPT (of X for Y). A perfectly competitive price ratio of P_X^*/P_Y^* could generate this allocation. Suppose, instead, that one of the goods, say, X, is produced under imperfectly competitive conditions whereas Y is produced under conditions of perfect competition. For good X, therefore, $MR_X < P_X^*$ whereas for Y, $MR_Y = P_Y^*$. The profit-maximizing output choice, then, is that combination of X and Y for which

$$RPT \text{ (X for Y)} = \frac{MC_X}{MC_Y} = \frac{MR_X}{P_Y^*} < \frac{P_X^*}{P_Y^*} = MRS \text{ (of X for Y)}, \quad (17.35)$$

where the inequality holds because of the presence of imperfect competition in the market for good X. But that will entail a choice of outputs such as that represented by point B, with less X and more Y being produced than is optimal, given the existing tastes and technology. Although production is efficient at B and supply and demand are in equilibrium, the price system has no longer led to a Pareto efficient outcome. At B there is a utility loss of $U_2 - U_1$ as a result of the misallocation.

A similar proof would hold for many other circumstances in which markets are imperfectly competitive. Market power creates a divergence between market price and the marginal figure that is relevant to the agent's decisions. Because of this divergence, market prices will not carry the appropriate information about relative marginal costs. The workings of the price system will be distorted, and an efficient allocation of resources cannot

FIGURE 17.4

THE PRODUCTION OF GOOD *X* UNDER IMPERFECT COMPETITION PREVENTS EFFICIENCY IN PRODUCTION AND EXCHANGE

If good *X* is produced under imperfect competition, the profit-maximizing firm will choose that output combination for which the *RPT* (of *X* for *Y*) is equal to MR_X/P_Y; this will be less than the ratio of these goods' market prices (P_X^*/P_Y^*). Production will take place at a point such as *B*, where the *RPT* is less than the individuals' marginal rates of substitution. Too little *X* will be produced as a result of imperfect competition in its market.

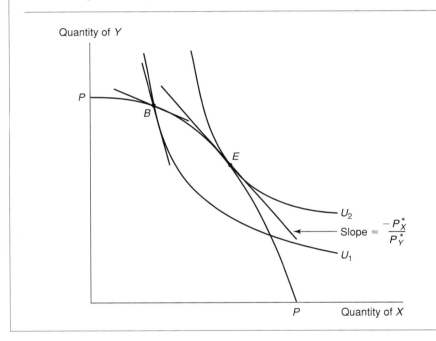

be achieved. In Part VI we will examine a number of models of imperfectly competitive markets in which such distortions occur.

Externalities   The competitive price system can also fail to allocate resources efficiently when there are interactions among firms and individuals that are not adequately reflected in market prices. Examples of such occurrences are numerous. Perhaps the prototype example is the case of a firm that pollutes the air with industrial smoke and other debris. Such a situation is termed an *externality*: It is an interaction between the firm's level of production and individuals' well-being that is not accounted for by the price system. A more complete discussion of the nature of externalities will be presented in Chapter 24, but here we can describe why the presence of such nonmarket interactions interferes with the ability of the price system to allocate resources efficiently.

The conditions for Pareto efficiency must be defined in a "social" sense when we recognize the possibility of externalities. For example, we would say that the *social rate of product transformation* (the rate at which society can transform one good into another) must be equal to the *social marginal rate of substitution* (the rate at which society is willing to trade one good for another) for there to be an optimal allocation of resources. The problem that arises in the presence of externalities is that economic agents pay attention to only *private* rates of transformation and substitution in their decisions. If private and social rates diverge, the perfectly competitive price system may not generate an efficient allocation.

Public Goods

A third possible failure of the price system to yield an optimal allocation of resources is related to the problem of externalities and stems from the existence of goods that must be provided on a "nonexclusive" basis. Such goods include national defense, inoculations against infectious diseases, criminal justice, and pest control. The distinguishing feature of these goods is that they provide benefits to all individuals: Once the goods are produced, it is impossible (or at least very costly) to exclude anyone from benefiting from them. Consequently, there is an incentive for each individual to adopt the position of a "free rider" by refusing to pay for the good in the hope that others will purchase it and thereby provide benefits to all. The pervasive nature of this incentive will ensure that resources are underallocated to nonexclusive goods. To avoid this underallocation, communities (or nations) may decide to have the government produce nonexclusive goods and finance this production through compulsory taxation. For that reason, nonexclusive goods frequently are termed *public goods*. In Chapter 24 we shall treat in detail the problems raised by the existence of such goods.

MARKET ADJUSTMENT AND INFORMATION

The efficiency properties of a competitive price system may also be affected by level of information in the marketplace. So far we have assumed that competitive prices are quickly established and are known with certainty to all market participants. In the next few sections we explore a few models that relax these assumptions. We begin by looking at how imperfect information may delay the establishment of market equilibrium. Then we turn to some more general issues about the nature of market equilibrium under imperfect information.

Establishing Competitive Equilibrium Prices

One of the most difficult informational problems faced by any competitive market is how an equilibrium price is discovered. What market signals do suppliers and demanders use to adjust their behavior toward equilibrium? Are temporary, nonequilibrium prices relied upon to make such decisions, or are other mechanisms available? In mathematical terms, suppose the competitive market price for some commodity starts at an arbitrary price, say, P_0. We know from Chapter 16 that under certain circumstances there exists an equilibrium price, P^*, for which

$$D(P^*) = S(P^*), \qquad (17.36)$$

where D and S are the demand and supply functions for the good. Now we wish to examine how market price moves from P_0 to P^*.

Walrasian Price Adjustment

An early model of equilibrium price adjustment was proposed by Walras.[5] In this scheme equilibrium prices are a goal toward which the market gropes. Changes in price are motivated by information from the market about the degree of *excess demand* at any particular price. Mathematically, the Walrasian adjustment mechanism specifies that the change in price over time is given by

$$\frac{dP}{dt} = k[D(P) - S(P)] = k[ED(P)] \qquad k > 0, \qquad (17.37)$$

where $ED(P)$ represents excess demand at price P. Price will increase if there is positive excess demand and will decrease if excess demand is negative. Such a mechanism is called a *tâtonnement* ("groping") *process*. This mechanism is pictured graphically in Figure 17.5. For any price above the equilibrium price (P^*), the *tâtonnement* process operates to lower price. Similarly, for prices less than P^* the process raises price. In Figure 17.5a the equilibrium price P^* is *stable;* there are forces that move P toward P^*. This may not always be the case, however, as Figure 17.5b illustrates. In this case the *tâtonnement* rule causes price to move away from its equilibrium level. It is easy to see that if the supply curve has a positive slope, the equilibrium price P^* is stable.

Another way to see the Walrasian result is to examine the excess demand function, $ED(P)$. Three possible shapes for the excess demand function are shown in Figure 17.6. For each of these shapes equilibrium prices exist at those points where excess demand equals 0. In Figure 17.6a the equilibrium price P_1 is a stable equilibrium in the Walrasian sense. If price initially starts above P_1, the Walrasian process will tend to move it downward toward P_1. Similarly, if the initial price is less than P_1, it will be adjusted upward. The

---

[5] L. Walras, *Elements of Pure Economics*, trans. W. Jaffee (Homewood, Ill.: Richard D. Irwin, 1954).

FIGURE 17.5

TWO POSSIBLE SUPPLY-DEMAND CONFIGURATIONS AND THEIR WALRASIAN STABILITY

The Walrasian definition of stability specifies that prices will adjust in response to excess demand. If at some price, quantity demanded exceeds quantity supplied, price is assumed to rise. Conversely, if quantity demanded is less than that supplied, price falls. In (a) these rules ensure that the equilibrium price P^* will be stable. Starting anywhere, there are forces moving price toward P^*. This is not true for the supply-demand configuration shown in (b). There the Walrasian mechanism will cause price to move away from P^*.

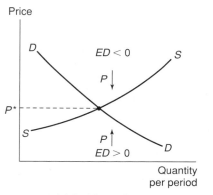

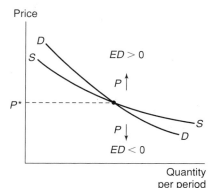

(a) Stable equilibrium (b) Unstable equilibrium

excess demand function in Figure 17.6b is unstable. The Walrasian process will tend to move price in the wrong direction. In Figure 17.6c there are multiple equilibria: P_1, P_2, and P_3 all cause excess demand to be 0. However, only P_1 and P_3 are stable in the Walrasian sense. There are no forces moving price toward P_2 (although if price started exactly at P_2, it would stay at this equilibrium position).

A Mathematical Derivation

In mathematical terms the Walrasian price adjustment procedure reflected in Equation 17.37 is a differential equation. To study the (local) behavior of such an equation in the vicinity of an equilibrium price, it is possible to use a Taylor approximation of the form

$$\frac{dp}{dt} \cong k[ED'(P^*)] \cdot (P - P^*). \tag{17.38}$$

This equation is called a first-order differential equation. An important theorem in the theory of such equations is that their solutions have the same

FIGURE 17.6

USING EXCESS DEMAND CURVES TO SHOW WALRASIAN STABILITY

Using the excess demand function $[ED(P) = D(P) - S(P)]$, we can investigate the stability of various equilibrium prices that occur whenever $ED(P) = 0$. However, only if the slope of the excess demand curve is negative $[ED'(P) < 0]$ at the equilibrium point will the Walrasian adjustment mechanism ensure stability. Notice, for example, that in (c) stable and unstable equilibria alternate.

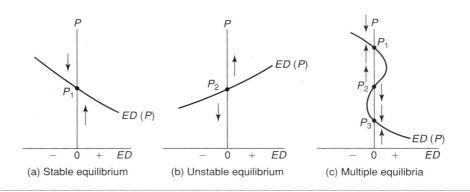

(a) Stable equilibrium   (b) Unstable equilibrium   (c) Multiple equilibria

stability properties as do the nonlinear equations that they approximate (Equation 17.37). Hence, for the purpose of our analysis of stability, we can study Equation 17.38, which is considerably easier to solve. Indeed, the general solution to this type of equation will be of the form

$$P(t) = (P_0 - P^*)e^{kED'(P^*)t} + P^*, \qquad (17.39)$$

where P_0 represents the initial price at time $t = 0$. For this system to be stable (that is, for $P(t)$ to approach P^* as t gets large), it must be the case that $ED'(P^*) < 0$. In words, an increase in price must reduce excess demand, and a fall in price must increase excess demand. This is the result illustrated in Figure 17.6. For a mathematical illustration, see Problem 17.8.

Marshallian Quantity Adjustment   The adjustment process we have just discussed views price as the motivating force in the adjustment of markets to equilibrium. Individuals and firms respond to price changes by moving along their respective demand and supply curves until an equilibrium price-quantity combination is reached. A somewhat different picture of the adjustment process was suggested by Marshall in his classic *Principles of Economics.*[6] There Marshall theorized that

---

[6] A. Marshall, *Principles of Economics*, 8th ed. (London: Macmillan & Co., 1920), pp. 287–288.

individuals and firms should be viewed as adjusting quantity in response to imbalances in quantities demanded and supplied and that price changes follow from these changes in quantity. If we let $D^{-1}(Q)$ represent the price that demanders are willing to pay for each quantity and $S^{-1}(Q)$ represent the price that suppliers require for each quantity (that is, their marginal cost), then the Marshallian adjustment mechanism can be represented by

$$\frac{dQ}{dt} = k[D^{-1}(Q) - S^{-1}(Q)] = k[ED^{-1}(Q)] \qquad k > 0. \qquad (17.40)$$

In words, movements in quantity toward equilibrium are motivated by discrepancies between the price individuals are willing to pay and the price firms wish to receive. When those two figures coincide, quantity adjustment ceases.

Transactions and Information Costs

The Walrasian and Marshallian adjustment processes represent mathematically elegant solutions to the market adjustment problem. But these solutions are largely devoid of economic content. Contrary to the other theoretical developments in this book, these adjustment processes do not represent any sort of optimizing behavior by economic agents. Rather, the differential equations have been plucked, more or less, out of the air. To develop a behaviorally oriented theory of market adjustment, one must examine the costs involved in reaching market equilibrium and illustrate how economic actions will seek to minimize those costs.

As a simple example, consider the question of whether market adjustments will be primarily of the Walrasian (price) or Marshallian (quantity) type. Presumably, the choice will be dictated by the types of transactions and information costs involved. If prices can easily be changed (say, by switching price tags) and if information about changed prices is readily disseminated among buyers and sellers, Walrasian price adjustment may predominate. Important examples are provided by auctions. In these cases, the auctioneer calls out tentative prices and can readily perceive how demanders react to them. Even in this simple case, however, a would-be buyer faces difficult decision problems because he or she does not know precisely what rival bidders will do. Whether a particular bidding sequence reaches a true equilibrium price for the item being auctioned may depend on the kinds of information shared by bidders (how much do they know about a potential oil-producing tract, for example) and on the bidding strategies used by the parties.[7]

---

[7] Prices set by auction are "equilibrium prices" in the sense that the good to be sold actually changes hands. But they may not represent an equilibrium in the sense that buyers' and sellers' decisions are, after the fact, optimal. For a discussion of the theory of auctions, see R. P. McAfee and J. McMillan, "Auctions and Bidding," *Journal of Economic Literature* (June 1987): 699–738.

Market situations that have characteristics markedly different from auctions may be more likely to exhibit Marshallian quantity adjustment. If prices are difficult to alter (perhaps because they are specified in long-term contracts) and if the quantity traded can be changed with little cost (say, by using inventory stockpiles), the information necessary to reach an equilibrium will come mainly from quantity flows. Macroeconomics frequently uses such observations, for example, to explain why employment rather than the wage rate tends to adjust to cyclical fluctuations in demand.

Ultimately, however, such speculation about the choice of adjustment mechanism is largely beside the point because neither the Walrasian nor the Marshallian mechanisms reflect actual behavior by economic agents. To devise behavioral models requires the adoption of the principle that some agent (typically the firm) sets a price and then adjusts that price in response to experience. Some general models of this type have been developed based on assumed patterns of search behavior by demanders (who are looking for bargains), but these models are too specialized to examine here.[8] Instead, we will move on to more tractable representations of the price determination process.

DISEQUILIBRIUM PRICING AND EXPECTATIONS

One problem that makes the specification of a realistic adjustment process difficult is that the traditional model pictures supply and demand decisions as being made simultaneously. There are two equations (the supply and demand functions) to be solved simultaneously for two unknowns (price and quantity). The theory offers no guidance on how demanders or suppliers behave in disequilibrium situations. If the simultaneity assumption could be relaxed (by assuming, say, that supply decisions are made first), this problem would be simplified. For example, if firms based their current output decisions on what they expected market prices to be, then output in the current period could be regarded as fixed; there would be no current-period supply response to changes in current prices. The analysis of pricing in the "very short run" would then be the relevant model to study. Price would adjust to equilibrate demand to the available supply, but it would have no influence on production in the current period. In the next period, however, the market price established in this period may affect expectations and output decisions; thus, there is some (lagged) response of output to price changes.

A Formal Model

To examine some of the issues that arise in modeling such expectations about price, assume that demanders respond to the current market price, which is

---

[8] For a survey, see F. Hahn, "Stability," in K. J. Arrow and M. D. Intriligator, eds., *Handbook of Mathematical Economics*, vol. 2 (Amsterdam: North-Holland Publishing Co., 1982), chap. 16.

known with certainty, but that suppliers must respond only to what they expect the market price to be. If we assume simple linear responses, demand is given by

$$Q_t^D = c - dP_t \qquad (17.41)$$

and supply by

$$Q_t^S = a + bE(P_t), \qquad (17.42)$$

where $E(P_t)$ is what suppliers expect market price to be at time t.[9]

The behavior of this model obviously will depend on how suppliers form price expectations. If, for example, suppliers are myopic and always expect the price in period $t - 1$ to prevail in period t, we would have

Adaptive Expectations

$$E(P_t) = P_{t-1}. \qquad (17.43)$$

In this case the model would become what has come to be known as the *cobweb model*. The situation is illustrated in Figure 17.7a. Initially, price is set at P_0, and this price dictates what will be produced in period 1 (Q_1). Demanders bid for Q_1 and in so doing establish the market price for period 1 (P_1). This new price then is used in firms' decisions to produce Q_2, and the process is repeated. In Figure 17.7a it appears that this price-quantity "cobweb" is stable—eventually, price works its way toward the equilibrium price P^*. Before reaching P^*, however, a number of disequilibrium (and inefficient) outcomes occur. With a more elastic supply curve, even stability is not assured, as Figure 17.7b illustrates. In this figure the price-quantity combinations dictated by the logic of the cobweb model result in explosive behavior—price moves ever further from equilibrium as time proceeds.[10] This type of wildly oscillating behavior is unlikely to characterize actual markets, however, since speculators might seek to enter such a market in order to take advantage of the observed patterns in price movements.

---

[9] This supply equation is a special case of a supply function of the form $Q_t^s = f(P_t \mid I_{t-1})$, where P_t is a random variable whose subjective distribution depends on the information available to the firm at time $t - 1$ (that is, I_{t-1}). In general, I_{t-1} will be to some degree under the firm's control. That is, it can invest in information acquisition in period $t - 1$ to provide a more accurate picture of the likely distribution of prices in period t. We will not examine that process here, however.

[10] Technically, these cobweb assumptions result in a difference equation explaining price movements. It is fairly easy to show through repeated substitution that

$$P_t = (P_0 - P^*)(-b/d)^t + P^*.$$

Hence, price is stable and approaches P^* providing $-b/d < 1$.

FIGURE 17.7

COBWEB MODEL OF PRICE DETERMINATION

In the cobweb model of lagged response to price by firms, a theory of nonequilibrium pricing can be established. Whether these prices will approach an equilibrium price level will depend on the relative slopes of the demand and supply curves. In the configuration shown in (a), convergence will take place, whereas in (b) it will not. A third possibility (not shown) would be for the supply and demand curves to have slopes so that the price perpetually oscillates about P^*.

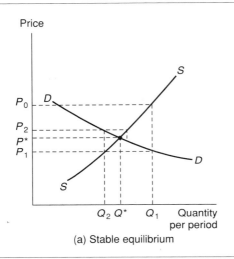

(a) Stable equilibrium

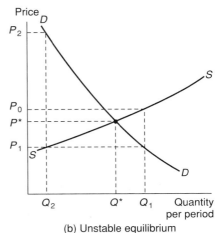

(b) Unstable equilibrium

Rational Expectations   A particularly intriguing hypothesis about the formation of price expectations was proposed by Muth in the early 1960s.[11] He suggested that one (and perhaps the only) method of forming expectations that is consistent with general optimizing behavior is to make such expectations on a "rational" basis by incorporating all available information about the market in question. Specifically, a supplier who knew the precise forms of the demand and supply curves could calculate the equilibrium price

$$P^* = \frac{c - d}{b + a} \tag{17.44}$$

and then use this to form the price expectation

$$E(P_t) = P^* = \frac{c - d}{b + a}. \tag{17.45}$$

[11] John Muth, "Rational Expectations and the Theory of Price Movements," *Econometrica* (July 1961): 315–335.

Using this expected price, supply will be at its equilibrium level, and the market will be free of the inefficient fluctuations observed in the cobweb model. In the absence of any other information or transactions costs, equilibrium will be established instantly.

The information requirements for the rational expectations solution are quite severe. Not only must the supplier know the precise values of the economic parameters a, b, c, and d, but it must also be assumed that no other random influences affect the supply or demand relationships. Models that relax both of these assumptions have been developed, principally in the field of macroeconomics.[12] As might be expected, the results of the rational expectations approach are not so simple once more realistic assumptions are employed, but the approach has revolutionized economists' thinking about expectations.[13]

EXAMPLE 17.4

PRICE EXPECTATIONS AND MARKET EQUILIBRIUM

Suppose that the demand for handmade violins is given by

$$Q_t^D = 10 - 3P_t, \qquad (17.46)$$

where Q_t^D is the number of violins demanded during a period (measured in thousands) and P is the price (measured in tens of thousands of dollars). Since producing a handmade violin takes longer than one period, makers base their decisions on what they expect the price to be:

$$Q_t^S = 2 + E(P_t). \qquad (17.47)$$

In equilibrium

$$E(P_t) = P_t \qquad (17.48)$$

and

$$P^* = 2 \qquad (17.49)$$

$$Q^* = 4.$$

With adaptive expectations, other price-quantity combinations might be observed. If, for example,

---

[12] See, for example, T. Sargent and N. Wallace, "Rational Expectations and the Theory of Economic Policy," *Journal of Monetary Economics* (April 1976): 169–183.

[13] In the theory of financial markets, for instance, the rational expectations notion leads to the "efficient market hypothesis"—that the current market price of an asset reflects all available information about that asset so that any future price movements must depend on the random and unpredictable arrival of new information.

TABLE 17.1

HYPOTHETICAL PRICE AND QUANTITY OF HANDMADE VIOLINS

PERIOD	QUANTITY (1,000)	PRICE ($10,000)
0	NA	1.00
1	3.00	2.33
2	4.33	1.89
3	3.89	2.04
4	4.04	1.99
5	3.99	2.00
6	4.00	2.00

$$E(P_t) = P_{t-1}, \tag{17.50}$$

it is a simple matter to compute the time pattern of prices from any initial price. If $P_0 = 1$, supply in period 1 is given by

$$Q_1 = 2 + P_0 = 3, \tag{17.51}$$

and P_1 is determined by the demand curve

$$3 = 10 - 3P_1 \tag{17.52}$$

or

$$P_1 = 7/3. \tag{17.53}$$

Proceeding in this way yields the time pattern of prices and quantities given in Table 17.1. Clearly, price approaches its equilibrium value fairly rapidly over time. Still though, one might question whether violin makers would continue to use simple adaptive expectations given the regular pattern in these figures. Indeed, the price-quantity points reported in Table 17.1 do not lie on the violin makers' supply curve. Since their expectations are always incorrect *ex post*, they are not making profit-maximizing output decisions in each period. Given the makers' informational disadvantage (that they must base supply decisions on expected prices), optimality would seem to require that they opt for the rational expectations price ($P = 2$) as the only one that would not yield disappointing results.

QUERY: Would the violin makers' situation be improved if they opted to base their expectations on the average price observed in the two previous periods

$$E(P_t) = 0.5(P_{t-1} + P_{t-2})?$$

Existence of imperfect information may not only affect the ability of markets to establish equilibrium prices, but it may also call into question the correspondence between competitive equilibria and Pareto efficiency. The proof of the efficiency of competitive prices assumed that these equilibrium prices were known to all economic actors. If some actors are not fully informed about prevailing prices or (what amounts to the same thing) if information about product quality is not freely available, Adam Smith's invisible hand may not be very effective. Incorrect decisions based on faulty information about price or quality can result in inefficient allocations.

INFORMATION AND INEFFICIENCT EQUILIBRIA

Asymmetric Information and the Lemons Model

One of the first formal models to incorporate imperfect information into a competitive framework was an examination of the market for used cars by G. A. Akerlof.[14] This model applies to any situation in which buyers and sellers of a good have differing ("asymmetric") amounts of information, including many of the models in Chapter 9. Here we will explicitly examine Akerlof's "lemons model," since it is representative of models in which the equilibrium outcome is Parieto inefficient.

To develop his model, Akerlof assumed that used cars come in a number of qualities, say, n. Each of these qualities has a price associated with it ($P_1 \ldots P_n$) representing the value these cars would have to buyers and sellers in a fully informed situation. The asymmetry in information in this problem arises from the fact that sellers of used cars have much more experience with their cars than do would-be buyers. Specifically, Akerlof assumed that sellers know precisely the value of the car they wish to sell, but buyers have no way of knowing a car's quality until they own it. Buyers base their evaluation of cars on the average quality of all cars available, $\overline{P}$. If demanders are to be satisfied, equilibrium price must be $\overline{P}$, since this is what they would pay for a car of average quality. At this price, quantity supplied, Q_s, will be given by

$$Qs = \sum_{P_i < \overline{P}} S_i(P_i), \qquad (17.54)$$

where S_i is the supply of cars of quality P_i, and the sum is taken only over qualities less than $\overline{P}$. For better quality cars, $P_i > \overline{P}$, a would-be seller would rather hold on to his or her car since it is worth more than (poorly informed) demanders are willing to pay. But in this situation, buyers are ultimately unsatisfied since the average quality of used cars traded is less than they expect, $\overline{P}$—only the poor-quality cars are brought to the market so the average quality of cars traded is lower than the overall average of the entire stock of used cars.

---

[14] G. A. Akerlof, "The Market for Lemons: Quality Uncertainty and the Market Mechanism," *Quarterly Journal of Economics* (August 1970): 485–500.

The inefficiency of Akerlof's lemons model arises from the fact that some Pareto optimal transactions do not occur. Both buyers and sellers would be willing to trade at a price in excess of $\overline{P}$ for a high-quality car. But the seller has no way to convince the buyer that his or her car is not a lemon. Indeed, matters may even deteriorate further if buyers learn over time that average quality falls short of $\overline{P}$ and drop their price offers accordingly. In this case, supply and quality will (according to Equation 17.54) fall even further, and an even larger number of Pareto optimal trades will be foregone.

Information and Equilibrium

The lemons example suggests that information about product quality can be acquired and provided in many different ways and that such information may not always be perfectly accurate. To develop models of how competitive markets operate in such situations is very difficult, and there are no universally accepted results. To illustrate some of the problems in building such models, consider the comparatively simple question of how a market equilibrium should be defined. Suppose the quantity demanded of a product can be represented by

$$\text{quantity demanded} = D(P, \alpha), \tag{17.55}$$

where α is the information used by the demander in making his or her decisions. Similarly, supply can be represented by

$$\text{quantity supplied} = S(P, \beta), \tag{17.56}$$

where β is the supplier's information set. As before, an equilibrium occurs where

$$D(P^*, \alpha) = S(P^*, \beta), \tag{17.57}$$

where P^* is the equilibrium price for this good given the information sets α and β. But these information sets themselves are not exogenously determined. Rather, as the used car example suggests, they are determined endogenously as part of demanders' and suppliers' overall decision processes. Furthermore, since the market equilibrium price, P^*, reflects these information sets, rational actors may draw additional information from this price itself. That is, actors may, to some extent, judge quality by price. A rational buyer of expensive cameras, for example, might reason that current prices reflect actual quality differences so he or she need not gain any more information before making a purchase. The fact that other buyers have read *Consumer Reports* is already reflected in the market price. If everyone adopts this position, however, there will not be sufficient pressure on the demand side of the market to assure that the assumption of efficient pricing is valid.

In these situations, then, the concept of market equilibrium is a complex one. It is possible to develop models in which no such equilibrium exists or in which multiple equilibria exist.[15] Hence, it is not surprising that there are no fundamental results about the nature of Pareto optimal allocations in such situations. It is clear that equilibrium allocations with imperfect information will generally be Pareto inferior to allocations with perfect information (as the lemons model suggests), but that conclusion is not an especially interesting one. That information is imperfect and costly to acquire is a fact of nature in all economic organizations. The relevant allocational question is which mechanisms produce Pareto efficient results from among all those that operate within a given informational environment. The informational environment poses a series of constraints on any economic system, and Pareto efficiency must be defined subject to these constraints. Competitive markets incorporate powerful incentives both to generate and to reveal information. But their Pareto efficiency in a variety of imperfect information contexts has not been clearly demonstrated.

Equilibrium and Efficiency

DISTRIBUTION

Although there are forces in competitive price systems that direct resources toward efficient allocations, there are no guarantees that these allocations will exhibit desirable distributions of welfare among individuals. As A. K. Sen has pointed out, an allocation of resources may be Pareto efficient "even when some people are rolling in luxury and others are near starvation as long as the starvers cannot be made better off without cutting into the pleasures of the rich. . . . In short, a society can be Pareto optimal and still be perfectly disgusting."[16] Although a formal treatment of social welfare economics is beyond the scope of this book, here we will look briefly at the nature of the distributional issue.

An Exchange Economy

To study distribution is its simplest setting, assume that there are only two people in society, Smith and Jones. Assume also that the total quantities of two goods (X and Y) to be distributed among these people are in fixed supply. Now we can use the Edgeworth box diagram introduced in Chapter 16 to illustrate all possible allocations of these goods between Smith and Jones. In Figure 17.8 the dimensions of the Edgeworth box are given by the total quantities of the goods available. Smith's indifference curves are drawn with origin O_S and Jones's indifference curves are drawn with origin O_J. Any point

---

[15] For a discussion, see J. E. Stiglitz, "The Causes and Consequences of the Dependence of Quality on Price," *Journal of Economic Literature* (March 1987): 1–48.

[16] A. K. Sen, *Collective Choice and Social Welfare* (San Francisco: Holden-Day, 1970), p. 22.

FIGURE 17.8

EDGEWORTH BOX DIAGRAM OF PARETO EFFICIENCY IN EXCHANGE

The points on the curve O_S, O_J are efficient in the sense that at these allocations Smith cannot be made better off without making Jones worse off, and vice versa. An allocation such as A, on the other hand, is inefficient because both Smith and Jones can be made better off by choosing to move into the shaded area. Notice that along O_S, O_J the *MRS* for Smith is equal to that for Jones. The line O_S, O_J is called the *contract curve*.

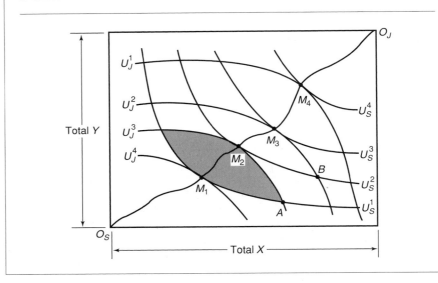

within the box represents a possible allocation of the goods to these two people, and we can use the indifference curves to evaluate the utility derived by each person from such allocations.

Mutually Beneficial
Transactions

Any point within the Edgeworth box (Figure 17.8) in which the *MRS* for Smith is unequal to that for Jones offers an opportunity for Pareto improvements. Consider the potential allocation A in Figure 17.8. This point lies on the point of intersection of Smith's indifference curve U_S^1 and Jones's indifference curve U_J^3. Obviously, the marginal rates of substitution (the slopes of the indifference curves) are not equal at A. Any allocation in the oval-shape shaded area in Figure 17.8 represents a mutually beneficial trade for these two people—they can both move to a higher level of utility by adopting a trade that moves them into this area. When the marginal rates of substitution of Smith and Jones are equal, however, such mutually beneficial trades are not available. The points M_1, M_2, M_3, and M_4 in Figure 17.8 indicate tangencies of these individuals' indifference curves, and movement away from such points must make at least one of the people worse off. A move from M_2 to A, for example, reduces Smith's utility from U_S^2 to U_S^1 even though Jones is made no worse off by the move. Alternatively, a move from M_2 to B makes Jones worse off, but keeps the utility level of Smith constant. In general, then, these points of tangency do not offer the promise of additional mutually beneficial trading and are therefore Pareto efficient.

The set of all the Pareto efficient allocations in an Edgeworth box diagram is called the *contract curve*. In Figure 17.8 this set of points is represented by the line running from O_S to O_J and includes the tangencies M_1, M_2, M_3, and M_4 (and many other such tangencies). Points off the contract curve (such as A or B) are inefficient, and mutually beneficial trades are possible. But, as its name implies, the contract curve represents the exhaustion of all such trading opportunities. Even a move along the contract curve (say, from M_1 to M_2) cannot represent a mutually beneficial trade since there will always be a winner (Smith) and a loser (Jones). These observations may be summarized as follows:

Contract Curve

DEFINITION

Contract Curve   In an exchange economy, all efficient allocations of the existing goods lie along a (multidimensional) *contract curve*. Points off that curve are necessarily inefficient, since individuals can be made unambiguously better off by moving to the curve. Along the contract curve, however, individuals' preferences are rivals in the sense that one individual's situation may be improved only if someone else is made worse off.

In our previous discussion we assumed that fixed quantities of the two goods could be allocated in any way conceivable. A somewhat different analysis would hold if the individuals participating in the exchange possessed specific quantities of the goods at the start. There would still be a very definite possibility that each person could benefit from voluntary trade, since it is unlikely that the initial allocations would be efficient ones. On the other hand, neither person would engage in a trade that would leave him or her worse off than would be the case without trading. Hence, only a portion of the contract curve can be regarded as allocations that might result from voluntary exchange.

Exchange with Initial Endowments

These ideas are illustrated in Figure 17.9. The initial endowments of Smith and Jones are represented by point A in the Edgeworth box. As before, the

FIGURE 17.9

EXCHANGE WITH INITIAL ENDOWMENTS

If individuals start with initial endowments (such as those represented by point A), neither would be willing to accept an allocation that promised a lower level of utility than point A does. Smith would not accept any allocation below U_S^A, and Jones would not accept any allocation below U_J^A. Therefore, not every point on the contract curve can result from free exchange. Only the efficient allocations between M_1 and M_2 are eligible if each individual is free to refrain from trading, and we require that the final allocation be efficient.

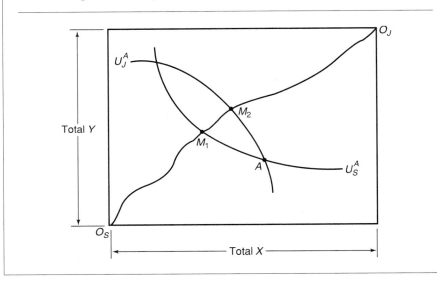

dimensions of the box are taken to be the total quantities of the two goods (X and Y) available. The contract curve of efficient allocations is represented by the line O_S, O_J. Let the indifference curve of Smith, which passes through point A, be called U_S^A and, similarly, let Jones's indifference curve through A be denoted by U_J^A. Notice that at point A, the individuals' indifference curves are not tangent, and therefore the initial endowments are not efficient. Neither Smith nor Jones will accept trading outcomes that give a utility level of less than U_S^A or U_J^A, respectively. It would be preferable for an individual to refrain from trading rather than accept such an inferior outcome. Thus, if we focus only on efficient allocations, only those between M_1 and M_2 on the contract curve can occur as a result of free exchange. The range of efficient outcomes from voluntary exchange has been narrowed by considering the initial endowments with which the individuals enter into trading. If the initial distribution of goods favors Jones, any final allocation will also favor Jones, since it is in Jones's interest to refuse to accept bargains that provide less utility.

This then is the distributional dilemma in its most abstract setting. If initial endowments are skewed in favor of some economic actors, the Pareto efficient allocations promised by the competitive price system will also tend to favor those actors. Voluntary transactions cannot overcome large differences in initial endowments and some sort of (possibly lump sum) transfers will be needed to attain more equal results. Designing such transfer schemes in ways that take account of the various economic incentives involved is a major problem in applied welfare policy. **The Distributional Dilemma**

EXAMPLE 17.5

A TWO-PERSON EXCHANGE ECONOMY

To fix these ideas, consider an exchange economy in which there are exactly 1000 soft drinks (X) and 1000 hamburgers (Y). If we let Smith's utility be represented by

$$U_S(X_S, Y_S) = X_S^{2/3} Y_S^{1/3} \qquad (17.58)$$

and Jones's utility by

$$U_J(X_J, Y_J) = X_J^{1/3} Y_J^{2/3}, \qquad (17.59)$$

we can compute the efficient ways of allocating soft drinks and hamburgers. Notice at the start that Smith has a relative preference for soft drinks, whereas Jones tends to prefer hamburgers, as reflected by the differing exponents in the utility functions of the two individuals. We might therefore expect that efficient allocations would give relatively more soft drinks to Smith and relatively more hamburgers to Jones.

To find the efficient points in this situation, suppose we let Smith start at any preassigned utility level, U_S. Our problem now is to choose X_S, Y_S, X_J, and Y_J to make Jones's utility as large as possible given Smith's utility constraint. Setting up the Lagrangian for this problem yields

$$\mathcal{L} = U_J(X_J, Y_J) + \lambda[U_S(X_S, Y_S) - \overline{U}_S]$$
$$= X_J^{1/3} Y_J^{2/3} + \lambda(X_S^{2/3} Y_S^{1/3} - \overline{U}_S). \qquad (17.60)$$

Remember now that Jones simply gets what Smith doesn't and vice versa. Hence,

$$X_J = 1000 - X_S$$

and (17.61)

$$Y_J = 1000 - Y_S.$$

Our Lagrangian is therefore only a function of the two variables X_S and Y_S:

$$\mathcal{L} = (1000 - X_S)^{1/3}(1000 - Y_S)^{2/3} + \lambda(X_S^{2/3}Y_S^{1/3} - \overline{U}_S). \quad (17.62)$$

The first-order conditions for a maximum are

$$\frac{\partial \mathcal{L}}{\partial X_S} = -\frac{1}{3}\left(\frac{1000 - Y_S}{1000 - X_S}\right)^{2/3} + \frac{2\lambda}{3}\left(\frac{Y_S}{X_S}\right)^{1/3} = 0$$

$$\frac{\partial \mathcal{L}}{\partial Y_S} = -\frac{2}{3}\left(\frac{1000 - X_S}{1000 - Y_S}\right)^{1/3} + \frac{\lambda}{3}\left(\frac{X_S}{Y_S}\right)^{2/3} = 0. \quad (17.63)$$

Moving the terms in λ to the right side of these equations and dividing the top equation by the bottom gives[17]

$$\frac{1}{2}\left(\frac{1000 - Y_S}{1000 - X_S}\right) = 2\left(\frac{Y_S}{X_S}\right) \quad (17.64)$$

or

$$\frac{X_S}{(1000 - X_S)} = \left(\frac{4Y_S}{1000 - Y_S}\right), \quad (17.65)$$

which is our required condition for efficiency. We can now use Equation 17.65 to calculate any number of Pareto efficient allocations. In Table 17.2 we have done so for a few values of X_S ranging from 0 to 1000 (that is, for situations in which Smith gets nothing to situations where she gets everything).

Pareto Efficiency. To illustrate why points off this contract curve are inefficient, consider an initial allocation in which Smith and Jones share X and Y equally. With 500 units of each item, both Smith and Jones receive a utility of 500 (assuming that such utility measurement is meaningful). But, by using your basic scientific calculator, it is a relatively simple matter to show that there are many allocations on the contract curve that offer more utility to both people. Table 17.2 shows that this is nearly true for the allocations where Smith gets 600 or 700 soft drinks, and the precise boundaries of such mutually beneficial trades can be easily calculated. For example, consider $X_S = 660$, $Y_S = 327$, $X_J = 340$, and $Y_J = 673$. For this allocation Smith's utility is 522 and Jones's is 536. They are clearly both better

---

[17] Notice that Equation 17.64 is a restatement of the condition that the individuals' marginal rates of substitution must be equal for an efficient allocation. That is, MRS (for Smith) $= (\partial U_S/\partial X)/(\partial U_S/\partial Y) = 2(Y/X)$ and MRS (for Jones) $= (\partial U_J/\partial X)/(\partial U_J/\partial Y) = 1/2(Y/X)$.

TABLE 17.2

PARETO EFFICIENT ALLOCATIONS OF 1000 SOFT DRINKS AND 1000 HAMBURGERS TO SMITH AND JONES

X_S	Y_S	$U_S =$ $X_S^{2/3} Y_S^{1/3}$	$X_J =$ $1000 - X_S$	$Y_J =$ $1000 - Y_S$	$U_J =$ $X_J^{1/3} Y_J^{2/3}$
0	0	0	1000	1000	1000
100	27	65	900	973	948
200	59	133	800	941	891
300	97	206	700	903	830
400	143	284	600	857	761
500	200	368	500	800	684
600	273	461	400	727	596
700	368	565	300	632	493
800	500	684	200	500	368
900	692	825	100	308	212
1000	1000	1000	0	0	0

off than at the initial alloction, and one might expect some sort of trading to take place that moves them toward the contract curve.

Effects of Initial Endowments. To see how initial endowments may restrict the range of Pareto efficient solutions in this economy, suppose Smith starts in a very favorable position with $X_S = 800$, $Y_S = 800$. Then Jones gets $X_J = 200$, $Y_J = 200$, and the initial utility levels are $U_S = 800$, $U_J = 200$. There are Pareto improvements that might be made from these initial endowments, but none of them will improve Jones's situation very much. For example, if we hold Smith's utility at 800, the efficient allocation $X_S = 884$, $Y_S = 657$, $X_J = 116$, $Y_J = 343$ will increase Jones's utility from 200 to 239. But that is the best that Jones can do given the constraint that Smith cannot be made worse off. The efficiency gains to Jones, while significant, do very little to move the overall allocation toward more equal outcomes.

QUERY: Would different preferences for the two people in this example offer greater scope for equalizing outcomes from voluntary transactions? Are there any preferences for Smith and Jones for which voluntary transactions would lead to equality even from very unequal initial allocations?

SUMMARY

In this chapter we have formalized Adam Smith's initial conjectures about the efficient properties of the "invisible hand" of competitive market forces. The equivalence between Pareto efficient allocations and perfectly competitive equilibria is the principal discovery of modern welfare economics. It provides the point of departure into practically all areas of normative, policy-oriented economics. Several major points were illustrated in our development of this fundamental relationship:

- Pareto's definition of an efficient allocation of resources—that no one person can be made better off without making someone else worse off—provides the basic focus for normative welfare theory.

- Productive or technical efficiency is a necessary though not sufficient condition for Pareto efficiency. Achieving technical efficiency (that is, being on the production possibility frontier) requires that three marginal conditions hold: (1) equality of rates of technical substitution across different outputs; (2) equality of marginal productivities among firms; and (3) equality of rates of product transformation across firms.

- Pareto efficiency requires both productive efficiency and efficiency in the choice of output mix. This latter goal can be attained by choosing that technically efficient output combination for which the rate of product transformation between any two goods is equal to individuals' marginal rate of substitution for these goods.

- Reliance on competitive equilibrium prices will yield a technically efficient allocation of resources because profit-maximizing firms will make choices that are consistent with the three marginal allocation rules. Existence of competitive equilibrium prices for outputs will also result in an efficient output mix. By so doing, the correspondence between Pareto efficiency and competitive equilibria is made complete.

- Violations of the competitive assumptions such as imperfect competition, externalities, or the existence of public goods may distort the allocation of resources away from Pareto efficiency.

- Imperfect information may affect the speed with which markets achieve equilibrium, perhaps yielding inefficient disequilibrium outcomes over the short term. Informational asymmetries may also affect the Pareto efficiency of competitive equilibria.

- Distributional outcomes under competitive markets may sometimes be considered undesirable from the perspective of equity. Initial endowments may constrain the range of outcomes achievable through voluntary transactions.

PROBLEMS

17.1

Suppose that Robinson Crusoe produces and consumes fish (F) and coconuts (C). Assume that during a certain period he has decided to work 200 hours and is indifferent as to whether he spends this time fishing or gathering coconuts. Robinson's production for fish is given by

$$F = \sqrt{L_F}$$

and for coconuts by

$$C = \sqrt{L_C},$$

where L_F and L_C are the number of hours spent fishing or gathering coconuts. Consequently,

$$L_C + L_F = 200.$$

Robinson Crusoe's utility for fish and coconuts is given by

$$\textbf{utility} = \sqrt{F \cdot C}.$$

a. If Robinson cannot trade with the rest of the world, how will he choose to allocate his labor? What will the optimal levels of F and C be? What will his utility be? What will be the RPT (of fish for coconuts)?

b. Suppose now that trade is opened and Robinson can trade fish and coconuts at a price ratio of $P_F/P_C = 2/1$. If Robinson continues to produce the quantities of F and C in part (a), what will he choose to consume, given the opportunity to trade? What will his new level of utility be?

c. How would your answer to part (b) change if Robinson adjusts his production to take advantage of the world prices?

d. Graph your results for parts (a), (b), and (c).

17.2

Consider an economy with just one technique available for the production of each good:

GOOD	FOOD	CLOTH
Labor per unit output	1	1
Land per unit output	2	1

a. Suppose that land is unlimited, but labor equals 100. Write and sketch the production possibility frontier.

b. Suppose that labor is unlimited but land equals 150. Write and sketch the production possibility frontier.

c. Suppose that labor equals 100 and land equals 150. Write and sketch the production possibility frontier. (*Suggestion:* What are the intercepts of the production possibility frontier? When is land fully employed? Labor? Both?)

d. Explain why the production possibility frontier of part (c) is concave.

e. Sketch the relative price of food as a function of its output in case (c).

f. If consumers insist on trading 4 units of food for 5 units of cloth, what is the relative price of food? Why?

g. Explain why production is exactly the same at a price ratio of $P_F/P_C = 1.1$ as at $P_F/P_C = 1.9$.

h. Suppose that capital is also required for producing food and clothing and that capital requirements per unit of food and per unit of clothing are 0.8 and 0.9, respectively. There are 100 units of capital

available. What is the production possibility curve in this case? Answer part (e) for this case.

17.3

In the country of Ruritania there are two regions, A and B. Two goods (X and Y) are produced in both regions. Production functions for region A are given by

$$X_A = \sqrt{L_X}$$
$$Y_A = \sqrt{L_Y}.$$

L_X and L_Y are the quantity of labor devoted to X and Y production, respectively. Total labor available in region A is 100 units. That is,

$$L_X + L_Y = 100.$$

Using a similar notation for region B, production functions are given by

$$X_B = \frac{1}{2}\sqrt{L_X}$$

$$Y_B = \frac{1}{2}\sqrt{L_Y}.$$

There are also 100 units of labor available in region B:

$$L_X + L_Y = 100.$$

a. Calculate the production possibility curves for regions A and B.

b. What condition must hold if production in Ruritania is to be allocated efficiently between regions A and B (assuming that labor cannot move from one region to the other)?

c. Calculate the production possibility curve for Ruritania (again assuming that labor is immobile between regions). How much total Y can Ruritania produce if total X output is 12?
Hint: A graphical analysis may be of some help here.

17.4

Suppose that all of the firms in Utopia obey the Pareto conditions for efficiency except General Widget (GW). That firm has a monopoly in production of widgets and is the only hirer of widget makers in the country. Suppose that the production function for widgets is

$$Q = 2L$$

(where L is the number of widget makers hired). If the demand for widgets is given by

$$P = 100 - Q$$

and the supply curve of widget makers by

$$w = 20 + 2L,$$

how many widgets should GW produce in order to maximize profits? At that output, what will L, w, and P be? How does this solution compare to that which would prevail if GW behaved in a competitive manner? Can you evaluate the gain to society of having GW be competitive?

17.5
Smith and Jones are stranded on a desert island. Each has in his possession some slices of ham (H) and cheese (C). Smith is a very choosy eater and will eat ham and cheese only in the fixed proportions of 2 slices of cheese to 1 slice of ham. His utility function is given by $U_S = \min(H, C/2)$.

Jones is more flexible in his dietary tastes and has a utility function given by $U_J = 4H + 3C$. Total endowments are 100 slices of ham and 200 slices of cheese.
a. Draw the Edgeworth box diagram that represents the possibilities for exchange in this situation. What is the only exchange ratio that can prevail in any equilibrium?
b. Suppose that Smith initially had $40H$ and $80C$. What would the equilibrium position be?
c. Suppose that Smith initially had $60H$ and $80C$. What would the equilibrium position be?
d. Suppose that Smith (much the stronger of the two) decides not to play by the rules of the game. Then what could the final equilibrium position be?

17.6
In Example 17.5 each individual has an initial endowment of 500 units of each good.
a. Express the demand of Smith and Jones for goods X and Y as functions of P_X and P_Y and their initial endowments.
b. Use the demand functions from part (a) together with the observation that total demand for each good must be 1000 to calculate the equilibrium

price ratio, P_X/P_Y, in this situation. What are the equilibrium consumption levels of each good by each person?

17.7
How would the answers to Problem 17.6 change for the following initial endowments?

	SMITH'S ENDOWMENT		JONES'S ENDOWMENT	
	X	Y	X	Y
a.	0	1000	1000	0
b.	600	600	400	400
c.	400	400	600	600
d.	1000	1000	0	0

Explain the reason for these varying results.

17.8
Suppose that the market demand for a particular product is given by

$$Q_D = -2P + 13$$

and the industry supply curve by

$$Q_s = 2P^2 - 12P + 21.$$

What are the equilibrium prices for this market? Which of these prices is stable by the Walrasian criterion?

17.9
Suppose that the demand curve for corn at time t is given by

$$Q_t = 100 - 2P_t$$

and that supply in period t is given by

$$Q_t = 70 + E(P_t),$$

where $E(P_t)$ is what suppliers expect the price to be in period t.
a. If in equilibrium $E(P_t) = P_t$, what are the price and quantity of corn in this market?
b. Suppose that suppliers are myopic and use last period's price as their expectation of this year's price [that is, $E(P_t) = P_{t-1}$]. If the initial market price of corn is $8, how long will it take for price to get within $.25 of the equilibrium price?

c. If farmers have "rational" expectations, how would they choose $E(P_t)$?

17.10

The used car supply in Metropolis consists of 10,000 cars. The value of these cars ranges from $5,000 to $15,000 with exactly one car being worth each dollar amount between these two figures. Used car owners are always willing to sell their cars for what they are worth. Demanders of used cars in Metropolis have no way of telling the value of a particular car. Their demand depends on the average value of cars in the market ($\overline{P}$) and on the price of the cars themselves (P) according to the equation

$$Q = 1.5\,\overline{P} - P.$$

a. If demanders base their estimate of $\overline{P}$ on the entire used car market, what will its value be and what will be the equilibrium price of used cars?

b. In the equilibrium described in part (a), what will be the average value of used cars actually traded in the market?

c. If demanders revise their estimate of $\overline{P}$ on the basis of the average value of cars actually traded, what will be the new equilibrium price of used cars? What is the average value of cars traded now?

d. Is there a market equilibrium in this situation at which the actual value of $\overline{P}$ is consistent with supply-demand equilibrium at a positive price and quantity?

SUGGESTED READINGS

Akerlof, G. A. "The Market for Lemons: Quality Uncertainty and the Market Mechanism." *Quarterly Journal of Economics* (August 1970): 488–500.
Early demonstration of the inefficiency of asymmetric information. Suggests many additional applications of the model.

Arrow, K. J., and F. H. Hahn. *General Competitive Analysis.* Amsterdam: North-Holland Publishing Co., 1978. Chaps. 1 and 2.
Comprehensive treatment of the efficiency of perfect competition. Heavy going in spots, but many literary sections too.

Bator, F. M. "The Simple Analytics of Welfare Maximization." *American Economic Review* (March 1957): 22–59.
Good graphical integration of productive and exchange efficiency.

Feldman, A. *Welfare Economics and Social Choice Theory.* Amsterdam: Martinus Nijhoff, 1980.
First two chapters give a good summary of efficiency notion in general equilibrium models.

Grossman, S., and J. Stiglitz. "On the Impossibility of Informationally Efficient Markets." *American Economic Review* (June 1980): 393–408.
Illustrates some difficulties in defining equilibrium in markets with efficient acquisition of information and where market prices incorporate all available information.

Sen, A. K. *Collective Choice and Social Welfare.* San Francisco: Holden-Day, 1970. Chaps. 1 and 2.
Basic reference on social choice theory. Early chapters have a good discussion of the meaning and limitations of the Pareto efficiency concept.

Spence, M. *Market Signalling.* Cambridge, Mass.: Harvard University Press, 1974.
Examines the consequences of markets in which information is imperfect and where participants try to signal product quality. Many applications, especially to the labor market.

MODELS OF IMPERFECT COMPETITION

One of the most important assumptions made throughout Part V was that both suppliers and demanders were price takers. All economic actors were assumed to exert no influence on prices, and therefore prices were treated as fixed parameters in their decisions. This behavioral assumption was crucial to most of our analysis, especially that related to the efficiency properties of the competitive price system. In this part we will explore the consequences of dropping the price-taking assumption for suppliers of goods.

We begin our examination of imperfect competition in Chapter 18 with the case of a single supplier of a good. Such a supplier is called a *monopoly*. This supplier faces the entire market demand curve for its product and can choose to operate at any point on that demand curve. That is, the monopoly supplier can choose whatever price-quantity combination on the demand curve it finds most profitable. Its activities are constrained only by the nature of the demand curve for its product, not by the behavior of rival producers. This then is the polar opposite case from perfect competition in which the existence of many suppliers enforces price-taking behavior on any one firm.

In Chapter 19 we move from the relatively simple case of monopoly to market structures involving a "few" firms. As we shall see, adding additional suppliers (even if we restrict ourselves to two-firm models of duopoly) makes matters much more complicated. In such cases any one firm does not face the total market demand curve, but, rather, faces a demand curve for its own output that will have properties determined in part by its rivals' behavior—the demand curve for GM cars depends in part on what Ford and Toyota do. To develop a realistic model, therefore, requires that some assumption be made about how one firm believes its rivals behave.

The issues of intrafirm rivalry and product differentiation introduced in Chapter 19 can also be approached formally as applications of the game theory tool that we introduced in Chapter 10. In Chapter 20 we survey some of these applications. We show how many strategic situations can be interpreted in game-theoretic terms and illustrate how the notion of market equilibrium has important analogies in these models.

CHAPTER 18

MODELS OF MONOPOLY

A *monopoly* is a single firm that serves an entire market. This single firm faces the market demand curve for its output. Using its knowledge of this demand curve, the monopoly makes a decision on how much to produce. Unlike the perfectly competitive firm's output decision (which has no effect on market price), the monopoly's output decision will, in fact, determine the good's price. In this sense monopoly markets and markets characterized by perfect competition are polar opposite cases.

At times it is more convenient to treat monopolies as having the power to set prices. Technically, a monopoly can choose that point on the market demand curve at which it prefers to operate. It may choose either market price or quantity, but not both. In this chapter we will usually assume that monopolies choose the quantity of output that maximizes profits and then settle for the market price that the chosen output level yields. It would be a simple matter to rephrase the discussion in terms of price setting, and in some places we shall do so. Given these conventions, we define a monopoly as follows:

DEFINITION

Monopoly   A *monopoly* is a single supplier to a market. This firm may choose to produce at any point on the market demand curve.

The reason a monopoly exists is that other firms find it unprofitable or impossible to enter the market. *Barriers to entry* are therefore the source of all monopoly power. If other firms could enter a market, the firm would, by definition, no longer be a monopoly. There are two general types of barriers to entry: technical barriers and legal barriers.

BARRIERS TO ENTRY

Technical Barriers to Entry

A primary technical barrier is that the production of the good in question may exhibit decreasing marginal (and average) costs over a wide range of output levels. The technology of production is such that relatively large-scale firms are low-cost producers. In this situation (which is sometimes referred to as *natural monopoly*) one firm may find it profitable to drive others out of the industry by price cutting. Similarly, once a monopoly has been established, entry will be difficult because any new firm must produce at relatively low levels of output and therefore at relatively high average costs. It is important to stress that the range of declining costs need only be "large" relative to the market in question. Declining costs on some absolute scale are not necessary. For example, the production and delivery of concrete does not exhibit declining marginal costs over a broad range of output when compared to the total U.S. market. However, in any particular small town, declining marginal costs may permit a monopoly to be established. The high costs of transportation in this industry tend to isolate one market from another.

Another technical basis of monopoly is special knowledge of a low-cost productive technique. But the problem for the monopoly that fears entry is keeping this technique uniquely to itself. When matters of technology are involved, this may be extremely difficult, unless the technology can be protected by a patent (see below). Ownership of unique resources, such as mineral deposits or land locations, or the possession of unique managerial talents may also be a lasting basis for maintaining a monopoly.

Legal Barriers to Entry

Many pure monopolies are created as a matter of law rather than as a matter of economic conditions. One important example of a government-granted monopoly position is in the legal protection of a productive technique by a patent. Xerox machines and Polaroid cameras are notable examples of highly successful products that were protected from competition (for a while) by a labyrinth of patents. Because the basic technology for these products was uniquely assigned to one firm, a monopoly position was established. The defense made of such a governmentally granted monopoly position is that the patent system makes innovation more profitable and therefore acts as an incentive to technical progress. Whether the benefits of such innovative behavior exceed the costs of having technological monopolies is an open question.

A second example of a legally created monopoly is the awarding of an exclusive franchise to serve a market. These franchises are awarded in cases of public utility (gas and electric) service, communications services, the post office, some television and radio station markets, and a variety of other situations. The argument usually put forward in favor of creating these franchised monopolies is that the industry in question is a natural monopoly: Average cost is diminishing over a broad range of output levels, and minimum average cost can be achieved only by organizing the industry as a monopoly. The public utility and communications industries are often considered to be good examples. Certainly, that does appear to be the case for local electricity and telephone service where a given network probably exhibits declining average cost up to the point of universal coverage. But recent deregulation actions in long-distance telephone service and suggestions for similar reforms in electricity generation show that even for these industries the natural monopoly rationale may not be all-inclusive. In other cases, franchises may be based largely on political rationales. This seems to be true for the postal service in the United States and for a number of nationalized industries (airlines, radio and television, banking) in other countries.

Creation of Barriers to Entry

Although some barriers to entry may be independent of the monopolist's own activities, other barriers may result directly from those activities. For example, firms may develop unique products or technologies and take extraordinary steps to keep these from being copied by competitors. Or firms may buy up unique resources to prevent potential entry. The De Beers cartel, for example, controls a high fraction of the world's diamond mines. Finally, a would-be monopolist may enlist government aid in devising barriers to entry. It may lobby for legislation that restricts new entrants so as to "maintain an orderly market" or for health and safety regulations that raise potential entrants' costs. Because the monopolist has both special knowledge of its business and significant incentives to pursue these goals, it may have considerable success in creating such barriers to entry.

The attempt by a monopolist to erect barriers to entry may involve real resource costs. Maintaining secrecy, buying unique resources, and engaging in political lobbying are all costly activities. A full analysis of monopoly should involve not only questions of cost minimization and output choice (as under perfect competition) but also an analysis of profit-maximizing entry barrier creation. However, we will not provide a detailed investigation of such questions here.[1] Instead, we will generally assume that the monopolist can do nothing to affect barriers to entry and that the firm's costs are therefore similar to what a competitive firm's costs would be. At times, however, we will mention some of the complications raised by the possibility of expenditures incurred to protect a monopolist's market. A more complete discussion of these "rent-seeking" expenditures is presented in Chapter 25.

---

[1] For a simple treatment, see R. A. Posner, "The Social Costs of Monopoly and Regulation," *Journal of Political Economy* 83 (August 1975): 807–827.

PROFIT MAXIMIZATION AND OUTPUT CHOICE

In order to maximize profits, a monopoly will choose to produce that output level for which marginal revenue is equal to marginal cost. Since the monopoly, in contrast to a perfectly competitive firm, faces a negatively sloped market demand curve, marginal revenue will be less than price. To sell an additional unit, the monopoly must lower its price on all units to be sold if it is to generate the extra demand necessary to absorb this marginal unit. The profit-maximizing output level for a firm is then the level Q^* in Figure 18.1. At that level marginal revenue is equal to marginal costs, and profits are maximized.

Given the monopoly's decision to produce Q^*, the demand curve D indicates that a market price of P^* will prevail. This is the price that demanders as a group are willing to pay for the output of the monopoly. In the market, an equilibrium price-quantity combination of P^*, Q^* will be

FIGURE 18.1

PROFIT MAXIMIZATION AND PRICE DETERMINATION FOR A MONOPOLY

A profit-maximizing monopolist produces that quantity for which marginal revenue is equal to marginal cost. In the diagram this quantity is given by Q^*, which will yield a price of P^* in the market. Monopoly profits can be read as the rectangle P^*EAC.

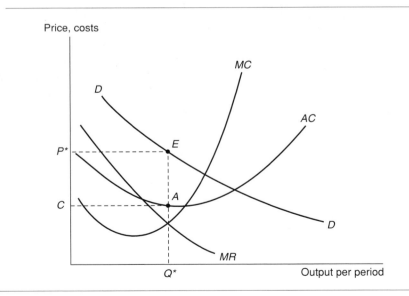

observed. Assuming $P^* > AC$, this output level will be profitable, and the monopolist will have no incentive to alter output levels unless demand or cost conditions change. Hence, we have the following principle:

OPTIMIZATION PRINCIPLE

Monopolist's Output   A monopolist will choose to produce that output for which marginal revenue equals marginal cost. Since the monopolist faces a downward-sloping demand curve, market price will exceed both marginal revenue and the firm's marginal cost at this output level.

In Chapter 13 we showed that the assumption of profit maximization implies that the gap between the price of a firm's output and its marginal cost is inversely related to the price elasticity of the demand curve facing the firm. Applying Equation 13.13 to the case of monopoly yields

The Inverse Elasticity Rule, Again

$$\frac{P - MC}{P} = -\frac{1}{e_{Q,P}},\qquad (18.1)$$

where now we use the elasticity of demand for the entire market ($e_{Q,P}$) since the monopoly is the sole supplier of the good in question. This observation leads to two general conclusions about monopoly pricing. First, a monopoly will only choose to operate in regions in which the *market* demand curve is elastic ($e_{Q,P} < -1$). If demand were inelastic, marginal revenue would be negative and could not therefore be equated to marginal cost (which presumably is always positive). Equation 18.1 also shows that $e_{Q,P} > -1$ implies an (implausible) negative marginal cost.

A second implication of Equation 18.1 is that the firm's "markup" over marginal cost (measured as a fraction of price) depends inversely on the elasticity of market demand. If, for example, $e_{Q,P} = -2$, Equation 18.1 shows that $P = 2MC$, whereas if $e_{Q,P} = -10$, $P = 1.11MC$. Notice also that if the elasticity of demand were constant along the entire demand curve, the proportional markup over marginal cost would remain unchanged in response to possible changes in input costs. Market price, therefore, moves proportionally to marginal cost—increases in marginal cost will prompt the monopoly to increase its price proportionally, and decreases in marginal cost will cause the monopoly to reduce its price proportionally. Even if elasticity is not constant along the demand curve, it seems clear from Figure 18.1 that increases in marginal cost will increase price (though not necessarily in the same proportion). So long as the demand curve facing the monopoly is downward sloping, upward shifts in *MC* will prompt the monopoly to reduce output and thereby obtain a higher price.[2]

Monopoly Profits   Total profits earned by the monopolist can be read directly from Figure 18.1. These are shown by the rectangle *P*EAC* and again represent the profit per unit (price minus average cost) times the number of units sold. These profits will be positive if market price exceeds average total cost. If $P^* < AC$, however, the monopolist can only operate at a long-term loss and will decline to serve the market.

Since no entry is possible into a monopoly market, the monopolist's positive profits can exist even in the long run. For this reason some authors refer to the profits that a monopoly earns in the long run as *monopoly rents*. These profits can be regarded as a return to that factor that forms the basis of the monopoly (a patent, a favorable location, or a dynamic entrepreneur, for example); hence, another possible owner might be willing to pay that amount in rent for the right to the monopoly. The potential for profits is the reason why some firms pay other firms for the right to use a patent and why concessioners at sporting events (and on some highways) are willing to pay for the right to the concession. To the extent monopoly rights are given away at below their true market value (as in radio and television licensing), the wealth of the recipients of those rights is increased.

Although a monopoly may earn positive profits in the long run,[3] the size of such profits will depend on the relationship between the monopolist's average costs and the demand for its product. Figure 18.2 illustrates two situations in which the demand, marginal revenue, and marginal cost curves are rather similar. As Equation 18.1 suggests, the price–marginal cost markup is about the same in these two cases. But average costs in Figure 18.2a are considerably lower than in Figure 18.2b. Although the profit-maximizing decisions are similar in the two cases, the level of profits ends up being quite different. In Figure 18.2a the monopolist's price (*P**) exceeds the average cost of producing *Q** (labeled *AC**) by a large extent, and significant profits are obtained. In Figure 18.2b, however, $P^* = AC^*$ and the monopoly earns zero economic profits, the largest amount possible in this case. Hence, large profits from a monopoly are not inevitable, and the actual extent of economic profits may not always be a good guide to the significance of monopolistic influences in a market.

---

[2] The comparative statics of a shift in the demand curve facing the monopolist are not so clear, however, and no unequivocal prediction about price can be made. For an analysis of this issue, see the discussion that follows and Problem 18.4.

[3] As in the competitive case, the profit-maximizing monopolist would be willing to produce at a loss in the short run as long as market price exceeds average variable cost.

FIGURE 18.2

MONOPOLY PROFITS DEPEND ON THE RELATIONSHIP BETWEEN
THE DEMAND AND AVERAGE COST CURVES

Both of the monopolies in this figure are equally "strong," if by this we mean they produce similar divergences between market price and marginal cost. However, because of the location of the demand and average cost curves, it turns out that the monopoly in (a) earns high profits whereas that in (b) earns no profits. Consequently, the size of profits is not a measure of the strength of a monopoly.

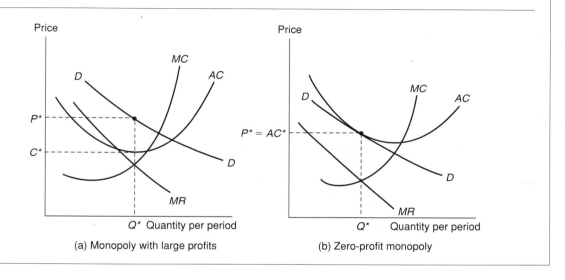

(a) Monopoly with large profits   (b) Zero-profit monopoly

In the theory of perfectly competitive markets we presented in Part V, it was possible to speak of an industry supply curve. We constructed this curve by allowing the market demand curve to shift and observing the supply curve that was traced out by the series of equilibrium price-quantity combinations. This type of construction is not possible for monopolistic markets. With a fixed market demand curve, the supply "curve" for a monopoly will be only one point, namely, that price-quantity combination for which $MR = MC$. If the demand curve should shift, the marginal revenue curve would also shift, and a new profit-maximizing output would be chosen. However, connecting the resulting series of equilibrium points on the market demand curves would have little meaning. This locus might have a very strange shape, depending on how the market demand curve's elasticity (and its associated MR curve) changes as the curve is shifted. In this sense the monopoly firm has no well-defined "supply curve."

There Is No Monopoly Supply Curve

EXAMPLE 18.1

MONOPOLY WITH LINEAR DEMAND

Suppose the market for Olympic-quality Frisbees (Q, measured in Frisbees bought per year) has a linear demand curve of the form

$$Q = 2,000 - 20P \tag{18.2}$$

or

$$P = 100 - Q/20 \tag{18.3}$$

and that the costs of a monopoly Frisbee producer are given by

$$TC = .05Q^2 + 10,000. \tag{18.4}$$

To maximize profits, this producer chooses that output level for which $MR = MC$:

$$P \cdot Q = 100Q - Q^2/20 \tag{18.5}$$

so

$$MR = 100 - Q/10 = MC = .1Q \tag{18.6}$$

and

$$Q^* = 500 \quad P^* = 75. \tag{18.7}$$

At the monopoly's preferred output level,

$$TC = .05(500)^2 + 10,000 = 22,500$$
$$AC = 22,500/500 = 45. \tag{18.8}$$

Using this information we can calculate profits by

$$\pi = (P^* - AC) \cdot Q^* = (75 - 45) \cdot 500 = 15,000. \tag{18.9}$$

Notice that at this equilibrium there is a large markup between price (75) and marginal cost ($MC = .1Q = 50$). As long as entry barriers prevent a new firm from producing Olympic-quality Frisbees, however, this gap and positive economic profits can persist indefinitely.

An Illustration of the Inverse Elasticity Rule. To see that the inverse elasticity rule holds, we need to compute the elasticity of demand at the monopoly's equilibrium point:

$$e_{Q,P} = \frac{\partial Q}{\partial P} \cdot \frac{P}{Q} = -20 \left(\frac{75}{500} \right) = -3. \tag{18.10}$$

So, by Equation 18.1

$$\frac{P - MC}{P} = \frac{1}{3}$$

or

$$P = \frac{3}{2} MC,$$

(18.11)

which is indeed the relationship between the equilibrium price (75) and the monopoly's marginal cost (50).

QUERY: How would an increase in fixed costs from 10,000 to 12,500 affect the monopoly's output plans? How would profits be affected? Suppose total costs were to shift to $TC = .075Q^2 + 10,000$. How would the equilibrium change?

In Chapter 17 we showed that the presence of monopoly can distort the efficiency properties of a competitive price system. Because a monopoly can affect market prices, it may be in its interest to restrict output in order to attain higher profits than are available at competitive prices. In this section we will offer a somewhat more complete analysis of this distortion using the partial equilibrium model of monopoly.

MONOPOLY AND RESOURCE ALLOCATION

In order to evaluate the allocational effect of a monopoly, we need a precisely defined basis of comparison. A particularly simple comparison is provided by the perfectly competitive, constant-cost industry. In this case, as we showed in Chapter 14, the industry's long-run supply curve will be infinitely elastic with price equal to both marginal and average cost. It is convenient to think of a monopoly as arising from the "capture" of such a competitive industry and to treat the individual firms that constitute the competitive industry as now being single plants in the monopolist's empire. A prototype case would be John D. Rockefeller's purchase of most of the U.S. petroleum refineries in the late nineteenth century and his decision to operate them as part of the Standard Oil monopoly. We can then compare the performance of this monopoly to the performance of the previously competitive industry to arrive at a statement about the welfare consequences of monopoly.

Basis of Comparison

FIGURE 18.3

ALLOCATIONAL AND DISTRIBUTIONAL EFFECTS OF MONOPOLY

Monopolization of this previously competitive market would cause output to be reduced from Q^* to Q^{**}. Consumer expenditures and productive inputs worth AEQ^*Q^{**} are reallocated to the production of other goods. Consumer surplus equal to $P^{**}BAP^*$ is transferred into monopoly profits. There is a deadweight loss given by BEA.

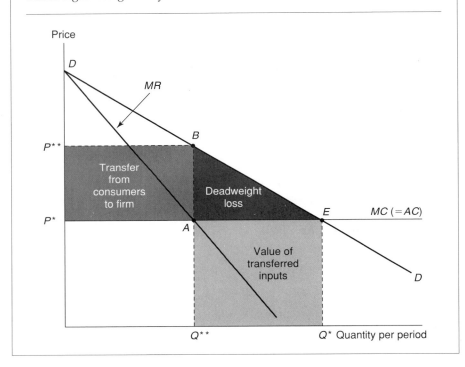

A Graphical Analysis   Figure 18.3 shows a simple linear demand curve for a product that is produced by a constant-cost industry.[4] If this market were competitive, output would be Q^*—that is, production would occur where price is equal to long-run average and marginal cost. Under a simple single-price

---

[4] Here we use the usual Marshallian demand curve on the presumption that income effects are relatively unimportant for the market we are analyzing. If income effects were significant, our analysis would be more nearly correct if we used an income-compensated demand curve instead.

monopoly, output would be Q^{**} since this is the level of production for which marginal revenue is equal to marginal cost. The restriction in output from Q^* to Q^{**} represents the misallocation brought about through monopolization. This is the result we showed previously in Figure 17.4. The total value of resources released by this output restriction is shown in Figure 18.3 as area AEQ^*Q^{**}. Essentially, the monopoly closes down some of the plants that operated in the competitive case. As we discussed previously, transferring these inputs elsewhere will cause these other goods to be overproduced relative to their Pareto efficient levels.

The restriction in output from Q^* to Q^{**} involves a total loss in consumer surplus of $P^{**}BEP^*$. Part of this loss is captured by the monopoly as profits. These profits are measured by $P^{**}BAP^*$, and they reflect a transfer of income from consumers to the firm. Whether such a transfer is regarded as desirable depends on prevailing societal norms about whether consumers or the monopoly are more deserving of such gains. As for any transfer, difficult issues of equity arise in attempting to assess social desirability. There is no ambiguity about the loss in consumers' surplus given by area BEA, however, since this loss is not transferred to anyone. It is a pure "deadweight" loss and represents the principal measure of the allocational harm of the monopoly.[5]

To illustrate the nature of this deadweight loss, consider Example 18.1, in which we calculated an equilibrium price of $75 and a marginal cost of $50. This gap between price and marginal cost is an indication of the efficiency-improving trades that are foregone through monopolization. Undoubtedly, there is a would-be buyer who is willing to pay, say, $60 for an Olympic Frisbee, but not $75. A price of $60 would more than cover all of the resource costs involved in Frisbee production, but the presence of the monopoly prevents such a mutually beneficial transaction between Frisbee users and the providers of Frisbee-making resources. For this reason, monopoly clearly does not lead to a Pareto optimal allocation of resources. Economists have made many attempts to estimate the overall cost of these deadweight losses in actual monopoly situations. Most of these estimates are rather small when viewed in the context of the whole economy.[6] Allocational losses are larger, however, for some narrowly defined industries.

---

[5] If the monopolized industry has a positively sloped long-run supply curve, some of the deadweight losses will also be reflected in reduced rents for inputs arising from the monopolist's restriction in output.

[6] The classic study is A. Harberger, "Monopoly and Resource Allocation," *American Economic Review* (May 1954): 77–87. Harberger estimates that such losses constitute about 0.1 percent of gross national product.

EXAMPLE 18.2

WELFARE LOSSES AND ELASTICITY

The allocational effects of monopoly can be characterized fairly completely in the case of constant marginal costs and a constant price elasticity demand curve. To do so, assume that constant marginal (and average) costs for a monopolist are given by C and that the (compensated) demand curve has a constant elasticity form of

$$Q = P^e, \tag{18.12}$$

where e is the price elasticity of demand ($e < -1$). We know that the competitive price in this market will be

$$P_c = C \tag{18.13}$$

and that the monopoly price is given by

$$P_m = \frac{C}{1 + \dfrac{1}{e}}. \tag{18.14}$$

The consumer surplus associated with any price (P_0) can be computed as

$$
\begin{aligned}
CS &= \int_{P_0}^{\infty} Q(P) dP \\
&= \int_{P_0}^{\infty} P^e dP \\
&= \frac{P^{e+1}}{e+1} \Bigg|_{P_0}^{\infty} \\
&= -\frac{P_0^{e+1}}{e+1}.
\end{aligned}
\tag{18.15}
$$

Hence, under perfect competition

$$CS_c = -\frac{C^{e+1}}{e+1}, \tag{18.16}$$

and, under monopoly,

$$CS_m = -\frac{\left(\dfrac{C}{1 + \dfrac{1}{e}}\right)^{e+1}}{e+1}. \tag{18.17}$$

Taking the ratio of these two surplus measures yields

$$\frac{CS_m}{CS_c} = \left(\frac{1}{1+\frac{1}{e}}\right)^{e+1}. \qquad (18.18)$$

If $e = -2$, for example, this ratio is $\frac{1}{2}$—consumer surplus under monopoly is half what it is under perfect competition. For more elastic cases this figure falls a bit (since output restrictions under monopoly are more significant). For elasticities closer to -1, the ratio increases.

Profits. The transfer from consumer surplus into monopoly profits can also be computed fairly easily in this case. Monopoly profits are given by

$$\pi_m = P_m Q_m - CQ_m = \left(\frac{C}{1+\frac{1}{e}} - C\right) Q_m$$

$$= \left(\frac{-\frac{C}{e}}{1+\frac{1}{e}}\right) \cdot \left(\frac{C}{1+\frac{1}{e}}\right)^e = -\left(\frac{C}{1+\frac{1}{e}}\right)^{e+1} \cdot \frac{1}{e}. \qquad (18.19)$$

Dividing this expression by Equation 18.16 yields

$$\frac{\pi_m}{CS_c} = \left(\frac{e+1}{e}\right)\left(\frac{1}{1+\frac{1}{e}}\right)^{e+1} = \left(\frac{e}{1+e}\right)^e. \qquad (18.20)$$

For $e = -2$, this ratio is $\frac{1}{4}$. Hence, one-fourth of the consumer surplus enjoyed under perfect competition is transferred into monopoly profits. The deadweight loss from monopoly in this case is therefore also $\frac{1}{4}$ of the level of consumer surplus under perfect competition.

QUERY: Suppose $e = -1.5$. What fraction of consumer surplus is lost through monopolization? How much is transferred into monopoly profits? Why do these results differ from the case $e = -2$?

The market power enjoyed by a monopoly may also be exercised along dimensions other than the market price of its product. If the monopoly has some leeway in the type, quality, or diversity of the goods it produces, it would not be surprising if the firm's decisions were to differ from those that might prevail under a competitive organization of the market. Whether a monopoly will produce higher-quality or lower-quality goods than would be

MONOPOLY AND PRODUCT QUALITY

produced under competition is unclear, however. It all depends on the nature of consumer demand and the firm's costs.

A Formal Treatment

Suppose consumers' willingness to pay for quality (X) is given by the inverse demand function $P(Q, X)$ where

$$\partial P/\partial Q < 0, \ \partial P/\partial X > 0.$$

If the costs of producing Q and X are given by $C(Q, X)$, the monopoly will choose Q and X to maximize

$$\pi = P(Q, X)Q - C(Q, X). \tag{18.21}$$

The first-order conditions for a maximum are

$$\frac{\partial \pi}{\partial Q} = P(Q, X) + Q\frac{\partial P}{\partial Q} - C_Q = 0 \tag{18.22}$$

$$\frac{\partial \pi}{\partial X} = Q\frac{\partial P}{\partial X} - C_X = 0. \tag{18.23}$$

The first of these equations repeats the usual rule that marginal revenue equals marginal cost for output decisions. The second equation states that when Q is appropriately set, the monopoly should choose that level of quality for which the marginal revenue attainable from increasing the quality of its output by one unit is equal to the marginal cost of making such an increase. As might have been expected, the assumption of profit maximization requires the monopolist to proceed to the margin of profitability along all of the dimensions it can. Notice, in particular, that the marginal demander's valuation of quality per unit is multiplied by the monopolist's output level.

The level of product quality that will be opted for under competitive conditions will be the one that maximizes net social welfare:

$$SW = \int_0^{Q^*} P(Q, X)dQ - C(Q, X), \tag{18.24}$$

where Q^* is the output level determined through the competitive process of marginal cost pricing given X. Differentiation of Equation 18.24 with respect to X yields the first-order condition for a maximum:

$$\frac{\partial SW}{\partial X} = \int_0^{Q^*} P_X(Q, X)dQ - C_X = 0. \tag{18.25}$$

The difference between the quality choice specified in Equation 18.23 and Equation 18.25 is that the former looks at the marginal valuation of one more unit of quality assuming Q is at its profit-maximizing level, whereas the latter looks at the marginal value of quality averaged across all output levels.[7] Therefore, even if a monopoly and a perfectly competitive industry chose the same output level, they might opt for differing quality levels since each is concerned with a different margin in its decision making. Only by knowing the specifics of the problem, however, is it possible to predict the direction of these differences. For an example, see Problem 18.10.

Durable Goods

Modeling the production of durable goods poses additional complications for the theory of monopoly. Not only does the firm's choice of optimal durability depend on the kinds of considerations raised in the previous section, but the fact that goods are long-lived means that the monopoly may face current competition from goods that it produced previously. In a very real sense, then, the monopoly creates its own competition and must take that into account in its production decisions.

In extreme cases the durable goods problem may enforce competitive behavior on a monopoly. Consider, for example, a monopolist producing a recyclable product such as aluminum or newsprint. If the recycling industry is itself perfectly competitive and is characterized by the same cost structure as the monopolist, both recycled and original output will be priced at marginal cost. Because the products are perfect substitutes, only the single competitive price can prevail in long-run equilibrium. To the extent that other durable goods approximate these conditions (that is, competitive pricing of used goods and perfect substitutability), monopolistic behavior is severely constrained.[8]

A profit-seeking monopolist can, however, adopt a number of alternative strategies to cope with the durable goods problem. It may, for example, opt for leasing its products in an effort to control the used product market (for many years IBM tried to follow this procedure in marketing its computers). Or the monopolist may seek to differentiate its products over time by encouraging rapid development of new products or the planned obsolescence of old ones. An examination of all of these possibilities, however, would take us too far afield.[9]

---

[7] The average valuation (AV) of product quality is given by

$$AV = \int_0^{Q^*} P_X(Q, X)dQ/Q.$$

Hence, $Q \cdot AV = C_X$ is the quality rule adopted to maximize net welfare under perfect competition.

[8] The possibility of competitive pricing by a durable goods monopolist is discussed in R. Coase, "Durability and Monopoly," *Journal of Law and Economics* (April 1972): 143–149.

[9] For a further discussion and a complete set of references, see J. Tirole, *The Theory of Industrial Organization* (Cambridge, Mass.: MIT Press, 1989), pp. 79–87.

PRICE DISCRIMINATION

In some circumstances a monopoly may be able to increase profits by departing from a single-price policy for its output. The possibility of selling identical goods at different prices is called price discrimination.[10]

DEFINITION

Price Discrimination   A monopoly engages in *price discrimination* if it is able to sell otherwise identical units of output at different prices.

Whether a price discrimination strategy is feasible depends crucially on the inability of buyers of the good to practice arbitrage. In the absence of transactions or information costs, the "law of one price" implies that a homogeneous good must sell everywhere for the same price. Consequently, price discrimination schemes are doomed to failure since demanders who can buy from the monopoly at lower prices will be more attractive sources of the good for those who must pay high prices than is the monopoly itself. Profit-seeking middlemen would destroy any discriminatory pricing scheme. When resale is costly (or can be prevented entirely), however, price discrimination becomes possible.

Perfect Price Discrimination

If each buyer can be separately identified by a monopolist, it may be possible to charge each the maximum price he or she would willingly pay for the good. This strategy of perfect (or "first degree") price discrimination would then extract all available consumer surplus, leaving demanders as a group indifferent to buying the monopolist's good or doing without it. The strategy is illustrated in Figure 18.4. The figure assumes that buyers are arranged in descending order of willingness to pay. The first buyer is willing to pay up to P_1 for Q_1 units of output, so the monopolist charges P_1 and obtains total revenues of $P_1 Q_1$ as indicated by the lightly shaded rectangle. A second buyer is willing to pay up to P_2 for $Q_2 - Q_1$ units of output, so the monopolist obtains total revenue of $P_2(Q_2 - Q_1)$ from this buyer. Notice that for this strategy to succeed, the second buyer must be unable to resell the output he or she buys at P_2 to the first buyer (who pays $P_1 > P_2$).

The monopolist will proceed in this way up to the point at which the marginal buyer is no longer willing to pay the good's marginal cost (labeled *MC* in Figure 18.4). Hence, total quantity produced will be Q^*. Total revenues collected will be given by the area DEQ^*0. All consumer surplus has been extracted by the monopolist and there is no deadweight loss in this situation.

---

[10] A monopoly may also be able to sell differentiated products at differential price-cost margins. Here, however, we treat only price discrimination for a monopoly that produces a single, homogeneous product.

FIGURE 18.4

PERFECT PRICE DISCRIMINATION

Under perfect price discrimination, the monopoly charges a different price to each buyer. It sells Q_1 units at P_1, $Q_2 - Q_1$ units at P_2, and so forth. In this case the firm will produce Q^*, and total revenues will be DEQ^*0.

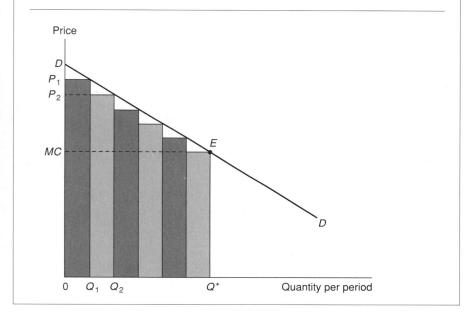

(Compare Figures 18.3 and 18.4.) The allocation of resources under perfect price discrimination is therefore efficient, though it does entail a large transfer from consumer surplus into monopoly profits.

EXAMPLE 18.3

PERFECT PRICE DISCRIMINATION

Consider again the Frisbee monopolist in Example 18.1. Since there are relatively few high-quality Frisbees sold, the monopolist may find it possible to discriminate perfectly among world-class flippers. In this case it will choose to produce that quantity for which the marginal buyer pays exactly the marginal cost of a Frisbee:

$$P = 100 - Q/20 = MC = .1Q. \tag{18.26}$$

Hence,

$$Q^* = 666$$

and, at the margin, price and marginal cost are given by

$$P = MC = 66.6. \tag{18.27}$$

Now we can compute total revenues by integration:

$$TR = \int_0^{Q^*} P(Q)dQ = 100Q - \frac{Q^2}{40} \Big|_0^{666}$$

$$= 55,511 \tag{18.28}$$

and total costs as

$$TC = .05Q^2 + 10,000 = 32,178. \tag{18.29}$$

Total profits are given by

$$\pi = TR - TC = 23,333, \tag{18.30}$$

which represents a substantial increase over the single-price policy examined in Example 18.1 (which yielded 15,000).

QUERY: What is the maximum price any Frisbee buyer pays in this case? Use this to obtain a geometric definition of profits.

Market Separation   Perfect price discrimination poses a considerable information burden for the monopoly—it must know the demand function for each potential buyer. A less stringent requirement would be to assume that the monopoly can separate its buyers into relatively few identifiable markets (such as "rural-urban," "domestic-foreign," or "prime-time–off-prime") and pursue a separate monopoly pricing policy in each market.[11] Knowledge of the price elasticities of demand in these markets is sufficient to pursue such a policy. The monopoly then sets price in each market according to the inverse elasticity rule. Assuming that marginal cost is the same in all markets, this results in a pricing policy in which

$$P_i \left(1 + \frac{1}{e_i} \right) = P_j \left(1 + \frac{1}{e_j} \right) \tag{18.31}$$

---

[11] Market-separating price discrimination is sometimes referred to as "third degree" price discrimination. We will take up "second degree" price discrimination in the next section.

or

$$\frac{P_i}{P_j} = \frac{\left(1 + \dfrac{1}{e_j}\right)}{\left(1 + \dfrac{1}{e_i}\right)},$$ (18.32)

where P_i and P_j are the prices charged in markets i and j which have price elasticities given by e_i and e_j. An immediate consequence of this pricing policy is that the profit-maximization price will be higher in markets in which demand is less elastic. If, for example, $e_i = -2$ and $e_j = -3$, Equation 18.32 shows that $P_i/P_j = 4/3$—prices will be one-third higher in the less elastic market.

Figure 18.5 illustrates this result for two markets which the monopoly can serve at constant marginal cost (MC). Demand is less elastic in market 1 than

FIGURE 18.5

SEPARATED MARKETS RAISE THE POSSIBILITY OF PRICE DISCRIMINATION

If two markets are separate, a monopolist can maximize profits by selling his or her product at different prices in the two markets. This would entail choosing that output for which $MC = MR$ in each of the markets. The diagram shows that the market that has a less elastic demand curve will be charged the higher price by the price discriminator.

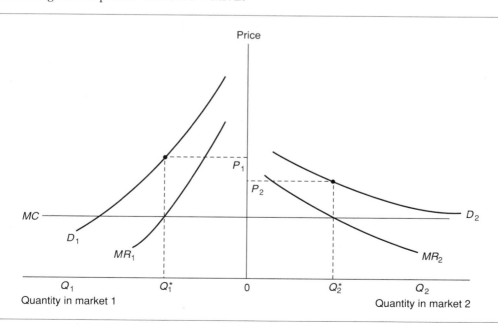

in market 2, hence, the gap between price and marginal revenue is larger in the former market. Profit maximization requires that the firm produce Q_1^* in market 1 and Q_2^* in market 2, resulting in a higher price in the less elastic market. So long as arbitrage between the two markets can be prevented, this price difference can persist. The two-price discriminatory policy is clearly more profitable for the monopoly than would be a single-price policy, since the firm could always opt for such a policy should market conditions warrant that choice.

The welfare consequences of third-degree price discrimination is in principle ambiguous. Relative to a single-price policy, the discriminating policy requires raising price in the less elastic market and reducing it in the more elastic one. Hence, the changes have an offsetting effect on total allocational losses. A more complete analysis suggests the intuitively plausible conclusion that the multiple-price policy will be allocationally superior to a single-price policy only in situations in which total output is increased through discrimination. Example 18.4 illustrates the simple case of linear demand curves for which the multiple-price policy always results in allocational losses.[12]

EXAMPLE 18.4

THIRD-DEGREE PRICE DISCRIMINATION

Suppose the demand curves in two separated markets are given by

$$Q_1 = 24 - P_1$$

and

$$Q_2 = 24 - 2P_2 \tag{18.33}$$

and that a monopoly can serve both of these markets at a constant marginal cost of 6. Profit maximization in the two markets requires

$$MR_1 = 24 - 2Q_1 = 6 = MR_2 = 12 - Q_2, \tag{18.34}$$

so the optimal choices are

$$Q_1 = 9$$

$$Q_2 = 6. \tag{18.35}$$

Prices that prevail in the two markets are then[13]

---

[12] For a detailed discussion, see R. Schmalensee, "Output and Welfare Implications of Monopolistic Third-Degree Price Discrimination," *American Economic Review* (June 1981): 242–247.

[13] At these prices, $e_1 = -15/9$, $e_2 = -2(9/6) = -3$. Hence, these choices obey Equation 18.32, since $P_1/P_2 = 5/3$.

$$P_1 = 15$$

$$P_2 = 9. \tag{18.36}$$

Profits for the monopoly following two-price policy are

$$\pi = (P_1 - 6)Q_1 + (P_2 - 6)Q_2 = 81 + 18 = 99. \tag{18.37}$$

The allocational impact of this policy can be evaluated by calculating the deadweight losses in the two markets. Since demand in market 1 at $P = MC = 6$ is 18 and competitive output would be 12 in market 2, such losses are given by

$$DW_1 = .5(P_1 - MC)(18 - Q_1) = .5(15 - 6)(18 - 9) = 40.5 \tag{18.38}$$

and

$$DW_2 = .5(P_2 - MC)(12 - Q_2) = .5(9 - 6)(12 - 6) = 9. \tag{18.39}$$

Single-Price Policy. If this monopoly were to pursue a single-price policy, it would use the market demand function

$$Q = Q_1 + Q_2 = 48 - 3P \tag{18.40}$$

to compute marginal revenue as

$$MR = 16 - \tfrac{2}{3}Q. \tag{18.41}$$

Hence, profit maximization requires $Q = 15$, which implies a market price of 11. A single-price policy requires lowering price in market 1 and raising price in market 2. This policy is clearly less profitable than the two-price policy $[\pi = (P - 6)(Q) = 75]$, and the fact that output is unchanged under the policy suggests that deadweight losses are smaller with one price. An explicit calculation shows this:

$$DW = .5(P - 6)(30 - Q) = .5(11 - 6)(15) = 37.5, \tag{18.42}$$

about 25 percent smaller than the allocational losses experienced under a two-price policy.

QUERY: In the case of linear demand, do single-price and two-price policies always result in the same monopoly output? What can you conclude about allocational losses in these two cases?

The examples of price discrimination examined in the previous section require the monopoly to separate demanders into a number of categories and choose a profit-maximizing price for each such category. An alternate approach would be for the monopoly to choose a (possibly rather complex) price schedule that provides incentives for demanders to separate

DISCRIMINATION THROUGH PRICE SCHEDULES

themselves depending on how much they wish to buy. Such schemes include quantity discounts, minimum purchase requirements or "cover" charges, and tie-in sales. These would be adopted by a monopoly if they yielded greater profits than would a single-price policy, after accounting for any possible costs of implementing the price schedule. Since the schedules will result in demanders paying different prices for identical goods, this form of (second degree) price discrimination is also feasible only when there are no arbitrage possibilities.

Two-Part Tariffs

One form of pricing schedule that has been extensively studied is a linear two-part tariff under which demanders must pay a fixed fee for the right to consume a good and a uniform price for each unit consumed. The prototype case, first studied by Walter Oi, is an amusement park (perhaps Disneyland) that sets a basic entry fee coupled with a stated marginal price for each amusement used.[14] Mathematically, this scheme can be represented by the tariff any demander must pay

$$T(Q) = A + PQ, \tag{18.43}$$

where A is the fixed fee and P is the marginal price to be paid. The monopolist's goal then is to choose A and P to maximize profits, given the demand for this product. Since the average price paid by demanders is given by

$$\overline{P} = \frac{T}{Q} = \frac{A}{Q} + P, \tag{18.44}$$

this tariff is feasible only when those who pay low average prices (those for whom Q is large) cannot resell the good to those who must pay high average prices (those for whom Q is small).

One feasible approach to establishing the parameters of this linear tariff would be for the firm to set $P = MC$ and then set A so as to extract the maximum consumer surplus from a given set of buyers. One might imagine buyers being arrayed according to willingness to pay. The choice of $P = MC$ would then maximize consumer surplus for this group, and A could be set equal to the surplus enjoyed by the least eager buyer. He or she would then be indifferent about buying the good, but all other buyers would experience net gains from the purchase.

---

[14] W. Y. Oi, "A Disneyland Dilemma: Two-Part Tariffs for a Mickey Mouse Monopoly," *Quarterly Journal of Economics* (February 1971): 77–90. Interestingly, the Disney empire once used a two-part tariff but abandoned it because the costs of administering the payment schemes for individual rides became too high. Like other amusement parks, Disney moved to a single-admissions-price policy (which still provided them with ample opportunities for price discrimination).

This feasible tariff might not be the most profitable, however. Consider the effects on profits of a small increase in P above MC. This would result in no net change in the profits earned from the least willing buyer. Quantity demanded would drop slightly at the margin where $P = MC$ and some of what had previously been consumer surplus (and therefore part of the fixed fee, A) would be converted into variable profits since now $P > MC$. For all other demanders, profits would be increased by the price rise. Although each will pay a bit less in fixed charges, profits per unit bought will rise to a greater extent.[15] In some cases it is possible to make an explicit calculation of the optimal two-part tariff. Example 18.5 provides an illustration. More generally, however, optimal schedules will depend on a variety of contingencies. Some of the possibilities are examined in the extensions to this chapter.

EXAMPLE 18.5

A PROFIT-MAXIMIZING TWO-PART TARIFF

In Example 18.4 we looked at the possibility for third-degree price discrimination in two separated markets characterized by the demand curves

$$Q_1 = 24 - P_1$$

and

$$Q_2 = 24 - 2P_2.$$

(18.45)

If the monopoly opts for pricing at marginal cost ($MC = 6$) it will sell 18 units in market 1 and 12 units in market 2. Consumer surplus earned in market 2 will be

$$S_2 = \tfrac{1}{2}(Q_2)(P_2^{\max} - 6),$$

(18.46)

where $P_2^{\max}$ is the price at which quantity demanded reaches zero in market 2 ($P_2^{\max} = 12$ here). Hence,

$$S_2 = \tfrac{1}{2}(12)(12 - 6) = 36$$

(18.47)

and the monopoly charges this as an entry fee. Given this two-part tariff $[T(Q) = 36 + 6Q]$, total profits amount to 72, a figure less than that available from either of the policies examined in Example 18.4.

---

[15] This follows since $Q_i(mc) > Q_1(mc)$, where $Q_i(mc)$ is the quantity demanded when $P = MC$ for all except the least willing buyer (person 1). Hence, the gain in profits from an increase in price above MC, $\Delta PQ_i(mc)$, exceeds the loss in profits from a smaller fixed fee, $\Delta PQ_1(mc)$.

The Optimal Tariff. More generally, the optimal two-part tariff can be computed in this problem by recognizing that profits consist of two components: (1) The fixed lump-sum fee collected from both markets; and (2) the profits on each unit sold. Assuming that the lump-sum fee is set equal to total consumer surplus in market 2, total profits are

$$\pi = 2S_2 + (P - MC)(Q)$$
$$= Q_2(12 - P) + (P - 6)(Q)$$
$$= (24 - 2P)(12 - P) + (P - 6)(48 - 3P)$$
$$= 18P - P^2. \tag{18.48}$$

Maximization of this expression yields

$$P^* = 9$$

and

$$S_2 = 9. \tag{18.49}$$

Hence, the profit-maximizing tariff is

$$T(Q) = 9 + 9Q. \tag{18.50}$$

According to Equation 18.48, total profits yielded by this tariff are

$$\pi = 2 \cdot 9 + (9 - 6)(21) = 81, \tag{18.51}$$

so the two-part tariff is more profitable than the single-price strategy for the monopoly but not so profitable as the third-degree price discrimination strategy in Example 18.4 (for which profits were 99). Still, the monopoly might opt for the two-part tariff since it does not require the sort of formal market separation that third-degree discrimination requires. Even with market separation, the monopoly may opt for the linear tariff if law or custom prohibits different prices in the two markets.

QUERY: What pricing strategy should the monopoly pursue if it can choose a different two-part tariff for each market?

REGULATION OF MONOPOLIES

The regulation of natural monopolies is an important subject in applied economic analysis. The utility, communications, and transportation industries are highly regulated in most countries, and devising regulatory procedures that cause these industries to operate in a desirable way is an important practical problem. Here we will examine a few aspects of the regulation of monopolies that relate to pricing policies.

Many economists believe that it is important for the prices charged by regulated monopolies to reflect marginal costs of production accurately. In this way the deadweight loss may be minimized. The principal problem raised by an enforced policy of marginal cost pricing is that it will require true natural monopolies to operate at a loss. Natural monopolies, by definition, exhibit decreasing average costs over a broad range of output levels. The cost curves for such a firm might look like those shown in Figure 18.6. In the absence of regulation the monopoly would produce output level Q_A and receive a price of P_A for its product. Profits in this situation are given by the rectangle $P_A ABC$. A regulatory agency might instead set a price of P_R for the monopoly. At this price, Q_R is demanded, and the marginal cost of producing this output level is also P_R. Consequently, marginal cost pricing has been achieved. Unfortunately, because of the declining nature of the firm's average cost curve, the price P_R (= marginal cost) falls below average costs. With this

Marginal Cost Pricing and the Natural Monopoly Dilemma

FIGURE 18.6

PRICE REGULATION FOR A DECREASING COST MONOPOLY

Because natural monopolies exhibit decreasing costs, marginal costs fall below average costs. Consequently, enforcing a policy of marginal cost pricing will entail operating at a loss. A price of P_R, for example, will achieve the goal of marginal cost pricing but will necessitate an operating loss of $GFEP_R$.

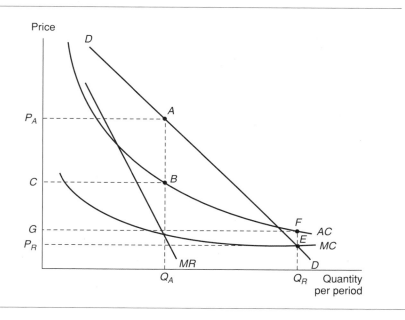

regulated price, the monopoly must operate at a loss of $GFEP_R$. Since no firm can operate indefinitely at a loss, this poses a dilemma for the regulatory agency: Either it must abandon its goal of marginal cost pricing, or the government must subsidize the monopoly forever.

Two-Tier Pricing Systems

One way out of the marginal cost pricing dilemma is the implementation of a discriminatory pricing system. Under such a system the monopoly is permitted to charge some users a high price while maintaining a low price for marginal users. In this way the demanders paying the high price in effect subsidize the losses of the low-price customers. Such a pricing scheme is shown in Figure 18.7. Here the regulatory commission has decided that some users will pay a relatively high price, P_1. At this price, Q_1 is demanded. Other users (presumably those who would not buy the good at the P_1 price) are

FIGURE 18.7

TWO-TIER PRICING SCHEDULE

By charging a high price (P_1) to some users and a low price (P_2) to others, it may be possible for a regulatory commission to (1) enforce marginal cost pricing and (2) create a situation where the profits from one class of user (P_1DBA) subsidize the losses of the other class ($BFEC$).

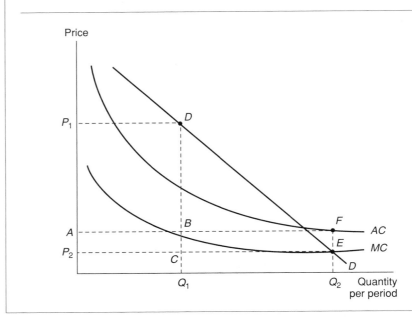

offered a lower price, P_2. This lower price generates additional demand of $Q_2 - Q_1$. Consequently, a total output of Q_2 is produced at an average cost of A. With this pricing system, the profits on the sales to high-price demanders (given by the rectangle P_1DBA) balance the losses incurred on the low-priced sales ($BFEC$). Furthermore, for the "marginal user," the marginal cost pricing rule is being followed: It is the "intramarginal" user who subsidizes the firm so that it does not operate at a loss. Although in practice it may not be so simple to establish pricing schemes that maintain marginal cost pricing and cover operating costs, many regulatory commissions do use price schedules that intentionally discriminate against some users (for example, businesses) to the advantage of others (consumers).

Rate of Return Regulation

Another approach that is followed in many regulatory situations is to permit the monopoly to charge a price above marginal cost that is sufficient to earn a "fair" rate of return on investment. Much analytical effort is then devoted to defining the "fair" rate concept and to developing ways in which it might be measured. From an economic point of view, some of the most interesting questions about this procedure concern how the regulatory activity affects the firm's input choices. If, for example, the rate of return allowed to firms exceeds what owners might obtain on investment under competitive circumstances, there will be an incentive to use relatively more capital input than would truly minimize costs. Or if regulators typically delay in making rate decisions, firms may be given incentives to minimize costs that would not otherwise exist. We will now briefly examine a formal model of such possibilities.[16]

A Formal Model

Suppose a regulated utility has a production function of the form

$$Q = f(K, L). \tag{18.52}$$

This firm's actual rate of return on capital is then defined as

$$s = \frac{Pf(K, L) - wL}{K}, \tag{18.53}$$

where P is the price of the firm's output (which depends on Q) and w is the wage rate for labor input. If s is constrained by regulation to be equal to, say, $\bar{s}$, then the firm's problem is to maximize profits

$$\pi = Pf(K, L) - wL - vK \tag{18.54}$$

---

[16] This model is based on H. Averch and L. L. Johnson, "Behavior of the Firm under Regulatory Constraint," *American Economic Review* (December 1962): 1052–1069.

subject to this regulatory constraint. Setting up the Lagrangian expression for this problem yields

$$\mathcal{L} = Pf(K, L) - wL - vK + \lambda[wL + \bar{s}K - Pf(K, L)]. \qquad (18.55)$$

Notice that if $\lambda = 0$, regulation is ineffective and the monopoly behaves like any profit-maximizing firm. If $\lambda = 1$, Equation 18.55 reduces to

$$\mathcal{L} = (\bar{s} - v)K, \qquad (18.56)$$

which, assuming $\bar{s} > v$ (which it must be if the firm is not to earn less than the prevailing rate of return on capital elsewhere), means that this monopoly will hire infinite amounts of capital—an implausible result. Hence, $0 < \lambda < 1$. The first-order conditions for a maximum are

$$\frac{\partial \mathcal{L}}{\partial L} = Pf_L - w + \lambda(w - Pf_L) = 0$$

$$\frac{\partial \mathcal{L}}{\partial K} = Pf_K - v + \lambda(\bar{s} - Pf_K) = 0 \qquad (18.57)$$

$$\frac{\partial \mathcal{L}}{\partial \lambda} = wL + \bar{s}K - Pf(K, L) = 0.$$

The first of these conditions implies that the regulated monopoly will hire additional labor input up to the point at which $Pf_L = w$—a result that holds for any profit-maximizing firm. For capital input, however, the second condition implies

$$(1 - \lambda)Pf_K = v - \lambda\bar{s} \qquad (18.58)$$

or

$$Pf_K = \frac{v - \lambda\bar{s}}{1 - \lambda} = v - \frac{\lambda(\bar{s} - v)}{1 - \lambda}. \qquad (18.59)$$

Since $\bar{s} > v$ and $\lambda < 1$, Equation 18.59 implies

$$Pf_K < v. \qquad (18.60)$$

The firm will hire more capital (and achieve a lower marginal productivity of capital) than it would under unregulated conditions. "Overcapitalization" may therefore be a regulatory-induced misallocation of resources for some utilities. Although we shall not do so here, it is possible to examine other regulatory questions using this general analytical framework.

DYNAMIC VIEWS OF MONOPOLY

The static view that monopolistic practices distort the allocation of resources provides the principal economic rationale for favoring antimonopoly policies. Not all economists believe that the static analysis should be determinant, however. Some authors, most notably J. A. Schumpeter, have stressed the beneficial role that monopoly profits can play in the process of economic development.[17] These authors place considerable emphasis on innovation and the ability of particular types of firms to achieve technical advances. In this context the profits that monopolistic firms earn provide funds that can be invested in research and development. Whereas perfectly competitive firms must be content with a normal return on invested capital, monopolies have "surplus" funds with which to undertake the risky process of research. More important, perhaps, the possibility of attaining a monopolistic position, or the desire to maintain such a position, provides an important incentive to keep one step ahead of potential competitors. Innovations in new products and cost-saving production techniques may be integrally related to the possibility of monopolization. Without such a monopolistic position, the full benefits of innovation could not be obtained by the innovating firm.

Schumpeter stresses the point that the monopolization of a market may make it less costly for a firm to plan its activities. Being the only source of supply for a product eliminates many of the contingencies that a firm in a competitive market must face. For example, a monopoly may not have to spend as much on selling expenses (advertising, brand identification, and visiting retailers, for example) as would be the case in a more competitive industry. Similarly, a monopoly may know more about the specific demand curve for its product and may more readily adapt to changing demand conditions. Of course, whether any of these purported benefits of monopolies outweigh their allocational and distributional disadvantages is an empirical question. Issues of innovation and cost savings cannot be answered by recourse to *a priori* arguments. Detailed investigation of real-world markets is a necessity.

---

[17] See, for example, J. A. Schumpeter, *Capitalism, Socialism and Democracy,* 3d ed. (New York: Harper & Row, 1950), especially chap. 8.

SUMMARY

In this chapter we have examined models of markets in which there is only a single monopoly supplier. Unlike the competitive case that we investigated in Part V, monopoly firms do not exhibit price-taking behavior. Instead, the monopolist can choose the price-quantity combination on the market demand curve that is most profitable. A number of consequences then follow from this market power:

- The most profitable level of output for the monopolist is that one for which marginal revenue is equal to marginal cost. At this output level, price will exceed marginal cost. The profitability of the monopolist will depend on the relationship between price and average cost.

- Relative to perfect competition, monopoly involves

a loss of consumer surplus for demanders. Some of this is transferred into monopoly profits, whereas some of the loss in consumer supply represents a deadweight loss of overall economic welfare. It is a sign of Pareto inefficiency.

■ Monopolists may opt for different levels of quality than would perfectly competitive firms. Durable goods monopolists may be constrained by markets for used goods.

■ A monopoly may be able to increase its profits

further through price discrimination—that is, charging different prices to different categories of buyers. The ability of the monopoly to practice price discrimination depends on its ability to prevent arbitrage among buyers.

■ Governments often choose to regulate natural monopolies (firms with diminishing average costs over a broad range of output levels). The type of regulatory mechanisms adopted can affect the behavior of the regulated firm.

PROBLEMS

18.1

A monopolist can produce at constant average and marginal costs of $AC = MC = 5$. The firm faces a market demand curve given by $Q = 53 - P$.

a. Calculate the profit-maximizing price-quantity combination for the monopolist. Also calculate the monopolist's profits.

b. What output level would be produced by this industry under perfect competition (where price = marginal cost)?

c. Calculate the consumer surplus obtained by consumers in case (b). Show that this exceeds the sum of the monopolist's profits and the consumer surplus received in case (a). What is the value of the "deadweight loss" from monopolization?

18.2

A monopolist faces a market demand curve given by

$$Q = 70 - P.$$

a. If the monopolist can produce at constant average and marginal costs of $AC = MC = 6$, what output level will the monopolist choose in order to maximize profits? What is the price at this output level? What are the monopolist's profits?

b. Assume instead that the monopolist has a cost structure where total costs are described by

$$TC = .25Q^2 - 5Q + 300.$$

With the monopolist facing the same market demand and marginal revenue, what price-quantity combination will be chosen now to maximize profits? What will profits be?

c. Assume now that a third cost structure explains the monopolist's position with total costs given by

$$TC = .0133Q^3 - 5Q + 250.$$

Again, calculate the monopolist's price-quantity combination that maximizes profits. What will profit be? (*Hint:* Set $MC = MR$ as usual and use the quadratic formula to solve the second-order equation for Q.)

d. Graph the market demand curve, the MR curve, and the three marginal cost curves from parts (a), (b), and (c). Notice that the monopolist's profit-making ability is constrained by (1) the market demand curve (along with its associated MR curve) and (2) the cost structure underlying production.

18.3

A single firm monopolizes the entire market for widgets and can produce at constant average and marginal costs of

$$AC = MC = 10.$$

Originally, the firm faces a market demand curve given by

$$Q = 60 - P.$$

a. Calculate the profit-maximizing price-quantity combination for the firm. What are the firm's profits?

b. Now assume that the market demand curve shifts outward (becoming steeper) and is given by

$$Q = 45 - .5P.$$

What is the firm's profit-maximizing price-quantity combination now? What are the firm's profits?

c. Instead of the assumptions of part (b), assume that the market demand curve shifts outward (becoming flatter) and is given by

$$Q = 100 - 2P.$$

What is the firm's profit-maximizing price-quantity combination now? What are the firm's profits?

d. Graph the three different situations of parts (a), (b), and (c). Using your results, explain why there is no real supply curve for a monopoly.

18.4

Suppose that the market for Hula Hoops is monopolized by a single firm.

a. Draw the initial equilibrium for such a market.

b. Suppose now that the demand for Hula Hoops shifts outward slightly. Show that, in general (contrary to the competitive case), it will not be possible to predict the effect of this shift in demand on the market price of Hula Hoops.

c. Consider three possible ways in which the price elasticity of demand might change as the demand curve shifts—it might increase, it might decrease, or it might stay the same. Consider also that marginal costs for the monopolist might be rising, falling, or constant in the range where $MR = MC$. Consequently, there are nine different combinations of types of demand shifts and marginal cost slope configurations. Analyze each of these to determine for which it is possible to make a definite prediction about the effect of the shift in demand on the price of Hula Hoops.

18.5

Suppose that a monopoly market has a demand function in which quantity demanded depends not only on market price (P) but also on the amount of advertising the firm does (A, measured in dollars). The specific form of this function is

$$Q = (20 - P)(1 + 0.1A - 0.01A^2).$$

The monopolistic firm's cost function is given by

$$TC = 10Q + 15 + A.$$

a. Suppose that there is no advertising ($A = 0$). What output will the profit-maximizing firm choose? What market price will this yield? What will be the monopoly's profits?

b. Now let the firm also choose its optimal level of advertising expenditure. In this situation, what output level will be chosen? What price will this yield? What will the level of advertising be? What are the firm's profits in this case?

Hint: Part (b) can be worked out most easily by assuming that the monopoly chooses the profit-maximizing price rather than quantity.

18.6

Suppose that a monopoly produces its output in several different plants and that these plants have differing cost structures. How should the firm decide how much total output to produce? How should it distribute this output among its plants in order to maximize profits?

18.7

Suppose that a monopoly can produce any level of output it wishes at a constant marginal (and average) cost of $5 per unit. Assume that the monopoly sells its goods in two different markets that are separated by some distance. The demand curve in the first market is given by

$$Q_1 = 55 - P_1,$$

and the demand curve in the second market is given by

$$Q_2 = 70 - 2P_2.$$

a. If the monopolist can maintain the separation between the two markets, what level of output should be produced in each market, and what price will prevail in each market? What are total profits in this situation?

b. How would your answer change if it only cost demanders $5 to transport goods between the two markets? What would be the monopolist's new profit level in this situation?

c. How would your answer change if transportation costs were zero and the firm was forced to follow a single-price policy?

d. Suppose the firm could adopt a linear two-part tariff under which marginal prices must be equal in the two markets but lump-sum entry fees might vary. What pricing policy should the firm follow?

18.8

Suppose a perfectly competitive industry can produce widgets at a constant marginal cost of $10 per unit. Monopolized marginal costs rise to $12 per unit because $2 per unit must be paid to lobbyists to retain the widget producers' favored position. Suppose the market demand for widgets is given by

$$Q_D = 1,000 - 50P.$$

a. Calculate the perfectly competitive and monopoly outputs and prices.
b. Calculate the total loss of consumer surplus from monopolization of widget production.
c. Graph your results and explain how they differ from the usual analysis.

18.9

Suppose the government wished to combat the undesirable allocational effects of a monopoly through the use of a subsidy.
a. Why would a lump-sum subsidy not achieve the government's goal?
b. Use a graphical proof to show how a per-unit-of-output subsidy might achieve the government's goal.

c. Suppose the government wishes its subsidy to maximize the difference between the total value of the good to consumers and the good's total cost. Show that to achieve this goal it should set

$$\frac{t}{P} = -\frac{1}{e_{Q,P}},$$

where t is the per-unit subsidy and P is the competitive price. Explain your result intuitively.

18.10

Suppose a monopolist produces alkaline batteries that may have various useful lifetimes (X). Suppose also that consumers' (inverse) demand depends on batteries' lifetimes and quantity (Q) purchased according to the function

$$P(Q, X) = g(X \cdot Q),$$

where $g' < 0$. That is, consumers care only about the product of quantity times lifetime. They are willing to pay equally for many short-lived batteries or few long-lived ones. Assume also that battery costs are given by

$$C(Q, X) = C(X)Q,$$

where $C'(X) > 0$. Show that in this case the monopoly will opt for the same level of X as does a competitive industry even though levels of output and prices may differ. Explain your result.
(*Hint*: Treat XQ as a composite commodity.)

SUGGESTED READINGS

Averch, H., and L. L. Johnson. "Behavior of the Firm under Regulatory Constraint." *American Economic Review* 52 (1962): 1052–1069.
Article introducing the idea of firm behavior with a regulatory constraint. Very readable.

Coase, R. H. "Some Notes on Monopoly Price." *Review of Economic Studies* 5 (1937–1938): 17–31.
Early thoughts about the sustainability of a monopolist's price.

Harberger, A. "Monopoly and Resource Allocation." *American Economic Review* 44 (May 1954): 77–87.
Empirical estimate of the deadweight loss from monopoly in the 1920s.

Posner, R. A. "The Social Costs of Monopoly and Regulation." *Journal of Political Economy* 83 (1975): 807–827.
An analysis of the probability that monopolies may spend resources on the creation of barriers to entry and therefore may have higher costs than perfectly competitive firms.

Schumpeter, J. A. *Capitalism, Socialism and Democracy.* 3d ed. New York: Harper & Row, 1950.
Classic defense of the role of the entrepreneur and economic profits in the economic growth process.

Stigler, G. J. "The Theory of Economic Regulation." *The Bell Journal of Economics and Management Science* 2 (Spring 1971): 3.

Early development of the "capture" hypothesis of regulatory behavior—that the industry captures the agency supposed to regulate it and uses that agency to enforce entry barriers and further enhance profits.

Tirole, J. *The Theory of Industrial Organization.* Cambridge, Mass.: MIT Press, 1989. Chaps. 1–3.
A complete analysis of the theory of monopoly pricing and product choice.

EXTENSIONS

Optimal Outlay Schedules

In Chapter 18 we examined a few simple illustrations of ways in which a monopoly may increase profits by practicing second-degree price discrimination—that is, by establishing price (or "outlay") schedules that prompt buyers to separate themselves into distinct market segments. Here we will pursue this topic a bit further, since the study of optimal outlay schedules has a wide variety of applications to many areas of microeconomic theory.

Structure of the Problem

In order to examine issues related to price schedules in a simple context for each demander, we define the "valuation function" as

$$V_i(q) = P_i(q) \cdot q + S_i, \qquad \text{(i)}$$

where $P_i(q)$ is the inverse demand function for individual i and S_i is consumer surplus. Hence, V_i represents the total value to individual i of undertaking transactions of amount q, which includes total spending on the good plus the value of consumer surplus obtained. Here we will assume that there are only two demanders[1] or homogeneous groups of demanders and that person 1 has stronger preferences for this good than person 2 in the sense that

$$V_1(q) > V_2(q) \qquad \text{(ii)}$$

for all values of q. The monopolist is assumed to have constant marginal costs (denoted by c) and chooses an outlay (revenue) schedule, $T(q)$, that maximizes profits given by

$$\pi = T(q_1) + T(q_2) - c(q_1 + q_2), \qquad \text{(iii)}$$

where q_i represents the quantity chosen by person i. In selecting a price schedule that successfully differentiates among consumers, the monopolist faces two "incentive compatibility" constraints. To ensure that the low-demand person (2) is actually served, it is necessary that

$$V_2(q_2) - T(q_2) \geq 0. \qquad \text{(iv)}$$

That is, person 2 must derive a net benefit from his or her optimal choice, q^2. Person 1, the high-demand individual, must also obtain a net gain from his or her chosen consumption level (q_1) and must prefer this choice to the output choice made by person 2:

$$V_1(q_1) - T(q_1) \geq V_1(q_2) - T(q_2). \qquad \text{(v)}$$

If the monopolist does not recognize this constraint, it may find that person 1 opts for the portion of the price schedule intended for person 2, thereby destroying the goal of obtaining self-selected market separation. Given this general structure, we can proceed to illustrate a number of interesting features of the monopolist's problem.

E18.1 Pareto Superiority

Permitting the monopolist to depart from a simple, single-price scheme offers the possibility of adopting

---

[1] Generalizations to many demanders are nontrivial. For a discussion, see Wilson (1993), Chapters 2–5.

"Pareto superior" outlay schedules under which all parties to the transaction are made better off. For example, suppose the monopolist's profit-maximizing price is P_M. At this price, person 2 consumes q_2^M and receives a net value from this consumption of

$$V_2(q_2^M) - P_M q_2^M. \qquad \text{(vi)}$$

An outlay schedule for which

$$T(q) = P_M q \text{ for } q \leq q_2^M$$

and

$$T(q) = A + \overline{P}q \text{ for } q > q_2^M, \qquad \text{(vii)}$$

where $A > 0$ and $c < \overline{P} < P_M$ may yield both increased profits for the monopolist and increased welfare for person 1. Specifically, consider values of A and $\overline{P}$ such that

$$A + \overline{P}q_1^M = P_M q_1^M$$

or

$$A = (P_M - \overline{P})q_1^M, \qquad \text{(viii)}$$

where q_1^M represents consumption of person 1 under a single-price policy. In this case then, A and $\overline{P}$ are set so that person 1 can still afford to buy q_1^M under this new price schedule. Because $\overline{P} < P_M$, however, he or she will opt for $q_1^* > q_1^M$. Since person 1 could have bought q_1^M but chose q_1^* instead, he or she must be better off under the new schedule. The monopoly's profits are now given by

$$\pi = A + \overline{P}q_1 + P_M q_2^M - c(q_1 + q_2^M) \qquad \text{(ix)}$$

and

$$\pi - \pi_M = A + \overline{P}q_1 - P_M q_1^M - c(q_1 - q_1^M), \qquad \text{(x)}$$

where π_M is the monopoly's single-price profits $[= (P_M - c)(q_1^M + q_2^M)]$. Substitution for A from Equation viii shows

$$\pi - \pi_M = (\overline{P} - c)(q_1 - q_1^M) > 0. \qquad \text{(xi)}$$

Hence, this new price schedule also provides more profits to the monopoly, some of which might be shared with person 2. The price schedule is Pareto superior to a single monopoly price. The notion that multipart schedules may be Pareto superior has been used not only in the study of price discrimination, but also in the design of optimal tax schemes and auction mechanisms (see Willig, 1978).

Pricing a Farmland Reserve

The potential Pareto superiority of complex outlay schedules was used by R. B. W. Smith (1995) to estimate a least cost method for the U.S. government to finance a Conservation Reserve Program for farmland. The specific plan the author studies would maintain a 34-million-acre reserve out of production in any given year. He calculates that use of carefully constructed (nonlinear) outlay schedules for such a program might cost only $1 billion annually.

E18.2 Tied Sales

Sometimes a monopoly will market two goods together. This situation poses a number of possibilities for discriminatory pricing schemes. Consider, for example, laser printers that are sold with toner cartridges or Polaroid cameras sold with patented film. Here the pricing situation is similar to that examined in Chapter 18—usually consumers buy only one unit of the basic product (the printer or camera) and thereby pay the "entry" fee. Then they consume a variable number of tied products (toner and film). Since our analysis in Chapter 18 suggests that the monopoly will choose a price for its tied product that exceeds marginal cost, there will be a welfare loss relative to a situation in which the tied good is produced competitively. Perhaps for this reason, tied sales are prohibited by law in some cases. Prohibition may not necessarily increase welfare, however, if the monopoly declines to serve low-demand consumers in the absence of such a practice (Oi, 1971).

Automobiles and Wine

One way in which tied sales can be accomplished is through creation of a multiplicity of quality variants that appeal to different classes of buyers. Automobile companies have been especially ingenious at devising quality variants of their basic models (for example, the Honda Accord comes in DX, LX, EX, and SX configurations) that act as tied goods in separating buyers into various market niches. A 1992 study by J. E. Kwoka examines one specific U.S. manufacturer (Chrysler) and shows how market segmentation is achieved through quality variation. The author calculates that significant transfer from consumer surplus to firms occurs as a result of such segmentation.

Generally, this sort of price discrimination in a tied good will be infeasible if that good is also produced under competitive conditions. In such a case the tied good will sell for marginal cost, and the only possibilities for discriminatory behavior open to the monopolist is in the pricing of its basic good (that is, by varying "entry fees" among demanders). In some special cases, however, choosing to pay the entry fee will confer monopoly power in the tied good on the monopolist even though it is otherwise produced under competitive conditions. For example, Locay and Rodriguez (1992) examine the case of restaurants' pricing of wine. Here group decisions to patronize a particular restaurant may confer monopoly power to the restaurant owner in the ability to practice wine price discrimination among buyers with strong grape preferences. The owner is constrained by the need to attract groups of customers to the restaurant, however, so the power to price discriminate is less than under the pure monopoly scenario.

References

Kwoka, J. E. "Market Segmentation by Price-Quality Schedules: Some Evidence from Automobiles." *Journal of Business* (October 1992): 615–628.

Locay, L., and A. Rodriguez. "Price Discrimination in Competitive Markets." *Journal of Political Economy* (October 1992): 954–968.

Oi, W. Y. "A Disneyland Dilemma: Two-Part Tariffs on a Mickey Mouse Monopoly." *Quarterly Journal of Economics* (February 1971): 77–90.

Smith, R. B. W. "The Conservation Reserve Program as a Least Cost Land Retirement Mechanism." *American Journal of Agricultural Economics* (February 1995): 93–105.

Willig, R. "Pareto Superior Non-Linear Outlay Schedules." *Bell Journal of Economics* (January 1978): 56–69.

Wilson, W. *Nonlinear Pricing*. Oxford: Oxford University Press, 1993.

CHAPTER 19

TRADITIONAL MODELS OF
IMPERFECT COMPETITION

In this chapter we examine models of price determination in markets that fall between the polar extremes of perfect competition and monopoly. Although no single model can be used to explain all possible forms of such imperfect competition, we will examine a few of the basic elements that are common to many of the models that are in current use. To that end we will focus on three specific topics: (1) pricing of homogeneous goods in markets in which there are relatively few firms; (2) product differentiation and advertising in such markets; and (3) the effect that entry and exit possibilities have on long-run outcomes in imperfectly competitive markets. In a sense then, this chapter concerns how the stringent assumptions of the perfectly competitive model can be relaxed and what the results of changing those assumptions are. For this study, the perfectly competitive model provides a useful benchmark since departures from the competitive norm may involve efficiency losses. Two specific criteria we will use in this comparison are (1) whether prices under imperfect competition equal marginal costs and (2) whether, in the long run, production occurs at minimum average cost. We will see that often imperfectly competitive markets will lack one or both of these desirable features of perfect competition. Many of these same topics are reexamined from the perspective of game theory in Chapter 20.

PRICING UNDER HOMOGENEOUS OLIGOPOLY

In this section we will examine the general theory of price determination in markets in which relatively few firms produce a single homogeneous product. As before, we will assume that the market is perfectly competitive on the demand side; that is, there are assumed to be many demanders, each of whom is a price taker. We will also assume that there are no transactions or information costs, so that the good in question obeys the law of one price and we may speak unambiguously of *the* good's price.

Later in this chapter we will relax this assumption when we consider product differentiation. In this section we will also assume that there are a fixed number of n identical firms (where n is taken to be a relatively small number). Later, we will consider a specific numerical example of duopoly (in which $n = 2$), but for the moment there is no reason to restrict our analysis to any specific number, since the method of analysis will not, for the most part, depend on what n happens to be. Throughout this section we will assume that n is fixed, but later in the chapter we will allow n to vary through entry and exit in response to firms' profitability.

The output of each firm in our model will be denoted by q_i $(i = 1 \ldots n)$. Since firms are assumed to be identical, symmetry in costs will usually require that these outputs are all equal, although it would be a simple matter to allow for some differences among firms. The inverse demand function for the good being examined will be denoted by $f(Q)$, and this shows the price, P, that demanders as a group are willing to pay for any particular level of industry output. That is,

Basic Structure of the Model

$$P = f(Q) = f(q_1 + q_2 + \cdots + q_n). \qquad (19.1)$$

Each firm's decision problem is to maximize its own profits (π_i), given this market price of the good and the firm's total costs, which are denoted by $TC_i(q_i)$. Hence, the firm's goal is to maximize

$$\begin{aligned}
\pi_i &= Pq_i - TC_i(q_i) \\
&= f(Q)q_i - TC_i(q_i) \qquad (19.2) \\
&= f(q_1 + q_2 + \cdots + q_n)q_i - TC_i(q_i).
\end{aligned}$$

Most of the issues to be discussed in this section ultimately center around how firms are assumed to make this profit-maximizing output choice. In perhaps overly simple mathematical terms, the results will depend on precisely what is assumed about how Equation 19.2 is to be differentiated to solve for a profit maximum. In economic terms, the central question concerns how the firm assumes other firms react to its decisions.

Four possible models will be examined here. These are summarized in the following definitions. We will see that these different models yield rather different results and that equilibria arising from the conjectural variations model are generally indeterminate except in a few special cases.

DEFINITIONS

Oligopoly Pricing Models   *Quasi-competitive model:* Assumes price-taking behavior by all firms (P is treated as fixed).

Cartel model: Assumes firms can collude perfectly in choosing industry output.
Cournot model: Assumes that firm i treats firm j's output as fixed in its decisions $(\partial q_j / \partial q_i = 0)$.
Conjectural variations model: Assumes that firm j's output will respond to variations in firm i's output $(\partial q_j / \partial q_i \neq 0)$.

Quasi-Competitive Model

As was the case under perfect competition, each firm in the quasi-competitive model is a price taker. That is, each firm assumes (probably incorrectly) that its decisions will not affect market price. In this case the first-order condition for profit maximization is that

$$\frac{\partial \pi_i}{\partial q_i} = P - \frac{\partial TC_i(q_i)}{\partial q_i} = 0 \tag{19.3}$$

or

$$P = MC_i(q_i) \quad (i = 1, n). \tag{19.4}$$

These n supply equations, together with the market-clearing demand equation,

$$P = f(Q) = f(q_1 + q_2 + \cdots + q_n), \tag{19.5}$$

will ensure that this market arrives at the short-run competitive solution. That solution is illustrated for the case of constant marginal costs as point C in Figure 19.1. Even though n may be a small number, the assumption of price-taking behavior in this case results in a competitive outcome.

Cartel Model

Of course, the assumption of price-taking behavior may be particularly inappropriate in oligopolistic industries in which each firm recognizes that its decisions have an obvious effect on price. An alternative assumption would be that firms as a group recognize that they can affect price and manage to coordinate their decisions so as to achieve monopoly profits. In this case the cartel acts as a multiplant monopoly and chooses $q_1, q_2, \ldots, q_n$ so as to maximize total industry profits.

$$\pi = PQ - [TC_1(q_1) + TC_2(q_2) + \cdots + TC_n(q_n)] \tag{19.6}$$

$$= f(q_1 + q_2 + \cdots + q_n)[q_1 + q_2 + \cdots + q_n] - \sum_{i=1}^{n} TC_i(q_i). \tag{19.7}$$

The first-order conditions for a maximum are that

FIGURE 19.1

ALTERNATIVE SOLUTIONS TO THE OLIGOPOLISTIC PRICING PROBLEM

Market equilibrium under an oligopoly can occur at many points on the demand curve. In this figure (which assumes that marginal costs are constant over all output ranges), the quasi-competitive equilibrium occurs at point C, the cartel equilibrium at point M, and the Cournot solution at point A. Many other solutions may occur between points M and C, depending on the specific assumption made about firms' strategic interrelationships.

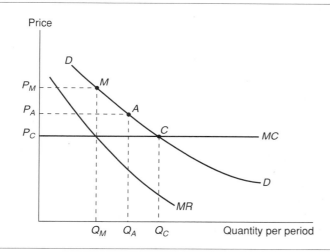

$$\frac{\partial \pi}{\partial q_i} = P + (q_1 + q_2 + \cdots + q_n)\frac{\partial P}{\partial q_i} - MC_i(q_i) = 0 \qquad (19.8)$$

$$= MR(Q) - MC_i(q_i) = 0. \qquad (19.9)$$

Notice that MR can be written as a function of the combined output of all firms, since its value is the same no matter which firm's output level is changed. At the profit-maximizing point this common marginal revenue will be equated for each firm's marginal production cost. Assuming these marginal costs are equal and constant for all firms, the output choice is indicated by point M in Figure 19.1. Because this coordinated plan requires a specific output level for each firm, the plan will also dictate how monopoly profits earned by the cartel are to be shared. In the aggregate these profits will be as large as possible, given the market demand curve and the industry's cost structure.

Viability of the Cartel Solution

There are three problems with this cartel solution. First, and most obviously, such monopolistic decisions may be illegal. In the United States, for example, Section I of the Sherman Act (1890) outlaws "conspiracies in restraint of trade," so would-be cartel members may expect a visit from the FBI. Similar laws exist in many other countries. A second problem with the cartel solution is that it requires that a considerable amount of information be available to the directors of the cartel—specifically, they must know the market demand function and each individual firm's marginal cost function. This information may be costly to obtain, and some cartel members may be reluctant to provide it. Finally, and most important, the cartel solution may be fundamentally unstable. Since each cartel member will produce an output level for which $P > MC_i$, each will have an incentive to expand output. If the directors of the oligopoly are not able to police such "chiseling," the monopolistic solution may collapse. The difficulties of the OPEC cartel in dictating output levels to its members during the mid-1980s attest to these problems. In Chapter 20 we will examine the stability of cartel pricing strategies in more detail.

Cournot Solution

One of the first researchers to develop a model of markets containing few firms was the French economist Augustin Cournot, who presented a formal analysis of duopoly behavior in 1838.[1] In our notation Cournot assumed that each firm recognizes that its own decisions about q_i affect price but that any one firm's output decisions do not affect those of any other firm. That is, each firm recognizes that $\partial P / \partial q_i \neq 0$ but assumes that $\partial q_j / \partial q_i = 0$ for all $j \neq i$. Using these assumptions, the first-order conditions for a profit maximum in our model are

$$\frac{\partial \pi_i}{\partial q_i} = P + q_i \frac{\partial P}{\partial q_i} - MC_i(q_i) = 0 \tag{19.10}$$

(for all $i = 1, n$). Notice from this equation that the firm assumes that changes in q_i affect its total revenue only through their direct effect on the market price of its own sales. Hence, the equation differs both from the cartel solution (where the effect of a change in price on total industry revenues is taken into account—see Equation 19.8) and from the conjectural variations case, to be discussed next, in which indirect effects of firm i's output on firm j's output are taken into account. In general, the n equations in 19.10, together with the market-clearing demand Equation 19.5, will permit an equilibrium solution for the variables $q_1, q_2, \ldots, q_n$ and P. An examination of the profit-maximizing Equation 19.10 shows that as long as marginal costs are increasing (as they

---

[1] A. Cournot, *Researches into the Mathematical Principles of the Theory of Wealth*, trans. N. T. Bacon (New York: Macmillan Co., 1897).

generally must be for a true profit maximum), each firm's output in the Cournot solution will exceed the cartel output, since the "firm-specific" marginal revenue in that equation is larger than the market–marginal revenue notion in Equation 19.8. On the other hand, the firm's output will fall short of the competitive output since the term $q_i \cdot \partial P / \partial q_i$ in Equation 19.10 is negative. Market equilibrium will therefore occur at a point such as A in Figure 19.1. At this point price exceeds marginal cost, but output is higher and industry profits lower than in the monopoly case.

In general, it might also be supposed that the greater the number of firms in the industry, the closer the equilibrium point will be to the competitive point C. With a larger number of firms the term $q_i \cdot \partial P / \partial q_i$ in Equation 19.10 tends to approach zero, and the equation therefore comes to resemble the quasi-competitive solution represented by Equation 19.3. For an illustration[2] of this limit property of the Cournot model, see Example 19.1 later in the chapter.

So far our models of oligopolistic price determination have not allowed for strategic interactions among firms. In markets with few firms, that is a particularly untenable assumption. Ford must obviously take some account of how General Motors will respond to its pricing and output decisions; all other software companies must worry about what Microsoft will do; and members of the OPEC cartel must be concerned with new oil exploration throughout the world. The problem faced by economic theorists is how to capture these strategic considerations in some sort of tractable analytical model. One approach relies on game theory to examine strategic choices in a simplified setting. In Chapter 20 we will illustrate how such tools can be applied to the analysis of duopolistic markets. Here we explore some of the ways in which strategic concerns can be integrated into the models we have already developed.

The primary way of building strategic concerns into our model is by considering the assumptions that might be made by one firm about other firms' behavior. In mathematical terms we wish to examine the possible assumptions that firm i might make about how its decisions might affect those of firm j. Specifically, for each firm i we are concerned with the assumed value of the derivative $\partial q_j / \partial q_i$ for all firms j other than firm i itself. Because the value of this derivative will be speculative, models based on various assumptions about its value are termed "conjectural variations" models; that

Conjectural Variations Model

---

[2] For a formal discussion of these issues, see J. Friedman, "Oligopoly Theory," in K. J. Arrow and M. D. Intriligator, eds., *Handbook of Mathematical Economics,* vol. 2 (Amsterdam: North-Holland Publishing Co., 1982).

is, they are concerned with firm i's "conjectures" about firm j's output variations.

Thus far in our models we have assumed that $\partial q_j / \partial q_i = 0$ for all $j \neq i$. We therefore have assumed no strategic interaction among firms. Once this assumption is relaxed, each firm's profit-maximizing decision becomes very complex. Now the first-order condition for maximizing Equation 19.2 becomes

$$\frac{\partial \pi_i}{\partial q_i} = P + q_i \left[\frac{\partial P}{\partial q_i} + \sum_{j \neq i} \frac{\partial P}{\partial q_j} \cdot \frac{\partial q_j}{\partial q_i} \right] - MC_i(q_i) = 0. \tag{19.11}$$

That is, the firm must now not only be concerned with how its own output affects market price directly but also must consider how variations in its own output will affect market price through their effect on other firms' output decisions. Because any number of plausible assumptions might be made about such responses, there is no generally accepted theory of the type of equilibrium that is likely to emerge from the responses given by Equation 19.11. A few interesting models have been developed for the duopoly case, and we will demonstrate a simple numerical example of these later in this chapter. And next we will examine a particular formulation of Equation 19.11 that yields a simple "price leadership" model. But these two examples are quite specific cases that fail to capture all of the intricacies that may occur in the conjectural variations model in its full generality.

Price Leadership Model

One tractable form of the conjectural variations model is based on the assumption that the market in question is composed of a single price leader and a fringe of quasi-competitive competitors. Assuming that the leader is firm 1, a mathematical representation of this market would include a price-taking reaction such as that given by Equation 19.4 for firms $2 \ldots n$, with only firm 1 requiring a complex reaction function of the type given by Equation 19.11. A graphical analysis of such a market is provided by Figure 19.2. The demand curve in the figure represents the total demand curve for the industry's product, and the supply curve SC represents the supply decisions of all the $n - 1$ firms in the competitive fringe. It is simply the horizontal sum of their short-run marginal cost curves. Using these two curves, the demand curve ($D'D'$) facing the industry leader is derived as follows. For a price of P_1 or above, the leader will sell nothing, since the competitive fringe would be willing to supply all that is demanded. For prices below P_2 the leader has the market to itself, since the fringe is not willing to supply anything. Between P_2 and P_1 the curve $D'D'$ is constructed by subtracting what the fringe will supply from total market demand; that is, the leader gets that portion of demand not taken by the fringe firms.

FIGURE 19.2

FORMAL MODEL OF PRICE LEADERSHIP BEHAVIOR

The curve $D'D'$ shows the demand curve facing the price leader; it is derived by subtracting what is produced by the competitive fringe of firms (SC) from market demand (DD). Given $D'D'$, the firm's profit-maximizing output level is Q_L, and a price of P_L will prevail in the market.

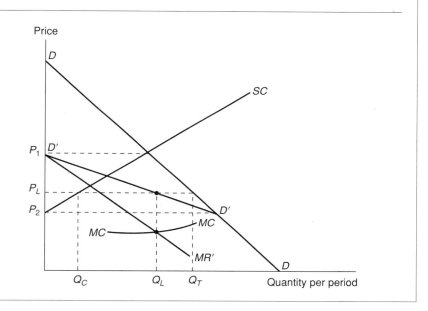

Given the demand curve $D'D'$, the leader can construct its marginal revenue curve (MR') and then refer to its own marginal cost curve (MC) to determine the profit-maximizing output level, Q_L. Market price then will be P_L. Given that price, the competitive fringe will produce Q_C, and total industry output will be $Q_T(= Q_C + Q_L)$.

Of course, this model does not answer such important questions as how the price leader in an industry is chosen or what happens when a member of the fringe decides to challenge the leader for its position and profits. But the model does illustrate one tractable example of the conjectural variations model that may explain pricing behavior in some instances. For example, it has been argued that the model may at times have offered an appropriate explanation for pricing in markets such as those for prime commercial loans (here the major money center banks are the "leaders"), standardized steel products (U.S. Steel is the leader), and, perhaps, the

OPEC cartel (where Saudi Arabia by virtue of politics and geology can play the role of leader). Of course, all such purported examples require substantial empirical investigation to determine the validity and scope of the price leadership model.

EXAMPLE 19.1

COURNOT'S NATURAL SPRING DUOPOLY

As a numerical example of some of these ideas, we will consider a very simple case in which there are no production costs and only two firms. Following Cournot's nineteenth-century example of two natural springs, we assume each spring owner has a large supply of (possibly healthful) water and faces the problem of how much to provide to the market. The demand for spring water is given by the linear demand curve

$$Q = q_1 + q_2 = 120 - P \tag{19.12}$$

and is illustrated in Figure 19.3. We will now examine various market equilibria along this demand curve.

Quasi-Competitive Solution. Since each firm has zero marginal costs, the quasi-competitive solution will result in a market price of zero. Total demand will be 120. In this particular example the division of output between the two springs is indeterminate, since each has zero marginal cost over all output ranges. The quasi-competitive output level is indicated by point C in Figure 19.3.

Cartel Solution. The cartel solution to this example can be found by maximizing total industry revenue (and profits):

$$\pi = PQ = 120Q - Q^2. \tag{19.13}$$

The first-order condition for a maximum is

$$\frac{\partial \pi}{\partial Q} = 120 - 2Q = 0$$

or

$$Q = 60$$

$$P = 60 \tag{19.14}$$

$$\pi = 3,600.$$

Again, the precise division of these output levels and profits between the two springs is indeterminate. The cartel solution is indicated by point M in Figure 19.3.

FIGURE 19.3

SOLUTIONS TO THE DUOPOLY PROBLEM

Given the demand curve $Q = 120 - P$, the points M, A, S, and C represent, respectively, the cartel, Cournot, Stackelberg, and quasi-competitive solutions to the duopoly problem.

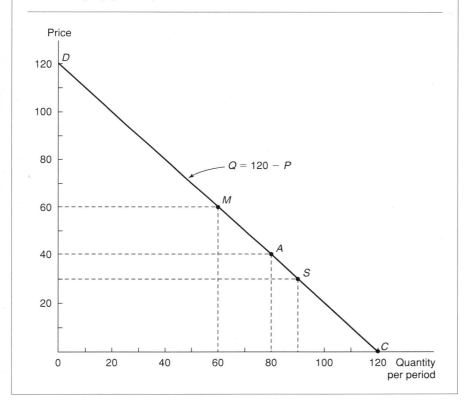

Cournot Solution. From Equation 19.12 it is easy to see that the two firms' revenues (and profits) are given by

$$\pi_1 = Pq_1 = (120 - q_1 - q_2)q_1 = 120q_1 - q_1^2 - q_1q_2$$
$$\pi_2 = Pq_2 = (120 - q_1 - q_2)q_2 = 120q_2 - q_2^2 - q_1q_2 .$$

(19.15)

If each spring owner assumes the other will not react to his or her own output decisions, $\partial q_1 / \partial q_2 = \partial q_2 / \partial q_1 = 0$, and the first-order conditions for a maximum are

$$\frac{\partial \pi_1}{\partial q_1} = 120 - 2q_1 - q_2 = 0$$

$$\frac{\partial \pi_2}{\partial q_2} = 120 - 2q_2 - q_1 = 0.$$

(19.16)

Equations 19.16 are called "reaction functions" since they show how each firm reacts to the other's output level. In equilibrium these equations must be mutually consistent—that is, each firm must produce what the other thinks it will. Given this assumption, Equations 19.16 can be solved simultaneously for the equilibrium values of q_1 and q_2 to yield

$$q_1 = q_2 = 40$$

$$P = 120 - (q_1 + q_2) = 40$$

$$\pi_1 = \pi_2 = Pq_1 = Pq_2 = 1{,}600.$$

(19.17)

More will be supplied under the Cournot assumptions than under the cartel case, and industry profits (3,200) will be somewhat lower than when output decisions are fully coordinated. This Cournot solution is denoted by point A in Figure 19.3. In this particular case it is easy to show that as more firms are introduced into the analysis, the equilibrium moves toward the competitive point.[3] For a somewhat more realistic case that also yields this solution, see Problem 19.2.

QUERY: Given that one spring owner's output is 40 in the Cournot model, why can't the other owner gain by producing more than 40 units of output? Does this conclusion conflict with our discussion of cartels where we expected chiseling whenever $P > MC$? (See Chapter 20 for a further discussion of this point.)

---

[3] With n firms Equation 19.16 becomes

$$\frac{\partial \pi_i}{\partial q_i} = 120 - 2q_i - \sum_{j \neq i} q_j = 0 \quad (i = 1, n).$$

Assuming, by symmetry, that all the q's are equal to $\bar{q}$, we have

$$\frac{\partial \pi_i}{\partial q_i} = 120 - (n + 1)\bar{q} = 0.$$

Hence, $\bar{q} = 120/(n + 1)$ and total output $= n\bar{q} = [n/(n + 1)](120)$, which approaches 120 (the competitive output) for large values of n.

EXAMPLE 19.2

STACKELBERG LEADERSHIP MODEL

The assumption of a constant marginal cost makes the price leadership model inappropriate for Cournot's spring problem. In this case the "competitive fringe" would simply take the entire market by pricing at marginal cost (here zero), with no room left in the market for the price leader. There is, however, the possibility for a different type of strategic leadership, a possibility first recognized by the German economist Heinrich von Stackelberg.[4] Von Stackelberg examined the consequences of assuming that one firm (say, firm 1) recognized how the other firm makes its output decisions. That is, he assumed that firm 1 knows (from Equation 19.16) that firm 2 chooses q_2 so that

$$q_2 = \frac{120 - q_1}{2}. \tag{19.18}$$

Firm 1 can now calculate the conjectural variation,

$$\frac{\partial q_2}{\partial q_1} = -\frac{1}{2}. \tag{19.19}$$

In words, firm 2 reduces its output by ½ unit for each unit increase in q_1. Firm 1's profit-maximization problem can be rewritten to take account of this reaction:

$$\pi_1 = Pq_1 = 120q_1 - q_1^2 - q_1q_2 \tag{19.20}$$

and

$$\frac{\partial \pi_1}{\partial q_1} = 120 - 2q_1 - q_1\frac{\partial q_2}{\partial q_1} - q_2 = 0$$

$$= 120 - \frac{3}{2}q_1 - q_2 = 0. \tag{19.21}$$

Solving this equation simultaneously with firm 2's reaction function (Equation 19.18) yields equilibrium values different from those in the Cournot model:

$$q_1 = 60$$

$$q_2 = 30$$

---

[4] H. von Stackelberg, *The Theory of the Market Economy*, trans. A. T. Peacock (New York: Oxford University Press, 1952).

$$P = 120 - (q_1 + q_2) = 30 \qquad (19.22)$$
$$\pi_1 = Pq_1 = 1{,}800$$
$$\pi_2 = Pq_2 = 900.$$

Firm 1 has been able to increase its profits by using its knowledge of firm 2's reactions. Firm 2's profits have been seriously eroded in this process. This solution is shown as point S on the demand curve presented in Figure 19.3.

Choice of the Leader and Ruinous Competition. One ambiguous feature of the Stackelberg model is how the leader is chosen. If each firm assumes that the other is a follower, each will produce 60 and will be disappointed at the final outcome (with total output of 120, market price, in the present example, will fall to zero). On the other hand, if each acts as a follower, the situation reverts to the Cournot equilibrium. From the Stackelberg perspective, however, the Cournot equilibrium is unstable: Each firm can perceive the benefits of being a leader and may try to choose its output accordingly. As we will see in Chapter 20, we need to explore the game theoretic aspects of this problem further if we are to evaluate all of the possibilities that may arise.

QUERY: Why does the first spring owner's decision to increase output raise profits here whereas it did not in the case proposed in the query to Example 19.1?

PRODUCT DIFFERENTIATION

Up to this point we have been assuming that the oligopolistic firms being examined produce a homogeneous output. Demanders therefore were assumed to be indifferent about which firm's output they bought, and the law of one price was assumed to hold in the market. Such an assumption is widely at variance with many real-world markets. Firms often devote considerable resources to differentiating their products from those of their competitors through such devices as quality and style variations, warranties and guarantees, special service features, and product advertising. All of these activities require firms to employ additional resources, and firms will choose to do so if profits are thereby increased. Such attempts at product variation also will result in a relaxation of the law of one price, since now the market will consist of goods that vary from firm to firm and demanders may have preferences about which supplier to patronize. That possibility introduces a certain fuzziness into what we mean by the "market for a good," since now there are many closely related, but not identical, products being produced.

For example, once it is recognized that toothpaste brands vary somewhat from supplier to supplier, should we consider all these products to be in the same market? Or should we differentiate, say, among fluoridated products, gels, striped toothpaste, smokers' toothpaste, and so forth? Or, consider the problem of spatial differentiation. Since demanders will be closer to some sellers than to others, they may view nearby sellers more favorably because buying from them involves lower transportation charges. Here we will assume that the market is composed of n firms, each producing a slightly different product, but that these products can usefully be considered a single-product group. This notion can be made more precise as follows:

DEFINITION

Product Group The outputs of a set of firms constitute a *product group* if the substitutability in demand among the products (as measured by the cross-price elasticity) is very high relative to the substitutability between those firms' outputs and other goods generally.

Although this definition has its own ambiguities (arguments about the definition of a product group often dominate antitrust proceedings, for example), it should suffice for our purposes.[5] Now we will proceed to offer a formal but simplified analysis of pricing within the market for such a product group.

Again we will assume that there are n firms competing in a particular product group. Now, however, each firm can choose the amount it spends on attempting to differentiate its product from those of its competitors. We will denote the resources used by the ith firm for this purpose by z_i, which might include spending on special options, quality, brand advertising, or moving to a favorable location. The firm's costs now are given by

Firms' Choices

$$\text{total costs} = TC_i(q_i, z_i). \qquad (19.23)$$

Because there are n slightly different goods in the product group, we must allow for the possibility of different market prices for each of these goods. Such prices will be denoted by $P_1, \ldots, P_n$ (although some of these may be equal). The demand facing the ith firm shows how price received depends on quantity produced by that firm (q_i), on prices being charged by all other

---

[5] A more precise definition might be built around the "attribute" concept introduced in Chapter 6. Under this approach, goods that share a common set of attributes would constitute a product group.

firms (P_j for $j \neq i$), and on the ith firm's and all other firms' attempts to differentiate their products (z_j, $j = 1$, n). In its most general form then,

$$P_i = g(q_i, P_j, z_i, z_j),\qquad(19.24)$$

where the terms P_j and z_j are intended to include all other prices and differentiation activities, respectively. Presumably, $\partial g/\partial q_i \leq 0$, $\partial g/\partial P_j \geq 0$, $\partial g/\partial z_i \geq 0$, and $\partial g/\partial z_j \leq 0$. That is, the demand curve facing the individual firm is downward sloping and is shifted outward by price increases by its competitors. Product differentiation activities by the ith firm may also shift demand outward, whereas such activities by competitors will shift demand inward.

The ith firm's profits are given by

$$\pi_i = P_i q_i - TC_i(q_i, z_i),\qquad(19.25)$$

and in the simple case where $\partial z_j/\partial q_i$, $\partial z_j/\partial z_i$, $\partial P_j/\partial q_i$, and $\partial P_j/\partial z_i$ are all zero, the first-order conditions for a maximum are

$$\frac{\partial \pi_i}{\partial q_i} = P_i + q_i\frac{\partial P_i}{\partial q_i} - \frac{\partial TC_i}{\partial q_i} = 0\qquad(19.26)$$

$$\frac{\partial \pi_i}{\partial z_i} = q_i\frac{\partial P_i}{\partial z_i} - \frac{\partial TC_i}{\partial z_i} = 0.\qquad(19.27)$$

Equation 19.26 is a restatement of the marginal revenue equals marginal cost condition for a profit maximum. Equation 19.27 shows that, as for any input, additional differentiation activities should be pursued up to the point at which the additional revenues they generate are equal to their marginal costs.[6]

Market Equilibrium   Although this description of firms' choices seems straightforward, these choices are actually quite complex. Since the demand curve facing any one firm depends on the prices and product differentiation activities of its competitors, that demand curve may shift frequently, and its position at any particular time may only be partly understood. As in the Cournot model, the firm must make some assumptions in order to make decisions. And, as in the conjectural variations model, whatever one firm decides to do may affect its competitors' actions. Hence, the differentiated oligopoly model poses even more complex strategic issues than did the models we examined for the homogeneous good case. Not surprisingly, few definitive conclusions can be reached about the nature of the market equilibria that result from such a situation. We illustrate one type of equilibrium in spatially differentiated

---

[6] For an alternative statement, see Problem 19.4.

markets in Example 19.3 and take up Chamberlin's model of monopolistic competition later in this chapter. Several of the game theory models described in Chapter 20 also offer insights about product differentiation.

EXAMPLE 19.3

SPATIAL DIFFERENTIATION

To develop a simple model of product differentiation, consider the case of ice cream stands located on a beach—a problem first studied by H. Hotelling in the 1920s.[7] Figure 19.4 shows this (linear) beach together with two ice cream stands located at points A and B. Assume demanders are located uniformly along the beach, one at each unit of length and that each buys exactly one ice cream cone per period. Ice cream cones are assumed to be costless to produce, but carrying them back to one's beach umbrella results in a cost c per unit of distance traveled (since the ice cream melts). If we let P_A be stand A's price and P_B be stand B's price, a person located at point E will be indifferent between stands A and B if

$$P_A + cx = P_B + cy. \tag{19.28}$$

As Figure 19.4 shows,

$$a + x + y + b = L, \tag{19.29}$$

FIGURE 19.4

SPATIAL DIFFERENTIATION AND PRICING

Ice cream stands are located at points A and B along a linear beach of length L. In equilibrium, consumers to the left of E will patronize stand A, those to the right will patronize stand B. Different prices will prevail at the two stands. If the stands can relocate, they may move to the center of the beach or to the ends depending on the strategic assumptions made.

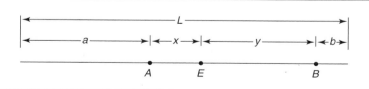

---

[7] H. Hotelling, "Stability in Competition," *The Economic Journal* (January 1929): 41–57.

where L is the length of the beach. The coordinate of point E is therefore

$$x = \frac{P_B - P_A + cy}{c} \tag{19.30}$$

$$= \frac{P_B - P_A}{c} + L - a - b - x \tag{19.31}$$

or

$$x = \frac{1}{2}\left(L - a - b + \frac{P_B - P_A}{c}\right) \tag{19.32}$$

and

$$y = \frac{1}{2}\left(L - a - b + \frac{P_A - P_B}{c}\right). \tag{19.33}$$

Profits for the two firms are

$$\pi_A = P_A(a + x) = \frac{1}{2}(L + a - b) P_A + \frac{P_A P_B - P_A^2}{2c} \tag{19.34}$$

and

$$\pi_B = P_B(b + y) = \frac{1}{2}(L - a + b) P_B + \frac{P_A P_B - P_B^2}{2c}. \tag{19.35}$$

Each firm will choose its own price so as to maximize profits:

$$\frac{\partial \pi_A}{\partial P_A} = \frac{1}{2}(L + a - b) + \frac{P_B}{2c} - \frac{P_A}{c} = 0 \tag{19.36}$$

$$\frac{\partial \pi_B}{\partial P_B} = \frac{1}{2}(L - a + b) + \frac{P_A}{2c} - \frac{P_B}{c} = 0.$$

These can readily be solved for

$$P_A = c\left(L + \frac{a - b}{3}\right)$$
$$\tag{19.37}$$
$$P_B = c\left(L - \frac{a - b}{3}\right).$$

In general, these prices will depend on the precise location of the two stands and will differ from each other. For example, if we assume that the beach is 100 yards long, $a \doteq 40$ yards, $b = 10$ yards, and $c = \$.01$ per yard, then

$$P_A = .01\left(100 + \frac{30}{3}\right)$$

$$= \$1.10 \tag{19.38}$$

$$P_B = .01\left(100 - \frac{30}{3}\right)$$

$$= \$.90$$

These price differences arise only from the locational aspects of this problem, since cones themselves are identical and costless. Because A is somewhat more favorably located than B, it can charge a higher price for its cones without losing too much business to B. Using Equation 19.32 shows

$$x = \frac{1}{2}(100 - 40 - 10 - 20) = 15 \tag{19.39}$$

so that stand A sells 55 cones (despite its higher price) whereas B sells only 45. At point E a consumer is indifferent between walking 15 yards to A and paying \$1.10 or walking 35 yards to B and paying \$.90. The solution is inefficient in that a consumer slightly to the right of E would incur a shorter walk by patronizing A, but chooses B because of A's power to set higher prices.

Locational Choices.   Perhaps the most important insights to be gained from this example arise if we allow the ice cream stands to change their locations at zero cost. That is, we allow the firms to change the nature of the product they are offering (theoretically, location plays the role of z_i in Equation 19.27). Analysis of this possibility formally raises a number of complexities, so an intuitive discussion may suffice. If we focus only on the number of ice cream cones sold, it seems clear that each stand has an incentive to move to the center of the beach. Any stand that opts for an off-center position is subject to its rival moving between it and the center and taking a large share of the market. This effect resembles the tendency of political candidates to move toward the center on controversial issues—opting for an off-center position makes a candidate vulnerable to moves that allow his or her rival to take a majority of the vote. In the case of product differentiation, such motives tend to encourage a similarity of products.

But the ice cream cone firms here care more about profits than market share. Moving closer to one's rival causes a decline in consumers' willingness to pay for locational advantages; hence, profits will fall from such a move. Ultimately, therefore, the firms' optimal locational decisions will depend on the specifics of consumers' demands for spatially differentiated products, and, in some cases, maximal differentiation (location at the ends of the beach) may be the result.[8] Whatever the locational choices that result in a sustainable

---

[8] See C. d'Aspremont, J. Gabszewicz, and J. Thisse, "On Hotelling's Stability in Competition," *Econometrica* (September 1979): 1145–1151.

equilibrium, it seems unlikely that the firms would opt for the socially optimal locations that minimize total travel cost.[9]

QUERY: In this problem would it matter if ice cream cones could be produced at constant marginal cost? Suppose cone production were subject to increasing marginal cost?

ENTRY

The possibility of new firms entering an industry plays an important role in the development of the theory of perfectly competitive price determination. It ensures that any long-run profits will be eliminated by new entrants and that firms will produce at the low points of their long-run average cost curves. Under conditions of oligopoly, the first of these forces continues to operate. To the extent that entry is possible, long-run profits are constrained. If entry is completely costless, long-run economic profits will be zero (as in the competitive case).

Zero-Profit Equilibrium

Whether firms in an oligopolistic industry with free entry will be directed to the low point of their average cost curves depends on the nature of the demand curve facing them. If firms are price takers, the analysis given for the competitive case carries over directly: Since $P = MR = MC$ for profit maximization with price taking and since $P = AC$ if entry is to result in zero profits, production will take place where $MC = AC$ (that is, at minimum average cost).

If oligopolistic firms have some control over the price they receive (perhaps because each produces a slightly differentiated product), each firm will face a downward-sloping demand curve and the competitive analysis may not hold. Entry still may reduce profits to zero, but now production at minimum average cost is not assured. This situation is illustrated in Figure 19.5. Initially, the demand curve facing the firm is given by dd, and economic profits are being earned. New firms will be attracted by these profits, and their entry will shift dd inward (because there are now a larger number of firms to contend with a given market demand curve). Indeed, entry can reduce profits to zero by shifting the demand curve to $d'd'$. The level of output that maximizes profits with this demand curve (q') is not, however, the same as that level at which average costs are minimized (q_m). Rather, the firm will

---

[9] Total walking costs to A are

$$\int_0^a z\,dz + \int_0^x z\,dz = (a^2 + x^2)/2.$$

Similarly, costs of walking to B are $(b^2 + y^2)/2$. The sum of these is minimized when

$$a = x = b = y = L/4.$$

FIGURE 19.5

ENTRY REDUCES PROFITABILITY IN AN OLIGOPOLY

Initially, the demand curve facing the firm is dd. Marginal revenue is given by mr, and q^* is the profit-maximizing output level. If entry is costless, new firms attracted by the possibility for profits may shift the firm's demand curve inward to $d'd'$, where profits are zero. At output level q', average costs are not a minimum, and the firm exhibits excess capacity given by $q_m - q'$.

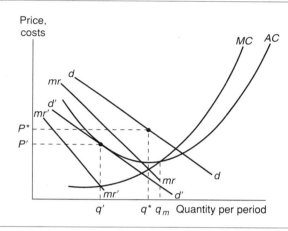

produce less than that "efficient" output level and will exhibit "excess capacity," given by $q_m - q'$. Some economists have hypothesized that this outcome characterizes industries such as service stations, convenience stores, and fast-food franchisers, where product differentiation is prevalent but entry is relatively costless.

EXAMPLE 19.4

MONOPOLISTIC COMPETITION

The zero-profit equilibrium illustrated in Figure 19.5 was first described by Edward Chamberlin, who termed his model "monopolistic competition."[10] In this model, each firm produces a slightly differentiated product and entry

[10] See E. Chamberlin, *The Theory of Monopolistic Competition* (Cambridge, Mass.: Harvard University Press, 1933).

is costless. As a numerical example, suppose there are n firms in a market and that each firm has the same total cost schedule of the form:

$$c_i = 9 + 4q_i . \tag{19.40}$$

Each firm also faces a demand curve for its product of the form:

$$q_i = -0.01(n - 1)p_i + 0.01 \sum_{j \neq i} p_j + \frac{303}{n} , \tag{19.41}$$

where p_j is the prices charged by other firms and n is the number of firms in the industry. Notice that the demand curve for each firm is a downward-sloping function of its own price and depends positively on the prices charged by its competitors. Here we will define an equilibrium for this industry to be a situation in which prices must be equal ($p_i = p_j$ for all i and j). Other models allow some price dispersion to exist even in equilibrium, perhaps because of spatial or other types of differentiation. Since in our equilibrium $p_i = p_j$, it is clear that $q_i = 303/n$ and $Q = nq_i = 303$. This solution holds for any n.

Equilibrium Market Structure. To find equilibrium n, we first examine each firm's profit-maximizing choice of p_i. Since

$$\pi_i = p_i q_i - c_i , \tag{19.42}$$

the first-order condition for a maximum is

$$\frac{\partial \pi_i}{\partial p_i} = -.02(n - 1)p_i + .01 \sum_{j \neq i} p_j + \frac{303}{n}$$

$$+ .04(n - 1) = 0, \tag{19.43}$$

so

$$p_i = \frac{.5 \sum_{j \neq i} p_j}{n - 1} + \frac{303}{.02(n - 1)n} + 2. \tag{19.44}$$

Applying the equilibrium condition $p_j = p_i$ yields

$$p_i = \frac{30,300}{(n - 1)(n)} + 4. \tag{19.45}$$

Notice that price approaches marginal cost (4) as n gets large here. Hence, this model has a competitive solution as a limiting case. Equilibrium n is determined by the zero-profit condition (since entry is unconstrained)

$$p_i q_i - c_i = 0. \tag{19.46}$$

Substituting into this expression the value for p_i found in Equation 19.44 and the value for q calculated in Equation 19.41 gives

$$\frac{30{,}300 \cdot 303}{n^2(n-1)} + \frac{4(303)}{n} = 9 + \frac{4(303)}{n} \qquad (19.47)$$

or $n = 101$. The final equilibrium is therefore

$$p_i = p_j = 7$$

$$q_i = 3 \qquad (19.48)$$

$$\pi_i = 0.$$

Nature of the Equilibrium.   In the equilibrium calculated in Equation 19.48, each firm has $p_i = AC_i$ but $p_i > MC_i = 4$. In addition, since

$$AC_i = 4 + \frac{9}{q_i}, \qquad (19.49)$$

each firm has diminishing average costs throughout all output ranges, so production does not occur at minimum average cost. Each firm's zero-profit equilibrium would therefore resemble Figure 19.5. The features of this equilibrium prompted Chamberlin's hypothesis that monopolistic competition is Pareto inefficient.

If each potential entrant faces a demand function similar to that in Equation 19.41, the equilibrium described in Equation 19.48 is sustainable. No new firm would find it profitable to enter this industry. This view of sustainability may be too narrow, however. By adopting a fairly large-scale production plan, a potential entrant could achieve relatively low average costs in this model (with $q = 9$, $AC = 5$, for example). This low average cost gives the potential entrant considerable leeway in pricing its product so as to tempt customers of existing firms to switch allegiances.[11]

QUERY: What is the Pareto efficient solution for this market? How might the efficient solution depend on the nature of demanders' utility?

The conclusion that the Chamberlin zero-profit equilibrium pictured in Figure 19.5 is sustainable in the long run has been challenged by several economists.[12] They argue that the model neglects the effects of *potential entry*

**Contestable
Markets and
Industry Structure**

---

[11] More generally, Chamberlin's model of monopolistic competition can be viewed as seriously incomplete because it does not specify the precise reasons why the demand curve facing each firm is downward sloping. Assuming that the slope arises from some sort of brand name, reputational, or locational differences among goods, a more complete model should address firms' choices among such strategies.

[12] See W. J. Baumol, "Contestable Markets: An Uprising in the Theory of Industry Structure," *American Economic Review* (March 1982): 1–19, and W. J. Baumol, J. C. Panzar, and R. D. Willig, *Contestable Markets and the Theory of Industry Structure* (San Diego, Calif.: Harcourt Brace Jovanovich, 1982).

on market equilibrium by focusing only on the behavior of actual entrants. They therefore reintroduce to economics the distinction, first made by H. Demsetz, between competition *in* the market and competition *for* the market by showing that the latter concept provides a more appropriate perspective for analyzing the free entry assumption.[13] Within this broader perspective the "invisible hand" of competition becomes even more constraining on firms' behavior, and perfectly competitive equilibria are more likely to emerge.

The expanded examination of entry begins by defining a "perfectly contestable market":

DEFINITION

Perfectly Contestable Market   A market is *perfectly contestable* if entry and exit are absolutely free. Equivalently, a perfectly contestable market is one in which no outside potential competitor can enter by cutting price and still make profits (since if such profit opportunities existed, potential entrants would take advantage of them).

A perfectly contestable market then drops the perfectly competitive assumption of price-taking behavior but expands a bit upon the concept of free entry by permitting potential entrants to operate in a hit-and-run manner, snatching up whatever profit opportunities are available. Such an assumption, as we will point out below, is not necessarily accurate in many market situations, but it does provide a different starting place for a simplified theory of pricing.

The equilibrium illustrated in Figure 19.5 is unsustainable in a perfectly contestable market, provided that two or more firms are already in the market. In such a case a potential hit-and-run entrant could turn a quick profit by taking all the first firm's sales by selling q' at a price slightly below P' and making up for the loss this would entail by selling a further marginal increment in output to the other firm(s)' customers at a price in excess of marginal cost. That is, because the equilibrium in Figure 19.5 has $P > MC$, it permits a would-be entrant to take away one zero-profit firm's market and encroach a bit on other firms' markets where, at the margin, profits are attainable. The only type of market equilibrium that would be impervious to such hit-and-run tactics would be one in which firms earn zero profits and price at marginal costs. And as we saw in Chapter 14, this requires that firms produce at the low points of their long-run average cost curves where $P = MC = AC$. Even in the absence of price-taking behavior in markets with relatively few firms, perfect contestability provides an "invisible hand" that guides market equilibrium to a competitive-type result.

---

[13] H. Demsetz, "Why Regulate Utilities?" *Journal of Law and Economics* (April 1968): 55–65.

This perfectly contestable analysis can be taken one step further by showing how industry structure is determined. If, as in Chapter 14, we let q^* represent that output level for which average costs are minimized and Q^* represent the total market demand for the commodity when price equals minimal average cost, then the equilibrium number of firms in the industry is given by

Market Structure

$$n = \frac{Q^*}{q^*},$$ (19.50)

and contrary to the perfectly competitive case, this number may be relatively small. In Figure 19.6, for example, exactly four firms fulfill the market demand for Q^*, and the perfectly contestable assumption will ensure competitive behavior, even though these firms may recognize strategic relationships among themselves. The ability of potential entrants to seize any possible opportunities for profit sharply constrains the types of behavior that are possible and thereby provides a determinate equilibrium market structure.

FIGURE 19.6

PERFECT CONTESTABILITY AND INDUSTRY STRUCTURE

In a perfectly contestable market, equilibrium requires that $P = MC = AC$. The number of firms is completely determined by market demand (Q^*) and by the output level that minimizes average cost (q^*).

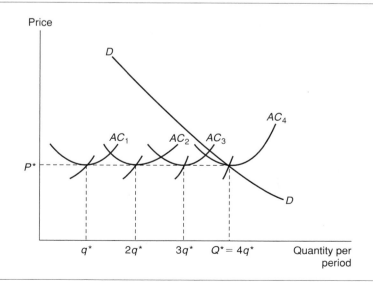

Barriers to Entry   All of the analysis presented so far in this section has been predicated on the assumptions of free entry and exit. When various barriers prevent such flexibility, these results must be modified. Possible barriers to entry in the oligopoly case include many of those already discussed in connection with monopoly in the previous chapter. They also include those arising specifically out of some features of oligopolistic markets. Product differentiation, for example, may raise entry barriers by promoting strong brand loyalty. Or producers may so proliferate their brands that no room remains for would-be entrants to do anything different (this has been alleged to be true in the ready-to-eat breakfast cereal industry). The possibility of strategic pricing decisions may also deter entry if existing firms can convince firms wishing to enter that it would be unprofitable to do so. Firms may, for a time, adopt lower, entry-deterring prices in order to accomplish this goal, with the intent of raising prices once potential entrants disappear (assuming they do).

Finally, the completely flexible type of hit-and-run behavior assumed in the contestable markets theory may be subject to two other types of barriers in the real world. First, some types of capital investments made by firms may not be reversible. A firm cannot build an automobile assembly plant for a week's use and then dismantle it at no loss. In this case there are exit costs that will make recurrent raids on the industry unprofitable. Of course, in other cases, such as the trucking industry, capital may be easily rented for short periods and exit will then pose few costs. Second, the contestable markets model requires that quantity demanded respond instantly to price differentials. If, instead, demanders only switch slowly to a new product, potential entrants cannot attain market penetration quickly, and their ability to discipline firms in the market will be constrained. The importance of all such restrictions for market behavior is ultimately an empirical question.

EXAMPLE 19.5

A CONTESTABLE NATURAL MONOPOLY

Suppose that the total cost of producing electric power (Q, measured in thousands of kilowatt hours) is given by

$$TC = 100Q + 8,000. \tag{19.51}$$

Obviously, this function exhibits declining average cost over all output ranges, so electricity production is a natural monopoly. The demand for electricity depends on its price (in dollars per thousand kilowatt hours) according to

$$Q_D = 1,000 - 5P. \tag{19.52}$$

If a single electricity producer behaves as a monopolist, it will choose a profit-maximizing quantity by

$$MR = 200 - \frac{2Q}{5} = MC = 100 \tag{19.53}$$

or

$$Q_m = 250$$

$$P_m = 150. \tag{19.54}$$

At this monopoly choice, profits will be 4,500 $(= TR - TC = 37,500 - 33,000)$. These profits provide a tempting target for would-be entrants into the electric industry. If there are no entry barriers (the existing company does not have an exclusive franchise, for example), such an entrant can offer electricity customers a lower price and still cover costs. The monopoly solution in Equations 19.54 may not therefore represent a viable equilibrium.

A Contestable Solution. If electricity production is fully contestable, the only price viable under the threat of potential entry is average cost. Only with average cost pricing will potential entrants have no incentive to threaten the monopolist's position. We can find this equilibrium by

$$Q = 1,000 - 5P = 1,000 - 5(AC)$$
$$= 1,000 - 5\left(100 + \frac{8,000}{Q}\right), \tag{19.55}$$

which results in the quadratic expression

$$Q^2 - 500Q + 40,000 = 0. \tag{19.56}$$

Factoring gives

$$(Q - 400)(Q - 100) = 0, \tag{19.57}$$

but only the $Q = 400$ solution is a sustainable entry deterrent. Under contestability, therefore, the market equilibrium is

$$Q_c = 400$$

$$P_c = 120. \tag{19.58}$$

Contestability has increased consumer welfare considerably from what it was under the monopoly solution. Indeed, the contestable solution is precisely what might have been chosen by a regulatory commission interested in average cost pricing.

QUERY: Is consumer surplus as large as possible in this case given the constraint that no subsidies are being provided to electric power producers? How might consumer surplus be increased further through an appropriate subsidy?

SUMMARY

Many markets fall between the polar extremes of perfect competition and monopoly. In this chapter we have begun our examination of such markets by introducing some of the most widely used models. We have seen that in such imperfectly competitive markets, each firm must take its rivals' actions into account in making decisions, and this adds a considerable conjectural element to the analysis. In Chapter 20 we will continue to explore these interrelations through the use of game theory models. Here we reached for general conclusions about modeling markets with relatively few firms:

- Markets with few firms offer potential profits through the formation of a monopoly cartel. Such cartels may, however, be unstable and costly to maintain because each member has an incentive to chisel on price.

- In markets with few firms, output and price decisions are interdependent. Each firm must

consider its rivals' decisions. Modeling such interdependence is difficult because of the need to consider conjectural variations.

- The Cournot model provides a tractable approach to oligopoly markets, but neglects important strategic issues.

- Product differentiation can be analyzed in a standard profit-maximization framework. With differentiated products, the law of one price no longer holds, and firms may have somewhat more leeway in their pricing decisions.

- Entry conditions are important determinants of the long-run sustainability of various market equilibria. With perfect contestability, equilibria may resemble perfectly competitive ones even though there are relatively few firms in the market.

PROBLEMS

19.1

Assume for simplicity that a monopolist has no costs of production and faces a demand curve given by

$$Q = 150 - P.$$

a. Calculate the profit-maximizing price-quantity combination for this monopolist. Also calculate the monopolist's profits.
b. Suppose a second firm enters the market. Let q_1 be

the output of the first firm and q_2 the output of the second. Market demand is now given by

$$q_1 + q_2 = 150 - P.$$

Assuming that this second firm also has no costs of production, use the Cournot model of duopoly to determine the profit-maximizing level of production for each firm as well as the market price. Also calculate each firm's profits.

c. How do the results from parts (a) and (b) compare to the price and quantity that would prevail in a perfectly competitive market? Graph the demand and marginal revenue curves and indicate the three different price-quantity combinations on the demand curve.

19.2

A monopolist can produce at constant average (and marginal) costs of $AC = MC = 5$. The firm faces a market demand curve given by

$$Q = 53 - P.$$

a. Calculate the profit-maximizing price-quantity combination for this monopolist. Also calculate the monopolist's profits.
b. Suppose that a second firm enters the market. Let q_1 be the output of firm 1 and q_2 the output of firm 2. Market demand now is given by

$$q_1 + q_2 = 53 - P.$$

Assuming that firm 2 has the same costs as firm 1, calculate the profits of firms 1 and 2 as functions of q_1 and q_2.
c. Suppose (after Cournot) that each of these two firms chooses its level of output so as to maximize profits on the assumption that the other's output is fixed. Calculate each firm's "reaction function," which expresses desired output of one firm as a function of the other's output.
d. On the assumption in part (c), what is the only level for q_1 and q_2 with which both firms will be satisfied (what q_1, q_2 combination satisfies both reaction curves)?
e. With q_1 and q_2 at the equilibrium level specified in part (d), what will be the market price, the profits for each firm, and the total profits earned?
f. Suppose now that there are n identical firms in the industry. If each firm adopts the Cournot strategy toward all its rivals, what will be the profit-maximizing output level for each firm? What will be the market price? What will be the total profits earned in the industry? (All these will depend on n.)
g. Show that when n approaches infinity, the output levels, market price, and profits approach those that would "prevail" in perfect competition.

19.3

Use the analysis developed in this chapter to explain the following industrial behavior:
a. Banks announce a widely publicized prime rate and change it only occasionally.
b. Apple and IBM computers are not compatible.
c. Insurance companies continue to solicit automobile insurance business in spite of their plea that "we lose money on every policy we write."
d. U.S. automobiles were of very low quality in the 1960s and 1970s, but quality improved in the late 1980s.

19.4

Suppose that a firm's costs for dollars spent on product differentiation (or advertising) activities (z) and quantity (q) can be written as

$$TC = g(q) + z \quad g'(q) > 0$$

and that its demand function can be written as

$$q = q(P, z).$$

Show that the firm's profit-maximizing choices for P and z will result in spending a share of total revenues on z given by

$$\frac{z}{Pq} = -\frac{e_{q,z}}{e_{q,P}}.$$

(This condition was derived by R. Dorfman and P. Steiner in "Optimal Advertising and Optimal Quality," *American Economic Review* [December 1954]: 826–836.)

19.5

One way of measuring the size distribution of firms is through the use of the Herfindahl Index, which is defined as

$$H = \sum \alpha_i^2,$$

where α_i is the share of firm i in total industry revenues. Show that if all firms in the industry have constant returns-to-scale production functions and follow Cournot output decisions (Equation 19.10), the ratio of total industry profits to total revenue will equal the Herfindahl Index divided by the price elasticity of demand. What does this result imply about the relationship between industry concentration and industry profitability?

19.6

In the Clorox case, Procter & Gamble was alleged to be a potential entrant into the liquid bleach market. Can you devise a way to use firms' cost curves and the demand curves facing the firms to differentiate among actual entrants? Potential entrants? Nonentrants? Use your analysis to suggest what the court should have looked for in this antitrust case.

19.7

Suppose that the demand for crude oil is given by

$$Q = -2,000P + 70,000,$$

where Q is the quantity of oil in thousands of barrels per year and P is the dollar price per barrel. Suppose also that there are 1,000 identical small producers of crude oil, each with marginal costs given by

$$MC = q + 5,$$

where q is the output of the typical firm.

a. Assuming that each small oil producer acts as a price taker, calculate the market supply curve and the market equilibrium price and quantity.

b. Suppose a practically infinite supply of crude oil is discovered in New Jersey by a would-be price leader and that this oil can be produced at a constant average and marginal cost of $15 per barrel. Assuming that the supply behavior of the competitive fringe described in part (a) is not changed by this discovery, how much should the price leader produce in order to maximize profits? What price and quantity will now prevail in the market?

c. Graph your results. Does consumer surplus increase as a result of the New Jersey oil discovery?

How does consumer surplus after the discovery compare to what would exist if the New Jersey oil were supplied competitively?

19.8

Suppose a firm is considering investing in research that would lead to a cost-saving innovation. Assuming the firm can retain this innovation solely for its own use, will the additional profits from the lower (marginal) costs be greater if the firm is a competitive price taker or if the firm is a monopolist? Develop a careful graphical argument. More generally, develop a verbal analysis to suggest whether competitive or monopoly firms are more likely to adopt cost-saving innovations. (For an early analysis of this issue, see W. Fellner, "The Influence of Market Structure on Technological Progress," *Quarterly Journal of Economics* [November 1951]: 560–567.)

19.9

The demand for telephones in a midsize city is given by

$$Q = 1,000 - 50P,$$

where Q is the number of homes buying service (in thousands) and P is the monthly connect charge (in dollars). Phone system costs are given by

$$TC = 500 \, ln \, (.1Q - 20) \text{ for } Q > 200.$$

a. Is telephone production a natural monopoly in this city?

b. What output level will an unregulated monopoly produce in this situation? What price will be charged? What will monopoly profits be?

c. If there is active (contestable) competition for the city franchise, what price will prevail?

SUGGESTED READINGS

Bain, J. S. *Barriers to New Competition.* Cambridge, Mass.: Harvard University Press, 1956.
Classic treatment of the theory of entry barriers together with some empirical detail.

Baumol, W. J. "Contestable Markets: An Uprising in the Theory of Industry Structure." *American Economic Review* (March 1982): 1–19.

AEA presidential address summarizing Baumol's and others' research on the theory of multiproduct firms and contestable markets.

Baumol, W. J., J. C. Panzar, and R. D. Willig. *Contestable Markets and the Theory of Industry Structure.* San Diego, Calif.: Harcourt Brace Jovanovich, 1982.

Detailed theoretical treatment of recent theories of contestable markets.

Rothschild, M. "Models of Market Organization with Imperfect Information: A Survey." *Journal of Political Economy* (November/December 1973): 1283–1908.
Nice survey of the theory of the relationship between imperfect competition in markets and the absence of full market information.

Scherer, F. M. *Industrial Market Structure and Economic Performance.* 2d ed. Chicago: Rand McNally, 1980.
Major industrial organization text. Encyclopedic coverage. Not as analytical as the more recent Tirole text.

Schmalensee, R. *The Economics of Advertising.* Amsterdam: North-Holland Publishing Co., 1972. Chap. 1.
Good summary of theories of advertising together with some empirical investigations (especially of cigarette advertising).

Spence, M. "Contestable Markets and the Theory of Industrial Structure." *Journal of Economic Literature* (September 1983): 981–990.
Brief, readable review of contestable markets theory.

Stiglitz, J., and G. F. Mathewson, eds. *New Developments in the Analysis of Market Structure.* Cambridge, Mass.: MIT Press, 1986.
Contains a number of useful review articles and discussions. Especially recommended are those by Baumol et al. (Contestability), Schmalensee (Advertising), and Stiglitz (Competition and Research and Development Incentives).

Tirole, J. *The Theory of Industrial Organization.* Cambridge, Mass.: MIT Press, 1988.
Complete treatment of a variety of models of imperfect competition. Particularly useful sections on product differentiation and nonprice competition.

CHAPTER 20

GAME THEORY MODELS OF PRICING

$\mathbf{M}$any of the strategic issues that arise under imperfect competition can be addressed using models from game theory. In this chapter, therefore, we reintroduce the concepts of games, strategies, and equilibrium first presented in Chapter 10. Here our purpose will be to use these tools to study pricing in imperfectly competitive markets. For the most part we will deal only with two-player games (that is, duopolies). Many of the results can be easily generalized to games with many players, however.

PRICING IN STATIC GAMES

We begin our analysis by looking at the simplest duopoly. Suppose there are two firms, A and B, each producing the same good at a constant marginal cost, c. The strategies for each firm consist of choosing prices, P_A and P_B, subject only to the condition that P_A and P_B must exceed c (no firm would opt to play a game that promised a certain loss). Payoffs in this game will be determined by demand conditions. Because output is homogeneous and marginal costs are constant, the firm with the lower price will gain the entire market. For simplicity we assume that if $P_A = P_B$, the firms share the market equally.

Bertrand-Nash Equilibrium

In this simple case the only Nash equilibrium is $P_A = P_B = c$. That is, the Nash equilibrium is the competitive solution even though there are only two firms. To see why, suppose firm A chooses a price greater than c. The profit-maximizing response for firm B is to choose a price slightly less than P_A and corner the entire market. But B's price, if it exceeds c, still cannot be a Nash equilibrium, since it provides A with further incentives for price cutting. Only by choosing $P_A = P_B = c$ will the two firms in this market have achieved a Nash equilibrium. This pricing strategy is sometimes referred to as a "Bertrand equilibrium" after the French economist who discovered it.[1]

The simplicity and definiteness of the Bertrand result depend crucially on the assumptions underlying the model. If firms do not have equal costs (see Problem 20.1) or if the goods produced by the two firms are not perfect substitutes, the competitive result no longer holds. Other duopoly models that depart from the Bertrand result treat price competition as only the final stage of a two-stage game in which the first stage involves various types of entry or investment considerations for the firms. In Example 19.1 we examined Cournot's example of a natural spring duopoly in which each spring owner chose how much water to supply. In the present context we might assume that each firm in a duopoly must choose a certain capacity output level. Marginal costs are constant up to that level and infinite thereafter. It seems clear that a two-stage game in which firms choose capacity first (and then price) is formally identical to the Cournot analysis. The quantities chosen in the Cournot equilibrium represent a Nash equilibrium since each firm correctly perceives what the other's output will be. Once these capacity decisions are made, the only price that can prevail is that for which total quantity demanded is equal to the combined capacities of the two firms.

Capacity Constraints: The Cournot Equilibrium

To see why Bertrand-type price competition will result in such a solution, suppose capacities are given by $\overline{q_A}$ and $\overline{q_B}$ and that

$$\overline{P} = D^{-1}(\overline{q_A} + \overline{q_B}),\qquad(20.1)$$

where D^{-1} is the inverse demand function for the good. A situation in which

$$P_A = P_B < \overline{P}\qquad(20.2)$$

is not a Nash equilibrium. With this price, total quantity demanded exceeds $\overline{q_A} + \overline{q_B}$ so any one firm could increase its profits by raising price a bit and still selling $\overline{q_A}$. Similarly,

$$P_A = P_B > \overline{P}\qquad(20.3)$$

is not a Nash equilibrium since now total sales fall short of $\overline{q_A} + \overline{q_B}$. At least one firm (say, firm A) is selling less than its capacity. By cutting price slightly, firm A can increase its profits by taking all possible sales up to $\overline{q_A}$. Of course,

---

[1] J. Bertrand, "Théorie Mathematique de la Richess Sociale," *Journal de Savants* (1883): 499–508.

B will respond to a loss of sales by dropping its price a bit too. Hence, the only Nash equilibrium that can prevail is the Cournot result:[2]

$$P_A = P_B = \overline{P}. \qquad (20.4)$$

In general, this price will fall short of the monopoly price but will exceed marginal cost (as was the case in Example 19.1). Results of this two-stage game are therefore indistinguishable from those arising from the Cournot model of the previous chapter.

The contrast between the Bertrand and Cournot games is striking—the former predicts competitive outcomes in a duopoly situation, whereas the latter predicts monopoly-like inefficiencies. This suggests that actual behavior in duopoly markets may exhibit a wide variety of outcomes depending on the precise way in which competition occurs. The principal lesson of the two-stage Cournot game is that, even with Bertrand price competition, decisions made prior to this final stage of a game can have an important impact on market behavior. This lesson will be reflected again in some of the game theory models of entry we describe later in this chapter.

REPEATED GAMES AND TACIT COLLUSION

In Chapter 10 we showed that players in infinitely repeated games may be able to adopt subgame perfect Nash equilibrium strategies that yield more favorable outcomes than simply repeating a less favorable Nash equilibrium indefinitely. From the perspective of duopoly theory, the issue is whether firms must endure the Bertrand equilibrium ($P_A = P_B = c$) in each period of a repeated game or might they be able to achieve more profitable outcomes through tacit collusion.[3]

With any finite number of replications, it seems clear that the Bertrand result remains unchanged. Any strategy in which firm A, say, chooses $P_A > c$ in period T (the final period) offers B the option of choosing $P_A > P_B > c$. Hence A's threat to charge P_A in period T is noncredible. Since a similar argument applies to any period prior to T, it seems clear that the only subgame perfect equilibrium in the finitely repeated price game is the perfectly competitive one in which both firms set price equal to marginal cost in every period.

If the pricing game is to be repeated over infinitely many periods, however, twin "trigger" strategies become feasible. Under these strategies

---

[2] For completeness, it should also be noted that no situation in which $P_A \neq P_B$ can be an equilibrium, since the low-price firm has an incentive to raise price and the high-price firm wishes to cut price.

[3] Explicit collusion between firms is ruled out here because we are considering only noncooperative games.

each firm, say firm A, chooses $P_A = P_M$ (where P_M is the monopoly price), providing firm B chose $P_B = P_M$ in the prior period. If B has cheated in the previous period (by setting P_B slightly below $P_A = P_M$ and obtaining all monopoly profits for itself), firm A opts for competitive pricing ($P_A = c$) in all future periods.

To determine whether these twin trigger strategies constitute a subgame perfect equilibrium, we must ask whether they constitute a Nash equilibrium in every period (every subgame). Suppose after the pricing game has been proceeding for several periods firm B is thinking about cheating. It knows that by choosing $P_B < P_A = P_M$ it can obtain (almost all) of the single period monopoly profits, π_M, for itself. On the other hand, if B continues to collude tacitly with A, B will earn its share of the profit stream

$$(\pi_M + \delta\pi_M + \delta^2\pi_M + \ldots + \delta^n\pi_M + \ldots)/2, \quad (20.5)$$

where δ is the discount factor applied to future profits. Since the value of this infinite stream of profits is given by $(\pi_M/2)[1(1 - \delta)]$, such cheating will be unprofitable providing

$$\pi_M < (\pi_M/2)[1/(1 - \delta)]. \quad (20.6)$$

Some algebraic manipulation shows that this inequality holds whenever

$$\delta > \frac{1}{2}. \quad (20.7)$$

That is, providing the firms are not too impatient in the ways in which they discount future profits, the trigger strategies represent a subgame perfect Nash equilibrium of tacit collusion. Example 20.1 provides a numerical example.[4]

EXAMPLE 20.1

TACIT COLLUSION

Suppose only two firms produce steel bars suitable for jailhouse windows. Bars are produced at a constant average and marginal cost of $10, and the demand for bars is given by

$$Q = 5,000 - 100P. \quad (20.8)$$

Under Bertrand competition, each firm will charge a price of $10 and a total of 4,000 bars will be sold. Since the monopoly price in this market is $30, each

---

[4] Many other supracompetitive price levels are also sustainable under the trigger strategy for suitable values of δ.

firm has a clear incentive to consider collusive strategies. With the monopoly price, total profits each period are \$40,000 (each firm's share of total profits is \$20,000) so any one firm will consider a next-period price cut only if

$$\$40,000 > \$20,000 \, (1/1 - \delta). \tag{20.9}$$

If we consider the pricing period in this model to be one year and a reasonable value of δ to be 0.8,[5] the present value of each firm's future profit share is \$100,000, so there is clearly little incentive to cheat on price. Alternatively, each firm might be willing to incur costs (say, by monitoring the other's price or by developing a "reputation" for reliability) of up to \$60,000 in present value to maintain the agreement.

Tacit Collusion with More Firms. Viability of a trigger price strategy may depend importantly on the number of firms. With eight producers of steel bars, the gain from cheating on a collusive agreement is still \$40,000 (assuming the cheater can corner the entire market). The present value of a continuing agreement is only \$25,000 (= \$40,000 ÷ 8 · $\frac{1}{2}$) so the trigger price strategy is not viable for any one firm. Even with three or four firms or less responsive demand conditions, the gain from cheating may exceed whatever the costs may be required to make tacit collusion work. Hence, the commonsense idea that tacit collusion is easier with fewer firms is supported by this model.

QUERY: How does the (common) discount factor, δ, determine the maximum number of firms that can successfully collude in this problem? What is the maximum if $\delta = .8$? How about the case when $\delta = .9$? Explain your results intuitively.

Generalizations and Limitations

The contrast between the competitive results of the Bertrand model and the monopoly results of the (infinite time period) collusive model suggests that the viability of tacit collusion in game theory models is very sensitive to the particular assumptions made. Two assumptions in our simple model of tacit collusion are especially important: (1) that firm B can easily detect whether firm A has cheated; and (2) that firm B responds to cheating by adopting a harsh response that not only punishes firm A, but also condemns firm B to zero profits forever. In more general models of tacit collusion, these assumptions can be relaxed by, for example, allowing for the possibility that it may be difficult for firm B to recognize cheating by A. Some models

---

[5] Since $\delta = (1/1 + r)$ where r is the interest rate, $\delta = .8$ implies an r of 0.25 (that is, 25 percent per year).

examine alternative types of punishment B might inflict on A—for example, B could cut price in some other market in which A also sells. Other categories of models explore the consequences of introducing differentiated products into models of tacit collusion or of incorporating other reasons why the demand for a firm's product may not respond instantly to price changes by its rival. As might be imagined, results of such modeling efforts are quite varied.[6] In all such models, the notions of Nash and subgame perfect equilibria continue to play an important role in identifying whether tacit collusion can arise from strategic choices that appear to be viable.

ENTRY, EXIT, AND STRATEGY

Our treatment of entry and exit in competitive and noncompetitive markets in previous chapters left little room for strategic considerations. A potential entrant was viewed as being concerned only with the relationship between prevailing market price and its own (average or marginal) costs. We assumed that making that comparison involved no special problems. Similarly, we assumed firms will promptly leave a market they find to be unprofitable. Upon closer inspection, however, the entry and exit issue can become considerably more complex. The fundamental problem is that a firm wishing to enter or leave a market must make some conjecture about how its action will affect market price in subsequent periods. Making such conjectures obviously requires the firm to consider what its rivals will do. What appears to be a relatively straightforward decision comparing price and cost may therefore involve a number of possible strategic ploys, especially when a firm's information about its rivals is imperfect.

Sunk Costs and Commitment

Many game-theoretic models of the entry process stress the importance of a firm's *commitment* to a specific market. If the nature of production requires firms to make specific capital investments in order to operate in a market and if these cannot easily be shifted to other uses, a firm that makes such an investment has committed itself to being a market participant. Expenditures on such investments are called sunk costs, defined more formally as follows:

DEFINITION

Sunk Costs *Sunk costs* are one-time investments that must be made in order to enter a market. Such investments allow the firm to produce in the market but have no residual value if the firm exits the market.

---

[6] See J. Tirole, *The Theory of Industrial Organization* (Cambridge, Mass: MIT Press, 1988), chap. 6.

Investments in sunk costs might include expenditures such as unique types of equipment (for example, a newsprint-making machine) or job-specific training for workers (developing the skills to use the newsprint machine). Sunk costs have many characteristics similar to what we have called "fixed costs" in that both these costs are incurred even if no output is produced. Rather than being incurred periodically as are many fixed costs (heating the factory), however, sunk costs are incurred only once in connection with the entry process.[7] When the firm makes such an investment, it has committed itself to the market, and that may have important consequences for its strategic behavior.

Sunk Costs, First-Mover Advantages, and Entry Deterrence

Although at first glance it might seem that incurring sunk costs by making the commitment to serve a market puts a firm at a disadvantage, in most models that is not the case. Rather, one firm can often stake out a claim to a market by making a commitment to serve it and in the process limit the kinds of actions its rivals find profitable. Many game theory models, therefore, stress the advantage of moving first, as the following example illustrates.

EXAMPLE 20.2

FIRST-MOVER ADVANTAGE IN COURNOT'S NATURAL SPRINGS

Let's return again to Cournot's natural spring duopoly that we studied in Examples 19.1 and 19.2. Under the Stackelberg version of this model, each firm has two possible strategies—to be a leader (produce $q_i = 60$) or a follower (produce $q_i = 30$). Payoffs under these strategies were defined in Example 19.2 and are repeated in Table 20.1.

As we noted before, here the leader-leader strategy choice for each firm proves to be disastrous. A follower-follower choice (the Cournot equilibrium) is profitable to both firms, but this choice is unstable because it gives each firm an incentive to cheat. This game is not like the Prisoner's Dilemma (see Chapter 10), however, because the leader-leader option is not a Nash equilibrium—if firm A knows that B will adopt a leader strategy, its best move is to be a follower.

---

[7] Mathematically, the notion of sunk costs can be integrated into the per-period total cost function as

$$TC_t = S + F_t + cq_t,$$

where S is the per-period amortization of sunk costs (for example, the interest paid for funds used to finance specific capital investments). F is per-period fixed costs, c is marginal cost, and q_t is per-period output. If $q_t = 0$, $TC_t = S + F_t$, but if the production period is long enough, some or all of F_t may also be avoidable. No portion of S is avoidable, however.

TABLE 20.1

PAYOFF MATRIX FOR THE STACKELBERG MODEL

		B's STRATEGIES	
		LEADER ($q_B = 60$)	FOLLOWER ($q_B = 30$)
A's STRATEGIES	LEADER ($q_A = 60$)	A: 0 B: 0	A: $1,800 B: $ 900
	FOLLOWER ($q_A = 30$)	A: $ 900 B: $1,800	A: $1,600 B: $1,600

It is this feature of the springs duopoly game that gives rise to a first-mover advantage. With simultaneous moves, either of the two leader-follower pairs represents a Nash equilibrium. But, if one firm (say B) has the opportunity to move first, it can (by choosing $q_B = 60$) dictate which of the two Nash equilibria are chosen. B's ability to choose a large plant capacity first forces A into the follower role.

QUERY: Suppose the springs duopoly game were repeated many times (say, by the same rivals entering many different markets), what kinds of additional outcomes might be observed?

Other situations in which a first mover might have an advantage include investing in research and development or pursuing product differentiation strategies. In international trade theory, for example, it is sometimes claimed that protection or subsidization of a domestic industry may allow it to enter an industry first, thereby gaining strategic advantage. Similarly, pursuit of "brand proliferation" strategies by existing toothpaste or breakfast cereal companies may make it more difficult for those who come later to develop a sufficiently different product to warrant a place in the market. The success of such first-mover strategies is by no means assured, however. Careful modeling of the strategic situation is required in order to identify whether moving first does offer any real advantages.

Entry Deterrence

In some cases first-mover advantages may be large enough to deter all entry by rivals. Intuitively, it seems plausible that the first mover could make the strategic choice to have a very large capacity and thereby discourage all other firms from entering the market. The economic rationality of such a decision is not clear-cut, however. In the springs duopoly model, for example, the only sure way for one spring owner to deter all entry is to satisfy the total market demand at the firm's marginal and average cost—that is, one firm would have to offer $q = 120$ at a price of zero to have a fully successful entry deterrence strategy. Obviously, such a choice results in zero profits for the incumbent firm and would not represent profit maximization. Instead, it would be better for that firm to accept some entry by following the Stackelberg leadership strategy.

With economies of scale in production, the possibility for profitable entry deterrence is increased. If the firm that is to move first can adopt a large-enough scale of operation, it may be able to limit the scale of the potential entrant. The potential entrant will therefore experience such high average costs that there would be no advantage to its entering the market. Example 20.3 illustrates this possibility in the case of Cournot's natural springs. Whether this example is of general validity depends, among other factors, on whether the market is contestable. If other firms with large scales of operations elsewhere can take advantage of prices in excess of marginal cost to practice hit-and-run entry, the entry deterrence strategy will not succeed.

EXAMPLE 20.3

ENTRY DETERRENCE IN COURNOT'S NATURAL SPRING

If the natural spring owners in our previous examples experience economies of scale in production, entry deterrence becomes a profitable strategy for the first firm to choose capacity. The simplest way to incorporate economies of scale into the Cournot model is to assume each spring owner must pay a fixed cost of operations. If that fixed cost is given by $784 (a carefully chosen number!), it is clear that the Nash equilibrium leader-follower strategies remain profitable for both firms (see Table 20.1). When firm A moves first and adopts the leader's role, however, B's profits are rather small $(900 - 784 = 116)$, and this suggests that firm A could push B completely out of the market simply by being a bit more aggressive.

Since B's reaction function (Equation 19.18) is unaffected by considerations of fixed costs, firm A knows that

$$q_B = \frac{120 - q_A}{2} \tag{20.10}$$

and that market price is given by

$$P = 120 - q_A - q_B. \tag{20.11}$$

Hence, A knows that B's profits are

$$\pi_B = Pq_B - 784, \tag{20.12}$$

which, when B is a follower (that is, when B moves second), depends only on q_A. Substituting Equation 20.10 into 20.12 yields

$$\pi_B = \left(\frac{120 - q_A}{2}\right)^2 - 784. \qquad (20.13)$$

Consequently, firm A can ensure nonpositive profits for firm B by choosing

$$q_A \geq 64. \qquad (20.14)$$

With $q_A = 64$, firm A becomes the only supplier of natural spring water. Since market price is \$56 $(= 120 - 64)$ in this case, firm A's profits are

$$\pi_A = (56 \cdot 64) - 784 = 2{,}800, \qquad (20.15)$$

a significant improvement over the leader-follower outcome. The ability to move first coupled with the fixed costs assumed here therefore makes entry deterrence a feasible strategy in this case.

QUERY: Why is the time pattern of play in this game crucial to the entry deterrence result? How does the result here contrast with our analysis of a contestable monopoly in Example 19.5?

ENTRY AND INCOMPLETE INFORMATION

So far our discussion of strategic considerations in entry decisions has focused on issues of sunk costs and output commitments. Prices were assumed to be determined through auction or Bertrand processes only after such commitments were made. A somewhat different approach to the entry deterrence question concerns the possibility of an incumbent monopoly accomplishing this goal through its pricing policy alone. That is, are there situations where a monopoly might purposely choose a low ("limit") price policy with the goal of deterring entry into its market?

In most simple cases, the limit pricing strategy does not seem to yield maximum profits nor to be sustainable over time. If an incumbent monopoly opts for a price of $P_L < P_M$ (where P_M is the profit-maximizing price), it is obviously hurting its current-period profits. But this limit price will deter entry in the future only if P_L falls short of the average cost of any potential entrant. If the monopoly and its potential entrant have the same costs (and if capacity choices do not play the role they did in the previous example), the only limit price that is sustainable in the presence of potential entry is $P_L = AC$, adoption of which would obviously defeat the purpose of being a monopoly since profits would be zero. Hence, the basic monopoly model offers little room for entry deterrence through pricing behavior—either there are barriers to entry that allow the monopoly to sustain P_M, or there are no such barriers, in which case competitive pricing prevails.

Limit Pricing and Incomplete Information

Believable models of limit pricing behavior must therefore depart from traditional assumptions. The most important set of such models are those involving incomplete information. If an incumbent monopoly knows more about a particular market situation than does a potential entrant, it may be able to take advantage of its superior knowledge to deter entry. As an example, consider the game tree illustrated in Figure 20.1. Here firm A, the incumbent monopolist, may have either "high" or "low" production costs as a result of past decisions. Firm A does not actually choose its costs currently but, since these costs are not known to B, we must allow for the two possibilities. Clearly, the profitability of B's entry into the market depends on A's costs—with high costs B's entry is profitable ($\pi_B = 3$), whereas if A has low costs, entry is unprofitable ($\pi_B = -1$). What is B to do? One possibility would be for B to use whatever information it does have to develop a subjective probability estimate of A's true cost structure. That is, B must assign probability estimates to the states of nature "low cost" and "high cost." If B assumes there is a probability ρ that A has high cost and $(1 - \rho)$ that it has low cost, entry will yield positive expected profits provided

$$E(\pi_B) = \rho(3) + (1 - \rho)(-1) > 0, \tag{20.16}$$

which holds for

FIGURE 20.1

AN ENTRY GAME

Firm A has either a "high" or a "low" cost structure that cannot be observed by B. If B assigns a subjective probability (ρ) to the possibility that A is high cost, it will enter providing $\rho > \frac{1}{4}$. Firm A may try to influence B's probability estimate.

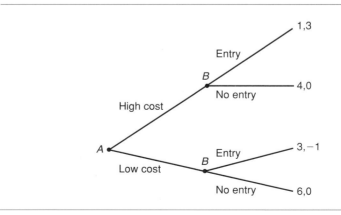

$$\rho > \frac{1}{4}. \qquad\qquad (20.17)$$

The particularly intriguing aspects of this game concern whether A can influence B's probability assessment. Clearly, regardless of its true costs, firm A is better off if B adopts the no-entry strategy, and one way to ensure that is for A to make B believe that $\rho < \frac{1}{4}$. As an extreme case, if A can convince B that it is a low-cost producer with certainty ($\rho = 0$), B will clearly be deterred from entry even if the true cost situation is otherwise. For example, if A chooses a low-price policy when it serves the market as a monopoly, this may signal to B that A's costs are low and thereby deter entry. Such strategy might be profitable for A even though it would require it to sacrifice some profits if its costs are actually high. This provides a possible rationale for low limit pricing as an entry deterrence strategy.

Unfortunately, as we saw in Chapter 10, examination of the possibilities for signaling equilibria in situations of asymmetric information raises many complexities. Since firm B knows that A may create false signals and firm A knows that B will be wary of its signals, a number of solutions to this game seem possible. The viability of limit pricing as a strategy for achieving entry deterrence depends crucially on the types of informational assumptions that are made.[8]

Predatory Pricing

Tools used to study limit pricing can also shed light on the possibility for "predatory" pricing. Ever since the formation of the Standard Oil monopoly in the late nineteenth century, part of the mythology of American business has been that John D. Rockefeller was able to drive his competitors out of business by charging ruinously low (predatory) prices. Although both the economic logic and the empirical facts behind this version of the Standard Oil story have generally been discounted,[9] the possibility of encouraging exit through predation continues to provide interesting opportunities for theoretical modeling.

The structure of many models of predatory behavior is similar to that used in limit pricing models—that is, the models stress incomplete information. An incumbent firm wishes to encourage its rival to exit the market, so it takes

---

[8] For an examination of some of these issues, see P. Milgrom and J. Roberts, "Limit Pricing and Entry under Conditions of Incomplete Information: An Equilibrium Analysis," *Econometrica* (March 1982): 443–460.

[9] J. S. McGee and others have pointed out that predatory pricing was a far less profitable strategy for Rockefeller than simply buying up his rivals at market price (which seems to have been what occurred). See J. S. McGee, "Predatory Pricing: The Standard Oil (NJ) Case," *Journal of Law and Economics* (1958): 137–169; and "Predatory Pricing Revisited," *Journal of Law and Economics* (October 1980): 289–330. Recent literature has examined whether predatory pricing can affect a rival firm's market value.

actions intended to affect the rival's view of the future profitability of market participation. The incumbent may, for example, adopt a low-price policy in an attempt to signal to its rival that its costs are low—even if they are not. Or the incumbent may adopt extensive advertising or product differentiation activities with the intention of convincing its rival that it has economies of scale in undertaking such activities. Once the rival is convinced that the incumbent firm possesses such advantages, it may recalculate the expected profitability of its production decisions and decide to exit the market. Of course, as in the limit pricing models, such successful predatory strategies are not a foregone conclusion. Their viability depends crucially on the nature of the informational asymmetries in the market.

GAMES OF INCOMPLETE INFORMATION

The illustrations in the previous section suggest the desirability of extending game theory models to include cases of incomplete information. In this section we provide a brief survey of some of the ways in which this has been done.

Player Types and Beliefs

To generalize game theoretic ideas to reflect incomplete information, we need to introduce some new terminology. When the nature of a game's incomplete information concerns asymmetries in the information the players have about each other, this is accomplished through the introduction of player characteristics or "types."[10] Each player in a game can be one of a number of possible such types (denoted by t_A and t_B for our two players). Player types may vary along several dimensions, but for our discussion we will confine our attention to differing potential payoff (profit) functions. Usually it will be assumed that each player knows his or her own payoffs, but does not know the opponent's payoffs with certainty. Hence, each player must make some conjectures about what the opponent's payoffs are in order to evaluate his or her own strategic choices.

Each player's conjectures about the opponent's player types are represented by belief functions B_A (t_B). These beliefs consist of player A's (say) probability estimates of the likelihood that the opponent B is of various types. As in the game tree in Figure 20.1, one player's beliefs are used to express the likelihood that the other player is on particular branches of the tree. Games of incomplete information are sometimes termed "Bayesian games" because of their use of subjective probability beliefs that were first studied by the statistician Thomas Bayes in the eighteenth century.

---

[10] Information about a game may also be subject to uncertainty if a player does not know its history (that is, what moves the opponent has made in the past). Such games are termed games of "imperfect" information.

Given these new tools, we can generalize the notation presented in Chapter 10 for a game (see Equation 10.1) as:

$$G[S_A, S_B, t_A, t_B, B_A, B_B, U_A(a,b,t_A,t_B), U_B(a,b,t_A,t_B)], \qquad (20.18)$$

where the payoffs to A and B depend not only on the strategies chosen ($a \subset S_A$, $b \subset S_B$) but also on the player types. Now we need to generalize the notion of Nash equilibrium to take this more complex game structure into account.

For static (one-period) games, it is fairly simple to generalize the Nash equilibrium concept to reflect incomplete information. Because each player's payoffs depend on the (unknown) player type of the opponent, we must introduce an expected utility criteria. A strategy pair—a^*, b^*—will be a Bayesian-Nash equilibrium providing that a^* maximizes A's expected utility when B plays b^* and vice versa. Specifically, Equations 10.2 should be modified as:

Bayesian-Nash Equilibrium

$$E[U_A(a^*,b^*,t_A,t_B)] = \sum_{t_B} B_A(t_B) U(a^*,b^*,t_A,t_B)$$
$$\geq E[U_A(a',b^*,t_A,t_B)] \text{ for all } a' \subset S_A$$

and

$$E[U_B(a^*,b^*,t_A,t_B)] = \sum_{t_A} B_B(t_A) U(a^*,b^*,t_A,t_B)$$
$$\geq E[U_B(a^*,b',t_A,t_B)] \text{ for all } b' \subset S_B.$$

$$(20.19)$$

Notice here that the payoffs to each player depend on both players' types, but that A's expectations concern only his or her beliefs about B (since player A knows his or her own type). Similarly, player B knows his or her own type but must consider subjective expectations about A. Although the notation in Equation 20.19 is formidable, most applications are straightforward, involving only a few player types, as Example 20.4 illustrates.

EXAMPLE 20.4

A BAYESIAN-COURNOT EQUILIBRIUM

Suppose duopolists compete for a market in which demand is given by

$$P = 100 - q_A - q_B. \qquad (20.20)$$

Suppose first that $MC_A = MC_B = 10$. Then it is a simple matter to show that the Nash (Cournot) equilibrium is $q_A = q_B = 30$ and payoffs are given by $\pi_A = \pi_B = 900$.

Imperfect Information. To give this game a Bayesian flavor, assume now that $MC_A = 10$, but MC_B may be either high ($MC_B = 16$) or low ($MC_B = 4$). Suppose also that A assigns equal probabilities to these two "types" for B so that the expected marginal cost for B remains 10.

Let's start to analyze this problem by considering firm B. Since B knows that there is only a single A type, it does not have to consider expectations. It chooses q_B to maximize.

$$\pi_B = (P - MC_B)\,(q_B) = (100 - MC_B - q_A - q_B)\,(q_B), \qquad (20.21)$$

and the first-order condition for a maximum is

$$q_B^* = (100 - MC_B - q_A)/2. \qquad (20.22)$$

Notice that q_B^* depends on firm B's marginal cost, which only it knows with certainty. With high marginal costs its optimal choice is

$$q_{BH}^* = (84 - q_A)/2, \qquad (20.23)$$

and with low marginal costs its optimal choice is

$$q_{BL}^* = (96 - q_A)/2. \qquad (20.24)$$

Firm A must take into account that B could be either high or low cost. Its expected profits are given by

$$\pi_A = .5(100 - MC_A - q_A - q_{BH})(q_A) + .5(100 - MC_A - q_A - q_{BL})(q_A)$$

$$= (90 - q_A - .5q_{BH} - .5q_{BL})q_A. \qquad (20.25)$$

The first-order condition for a profit maximum is therefore

$$q_A^* = (90 - .5q_{BH} - .5q_{BL})/2, \qquad (20.26)$$

and Equations 20.23, 20.24, and 20.26 must be solved simultaneously for q_{BH}^*, q_{BL}^*, and q_A^*. A bit of algebraic manipulation yields the Bayesian-Nash equilibrium:

$$q_A^* = 30$$

$$q_{BH}^* = 27 \qquad (20.27)$$

$$q_{BL}^* = 33.$$

These strategic choices constitute an *ex ante* equilibrium. After the game is played, only one market equilibrium will prevail, depending on whether firm B actually has high or low costs. But the concept of Bayesian-Nash equilibrium clarifies how the game will be played.

QUERY: In this case q_A^* in the Bayesian-Nash equilibrium is the same value as in the Cournot equilibrium with firm B's marginal cost equal to its expected value, 10. Why does this occur? Would you expect that in general expected values could be used in calculating Bayesian-Nash equilibria?

Proof of the existence of Bayesian-Nash equilibria closely parallels our discussion in Chapter 10. The previous proof is generalized by treating each player type in a static Bayesian game as a distinct player. With such an enlarged cast of players, the prior proof suggests the existence of a pure strategy Nash equilibrium in games with continuous strategies and the existence of a mixed strategy equilibrium for games where each player type has a finite set of discrete strategies. The strategy choices that comprise a Nash equilibrium in this expanded game of certainty will also constitute a Bayesian-Nash equilibrium given the beliefs of the players about the likelihood of various player types.

Existence of Equilibrium

One important way in which the concept of Bayesian-Nash equilibrium is used is in the study of the performance of various economic mechanisms; most notably, auctions. By examining equilibrium solutions under various possible auction rules, it has been possible for game theorists to devise procedures that yield desirable results in terms of obtaining high prices for goods being sold and ensuring that the goods end up in the hands of those who value them most highly. Features of auctions such as multiple bidding rounds, reservation prices, or second-price designs (where the auction winner pays the second highest bid price) can be quite complicated. Game theoretic tools help to illuminate the underlying operations of such features and to determine whether they encourage auction participants to reveal this true value for the good being sold. Although a thorough study of auction theory is beyond the scope of this book,[11] Example 20.5 illustrates some of the features of such models.

Mechanism Design and Auctions

EXAMPLE 20.5

AN OIL TRACT AUCTION

Suppose two firms are bidding for a tract of land that may have oil underground. Each firm has done some preliminary geological work and has decided on a potential value for the tract (V_A and V_B, respectively). The seller of the tract would obviously like to obtain the largest price possible for the land, which, in this case, would be the larger of V_A or V_B. Will a simple sealed bid auction accomplish this goal?

To develop this problem as a Bayesian game, we first need to model each firm's beliefs about the other's valuations. For simplicity, assume $0 \leq V_i \leq 1$

---

[11] For a survey, see R. P. M. McAfee and J. McMillan, "Auctions and Bidding," *Journal of Economic Literature* (June 1987): 699–738.

and that each firm assumes that all possible values for the other firm's valuation are equally likely. In statistical terms, we assume that firm A believes that V_B is uniformly distributed over the interval [0, 1], and vice versa. Each firm must now decide on its bid (b_A and b_B). The gain from the auction for firm A, say, is

and[12]
$$V_A - b_A \text{ if } b_A > b_B$$
$$0 \text{ if } b_B > b_A. \tag{20.28}$$

To derive explicit bidding strategies for each player, assume each opts to bid a fraction, k_i ($k_i \leq 1$) of the valuation. That is,

$$b_i = k_i V_i \quad i = A, B \tag{20.29}$$

Firm A's expected gain from the sale is then

$$\pi_A = (V_A - b_A) \cdot \text{Prob}(b_A > b_B) \tag{20.30}$$

and

$$\text{prob}(b_A > b_B) = \text{prob}(b_A > k_B V_B) = \text{prob}(b_A/k_B > V_B) = b_A/k_B, \tag{20.31}$$

where the final equality follows because of A's beliefs about how V_B is distributed. Hence,

$$\pi_A = (V_A - b_A) \cdot b_A/k_B, \tag{20.32}$$

which is maximized when

$$b_A = V_A/2. \tag{20.33}$$

A similar chain of logic would conclude

$$b_B = V_B/2 \tag{20.34}$$

so the firm with the highest valuation will win the oil tract and pay a price that is only 50 percent of that geological valuation. The auction we have described so far does not therefore result in a truthful revelation of the bidders' valuations.

Effect of Additional Bidders. The presence of additional bidders improves the situation, however. With $n - 1$ other bidders, firm A's expected gains become

$$\pi_A = (V_A - b_A) \cdot \text{Prob}(b_A > b_i, i = 1 \ldots n - 1) \tag{20.35}$$

and (again assuming away the problem of equal bids)

$$\pi_A = 0 \cdot \text{Prob}(b_A < b_i \text{ for any } i). \tag{20.36}$$

---

[12] To simplify the analysis we assume that the probability $b_A = b_B$ is zero.

If firm A continues to believe that its rival's valuations are uniformly distributed over the [0, 1] interval,

$$\text{Prob}(b_A > b_i, i = 1 \ldots n)$$

$$= \text{Prob}(b_A > k_i V_i \quad i = 1 \ldots n) \tag{20.37}$$

$$= \prod_{i=1}^{n-1} (b_A/k_i) = b_A^{n-1}/k^{n-1},$$

where, by symmetry, we let $k = k_i$ for all i. Hence,

$$\pi_A = (V_A - b_A)(b_A^{n-1}/k^{n-1}), \tag{20.38}$$

and the first-order condition for a maximum is

$$\pi_A = \left(\frac{n-1}{n}\right)V_A. \tag{20.39}$$

So, as the number of bidders expands, there are increasing incentives for a truthful revelation of each firm's valuation. In the language of auction theory, sealed bid auctions are "incentive compatible," providing there are enough bidders.

QUERY: Could a seller mitigate the low valuations that arise when there are few bidders by specifying a reservation price, r, such that no sale is made if the maximal bid falls below r?

Multiperiod and repeated games may also be characterized by incomplete information. As suggested by our informal discussion of the game depicted in Figure 20.1, the interesting additional feature of these games is that a player may be able to make inferences about the type of his or her opponent from the strategic choices the opponent makes. Hence, it is necessary for players to update beliefs by incorporating the new information provided by each round of play in the game. Of course, each player is aware that his or her opponent will be doing such updating, so that too must be taken into account in deciding on a strategy. By using the method of backward induction, it is often possible to derive equilibrium strategies in such games that mirror the notion of subgame perfection that we introduced in the context of repeated games with perfect information. Examination of these equilibrium concepts is an important area of current research in game theory.[13]

Dynamic Games with Incomplete Information

---

[13] For a summary, see D. Fudenberg and J. Tirole, *Game Theory* (Cambridge: MIT Press, 1991), Chaps. 8–10.

SUMMARY

In this chapter we have illustrated how game theory concepts can be used to examine pricing in duopoly markets. Some of the principal results are:

- In a simple single-period game, the Nash-Bertrand equilibrium implies competitive pricing with price equal to marginal cost. The Cournot equilibrium (with $p > mc$) can be interpreted as a two-stage game in which firms first select a capacity constraint.

- Tacit collusion is a possible subgame perfect equilibrium in an infinitely repeated game. The likelihood of such equilibrium collusion dimin-

ishes with larger numbers of firms, however, since the incentive to chisel on price increases.

- Some games offer first-mover advantages. In cases involving increasing returns to scale, such advantages may result in the deterrence of all entry.

- Games of incomplete information arise when players do not know their opponents' payoff functions and must make some conjectures about them. In such Bayesian games, equilibrium concepts involve straightforward generalizations of the Nash and subgame perfect notions encountered in games of complete information.

PROBLEMS

20.1

Suppose firms A and B each operate under conditions of constant average and marginal cost, but that $MC_A = 10$, $MC_B = 8$. The demand for the firms' output is given by

$$Q_D = 500 - 20P.$$

a. If the firms practice Bertrand competition, what will be the market price under a Nash equilibrium?
b. What will the profits be for each firm?
c. Will this equilibrium be Pareto efficient?

20.2

Suppose the two firms in a duopoly pursue Cournot competition as described in Equation 19.10. Suppose each firm operates under conditions of increasing marginal cost but that firm A has a larger scale of operations than does firm B in the sense that $MC_A < MC_B$ for any given output level. In a Nash equilibrium, will marginal cost necessarily be equalized across the two firms? Will total output be produced as cheaply as possible?

20.3

In the ice cream stand example of Chapter 19, assume each stand has five possible locational strategies—

locating 0, 25, 50, 75, or 100 yards from the left end of the beach. Describe the payoff matrix for this game, and explain whether it has an equilibrium strategy pair.

20.4

Two firms (A and B) are considering bringing out competing brands of a healthy cigarette. Payoffs to the companies are as shown in the table (A's profits are given first):

		FIRM *B*	
		PRODUCE	DON'T PRODUCE
FIRM *A*	**PRODUCE**	3, 3	5, 4
	DON'T PRODUCE	4, 5	2, 2

a. Does this game have a Nash equilibrium?
b. Does this game present any first-mover advantages for either firm A or firm B?
c. Would firm B find it in its interest to bribe firm A enough to stay out of the market?

20.5

The world's entire supply of kryptonite is controlled by 20 people, with each having 10,000 grams of this potent mineral. The world demand for kryptonite is given by

$$Q = 10,000 - 1,000P,$$

where P is the price per gram.

a. If all owners could conspire to rig the price of kryptonite, what price would they set, and how much of their supply would they sell?

b. Why is the price computed in part (a) an unstable equilibrium?

c. Does a price for kryptonite exist that would be a stable equilibrium in the sense that no firm could gain by altering its output from that required to maintain this market price?

20.6

The Wave Energy Technology (WET) company has a monopoly on the production of vibratory waterbeds. Demand for these beds is relatively inelastic—at a price of $1,000 per bed, 25,000 will be sold, whereas at a price of $600, 30,000 will be sold. The only costs associated with waterbed production are the initial costs of building a plant. WET has already invested in a plant capable of producing up to 25,000 beds, and this sunk cost is irrelevant to its pricing decisions.

a. Suppose a would-be entrant to this industry could always be assured of half the market but would have to invest $10 million in a plant. Construct the payoff matrix for WET's strategies ($P = 1,000$ or $P = 600$) against the entrant's strategies (enter, don't enter). Does this game have a Nash equilibrium?

b. Suppose WET could invest $5 million in enlarging its existing plant to produce 40,000 beds. Would this strategy be a profitable way to deter entry by its rival?

20.7

Pursuing the Query of Example 20.1 a bit further, calculate an explicit expression for the minimum value for δ as a function of the number of firms (n) seeking tacit collusion through trigger strategies. Explain also how the maximum attainable profits ($\pi^* < \pi_m$) varies as a function of δ and n when δ is too small to permit the attainment of π_m.

20.8

Suppose that demand for steel bars in Example 20.1 fluctuates with the business cycle. During expansions demand is

$$Q = 7,000 - 100P,$$

and during recessions demand is

$$Q = 3,000 - 100P.$$

Assume also that expansions and recessions are equally likely and that firms know what the economic conditions are before setting their price.

a. What is the lowest value of δ that will permit the sustaining of a trigger price strategy that maintains the appropriate monopoly price during both recessions and expansions?

b. If δ falls slightly below the value calculated in part (a), how should the trigger price strategies be adjusted to retain profitable tacit collusion?

20.9

Suppose that in the Bayesian-Cournot model described in Example 20.4 the firms have identical marginal costs (10) but that information about demand is asymmetric. Specifically, assume firm A knows the demand function (Equation 20.20) but that firm B believes that demand may be either

$$P = 120 - q_A - q_B$$

or

$$P = 80 - q_A - q_{B'}$$

each with probability of 0.5. Assuming that the firms must announce their quantities simultaneously, what is the Bayesian-Nash equilibrium for this situation?

20.10

Using either an intuitive analysis or a mathematical presentation, discuss how the Bayesian-Nash equilibrium in the oil tract auction (Example 20.5) would be altered if the assumed distribution of valuations was not uniform over the interval [0, 1], but instead was characterized by a symmetric, peaked distribution. Would you expect higher bids in the two-bidder auction than in the case of uniform distributions?

SUGGESTED READINGS

Fudenberg, D., and J. Tirole. *Game Theory.* Cambridge, Mass.: MIT Press, 1991.
The later chapters provide extensive illustrations of dynamic games of imperfect information.

Gibbons, R. *Game Theory for Applied Economists.* Princeton: Princeton University Press, 1992.
Illustrates a number of game-theoretic models relevant to topics such as bargaining, bank runs, auctions, and monetary policy. Chapter 4 on signaling equilibria is especially helpful.

"Symposium on Auctions," *Journal of Economic Perspectives* (Summer 1989): 3–50.
A collection of four papers on auction theory in practice. Milgrove's overview and Riley's paper on expected revenue provide good extensions of the brief material in this chapter.

Tirole, J. *The Theory of Industrial Organization.* Cambridge, Mass.: MIT Press, 1988.
Game theory is used throughout Part II of this classic text. The final chapter of the book provides a convenient "user's manual" for the subject.

EXTENSIONS

Strategic Substitutes and Complements

One way to conceptualize the relationships between the choices of firms in an imperfectly competitive market is to introduce the ideas of strategic substitutes and complements. By drawing analogies to similar definitions from consumer and producer theory, game theorists define firms' activities to be *strategic substitutes* if an increase in the level of an activity (say, output, price, or spending on product differentiation) by one firm is met by a decrease in that activity by its rival. On the other hand, activities are *strategic complements* if an increase in an activity by one firm is met by an increase in that activity by its rival.

To make these ideas precise, suppose that profits for firm A (π^A) depend on the level of an activity it uses itself (S_A) and on use of a similar activity by its rival. The firm's goal, therefore, is to maximize $\pi^A(S_A, S_B)$.

E20.1 Optimality Conditions and Reaction Functions

The first-order condition for A's choice of its own strategic activity is

$$\pi_1^A(S_A, S_B) = 0, \tag{i}$$

where the subscripts for π represent partial derivatives with respect to its various arguments. For a maximum we also require that

$$\pi_{11}^A(S_A, S_B) \leq 0. \tag{ii}$$

Obviously, the optimal choice of S_A specified by Equation i will differ for different values of S_B. We can record this relationship by A's reaction function (R_A)

$$S_A = R_A(S_B). \tag{iii}$$

The strategic relationship between S_A and S_B is implied by this reaction function. If $R_A' > 0$, S_A and S_B are strategic complements. If $R_A' < 0$, S_A and S_B are strategic substitutes.

E20.2 Inferences from the Profit Function

It is usually more convenient to use the profit function directly to examine strategic relationships. Substituting Equation iii into the first-order condition i gives

$$\pi_1^A = \pi_1^A[R_A(S_B), S_B] = 0. \tag{iv}$$

Partial differentiation with respect to S_B yields

$$\pi_{11}^A R_A' + \pi_{12}^A = 0. \tag{v}$$

Therefore,

$$R'_A = \frac{-\pi^A_{12}}{\pi^A_{11}}$$

so, in view of the second-order condition (ii), $\pi^A_{12} > 0$ implies $R'_A > 0$ and $\pi^A_{12} < 0$ implies $R'_A > 0$. Strategic relationships can therefore be inferred directly from the derivatives of the profit function.

E20.3 The Cournot Model

In the Cournot model, profits are given as a function of the two firms' quantities as

$$\pi^A = \pi^A(q_A, q_B) = q_A P(q_A + q_B) - TC(q_A). \quad \text{(vi)}$$

In this case

$$\pi^A_1 = q_A P' + P - TC' = 0 \quad \text{(vii)}$$

and

$$\pi^A_{12} = q_A P'' + P'. \quad \text{(viii)}$$

Since $P' < 0$, the sign of π^A_{12} will depend on the concavity of the demand curve (P''). With a linear demand curve, $P'' = 0$ so π^A_{12} is clearly negative. Quantities are strategic substitutes in the Cournot model with linear demand. This will generally be true unless the demand curve is relatively convex ($P'' > 0$). For a more detailed discussion, see Bulow, Geanakoplous, and Klemperer (1985).

Voluntary Export Restraints

Several authors have used the strategic substitute concept in the Cournot model to examine models of trade restrictions. In these models domestic and foreign producers are treated as two "firms" vying for the domestic market. Under (Bertrand) price competition, a competitive model might be used to explain pricing in such a market, as we did in Chapter 17. But the presence of trade barriers may alter the nature of such competition. For example, a number of recent papers have focused on the potential strategic role of "voluntary" export restraints (VERs) such as those negotiated between the United States, Hong Kong, and Taiwan over footware or between the United States and Japan over automobiles. Traditionally VERs have been viewed as virtually identical to import quotas—a restriction that would harm import-ing firms. But Karikari (1991) and others have challenged this view by noting that the pegging of import quantities (as with VERs) may aid in the establishment of a Cournot equilibrium in situations that would otherwise be unstable. Hence, voluntary export restraints may indeed by "voluntary" because they yield supracompetitive profits to both parties.

E20.4 Strategic Relationship between Prices

If we view the duopoly problem as one of setting prices, both q_A and q_B will be functions of prices charged by the two firms:

$$q_A = D^A(P_A, P_B)$$
$$q_B = D^B(P_A, P_B). \quad \text{(ix)}$$

Using this notation,

$$\pi^A = P_A q_A - TC(q_A)$$
$$= P_A D^A(P_A, P_B) - TC[D^A(P_A, P_B)]. \quad \text{(x)}$$

Hence,

$$\pi^A_1 = P_A D^A_1 + D^A - TC' D^A_1 \quad \text{(xi)}$$

and

$$\pi^A_{12} = P_A D^A_{12} + D^A_2 - TC' D^A_{12} - TC'' D^A_2 D^A_1. \quad \text{(xii)}$$

Obviously, interpreting this mass of symbols is no easy task. In the special case of constant marginal cost ($TC' = 0$) and linear demand ($D^A_{12} = 0$), the sign of π^A_{12} is given by the sign of D^A_2 —that is, how increases in P_B affect q_A. In the usual case when the two goods are themselves substitutes, $D^A_2 > 0$, so $\pi^A_{12} > 0$. That is, prices are strategic complements. Firms in such a duopoly would either raise or lower prices together (see Tirole, 1988).

Cartels and Price Wars

Use of these concepts may aid in understanding the behavior of cartels. For example, Porter (1983) develops a model of the Joint Executive Committee, a cartel of railroads that controlled eastbound grain shipments from Chicago during the 1880s. One oddity of the shipping price data is that they illustrate periodic, sharp price drops. The author rejects the notion that these were caused by slumps in demand. For example, the price declines did not appear to be associated with shipping prices on Great Lakes' steamers, a primary substitute for the railroads. Instead, the price declines appeared to be one component of the cartel's internal enforcement mechanism. Price wars were motivated by unpredictable declines in the market share of one or two market participants who used such declines as a sign of the need to reestablish market discipline. By "cheating" on their pricing, they signaled this need to other cartel participants. Hence, price wars were an important component of an overall strategy to ensure cartel stability.

References

Bulow, J., G. Geanakoplous, and P. Klemperer. "Multimarket Oligopoly: Strategic Substitutes and Complements." *Journal of Political Economy* (June 1985): 488–511.

Karikari, J. A. "On Why Voluntary Export Restraints are Voluntary." *Canadian Journal of Economics* (February 1991): 228–233.

Porter, R. H. "A Study of Cartel Stability: The Joint Executive Committee 1880–1886." *Bell Journal of Economics* (Autumn 1983): 301–314.

Tirole, J. *The Theory of Industrial Organization.* Cambridge, Mass.: MIT Press, 1988, pp. 326–336.

PRICING IN INPUT MARKETS

In this part we examine models that seek to explain how prices for inputs are determined. We begin in Chapter 21 by showing how the demand for any factor of production is derived from the demand for the goods it produces. Profit-maximizing firms play the role of intermediary in bringing together individuals' demands for economic goods with input suppliers' abilities to produce those goods—if no one wants a good, firms will not hire anyone to produce it.

As in our examination of markets for goods, we use this notion of derived demand to study input pricing in two different cases. First we treat the firm as a price taker in input markets—that is, we assume that firms cannot affect factor prices through their actions. Then we examine input pricing in imperfectly competitive markets. In these sections we relax the price-taker assumption in several different ways and illustrate the implications of those relaxations for factor pricing. As we show, the results of this analysis closely mirror those we obtained in our study of monopoly.

The development of Chapter 21 is quite general in that it applies to any factor of production. In Chapters 22 and 23 we take up several issues specifically related to pricing in the labor and capital markets. Chapter 22 discusses three particular aspects of the supply and demand for labor services. First, we analyze the simple labor supply decision for a single individual and develop a market supply of labor curve in much the same way we developed a market demand curve in Part II. Next, we briefly discuss occupational choice and the concept of *compensating wage differentials*. Finally, we take note of the fact that important portions of the labor market are characterized by the presence of unions, and we show how these organizations can be incorporated into the general theory of labor pricing.

In Chapter 23 the market for capital is examined. The central purpose of the chapter is to emphasize the interconnection between capital and the allocation of resources over time. An economy's stock of capital represents some output that was produced in the past but was not consumed, and we shall analyze the choices that were made in this process. Some care is also taken to integrate the theory of capital into the models of firms' behavior that we developed in Part IV. A brief appendix to Chapter 23 presents some useful mathematical results about interest rates.

In *The Principles of Political Economy and Taxation,* Ricardo wrote

> The produce of the earth . . . is divided among three classes of the community, namely, the proprietor of the land, the owner of the stock of capital necessary for its cultivation, and the laborers by whose industry it is cultivated. To determine the laws which regulate this distribution is the principal problem in Political Economy.[1]

The purpose of Part VII is to illustrate how the study of these "laws" has advanced since Ricardo's time.

---

[1] D. Ricardo, *The Principles of Political Economy and Taxation* (1817; reprinted, London: J. M. Dent and Son, 1965), p. 1.

CHAPTER 21

FIRMS' DEMANDS FOR INPUTS

In this chapter we will examine several general models of the pricing of inputs. For the most part we will study how differences in the nature of firms' demands for inputs can affect their prices and will devote relatively little attention to the supply side of the market. Chapters 22 and 23 are concerned with issues related to the supply of labor and capital, respectively, so we will postpone any very explicit treatment of factor supply until then.

In Chapter 13 we showed that a firm's hiring of inputs is directly related to its desire to maximize profits. No firm hires workers or rents equipment simply to provide its managers with companionship. Rather, hiring of inputs is a primary component of the profit-maximization process. Specifically, as we showed in Chapter 13, any firm's profits (π) can be expressed as the difference between total revenues (TR) and total costs (TC), each of which can be regarded as functions of the inputs used (say, capital, K, and labor, L):

PROFIT MAXIMIZATION AND DERIVED DEMAND

$$\pi = TR(K, L) - TC(K, L). \qquad (21.1)$$

The first-order conditions for a profit maximum are

$$\frac{\partial \pi}{\partial K} = \frac{\partial TR}{\partial K} - \frac{\partial TC}{\partial K} = 0$$

$$\frac{\partial \pi}{\partial L} = \frac{\partial TR}{\partial L} - \frac{\partial TC}{\partial L} = 0 \qquad (21.2)$$

or

$$\frac{\partial TR}{\partial K} = \frac{\partial TC}{\partial K}$$

and

$$\frac{\partial TR}{\partial L} = \frac{\partial TC}{\partial L}. \qquad (21.3)$$

In words, Equations 21.3 report the rather obvious result that any profit-maximizing firm should hire additional units of each factor of production up to the point at which the extra revenue yielded by hiring one more unit is equal to the extra cost of hiring that unit.

Marginal Revenue Product

All of the derivatives in Equations 21.3 are given special names in the theory of input demand. Expressions for the change in revenue with respect to a change in an input (that is, the terms on the left in Equations 21.3) are termed the *marginal revenue product* (*MRP*) for that input. By recognizing that the hiring of an extra unit of an input results in extra revenue only through the output (q) it yields, we can gain some further insights into the nature of this concept. For the case of labor input, for example, we have

$$MRP_L = \frac{\partial TR(q)}{\partial L} = \frac{\partial TR(q)}{\partial q} \cdot \frac{\partial q}{\partial L} = MR \cdot MP_L, \qquad (21.4)$$

where MR is the marginal revenue for the firm's output and MP_L is the marginal physical product of labor. Suppose that, at current production levels, hiring an extra apple picker for one hour would yield three extra bushels of apples and that the marginal revenue yielded from selling a bushel of apples is $4. Then the extra revenue yielded to an orchard owner from hiring an extra hour of an apple picker's time would be $12—that is, the marginal revenue product of labor is $12. An identical argument would follow for the hiring of any other input. We have, therefore, developed the following definition:

DEFINITION

Marginal Revenue Product The *marginal revenue product* (*MRP*) from hiring an extra unit of any input is the extra revenue yielded by selling what that extra input produces. It can be found by multiplying the input's marginal physical productivity times the marginal revenue obtainable from the firm's output in the market for goods:

$$MRP = MR \cdot MP. \qquad (21.5)$$

Marginal Expense

Equations 21.3 show that an additional unit of input should be hired up to the point at which the inputs' *MRP* is equal to the additional cost of hiring that unit. If the supply curves facing the firm for the inputs it hires are infinitely elastic at prevailing prices (that is, if the firm can hire all it wants without affecting input prices), this extra cost is simply the inputs' price. If our orchard owner can hire any number of pickers at a market wage of $10 per hour, then the *marginal expense* of hiring labor is given by this market wage. In this case it would indeed make sense to hire the worker since his or her MRP_L ($12) exceeds this market wage. If input supply is not infinitely elastic, however, a firm's hiring decisions may have some effect on input prices. In this case, as we will show later in this chapter, the marginal expense of hiring another unit of input will exceed its market price because the firm's hiring will drive up input prices. For the moment, however, we will not examine this possibility and will instead assume the firm is a price taker for the inputs it buys. That is,

$$\frac{\partial TC}{\partial K} = v$$

$$\frac{\partial TC}{\partial L} = w,$$

(21.6)

where v and w are the prevailing per-unit hiring costs of capital and labor. The first-order conditions for profit maximization therefore become

$$MRP_K = v$$

$$MRP_L = w.$$

(21.7)

Before turning to examine the implications of Equations 21.7 for the firm's demand for inputs, we present an alternative derivation of these profit-maximizing conditions that offers additional insights into the relationship between the firm's input and output choices. In Chapter 12 we examined a model in which the firm was assumed to minimize the costs of producing any level of its output (say, q_0). The Lagrangian expression associated with this minimization problem is

An Alternative Derivation

$$\mathcal{L} = vK + wL + \lambda[q_0 - f(K, L)],$$

(21.8)

where $f(K, L)$ is the firm's production function. Assuming again that the firm's input choices do not affect the input prices, v and w, the first-order conditions for a minimum are

$$\frac{\partial \mathcal{L}}{\partial K} = v - \lambda \frac{\partial f}{\partial K} = 0$$

$$\frac{\partial \mathcal{L}}{\partial L} = w - \lambda \frac{\partial f}{\partial L} = 0$$

(21.9)

$$\frac{\partial \mathcal{L}}{\partial \lambda} = q_0 - f(K, L) = 0.$$

The first two of these equations can be written as

$$\lambda \frac{\partial f}{\partial K} = \lambda MP_K = v$$

$$\lambda \frac{\partial f}{\partial L} = \lambda MP_L = w.$$

(21.10)

But, as we pointed out in Chapter 12, the Lagrangian multiplier, λ, can be interpreted as marginal cost (MC) in this problem because it reflects the change in the objective (total costs) for a one-unit change in the constraint (output $- q_0$). Using this interpretation, we have

$$MC \cdot MP_K = v$$
$$MC \cdot MP_L = w. \tag{21.11}$$

Output choices can now be incorporated into this theory of input choice by introducing the old reliable $MR = MC$ rule for profit maximization:

$$MR \cdot MP_K = v$$
$$MR \cdot MP_L = w, \tag{21.12}$$

which is precisely the result we developed earlier. This approach makes especially clear that the firm's demand for any input stems not only from its desire to minimize costs but also from the firm's desire to make profit-maximizing output choices. As we shall see, examining how firms react to changes in input prices requires that we take account of both of these motivations.

Price Taking in the Output Market: Marginal Value Product

A final observation that might be made about profit-maximizing input choices concerns the possibility that the firm may exhibit price-taking behavior in the market for its output. In this case marginal revenue is identical to market price, and Equations 21.12 become

$$P \cdot MP_K = v$$
$$P \cdot MP_L = w. \tag{21.13}$$

The terms on the left of these equations represent a special case of the marginal revenue product notion in which the physical quantity of output produced by one extra unit of an input is valued at its market price. Although for price takers there is no distinction between this concept and the MRP, for firms that are not price takers, $MR < P$ so it does make a difference whether one values an input's physical productivity at the firm's marginal revenue or at market price for the output being produced. Sometimes the term *marginal value product* is used to refer to this valuation by market price, but we will not use that term here. Instead, we will only use the marginal revenue product concept in referring to the elements that influence a firm's demand for inputs. For the most part, however, we will also assume price-taking behavior in the goods market so there is no necessity to make the distinction.

In this section we use the profit-maximization assumption to study the comparative statics of input demand. Specifically, we shall look at the demand for labor (the analysis for capital would be symmetric) and ask about the direction and size of $\partial L/\partial w$. As we have indicated previously, it is likely this derivative will be negative (a decrease in w will cause more labor to be hired), but now we are in a position to give a detailed treatment of the issue.

COMPARATIVE STATICS OF INPUT DEMAND

One reason for expecting $\partial L/\partial w$ to be negative is based on the presumption that the marginal physical product of labor declines as the quantity of labor employed increases. A decrease in w means that more labor must be hired to bring about the equality $w = P \cdot MP_L$: A fall in w must be met by a fall in MP_L (since P is fixed), and this can be brought about by increasing L. That this argument is strictly correct for the case of one input can be shown as follows. Write the total differential of the profit-maximizing Equation 21.13 as

Single-Input Case

$$dw = P \cdot \frac{\partial MP_L}{\partial L} \cdot \frac{\partial L}{\partial w} \cdot dw$$

or

$$1 = P \cdot \frac{\partial MP_L}{\partial L} \cdot \frac{\partial L}{\partial w} \tag{21.14}$$

or

$$\frac{\partial L}{\partial w} = \frac{1}{P \cdot \partial MP_L/\partial L}.$$

If we assume that $\partial MP_L/\partial L < 0$ (that is, that MP_L decreases as L increases), we have

$$\frac{\partial L}{\partial w} < 0. \tag{21.15}$$

A *ceteris paribus* fall in w will cause more labor to be hired (and, parenthetically, this also will cause more output to be produced).

EXAMPLE 21.1

SINGLE-INPUT DEMAND

Suppose that the number of pounds of truffles harvested in a particular forest during one season is given by

$$Q = 100\sqrt{L}, \tag{21.16}$$

where L is the number of searchers hired to look for the fragrant fungi. Assuming truffles sell for $50 per pound, total revenue for the forest owner is

$$TR = P \cdot Q = 5{,}000\sqrt{L}, \tag{21.17}$$

and the marginal revenue product is given by

$$\frac{\partial TR}{\partial L} = 2{,}500L^{-1/2}. \tag{21.18}$$

If truffle searchers' seasonal wages are $500, the owner will determine L by

$$500 = 2{,}500L^{-1/2} \tag{21.19}$$

or

$$L = 25. \tag{21.20}$$

With 25 searchers, the marginal revenue product is $500, which is precisely what the owner must pay in wages. The 25 workers find a total of 500 pounds of truffles during the season. At a lower wage rate of $250, the owner would hire 100 searchers since the lower marginal revenue product obtained from such a large workforce would be justified by the lower wage. Notice that at the lower wage, truffle output expands to 1,000 during the season.

QUERY: How would the forest owner's hiring change if truffle prices rose to $60 per pound? Explain the reasons for this result.

Two-Input Case   For the case of two (or more) inputs, the story is more complex. The assumption of a diminishing marginal physical product of labor can be misleading here. If w falls, there will not only be a change in L but also a change in K as a new cost-minimizing combination of inputs is chosen. When K changes, the entire MP_L function changes (labor now has a different amount of capital to work with), and the simple argument we used above cannot be made. In the remainder of this section we will use a graphic approach to suggest why, even in the two-input case, $\partial L/\partial w$ must be negative. A more precise, mathematical analysis is presented in the next section.

Substitution Effect   In some ways, analyzing the two-input case is similar to the analysis of the individual's response to a change in the price of a good that was presented in Chapter 5. When w falls, we can decompose the total effect on the quantity of L hired into two components. The first of these might be called the *substitution effect*. If q is held constant at q_1, there will be a tendency to substitute L for K in the productive process. This effect is illustrated in Figure 21.1a. Since the condition for minimizing the cost of producing q_1 requires that $RTS = w/v$, a fall in w will necessitate a movement from input combination A to combination B. Because the isoquants have been assumed to exhibit a diminishing RTS, it is clear from the diagram that this substitution

FIGURE 21.1

THE SUBSTITUTION AND OUTPUT EFFECTS OF A DECREASE IN THE PRICE OF A FACTOR

When the price of labor falls, two analytically different effects come into play. One of these, the substitution effect, would cause more labor to be purchased if output were held constant. This is shown as a movement from point A to point B in (a). At point B the cost-minimizing condition ($RTS = w/v$) is satisfied for the new, lower w. This change in w/v will also shift the firm's expansion path and its marginal cost curve. A normal situation might be for the MC curve to shift downward in response to a decrease in w as shown in (b). With this new curve (MC') a higher level of output (q_2) will be chosen. Consequently, the hiring of labor will increase (to L_2), also from this output effect.

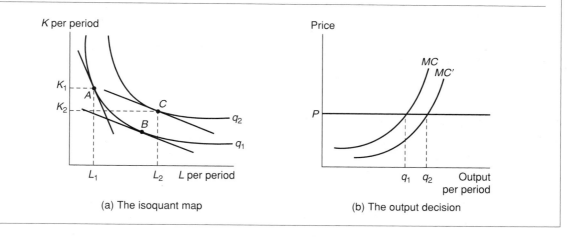

(a) The isoquant map

(b) The output decision

effect must be negative: A decrease in w will cause an increase in labor hired if output is held constant.

Output Effect

It is not correct, however, to hold output constant. It is in considering a change in q (the *output effect*) that the analogy to the individual's utility-maximization problem breaks down. Consumers have budget constraints, but firms do not. Firms produce as much as the available demand allows. In order to investigate what happens to the quantity of output produced, we must investigate the firm's profit-maximizing output decision. A change in w, because it changes relative factor costs, will shift the firm's expansion path. Consequently, all the firm's cost curves will be shifted, and probably some output level other than q_1 will be chosen. In Figure 21.1b what might be considered the "normal" case has been drawn. It has been assumed that with this new expansion path, the marginal cost curve for the firm has shifted downward to MC'. Consequently, the profit-maximizing level of output rises from q_1 to q_2. The profit-maximizing condition ($P = MC$) is now satisfied at a higher level of output. Returning to Figure 21.1a, this increase in output will cause even more L to be demanded, providing L is not an inferior input (see below). The result of both the substitution and output effects will be to move the input choice to point C on the firm's isoquant map. Both effects work to increase the quantity of labor hired in response to a decrease in the real wage.

The analysis provided in Figure 21.1 assumed that the market price (or marginal revenue if this does not equal price) of the good being produced remained constant. This would be an appropriate assumption if only one firm in an industry experienced a fall in unit labor costs. However, if (as seems more likely) the decline were industrywide, a slightly different analysis would be required. In that case *all* firms' marginal cost curves would shift outward, and hence the industry supply curve would shift also. Assuming that demand is downward sloping, this will lead to a decline in product price. Output for both the industry and for the typical firm will still increase and, as before, more labor will be hired. Since this latter, industrywide output effect arising from shifts in the market supply curve is more commonly used, it is the one we will use in our subsequent mathematical development.

Cross-Price Effects

We have shown that at least in simple cases, $\partial L/\partial w$ is unambiguously negative: Both substitution and output effects cause more labor to be hired when the wage rate falls. From Figure 21.1 it should be clear that no definite statement can be made about how capital usage responds to the wage change. That is, the sign of $\partial K/\partial w$ is indeterminate. In the simple two-input case, a fall in the wage will cause a substitution away from capital; that is, less capital will be used to produce a given output level. But the output effect will cause more capital to be demanded as part of the firm's increased production plan. So, substitution and output effects in this case work in opposite directions, and no definite conclusion about the sign of $\partial K/\partial w$ is possible.

A Summary of Substitution and Output Effects

The results of this discussion can be summarized by the following principle:

OPTIMIZATION PRINCIPLE

Substitution and Output Effects in Input Demand   When the price of an input falls, two effects cause the quantity demanded of that input to rise:

1. The *substitution effect* causes any given output level to be produced using more of the input; and
2. The fall in costs causes more of the good to be sold, thereby creating an additional *output effect* that increases demand for the input.

For a rise in input price, both substitution and output effects cause the quantity of an input demanded to decline.

We will now provide a more precise development of these concepts using a mathematical approach to the analysis.

MATHEMATICAL DERIVATION

As we showed in Chapter 13, general input demand functions generated by considering the firm's profit-maximizing decision can be stated for the two-input case as

$$L = L(P, w, v)$$
$$K = K(P, w, v), \tag{21.21}$$

where P is the product price. The presence of this term in the demand function again illustrates the close connection between product demand and the derived demand for inputs. Here we will examine how changes in input prices affect these demands.[1] For simplicity, we will focus only on labor demand, since the argument for capital (or for any other variable input) would be identical. As in our graphic analysis, we start by dividing $\partial L/\partial w$ into two components: (1) the change in L induced by the change in w, holding output constant; and (2) the change in L induced by changes in output. Hence,

$$\frac{\partial L}{\partial w} = \frac{\partial L}{\partial w} \ \text{(q constant)} \quad + \frac{\partial L}{\partial w} \ \text{(from changes in q)}. \tag{21.22}$$

We now examine each of these terms separately.

Constant Output Demand Functions and Shephard's Lemma

We have already discussed the first term on the right of Equation 21.22 in connection with an analysis of cost minimization. In Chapter 12 we demonstrated Shephard's lemma, which uses the envelope theorem to show that the constant output demand function for L can be found simply by partially differentiating total costs with respect to w (see footnote 7 in that chapter). That is,

$$\frac{\partial TC}{\partial w} = L'(q, w, v), \tag{21.23}$$

---

[1] In general, $\partial L/\partial P$ and $\partial K/\partial P$ will be positive, since, assuming a positively sloped marginal cost curve, an increase in product price will increase output and the derived demand for both inputs. In the inferior input case, however, this analysis will not hold, since an increase in output will actually cause less of the inferior input to be purchased.

where the function L' permits output to be held constant in studying labor demand. Two arguments suggest why $\partial L'/\partial w$ will be negative. In the two-input case the assumption that the rate of technical substitution diminishes for southeasterly movements along an isoquant, combined with the assumption of cost minimization, requires that w and L move in opposite directions when output is held constant. That result has already been demonstrated graphically in Figure 21.1a. Second, even in the many-input case it can be shown that $\partial L'/\partial w = \partial^2 TC/\partial w^2$ must be negative if costs are truly minimized.[2] Hence, the substitution effect in input demand theory is unambiguously negative.

Output Effects   Derivation of the output effect in Equation 21.22 is considerably more tedious, and we will provide only a heuristic proof here.[3] To do so we make use of a "chain rule" type of argument to examine the causal links that determine how changes in w affect the demand for L through induced output changes. Specifically, we can write

$$\frac{\partial L}{\partial w} \text{ (from changes in } q) = \frac{\partial L}{\partial q} \cdot \frac{\partial q}{\partial P} \cdot \frac{\partial P}{\partial MC} \cdot \frac{\partial MC}{\partial w} \qquad (21.24)$$

to record the way in which w affects L through its effect on marginal costs, product prices, and market demand. Evaluation of the middle two terms on the right side of Equation 21.24 is straightforward. Since $P = MC$ for profit maximization under perfect competition, $\partial P/\partial MC = 1$. The derivative $\partial q/\partial P$ shows how market demand (or, more precisely, the firm's share of that demand) responds to price changes. In the usual case, $\partial q/\partial P < 0$. This term indicates how behavior in the goods market affects input demand. As we will see in the next section, the price elasticity of demand for goods therefore plays an important role in determining the price elasticity of demand for inputs.

Evaluation of the terms $\partial L/\partial q$ and $\partial MC/\partial w$ in Equation 21.24 is tedious. But we have already shown (in footnote 8 of Chapter 12) that both these terms must have the same sign. Hence, their product must be positive. Overall then, the right-hand side of Equation 21.24 must be negative because of the negatively sloped market demand curve for the good being produced.

---

[2] For a proof, see E. Silberberg, *The Structure of Economics: A Mathematical Analysis* (New York: McGraw-Hill Book Co., 1978), chap. 8. Silberberg also uses Shephard's lemma to show that cross-price effects in input demand functions are equal. That is, for the two-input case, $\partial L'/\partial v = \partial^2 TC/\partial w \partial v = \partial^2 TC/\partial v \partial w = \partial K'/\partial w$ (where K' is the constant output demand function for capital). An analogous proof holds for the many-input case.

[3] For a detailed proof, see C. E. Ferguson, *The Neoclassical Theory of Production and Distribution* (Cambridge: Cambridge University Press, 1969), pp. 136–153.

As in our graphic analysis, the mathematical conclusion is that $\partial L/\partial w$ must be negative because both substitution and output effects operate in the same direction. The ambiguity that arises in the Slutsky equation in the theory of demand for goods does not arise in the theory of demand for inputs. Because input demands are themselves derived from the demand for the goods being produced by profit-maximizing firms, the types of responses to price changes that might occur are somewhat constrained.

EXAMPLE 21.2

DECOMPOSING INPUT DEMAND

In Chapter 13 we examined the input demand and short-run supply decisions for a hamburger emporium with a seating capacity of 16 square meters. We showed (in Equation 13.39) that the short-run supply function for this firm is

$$q = \frac{40(10P)}{(vw)^{.5}} \tag{21.25}$$

and that the demand for labor is

$$L = \frac{(10P)^2}{v^{.5}w^{1.5}} . \tag{21.26}$$

As we showed, if $w = v = \$4$ and $P = \$1$, this firm will supply 100 hamburgers per hour and will hire 6.25 workers each hour. If w rises to $\$9$ with P and v unchanged, the firm will produce 66.6 hamburgers per hour using only 1.9 workers.

Disaggregating Substitution and Output Effects. To examine the substitution and output effects present in this problem, suppose that the firm had continued to produce 100 hamburgers per hour even though the wage rose to $\$9$. As we showed in Chapter 13, cost minimization requires that

$$\frac{K}{L} = \frac{w}{v} = \frac{9}{4} . \tag{21.27}$$

Using the original production function

$$q = 100 = 10K^{.25}L^{.25}F^{.5} \tag{21.28}$$

together with the cost-minimization requirement (and $F = 16$) implies

$$10 = 4(9/4L)^{.25}L^{.25}, \tag{21.29}$$

which yields a value for L of approximately 4.17. Even if output were held constant at 100 hamburgers, employment would decline from 6.25 to 4.17 as the firm substitutes capital (grills) for labor. This is the substitution effect. The additional reduction in hiring from 4.17 workers to 1.9 reflects the decline in hourly hamburger output from 100 to 66.6.

Constant Output Demand Function. To analyze this situation a bit more formally, we can compute the constant output demand for labor function using Shephard's lemma. Total costs for the hamburger firm are

$$TC = vK + wL + R, \tag{21.30}$$

where R is the fixed rental rate for space. Substituting the input demand functions for K and L into this expression and using the supply function (Equation 21.25) we can calculate the total cost function:

$$TC = \frac{q^2 v^{.5} w^{.5}}{800} + R. \tag{21.31}$$

Applying Shephard's lemma yields

$$L' = \frac{\partial TC}{\partial w} = \frac{q^2 v^{.5} w^{-.5}}{1,600}. \tag{21.32}$$

For $q = 100$ we have

$$L' = 6.25 v^{.5} w^{-.5}, \tag{21.33}$$

which for $v = \$4$, $w = \$4$ yields $L' = 6.25$; and for $v = \$4$, $w = \$9$ yields $L' = 4.17$ as we derived earlier. Notice how the (constant output) input demand function (Equation 21.32) allows us to hold output (q) constant in our analysis, whereas the total demand function for L (Equation 21.26) implicitly allows output to change. The total input demand function therefore provides a larger impact from a wage change.

QUERY: The "output elasticity" of demand for labor in Equation 21.32 is 2—a 10 percent increase in output requires a 20 percent increase in labor input. Why is this figure so different from unity in this example?

RESPONSIVENESS OF INPUT DEMAND TO CHANGES IN INPUT PRICES

The previous analysis provides a basis for explaining the degree to which input demand will respond to changes in input prices; that is, it helps to explain the price elasticity of demand for inputs. Suppose, for example, that the wage rate rises. We already know that less labor will be demanded. Now we wish to investigate whether this decrease in quantity demanded will be large or small. First, consider the substitution effect. The decrease in hiring of labor will depend on how easy it is for firms to substitute other factors of production for labor. In the terminology of Chapters 11 and 12, the size of the effect will depend on the elasticity of substitution that characterizes a firm's production function. Some firms may find it relatively simple to substitute machines for workers, and for these firms the quantity of labor demanded will decrease substantially. Other firms may produce with a fixed-proportions technology, and for them substitution will be impossible.

In addition to depending on technical properties of the production function, the size of the substitution effect will depend on the length of time that is allowed for adjustment. In the short run, firms may have a stock of machinery that requires a relatively set complement of workers. Consequently, the short-run substitution possibilities are slight. Over the long run, however, the firm may be able to adapt its machinery so as to use less labor per machine; the possibilities of substitution may therefore be substantial. For example, a rise in the wages of coal miners will have little short-run substitution effect, since existing coal-mining equipment requires a fixed complement of workers. In the long run, however, there is clear evidence that mining can be made more capital intensive by designing more complex machinery. In the long run, capital can be substituted for labor.

Timing of Substitution

An increase in the wage rate will also raise firms' costs. As we have seen, this will cause the price of the good being produced to rise, and individuals will reduce their purchases of that good. This reduction in purchases is called the output effect: Because less output is being produced, less labor will be demanded. The output effect will in this way reinforce the substitution effect. In order to investigate the likely size of the output effect, we must know (1) how large the increase in costs brought about by the wage rate increase is and (2) how much quantity demanded will be reduced by a rising price. The size of the first of these components will depend on how "important" labor is in total production costs, whereas the size of the second will depend on how price elastic demand for the product is. In industries for which labor costs are a major portion of total costs and for which demand is very elastic, output effects will be large. For example, an increase in wages for restaurant workers is likely to induce a large output effect in the demand for such workers, since labor costs are a significant portion of restaurant operating costs and the demand for meals eaten out is relatively price elastic. An increase in wages will cause a big price rise, and this will cause individuals to reduce sharply the meals they eat out. On the other hand, output effects in the demand for pharmaceutical workers are probably small, since direct

Output Effect

labor costs are a small fraction of drug production costs and the demand for drugs is price inelastic. Wage increases will have only a small effect on costs, and any increases in price that do result will not cause demand for drugs to be reduced significantly.

A Summary   Our general conclusion then is that the price elasticity of demand for any input will be greater (in absolute value),

1. The larger is the elasticity of substitution of that input for other inputs;
2. The larger is the share of total cost represented by expenditures on that input; and
3. The larger is the price elasticity of demand for the good being produced.

Similar conclusions hold for the cross-price elasticity of demand for an input with respect to changes in some other input price. These relations are examined in the next example and pursued in more detail in the extensions to this chapter.

EXAMPLE 21.3

ELASTICITIES OF DEMAND FOR INPUTS

The labor demand functions calculated in Example 21.2 provide particularly simple examples for calculating the wage elasticity of demand for labor. They also can be readily generalized to cases more complex than the Cobb-Douglas.

Substitution Elasticities. In Equation 21.32 we calculated the constant output demand for labor function for Hamburger Heaven as

$$L' = \frac{q^2 v^{.5} w^{-.5}}{1,600}. \tag{21.34}$$

This function makes clear that the constant output wage elasticity of demand (for reasons we describe in the extensions, this is denoted by η_{LL}) is

$$\eta_{LL} = \frac{\partial L'}{\partial w} \cdot \frac{w}{L'} = \frac{\partial lnL'}{\partial lnw} = -0.5. \tag{21.35}$$

In this example we were examining short-run supply decisions and there were substantial fixed costs involved. These costs are, however, irrelevant to the firm's substitution decisions and drop out when the constant output demand function is calculated. In order to generalize our result, we focus only on variable costs: this also permits extending the analysis to the long run when all costs are variable.

In the Hamburger Heaven case, labor costs represent half of all variable costs (see the production function in Equation 13.30). Using s_L to denote this share of labor costs in variable costs, it is clear from the derivative in Equation 21.32 that

$$\eta_{LL} = s_L - 1 = -(1 - s_L) = -0.5. \tag{21.36}$$

This result is in fact a special case of the result shown in the extensions that

$$\eta_{LL} = -(1 - s_L)\sigma, \tag{21.37}$$

where σ is the elasticity of substitution of the production function. For the Cobb-Douglas case examined here, $\sigma = 1$ so Equation 21.37 reduces to 21.36. More generally, as might be expected, the larger is σ, the larger (in absolute value) will be η_{LL}, the substitution effect in labor demand.

Output Elasticities. Quantifying output effects in input demand requires examining the chain of events that cause output to change when the wage changes. This sequence has already been stated in Equation 21.24. Phrasing it in elasticity terms yields

$$e_{L,w} \text{ (from changes in } q) = e_{L,q} \cdot e_{q,P} \cdot e_{P,MC} \cdot e_{MC,w}. \tag{21.38}$$

There are two ways of interpreting this equation, depending on whether all firms or just one firm experience changes in w, and hence, whether or not price changes. In the case studied in Example 21.2, output price was assumed constant, so the middle two terms in Equation 21.38 require some reinterpretation. The terms have a product of -1 since, in this particular example, marginal costs are a linear function of q as shown by Equation 21.31. That equation also shows that $e_{MC,w} = 0.5$. Since the production function used in Example 21.2 (Equation 21.28) exhibits diminishing returns to scale for the short run, $e_{L,q} = 1/e_{q,L} = 2$ for movements along the expansion path (when, as in Equation 21.29, both variable inputs increase together). In summary then,

$$e_{L,w} \text{ (from changes in } q) = (2)(-1)(.5) = -1. \tag{21.39}$$

The total elasticity of demand (including substitution and output effects) is

$$e_{L,w} = -0.5 - 1.0 = -1.5 \tag{21.40}$$

as can be verified directly from the demand Equation 21.26.

When wage changes affect all firms, Equation 21.38 must be reinterpreted once again. In the long run, with constant returns to scale,

$$e_{L,q} = 1$$
$$e_{P,MC} = 1 \tag{21.41}$$
$$e_{MC,w} = s_L,$$

so the output effect can be written as

$$e_{L,w} \text{ (from changes in } q) = s_L e_{q,P} \qquad (21.42)$$

and the total wage elasticity of demand is

$$e_{L,w} = \eta_{LL} + s_L e_{q,P} = -(1 - s_L)\sigma + s_L e_{q,P}. \qquad (21.43)$$

Since each firm maintains a constant share of industry output, $e_{q,P}$ is identical to the market elasticity of demand for these firms' outputs ($e_{Q,P}$). Hence, Equation 21.43 shows explicitly how $e_{L,w}$ depends on the various factors listed previously. For example, if labor constitutes 75 percent of the costs in an industry characterized by a Cobb-Douglas production function and the elasticity of demand for the industry's output is –2, $e_{L,w}$ will be [$= -.25 + .75(-2)] = -1.75$. Notice that in this case the wage elasticity is largely determined by the elasticity of demand for the good labor produces. On the other hand, for an input that constitutes a small share of total costs, the demand elasticity will be determined mainly by the elasticity of substitution of that input for other inputs.

QUERY: If hamburgers have a unitary elasticity of demand, what is the wage elasticity of demand for labor input for each hamburger emporium like Hamburger Heaven?

MARGINAL PRODUCTIVITY ANALYSIS AND THE DETERMINANTS OF FACTOR SHARES

As the quotation from Ricardo in the introduction to Part VII indicated, the analysis of the determinants of the share of total output accruing to each factor of production has been of central concern in the development of economic theory. An early policy question that provided the impetus for much of this analysis was the debate in England over the repeal of the Corn Laws, which we examined in Chapter 16. The debate over repeal centered attention on the fact that, under these laws, protected landowners in England received a larger share of the nation's income than they would if the laws were repealed. In order to discuss adequately the possible effects of repeal on the factor distribution of income, it was necessary to develop a theory of factor shares. The examination of this problem relied on Ricardo's earlier analysis of rent. More recent examinations have used the theory of input demand developed in this chapter.

Competitive Determination of Income Shares

Assume that there is only one firm (perhaps "the economy") producing a homogeneous output using labor and capital. The production function for the firm is given by $Q = f(K, L)$, and this output sells at price P in the market. The total income received by labor from the productive process during one period is wL, whereas the total income accruing to capital is vK (where v is the rental rate on capital). If the firm in question is a profit maximizer and if it operates as if it were in a perfectly competitive market, it will choose capital and labor so that the marginal revenue product of each factor is equal to its price. Hence,

$$\text{labor's share} = \frac{wL}{PQ} = \frac{P \cdot MP_L \cdot L}{PQ} = \frac{MP_L \cdot L}{Q} \tag{21.44}$$

and

$$\text{capital's share} = \frac{vK}{PQ} = \frac{P \cdot MP_K \cdot K}{PQ} = \frac{MP_K \cdot K}{Q}.$$

The shares of capital and labor therefore are determined by purely technical properties of the production function relating the quantities of those inputs used and their respective marginal physical products. If we knew the exact form of the production function, we could predict the behavior of the factor shares.[4]

If we are willing to assume that factor markets are perfectly competitive (or perhaps a reasonable approximation thereof), the concept of the elasticity of substitution can be quite useful in analyzing the behavior of factor shares. Recall that the elasticity of substitution was defined as

Factor Shares and the Elasticity of Substitution

$$\sigma = \frac{\text{percent}\Delta(K/L)}{\text{percent}\Delta(w/v)}, \tag{21.45}$$

and we can use this parameter to study changes in relative factor shares. If $\sigma = 1$, Equation 21.45 says that w/v will change in exactly the same proportion

---

[4] The competitively determined factor share can also be given an interpretation as the elasticity of output with respect to the input in question. For example, in the case of labor,

$$e_{Q, L} = \frac{\partial f}{\partial L} \cdot \frac{L}{Q} = \frac{MP_L \cdot L}{Q} = \text{labor's share.}$$

This fact is often used in empirical studies of technical change (see Chapter 11). If the production function exhibits constant returns to scale, these shares will sum to 1.

Proof: If $f(K, L)$ exhibits constant returns to scale, we know that

$$f(tK, tL) = t \cdot f(K, L) \quad \text{for any } t > 0.$$

Differentiating this with respect to t gives

$$f_1 K + f_2 L = f(K, L)$$

or

$$MP_K \cdot K + MP_L \cdot L = f(K, L) = Q.$$

Multiplying this equation by P and using the demand relations in Equations 21.13 shows that these shares do indeed sum to 1.

that K/L does. In this case, therefore, the relative shares of capital and labor (vK/wL) will stay constant. Any increase in the capital-labor ratio over time will be exactly counterbalanced by an increase in MP_L/MP_K (= RTS), and this will be manifested by an identical increase in w/v.

For $\sigma > 1$, the percentage increase in K/L will exceed the percentage increase in w/v, and hence the share of capital in total income will rise as the capital-labor ratio increases. The opposite result occurs when $\sigma < 1$ (when substitution is relatively "difficult"). Capital's share will tend to decline in this case because the relative price of labor is rising rapidly in response to an increasing amount of capital per worker.

The elasticity of substitution is therefore a useful conceptual tool for understanding the effect of changing input proportions on factor shares. If factor substitution is relatively easy, the more rapidly expanding input will increase its share of total income. But this need not be the case. If substitution is difficult, the changing relative factor rewards that result from changed input proportions can reverse this result. Empirically, it seems to be the case that the shares of labor and capital income in total income have been relatively constant over time. This is one reason why the Cobb-Douglas production function is of considerable interest. Since this is the production function for which $\sigma = 1$, it is in general accord with the observed constancy of income shares.[5]

MONOPSONY IN THE INPUT MARKET

In many situations firms are not price takers for the inputs they buy. That is, the supply curve for, say, labor faced by the firm is not infinitely elastic at the prevailing wage rate. It frequently may be necessary for the firm to offer a wage above that currently prevailing if it is to attract more employees. In order to study such situations, it is most convenient to examine the polar case of *monopsony* (a single buyer) in the labor market. If there is only one buyer in the labor market, this firm faces the entire market supply curve. In order to increase its hiring of labor by one more unit, it must move to a higher point

---

[5] Constancy of factor shares can be shown directly with the Cobb-Douglas production function:

$$Q = AK^\alpha L^\beta,$$

where $\alpha + \beta = 1$. Since

$$MP_L = \frac{\partial Q}{\partial L} = \beta A K^\alpha L^{\beta - 1},$$

$$\text{labor's share} = s_L = \frac{P \cdot MP_L \cdot L}{PQ} = \frac{(\beta A K^\alpha L^{\beta - 1}) \cdot L}{A K^\alpha L^\beta} = \beta.$$

A similar proof shows that capital's share = α, and hence the shares are constants independent of the total supplies of labor and capital.

on this supply curve. This will involve paying not only a higher wage to the "marginal worker" but also additional wages to those workers already employed. The marginal expense associated with hiring the extra unit of labor (ME_L) therefore exceeds its wage rate. We can show this result mathematically as follows. The total cost of labor to the firm is wL. Hence, the change in those costs brought about by hiring an additional worker is

$$ME_L = \frac{\partial wL}{\partial L} = w + L\frac{\partial w}{\partial L}. \qquad (21.46)$$

In the competitive case, $\partial w/\partial L = 0$ and the marginal expense of hiring one more worker is simply the market wage, w. However, if the firm faces a positively sloped labor supply curve, $\partial w/\partial L > 0$ and the marginal expense exceeds the wage. These ideas are summarized in the following definition:

DEFINITION

Marginal Input Expense The *marginal expense* associated with any input (ME) is the increase in total costs of the input that results from hiring one more unit. If the firm faces an upward-sloping supply curve for the input, the marginal expense will exceed the market price of the input.

A profit-maximizing firm will hire any input up to the point at which its marginal revenue product is just equal to its marginal expense. This is simply a generalization of our previous discussion of marginalist choices to cover the case of monopsony power in the labor market. As before, any departure from such choices will result in lower profits for the firm. If, for example, $MRP_L > ME_L$, the firm should hire more workers, since such an action would increase revenues more than costs. Alternatively, if $MRP_L < ME_L$, employment should be reduced, since that would lower costs more rapidly than revenues.

The monopsonist's choice of labor input is illustrated in Figure 21.2. The firm's demand curve for labor (D) is drawn negatively sloped, as we have shown it must be.[6] Here also the ME_L curve associated with the labor

Graphical Analysis

---

[6] Figure 21.2 is intended only as a pedagogic device and cannot be rigorously defended. In particular, the curve labeled D, although it is supposed to represent the "demand" (or marginal revenue product) curve for labor, has no precise meaning for the monopsonist buyer of labor, since we cannot construct this curve by confronting the firm with a fixed wage rate. Instead, the firm views the entire supply curve, S, and uses the auxiliary curve ME_L to choose the most favorable point on S. In a strict sense, there is no such thing as the monopsonist's demand curve. This is analogous to the case of a monopoly, for which we could not speak of a monopolist's "supply curve."

FIGURE 21.2

PRICING IN A MONOPSONISTIC LABOR MARKET

If a firm faces a positively sloped supply curve for labor (S), it will base its decisions on the marginal expense of additional hiring (ME_L). Because S is positively sloped, the ME_L curve lies above S. The curve S can be thought of as an "average cost of labor curve," and the ME_L curve is marginal to S. At L_1 the equilibrium condition $ME_L = MRP_L$ holds, and this quantity will be hired at a market wage rate w_1. Notice that the monopsonist buys less labor than would be bought if the labor market were perfectly competitive (L^*).

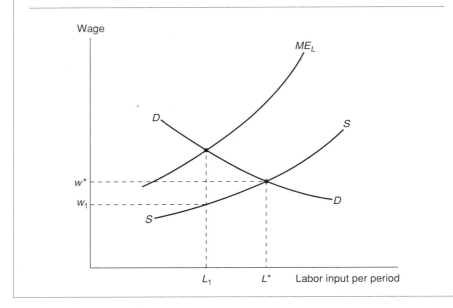

supply curve (S) is constructed in much the same way that the marginal revenue curve associated with a demand curve can be constructed. Because S is positively sloped, the ME_L curve lies everywhere above S. The profit-maximizing level of labor input for the monopsonist is given by L_1, for at this level of input the profit-maximizing requirement of Equation 21.3 holds. At L_1 the wage rate in the market is given by w_1. Notice that the quantity of labor demanded falls short of that which would be hired in a perfectly competitive labor market (L^*). The firm has restricted input demand by virtue of its monopsonistic position in the market. The formal similarities between this analysis and that of monopoly presented in

Chapter 18 should be clear. In particular, the "demand curve" for a monopsonist consists of a single point given by L_1, w_1. The monopsonist has chosen this point as the most desirable of all those points on the supply curve, S. A different point will not be chosen unless some external change (such as a shift in the demand for the firm's output or a change in technology) affects labor's marginal revenue product.[7]

EXAMPLE 21.4

MONOPSONISTIC HIRING

To illustrate these concepts in a very simple context, suppose a coal mine's workers can dig two tons of coal per hour and that coal sells for $10 per ton. The marginal revenue product of a coal miner is therefore $20 per hour. If the coal mine is the only hirer of miners in a local area and faces a labor supply curve of the form

$$L = 50w, \tag{21.47}$$

this firm must recognize that its hiring decisions affect wages. Expressing the total wage bill as a function of L,

$$wL = \frac{L^2}{50}, \tag{21.48}$$

permits the mine operator (perhaps only implicitly) to calculate the marginal expense associated with hiring miners:

$$ME_L = \frac{\partial wL}{\partial L} = \frac{L}{25}. \tag{21.49}$$

Equating this to miners' marginal revenue product of $20 implies that the mine operator should hire 500 workers per hour. At this level of employment the wage will be $10 per hour—only half the value of the workers' marginal revenue product. If the mine operator had been forced by market competition to pay $20 per hour, regardless of the number of miners hired, market equilibrium would have been established with $L = 1,000$ rather than the 500 hired under monopsonistic conditions.

---

[7] For a detailed discussion of the comparative statics analysis of factor demand in the monopoly and monopsony cases, see W. E. Diewert, "Duality Approaches to Microeconomic Theory" in K. J. Arrow and M. D. Intriligator, eds., *Handbook of Mathematical Economics*, vol. 2 (Amsterdam: North-Holland Publishing Co., 1982), pp. 584–590.

QUERY: Suppose the price of coal rises to $15. How would this affect the monopsonist's hiring and the wages of coal miners? Would the miners benefit fully from the increase in their *MRP*?

Wage Discrimination in Hiring

If a monopsony can segregate the supply of a factor into two or more distinct markets, it may be able to increase profits. For example, a monopsony may be able to discriminate in hiring between men and women. Because the firm can readily identify which market a prospective employee belongs to, it will find it profitable to pay different wages in the two markets. Such a situation is shown in Figure 21.3. The assumptions that men and women are equally productive and that the firm has a constant marginal revenue product of labor no matter how much labor is hired are shown by the horizontal MRP_L

FIGURE 21.3

DISCRIMINATION IN HIRING BY A MONOPSONIST

By separating the labor market, say, between men and women, a monopsonist will minimize labor costs by choosing quantities of labor such that the marginal revenue product of labor is equal to the marginal expense in each market. In this diagram the wages of women (w_w) will be below the wages of men (w_m), even though the marginal revenue product for both types of labor is identical.

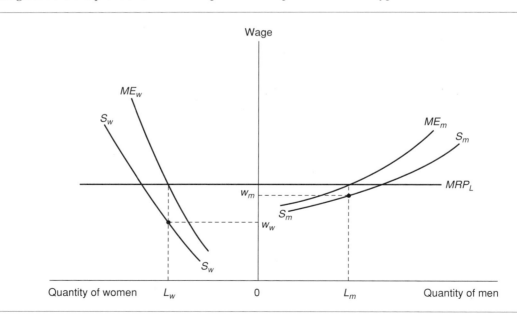

curve. The supply curves for men and women share the same vertical axis in the figure. Given these supply curves, the firm will choose that quantity of labor in each market for which the marginal expense (ME_L) is equal to labor's marginal revenue product. Consequently, the firm will hire L_m from the men's market and L_w from the women's. The wage rates in the two markets will be w_m and w_w, respectively. The way we have drawn Figure 21.3, men's wages will exceed women's, and this happens because women's labor supply is relatively inelastic.

A similar analysis can be developed for any situation in which a monopsony can separate the market for its inputs into two or more parts. In order to do so, it must be able to identify workers as belonging to particular markets so that its segmentation strategy will work: It must know how much of each kind of worker it is hiring. For this reason, wage discrimination along easily identifiable lines (sex, race, or age) might be expected to occur. Whether existing wage differences along such lines can be explained by such a model is doubtful, however, since most labor markets seem to be more subject to the forces of competition than that depicted in Figure 21.3. As in our discussion of price discrimination, competition reduces the scope for violating the law of one price.

MONOPOLY IN THE SUPPLY OF INPUTS

Another way in which imperfect competition may occur in input markets is that the suppliers of the input may be able to form a monopoly. Examples of such monopolies include labor unions in "closed shop" industries, production cartels for certain types of capital equipment, and firms (or countries) that control unique supplies of natural resources. Analysis of such situations proceeds in a way similar to that used for any monopoly: The monopoly supplier may choose any point on the input demand curve it faces. For example, a monopolistic input supplier could maximize its revenues from selling inputs by choosing to produce that output level for which marginal revenue is zero. Or it could choose any other level of factor supply that yields a desirable outcome.[8] To the extent that this choice results in input prices in excess of opportunity costs, monopoly rents will be earned. Those rents will persist as long as entry into the input market can be restricted.

Bilateral Monopoly

If both the supply and demand sides of an input market are monopolized, the market outcome will be indeterminate. Each participant can set bounds on the range of outcomes that may result, but the actual outcome will depend

---

[8] Several alternative goals of a monopolistic union are described in Chapter 22.

FIGURE 21.4

BILATERAL MONOPOLY

A monopoly supplier of an input would prefer equilibrium E_1, whereas a monopsony demander of the input would prefer equilibrium E_2. Here the market outcome is indeterminate and must be settled through bargaining.

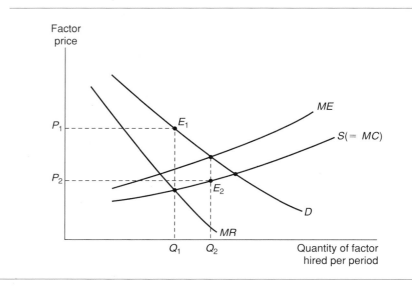

on the bargaining skills of the parties. Figure 21.4 illustrates a market in which a monopolistic supplier of some input (say, a rare metal used to produce an alloy) faces a monopsonistic buyer of the input (the only producer of the alloy). The monopolist's preferred point occurs where its marginal production cost (MC) equals the marginal revenue (MR) associated with the demand for the rare metal. At that point Q_1 would be produced at a price of P_1. The monopolist's preferred equilibrium is denoted by E_1. The monopsony, on the other hand, would prefer to trade amount Q_2 at a price of P_2, since that equilibrium (E_2) maximizes its profits.

Thus, in the bilateral monopoly situation illustrated in Figure 21.4, the desires of buyer and seller are in conflict. Neither point E_1 nor point E_2 is the equilibrium outcome, and the parties must bargain with each other to reach a solution. Although the analysis provided in the figure can place bounds on the likely outcome of such bargaining, arriving at a specific solution would require the development of a formal model of the bargaining process. Often such models draw on some of the tools of game theory that were introduced in Chapters 10 and 20 (see the discussion in Chapter 22 also).

SUMMARY

In this chapter we used the model of a profit-maximizing firm to examine that firm's demand for the inputs it uses. We illustrated several applications of our general result (first derived in Chapter 13) that the firm will hire any input up to the point at which the marginal revenue product (MRP) of the last unit hired is equal to the marginal expense (ME) of hiring that unit:

- The marginal revenue product from hiring extra units of an input is the combined influence of the marginal physical product of the input and the firm's marginal revenue in its output market.

- If the firm is a price taker for the inputs it buys, it is possible to analyze the comparative statics of its demand fairly completely. A rise in the price of an input will cause fewer units to be hired because of both substitution and output effects. The size of these effects will depend on the firm's technology and on the price responsiveness of the demand for its output.

- The marginal productivity theory of input demand can also be used to study the determinants of relative income shares accruing to various factors of production. The elasticity of substitution indicates how these shares change in response to changing factor supplies.

- If a firm has a monopsonistic position in an input market, it will recognize how its hiring affects input prices. The marginal expense associated with hiring additional units of an input will exceed that input's price, and the firm will reduce hiring below competitive levels to maximize profits. If the firm holds a monopsonistic position in several markets, it may be able to practice input price discrimination among them.

- If input suppliers form a monopoly against a monopsonistic demander, the result is indeterminate. In such a situation of bilateral monopoly, the market equilibrium chosen will depend on the bargaining of the two parties.

PROBLEMS

21.1
Suppose that the demand for labor is given by

$$L = -50w + 450$$

and the supply is given by

$$L = 100w,$$

where L represents the number of people employed and w is the real wage rate per hour.
a. What will be the equilibrium levels for w and L in this market?
b. Suppose that the government wishes to raise the equilibrium wage to $4 per hour by offering a subsidy to employers for each person hired. How much will this subsidy have to be? What will the new equilibrium level of employment be? How much total subsidy will be paid?

c. Suppose instead that the government declared a minimum wage of $4 per hour. How much labor would be demanded at this price? How much unemployment would there be?
d. Graph your results.

21.2
Assume that the market for rental cars (used for business purposes) is perfectly competitive with the demand for this capital input given by

$$K = 1,500 - 25v$$

and the supply given by

$$K = 75v - 500,$$

where K represents the number of cars rented by firms and v is the rental rate per day.

a. What will be the equilibrium levels for v and K in this market?
b. Suppose that following an oil embargo gas prices rise dramatically so that now business firms must take account of gas prices in their car rental decisions. Their demand for rental cars is now given by

$$K = 1,700 - 25v - 300g,$$

where g is the per-gallon price of gasoline. What will be the equilibrium levels for v and K if $g = \$2$? If $g = \$3$?
c. Graph your results.
d. Since the oil embargo brought about decreased demand for rental cars, what might be the implication for other capital input markets as a result? For example, employees may still need transportation, so how might the demand for mass transit be affected? Since businesspeople also rent cars to attend meetings, what might happen in the market for phone equipment as employees drive less and use the phone more? Can you think of any other factor input markets that might be affected?

21.3
A landowner has three farms (A, B, and C) of differing fertility. The levels of output for the three farms with one, two, and three laborers employed are as given:

NUMBER OF LABORERS	LEVEL OF OUTPUT		
	FARM A	FARM B	FARM C
1	10	8	5
2	17	11	7
3	21	13	8

For example, if three laborers are hired, one for each farm, the total output would be $10 + 8 + 5 = 23$. This would represent a poor allocation of labor, since if the Farm C laborer were assigned to help on Farm A, the total output would be $17 + 8 = 25$.

a. If market conditions caused the landowner to hire five laborers, what would be the most productive allocation of that labor? How much would be produced? What is the marginal product of the last worker?
b. If that farm output is sold in a perfectly competitive market with one unit of output priced at $1, and

labor market equilibrium occurs when five workers are hired, what wage is paid? How much profit does the landowner receive?

21.4
The mowing of lawns requires only labor (gardeners) and capital (lawn mowers). These factors must be used in the fixed proportions of one worker to one lawn mower, and production exhibits constant returns to scale. Suppose that the wage rate of gardeners is $2 per hour, that lawn mowers rent for $5 per hour, and that the price elasticity of demand for mowed lawns is -2.

a. What is the wage elasticity of demand for gardeners (that is, what is $\partial L / \partial w \cdot w/L$)?
b. What is the elasticity of demand for lawn mowers with respect to their rental rate (that is, $\partial K / \partial v \cdot v/K$)?
c. What is the cross elasticity of demand for lawn mowers with respect to the wage rate (that is, $\partial K / \partial w \cdot w/K$)?

21.5
Assume that the quantity of envelopes licked per hour by Sticky Gums, Inc., is $Q = 10,000\sqrt{L}$, where L is the number of laborers hired per hour by the firm. Assume further that the envelope-licking business is perfectly competitive with a market price of $.01 per envelope.

a. How much labor would be hired at a competitive wage of $10? $5? $2? Use your results to sketch a demand curve for labor.
b. Assume that Sticky Gums hires its labor at an hourly wage of $10. What quantity of envelopes will be licked when the price of a licked envelope is $.10, $.05, $.02? Use your results to sketch a supply curve for licked envelopes.

21.6
Suppose there are a fixed number of 1,000 identical firms in the perfectly competitive concrete pipe industry. Each firm produces the same fraction of total market output, and each firm's production function for pipe is given by

$$q = \sqrt{KL}.$$

Suppose also that the market demand for concrete pipe is given by

$$Q = 400,000 - 100,000P,$$

where Q is total concrete pipe.

a. If $w = v = \$1$, in what ratio will the typical firm use K and L? What will be the long-run average and marginal cost of pipe?
b. In long-run equilibrium what will be the market equilibrium price and quantity for concrete pipe? How much will each firm produce? How much labor will be hired by each firm and in the market as a whole?
c. Suppose the market wage, w, rose to $\$2$ while v remained constant at $\$1$. How will this change the capital-labor ratio for the typical firm, and how will it affect its marginal costs?
d. Under the conditions of part (c), what will the long-run market equilibrium be? How much labor will now be hired by the concrete pipe industry?
e. How much of the change in total labor demand from part (b) to part (d) represented the substitution effect resulting from the change in wage and how much represented the output effect?

21.7

In the early 1960s President John Kennedy's Council of Economic Advisers recommended the institution of "Wage-Price Guideposts." The basic idea of the guideposts was to require wages in all industries to increase at the rate at which the national level of output per worker increases (about 3.2 percent per year). Some industries would have had rates of productivity increase of less than 3.2 percent. These industries were to be permitted to increase prices to the extent that their productivity increase fell short of the national average. On the other hand, firms that had productivity increases in excess of the national average were expected to reduce their prices to the extent of this excess.

Adherence to these rules was intended to keep prices constant on a nationwide basis. There were numerous exceptions to these general principles, but assume for the purposes of this problem that these were not important. Assuming the Wage-Price Guideposts were legislated as an unbreakable law, answer the following questions:

a. What would happen to the relative factor shares in each industry over time?
b. What does this implicitly assume about the elasticity of substitution in all industries?
c. What effect would this legislation have on the investment of new capital if industries did not obey the assumption discussed in part (b)?

d. In regard to your answer to part (c), what effects do you think the guideposts would have on economic growth?

21.8

Carl the clothier owns a large garment factory on an isolated island. Carl's factory is the only source of employment for most of the islanders, and thus Carl acts as a monopsonist. The supply curve for garment workers is given by

$$L = 80w,$$

where L is the number of workers hired and w is their hourly wage. Assume also that Carl's labor demand (marginal revenue product) curve is given by

$$L = 400 - 40MRP_L.$$

a. How many workers will Carl hire in order to maximize his profits and what wage will he pay?
b. Assume now that the government implements a minimum wage law covering all garment workers. How many workers will Carl now hire and how much unemployment will there be if the minimum wage is set at $\$4$ per hour?
c. Graph your results.
d. How does a minimum wage imposed under monopsony differ in results as compared with a minimum wage imposed under perfect competition (assuming the minimum wage is above the market-determined wage)?

21.9

The Ajax Coal Company is the only hirer of labor in its area. It can hire any number of female workers or male workers it wishes. The supply curve for women is given by

$$L_f = 100w_f$$

and for men by

$$L_m = 9w_m^2,$$

where w_f and w_m are the hourly wage rates paid to female and male workers, respectively. Assume that Ajax sells its coal in a perfectly competitive market at $\$5$ per ton and that each worker hired (both men and women) can mine 2 tons per hour. If the firm wishes to maximize profits, how many female and male workers should be hired, and what will the wage rates for these two groups be? How much will Ajax earn in profits per hour on its mine machinery? How will that result compare to one in which Ajax was constrained (say, by market forces) to pay all workers the same wage based on the value of their marginal products?

21.10

The town of Podunk has decided to provide security services to its residents by hiring workers (L) and guard dogs (D). Security services (S) are produced according to the production function

$$S = \sqrt{LD},$$

and residents of the town wish to consume 10 units of such services per period.

a. Suppose that L and D both rent for $1 per period. How much of each input should the town hire to produce the desired services at minimal cost? What will that cost be?

b. Suppose now that Podunk is the only hirer of people who work with guard dogs and that the supply curve for such workers is given by

$$L = 10w,$$

where w is the per-period wage of guard dog handlers. If dogs continue to rent for $1 per period, how much of each input should the town hire to produce the desired services at minimal cost? What will those costs be? What will the wage rate of dog handlers be?

SUGGESTED READINGS

Becker, G. *The Economics of Discrimination*. 2d ed. Chicago: University of Chicago Press, 1971.
First theoretical analysis of economic discrimination. Shows that under competitive conditions discrimination may harm the discriminator as well.

Berck, P., and K. Sydsaeter. *Economists' Mathematical Manual*. Berlin: Springer-Verlag, 1993.
Chapter 25 contains a nice summary of functional forms for input demand equations.

Diewert, W. E. "Duality Approaches to Microeconomic Theory." In K. J. Arrow and M. D. Intriligator, eds., *Handbook of Mathematical Economics*, vol. 2. Amsterdam: North-Holland Publishing Co., 1982, pp. 537–584.
Advanced use of duality to study input demand.

Douglas, P. H. *The Theory of Wages*. New York: Crowell-Collier and Macmillan, 1934.
First use of the Cobb-Douglas production function to analyze input shares in the United States.

Ferguson, C. E. " 'Inferior Factors' and the Theories of Production and Input Demand." *Economica* n.s. 35 (1968): 140–150.

Detailed treatment of inferior inputs and why they pose no special problems for input demand theory.

Fuss, M., and D. McFadden, eds. *Production Economics: A Dual Approach to Theory and Application*. Amsterdam: North-Holland Publishing Co., 1980.
Sophisticated development of the relationship between production functions and input demand functions.

Hamermesh, D. *Labor Demand*. Princeton: Princeton University Press, 1993.
Comprehensive review of both theoretical and empirical issues in the demand for labor. Especially strong in analyzing the demand for different types of labor.

Robinson, J. "Euler's Theorem and the Problem of Distribution." *Economic Journal* 44 (1934): 398–421.
Discussion of the "adding-up" problem and some criticisms of using Euler's theorem to solve it.

Silberberg, E. *The Structure of Economics: A Mathematical Analysis*. New York: McGraw-Hill Book Company, 1978. Chaps. 8 and 10.
Extensive use of duality and Shephard's lemma to derive input demand results.

EXTENSIONS

The Elasticity of Demand for Labor

In these extensions we show explicitly how the elasticity of demand for labor (or any other input) is related to a firm's underlying production and cost functions. Following convention we will denote the (constant output) wage elasticity of demand for labor as

$$\eta_{LL} = \frac{\partial L}{\partial w} \cdot \frac{w}{L} \quad (q \text{ constant})$$

and the cross-elasticity of labor demand for changes in the capital rental rate as

$$\eta_{LK} = \frac{\partial L}{\partial v} \cdot \frac{v}{L} \quad (q \text{ constant}).$$

For the most part our discussion will focus on cases in which production depends only on two inputs (K and L), but in the final extension we show how the results can be generalized.

E21.1 Basic Demand Relations

Suppose the total cost function can be written as

$$TC(w, v, q) = qC(w, v), \quad \text{(i)}$$

where $C(w, v)$ is a unit cost function that is homogeneous of degree one in w and v (this is true for all the cost functions we introduced in the extensions to Chapter 12, for example). Shephard's lemma shows that the constant output demand functions are given by

$$L' = qC_w$$
and
$$K' = qC_v. \quad \text{(ii)}$$

These results together with

$$wC_{ww} + vX_{ww} = 0 \quad \text{(iii)}$$

(which follows from Euler's theorem for homogeneous functions) and the definition

$$\sigma = \frac{CC_{ww}}{C_w C_v} \quad \text{(iv)}$$

(see the extensions to Chapter 12) can be used to prove that in the two-factor case

$$\eta_{LL} = -(1 - s_L)\sigma$$
$$\eta_{LK} = (1 - s_L)\sigma, \quad \text{(v)}$$

where s_L ($= wL/qC$) is labor's share of total costs.

For the three cost functions introduced in the extensions to Chapter 12, it is easy to see that the constant output wage elasticity of demand for labor is:

COST FUNCTION	η_{LL}
Cobb-Douglas	$-(1 - s_L)$
CES	$-(1 - s_L)\sigma$
Translog	$(2\beta_2 + s_L^2 - s_L)/s_L$
	$= (1 - s_L)\left(\dfrac{2\beta_2 + s_L(s_L - 1)}{s_L(1 - s_L)}\right)$
	$= (1 - s_L)\sigma,$

where the notation here follows that used in the extensions to Chapter 12.

Empirical Evidence and Tax Incidence

Economists have estimated η_{LL} in many ways ranging from the use of economywide data to the use of data on only a few industries in specific geographic locales. Hamermesh (1993) summarizes many of these studies. He concludes that most values for η_{LL} fall in the range $-.15$ to $-.75$, with $-.30$ representing a reasonable median value. Interestingly, as equation v shows, the .30 value is consistent with a typical value for labor's share ($s_L = .70$) and a Cobb-Douglas production function ($\sigma = 1$). The fact that empirical estimates of the wage elasticity of demand for labor tend to exceed substantially (in absolute value) estimates of the wage elasticity of labor supply implies that the incidence of employment taxes (such as those that finance Social Security in the United States) falls largely on workers. Direct empirical evidence on whether such taxes are largely shifted to workers is somewhat ambiguous, however.

E21.2 Output Effects

We can use the procedure followed in E21.1 to show that the total wage elasticity of demand for labor (including output effects) is given by

$$e_{L,w} = -(1 - s_L)\sigma + s_L e_{q,P},\qquad \text{(vi)}$$

where $e_{q,P}$ is the price elasticity of demand for the firm's output. This proof assumes that the industry in question is in long-run competitive equilibrium so that $P = MC = AC$ (which is C, given the notation used previously).

Minimum Wages and Teenagers

Equation vi provides the basis for economists' concerns that increasing minimum wage requirements may lessen the demand for low-wage workers, especially teenagers. Although the effects of minimum wage rates may be ameliorated by the facts that they affect the wages of relatively few workers and that the laws may be unenforced in some cases, it is still possible that the impact could be important. This would be especially true if teens are hired by firms with high price elasticities of demand for their output (for example, fast-food producers).

Such concerns have been subject to major challenges in recent years. While earlier studies suggested that minimum wage elasticities for teenage workers might be in the −.1 to −.3 range (Hamermesh [1993], page 187), more recent studies have found much smaller effects. For example, Wellington (1991) finds many elasticities in the range 0 to −.1 and attributes such results to the declining real value of the minimum wage during the 1980s. More controversially, Card and Krueger's (1993) influential study, based in part on fast-food employment trends in New Jersey and Pennsylvania, concludes that rising minimum wages may even have had a positive effect on teen employment. Most economists remain skeptical of this claim, however (Kennan, 1995).

E21.3 The Many-Input Case

For the many-input case, it can be shown that

$$\eta_{ij} = \frac{\partial X_i}{\partial w_j} \cdot \frac{w_j}{X_i} = s_j \sigma_{ij}\qquad \text{(vii)}$$

(see Hamermesh, 1993).

This general equation applies directly to the cross-elasticity of demand for labor (η_{LK}) in the two-input case, but the own wage elasticity (η_{LL}) derived previously requires some modification to allow for different elasticity of substitution concepts.

Since (constant output) factor demand equations are homogeneous of degree zero in all input prices, Euler's theorem implies

$$\sum_{j=1}^{n} \eta_{ij} = 0.\qquad \text{(viii)}$$

Because $\eta_{ii} < 0$, we can conclude that the signs of η_{ij} for $i \neq j$ are predominantly positive. Most inputs are net substitutes.

Immigration

One topic for which possible substitutability among inputs has been intensively studied is the impact of immigration on the wages of domestic workers. Although immigrants may be close substitutes for low-wage domestic workers, a large negative impact from increased immigration is not a foregone conclusion. Wages may also be affected by international trade patterns and immigration may itself set up countervailing trends (for example, domestic immigration into an area may decline as foreign immigration rises). Friedberg and Hunt (1995) summarize a number of econometric studies of these effects and conclude that immigration effects on wages are relatively small—at current levels, a 10 percent increase in immigration into an area might reduce wages by less than 1 percent. Results from several "natural experiments" such as the 1980 Mariel boatlift of Cubans to Miami or the return of Europeans to France following Algerian independence in 1962 also tend to show relatively modest effects.

References

Card, D. E., and A. B. Krueger. *Myth and Measurement: The New Economics of the Minimum Wage.* Princeton: Princeton University Press, 1993.

Friedberg, R. M., and J. Hunt. "The Impact of Immigrants on Host Country Wages, Employment, and Growth." *Journal of Economic Perspectives* (Spring 1995): 23–44.

Hamermesh, D. S. *Labor Demand.* Princeton: Princeton University Press, 1993.

Kennan, J. "The Elusive Effects of the Minimum Wage." *Journal of Economic Literature* (December 1995): 1949–1965.

Wellington, A. "Effects of Minimum Wages in the Employment Status of Youth." *Journal of Human Resources* (Winter 1991): 27–46.

CHAPTER 22

LABOR SUPPLY

In this chapter we examine some aspects of input pricing that are related particularly to the labor market. Because we have already discussed questions about the demand for labor (or any other input) in some detail, we will be concerned primarily with analyzing the supply of labor.

ALLOCATION OF TIME

In Part II we analyzed the way in which an individual chooses to allocate a fixed amount of income among a variety of available goods. Individuals must make similar choices in deciding how they will spend their time. The number of hours in a day (or in a year) is absolutely fixed, and time must be used as it "passes by." Given this fixed amount of time, any individual must decide how many hours to work; how many hours to spend consuming a wide variety of goods, ranging from cars and television sets to operas; how many hours to devote to self-maintenance; and how many hours to sleep. By studying how individuals choose to divide their time among these activities, economists are able to understand the labor supply decision.

Simple Two-Good Model

For simplicity we start by assuming that there are only two uses to which an individual may devote his or her time—either engaging in market work at a real wage rate of w per hour or not working. We shall refer to nonwork time as "leisure," but this word is not meant to carry any connotation of idleness. Time that is not spent in market work can be devoted to work in the home, to self-improvement, or to consumption (it takes time to use a television set or a bowling ball).[1] All of those activities contribute to an individual's

---

[1] Perhaps the first formal theoretical treatment of the allocation of time was given by G. S. Becker in "A Theory of the Allocation of Time," *Economic Journal* 75 (September 1965): 493–517.

well-being, and time will be allocated to them in what might be assumed to be a utility-maximizing way.

More specifically, assume that an individual's utility during a typical day depends on consumption during that period (C) and on hours of leisure enjoyed (H):

$$\text{utility} = U(C, H). \tag{22.1}$$

Notice that in writing this utility function, we have used two "composite" goods, consumption and leisure. The reader should recognize that utility is in fact derived by devoting real income and time to the consumption of a wide variety of goods and services.[2] In seeking to maximize utility, the individual is bound by two constraints. The first of these concerns available time. If we let L represent hours of work, then

$$L + H = 24. \tag{22.2}$$

That is, the day's time must be allocated either to work or to nonwork. A second constraint records the fact that the individual can purchase consumption items only by working (later in this chapter we will allow for the availability of nonlabor income). If the real hourly market wage rate that the individual can earn is given by w, the income constraint is given by

$$C = wL. \tag{22.3}$$

Combining the two constraints, we have

$$C = w(24 - H) \tag{22.4}$$

or

$$C + wH = 24w. \tag{22.5}$$

This combined constraint has an important interpretation. Any individual has a "full income" given by $24w$. That is, an individual who worked all the time would have this much command over real consumption goods each day. Individuals may spend their full income either by working (for real income and consumption) or by not working and thereby enjoying leisure. Equation 22.5 shows that the opportunity cost of consuming leisure is w per hour: It is equal to earnings foregone by not working.

The individual's problem then is to maximize utility, subject to the full income constraint. Setting up the Lagrangian expression

Utility Maximization

---

[2] This observation leads to the consideration of how such activities are produced in the home. For a survey, see R. Gronau, "Home Production: A Survey" in O. C. Ashenfelter and R. Layard, eds., *Handbook of Economics*, vol. 1 (Amsterdam: North-Holland Publishing Co., 1986), pp. 273–304.

$$\mathcal{L} = U(C, H) + \lambda(24w - C - wH), \tag{22.6}$$

the first-order conditions for a maximum are

$$\frac{\partial \mathcal{L}}{\partial C} = \frac{\partial U}{\partial C} - \lambda = 0$$

$$\frac{\partial \mathcal{L}}{\partial H} = \frac{\partial U}{\partial H} - w\lambda = 0. \tag{22.7}$$

Dividing the two lines in Equation 22.7, we get

$$\frac{\partial U/\partial H}{\partial U/\partial C} = w = MRS(H \text{ for } C). \tag{22.8}$$

Hence, we have derived the following principle:

OPTIMIZATION PRINCIPLE

Utility-Maximizing Labor Supply Decision   In order to maximize utility, given the real wage, w, the individual should choose to work that number of hours for which the marginal rate of substitution of leisure for consumption is equal to w.

Of course, the result derived in Equation 22.8 is only a necessary condition for a maximum. As in Chapter 5, this tangency will be a true maximum provided that the *MRS* of leisure for consumption is diminishing.

Income and Substitution Effects of a Change in w

A change in the real wage rate (w) can be analyzed in a manner identical to that used in Chapter 5. When w rises, the "price" of leisure becomes higher—the individual must give up more in lost wages for each hour of leisure consumed. The substitution effect of an increase in w on the hours of leisure therefore will be negative. As leisure becomes more expensive, there is reason to consume less of it. However, the income effect will be positive—since leisure is a normal good, the higher income resulting from a higher w will increase the demand for leisure. Thus, the income and substitution effects work in opposite directions. It is impossible to predict on *a priori* grounds whether an increase in w will increase or decrease the demand for leisure time. Since leisure and work are mutually exclusive ways to spend one's time, it is also impossible to predict what will happen to the number of hours worked. The substitution effect tends to increase hours worked when w increases, whereas the income effect, because it increases the demand for leisure time, tends to decrease the number of hours worked. Which of these two effects is the stronger is an important empirical question.[3]

The two possible reactions to a change in w are illustrated in Figure 22.1. In both graphs the initial wage is w_0, and the initial optimal choices of C and H are given by the point C_0, H_0. When the wage rate increases to w_1, the optimal combination moves to point C_1, H_1. This movement can be

A Graphical Analysis

FIGURE 22.1

INCOME AND SUBSTITUTION EFFECTS OF A CHANGE IN THE REAL WAGE RATE w

Since the individual is a supplier of labor, the income and substitution effects of an increase in the real wage rate (w) work in opposite directions in their effects on the hours of leisure demanded (or on hours of work). In (a) the substitution effect (move- ment to point S) outweighs the income effect, and a higher wage causes hours of leisure to decline to H_1. Hours of work therefore increase. In (b) the income effect is stronger than the substitution effect, and H increases to H_1. In this case hours of work decline.

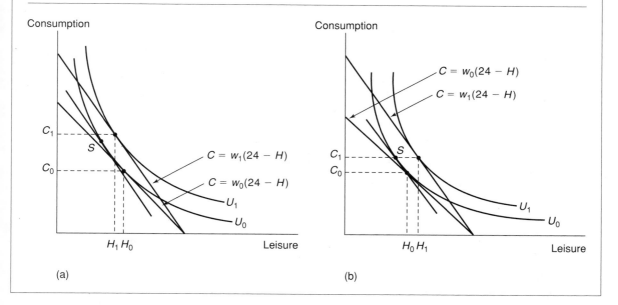

(a)

(b)

---

[3] If the family is taken to be the relevant decision unit, even more complex questions arise about the income and substitution effects that changes in the wages of one family member, say, the husband, will have on the labor force behavior of other family members, such as the wife.

considered as the result of two effects. The substitution effect can be represented by the movement of the optimal point from C_0, H_0 to S and the income effect by the movement from S to C_1, H_1. In the two panels of Figure 22.1, these two effects combine to produce different results. In panel (a) the substitution effect of a change in w outweighs the income effect, and the individual demands less leisure ($H_1 < H_0$). Another way of saying this is that the individual will work longer hours when w rises.

In panel (b) of Figure 22.1 the situation is reversed. The income effect of a change in w more than offsets the substitution effect, and the demand for leisure increases ($H_1 > H_0$). The individual works shorter hours when w rises. In the cases examined in Chapter 5 this would have been considered an unusual result—when the "price" of leisure rises, the individual demands more of it. For the case of normal consumption goods, the income and substitution effects work in the same direction. Only for "inferior" goods do they differ in sign. In the case of leisure and labor, however, the income and substitution effects always work in opposite directions. An increase in w makes an individual better off because he or she is a *supplier* of labor. In the case of a consumption good, individuals are made worse off when a price rises because they are *consumers* of that good. We can summarize this analysis as follows:

OPTIMIZATION PRINCIPLE

Income and Substitution Effects of a Change in the Real Wage   When the real wage rate increases, a utility-maximizing individual may increase or decrease hours worked. The substitution effect will tend to increase hours worked as the individual substitutes earnings for leisure, which is now relatively more costly. On the other hand, the income effect will tend to reduce hours worked as the individual uses his or her increased purchasing power to buy more leisure hours.

We now turn to examine a mathematical development of these responses that provides additional insights into the labor supply decision.

A MATHEMATICAL ANALYSIS OF LABOR SUPPLY

In order to derive a mathematical statement of labor supply decisions, it is helpful first to amend the individual's budget constraint slightly to allow for the presence of nonlabor income. To do so, we rewrite Equation 22.3 as

$$C = wL + N, \tag{22.9}$$

where N is real nonlabor income and may include such items as dividend and interest income, receipt of government transfer benefits, or simply gifts from other persons. Indeed, N could stand for lump-sum taxes paid by the individual, in which case its value would be negative.

Maximization of utility subject to this new budget constraint would yield results virtually identical to those already derived. That is, the necessary condition for a maximum described in Equation 22.8 would continue to hold as long as the value of N is unaffected by the labor-leisure choices being made; that is, so long as N is a "lump-sum" receipt or loss of income,[4] the only effect of introducing nonlabor income into the analysis is to shift the budget constraints in Figure 22.1 outward or inward in a parallel manner without affecting the trade-off rate between earnings and leisure.

This discussion suggests that we can write the individual's labor supply function as $L(w, N)$ to indicate that the number of hours worked will depend both on the real wage rate and on the amount of real nonlabor income received. On the assumption that leisure is a normal good, $\partial L/\partial N$ will be negative; that is, an increase in N will raise the demand for leisure and (since there are only 24 hours in the day) reduce L. To study wage effects on labor supply ($\partial L/\partial w$), we will find it helpful first to consider the dual problem to the individual's primary utility-maximization problem.

As we showed in Chapter 5, related to the individual's primary problem of utility maximization given a budget constraint is the dual problem of minimizing the expenditures necessary to attain a given utility level. In the present context, this problem can be phrased as choosing values for consumption (C) and leisure time ($H = 24 - L$) so that the amount of additional spending,

Dual Statement of the Problem

$$E = C - wL, \tag{22.10}$$

required to attain a given utility level [say, $U_0 = U(C, H)$] is as small as possible. As in Chapter 5, solving this minimization problem will yield exactly the same solution as solving the utility-maximization problem.

Now we can apply the envelope theorem to the minimum value for these extra expenditures calculated in the dual problem. Specifically, a small change in the real wage will change the minimum expenditures required by

$$\frac{\partial E}{\partial w} = -L. \tag{22.11}$$

---

[4] In many situations, however, N itself may depend on labor supply decisions. For example, the value of welfare or unemployment benefits a person can receive depends on his or her earnings, as does the amount of income taxes paid. In such cases the slope of the individual's budget constraint will no longer be reflected by the real wage but must instead reflect the *net* return to additional work after taking increased taxes and reductions in transfer payments into account. For some examples, see the problems at the end of this chapter.

Intuitively, each \$1 increase in w reduces the required value of E by \$$L$, since that is the extent to which labor earnings are increased by the wage change. This result is very similar to Shephard's lemma in the theory of production (see Chapters 12 and 21): Here the result shows that a labor supply function can be calculated from the expenditure function by partial differentiation. Since utility is held constant in the dual expenditure minimization approach, this function should be interpreted as a "compensated" (constant utility) labor supply function, which we will denote by $L'(w, U)$ to differentiate it from the uncompensated labor supply function $L(w, N)$ introduced earlier.

Slutsky Equation of Labor Supply Now we can use these concepts to derive a Slutsky-type equation that reflects the substitution and income effects that result from changes in the real wage. We begin by recognizing that the expenditures being minimized in the dual problem of Equation 22.11 play the role of nonlabor income in the primal utility-maximization problem. Hence, by definition, at the optimal point we have

$$L'(w, U) = L[w, E(w, U)] \equiv L(w, N). \tag{22.12}$$

Partial differentiation of both sides of Equation 22.12 with respect to w yields

$$\frac{\partial L'}{\partial w} = \frac{\partial L}{\partial w} + \frac{\partial L}{\partial E} \cdot \frac{\partial E}{\partial w}, \tag{22.13}$$

and using the envelope relation from Equation 22.11, we have

$$\frac{\partial L'}{\partial w} = \frac{\partial L}{\partial w} - L \frac{\partial L}{\partial E} = \frac{\partial L}{\partial w} - L \frac{\partial L}{\partial N}. \tag{22.14}$$

Introducing a slightly different notation for the compensated labor supply function,

$$\frac{\partial L'}{\partial w} = \frac{\partial L}{\partial w} \bigg|_{U = U_0}, \tag{22.15}$$

and rearranging terms gives the final Slutsky equation for labor supply:

$$\frac{\partial L}{\partial w} = \frac{\partial L}{\partial w} \bigg|_{U = U_0} + L \frac{\partial L}{\partial N}. \tag{22.16}$$

In words (as we have previously shown), the change in labor supplied in response to a change in the real wage can be disaggregated into the sum of a substitution effect in which utility is held constant and an income effect that is analytically equivalent to an appropriate change in nonlabor income. Since the substitution effect is positive (a higher wage increases the amount of work chosen when utility is held constant) and the term $\partial L/\partial N$ is negative, this derivation shows that the substitution and income effects work in opposite directions. The mathematical development supports the earlier conclusions from our graphical analysis. The mathematical development also suggests that the importance of negative income effects may be greater the greater is labor supply, L, a possibility we will examine later.

EXAMPLE 22.1

COBB-DOUGLAS LABOR SUPPLY

The Cobb-Douglas utility function provides an instructive example of these offsetting substitution and income effects in labor supply decisions. Suppose that hourly utility is a function of consumption and leisure of the form

$$U = \sqrt{CH}. \tag{22.17}$$

The individual is constrained by a budget constraint

$$C = wL + N \tag{22.18}$$

and by a time constraint

$$H = 1 - L, \tag{22.19}$$

where, for simplicity, we have set maximum work time equal to 1 (hour). Combining these equations, we can express utility as a function of labor supply choice only:

$$U^2 = CH = (wL + N)(1 - L)$$
$$= wL - wL^2 + N - NL. \tag{22.20}$$

Differentiation of U^2 with respect to L yields the first-order condition for a utility maximum

$$\frac{\partial U^2}{\partial L} = w - 2wL - N = 0 \tag{22.21}$$

or

$$L = \frac{1}{2} - \frac{N}{2w}. \tag{22.22}$$

This, then, is the individual's labor supply function. If $N = 0$, this individual will work $\frac{1}{2}$ of each hour no matter what the wage is—that is, if $N = 0$, the substitution and income effects of a change in w precisely offset each other and leave L unaffected.

Examining Income and Substitution Effects. A more complete analysis of why this is so requires that we examine the income and substitution effects separately. Calculation of the income effect in the Slutsky Equation 22.16 is straightforward using the optimal choice in Equation 22.22:

$$L \cdot \frac{\partial L}{\partial N} = \left(\frac{1}{2} - \frac{N}{2w}\right)\left(-\frac{1}{2w}\right) = -\frac{1}{4w} + \frac{N}{4w^2}. \tag{22.23}$$

If $N = 0$, this income effect will be simply

$$L \cdot \frac{\partial L}{\partial N} = -\frac{1}{4w},$$

where the negative sign indicates that the income effect of an increase in w will reduce L, since leisure is a normal good.

Calculation of the substitution effect in the Slutsky equation is a rather messy process. First, one must derive an expression for indirect utility as a function of w and N (the two exogenous elements in the individual's budget constraint) and then use this to eliminate N from the optimal labor supply choice given by Equation 22.22. Luckily, your author has made this calculation for you:[5]

$$L'(w, U) = 1 - \frac{U}{\sqrt{w}}. \tag{22.24}$$

This constant utility labor supply function shows that if only substitution effects are allowed, $\partial L'/\partial w$ is definitely positive:

$$\frac{\partial L'}{\partial w} = \frac{U}{2w^{3/2}}. \tag{22.25}$$

Replacing U with its indirect representation in terms of w and N in Equation 22.25 (see footnote 5) now yields

$$\frac{\partial L'}{\partial w} = \frac{1}{4w} + \frac{N}{4w^2}. \tag{22.26}$$

Hence, if $N = 0$,

$$\frac{\partial L'}{\partial w} = \frac{1}{4w}, \tag{22.27}$$

and the Slutsky equation

$$\frac{\partial L}{\partial w} = \frac{\partial L'}{\partial w} + L\frac{\partial L}{\partial N} = \frac{1}{4w} - \frac{1}{4w} = 0 \tag{22.28}$$

---

[5] The indirect utility function is

$$U = \frac{\sqrt{w}}{2} + \frac{N}{2\sqrt{w}}.$$

shows that the substitution and income effects are precisely offsetting in this Cobb-Douglas case.

QUERY: How do the mathematical results of this problem compare to the intuitive idea that with the Cobb-Douglas utility function a person always spends a constant fraction of income on each good regardless of price?

EXAMPLE 22.2

EFFECTS OF NONLABOR INCOME

If $N \neq 0$ (the individual has some nonlabor income), the precise offsetting of income and substitution effects shown in Example 22.1 would not occur. The explanation for this is that this individual will always choose to spend half of his or her nonlabor income on leisure. But leisure "costs" w per hour, and a rise in w will mean that less leisure can be "bought" with a fixed number of N dollars. If, for example, $N = \$2$ per hour and w is $\$10$ per hour, Equation 22.22 shows that this individual will work

$$L = \tfrac{1}{2} - \tfrac{2}{20} = \tfrac{4}{10}. \tag{22.29}$$

This person spends $\$1$ of his or her nonlabor income on leisure each hour. At a wage of $\$10$, this $\$1$ will buy $\tfrac{1}{10}$ of an hour of leisure. If, on the other hand, $w = \$5$, the $\$1$ would buy $\tfrac{2}{10}$ of an hour and

$$L = \tfrac{1}{2} - \tfrac{2}{10} = \tfrac{3}{10}. \tag{22.30}$$

With nonlabor income, therefore, the income and substitution effects are not offsetting—the substitution effect dominates, and a fall in wages reduces hours of work.

Changes in Nonlabor Income and the Effects of Subsidies. Clearly, the effect of an increase in N in this problem is to reduce hours of work. With $N = \$4$ and $w = \$10$, for example, $\tfrac{3}{10}$ of an hour of work is supplied. For $N = \$10$, hours of work would fall to zero. If N is interpreted as an income subsidy from the government, this model then provides some support for the purported negative labor supply effects of income maintenance programs.

QUERY: Suppose the government sets N at $\$4$ but reduces N by half of each dollar earned; that is,

$$N = 4 - \frac{wL}{2}.$$

Would this scheme increase or decrease labor supply relative to a flat grant of $\$4$ regardless of labor supply?

INDIVIDUAL SUPPLY CURVE FOR LABOR

Using the analysis of the previous sections, we now can discuss individual labor supply in detail. In Figure 22.2 we have drawn an individual's supply of labor curve by calculating the number of hours he or she is willing to work at every possible real wage rate. Such a curve might resemble that shown in Figure 22.2a. There the individual's labor supply curve is drawn with a positive slope: At higher real wage rates the individual chooses to work longer hours. The substitution effect of a higher wage outweighs the income effect. This need not always be the case, however, as Figure 22.2b demonstrates. There the supply curve is "backward bending"—once real wages exceed a certain level, even higher wage rates induce the individual to work fewer hours. Such a curve is entirely consistent with the theory of the allocation of time we have developed. At relatively high wage rates and hours of work, a further increase in the wage may cause individuals to choose to work fewer hours, since the income effect may come to outweigh the substitution effect. The individual uses the higher real wage rate to "buy" more leisure.

FIGURE 22.2

TWO SHAPES FOR AN INDIVIDUAL'S SUPPLY CURVE FOR LABOR

In (a) a higher real wage induces the individual to supply more labor. The substitution effect of the higher wage outweighs the income effect. In (b), on the other hand, the supply curve of labor is backward bending. For relatively high wage rates, the income effect of a higher wage outweighs the substitution effect and causes the individual to demand more leisure.

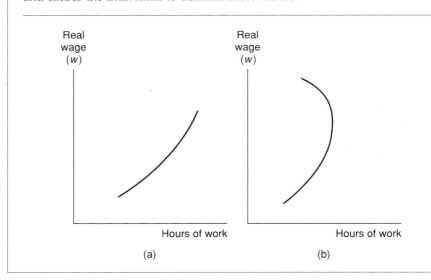

(a)   (b)

An important empirical question is which of these curves best reflects individual labor supply decisions. Although there is substantial evidence that short-run labor supply curves have a positive slope (consider, for example, the positive effect of offering higher overtime wages on hours of work), it appears that in the long run individual supply curves at times may have been backward bending. In 1890 the average work week in the United States in the manufacturing industry was about 60 hours. Real wages in 1890 were about $3.25 per hour (in terms of 1990 consumption prices). By 1929 the work week in manufacturing had dropped to 40 hours, in spite of the fact that real wages had risen to about $5.85 per hour. American workers chose to take some of their increasing incomes in the form of leisure, and this is consistent with the notion of a backward-bending supply curve. Since 1929, real wages in manufacturing have continued to rise (to about $10.60 per hour in 1993), but the work week has not fallen below 40 hours per week. It appears that in recent years the substitution effect of higher wages has almost exactly balanced the income effect, at least for manufacturing workers.

MARKET SUPPLY CURVE FOR LABOR

We can construct a market supply of labor curve from individual supply curves by horizontal summation. At each possible wage rate we would add together the quantity of labor offered by each individual in order to arrive at a market total. One particularly interesting aspect of this procedure is that as the wage rate rises, more individuals may be induced to enter the labor force. Figure 22.3 illustrates this possibility for the simple case of two individuals. For a real wage below w_1 neither individual chooses to work. Consequently, the market supply curve of labor (Figure 22.3c) shows that no labor is supplied at real wages below w_1. A wage in excess of w_1 causes individual 1 to enter the labor market. However, as long as wages fall short of w_2, individual 2 will not work. Only at a wage rate above w_2 will both individuals participate in the labor market. In general, the possibility of the entry of new workers makes the market supply of labor somewhat more responsive to wage rate increases than would be the case if the number of workers was assumed to be fixed.

The most important example of higher real wage rates inducing increased labor force participation is the labor force behavior of married women in the United States in the post–World War II period. Since about 1950 the percentage of working married women has increased from 32 percent to over 60 percent; economists attribute this, at least in part, to the increasing wages that women are able to earn. In recent years a substantial portion of the annual increase in the size of the labor force has been provided by the increasing tendency for married women to work. Both recent attitudinal changes and possible increases in real wage rates suggest that this trend will continue.

FIGURE 22.3

CONSTRUCTION OF THE MARKET SUPPLY CURVE FOR LABOR

As the real wage rises, there are two reasons why the supply of labor may increase. First, higher real wages may cause each individual in the market to work more hours. Second, higher wages may induce more individuals (for example, individual 2) to enter the labor market.

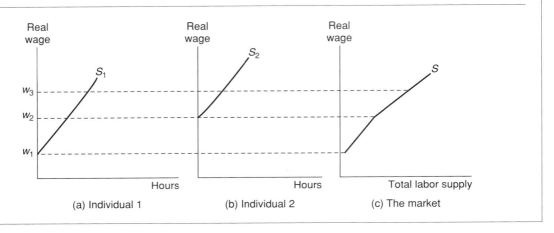

(a) Individual 1   (b) Individual 2   (c) The market

OTHER USES OF THE TIME ALLOCATION MODEL

Although we have applied the time allocation model only to the case of choices between labor and leisure time, the model itself is quite general. Choices that individuals must make among competing uses of time can usually be analyzed within a utility-maximization framework, and it is often possible to gain considerable insights by proceeding in this way. Here we shall briefly discuss three such additional applications: job search theory, the economics of childbearing, and transportation choices. Each of those applications builds on the observation that the opportunity cost of time not working is given by the market wage rate.

Job Search Theory

In seeking new jobs individuals are often faced with considerable uncertainty about available openings. Consequently, they must invest some time (and possibly other resources such as phone calls or placing of advertisements) in finding a suitable job match. To the extent that individuals must reduce potential work time to accommodate their job search plans, the hourly cost of searching can be approximated by the market wage. The higher an individual's market wage, the more likely he or she would be to adopt search techniques that economize on time (such as using an employment agency). If, on the other hand, search time is subsidized (say, by receipt of unemployment insurance benefits), it is possible that search time may be prolonged in the hope of finding a better job.[6]

The Economics of Childbearing

Individuals' decisions to have children are affected by a number of social, religious, and economic factors. Economists have tended to focus primarily on the costs associated with having children and how those costs vary among individuals. One of the most important of those costs is the foregone wages of parents who choose to care for their children rather than to pursue market employment. Indeed, by some estimates, this cost is far in excess of all other costs of childbearing combined. That type of calculation has led some authors to speculate that the increase in real wages for women in the United States since World War II is a principal reason for the decline in the birthrate during that period. Since children have become relatively more expensive, people have chosen to "consume" fewer of them. Similarly, the fact that birthrates in North America and Western Europe are lower than in the less-developed parts of the world might be attributed to wage rate differences (and hence cost of children differences) between these regions.[7]

Transportation Choices

In choosing among alternative transportation modes, individuals will take both time and dollar costs into account. Transportation planners are particularly interested in how individuals respond to differences in such costs so that they can predict the effect on demand of improvements in highways or in public transit systems. Most studies have found that individuals are quite sensitive to time costs, especially those associated with walking or waiting.[8] From examinations of individuals' trade-offs between time and dollar costs, those studies generally conclude that individuals value transit time at between 50 percent and 100 percent of their market wage. These findings then offer further support for the time allocation model.

---

[6] For a theoretical treatment of some of these issues, see the discussion of search theory in the extensions to Chapter 10.

[7] For a seminal contribution to the economics of fertility, see G. Becker, "An Economic Analysis of Fertility" in *Demographic and Economic Change in Developed Countries* (Princeton, N.J.: Princeton University Press, 1960).

[8] See, for example, T. A. Domencich and D. McFadden, *Urban Travel Demand* (Amsterdam: North-Holland Publishing Co., 1975).

**OCCUPATIONAL
CHOICE AND
COMPENSATING
WAGE
DIFFERENTIALS**

Wage rates differ greatly among individuals and among jobs. There are three economic reasons why these differentials arise. First, workers have different levels of skills. These differences in skills may cause some workers to be more productive than others; in a competitive market for labor, those with greater skills will earn higher wages. Second, some workers may receive wages that are essentially a monopoly rent. If workers can successfully limit access to certain jobs, they may succeed in improving their own wages. Finally, wage rates may differ among jobs because some jobs are more pleasant than others. More enjoyable jobs will attract a large supply of applicants, and this may cause the wage rates to be lower than in less desirable ones. In this section we shall restrict our attention to this third reason for wage differentials. Even though we shall implicitly assume that all workers are equally skilled and that there are no monopolistic elements in the wage-setting process, wage differentials can (and do) arise, and we wish to examine this possibility.

The notion that differing characteristics of jobs may lead to differential wages has long been noted by economists. In *The Wealth of Nations,* for example, Adam Smith noted that

> the whole of the advantages and disadvantages of the different employments of labour . . . must, in the same neighbourhood, be either equal or continually tending to equality. If in the same neighbourhood there is any employment either more or less advantageous than the rest, so many people would crowd into it in the one case, and so many would desert it in the other, that its advantages would soon return to the level of other employments. . . .
>
> [But] pecuniary wages . . . are everywhere in Europe extremely different according to the different employments of labour . . . this difference arises partly from certain circumstances in the employments themselves, which, either really, or at least in the imaginations of men, make up for a small pecuniary gain in some and counter-balance a great one in others. . . .[9]

Smith then stressed the difference between the "whole advantages and disadvantages" of a particular job and the wages paid for the job. Even with perfect freedom of access to jobs and no skill differentials, wage rate differences can persist because of differences in the attractiveness of certain jobs. The market operates to equate the total attractiveness of jobs, not the pecuniary rewards of these jobs. Economists refer to those wage rate differences that relate to the amenities of various jobs as *compensating differentials* because higher wages are presumed to compensate for unpleasant working conditions.

---

[9] A. Smith, *The Wealth of Nations* (New York: Random House, Modern Library Edition, 1937), chap. 10, p. 1.

FIGURE 22.4

COMPENSATING WAGE DIFFERENTIALS

The demand curve for labor is assumed to be the same for both a "pleasant" job and an "unpleasant" one. However, the supply curves (S_p and S_u, respectively) differ for the two types of jobs. This causes wages to differ between the jobs. The higher wage rate for the unpleasant job (w_u) is said to "compensate" for the nature of the job.

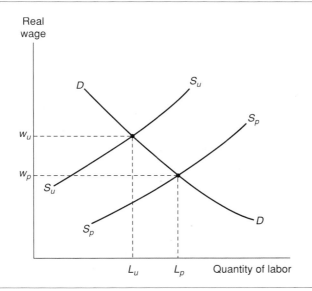

Figure 22.4 illustrates a simple example of the way in which compensating differentials might arise. It assumes that there are two jobs: one "pleasant" and the other "unpleasant." The demand curve of firms for workers to fill those jobs is assumed to be the same for both jobs. There are no differences in the skills of workers that might lead to differing demand conditions. The demand curve for both jobs is represented by the curve *DD*. Because the jobs differ in attractiveness, the supply of labor to them will differ. The curve S_u represents the supply curve to the unpleasant job, and the equilibrium wage is given by w_u. At this wage, firms in the unpleasant industry will demand L_u labor-hours of labor input, and this is what individuals are willing to supply. Similarly, the curve S_p represents the supply curve of workers to the pleasant job. This curve lies to the right of the S_u curve because of the differences in the jobs: At any given wage individuals are willing to supply

more labor to the pleasant job. By the interaction of supply and demand, an equilibrium wage rate of w_p will be established for the pleasant job. This wage will be below w_u, and the difference between w_u and w_p is a wage differential that compensates for the unpleasantness of the first job. The equilibrium shown in Figure 22.4 is stable: There is no incentive for a worker to transfer from one job to the other. The net advantages of the two jobs have been equalized.

LABOR UNIONS

Workers may at times find it advantageous to join together in a labor union in order to pursue goals that can more effectively be accomplished by a group. If association with a union were wholly voluntary, it could be assumed that every union member derives a positive benefit from belonging. Compulsory membership (the "closed shop"), however, is frequently enforced in order to maintain the viability of the union organization. If all workers were left on their own to decide on membership, their rational decision might be not to join the union, and hence avoid dues and other restrictions. However, they would benefit from the higher wages and better working conditions that have been won by the union. What appears to be rational from each individual worker's point of view may prove to be irrational from a group's point of view, since the union is undermined by "free riders." Compulsory membership therefore may be a necessary means of maintaining an effective union coalition.[10]

Unions' Goals

As in our discussion of the theory of the firm, we shall start our analysis of union behavior by defining the goals toward which a union strives. A first assumption we might make is that the goals of a union are in some sense an adequate representation of the goals of its members. This assumption avoids the problem of union leadership and disregards the personal aspirations of those leaders, which may be in conflict with rank-and-file goals. Union leaders therefore are assumed to be conduits for expressing the desires of the membership.[11] In the United States union goals have tended to be oriented toward "bread-and-butter" issues. The programs of major unions have not

---

[10] For a more complete discussion of the issues raised in this and later sections, see J. Dunlop, *Wage Determination under Trade Unions* (New York: Crowell-Collier and Macmillan, 1944). For a more recent analysis, see H. S. Farber, "The Analysis of Union Behavior" in O. C. Ashenfelter and R. Layard, eds., *Handbook of Labor Economics*, vol. 2 (Amsterdam: North-Holland Publishing Co., 1986), pp. 1039–1089.

[11] Much recent analysis, however, revolves around whether "potential" union members have some voice in setting union goals and how union goals may affect the desires of workers with differing amounts of seniority on the job.

emphasized the promotion of radical social change, except briefly in the early 1900s. Rather, unions have attempted to exert an effect solely in the labor market, and in this they have had some success.

In some respects, strong unions can be analyzed in the same way as a monopoly firm. The union faces a demand curve for labor; because it is the sole source of supply, it can choose at which point on this curve it will operate. The point that is actually chosen by the union will obviously depend on what particular goals it has decided to pursue. Three possible choices are illustrated in Figure 22.5. For example, the union may choose to offer that quantity of labor that maximizes the total wage bill $(w \cdot L)$. If this is the case, it will offer that quantity for which the "marginal revenue" from labor demand is equal to 0. This quantity is given by L_1 in Figure 22.5, and the wage rate associated with this quantity is w_1. The point E_1 is therefore the preferred wage-quantity combination. Notice that at wage rate w_1 there may be an excess supply of labor, and the union must somehow allocate those jobs that are available to those workers who

FIGURE 22.5

THREE POSSIBLE POINTS ON THE LABOR DEMAND CURVE THAT A MONOPOLISTIC UNION MIGHT CHOOSE

A union has a monopoly in the supply of labor. It therefore may choose that point on the demand curve for labor that it most prefers. Three such points are shown in the figure. At point E_1 total labor payments $(w \cdot L)$ are maximized; at E_2 the economic rent that workers receive is maximized; and at E_3 the total amount of labor services supplied is maximized.

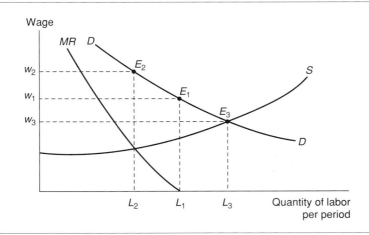

want them. Since it may be difficult to initiate transfers between workers with jobs and those without jobs, this equilibrium may be unstable within the union itself.

Another possible goal that the union may pursue would be to choose the quantity of labor that would maximize the total economic rent (that is, wages less opportunity costs) obtained by those members who are employed. This would necessitate choosing that quantity of labor for which the additional total wages obtained by having one more employed union member (the marginal revenue) are equal to the extra cost of luring that member into the market. The union therefore should choose that quantity, L_2, at which the marginal revenue curve crosses the supply curve.[12] The wage rate associated with this quantity is w_2, and the desired wage-quantity combination is labeled E_2 in the diagram. With the wage w_2, many individuals who desire to work at the prevailing wage are left unemployed. Perhaps the union may "tax" the large economic rent earned by those who do work in order to transfer income to those who don't.

A third possibility would be for the union to aim for maximum employment of its members. This would involve choosing the point w_3, L_3, which is precisely the point that would result if the market were organized in a perfectly competitive way. No employment greater than L_3 could be achieved, since the quantity of labor that union members supply would be reduced for wages less than w_3.

EXAMPLE 22.3

MODELING A UNION

In Example 21.4 we examined a monopsonistic hirer of coal miners who faced a supply curve given by

$$L = 50w. \tag{22.31}$$

In order to study possibilities for unionization to combat this monopsonist, assume (contrary to Example 21.4) that the monopsonist has a downward-sloping marginal revenue product for labor curve of the form

$$MRP = 70 - .1L. \tag{22.32}$$

---

[12] Mathematically, the union's goal is to choose L so as to maximize $wL -$ (area under S), where S is the compensated supply curve for labor and reflects workers' opportunity costs in terms of foregone leisure.

It is easy to show that without an effective union the monopsonist in this situation will choose the same wage-hiring combination it did in Example 21.4—500 workers will be hired at a wage of $10.

If the union can establish control over labor supply to the mine owner, several other options become possible. The union could press for the competitive solution, for example. A contract of $L = 583$, $w = 11.66$ would equate supply and demand. Alternatively, the union could act as a monopolist facing the demand curve given by Equation 22.32. It could calculate the marginal increment yielded by supplying additional workers as

$$\frac{d(L \cdot MRP)}{dL} = 70 - .2L. \tag{22.33}$$

The intersection between this "marginal revenue" curve and the labor supply curve (which indicates the "marginal opportunity cost" of workers' labor supply decisions) yields

$$\frac{L}{50} = 70 - .2L \tag{22.34}$$

or

$$3,500 = 11L. \tag{22.35}$$

Such a calculation would therefore suggest a contract of $L = 318$ and a wage (MRP) of $38.20. The fact that both the competitive and union monopoly supply contracts differ significantly from the monopsonist's preferred contract indicates that the ultimate outcome here is likely to be determined through bilateral bargaining. Notice also that wages differ significantly depending on which side has market power.

QUERY: Which, if any, of the wage contracts described in this example might represent a Nash equilibrium as described in Chapters 10 and 20?

EXAMPLE 22.4

A UNION BARGAINING MODEL

Game theory can also be used to gain insights into the impact of unions. As a simple illustration, suppose that a union and a firm engage in a two-stage game. In the first stage, the union sets the wage rate that its workers will accept. Given this wage, the firm then chooses its employment level. This two-stage game can be solved by backward induction. Given the wage, specified by the union, w, the firm's second-stage problem is to maximize

$$\pi = TR(L) - wL, \tag{22.36}$$

where TR is the total revenue function of the firm expressed as a function of employment. The first-order condition for a maximum here (assuming that the wage is fixed) is the familiar

$$TR'(L) = w. \tag{22.37}$$

Assuming L^* solves Equation 22.37, the union's goal is to choose w to maximize utility

$$U(w, L) = U[w, L^*(w)] \tag{22.38}$$

and the first-order condition for a maximum is

$$U_1 + U_2L' = 0 \tag{22.39}$$

or

$$U_1/U_2 = L'. \tag{22.40}$$

In words, the union should choose w so that its *MRS* is equal to the slope of the firm's labor demand function. The w^*, L^* combination resulting from this game is clearly a Nash equilibrium.

Efficiency of the Labor Contract.   The labor contract w^*, L^* is Pareto inefficient. To see that, notice that Equation 22.40 implies that small movements along the firm's labor demand curve (L) leave the union equally well off. But the envelope theorem implies that a decline in w must increase profits to the firm. Hence, there must exist a contract, w', L' (where $w' < w^*$, $L' > L^*$), with which both the firm and union are better off.

The inefficiency of the labor contract in this two-stage game is similar to the inefficiency of some of the repeated Nash equilibria that we studied in Chapters 10 and 20. This suggests that, with repeated rounds of contract negotiations, trigger strategies might be developed that form a subgame perfect equilibrium and maintain Pareto superior outcomes. For a simple example, see Problem 22.9.[13]

QUERY: Suppose that the firm's total revenue function differed depending on whether the economy was in an expansion or a recession. What kinds of labor contract might be Pareto optimal?

---

[13] A much more complete discussion of game-theoretic models of repeated games and wage bargaining is provided in M. Espinosa and C. Rhee, "Efficient Wage Bargaining as a Repeated Game," *Quarterly Journal of Economics* (September 1989): 565–588.

SUMMARY

This chapter was primarily concerned with the question of labor supply by individuals. By treating work as one of a number of possible ways that an individual might allocate his or her time, the analysis of labor supply was shown to be a further application of the general theory of utility maximization. Some of the results stemming from this approach were:

- A utility-maximizing individual will choose to work that number of hours for which the marginal rate of substitution of leisure for consumption is equal to his or her real wage rate.

- An increase in the real wage creates income and substitution effects that operate in different directions in their effect on labor supply. This result can be shown using a Slutsky-type equation similar to that developed in Chapter 5.

- The theory of time allocation is relevant to a number of other economic decisions in addition to the labor supply decision. Since most activities require time to complete them, the notion that they have both market prices and time prices has far-reaching consequences for economic theory.

- Jobs may differ in their relative attractiveness, and this may give rise to compensating wage differentials. Such differentials represent equilibrium market outcomes and can persist until supply or demand conditions in the various job markets change.

- Unions can be treated analytically as monopoly suppliers of labor. Labor market equilibrium in the presence of unions will depend on what goals the union chooses to pursue in this supply decision and in the bargaining between unions and firms.

PROBLEMS

22.1
Suppose there are 8,000 hours in a year (actually there are 8,760) and that an individual has a potential market wage of $5 per hour.
a. What is the individual's full income? If he or she chooses to devote 75 percent of this income to leisure, how many hours will be worked?
b. Suppose a rich uncle dies and leaves the individual an annual income of $4,000 per year. If he or she continues to devote 75 percent of full income to leisure, how many hours will be worked?
c. How would your answer to part (b) change if the market wage were $10 per hour instead of $5 per hour?
d. Graph the individual's supply of labor curve implied by parts (b) and (c).

22.2
Mr. Peabody has a utility function $U = \sqrt{C \cdot H}$ and is maximizing his utility at $U = 20$ when he works 14 hours a day. Would he be willing to give up an hour

of his leisure to drive Mrs. Atterboy to the wrestling match if she offered him $5?

22.3
Using the concept of the opportunity cost of time, discuss the following:
a. Which persons might you expect to pay the higher fares to fly the faster Concorde to Europe?
b. Which individuals do you expect would be more likely to stand in long lines and even camp out overnight to purchase tickets to a sporting event?
c. Are greens fees a larger fraction of the total cost of a golf game for a prospering physician or a peanut vendor?
d. How would the degree of traffic congestion affect which individuals drive to work and which take mass transit?

22.4
An individual receives utility from daily income (Y), given by

$$U(Y) = 100Y - \frac{1}{2}Y^2.$$

The only source of income is earnings. Hence, $Y = wL$, where w is the hourly wage and L is hours worked per day. The individual knows of a job that pays $5 per hour for a certain 8-hour day. What wage must be offered for a construction job where hours of work are random with a mean of 8 hours and a standard deviation of 6 hours to get the individual to accept this more "risky" job?

Hint: This problem makes use of the statistical identity

$$E(X^2) = \text{Var } X + E(X)^2,$$

where E means "expected value."

22.5
A family with two adult members seeks to maximize a utility function of the form

$$U(C, H_1, H_2),$$

where C is family consumption and H_1 and H_2 are hours of leisure of each family member. Choices are constrained by

$$C = w_1(24 - H_1) + w_2(24 - H_2) + N,$$

where w_1 and w_2 are the wages of each family member and N is nonlabor income.
a. Without attempting a mathematical presentation, use the notions of substitution and income effects to discuss the likely signs of the cross-substitution effects $\partial H_1 / \partial w_2$ and $\partial H_2 / \partial w_1$.
b. Suppose that one family member (say, individual 1) can work in the home, thereby converting leisure hours into consumption according to the function

$$C_1 = f(H_1),$$

where $f' > 0$, $f'' < 0$. How might this additional option affect the optimal division of work among family members?

22.6
A welfare program for low-income people offers a family a basic grant of $6,000 per year. This grant is reduced by $.75 for each $1 of other income the family has.

a. How much in welfare benefits does the family receive if it has no other income? If the head of the family earns $2,000 per year? How about $4,000 per year?
b. At what level of earnings does the welfare grant become zero?
c. Assume that the head of this family can earn $4 per hour and that the family has no other income. What is the annual budget constraint for this family if it does not participate in the welfare program? That is, how are consumption (C) and hours of leisure (H) related?
d. What is the budget constraint if the family opts to participate in the welfare program? (Remember, the welfare grant can only be positive.)
e. Graph your results from parts (c) and (d).
f. Suppose the government changes the rules of the welfare program to permit families to keep 50 percent of what they earn. How would this change your answer to parts (d) and (e)?
g. Using your results from part (f), can you predict whether the head of this family will work more or less under the new rules described in part (f)?

22.7
Suppose that a union has a fixed supply of labor to sell. If the union desires to maximize the total wage bill, what wage rate will it demand? How would your answer change if unemployed workers were paid unemployment insurance at the rate u per worker and the union now desired to maximize the sum of the wage bill and the total amount of unemployment compensation?

22.8
Universal Fur is located in Clyde, Baffin Island, and sells high-quality fur bow ties throughout the world at a price of $5 each. The production function for fur bow ties (Q) is given by

$$Q = 240X - 2X^2,$$

where X is the quantity of pelts used each week. Pelts are supplied only by Dan's Trading Post, which obtains them by hiring Eskimo trappers at a rate of $10 per day. Dan's weekly production function for pelts is given by

$$X = \sqrt{L},$$

where L represents the number of days of Eskimo time used each week.

a. For a quasi-competitive case in which both Universal Fur and Dan's Trading Post act as price takers for pelts, what will be the equilibrium price (P_X) and how many pelts will be traded?

b. Suppose Dan acts as a monopolist, while Universal Fur continues to be a price taker. What equilibrium will emerge in the pelt market?

c. Suppose Universal Fur acts as a monopsonist but that Dan acts as a price taker. What will the equilibrium be?

d. Graph your results and discuss the type of equilibrium that is likely to emerge in the bilateral monopoly bargaining between Universal Fur and Dan.

22.9
Following in the spirit of the labor market game described in Example 22.4, suppose that the firm's total revenue function is given by

$$TR = 10L - L^2$$

and that the union's utility is simply a function of the total wage bill

$$U(w, L) = wL.$$

a. What is the Nash equilibrium wage contract in the two-stage game described in Example 22.4?

b. Show that the alternative wage contract $w' = L' = 4$ is Pareto superior to the contract identified in part (a).

c. Under what conditions would the contract described in part (b) be sustainable as a subgame perfect equilibrium?

SUGGESTED READINGS

Ashenfelter, O. C., and R. Layard. *Handbook of Labor Economics* (2 volumes). Amsterdam: North-Holland Publishing Co., 1986.
Collection of survey articles on many of the topics touched on in this chapter. Particularly thorough articles on men's and women's labor supply and on the economics of unions.

Becker, G. S. "An Economic Analysis of Fertility." In *Demographic and Economic Change in Developed Countries*, National Bureau Conference Series No. 11. Princeton, N.J.: Princeton University Press, 1960.
First economic approach to the theory of childbearing.

_____. "A Theory of the Allocation of Time." *Economic Journal* 75 (September 1965): 493–517.
Fundamental work on time allocation including both labor supply and consumption decisions.

Killingsworth, Mark R. *Labor Supply*. Cambridge: Cambridge University Press, 1983.

A complete survey of the literature. Interesting observations on family labor supply.

Moffitt, R. A., and K. C. Kehrer. "The Effect of Tax and Transfer Programs on Labor Supply: The Evidence from the Income Maintenance Experiments." In R. G. Ehrenberg, ed., *Research in Labor Economics*, vol. 4. Greenwich, Conn.: JAI Press, 1981, pp. 103–150.
Complete survey of the experimental evidence in labor supply, especially in relationship to the effects of transfer programs.

Parsley, C. J. "Labor Unions and Wages: A Survey." *Journal of Economic Literature* (March 1980): 1–31.
A survey of the empirical literature with an extensive bibliography.

Rees, A. "The Effects of Unions on Resource Allocation." *Journal of Law and Economics* 6 (October 1963): 69–78.
Classic paper on the allocational effects of unions.

CHAPTER 23

CAPITAL

In this chapter we provide an introduction to the theory of capital. In many ways that theory resembles our analysis of input pricing in general—the principles of profit maximizing input choice do not change. But capital theory adds an important time dimension to economic decision-making and our goal here is to explore that extra dimension. We begin with a broad characterization of the capital accumulation process and the notion of the rate of return. Then we turn to more specific models of economic behavior over time.

CAPITAL AND THE RATE OF RETURN

When we speak of the capital stock of an economy, we mean the sum total of machines, buildings, and other reproducible resources that are in existence at some point in time. These assets represent some part of an economy's past output that was not consumed, but was instead set aside to be used for production in the future. All societies, from the most primitive to the most complex, engage in capital accumulation. Hunters in a primitive society taking time off from hunting to make arrows, individuals in a modern society using part of their incomes to buy houses, or governments taxing citizens in order to purchase dams and post office buildings are all engaging in essentially the same sort of activity: Some portion of current output is being set aside for use in producing output in future periods. Present "sacrifice" for future gain is the essential aspect of capital accumulation.

Rate of Return

The process of capital accumulation is pictured schematically in Figure 23.1. In both panels of the figure, society is initially consuming level C_0 and has been doing so for some time. At time t_1 a decision is made to withhold some output (amount s) from current consumption for one period. Starting in period t_2 this withheld consumption is in some way put to use producing

FIGURE 23.1

TWO VIEWS OF CAPITAL ACCUMULATION

In (a), society withdraws some current consumption (s) in order to gorge itself (with x extra consumption) in the next period. The one-period rate of return would be measured by $x/s - 1$. The society in (b) takes a more long-term view and uses s to increase its consumption perpetually by y. The perpetual rate of return would be given by y/s.

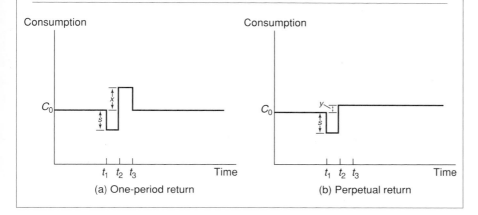

(a) One-period return   (b) Perpetual return

future consumption. An important concept connected with this process is the *rate of return*, which is earned on that consumption that is put aside. In panel (a), for example, all of the withheld consumption is used to produce additional output only in period t_2. Consumption is increased by amount x in period t_2 and then returns to the long-run level C_0. Society has saved in one year in order to splurge in the next year. The (one-period) rate of return from this activity would be defined as follows:

DEFINITION

Single Period Rate of Return The *single period rate of return* (r_1) on an investment is the extra consumption provided in period 2 as a fraction of the consumption foregone in period 1. That is,

$$r_1 = \frac{x - s}{s} = \frac{x}{s} - 1. \tag{23.1}$$

If $x > s$ (if more consumption comes out of this process than went into it), we would say that the one-period rate of return to capital accumulation is positive. For example, if withholding 100 units from current consumption permitted society to consume an extra 110 units next year, the one-period rate of return would be

$$\frac{110}{100} - 1 = 0.10$$

or 10 percent.

In panel (b) of Figure 23.1, society is assumed to take a more long-term view in its capital accumulation. Again, an amount s is set aside at time t_1. Now, however, this set-aside consumption is used to raise the consumption level for all periods in the future. If the permanent level of consumption is raised to $C_0 + y$, we define the perpetual rate of return as follows:

DEFINITION

Perpetual Rate of Return The *perpetual rate of return* (r_∞) is the permanent increment to future consumption expressed as a fraction of the initial consumption foregone. That is,

$$r_\infty = \frac{y}{s}. \tag{23.2}$$

If capital accumulation succeeds in raising C_0 permanently, r_∞ will be positive. For example, suppose that society set aside 100 units of output in period t_1 to be devoted to capital accumulation. If this capital would permit output to be raised by 10 units for every period in the future (starting at time period t_2), the perpetual rate of return would be 10 percent.

When economists speak of the rate of return to capital accumulation, then, they have in mind something between these two extremes. Somewhat loosely we shall speak of the rate of return as being a measure of the terms at which consumption today may be turned into consumption tomorrow (this will be made more explicit soon). A natural question to ask is how the economy's rate of return is determined. Again, the answer must somehow revolve around the supply and demand for present and future goods. In the next section we present a simple two-period model in which this supply-demand interaction is demonstrated.

DETERMINATION OF THE RATE OF RETURN

In this section we will describe how operation of supply and demand in the market for "future" goods establishes an equilibrium rate of return. We begin by analyzing the connection between the rate of return and the "price" of future goods. Then we show how individuals and firms are likely to react to this price. Finally, these actions are brought together (as we have done for the analysis of other markets) to demonstrate the determination of an equilibrium price of future goods and to examine some of the characteristics of that solution.

For most of our analysis in this chapter, we will assume that there are only two periods to be considered—the current period (to be denoted by the subscript 0) and the next period (denoted by the subscript 1). We will use r to denote the (one-period) rate of return between these two periods. Hence, as defined in the previous section then,

Rate of Return and Price of Future Goods

$$r = \frac{\Delta C_1}{\Delta C_0} - 1, \tag{23.3}$$

where we use the Δ notation to refer to the change in consumption in the two periods. Rewriting Equation 23.3 yields

$$\frac{\Delta C_1}{\Delta C_0} = 1 + r \tag{23.4}$$

or

$$\frac{\Delta C_0}{\Delta C_1} = \frac{1}{1 + r}. \tag{23.5}$$

But the term on the left of Equation 23.5 simply records how much C_0 must be foregone if C_1 is to be increased by one unit; that is, the expression represents the relative "price" of one unit of C_1 in terms of C_0. So we have defined the price of future goods:

DEFINITION

Price of Future Goods The relative *price of future goods* (P_1) is defined to be the quantity of present goods that must be foregone to increase future consumption by one unit. That is,

$$P_1 = \frac{\Delta C_0}{\Delta C_1} = \frac{1}{1 + r}. \tag{23.6}$$

We now proceed to develop a demand-supply analysis of the determination of P_1. By so doing we also will have developed a theory of the determination of r, the rate of return in this simple model.

The theory of the demand for future goods is one further application of the utility-maximization model developed in Part II of this book. Here the individual's utility depends on present and future consumption [that is, utility = $U(C_0, C_1)$], and he or she must decide how much of current wealth

Demand for Future Goods

FIGURE 23.2

INDIVIDUAL'S INTERTEMPORAL UTILITY MAXIMIZATION

When faced with the intertemporal budget constraint $W = C_0 + P_1 C_1$, the individual will maximize utility by choosing to consume C_0^* currently and C_1^* in the next period. A fall in P_1 (an increase in the rate of return, r) will cause C_1 to rise, but the effect on C_0 is indeterminate since substitution and income effects operate in opposite directions (assuming that both C_0 and C_1 are normal goods).

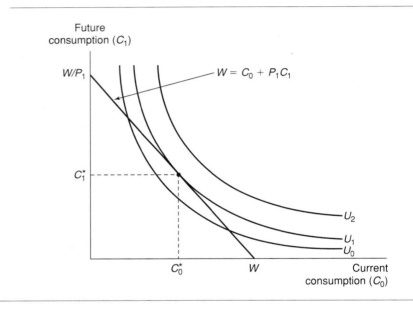

(W) to allocate to these two goods.[1] Wealth not spent on current consumption can be invested at the rate of return r in order to obtain consumption next period. As before, P_1 reflects the present cost of future consumption, and the individual's budget constraint is given by

$$W = C_0 + P_1 C_1. \qquad (23.7)$$

This constraint is illustrated in Figure 23.2. If the individual chooses to spend all of his or her wealth on C_0, total current consumption will be W with no consumption occurring in period 2. Alternatively, if $C_0 = 0$, C_1 will be given

---

[1] For an analysis of the case where the individual has income in both periods, see Problem 23.1.

by $W/P_1 = W(1 + r)$. That is, if all wealth is invested at the rate of return r, current wealth will grow to $W(1 + r)$ in period 2.[2]

Utility Maximization

Imposition of the individual's indifference curve map for C_0 and C_1 onto the budget constraint in Figure 23.2 illustrates utility maximization. Here utility is maximized at the point C_0^*, C_1^*. The individual consumes C_0^* currently and chooses to save $W - C_0^*$ to consume next period. This future consumption can be found from the budget constraint as

$$P_1 C_1^* = W - C_0^* \qquad (23.8)$$

or

$$C_1^* = \frac{(W - C_0^*)}{P_1} \qquad (23.9)$$

$$= (W - C_0^*)(1 + r). \qquad (23.10)$$

In other words, wealth that is not currently consumed $(W - C_0^*)$ is invested at the rate of return, r, and will grow to yield C_1^* in the next period.

EXAMPLE 23.1

INTERTEMPORAL IMPATIENCE

Individuals' utility-maximizing choices over time will obviously depend on how they feel about the relative merits of consuming currently or waiting to consume in the future. One way of reflecting the possibility that people may exhibit some impatience in their choices is to assume that the utility from future consumption is implicitly discounted in the individual's mind. For example, we might assume that the utility function for consumption, $U(C)$, is the same in both periods (with $U' > 0$, $U'' < 0$), but that period 1's utility is discounted in the individual's mind by a "rate of time preference" of $1/(1 + \delta)$ (where $\delta > 0$). If the intertemporal utility function is also separable (for more discussion of this concept, see the extensions to Chapter 6), we can write

$$U(C_0, C_1) = U(C_0) + \frac{1}{1 + \delta} U(C_1). \qquad (23.11)$$

---

[2] This observation yields an alternative interpretation of the budget constraint given by Equation 23.7, which can be written in terms of the rate of return as

$$W = C_0 + \frac{C_1}{1 + r}.$$

This records the fact that it is the "present value" of C_1 that enters into the individual's current budget constraint. The concept of present value is discussed in more detail later in this chapter.

Maximization of this function subject to the intertemporal budget constraint

$$W = C_0 + \frac{C_1}{1 + r} \tag{23.12}$$

yields the following Lagrangian expression:

$$\mathcal{L} = U(C_0, C_1) + \lambda \left[W - C_0 - \frac{C_1}{1 + r} \right], \tag{23.13}$$

and the first-order conditions for a maximum are

$$\frac{\partial \mathcal{L}}{\partial C_0} = U'(C_0) - \lambda = 0$$

$$\frac{\partial \mathcal{L}}{\partial C_1} = \frac{1}{1 + \delta} U'(C_1) - \frac{\lambda}{1 + r} = 0 \tag{23.14}$$

$$\frac{\partial \mathcal{L}}{\partial \lambda} = W - C_0 - \frac{C_1}{1 + r} = 0.$$

Dividing the first and second of these and rearranging terms gives[3]

$$U'(C_0) = \frac{1 + r}{1 + \delta} U'(C_1). \tag{23.15}$$

Since the utility function for consumption was assumed to be the same in two periods, we can conclude that $C_0 = C_1$ if $r = \delta$, that $C_0 > C_1$ if $\delta > r$ [since to obtain $U'(C_0) < U'(C_1)$ requires $C_0 > C_1$], and that $C_0 < C_1$ for $r > \delta$. Whether this individual's consumption increases or decreases from period 0 to period 1 therefore will depend on exactly how impatient he or she is. Even though a consumer may have a preference for present goods ($\delta > 0$), he or she may still consume more in the future than in the present if the rate of return received on savings is high enough.

QUERY: If two individuals are equally impatient but face different rates of return, which will exhibit the greatest increase of C_1 over C_0?

Effects of Changes in r A comparative statics analysis of the equilibrium illustrated in Figure 23.2 is straightforward. If P_1 falls (that is, if r rises), both income and substitution effects will cause more C_1 to be demanded, except in the unlikely event that C_1 is an inferior good. Hence, the demand curve for C_1 will be downward sloping. An increase in r effectively lowers the price of C_1, and consumption of that good thereby increases. This demand curve is labeled D in Figure 23.3.

---

[3] Equation 23.15 is sometimes called the "Euler equation" for intertemporal utility maximization.

FIGURE 23.3

DETERMINATION OF THE EQUILIBRIUM PRICE OF FUTURE GOODS

The point P_1^*, C_1^* represents an equilibrium in the market for future goods. The equilibrium price of future goods determines the rate of return via Equation 23.16.

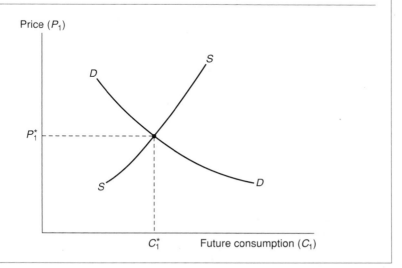

Before leaving our discussion of individuals' intertemporal decisions, we should point out that our analysis does not permit an unambiguous statement to be made about the sign of $\partial C_0 / \partial P_1$. In Figure 23.2 substitution and income effects work in opposite directions, and no definite prediction is possible. A fall in P_1 will cause the individual to substitute C_1 for C_0 in his or her consumption plans. But the fall in P_1 raises the real value of wealth, and the income effect causes both C_0 and C_1 to increase. Phrased somewhat differently, the model illustrated in Figure 23.2 does not permit a definite prediction about how changes in the rate of return affect current-period wealth accumulation (saving). A higher r produces substitution effects that favor more saving and income effects that favor less. Ultimately therefore, the direction of the effect must be an empirical question.

In one sense the analysis of the supply of future goods is quite simple. We can argue that an increase in the relative price of future goods (P_1) will induce firms to produce more of them, since the yield from doing so is now greater. This reaction is reflected in the positively sloped supply curve S in Figure 23.3. It might be expected that, as in our previous perfectly competitive

Supply of Future Goods

analysis, this supply curve reflects the increasing marginal costs (or diminishing returns) that firms experience when attempting to turn present goods into future ones through capital accumulation.

Unfortunately, delving deeper into the nature of capital accumulation runs into complications that have occupied economists for hundreds of years.[4] Basically, all of these derive from problems in developing a tractable model of the capital accumulation process. For our model of individual behavior this problem did not arise, since we could assume that the "market" quoted a rate of return to individuals so that they could adapt their behavior to it. We shall also follow this route when describing firms' investment decisions later in this chapter. But to develop an adequate model of capital accumulation by firms, we must describe precisely how C_0 is "turned into" C_1 and to do so would take us too far afield into the intricacies of capital theory. Instead, we will be content to draw the supply curve in Figure 23.3 with a positive slope on the presumption that such a shape is intuitively reasonable. Much of the subsequent analysis in this chapter may serve to convince the reader that this is indeed the case.

Equilibrium Price of Future Goods

Equilibrium in the market shown in Figure 23.3 is at P_1^*, C_1^*. At that point individuals' supply and demand for future goods are in balance, and the required amount of current goods will be put into capital accumulation in order to produce C_1^* in the future.[5]

There are a number of reasons to expect that P_1 will be less than 1; that is, it will cost less than the sacrifice of one current good to "buy" one good in the future. As we showed in Example 23.1, it might be argued that individuals require some reward for waiting. Everyday adages ("a bird in the hand is worth two in the bush," "live for today") and more substantial realities (the uncertainty of the future and the finiteness of life) suggest that individuals are generally impatient in their consumption decisions. Hence, capital accumulation such as that shown in Figure 23.3 will take place only if the current sacrifice is in some way worthwhile.

There are also supply reasons for believing P_1 will be less than 1. All of these involve the idea that capital accumulation is "productive": Sacrificing one good currently will yield more than one good in the future. Some simple examples of the productivity of capital investment are provided by such pastoral activities as the growing of trees or the aging of wine and cheese. Tree nursery owners and vineyard and dairy operators "abstain" from

---

[4] For a discussion of some of this debate, see M. Blaug, *Economic Theory in Retrospect*, rev. ed. (Homewood, Ill.: Richard D. Irwin, 1978), chap. 12.

[5] This is a much simplified form of an analysis originally presented by I. Fisher, *The Rate of Interest* (New York: Macmillan Co., 1907).

selling their wares in the belief that time will make them more valuable in the future. Although it is obvious that capital accumulation in a modern industrial society is more complex than growing trees (consider building a steel mill or an electric power system), economists believe the two processes have certain similarities. In both cases investing current goods makes the production process longer and more complex and therefore improves the overall productive power of other resources used in production.

The Equilibrium Rate of Return

We can now define the relationship of the rate of return (r) to what we have called the price of future goods by the formula

$$P_1^* = \frac{1}{1 + r}. \qquad (23.16)$$

Since we believe that P_1^* will be less than 1, the rate of return (r) will be positive. For example, if $P_1^* = .9$, r will equal approximately .11, and we would say that the rate of return to capital accumulation is "11 percent." By withholding one unit of current consumption, the consumption of future goods can be increased by 1.11. The rate of return and P_1 are equivalent ways of measuring the terms on which present goods can be turned into future goods.

Rate of Return, Real Interest Rates, and Nominal Interest Rates

The concept of the rate of return that we have been analyzing so far in this chapter is sometimes used synonymously with the related concept of the "real" interest rate. In this context both are taken to refer to the real return that is available from capital accumulation. The term "interest rate" is used much more widely in economics, and it is important to point out the difference between these other uses and the one employed here. Most importantly, interest rates observed in the real world will usually be nominal rates that reflect not only real returns to capital accumulation but also expected inflation rates as well. When the general price level is changing, borrowers and lenders will want to be compensated for such changes in purchasing power. Specifically, if overall prices are expected to increase by $\dot{P}_e$ between two periods (that is, a $\dot{P}_e$ of .10 would be a 10 percent inflation rate), we would expect the nominal interest rate (R) to be given by the equation

$$1 + R = (1 + r)(1 + \dot{P}_e), \qquad (23.17)$$

since a would-be lender would expect to be compensated for both the opportunity cost of not investing in real capital (r) and for the general rise in prices ($\dot{P}_e$). Expansion of Equation 23.17 yields

$$1 + R = 1 + r + \dot{P}_e + r\dot{P}_e, \tag{23.18}$$

and assuming $r \cdot \dot{P}_e$ is small, we have the simpler approximation

$$R = r + \dot{P}_e. \tag{23.19}$$

If the real rate of return is 4 percent (.04) and the expected rate of inflation is 10 percent (.10), the nominal interest rate would be approximately 14 percent (.14). The difference, therefore, between observed nominal interest rates and real interest rates may be substantial.

THE FIRM'S DEMAND FOR CAPITAL

Firms rent machines in accordance with the same principles of profit maximization that we derived in Chapter 21. Specifically, in a perfectly competitive market the firm will choose to hire that number of machines for which the marginal revenue product is precisely equal to their market rental rate. In this section we first investigate the determinants of this market rental rate, and we assume that all machines are rented. Later in the section, because most firms buy machines and hold them until they deteriorate rather than rent them, we shall examine the particular problems raised by that situation.

Determinants of Market Rental Rates

Consider a firm in the business of renting machines to other firms. Suppose that firm owns a machine (say, a car or a backhoe) that has a current market price of P. How much will the firm charge its clients for the use of the machine? The owner of the machine faces two kinds of costs: depreciation on the machine and the *opportunity cost* of having its funds tied up in a machine rather than in an investment earning the current available rate of return. If it is assumed that depreciation costs per period are a constant percentage (d) of the machine's market price and that the real interest rate is given by r, then the total costs to the machine owner for one period are given by

$$Pd + Pr = P(r + d). \tag{23.20}$$

If we assume that the machine rental market is perfectly competitive, no long-run profits can be earned by renting machines. The workings of the market will ensure that the rental rate per period for the machine (v) is exactly equal to the costs of the machine owner. Hence, we have the basic result that

$$v = P(r + d). \tag{23.21}$$

The competitive rental rate is the sum of foregone interest and depreciation costs that the machine's owner must pay. For example, suppose that the real interest rate is 5 percent (that is, 0.05) and that the physical depreciation rate is 15 percent (0.15). Suppose also that the current market price of the machine is $10,000. Then, in this simple model, the machine would have an annual rental rate of $2,000 [= $10,000 \times (0.05 + 0.15)$] per year; $500 of this would represent the opportunity cost of the funds invested in the machine, and the remaining $1,500 would reflect the physical costs of deterioration.

In the hypothetical case of a machine that does not depreciate ($d = 0$), Equation 23.21 can be written as

Nondepreciating Machines

$$\frac{v}{P} = r. \tag{23.22}$$

This equation says that in equilibrium an infinitely long-lived (nondepreciating) machine is equivalent to a perpetual bond (see the appendix to this chapter) and, hence, must "yield" the market rate of return. The rental rate as a percentage of the machine's price must be equal to r. If $v/P > r$, everyone would rush out to buy machines, since renting out machines would yield more than rates of return elsewhere. Similarly, if $v/P < r$, no one would be in the business of renting out machines, since more could be made on alternative investments. The reader also may notice that v/P is analogous to the concept of a perpetual rate of return, which we discussed in the first section of this chapter. An amount P is given up in order to receive a return of v for every period in the future. In our previous example, if the physical depreciation rate were 0, the annual rental rate for the machine would be $500 ($= 0.05 \times $10,000$). The owner of a machine, by renting out the machine to someone else, will earn 5 percent on the investment. This is exactly what the machine owner could earn on any other investment.

Our analysis so far has assumed that firms rent all of the machines they use. Although such rental does take place in the real world (for example, many firms are in the business of leasing airplanes, trucks, freight cars, and computers to other firms), more commonly firms own the machines they use. A firm will buy a machine and will use the services of the machine in combination with the labor it hires to produce output. The ownership of machines makes the analysis of the demand for capital somewhat more complex than that of the demand for labor. However, by recognizing the important distinction between a *stock* and a *flow*, we can show that these two demands are quite similar.

Ownership of Machines

A firm uses *capital services* to produce output. These services are a *flow* magnitude. It is the number of machine-hours that is relevant to the productive process (just as it is labor-hours), not the number of machines *per se*. Frequently, however, the assumption is made that the flow of capital services is proportional to the *stock* of machines (100 machines, if fully employed for 1 hour, can deliver 100 machine-hours of service); therefore, these two different concepts are used synonymously. If during a period a firm desires a certain number of machine-hours, this is usually taken to mean that the firm desires a certain number of machines. The firm's demand for capital services is also a demand for capital.

A profit-maximizing firm in perfect competition will choose its level of inputs so that the marginal revenue product from an extra unit of any input is equal to its cost. This result also holds for the demand for machine-hours. The cost of capital services is given by the rental rate (v) in Equation 23.21. This cost is borne by the firm whether it rents the machine in the open market or owns the machine itself. In the former case it is an explicit cost, whereas in the latter case it is an implicit cost, since the firm could rent its machine to someone else if it chose to do so. In either case the opportunity cost of machine usage is given by the market rental rate, v. The fact of ownership, to a first approximation, is irrelevant to the determination of cost. Hence, we can apply our prior analysis of input demand:

OPTIMIZATION PRINCIPLE

Demand for Capital   A profit-maximizing firm facing a perfectly competitive rental market for capital will hire additional capital input up to the point at which its marginal revenue product (MRP_K) is equal to the market rental rate, v. Under perfect competition the rental rate will reflect both depreciation costs and opportunity costs of alternative investments. Thus, we have

$$MRP_K = v = P(r + d). \tag{23.23}$$

Theory of Investment   If a firm obeys the profit-maximizing rule of Equation 23.23 and finds that it desires more capital services than can be provided by its currently existing stock of machinery, it has two choices. First, it may hire the additional machines that are needed in the rental market. This would be formally identical to its decision to hire additional labor. Second, the firm can buy new machinery to meet its needs. This second alternative is the one most often chosen; we call the purchase of new equipment by the firm *investment*.

Investment demand is an important component of "aggregate demand" in macroeconomic theory. Frequently, it is assumed that this demand for plant and equipment (that is, machines) is inversely related to the rate of interest, or what we have called the "rate of return." Using the analysis we developed in this part of the text, we can demonstrate the links in this argument. A fall in the interest rate (r) will, *ceteris paribus*, decrease the rental rate on capital (Equation 23.21). Because foregone interest represents an implicit cost for the owner of a machine, a fall in r in effect reduces the price (that is, the rental rate) of capital inputs. This fall in v implies that capital has become a relatively less expensive input, and as we showed in Chapter 21, this will prompt firms to increase their capital usage.

PRESENT DISCOUNTED VALUE APPROACH TO INVESTMENT DECISIONS

When a firm buys a machine, it is in effect buying a stream of net revenues in future periods. In order to decide whether to purchase the machine, the firm must compute the present discounted value of this stream.[6] Only by doing so will the firm have taken adequate account of the effects of foregone interest. This provides an alternative approach to explaining the investment decision.

Consider a firm in the process of deciding whether to buy a particular machine. The machine is expected to last n years and will give its owner a stream of monetary returns (that is, marginal revenue products) in each of the n years. Let the return in year i be represented by R_i. If r is the present interest rate, and if this rate is expected to prevail for the next n years, the present discounted value (PDV) of the net revenue flow from the machine to its owner is given by

$$PDV = \frac{R_1}{1 + r} + \frac{R_2}{(1 + r)^2} + \cdots + \frac{R_n}{(1 + r)^n}. \tag{23.24}$$

This present discounted value represents the total value of the stream of payments that is provided by the machine, once adequate account is taken of the fact that these payments occur in different years. If the PDV of this stream of payments exceeds the price (P) of the machine, the firm, and other similar firms, should make the purchase. Even when the effects of the interest payments that the firm could have earned on its funds had it not purchased the machine are taken into account, the machine promises to return more than its prevailing price. On the other hand, if $P > PDV$, the firm would be better off to invest its funds in some alternative that promises a rate of return of r. When account is taken of foregone interest, the machine does not pay for itself. Thus, in a competitive market the only equilibrium that can prevail is that in which the price of a machine is equal to the present discounted value of the net revenues from the machine. Only in this situation will there be neither an excess demand for machines nor an excess supply of machines. Hence, market equilibrium requires that

---

[6] See the appendix to this chapter for a discussion of present discounted value.

$$P = PDV = \frac{R_1}{1+r} + \frac{R_2}{(1+r)^2} + \cdots + \frac{R_n}{(1+r)^n}. \tag{23.25}$$

We shall now use this condition to show two situations in which the present discounted value criterion of investment reduces to the equilibrium conditions outlined earlier in this chapter.

Simple Case   Assume first that machines are infinitely long-lived and that the marginal revenue product (that is, R_i) is the same in every year. This uniform return also will equal the rental rate for machines (v), since that is what another firm would pay for the machine's use during any period. With these simplifying assumptions we may write the present discounted value from machine ownership as

$$
\begin{aligned}
PDV &= \frac{v}{(1+r)} + \frac{v}{(1+r)^2} + \cdots + \frac{v}{(1+r)^n} + \cdots \\[2mm]
&= v \cdot \left(\frac{1}{(1+r)} + \frac{1}{(1+r)^2} + \cdots + \frac{1}{(1+r)^n} + \cdots \right) \\[2mm]
&= v \cdot \left(\frac{1}{1 - 1/(1+r)} - 1 \right) \tag{23.26} \\[2mm]
&= v \cdot \left(\frac{1+r}{r} - 1 \right) \\[2mm]
&= v \cdot \frac{1}{r}.
\end{aligned}
$$

But since in equilibrium $P = PDV$, this says

$$P = v \cdot \frac{1}{r} \tag{23.27}$$

or

$$\frac{v}{P} = r, \tag{23.28}$$

as was shown in Equation 23.22. For this case the present discounted value criterion gives results identical to those outlined in the previous section.

General Case   Equation 23.21 can be derived for the more general case in which the rental rate on machines is not constant over time and in which there is some depreciation. This analysis is most easily carried out by using continuous time. Suppose that the rental rate for a *new* machine at any time s is given by

$v(s)$. Assume also that the machine depreciates exponentially at the rate of d.[7] The net rental rate (and the marginal revenue product) of a machine therefore declines over time as the machine gets older. In year s the net rental rate on an *old* machine bought in a previous year (t) would be

$$v(s)e^{-d(s - t)},\qquad(23.29)$$

since $s - t$ is the number of years over which the machine has been decaying. For example, suppose that a machine were bought in 1993. Its net rental rate in 1998 then would be the rental rate that is earned by new machines in 1998 [$v(1998)$] discounted by the factor e^{-5d} to account for the amount of depreciation that has taken place over the five years of the machine's life.

If the firm is considering buying the machine when it is new in year t, it should discount all of these net rental amounts back to that date. The present value of the net rental in year s discounted back to year t is therefore (if r is the interest rate)

$$e^{-r(s - t)}v(s)e^{-d(s - t)} = e^{(r + d)t}v(s)e^{-(r + d)s},\qquad(23.30)$$

since, again, $(s - t)$ years elapse from when the machine is bought until when the net rental is received. The present discounted value of a machine bought in year t is therefore the sum (integral) of these present values. This sum should be taken from year t (when the machine is bought) over all years into the future:

$$PDV(t) = \int_t^\infty e^{(r + d)t}v(s)e^{-(r + d)s}ds.\qquad(23.31)$$

Since in equilibrium the price of the machine at year t [$P(t)$] will be equal to this present value, we have the following fundamental equation:

$$P(t) = \int_t^\infty e^{(r + d)t}v(s)e^{-(r + d)s}ds.\qquad(23.32)$$

This rather formidable equation is simply a more complex version of Equation 23.25 and can be used to derive Equation 23.21. First rewrite the equation as

$$P(t) = e^{(r + d)t}\int_t^\infty v(s)e^{-(r + d)s}ds.\qquad(23.33)$$

---

[7] In this view of depreciation, machines are assumed to "evaporate" at a fixed rate per unit of time. This model of decay is in many ways identical to the assumptions of radioactive decay made in physics. There are other possible forms that physical depreciation might take; this is only the most mathematically tractable.

It is important to keep the concept of physical depreciation (depreciation that affects a machine's productivity) distinct from accounting depreciation. The latter concept is important only in that the method of accounting depreciation chosen may affect the rate of taxation on the profits from a machine. From an economic point of view, however, the cost of a machine is a sunk cost: Any choice on how to "write off" this cost is to some extent arbitrary.

Now differentiate with respect to t, using the rule for taking the derivative of a product:

$$\frac{dP(t)}{dt} = (r + d)e^{(r + d)t}\int_{t}^{\infty} v(s)e^{-(r + d)s}ds - e^{(r + d)t}v(t)e^{-(r + d)t}$$

(23.34)

$$= (r + d)P(t) - v(t).$$

Hence,

$$v(t) = (r + d)P(t) - \frac{dP(t)}{dt}.$$

(23.35)

This is precisely the result shown earlier in Equation 23.21, except that the term $-dP(t)/dt$ has been added. The economic explanation for the presence of this term is that it represents the capital gains that accrue to the owner of the machine. If the machine's price can be expected to rise, for example, the owner may accept somewhat less than $(r + d)P$ for its rental.[8] On the other hand, if the price of the machine is expected to fall [$dP(t)/dt < 0$], the owner will require more in rent than is specified in Equation 23.21. If the price of the machine is expected to remain constant over time, $dP(t)/dt = 0$ and the equations are identical. The result of this analysis is to show that there is a definite relationship among the price of a machine at any time, the stream of future profits that the machine promises, and the current rental rate for the machine.

EXAMPLE 23.2

CUTTING DOWN A TREE

As an example of the *PDV* criterion, consider the case of a forester who must decide when to cut down a growing tree. Suppose that the value of the tree at any time, t, is given by $f(t)$ (where $f'(t) > 0$, $f''(t) < 0$) and that L dollars were invested initially as payments to workers who planted the tree. Assume also that the (continuous) market interest rate is given by r. When the tree is planted, the present discounted value of the tree owner's profits is given by

$$PDV(t) = e^{-rt}f(t) - L,$$

(23.36)

which is simply the difference between (the present value of) revenues and present costs. The forester's decision, then, consists of choosing the harvest date, t, to maximize this value. As always, this value may be found by differentiation:

---

[8] For example, rental houses in suburbs with rapidly appreciating house prices will usually rent for less than the landlord's actual costs because the landlord also gains from price appreciation.

$$\frac{dPDV(t)}{dt} = e^{-rt}f'(t) - re^{-rt}f(t) = 0, \tag{23.37}$$

or dividing both sides by e^{-rt}:

$$f'(t) - rf(t) = 0; \tag{23.38}$$

therefore,

$$r = \frac{f'(t)}{f(t)}. \tag{23.39}$$

Two features of this optimal condition are worth noting. First, observe that the cost of the initial labor input drops out upon differentiation. This cost is (even in a literal sense) a "sunk" cost that is irrelevant to the profit-maximizing decision. Second, Equation 23.39 can be interpreted as saying that the tree should be harvested when the rate of interest is equal to the proportional rate of growth of the tree. This result makes intuitive sense. If the tree is growing more rapidly than the prevailing interest rate, its owner should leave his or her funds invested in the tree, since the tree provides the best return available. On the other hand, if the tree is growing less rapidly than the prevailing interest rate, the tree should be cut, and the funds obtained from its sale should be invested elsewhere at the rate r.

Equation 23.39 is only a necessary condition for a maximum. By differentiating Equation 23.38 again it is easy to see that it is also required that at the chosen value of t

$$f''(t) - rf'(t) < 0, \tag{23.40}$$

if the first-order conditions are to represent a true maximum. Since we assumed that $f'(t) > 0$ (the tree is always growing) and that $f''(t) < 0$ (the growth slows over time), it is clear that this condition holds.

A Specific Illustration. Suppose that trees grow according to the equation

$$f(t) = e^{.4\sqrt{t}}. \tag{23.41}$$

This equation always exhibits a positive growth rate $[f'(t) > 0]$ and, since

$$\frac{f'(t)}{f(t)} = \frac{.2}{\sqrt{t}}, \tag{23.42}$$

the tree's proportional growth rate diminishes over time. If the real interest rate were, say, .04, we can solve for the optimal harvesting age as

$$r = .04 = \frac{f'(t)}{f(t)} = \frac{.2}{\sqrt{t}} \tag{23.43}$$

or

$$\sqrt{t} = \frac{.2}{.04} = 5$$

so

$$t^* = 25. \tag{23.44}$$

Up to 25 years of age, the volume of wood in the tree is increasing at a rate in excess of 4 percent per year so the optimal decision is to permit the tree to stand. But, for $t > 25$, the annual growth rate falls below 4 percent, and the forester can find better investments—perhaps planting new trees.

A Change in the Interest Rate. If the real interest rate rises to 5 percent, Equation 23.43 would become

$$r = .05 = \frac{.2}{\sqrt{t}}, \tag{23.45}$$

and the optimal harvest age would be

$$t^* = \left(\frac{.2}{.05} \right)^2 = 16. \tag{23.46}$$

The higher real interest rate discourages investment in trees by prompting the forester to choose an earlier harvest date.[9]

QUERY: Suppose all prices (including those of trees) were rising at 10 percent per year. How would this change the optimal harvesting results in this problem?

OPTIMAL RESOURCE ALLOCATION OVER TIME

The theory of capital is concerned primarily with the allocation of resources over time. Firms and individuals are led to set aside some portion of current production as capital accumulation in order to produce more in future periods. Many economic problems are of this general type: Economic agents must make decisions about additions to or reductions in the level of some stock, and those decisions will affect both current and future well-being. In this section we shall examine how such decisions might be made in an optimal (that is, utility-maximizing) way.

The Mathematical Model of Optimal Control

Two variables are of primary interest for the problem of allocating resources over time: the stock being allocated (K) and a "control" variable (C) being used to effect increases or decreases in K. For our present discussion it is helpful to think of K as the capital stock, with C representing either the savings rate or total net investment, but many other interpretations arise in

---

[9] For further tree-related economics, see Problems 23.4 and 23.5.

economics. Since these variables obviously will take on different values in different periods, they should be denoted as functions of time [$K(t)$ and $C(t)$]. For most of our development, however, it will be convenient not to record this functional dependence on time explicitly.

Choices of K and C will yield benefits over time to the economic agents involved. Those benefits at any point of time will be denoted by $U(K, C, t)$. The agents' goal is to maximize

$$\int_0^T U(K, C, t)dt, \tag{23.47}$$

where T denotes the time period over which decisions are to be made.

There are two types of constraints in this problem. The first shows the rules by which K changes over time:

$$\frac{dK}{dt} = f(K, C, t). \tag{23.48}$$

Here the notation indicates that changes in K will depend on the level of that variable itself, on the control decisions made (C), and (possibly) on the particular point in time being observed. In order to avoid cumbersome notation, we shall adopt the convention of denoting the time derivative of any variable, X, by $\dot{X}$. Hence, the constraint given in Equation 23.48 will be written as

$$\frac{dK}{dt} = \dot{K} = f(K, C, t). \tag{23.49}$$

A second type of constraint in this maximization problem concerns initial and terminal conditions specified for the stock K. At the start of the problem, K will exist as a piece of historical data that cannot be altered, and at the conclusion of the planning period, some other type of requirement may be placed on K (for example, that K be zero). We shall write these end point constraints as

$$K(0) = K_0$$
$$K(T) = K_T, \tag{23.50}$$

where the particular value of the constants K_0 and K_T will depend on the nature of the problem being analyzed.

Maximum Principle: An Intuitive Approach

The dynamic optimization problem we have described requires that we find an optimum time path for the variables K and C. That is a considerably more difficult problem than other maximization problems discussed in this book, for which we required discovery of only a single optimal point rather than an entire time path of points. Our strategy for finding a solution is to convert the dynamic problem into a "single-period" problem and then show how the solution to that simplified problem for any arbitrary point in time solves the dynamic problem as well.

To convert the dynamic problem to a single-period problem, we start by recognizing that any current decision about how the stock of K should be changed will affect both current and future well-being. An optimal choice that uses C to effect current changes in K should balance the current costs of changing K against the future benefits of changing K and vice versa. To aid in this balancing process, we introduce a Lagrangian-type multiplier, $\lambda(t)$, which can be interpreted as the marginal change in future benefits brought about by a one-unit change in K. Therefore, $\lambda(t)$ is a measure of the (marginal) value of the stock K at the current time t. That variable (as in our other maximization problems) permits a solution that balances benefits and costs of current decisions.

Having in this way converted the dynamic problem to a single-period one, it remains to reformulate the solution in a dynamic context. That reformulation consists of showing how $\lambda(t)$ must change over time so as to (1) keep changes in K occurring in an optimal way and (2) assure that the end point conditions on K (Equation 23.50) are satisfied. Such a final solution will then provide a time path of values for C and K that maximizes the integral given in Equation 23.47. As an additional feature, the optimal solution will also provide a time path for the multiplier λ that will show how the marginal evaluation of K (that is, its price) changes over time.

A Mathematical Development

To proceed formally in the manner sketched in the previous section, we introduce the multiplier $\lambda(t)$ as a measure of the marginal value of the stock K at any instant. The total value of the stock is given by $\lambda(t)K$, and the rate of change in this value (that is, the value of gains or losses being experienced in the capital stock) is given by

$$\frac{d\lambda(t)K}{dt} = \lambda \frac{dK}{dt} + K \frac{d\lambda}{dt} = \lambda \dot{K} + K \dot{\lambda}. \tag{23.51}$$

Hence, the total net value of utility at any time (including any effect that current changes in $\dot{K}$ may have—this is what permits this single-period problem to reflect many periods) is given by

$$H = U(K, C, t) + \lambda \dot{K} + K \dot{\lambda}, \tag{23.52}$$

where we have labeled this expression "H" to indicate its similarity to the "Hamiltonian" function encountered in formal dynamic optimization theory.[10] The function H is in some ways similar to the Lagrangian expression we have used repeatedly to solve maximization problems elsewhere in this book.

---

[10] The usual Hamiltonian omits the final term in Equation 23.52. See L. S. Pontryagin et al., *The Mathematical Theory of Optimal Processes* (New York: Interscience Publishers, 1972).

The first-order condition for choosing C to maximize H is

$$\frac{\partial H}{\partial C} = \frac{\partial U(K, C, t)}{dC} + \lambda \frac{\partial \dot{K}}{\partial C} = 0, \tag{23.53}$$

since λ and K (as opposed to $\dot{K}$) are not dependent on the current value of C. Rewriting this first optimal condition yields

$$\frac{\partial U}{\partial C} = -\lambda \frac{\partial \dot{K}}{\partial C}. \tag{23.54}$$

In words, for C to be optimally chosen it must be the case that the marginal increase in U from increasing C is exactly balanced by any effect that such an increase has on decreasing the change in the stock of K (where such changes are evaluated at the margin by λ).

Having chosen C to maximize our augmented single-period measure of utility, it is now necessary to focus on how the marginal valuation of K (that is, λ) should change over time. We can do that by asking what level of K would maximize H. Of course, in actuality K is not a choice variable at any instant—its value is determined by past history. But by "pretending" that K is at its optimal value, we can infer what the behavior of λ must be. Differentiation of H with respect to K yields

$$\frac{\partial H}{\partial K} = \frac{\partial U}{\partial K} + \lambda \frac{\partial \dot{K}}{\partial K} + \dot{\lambda} = 0 \tag{23.55}$$

as a first-order condition for a maximum. Rearranging terms gives

$$-\dot{\lambda} = \frac{\partial U}{\partial K} + \lambda \frac{\partial \dot{K}}{\partial K}. \tag{23.56}$$

This expression can be interpreted as saying that any decline in the marginal valuation of K must equal the net productivity of K in either increasing U or increasing $\dot{K}$. The value of K should be changing in a way opposite to that in which K itself imparts the sum of present and future benefits.

Bringing together the two optimal conditions, we have

$$\frac{\partial H}{\partial C} = \frac{\partial U}{\partial C} + \lambda \frac{\partial \dot{K}}{\partial C} = 0$$

$$\frac{\partial H}{\partial K} = \frac{\partial U}{\partial K} + \lambda \frac{\partial \dot{K}}{\partial K} + \dot{\lambda} = 0. \tag{23.57}$$

These show how C and λ should evolve over time so as to keep K on its optimal path.[11] Once the system of equations is started in motion, the entire

---

[11] These are only first-order conditions for a maximum. We shall not discuss second-order conditions here.

time path of the relevant variables is determined. To provide a complete solution, it is also necessary to make sure that the path of K is "feasible" in that it obeys the end point conditions of Equation 23.50. This can usually be accomplished by adjusting the initial values for C and λ to some appropriate levels. The following example shows how this might be done.

EXAMPLE 23.3

EXHAUSTIBLE RESOURCES

Concern with rising energy prices during the 1970s caused economists to reexamine theories of the optimal use of natural resource stocks. Since that question necessarily involves examination of the optimal time pattern for the depletion of a fixed stock of some resource (for example, oil, coal, or iron ore), it can be examined using the control theory tools we have developed.[12]

Suppose that the (inverse) demand function for the resource in question is given by

$$P = P(C), \tag{23.58}$$

where P is the market price and C is the total quantity consumed during a period. For any output level C, the total utility from consumption is given by

$$U(C) = \int_0^C P(c)dc. \tag{23.59}$$

If the rate of time preference is given by r, the optimal pattern of resource usage will be the one that maximizes

$$\int_0^T e^{-rt}U(C)dt. \tag{23.60}$$

The constraints in this problem are again of two types. First, since the stock of the resource is fixed, that stock is reduced each period by the level of consumption:

$$\dot{K} = -C. \tag{23.61}$$

In addition to this rule for changes in K, the stock of resources must also obey the end point constraints:

$$K(0) = K_0$$

and

$$K(T) = K_T. \tag{23.62}$$

---

[12] The model developed here can be readily generalized to the case of renewable resources such as timber or fish.

Usually, the initial stock, K_0, will represent the quantity of current "known reserves" of the resource, whereas the terminal stock, K_T, will be zero (assuming that resources left in the ground have no value).

Setting up the Hamiltonian,

$$H = e^{-rt}(U) + \lambda \dot{K} + \dot{\lambda} K$$
$$= e^{-rt}(U) - \lambda C + \dot{\lambda} K, \tag{23.63}$$

yields the following first-order conditions for a maximum:

$$\frac{\partial H}{\partial C} = e^{-rt} \frac{\partial U}{\partial C} - \lambda = 0 \tag{23.64}$$

$$\frac{\partial H}{\partial K} = \dot{\lambda} = 0. \tag{23.65}$$

The second equation illustrates the important result that in this problem, the shadow price of the resource (λ) should stay constant over time. Because we are allocating a fixed stock, any path in which the resource had a higher shadow price in one period than in another could be improved upon (in terms of providing more utility) by reducing consumption in the period in which the shadow price is high and increasing consumption in the period in which it is low.[13]

Optimal Price Path. To interpret the first condition, Equation 23.59 can be used to show that

$$\frac{\partial U}{\partial C} = P(C). \tag{23.66}$$

This condition is very similar to those from most of the utility-maximizing models in Part II. Substituting this into Equation 23.64,

$$e^{-rt} P(C) = \lambda. \tag{23.67}$$

Since we know from our previous discussion that λ must be constant, this equation requires that the path for C be chosen so that market price rises at the rate r per period. That is precisely the sort of solution that would emerge in a competitive market. For any resource to provide an investment that is in equilibrium with other alternatives, its price must rise at the rate of interest. Any slower rate of price increase would prompt investors to put their funds into some alternative form of capital, whereas any faster rate

---

[13] One of the first authors to recognize this fundamental point was H. Hotelling, in his path-breaking article, "The Economics of Exhaustible Resources," *Journal of Political Economy* 39 (April 1931): 137–175.

would draw all available funds into investments in the resource. This result therefore suggests that at least in this simple case, competitive markets will allocate natural resources efficiently over time.

A Numerical Illustration. End-period constraints in the natural resource case are usually handled by examining those that relate to terminal-period stocks. If the resource stock is to be fully depleted, then it is required that the final-period price, $P(T)$, be such that demand becomes zero at that price. In most applications such a price can be found by setting it high enough so that substitutes for the resource in question totally dominate the market. For example, if it were known that solar power would totally replace petroleum energy sources in the year 2035 if oil in that year sold for more than $50 per barrel, then $50 would be the terminal price. Using that price together with Equation 23.67, the entire time path of prices can be computed [including the initial price $P(0)$]. With a real interest rate of 3 percent, equilibrium price in 1998 would be $50 \cdot e^{-.03(37)} = \$16.50$.

One final aspect of this resource-pricing problem should be noted. Throughout we have assumed that extraction costs are zero, but that should not be taken to imply that use of the resource itself is "costless." Current consumption of the resource implies lower future consumption, and this cost is no less real than actual production costs would be. Some authors refer to costs of this nature (those related to the fixed nature of the resource stock) as "user costs" or "scarcity costs." The costs are best measured by the shadow price of the resource stock, λ.

QUERY: Suppose extraction of oil is costly. How would this change the calculations made here?

SUMMARY

In this chapter we examined several aspects of the theory of capital with particular emphasis on integrating that theory with the theory of the firm's demand for capital inputs. Some of the results were:

- Capital accumulation represents the sacrifice of present for future consumption. The rate of return measures the terms at which this trade can be accomplished.

- The rate of return is established through mechanisms much like those that establish any equilibrium price. The equilibrium rate of return will be positive reflecting both individuals' relative preferences for present over future goods and the positive physical productivity of capital accumulation.

- The rate of return is an important element in the overall costs associated with capital ownership. It is an important determinant of the market rental rate on capital, v.

- Future returns on capital investments must be discounted at the prevailing real interest rate. Use of such present value notions provides an alterna-

tive way to approach studying the firm's investment decisions.

- Capital accumulation can be studied using the techniques of optimal control theory. Often such models will yield competitive-type results.

PROBLEMS

23.1

An individual has a fixed wealth (W) to allocate between consumption in two periods (C_1 and C_2). The individual's utility function is given by

$$U(C_1, C_2),$$

and the budget constraint is

$$W = C_1 + \frac{C_2}{1 + r},$$

where r is the one-period interest rate.

a. Show that in order to maximize utility, given this budget constraint, the individual should choose C_1 and C_2 so that the MRS (of C_1 for C_2) is equal to $1 + r$.

b. Show that $\partial C_2 / \partial r \geq 0$ but that the sign of $\partial C_1 / \partial r$ is ambiguous. If $\partial C_1 / \partial r$ is negative, what can you conclude about the price elasticity of demand for C_2?

c. How might your analysis of this problem be amended if the individual received income in each period (Y_1 and Y_2) such that the budget constraint is given by

$$Y_1 - C_1 + \frac{Y_2 - C_2}{1 + r} = 0?$$

23.2

Assume that an individual expects to work for 40 years and then retire with a life expectancy of an additional 20 years. Suppose also that the individual's earnings rise at a rate of 3 percent per year and that the interest rate is also 3 percent (the overall price level is constant in this problem). What (constant) fraction of income must the individual save in each working year to be able to finance a level of retirement income equal to 60 percent of earnings in the year just prior to retirement?

23.3

As scotch whiskey ages, its value increases. One dollar of scotch at year 0 is worth $V(t) = e^{2\sqrt{t} - 0.15t}$ dollars at time t. If the interest rate is 5 percent, after how many years should a person sell scotch in order to maximize the PDV of this sale?

23.4

As in Example 23.2, suppose that trees are produced by applying one unit of labor at time 0. The value of the wood contained in a tree is given at any time (t) by $f(t)$. If the market wage rate is w and the instantaneous rate is r, what is the PDV of this production process and how should t be chosen to maximize this PDV?

a. If the optimal value of t is denoted by t^*, show that the no-pure-profit condition of perfect competition will necessitate that

$$w = e^{-rt} f(t^*).$$

Can you explain the meaning of this expression?

b. A tree sold before t^* will not be cut down immediately. Rather, it still will make sense for the new owner to let the tree continue to mature until t^*. Show that the price of a u-year-old tree will be we^{ru} and that this price will exceed the value of the wood in the tree [$f(u)$] for every value of u except $u = t^*$ when these two values are equal.

c. Suppose that a landowner has a "balanced" woodlot with one tree of "each" age from 0 to t^*. What is the value of this woodlot? (*Hint:* It is the sum of the values of all trees in the lot.)

d. If the value of the woodlot is V, show that the instantaneous interest on V (that is, $r \cdot V$) is equal to the "profits" earned at each instant by the landowner, where by profits we mean the difference between the revenue obtained from selling a fully matured tree [$f(t^*)$] and the cost of planting a new one (w). This result shows that there is no pure profit in borrowing to buy a woodlot, since one would have to pay in interest at each instant exactly what would be earned from cutting a fully matured tree.

23.5

The calculations in Problem 23.4 assume that there is no difference between the decision on cutting a single tree and managing a woodlot. But managing a wood-lot also involves replanting, which should be explic-itly modeled. To do so, assume a lot owner is consid-ering planting a single tree at a cost w, harvesting the tree at t^*, planting another, and so forth forever. The discounted stream of profits from this activity is then

$$V = -w + e^{-rt}[f(t) - w] + e^{-r2t}[f(t) - w] \dots$$
$$e^{-rnt}[f(t - w)] + \dots$$

a. Show that the total value of this planned harvest-ing activity is given by

$$V = \frac{f(t) - w}{e^{rt} - 1} - w.$$

b. Find the value of t that maximizes V. Show that this value solves the equation

$$f'(t^*) = rf(t^*) + rV(t^*).$$

c. Interpret the results of part (b)—how do they reflect optimal usage of the "input" time? Why is the value of t^* specified in part (b) different from that in Example 23.2?

d. Suppose tree growth (measured in dollars) follows the logistic function

$$f(t) = 50/(1 + e^{10 - .1t}).$$

What is the maximum value of the timber available from this tree?

e. If tree growth is characterized by the equation given in part (d), what is the optimal rotation period if $r = .05$, $w = 0$? Does this period produce a "maximum sustainable" yield?

f. How would the optimal period change if r fell to .04?

[*Note:* The equation derived in part (b) is termed Faustmann's equation in forestry economics.]

23.6

This problem focuses on the interaction of the corpo-rate profits tax with firms' investment decisions.

a. Suppose (contrary to fact) that profits were defined for tax purposes as what we have called pure economic profits. How would a tax on such profits affect investment decisions?

b. In fact, profits are defined for tax purposes as

$$\pi' = PQ - wL - \text{depreciation,}$$

where depreciation is determined by governmental and industry guidelines that seek to allocate a machine's costs over its "useful" lifetime. If depre-ciation were equal to actual physical deterioration and if a firm were in long-run competitive equi-librium, how would a tax on π' affect the firm's choice of capital inputs?

c. Under the conditions of part (b), how would capital usage be affected by adoption of "accelerated depreciation" policies that specify depreciation rates in excess of physical deterioration early in a machine's life, but much lower depreciation rates as the machine ages?

d. Under the conditions of part (c), how might a decrease in the corporate profits tax affect capital usage?

23.7

A high-pressure life insurance salesman was heard to make the following argument: "At your age a $100,000 whole life policy is a much better buy than a similar term policy. Under a whole life policy you'll have to pay $2,000 per year for the first four years, but nothing more for the rest of your life. A term policy will cost you $400 per year, essentially forever. If you live 35 years, you'll pay only $8,000 for the whole life policy, but $14,000 for the term policy. Surely, the whole life is a better deal."

Assuming the salesman's life expectancy assump-tion is correct, how would you evaluate this argu-ment? Specifically, calculate the present discounted value of the premium costs of the two policies assuming that the interest rate is 10 percent.

23.8

Suppose an individual has W dollars to allocate between consumption this period (C_0) and consumption next period (C_1) and that the interest rate is given by r.

a. Graph the individual's initial equilibrium and indicate the total value of current-period savings ($W - C_0$).

b. Suppose that after the individual makes his or her savings decision (by purchasing one-period bonds), the interest rate falls to r'. How will this alter the individual's budget constraint? Show the new utility-maximizing position. Discuss how the individual's improved position can be interpreted as resulting from a "capital gain" on his or her initial bond purchases.

c. Suppose the tax authorities wish to impose an "income" tax based on the value of capital gains. If all such gains are valued in terms of C_0 as they are "accrued," show how those gains should be measured. Call this value G_1.

d. Suppose instead that capital gains are measured as they are "realized"—that is, capital gains are defined to include only that portion of bonds that is cashed in to buy additional C_0. Show how these realized gains can be measured. Call this amount G_2.

e. Develop a measure of the true increase in utility that results from the fall in r, measured in terms of C_0. Call this "true" capital gain G_3. Show that $G_3 < G_2 < G_1$. What do you conclude about the current policy that taxes only realized gains?

(*Note:* This problem is adapted from J. Whalley, "Capital Gains Taxation and Interest Rate Changes," *National Tax Journal* [March 1979]: 87–91.)

23.9

Example 23.3 assumed that oil was produced in a competitive market. Assuming that the other conditions of the example did not change, how would optimal resource use change if all oil were owned by a single monopoly firm?

23.10

Optimal control theory can be used to generalize the model of intertemporal consumption choice contained in Example 23.1. Consider the following simple life cycle model: An individual receives wages (w) each period and a return on his or her invested capital. Let k = capital, r = market interest rate at which the individual can borrow or lend. During each period, the individual chooses consumption (c) to maximize

$$\int_0^T U(c)e^{-\rho t}dt,$$

where ρ is the individual's rate of time preference. Given these assumptions, the intertemporal budget constraint for this problem is

$$\dot{k} = w + rk - c$$

with constraints on initial and final k of the form $k(0) = k(T) = 0$.

a. What are the necessary conditions for a maximum for this problem?

b. Under what conditions would optimal consumption rise over time? When would consumption fall over time?

c. Suppose $U(c) = ln(c)$, what is the optimal pattern of consumption?

d. More generally, suppose

$$U(c) = \frac{c^\delta}{\delta} \qquad \delta < 1.$$

What is the optimal time pattern for consumption? How does this compare to the special case in part (c)?

e. How does the optimal time pattern for consumption in this problem determine this individual's measured wealth at various points in the life cycle?

SUGGESTED READINGS

Blaug, M. *Economic Theory in Retrospect*. Rev. ed. Homewood, Ill.: Richard D. Irwin, 1978. Chap. 12. *Good review of an Austrian capital theory and of attempts to conceptualize the capital accumulation process.*

Dixit, A. K. *Optimization in Economic Theory*, 2nd edition. New York, Oxford University Press, 1990. *Extended treatment of optimal control theory in a fairly easy to follow format.*

Dorfman, R. "An Economic Interpretation of Optimal Control Theory." *American Economic Review* 59 (December 1969): 817–831.
Uses the approach of this chapter to examine optimal capital accumulation. Excellent intuitive introduction.

Harcourt, G. C. "Some Cambridge Controversies in the Theory of Capital." *Journal of Economic Literature* 7 (June 1969): 369–405.
Summarizes the "Cambridge Controversy" about the nature and measurability of capital.

Hotelling, H. "The Economics of Exhaustible Resources." *Journal of Political Economy* 39 (April 1931): 137–175.
Fundamental work on allocation of natural resources. Analyzes both competitive and monopoly cases.

Ramsey, F. P. "A Mathematical Theory of Saving." *Economic Journal* 38 (December 1928): 542–559.
One of the first uses of the calculus of variations to solve economic problems.

Samuelson, P. A. "Parable and Realism in Capital Theory: The Surrogate Producton Function." *Review of Economic Studies* 39 (June 1962): 193–206.
A discussion of how capital might be added up for use in an aggregate production function.

Scott, A. D. "Notes on User Cost." *Economic Journal* 63 (June 1953): 368–384.
Basic methodological note concerning scarcity costs.

Solow, R. M. *Capital Theory and the Rate of Return.* Amsterdam: North-Holland Publishing Co., 1964.
Lectures on the nature of capital. Very readable.

THE MATHEMATICS OF COMPOUND INTEREST

The purpose of this appendix is to gather together some simple results concerning the mathematics of compound interest. These results have applications in a wide variety of economic problems, ranging from macroeconomic policy to the optimal way to raise Christmas trees.

We assume that there is a current prevailing market interest rate of i per period, say, one year. This interest rate is assumed to be both certain and constant over all future periods.[1] If \$1 is invested at this rate, i, and the interest is then compounded (that is, future interest is paid on past interest earned), at the end of one period \$1 will be

$$\$1 \times (1 + i),$$

at the end of two periods \$1 will be

$$\$1 \times (1 + i) \times (1 + i) = \$1 \times (1 + i)^2,$$

and at the end of n periods \$1 will be

$$\$1 \times (1 + i)^n.$$

Similarly, \$N grows like

$$\$N \times (1 + i)$$

---

[1] The assumption of a constant i is obviously unrealistic. Since the problems introduced by considering an interest rate that varies from period to period greatly complicate the notation without adding a commensurate degree of conceptual knowledge, such an analysis is not undertaken here. In many cases the generalization to a varying interest rate is merely a trivial application of the notion that any multiperiod interest rate can be regarded as resulting from compounding several single-period rates. If we let r_{ij} be the interest rate prevailing between periods i and j (where $i < j$), then,

$$1 + r_{ij} = (1 + r_{i,i+1})(1 + r_{i+1,i+2}) \cdots (1 + r_{j-1,j}).$$

$$\$N \times (1 + i)^2$$

$$.$$
$$.$$
$$.$$

$$\$N \times (1 + i)^n.$$

PRESENT DISCOUNTED VALUE

The *present value* of $1 payable one period from now is

$$\frac{\$1}{(1 + i)}.$$

This is simply the amount that an individual would be willing to pay now for the promise of $1 at the end of one period. Similarly, the present value of $1 payable n periods from now is

$$\frac{\$1}{(1 + i)^n},$$

and the present value of $N payable n periods from now is

$$\frac{\$N}{(1 + i)^n}.$$

The *present discounted value* of a stream of payments $N_0, N_1, N_2, \ldots, N_n$ (where the subscripts indicate the period in which the payment is to be made) is

$$PDV = N_0 + \frac{N_1}{(1 + i)} + \frac{N_2}{(1 + i)^2} + \cdots + \frac{N_n}{(1 + i)^n}. \qquad \text{(23A.1)}$$

PDV is the amount that an individual would be willing to pay in return for a promise to receive the stream $N_0, N_1, N_2, \ldots, N_n$. It represents the amount that would have to be invested now if one wished to duplicate the payment stream.

Annuities and Perpetuities

An *annuity* is a promise to pay $N in each period for n periods, starting next period. The *PDV* of such a contract is

$$PDV = \frac{N}{(1 + i)} + \frac{N}{(1 + i)^2} + \cdots + \frac{N}{(1 + i)^n}. \qquad \text{(23A.2)}$$

Let $D = 1/(1 + i)$; then,

$$PDV = N(D + D^2 + \cdots + D^n)$$

$$= ND(1 + D + D^2 + \cdots + D^{n-1}) \qquad (23A.3)$$

$$= ND\left(\frac{1 - D^n}{1 - D}\right).$$

Notice that

$$\lim_{n \to \infty} D^n = 0.$$

Therefore, for an annuity of infinite duration,

$$PDV \text{ of infinite annuity} = \lim_{n \to \infty} PDV = ND\left(\frac{1}{1 - D}\right), \qquad (23A.4)$$

which, by the definition of D,

$$= N\left(\frac{1}{1 + i}\right)\left(\frac{1}{1 - 1/(1 + i)}\right)$$

$$= N\left(\frac{1}{1 + i}\right)\left(\frac{1 + i}{i}\right) = \frac{N}{i}. \qquad (23A.5)$$

This case of an infinite-period annuity is sometimes called a *perpetuity* or a *consol*. The formula simply says that the amount that must be invested if one is to obtain $N per period forever is simply N/i, since this amount of money would earn $N in interest each period ($i \cdot \$N/i = \$N$).

An n-period *bond* is a promise to pay $N each period, starting next period, for n periods. It also promises to return the principal (face) value of the bond at the end of n periods. If the principal value of the bond is $P (usually $1,000 in the U.S. bond market), then the present discounted value of such a promise is

The Special Case of a Bond

$$PDV = \frac{N}{(1 + i)} + \frac{N}{(1 + i)^2} + \cdots + \frac{N}{(1 + i)^n} + \frac{P}{(1 + i)^n}. \qquad (23A.6)$$

Again, let $D = 1/(1 + i)$; then,

$$PDV = ND + ND^2 + \cdots + (N + P)D^n. \qquad (23A.7)$$

Equation 23A.7 can be looked at in another way. Suppose that we knew the price at which the bond is currently trading, say, B. Then we could ask what value of i gives the bond a PDV equal to B. To find this i we set

$$B = PDV = ND + ND^2 + \cdots + (N + P)D^n. \qquad (23A.8)$$

Since B, N, and P are known, we can solve this equation for D and hence for i.[2] The i that solves the equation is called the *yield* on the bond and is the best measure of the return actually available from the bond. The yield of a bond represents the return available both from direct interest payments and from any price differential between the initial price (B) and the maturity price (P).

Notice that as i increases, PDV decreases. This is a precise way of formulating the well-known concept that bond prices (PDV's) and interest rates (yields) are inversely correlated.

CONTINUOUS TIME

Thus far this appendix has dealt with discrete time—the analysis has been divided into periods. Often it is more convenient to deal with continuous time. In such a case the interest on an investment is compounded "instantaneously" and growth over time is "smooth." This facilitates the analysis of maximization problems because exponential functions are more easily differentiated. Many financial intermediaries (for example, savings banks) have adopted (nearly) continuous interest formulas in recent years.

Suppose that i is given as the (nominal) interest rate per year but that half this nominal rate is compounded every six months. Then, at the end of one year, the investment of $1 would have grown to

$$\$1 \times \left(1 + \frac{i}{2}\right)^2. \tag{23A.9}$$

Notice that this is superior to investing for one year at the simple rate, i, because interest has been paid on interest; that is,

$$\left(1 + \frac{i}{2}\right)^2 > (1 + i). \tag{23A.10}$$

Consider the limit of this process—for the nominal rate of i per period, consider the amount that would be realized if i were in fact "compounded n times during the period"; let $n \to \infty$:

$$\lim_{n \to \infty} \left(1 + \frac{i}{n}\right)^n. \tag{23A.11}$$

---

[2] Since this equation is really an nth-degree polynomial, there are in reality n solutions (roots). Only one of these solutions is the relevant one reported in bond tables or on calculators. The other solutions are either imaginary or unreasonable. In the present example there is only one real solution.

TABLE 23A.1

**EFFECTIVE ANNUAL INTEREST RATES FOR SELECTED
CONTINUOUSLY COMPOUNDED RATES**

CONTINUOUSLY COMPOUNDED RATE	EFFECTIVE ANNUAL RATE
3.0%	3.05%
4.0	4.08
5.0	5.13
5.5	5.65
6.0	6.18
6.5	6.72
7.0	7.25
8.0	8.33
9.0	9.42
10.0	10.52

This limit exists and is simply e^i, where e is the base of natural logarithms (the value of e is approximately 2.72). It is important to note that $e^i > (1 + i)$—it is much better to have continuous compounding over the period than to have simple interest.

We can ask what continuous rate, r, yields the same amount at the end of one period as the simple rate i. We are looking for the value of r that solves the equation

$$e^r = (1 + i). \qquad (23A.12)$$

Hence,

$$r = ln(1 + i). \qquad (23A.12')$$

Using this formula it is a simple matter to translate from discrete interest rates into continuous ones. If i is measured as a decimal yearly rate, then r is a yearly continuous rate. Table 23A.1 shows the effective annual interest rate (i) associated with selected interest rates (r) that are continuously compounded.[3] Tables similar to 23A.1 often appear in the windows of savings banks advertising the "true" yields on their accounts.

---

[3] To compute the figures in Table 23A.1, interest rates are used in decimal rather than percent form (that is, a 5 percent interest rate is recorded as 0.05 for use in Equation 23A.12).

Continuous Growth One dollar invested at a continuous interest rate of r will become

$$V = \$1 \cdot e^{rT} \tag{23A.13}$$

after T years. This growth formula is a very convenient one to work with. For example, it is easy to show that the instantaneous relative rate of change in V is, as would be expected, simply given by r:

$$\textbf{relative rate of change} = \frac{dV/dt}{V} = \frac{re^{rt}}{e^{rt}} = r. \tag{23A.14}$$

Continuous interest rates also are convenient for calculating present discounted values. Suppose that we wished to calculate the *PDV* of \$1 to be paid T years from now. This would be given by[4]

$$\frac{\$1}{e^{rT}} = \$1 \cdot e^{-rT}. \tag{23A.15}$$

The logic of this calculation is exactly the same as that used in the discrete time analysis of this appendix: Future dollars are worth less than present ones.

One interesting application of continuous discounting occurs in calculating the *PDV* of \$1 per period paid in small installments at each instant of time from today (time 0) until period T. Since there would be an infinite number of payments, the mathematical tool of integration must be used to compute this result:

$$PDV = \int_0^T e^{-rt}dt. \tag{23A.16}$$

All this statement says is that we are adding all the discounted dollars over the time period 0 to T.

The value of this definite integral is given by

$$PDV = \left. \frac{-e^{-rt}}{r} \right|_0^T$$

$$= \frac{-e^{-rT}}{r} + \frac{1}{r}. \tag{23A.17}$$

If we let T go to infinity, this value becomes

---

[4] In physics this formula occurs as an example of "radioactive decay." If one unit of a substance decays continuously at the rate δ, then after T periods, $e^{-\delta T}$ will remain. This amount never exactly reaches zero no matter how large T is. Depreciation can be treated the same way in capital theory.

$$PDV = \frac{1}{r}, \qquad (23A.18)$$

as was the case for the infinitely long annuity considered in the discrete case.

Continuous discounting is particularly convenient for calculating the PDV of an arbitrary stream of payments over time. Suppose that $f(t)$ records the number of dollars to be paid during period t. Then the PDV of the payment at time T is

$$e^{-rT}f(T), \qquad (23A.19)$$

and the PDV of the entire stream from the present time (year 0) until year T is given by

$$\int_0^T f(t)e^{-rt}dt. \qquad (23A.20)$$

Frequently, economic agents may seek to maximize an expression such as that given in Equation 23A.20. Use of continuous time makes the analysis of such choices straightforward because standard calculus methods of maximization can be used.

LIMITS OF THE MARKET

Prior sections of this book have focused at length on the ways in which markets allocate resources. Although the equilibria described were not always efficient, they were arrived at through some type of interaction of the forces of supply and demand. Only on a few occasions (for example, in our discussion of the regulation of natural monopolies) have we analyzed how nonmarket actors (for example, government regulators) might affect observed outcomes. In this final part, we will move away somewhat from our examination of market forces and explore some situations where nonmarket influences may be important. We will show that, for some allocational questions, markets will perform relatively poorly and other economic institutions (most importantly, the government) may play decisive, though not necessarily better, allocational roles.

Chapter 24 addresses problems raised by goods that have externality or spillover effects. For these goods simple market transactions may not accurately reflect all of the economic consequences of consumption and production—some misallocations of resources may occur. In Chapter 24 we examine both externalities in the relations between two specific economic actors and externalities that arise in the provision of public goods when many parties may benefit from a good without paying for it.

Chapter 25, the final chapter in this text, focuses on public choice theory. In its most general statement, this theory is concerned with how governmental choices are made. A major portion of public choice theory is concerned with modeling the results of voting for governmental decisions. We show that the Pareto optimality of voting procedures is open to question in many important cases.

CHAPTER 24

EXTERNALITIES AND PUBLIC GOODS

In Chapter 17 we showed that a number of problems may interfere with the allocational efficiency of perfectly competitive markets. Here we will examine two of those problems, externalities and public goods, in more detail. This examination has two purposes. First, we wish to show clearly why the existence of externalities and public goods may distort the allocation of resources. In so doing it will be possible to illustrate some additional features of the type of information that is provided by competitive prices and some of the circumstances that may diminish the usefulness of that information. Our second reason for looking more closely at externalities and public goods is to suggest ways in which the allocational problems they pose might be mitigated. We will see that, at least in some cases, the efficiency of competitive market outcomes may be more robust than might at first have been anticipated.

Externalities occur because economic agents have effects on third parties that are not reflected in market transactions. Chemical makers spewing toxic fumes on their neighbors, jet planes waking up people, or motorists littering the highway are, from an economic point of view, all engaging in the same sort of activity—they are having a direct effect on the well-being of others that is outside direct market channels. Such activities might be contrasted to effects that take place directly through markets. When I choose to purchase a loaf of bread, for example, I (perhaps imperceptibly) raise the price of bread generally and that may affect the well-being of other bread buyers. But such effects, because they are reflected in market prices, are not true externalities

DEFINING EXTERNALITIES

and do not affect the market's ability to allocate resources efficiently.[1] Rather, the rise in the price of bread that results from my increased purchase is an accurate reflection of societal preferences, and the price rise helps to ensure that the right mix of products is produced. That is not the case for toxic chemical discharges, jet noise, or litter. In these cases, market prices (of chemicals, air travel, or disposable containers) may not accurately reflect social costs because they may take no account of the damage being done to third parties. Information being conveyed by the prices is fundamentally inaccurate, leading to a misallocation of resources.

As a summary, therefore, we have developed the following definition:

DEFINITION

Externality An *externality* occurs whenever the activities of one economic agent affect the activities of another agent in ways that are not reflected in market transactions.

Before analyzing in detail why failing to take externalities into account can lead to a misallocation of resources, we will examine a few examples that may clarify the nature of the problem.

Interfirm Externalities

To illustrate the externality issue in its simplest form, consider two firms—one producing good X and the other producing good Y—where each firm uses only a single input, labor. The production of good Y is said to have an external effect on the production of X if the output of X depends not only on the amount of labor chosen by the X-entrepreneur but also on the level at which the production of Y is carried on. Notationally, the production function for good X can be written as

$$X = f(L_X; Y), \tag{24.1}$$

where L_X denotes the amount of labor devoted to good X, and Y appears to the right of the semicolon in the equation to show that it is an effect on production over which the X-entrepreneur has no control.[2] As an example,

---

[1] Sometimes effects of one economic agent on another that take place through the market system are termed "pecuniary" externalities to differentiate such effects from the "technological" externalities we are discussing. Here the use of the term "externalities" will refer only to the latter type, since these are the only type with consequences for the efficiency of resource allocation by competitive markets.

[2] We shall find it necessary to redefine the assumption of "no control" considerably as the analysis of this chapter proceeds.

suppose that the two firms are located on a river, with firm X being downstream from Y. Suppose that firm Y pollutes the river in its productive process. Then the output of firm X may depend not only on the level of inputs it uses itself but also on the amount of pollutants flowing past its factory. The level of pollutants, in turn, is determined by the output of firm Y. In the production function shown by Equation 24.1, the output of firm Y would have a negative marginal physical productivity $\partial X/\partial Y < 0$. Increases in Y output would cause less X to be produced. In the next section we shall return to analyze this case more fully as it is representative of most simple types of externalities.

Beneficial Externalities

The relationship between two firms may be beneficial. Most examples of such positive externalities are rather bucolic in nature. Perhaps the most famous, proposed by J. Meade, involves two firms, one producing honey (raising bees) and the other producing apples.[3] Because the bees feed on apple blossoms, an increase in apple production will improve productivity in the honey industry. The beneficial effects of having well-fed bees is a positive externality to the beekeeper. In the notation of Equation 24.1, $\partial X/\partial Y$ would now be positive. In the usual perfectly competitive case, the productive activities of one firm have no direct effect on those of other firms: $\partial X/\partial Y = 0$.

Externalities in Utility

Externalities also can occur if the activities of an economic agent directly affect an individual's utility. Most common examples of environmental externalities are of this type. From an economic perspective it makes little difference whether such effects are created by firms (in the form, say, of toxic chemicals or jet noise) or by other individuals (litter or, perhaps, the noise from a loud radio). In all such cases the amount of such activities would enter directly into the individual's utility function in much the same way as firm Y's output entered into firm X's production function in Equation 24.1. As in the case of firms, such externalities may sometimes be beneficial (you may actually like the song being played on your neighbor's radio). So, again, a situation of no externalities can be regarded as simply the middle ground in which other agents' activities have no direct effect on individuals' utilities.

One special type of utility externality that is relevant to the analysis of social choices arises when one individual's utility depends directly on the

[3] J. Meade, "External Economies and Diseconomies in a Competitive Situation," *Economic Journal* 62 (March 1952): 54–67. We shall return to examine Meade's example later in this chapter.

utility of someone else. If, for example, Smith cares about Jones's welfare, we could write his or her utility function (U_S) as

$$\text{utility} = U_S(X_1, \ldots, X_n; U_J), \tag{24.2}$$

where $X_1, \ldots, X_n$ are the goods that Smith consumes and U_J is Jones's utility. If Smith is altruistic and wants Jones to be well off (as might happen if Jones were a close relative), $\partial U_S / \partial U_J$ would be positive. If, on the other hand, Smith were envious of Jones, it might be the case that $\partial U_S / \partial U_J$ would be negative; that is, improvements in Jones's utility make Smith worse off. The middle ground between altruism and envy would occur if Smith were indifferent to Jones's welfare ($\partial U_S / \partial U_J = 0$), and that is what we have usually assumed throughout this book (for a brief discussion, see the extensions to Chapter 3).

Public Goods Externalities

Goods that are "public" or "collective" in nature will be the focus for our analysis in the second half of this chapter. The defining characteristic of these goods is nonexclusion; that is, once the goods are produced (either by the government or by some private entity), they provide benefits to an entire group, perhaps to everyone. It is technically impossible to restrict these benefits to the specific group of individuals who pay for them, so the benefits are available to all. As we mentioned in Chapter 17, national defense provides the traditional example. Once a defense system is established, all individuals in society are protected by it whether they wish to be or not and whether they pay for it or not. Choosing the right level of output for such a good can be a tricky process, since market signals will be inaccurate.

EXTERNALITIES AND ALLOCATIVE EFFICIENCY

Traditionally, it has been argued that the presence of externalities such as those just described can cause a market to operate inefficiently. To illustrate this inefficiency, assume that two firms are located near each other and that one of these (Y) has a negative impact on the production of the other (X). Suppose that the production function of the pollution-producing firm is given by

$$Y = g(L_Y), \tag{24.3}$$

where L_Y is the quantity of labor devoted to Y production. The production function for good X (which exhibits an externality) was given by Equation 24.1. The Pareto conditions for an optimal allocation of labor require that the social marginal revenue product of labor ($SMRP_L$) be equal for both firms. If P_X and P_Y are the prices of good X and Y, respectively, the $SMRP$ of labor in the production of good X is given by

$$SMRP_L^X = P_X \frac{\partial f}{\partial L_X}. \tag{24.4}$$

Because of the productive externality, the statement of the $SMRP$ of labor in the production of Y is more complex. An additional unit of labor employed by firm Y will produce some extra Y. But it will also produce some extra pollution, and this will reduce the production of X. Consequently,

$$SMRP_L^Y = P_Y \cdot \frac{\partial g}{\partial L_Y} + P_X \cdot \frac{\partial f}{\partial Y} \cdot \frac{\partial Y}{\partial L_Y}, \tag{24.5}$$

where the second term represents the effect that hiring additional workers in plant Y has on the value of production in plant X. This effect will be negative if $\partial f / \partial Y < 0$. Efficiency then requires that

$$SMRP_L^X = SMRP_L^Y. \tag{24.6}$$

The decentralized calculations of the two firm managers will normally not bring this condition about. Firm X will hire labor up to the point at which its private marginal revenue product (MRP_L) is equal to the prevailing wage rate:

$$w = MRP_L^X = P_X \frac{\partial f}{\partial L_X}. \tag{24.7}$$

Firm Y will follow a similar course of action:

$$w = MRP_L^Y = P_Y \frac{\partial g}{\partial L_Y}. \tag{24.8}$$

The market therefore will equate private marginal revenue products, but this market equilibrium will ensure Pareto efficiency only if $\partial f / \partial Y = 0$ in Equation 24.5. In other words, as long as the externality exists, the managers' decisions will not bring about an optimal allocation. In our example we assumed that $\partial f / \partial Y < 0$, which implies that labor will be overallocated to the production of good Y. Labor's social marginal revenue product in the production of Y will fall short of its value in the production of X. The value of output could be increased by shifting labor from the production of Y into the production of X. If, on the other hand, we had assumed that $\partial f / \partial Y > 0$ (Meade's bees example), labor would have been underallocated to Y production.

EXAMPLE 24.1

PRODUCTION EXTERNALITIES

Suppose two newsprint producers are located along a river. The upstream firm (Y) has a production function of the form

$$Y = 2,000 L_Y^{1/2}, \tag{24.9}$$

where L_Y is the number of workers hired per day and Y is newsprint output in feet. The downstream firm (X) has a similar production function, but its output may be affected by the chemicals firm Y pours into the river:

$$X = 2{,}000L_X^{1/2}(Y - Y_0)^\alpha \quad \text{(for } Y > Y_0)$$
$$X = 2{,}000L_X^{1/2} \qquad \text{(for } Y \leq Y_0),$$

(24.10)

where Y_0 represents the river's natural capacity for pollutants. If $\alpha = 0$, Y's production process has no effect on firm X, whereas if $\alpha < 0$, increases in Y above Y_0 cause X's output to decline.

Assuming newsprint sells for $1 per foot and workers earn $50 per day, firm Y will maximize profits by setting this wage equal to labor's marginal value product:

$$50 = P \cdot \frac{\partial Y}{\partial L_Y} = 1{,}000L_Y^{-1/2}.$$

(24.11)

The solution then is $L_Y = 400$. If $\alpha = 0$ (there are no externalities), firm X will also hire 400 workers. Each firm will produce 40,000 feet of newsprint.

Effects of an Externality. When firm Y does have a negative externality $(\alpha < 0)$, its profit-maximizing hiring decision is not affected—it will still hire $L_Y = 400$ and produce $Y = 40{,}000$. But for firm X, labor's marginal product will be lower because of this externality. If $\alpha = -.1$ and $Y_0 = 38{,}000$, for example, profit maximization will require

$$50 = P \cdot \frac{\partial X}{\partial L_X} = 1{,}000L_X^{-1/2}(Y - 38{,}000)^{-.1}$$
$$= 1{,}000L_X^{-1/2}(2{,}000)^{-.1}$$
$$= 468L_X^{-1/2}.$$

(24.12)

Solving this equation for L_X shows that firm X now hires only 87 workers because of this lowered productivity. Output of firm X will now be

$$X = 2{,}000(87)^{1/2}(2{,}000)^{-.1} = 8{,}723.$$

(24.13)

Because of the externality $(\alpha = -.1)$, newsprint output will be lower than without the externality $(\alpha = 0)$.

Inefficiency. We can demonstrate that decentralized profit maximization is inefficient in this situation by imagining that firms X and Y merge and the manager must decide how to allocate the combined workforce. If one worker is transferred from firm Y to firm X, Y output becomes

$$Y = 2{,}000(399)^{1/2}$$
$$= 39{,}950$$

(24.14)

and for firm X

$$X = 2,000(88)^{1/2}(1,950)^{-.1}$$

$$= 8,796.$$

(24.15)

Total output has therefore increased by 23 feet of newsprint with no change in labor input. The previous allocation was inefficient because firm Y did not take the effect its hiring decisions have on firm X into account.

Marginal Productivity.   This can be illustrated in another way by computing the social marginal productivity of labor input to firm Y. If that firm were to hire one more worker, its own output would rise to

$$Y = 2,000(401)^{1/2} = 40,050.$$

(24.16)

As profit maximization requires, the (private) marginal value product of the 401st worker is equal to the wage. But increasing Y's output now also has an effect on firm X—its output declines by about 21 units. Hence, the social marginal value product of labor to firm Y actually only amounts to $29 ($50 – $21). That is why the manager of the merged firm would find it profitable to shift some workers.

QUERY: Suppose $\alpha = +.1$. What would that imply about the relationship between the firms? How would such an externality affect the allocation of labor?

The model we have been using to analyze externalities assumes that productive technologies and society's preferences regarding external costs are unchanging. Within the confines of this simple model,[4] there are still a number of potential solutions to the allocational problems posed. In this section we will examine two "traditional" solutions: taxation and internalization of costs. Then, in the next section, we will show that, in some circumstances, externalities can be accommodated by the normal workings of the market and the traditional solutions may be unnecessary.

TRADITIONAL WAYS OF COPING WITH EXTERNALITIES

The government could impose a suitable excise tax on the firm generating the external diseconomy. Presumably, this tax would cause the output of Y to be

Taxation

---

[4] For a more general treatment that allows for changing technologies to cope with externalities, see W. J. Baumol and W. E. Oates, *The Theory of Environmental Policy,* 2d ed. (Cambridge: Cambridge University Press, 1988).

cut back and would cause labor to be shifted out of the production of Y. This classic remedy to the externality problem was first put forward lucidly in the 1920s by A. C. Pigou;[5] although it has been somewhat modified, it remains one of the "standard" answers to the externality problem given by economists. The central issue for regulators becomes one of obtaining sufficient empirical information so that the correct tax can be imposed directly on the polluting firm.

The taxation solution is illustrated conceptually in Figure 24.1. Suppose that firm Y's marginal cost curve is given by MC and that the market demand curve for Y is given by DD (ignore the curve D' for the moment). Assume also that Y's social marginal cost curve is represented by MC'. This curve differs from MC by the amount of extra costs that the production of Y imposes on others (here only firm X) in the economy. From a social point of view the optimal output of Y would be Y_2. At this output level the marginal benefit of Y's production (what people are willing to pay for the good) is exactly equal to the social marginal cost. However, the market will cause output level Y_1 to be produced since, at this output, market price is equal to private marginal cost. Consequently, Y will be overproduced as we indicated previously.[6]

A per-unit tax of t would cause the effective demand curve for Y to shift to D'. With this new demand curve, the private profit-maximizing output will be Y_2, and this indeed will be the level of output that is socially optimal. At Y_2 the marginal external damage done by producing Y is given by the distance ad, which is precisely the amount (t) paid by the consumers of Y in the form of excise taxes. By taxing good Y the effective demand for the product has been reduced; individuals who use Y are now forced to pay for the damage that its production creates. This reduces demand and causes Y output to contract. Resources are shifted out of Y production, and an efficient allocation is established.

Merger and Internalization   A second traditional cure for the allocational distortions caused by the externality between X and Y would be for the two firms to merge. As we saw in Example 24.1, if a single firm were operating both plants X and Y, it would

---

[5] A. C. Pigou, *The Economics of Welfare,* 4th ed. (London: Macmillan & Co., 1946). Pigou also stresses the desirability of providing subsidies to firms that produce beneficial externalities.

[6] It will be convenient in our discussion to assume that firm Y acts as a perfectly *price-discriminating monopolist* in the market by selling each unit separately at the highest price it will bring. The assumption of a perfect price discriminator eliminates the need for introducing possible transfers of consumer surplus into this analysis, since there is in fact no such surplus. At the same time, the assumption assures that an efficient level of output will be produced ($P = MC$) as we showed in Chapter 18.

FIGURE 24.1

GRAPHICAL DEMONSTRATION OF THE COSTS OF AN EXTERNALITY

The demand for Y is given by the curve DD and the private marginal cost curve for Y by MC. The curve MC' records the social marginal cost of Y production. From society's point of view, therefore, Y_2 is the optimal output. However, the normal workings of the market will cause output level Y_1 to be produced. One way to force the market to allocate goods correctly would be to adopt an excise tax of amount t on the production of Y. The effect of the tax is to reduce the demand curve facing the firm from DD to $D'D'$, and this will shift the profit-maximizing level of output from Y_1 to Y_2.

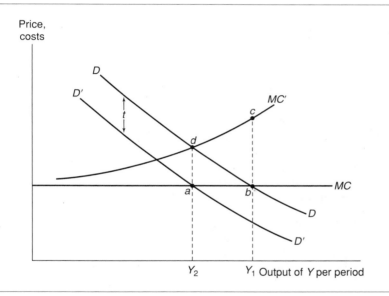

recognize the detrimental effect that Y production has on the production function for good X. In effect the firm $(X + Y)$ would now pay the full social marginal costs of Y production because it also produces X. In other words, the firm's manager would now take the marginal cost curve for Y production to be MC' and would produce at the point where

$$P_Y = MC',\qquad(24.17)$$

which is exactly what is required for efficiency. Economists would say that the externality in Y production has been internalized as a result of the merger.

EXAMPLE 24.2

A PIGOVIAN TAX

The inefficiency in Example 24.1 arises because the upstream newsprint producer (firm Y) takes no account of the effect that its production has on firm X. A suitably chosen tax on firm Y can cause it to reduce its hiring to a level at which the externality vanishes. Since the river can absorb the pollutants generated with an output of $Y = 38{,}000$, we might consider imposing a tax (t) on the firm's output that will encourage it to reduce output to this level. Since output will be 38,000 if $L_Y = 361$, we can calculate t from the labor demand condition:

$$(1 - t)MP_L = (1 - t)1{,}000(361)^{-.5} = 50 \tag{24.18}$$

or

$$t = .05. \tag{24.19}$$

Such a 5 percent tax would effectively reduce the price firm Y receives for its newsprint to $.95 and provide it with an incentive to reduce its hiring by 39 workers. Now, since the river can handle all of the pollutants Y produces, there is no externality in the production function of firm X. It will hire 400 workers and produce 40,000 feet of newsprint per day. Notice that total newsprint output is now 78,000, a significantly higher figure than would be produced in the untaxed situation. The taxation solution here provides a considerable improvement in the efficiency of resource allocation.

QUERY: The tax rate proposed here (0.05) seems rather small given the significant output gains obtained relative to the situation in Example 24.1. Can you explain why? Would a merged firm opt for $Y = 38{,}000$ even without a tax?

PROPERTY RIGHTS, ALLOCATION, AND THE COASE THEOREM

One important question we might still ask about this analysis is if firm Y's actions impose a cost on firm X, why doesn't firm X try to convince firm Y to cut back on its output? Presumably, the gain of such a cutback to firm X (area *abcd* in Figure 24.1) would exceed the loss of profits to firm Y (area *abd*—remember the assumption in footnote 6 that firm Y is a perfect price discriminator), and some bargaining arrangement might be worked out that would monetarily benefit both parties. Through such a bargain the benefits of internalization could be obtained without the necessity of a merger.

We can gain additional insights into these possibilities for bargaining by looking at the ways property rights are assigned in this case. We start with a definition:

Property Rights

DEFINITION

Property Rights   *Property rights* establish the legal owner of a resource and specify the ways in which the resource may be used.

Two major types of property rights specifications are "common" property and "private" property. Common property is, by definition, owned by "society at large": No individual may appropriate such a resource solely for his or her own use. Private property, on the other hand, is directly owned by individuals who have, within prevailing legal strictures, control over how it is used.

For the purposes of the two-firm externality example, it is interesting to consider the nature of the property right that might be attached to the river shared by the firms. Suppose that property rights were defined so as to give "ownership" of the river to one of the firms but that the firms were free to bargain over how the river might be used. It might be thought that if the ownership of the river were given to firm Y, pollution would result, whereas if the right were given to firm X, the river would remain pure. This might not be the case, however, because such a conclusion disregards the bargains that might be reached by the two parties. Indeed, if bargaining is costless, the two parties left on their own will arrive at the efficient output (Y_2), and this result will be independent of who "owns" the river. We now demonstrate this result, which is sometimes termed the Coase theorem, after the economist who first proposed it.[7]

The Coase Theorem and Allocation

   If, for example, firm Y owns the river, it must then impute some cost of this ownership into its cost function. What are the costs associated with river ownership? The opportunity cost doctrine provides the answer: The costs are what the river would bring in its next best alternative use. In the problem, only firm X has some alternative use for the river (to keep it clean); the amount that this firm would be willing to pay for a clean river is equal to the external damage done by the pollution. Consequently, if firm Y calculates its costs correctly, its marginal cost curve (including the cost of river ownership) becomes MC' in Figure 24.1. Firm Y therefore will produce Y_2 and sell the remaining rights of river use to firm X for a fee of some amount between *abd*

---

[7] See R. Coase, "The Problem of Social Cost," *Journal of Law and Economics* 3 (October 1960): 1–44.

(Y's lost profits from producing Y_2 rather than Y_1) and *abcd* (the maximum amount X would pay to avoid having Y increased from Y_2 to Y_1).

A similar allocation would result if firm X owned the rights to the river. In this case, firm Y would be willing to pay any amount up to the total profits it earns from production for the right to pollute the river. Firm X will accept these payments as long as they exceed the costs imposed on it by the river pollution. The ultimate result of bargaining will be for firm Y to offer a payment to firm X for the use of the river in dumping pollution associated with output level Y_2. Firm X will not sell the rights to dump any further pollution because what firm Y would be willing to pay falls short of the cost of additional pollution to firm X. Again, the efficient point can be reached by relying on free bargaining between the two firms. Notice that in both situations, some production of Y takes place, and there will be some pollution. Having no Y output (and no pollution) would be inefficient in the same sense that producing Y_1 is: Scarce resources would not be efficiently allocated. The example shows (by relying on the opportunity cost doctrine) that there is some "optimal" level of pollution and that this level may be achieved through bargains between the individuals involved.

Distributional Effects

There are distributional effects that do depend on who is assigned ownership of the river. If firm Y is given ownership of the river, its owners will be better off than they would be if firm X were the owner. Because, in our example, allocation will be unaffected by the way in which property rights are assigned,[8] any assessment of the desirability of certain assignments must be made on equity grounds. The price system, in principle, may be capable of solving certain simple externality problems of allocation, but, as always, the price system does not necessarily yield equity.[9]

Relevance of the Coase Theorem

It should be repeated that the results of this section depend crucially on the assumption that bargaining is costless. If there were costs associated with

---

[8] This conclusion requires that the changing distribution of wealth implied by different assignments of property rights has no effect on the allocation of goods. Loosely speaking, it is assumed that the demand and cost curves of Figure 24.1 will not shift in response to the changing distribution of wealth. It is assumed that "income effects" are unimportant.

[9] Matters of equity cannot be established here on *a priori* grounds but, rather, require a detailed examination of the welfare level of each agent. It would be inappropriate to argue, for example, that firm Y has an inalienable right to the use of the river or, conversely, that firm X has a basic right to clean water. Since firm Y's actions affect only firm X, no such *a priori* conclusions are possible. The desires of the two firms are symmetric, and any arguments about the intrinsic rights of one party can be applied symmetrically to the other. For some fascinating examples of this symmetry in legal cases, see Coase, "Problem of Social Cost," 1–44.

striking bargains, we would have to compare those costs to the potential allocational gains from Coase bargaining. Only in situations where those gains exceed necessary bargaining costs will Coase-type results hold. When bargaining costs are high, externalities will continue to distort the allocation of resources, and the assignment of property rights can have a major effect on that allocation. If major industries are given the right to spew noxious fumes into the atmosphere, for example, an efficient allocation is unlikely to emerge, since the costs of bringing together into an effective bargaining unit all the individuals harmed by such fumes are probably quite high. Nevertheless, development of the Coase theorem and the later research based on it has had a major impact on the way economists think about the relationship among externalities, property rights, and the efficient allocation of resources.

ATTRIBUTES OF PUBLIC GOODS

We now turn our attention to a related set of problems about the relationship between competitive markets and the allocation of resources—those raised by the existence of public goods. We begin by providing a precise definition of this concept and then examine why such goods pose allocational problems. We then briefly discuss potential ways in which such problems might be mitigated. In the next chapter, we offer a few warnings about the normative value of some of these prescriptions and stress the need for a positive, behavioral theory of government before attempting to draw policy conclusions about public goods production.

The most common definitions of public goods stress two attributes of such goods: nonexclusivity and nonrivalness. We now describe these attributes in detail.

Nonexclusivity

The first property that distinguishes public goods concerns whether individuals may be excluded from the benefits of consuming the good. For most private goods such exclusion is indeed possible: I easily can be excluded from consuming a hamburger if I don't pay for it. In some cases, however, such exclusion is either very costly or impossible. National defense is the standard example. Once a defense system is established, everyone in a country benefits from it whether they pay for it or not. Similar comments apply, on a more local level, to goods such as mosquito control or inoculation against disease programs. In these cases, once the programs are implemented, no one in the community can be excluded from those benefits whether he or she pays for them or not. Hence, we can divide goods into two categories according to the following definition:

DEFINITION

Exclusive Goods   A good is *exclusive* if it is relatively easy to exclude individuals from benefiting from the good once it is produced. A good is nonexclusive if it is impossible, or very costly, to exclude individuals from benefiting from the good.

Nonrivalry

A second property that characterizes some public goods is nonrivalry. A nonrival good is one for which additional units can be consumed at zero social marginal cost. For most goods, of course, consumption of additional amounts involves some marginal costs of production. Consumption of one more hot dog by someone, for example, requires that various resources be devoted to its production. For certain goods, however, this is not the case. Consider, for example, having one more automobile cross a highway bridge during an off-peak period. Since the bridge is already in place, having one more vehicle cross requires no additional resource and does not reduce consumption elsewhere. Similarly, having one more viewer tune in to a television channel involves no additional cost, even though this action would result in additional consumption taking place. Therefore, we have developed the following definition:

DEFINITION

Nonrival Goods   A good is *nonrival* if consumption of additional units of the good involves zero social marginal costs of production.

Typology of Public Goods

The concepts of nonexclusion and nonrivalry are in some ways related. Many goods that are nonexclusive are also nonrival. National defense and mosquito control are two examples of goods for which exclusion is not possible and additional consumption takes place at zero marginal cost. Many other instances might be suggested. The concepts, however, are not identical: Some goods may possess one property, but not the other. It is, for example, impossible (or at least very costly) to exclude some fishing boats from ocean fisheries, yet the arrival of another boat clearly imposes social costs in the form of a reduced catch for all concerned. Similarly, use of a bridge during off-peak hours may be nonrival, but it is possible to exclude potential users by erecting toll booths. Table 24.1 presents a cross-classification of goods by their possibilities for exclusion and their rivalry. Several examples of goods that fit into each of the categories are provided. Many of the examples other than those in the upper left corner of the table (exclusive, rival private goods) are often produced by the government. However, most economists focus on

TABLE 24.1

**EXAMPLES SHOWING THE TYPOLOGY
OF PUBLIC AND PRIVATE GOODS**

		EXCLUSIVE	
		YES	**NO**
RIVAL	**YES**	Hot dogs, automobiles, houses	Fishing grounds, public grazing land, clean air
	NO	Bridges, swimming pools, satellite television transmission (scrambled)	National defense, mosquito control, justice

nonexclusion as the defining characteristic of "public goods" since, as will be described below, those goods pose the most significant problems for resource allocation in a market economy. Nonrival goods often are privately produced (there are, after all, private bridges, swimming pools, and highways that consumers must pay to use) as long as nonpayers can be excluded from consuming them.[10] Hence, we will use the following narrow definition:

DEFINITION

Public Good   A good is a (pure) *public good* if, once produced, no one can be excluded from benefiting from its availability. Public goods usually also will be nonrival, but that need not always be the case.

Our definition of "public goods" offers a clear illustration of why private markets may not produce such goods in adequate amounts. Purchasers of exclusive private goods can appropriate the benefits of those goods entirely for themselves. Smith's pork chop, for example, yields no benefits to Jones. The resources that were used to produce the pork chop can be seen as

**EFFICIENT
PROVISION OF
PUBLIC GOODS**

---

[10] Nonrival goods that permit imposition of an exclusion mechanism are sometimes referred to as *club goods* since provision of such goods might be organized along the lines of private clubs. Such clubs might then charge a "membership" fee and permit unlimited use by members. The optimal size of a club is determined by the economies of scale present in the production process for the club good. For an analysis, see R. Cornes and T. Sandler, *The Theory of Externalities, Public Goods, and Club Goods* (Cambridge: Cambridge University Press, 1986).

contributing only to Smith's utility, and he or she is willing to pay whatever this is worth. The resource cost of a private good, then, can be "attributed" to a single individual. For a public good, this will not be the case. In buying a public good, an individual would not be able to appropriate all the benefits of the good. Since others cannot be excluded from benefiting from the good, society's utility obtained from the resources devoted to the public good will exceed the utility that accrues to the single individual who pays for the good. The resource cost cannot be attributed solely to the one purchaser. However, potential purchasers will not take the benefits that their purchases have for others into account in their expenditure decisions. Consequently, private markets will tend to underallocate resources to public goods.

The distinction between "pure" public goods and "pure" private goods can be made in a simple way by considering the conditions for efficiency that must hold in the two cases. We know that for the case of any two private goods, marginal rates of substitution must be identical for all individuals and that this common *MRS* must equal the rate at which the goods can be technically transformed in production (see Chapter 17). There is no ambiguity when we say that the social *MRS* must equal the social rate of product transformation. For the case of a (nonexclusive) public good, it is still possible to speak of the rate of product transformation of this good for some private good. Exactly the same kind of resource reallocation takes place between private and public producers as takes place between two private producers when the composition of output changes. In producing more national defense, some automobiles, say, will have to be given up, just as they would if society decided to produce more trucks. It is in defining the social marginal rate of substitution between a public good and some private good that important differences arise.

An Intuitive Analysis

Because public goods are provided on a nonexclusive basis to everyone, the social marginal utility of an additional unit of a public good is the sum of the marginal utilities of all persons benefiting from the public good. For example, suppose that a flood control plan were under consideration and assume that 100,000 individuals would benefit from the plan. Assume also that each individual would be willing to trade away the benefits that the flood control program promises in exchange for one car. Clearly, then, the social marginal rate of substitution of the flood control plan for automobiles is 1 to 100,000. In the aggregate, individuals would be willing to give up 100,000 automobiles in exchange for the benefits of flood prevention.

If left to the private market, however, the flood control program would not come into being. Suppose, for example, that the opportunity cost of producing the dams and dikes necessary for flood control is 50,000 automobiles; that is, a cutback in automobile production by 50,000 would free enough resources to produce the flood control system. Under these circumstances, it is clear that no private individuals would pay for the flood control program themselves. They would only be willing to trade 1 car for the benefits of the program, whereas production conditions would require that they be willing to trade 50,000 cars. Each individual would therefore opt for a privately owned automobile.

Such a decision is clearly inefficient from a social point of view. The social *MRS* of flood control for cars is 1 to 100,000, whereas the technical rate of product transformation is only 1 to 50,000. Looked at in a social context, flood control is a much better "buy" than automobiles; resources should be transferred into flood control up to the point at which the social *MRS* is brought into line with the technological *RPT* implied by the economy's productive abilities.

More formally, if we let MRS^i (*P* for *G*) represent the marginal rate of substitution of public goods (*P*) for private goods (*G*) for the *i*th person, then, by definition,

Mathematical Approach

$$MRS^i \text{ (P for G)} = \left(-\frac{dG}{dP}\right)^i = \frac{MU_P^i}{MU_G^i} \qquad (24.20)$$

and this expression indicates how many units of *G* this person is willing to give up for one more unit of *P*. Since an additional unit of *P* benefits all individuals in society, the social *MRS* (indicated by *SMRS*) can be found by adding up the total amount of private goods that all individuals would be willing to give up to get this unit.

$$SMRS \text{ (P for G)} = \sum_{i=1}^{n} \left(-\frac{dG}{dP}\right)^i = \sum_{i=1}^{n} MRS^i(P \text{ for } G) \qquad (24.21)$$

and the condition for an efficient allocation of resources requires that

$$RPT \text{ (P for G)} = SMRS \text{ (P for G)}, \qquad (24.22)$$

where *RPT* (*P* for *G*) is the rate of product transformation of the public good for the private good.[11]

The efficiency condition of Equation 24.22 cannot be achieved by the workings of the price system. Operation of even an "ideal" perfectly competitive market will only ensure that

---

[11] These conditions were first demonstrated in P. A. Samuelson, "The Pure Theory of Public Expenditure," *Review of Economics and Statistics* 36 (November 1954): 387–389, and in several later articles in the same journal.

$$RPT \ (P \ \text{for} \ G) = MRS^i(P \ \text{for} \ G)$$

$$= \frac{MU_P^i}{MU_G^i} < SMRS \ (P \ \text{for} \ G), \qquad (24.23)$$

where the final inequality sign holds as long as the public good provides some positive benefits to other individuals in addition to those provided to individual i. For this reason, competitive markets will tend to underallocate resources to the production of public goods.

A Graphical Analysis   Problems raised by the nonexclusive nature of public goods also can be demonstrated with partial equilibrium analysis by examining the demand curve associated with such goods. In the case of a private good, the market demand curve (see Chapter 7) was found by summing individuals' demands horizontally. At any price the quantities demanded by each individual are summed to calculate the total quantity demanded in the market. The market demand curve shows the marginal evaluation that individuals place on an

---

FIGURE 24.2

DERIVATION OF THE DEMAND FOR A PUBLIC GOOD

Since a public good is nonexclusive, the price that individuals are willing to pay for one more unit (their "marginal valuations") is equal to the sum of what each individual would pay. Hence, for public goods, market demand curves are derived by a vertical summation rather than the horizontal summation used in the case of private goods.

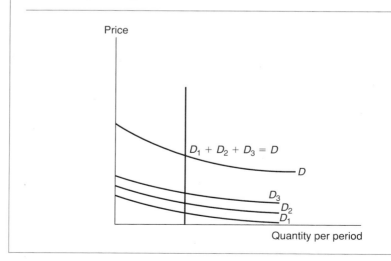

additional unit of output. For a public good (which is provided in fixed quantity to everyone), individual demand curves must be added vertically. To find out how society values some level of public good provision, we must ask how each individual values this level of output and then sum these valuations. This is illustrated conceptually in Figure 24.2. Here the total demand curve for the public good (D) is the vertical sum of each individual's demand curve. Each point on the D curve represents the social marginal evaluation of the particular level of public goods' expenditure. Producing one more unit of the public good would benefit everyone. To evaluate this benefit, all individuals' personal evaluations of the good must be summed. Because markets, by their nature, sum demand curves horizontally rather than vertically, Figure 24.2 again indicates why competitive markets may fail to provide public goods in adequate amounts.

EXAMPLE 24.3

PURCHASING A PUBLIC GOOD: THE ROOMMATES' DILEMMA

To illustrate the nature of the public goods problem, suppose that two Bohemian roommates with identical preferences derive utility from the number of paintings hung on their hovel's walls (X) and on the number of granola bars (Y) they eat. The specific form of the utility function is given by

$$U_i(X, Y_i) = X^{1/3}Y_i^{2/3} \quad \text{(for } i = 1, 2\text{).} \tag{24.24}$$

Notice that utility for each person depends on the total number of paintings hung and on the number of granola bars each person consumes individually. Enjoyment of paintings in this problem, therefore, constitutes a public good.

If we assume each roommate has $300 to spend and that $P_X = \$100$, $P_Y = \$.20$, we can explore the consequences of various expenditure allocations. We know from previous Cobb-Douglas examples that if each person lived alone, he or she would spend $\frac{1}{3}$ of income on paintings ($X = 1$) and $\frac{2}{3}$ on granola bars ($Y = 1,000$).

Public Goods Provision and Strategy. When the roommates live together, however, each must think about what the other will do. Each could, for example, assume the other will buy the paintings. In this case $X = 0$ and both people end up with a zero utility level. Alternatively, person 1 might assume that person 2 will buy no paintings. If that proves to be the case, he or she would choose to purchase one and receive a utility of

$$U_1(X, Y_1) = 1^{1/3}(1,000)^{2/3} = 100, \tag{24.25}$$

whereas person 2's utility would be

$$U_2(X, Y_2) = 1^{1/3}(1,500)^{2/3} = 131. \tag{24.26}$$

Clearly, person 2 has gained from his or her free rider position. Person 1's purchases provide an externality to person 2. Of course, person 2's purchases of paintings would also provide an externality to person 1 should he or she choose to be socially conscious.

Inefficiency of Allocation. That the solution obtained in Equations 24.25 and 24.26 (along with many other possibilities) is inefficient can be shown by calculating each person's marginal rate of substitution:

$$MRS_i = \frac{\partial U_i / \partial X}{\partial U_i / \partial Y_i} = \frac{Y_i}{2X}. \tag{24.27}$$

Hence, at the allocations described,

$$MRS_1 = \frac{1,000}{2} = 500$$

$$MRS_2 = \frac{1,500}{2} = 750. \tag{24.28}$$

The roommates in total would be willing to sacrifice 1,250 granola bars for one more painting—a sacrifice that would actually only cost them 500 bars. Relying on decentralized decision making in this case is inefficient—too few paintings are bought.

An Efficient Allocation. To calculate the efficient level of painting purchases, we must set the sum of each person's *MRS* equal to the goods' price ratio since such a sum correctly reflects the trade-offs the roommates living together would make:

$$MRS_1 + MRS_2 = \frac{Y_1}{2X} + \frac{Y_2}{2X} = \frac{Y_1 + Y_2}{2X} = \frac{P_X}{P_Y} = \frac{100}{.20}. \tag{24.29}$$

Consequently,

$$Y_1 + Y_2 = 1,000X, \tag{24.30}$$

which can be substituted into the combined budget constraint

$$.20(Y_1 + Y_2) + 100X = 600 \tag{24.31}$$

to obtain

$$X = 2$$

$$Y_1 + Y_2 = 2,000. \tag{24.32}$$

Allocating the Cost of Paintings. Assuming the roommates split the cost of the two paintings and use their remaining funds to buy granola bars, each will finally receive a utility of

$$U_i = 2^{1/3}1,000^{2/3} = 126. \qquad (24.33)$$

Although person 1 may not be able to coerce person 2 into such a joint sharing of cost, a 75–25 split provides a utility of

$$U_1 = 2^{1/3}750^{2/3} = 104$$
$$U_2 = 2^{1/3}1,250^{2/3} = 146, \qquad (24.34)$$

which is Pareto superior to the solution obtained when person 1 acts alone. Many other financing schemes would also yield allocations which are Pareto superior to those discussed previously. Which of these, if any, might be chosen depends on how well each roommate plays the strategic financing game.

QUERY: Show that in this example an efficient solution would be obtained if two people living separately decided to live together and pool their paintings. Would you expect that result to hold generally?

LINDAHL PRICING OF PUBLIC GOODS

Since pure public goods may not be produced in efficient quantities in competitive markets, economists have examined how such goods might be provided by the government and financed through taxation. One approach has been to investigate whether an efficient allocation of resources to public goods might come about voluntarily; that is, individuals would agree to be taxed in exchange for the benefits that the public good provides. Perhaps the clearest statement of how such an equilibrium might arise was provided by the Swedish economist Erik Lindahl in 1919.[12] In this section we will briefly examine Lindahl's solution, showing why it is at best a conceptual answer to the public goods question.

A Graphical Approach

Lindahl's argument can be illustrated graphically for a society with only two individuals (again the ever-popular Smith and Jones). In Figure 24.3 the curve labeled SS shows Smith's demand for a particular public good. Rather than using the price of the public good on the vertical axis, we instead have assumed that the share of the public good's cost that Smith must pay varies from 0 percent to 100 percent. The negative slope of SS simply indicates that at a higher tax price for the public good, Smith will demand a smaller quantity of it.

---

[12] Most of Lindahl's writings are not in English. Excerpts from them are reprinted in translation in R. A. Musgrave and A. T. Peacock, eds., *Classics in the Theory of Public Finance* (London: Macmillan, 1958).

FIGURE 24.3

LINDAHL EQUILIBRIUM IN THE DEMAND FOR PUBLIC GOODS

The curve *SS* shows that Smith's demand for a public good increases as the tax share that Smith must pay falls. Jones's demand curve for the public good (*JJ*) is constructed in a similar way. The point *C* represents a Lindahl equilibrium at which *OE* of the public good is supplied with Smith paying 60 percent of the cost. Any other quantity of the public good is not an equilibrium since either too much or too little funding would be available.

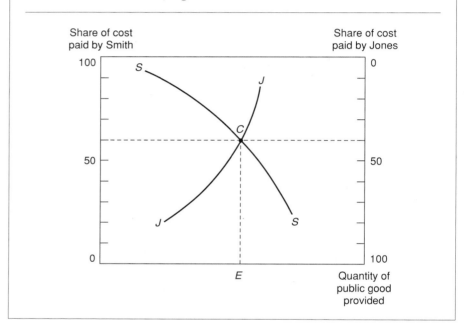

Jones's demand for the public good is derived in much the same way. Now, however, we record the proportion paid by Jones on the right-hand vertical axis of Figure 24.3 and reverse the scale so that moving up the axis results in a lower tax price paid. Given this convention Jones's demand for the public good (*JJ*) has a positive slope.

The two demand curves in Figure 24.3 intersect at *C*, with an output level of *OE* for the public good. At this output level Smith is willing to pay, say, 60 percent of the good's cost whereas Jones pays 40 percent. That point *C* is an equilibrium is suggested by the following argument. For output levels less than *OE*, the two individuals combined are willing to pay more than 100 percent of the public good's cost. Hence, they will vote to increase its level of production (but see the caveats to this statement at the end of this section).

For output levels greater than OE, the individuals are not willing to pay the total cost of the public good being produced and therefore may vote for reductions in the amount being provided. Only for output level OE is there an equilibrium where the tax shares pay precisely for the level of the public good's production undertaken by the government. That this Lindahl equilibrium also will be an efficient allocation of resources can be most conveniently demonstrated mathematically.

Assume, as before, that there are only two individuals (Smith and Jones) and two goods in society: pure public goods (P) and pure private goods (G). Denote the market prices of these goods by P_P and P_G, respectively. Let Smith's share of the public good's price be denoted by α. Then the tax price to Smith for each unit of public good provided is αP_P. Smith therefore will maximize utility by choosing those quantities of the two goods for which

Efficiency of the Lindahl Equilibrium

$$\frac{\alpha P_P}{P_G} = MRS_{Smith} \ (P \text{ for } G) = \frac{MU_{Smith}(P)}{MU_{Smith}(G)}. \tag{24.35}$$

Similarly, Jones will pay a tax share of $(1 - \alpha)$ and will maximize utility by choosing P and G so that

$$\frac{(1 - \alpha)P_P}{P_G} = MRS_{Jones} \ (P \text{ for } G) = \frac{MU_{Jones}(P)}{MU_{Jones}(G)}. \tag{24.36}$$

Producers now will produce private and public goods so as to maximize their profits, requiring that

$$\frac{P_P}{P_G} = RPT \ (P \text{ for } G). \tag{24.37}$$

Summing the utility-maximizing Equations 24.35 and 24.36 yields

$$MRS_{Smith} + MRS_{Jones} = \frac{MU_{Smith}(P)}{MU_{Smith}(G)} + \frac{MU_{Jones}(P)}{MU_{Jones}(G)}$$

$$= \frac{\alpha P_P}{P_G} + \frac{(1 - \alpha)P_P}{P_G} = \frac{P_P}{P_G} = RPT \ (P \text{ for } G), \tag{24.38}$$

where the final equality follows from the profit-maximizing condition 24.37. But these conditions are precisely those required for an efficient allocation of resources to public goods—compare Equation 24.22 to Equation 24.38. Consequently, we have shown that the Lindahl equilibrium represents an efficient allocation of resources. The tax shares introduced in that equilibrium play the role of "pseudo" prices that mimic the functioning of a competitive price system in achieving efficiency. Unfortunately, for reasons we shall now examine, this solution is at best only a conceptual one.

REVEALING THE DEMAND FOR PUBLIC GOODS: THE FREE RIDER PROBLEM

Deriving a Lindahl equilibrium requires knowledge of the optimal tax share (what we have called α) for each individual. A major problem arises in attempting to envision how such data might be collected. Although, through their voting patterns, individuals may provide some information about their preferences for public goods (a topic we take up in the next chapter), that information is usually too sketchy to permit tax shares to be computed because most voting methods do not record the intensity of individuals' preferences. As an alternative a government might choose to ask individuals how much they are willing to pay for particular packages of public goods, but the results of this poll might be extremely inaccurate. In responding to such a question, individuals may feel that they should understate their true preferences for fear they will ultimately have to pay what the good is worth to them in the form of taxes. From the individual's point of view, the proper strategy is to understate true preferences in the hope that others will bear the burden of paying for the good. Since no one can be excluded from enjoying the benefits of a traditional public good, as we saw in Example 24.3, the best position to occupy may be that of a free rider. Each individual, by acting in his or her own self-interest, may ensure that society (or any organization that produces public goods for its members) underestimates the demand for public goods and hence underallocates resources to their production.

Local Public Goods

Some economists have suggested that the public goods problem may be more tractable on a local than on a national level.[13] Because individuals are relatively mobile, they may indicate their preferences for local public goods by choosing to live in communities that offer them utility-maximizing public goods taxation packages. "Voting with one's feet" thereby provides a mechanism for revealing public goods demand in much the same way that "dollar voting" reveals private goods demand. Individuals who want high-quality schools or a high level of police protection can "pay" for them by choosing to live in highly taxed communities. Those who prefer not to receive such benefits can choose to live elsewhere. Similar arguments apply to other types of organizations (such as clubs) that offer packages of public goods for their members—individuals can choose which package of goods they prefer. Whether such actions can completely cope with the problem of revealing the demand for public goods (even on a local level) remains an unsettled question, however.

---

[13] See C. M. Tiebout, "A Pure Theory of Local Expenditures," *Journal of Political Economy* 64 (October 1956): 416–424.

SUMMARY

In this chapter we have examined difficulties that arise from externality (or spillover) effects involved in the consumption or production of certain types of goods. In some cases it may be possible to design mechanisms to cope with these externalities in a market setting, but important limits are involved in such solutions. Some specific issues we examined were:

- Externalities may cause a misallocation of resources because of a divergence between private and social marginal cost. Traditional solutions to this divergence include mergers among the affected parties and adoption of suitable (Pigovian) taxes or subsidies.

- If transactions costs are small, private bargaining among the parties affected by an externality may bring social and private costs into line. The proof that resources will be efficiently allocated under such circumstances is sometimes called the *Coase theorem*.

- Public goods provide benefits to individuals on a nonexclusive basis—no one can be prevented from consuming such goods. Such goods may often also be nonrival in that the marginal cost of serving another user is zero.

- Private markets will tend to underallocate resources to public goods because no single buyer can appropriate all of the benefits that such goods provide.

- A Lindahl optimal tax-sharing scheme can result in an efficient allocation of resources to the production of public goods. Computation of these tax shares requires substantial information that individuals have incentives to hide, however. Reliance on voluntary assent to tax-sharing schemes may therefore fall victim to the tendency of individuals to adopt the free rider position.

PROBLEMS

24.1

A firm in a perfectly competitive industry has patented a new process for making widgets. The new process lowers the firm's average cost curve, meaning this firm alone (although still a price taker) can earn real economic profits in the long run.

a. If the market price is $20 per widget and the firm's marginal cost curve is given by $MC = .4q$, where q is the daily widget production for the firm, how many widgets will the firm produce?

b. Suppose a government study has found that the firm's new process is polluting the air and estimates the social marginal cost of widget production by this firm to be $SMC = .5q$. If the market price is still $20, what is the socially optimal level of production for the firm? What should the rate of a government-imposed excise tax be in order to bring about this optimal level of production?

c. Graph your results.

24.2

On the island of Pago Pago there are 2 lakes and 20 anglers. Each angler can fish on either lake and keep the average catch on his particular lake. On Lake X the total number of fish caught is given by

$$F^X = 10L_X - \tfrac{1}{2}L_X^2,$$

where L_X is the number of people fishing on the lake. For Lake Y the relationship is

$$F^Y = 5L_Y.$$

a. Under this organization of society, what will be the total number of fish caught?

b. The chief of Pago Pago, having once read an economics book, believes that it is possible to raise the total number of fish caught by restricting the number of people allowed to fish on Lake X. What number should be allowed to fish on Lake X in order to maximize the total catch of fish? What is the number of fish caught in this situation?

c. Being basically opposed to coercion, the chief decides to require a fishing license for Lake X. If the licensing procedure is to bring about the optimal allocation of labor, what should the cost of a license be (in terms of fish)?

d. Does this example prove that a "competitive" allocation of resources may not be optimal?

24.3

Suppose that the oil industry in Utopia is perfectly competitive and that all firms draw oil from a single (and practically inexhaustible) pool. Assume that each competitor believes that he or she can sell all the oil he or she can produce at a stable world price of $10 per barrel and that the cost of operating a well for one year is $1,000.

Total output per year (Q) of the oil field is a function of the number of wells (N) operating in the field. In particular,

$$Q = 500N - N^2,$$

and the amount of oil produced by each well (q) is given by

$$q = \frac{Q}{N} = 500 - N.$$

a. Describe the equilibrium output and the equilibrium number of wells in this perfectly competitive case. Is there a divergence between private and social marginal cost in the industry?

b. Suppose now that the government nationalizes the oil field. How many oil wells should it operate? What will total output be? What will the output per well be?

c. As an alternative to nationalization, the Utopian government is considering an annual license fee per well to discourage overdrilling. How large should this license fee be if it is to prompt the industry to drill the optimal number of wells?

24.4

There is considerable legal controversy about product safety. Two extreme positions might be termed *caveat emptor* (let the buyer beware) and *caveat vendor* (let the seller beware). Under the former scheme producers would have no responsibility for the safety of their products: buyers would absorb all losses. Under the latter scheme this liability assignment would be reversed: firms would be completely responsible under law for losses incurred from unsafe products. Using simple supply and demand analysis, discuss how the assignment of such liability might affect the allocation of resources. Would safer products be produced if firms were strictly liable under law? How do possible information asymmetries affect your results?

24.5

Three types of contracts are used to specify the way in which tenants on a plot of agricultural land may pay rent to the landlord. Rent may be paid (1) in money (or a fixed amount of agricultural produce), (2) as a fixed proportionate share of the crop, or (3) in "labor dues" by agreeing to work on other plots owned by the landlord. How might these alternative contract specifications affect tenants' production decisions? What sorts of transactions costs might occur in the enforcement of each type of contract? What economic factors might affect the type of contract specified in different places or during different historical periods?

24.6

Suppose a monopoly produces a harmful externality. Use the concept of consumer surplus to analyze whether an optimal tax on the polluter would necessarily be a welfare improvement.

24.7

Suppose there are only two individuals in society. The demand curve for mosquito control for person A is given by

$$q_a = 100 - P.$$

For person B the demand curve for mosquito control is given by

$$q_b = 200 - P.$$

a. Suppose mosquito control is a pure public good: that is, once it is produced, everyone benefits from it. What would be the optimal level of this activity if it could be produced at a constant marginal cost of $120 per unit?

b. If mosquito control were left to the private market, how much might be produced? Does your answer depend on what each person assumes the other will do?

c. If the government were to produce the optimal amount of mosquito control, how much will this cost? How should the tax bill for this amount be allocated between the individuals if they are to share it in proportion to benefits received from mosquito control?

24.8

Suppose that there are N individuals in an economy with three goods. Two of the goods are pure (nonexclusive) public goods, whereas the third is an ordinary private good.

a. What conditions must hold for resources to be allocated efficiently between either of the public goods and the private good?

b. What conditions must hold for resources to be allocated efficiently between the two public goods?

24.9

Suppose that the production possibility frontier for an economy that produces one public good (P) and one private good (G) is given by

$$G^2 + 100P^2 = 5,000.$$

This economy is populated by 100 identical individuals, each with a utility function of the form

$$\text{utility} = \sqrt{G_i P},$$

where G_i is the individual's share of private good production ($= G/100$). Notice that the public good is nonexclusive and that everyone benefits equally from its level of production.

a. If the market for G and P were perfectly competitive, what levels of those goods would be produced? What would the typical individual's utility be in this situation?

b. What are the optimal production levels for G and P? What would the typical individual's utility level be? How should consumption of good G be taxed to achieve this result? (*Hint:* The numbers in this problem do not come out evenly, and some approximations should suffice.)

SUGGESTED READINGS

Alchian, A., and H. Demsetz. "Production, Information Costs, and Economic Organization." *American Economic Review* 62 (December 1972): 777–795.
Uses externality arguments to develop a theory of economic organizations.

Barzel, Y. *Economic Analysis of Property Rights.* Cambridge: Cambridge University Press, 1989.
Provides a graphical analysis of several economic questions that are illuminated through use of the property rights paradigm.

Cheung, S. N. S. "The Fable of the Bees: An Economic Investigation." *Journal of Law and Economics* 16 (April 1973): 11–33.
Empirical study of how the famous bee–orchard owner externality is handled by private markets in the state of Washington.

———. "Private Property Rights and Sharecropping." *Journal of Political Economy* 76 (December 1968): 1107–1122.

An analysis of the efficiency properties of various land tenancy arrangements.

Coase, R. H. "The Market for Goods and the Market for Ideas." *American Economic Review* 64 (May 1974): 384–391.
Speculative article about notions of externalities and regulation in the "marketplace of ideas."

———. "The Problem of Social Cost." *Journal of Law and Economics* 3 (October 1960): 1–44.
Classic article on externalities. Many fascinating historical-legal cases.

Cornes, R., and T. Sandler. *The Theory of Externalities, Public Goods, and Club Goods.* Cambridge: Cambridge University Press, 1986.
Good theoretical analysis of many of the issues raised in this chapter. Good discussions of the connections between returns to scale, excludability, and club goods.

Cropper, M. L., and W. E. Oates. "Environmental

Economics: A Survey." *Journal of Economic Literature* (June 1992): 675–740.
Complete survey article with particularly useful sections on applications of hedonic price theory.

Demsetz, H. "Toward a Theory of Property Rights." *American Economic Review, Papers and Proceedings* 57 (May 1967): 347–359.
Brief development of a plausible theory of how societies come to define property rights.

Posner, R. A. *Economic Analysis of Law.* 2d ed. Boston: Little Brown, 1977.
In many respects the "bible" of the law and economics movement. Posner's arguments are not always economically correct, but unfailingly interesting and provocative.

Samuelson, P. A. "The Pure Theory of Public Expenditures." *Review of Economics and Statistics* 36 (November 1954): 387–389.
Classic statement of the efficiency conditions for public goods production.

———. "Diagrammatic Exposition of a Theory of Public Expenditures." *Review of Economics and Statistics* 37 (November 1955): 350–356.
Diagrammatic treatment of the famous 1954 article.

Tiebout, C. M. "A Pure Theory of Local Expenditures." *Journal of Political Economy* 64 (October 1956): 416–424.
Primary reference on the local public goods concept and how such goods might be produced efficiently.

CHAPTER 25

PUBLIC CHOICE THEORY

In this chapter we look at the general theory of public choice. That is, we examine how economic choices are made in the public arena, by government. Our analysis is divided into three major parts. First, we adopt a theoretical perspective and examine possible welfare criteria for choosing among differing resource allocations. Here, we examine some very general results about the nature of social decision rules and introduce the principal negative "theorem" (due to K. J. Arrow), which states that no such decision rule can be completely satisfactory. The final two parts of the chapter are then devoted to the question of modeling individual voting and representative government, respectively. Consistent with our focus throughout this book, our primary concern will be to illustrate the connection (if any) between voting methods and resource allocation.

SOCIAL WELFARE CRITERIA

We will begin our study of public choice theory by examining some of the problems associated with devising welfare criteria for choosing among feasible allocations of resources. This subject is the most normative branch of microeconomics, since it necessarily involves making hard choices about the utility levels of different individuals. In choosing between two allocations, A and B, the problem arises that some individuals prefer A whereas others prefer B. In some way comparisons among people must be made in order to judge which allocation is preferable. As might be expected, there is no universally accepted criterion for making such choices. Very basic philosophical questions continue to perplex welfare economists. Our main purpose here is to illustrate these perplexities in order to provide a foundation for our more applied analysis of voting.

Social Welfare Criteria in an Exchange Model

The model of efficiency in exchange that we developed in Chapter 17 is useful for demonstrating the problems involved in establishing social welfare criteria. Consider the Edgeworth box diagram in Figure 25.1. Only those

FIGURE 25.1

EDGEWORTH BOX DIAGRAM OF EXCHANGE

This diagram is simply a redrawing of Figure 17.7. The curve O_S, O_J is the locus of efficient allocations of X and Y between Smith and Jones. Allocations of this locus are dominated by those on it in that both individuals can be made better off by moving to the contract curve.

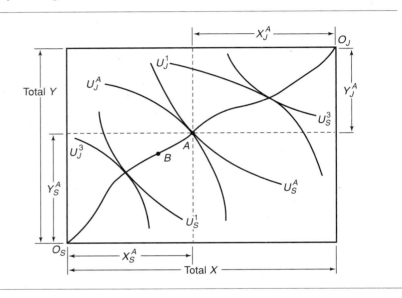

points on the contract curve are eligible to be considered as possible candidates for a social optimum. Points off the contract curve are dominated by points on the curve in the sense that both individuals can be made better off, and in so doing (presumably) social welfare could be improved. Along the contract curve the utilities of the two individuals (Smith and Jones) vary, and these utilities are directly competitive. Smith's utility can be increased only by decreasing Jones's. Given this set of efficient allocations, we now wish to discuss possible criteria for choosing among them.

If we are willing to make the heroic assumption that utility can be compared among individuals, we can use the possible utility combinations along the contract curve in Figure 25.1 to construct[1] the utility possibility frontier shown in Figure 25.2. The curve O_S, O_J records those utility levels for

---

[1] This construction is identical to that we used in Chapter 16 to derive the production possibility frontier.

FIGURE 25.2

UTILITY POSSIBILITY FRONTIER

Assuming measurability of utility, the utility possibility frontier can be derived from Figure 25.1. This curve (O_S, O_J) shows those combinations of utility that society can achieve. Two criteria for choosing among points on O_S, O_J might be: Choose "equal" utilities for Smith and Jones (point A); or choose the utilities so that their sum is the greatest (point B). Under the Rawls criterion, the efficient allocation B would be regarded as inferior to equal allocations between D and A.

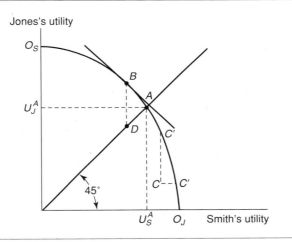

Smith and Jones that are obtainable from the fixed quantities of those goods that are available. Any utility combination (such as point C) that lies inside the curve O_S, O_J is inefficient in the sense that utilities could be unambiguously improved (for example, by moving to any point on the arc $C'C'$). This is simply a reflection of the way in which the contract curve is constructed. Using the utility possibility frontier, we can now rephrase the "problem" of welfare economics as being the development of criteria for selecting a point on this frontier.

Equality Criterion

A few simple criteria for choosing a point on O_S, O_J are easily shown. One possible principle would require complete equality: Smith and Jones should enjoy the same level of welfare. This social welfare criterion would necessitate choosing point A on the utility possibility frontier. Since point A corresponds to a unique point on the contract curve, the socially optimal allocation of goods has been determined by this choice. In Figure 25.1 this allocation is seen to require that Smith gets X_S^A and Y_S^A, whereas Jones gets X_J^A and Y_J^A. Notice that the goods X and Y are not necessarily distributed equally. It is equality of utilities that is required by the criterion, not equality of goods.

Utilitarian Criterion

A similar (though not necessarily identical) criterion would be to choose that point on the utility possibility frontier for which the sum of Smith's and Jones's utilities is the greatest. This would require that the optimal point (B) be chosen to maximize ($U_J + U_S$) subject to the constraint implied by the utility possibility frontier. As before, point B would imply a certain allocation of X and Y between Smith and Jones, and this allocation could be derived from Figure 25.1.

The Rawls Criterion

A final criterion we can examine was first posed by the philosopher John Rawls.[2] Rawls begins by envisioning society as being in an "initial position" in which no one knows what his or her final position (and ultimate utility) will be. He then asks what kind of welfare criterion would be adopted by people who find themselves in such a position. Posed in this way, selection of a welfare criterion is a problem in behavior under uncertainty, since no one knows exactly how the criterion chosen will affect his or her personal well-being. From his initial premise Rawls concludes that individuals would be very risk averse in their selection of a criterion. Specifically, he asserts that members of society would choose to depart from perfect equality only on the condition that the worst-off person under an unequal distribution of utilities would actually be better off than under equality. In terms of Figure 25.2 unequal distributions such as B would be permitted only when the attainable equal distributions (which lie along the 45° line) were below point D. Equal distributions that lie between D and A are, according to Rawls, superior to B because the worse-off individual (Smith) is better off there than under allocation B. The Rawls criterion therefore suggests that many efficient allocations may not be socially desirable and that societies may choose equality even at considerable efficiency costs. Such a conclusion is not universally shared by economists, many of whom argue that the criteria proposed are unnecessarily risk averse. Individuals in the initial position may instead prefer to gamble that they will be the winners under an unequal final distribution, and such motives may dominate if the likelihood of being the worse-off individual is small.[3] Still, Rawls's conception of using the "initial position" methodology to conceptualize how individuals might

---

[2] J. Rawls, *A Theory of Justice* (Cambridge, Mass.: Harvard University Press, 1971).

[3] See, for example, K. J. Arrow, "Some Ordinalist-Utilitarian Notes on Rawls's Theory of Justice," *Journal of Philosophy* (May 1973): 245–263.

FIGURE 25.3

USING A SOCIAL WELFARE FUNCTION TO FIND THE SOCIAL OPTIMUM

If we can postulate the existence of a social welfare function having the indifference curves W_1, W_2, and W_3, it is possible to conceptualize the problem of social choice. It is clear that efficiency (being on O_S, O_J) is necessary for a welfare optimum, but this is not sufficient, as may be seen by comparing points D and F.

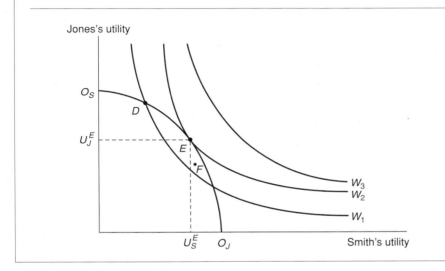

make social decisions is an intriguing one that has been widely used in other investigations.

A more general approach to social welfare (which as special cases includes the three criteria we discussed above) can be obtained by examining the concept of a social welfare function.[4] This function might depend only on Smith's and Jones's utility levels:

$$\text{social welfare} = W(U_S, U_J). \qquad (25.1)$$

The social choice problem, then, is to allocate X and Y between Smith and Jones so as to maximize W. This procedure is pictured in Figure 25.3. The

SOCIAL WELFARE FUNCTIONS

---

[4] This concept was first developed by A. Bergson in "A Reformulation of Certain Aspects of Welfare Economics," *Quarterly Journal of Economics* 52 (February 1938): 310–334.

curves labeled W_1, W_2, and W_3 represent social indifference curves, in that society is indifferent about which utility combination on a particular curve is chosen.[5] These indifference curves for the function W are drawn convex on the normative assumption that "society" exhibits a diminishing rate of substitution of Smith's utility for Jones's. This assumption would seem to be reasonable if society is basically egalitarian and is progressively less willing to make Smith better off at the expense of making Jones worse off. Point E is the optimal point of social welfare, in that this is the highest level of W achievable with the given utility possibility frontier. As before, it is necessary to go from point E to the Edgeworth box diagram in order to determine the socially optimal allocation of goods.

Conflicts between Efficiency and Equity

Figure 25.3 demonstrates a conceptual way of choosing a distribution of utilities that maximizes social welfare. The figure again illustrates the important distinction to be made between the goals of equity and efficiency. All of the points on O_S, O_J are efficient by the Pareto criterion. However, some of the efficient points represent far more socially desirable distributions than do others. As with the Rawls criterion, there are in fact many inefficient points (such as F) that are socially preferred to efficient points (such as D). It sometimes may be in society's interest to choose seemingly inefficient allocations of resources if the truly optimal allocation (point E) is unattainable. In order to satisfy societal concepts of equity, it may make sense to accept some inefficiency.

EXAMPLE 25.1

EQUITABLE SHARING

A father arrives home carrying an eight-piece pizza. How should he share it between his two ravenous teenagers? Suppose teen 1 has a utility of pizza function of the form

$$U_1 = 2\sqrt{X_1}, \tag{25.2}$$

and teen 2 (the larger of the two) has a utility function of the form

$$U_2 = \sqrt{X_2}. \tag{25.3}$$

---

[5] Under the "equality" criterion the social welfare function would have L-shaped indifference curves, whereas under the "maximum sum of utilities" criterion the indifference curves would be parallel straight lines with a slope of -1.

The least-resistance option would be to share the pizza equally—four slices each. In this case $U_1 = 4$, $U_2 = 2$. Alternatively, a benevolent father recognizes teen 2's greater needs and opts for an allocation that provides equal utility. In this case $X_1 = 1.6$, $X_2 = 6.4$, $U_1 = U_2 = 2.53$. As a third simple alternative, a utilitarian father might seek to maximize the sum of his teens' utility by choosing $X_1 = 6.4$, $X_2 = 1.6$, $U_1 = 5.06$, $U_2 = 1.26$ and $U_1 + U_2 = 6.32$.

A Probabilistic Father. A father familiar with probability theory might turn this whole problem over to the teens to decide. But since the teens' desires are directly competitive, it is unlikely that they will arrive at a unanimous decision with full information. If, however, the father offers the three possible allocations listed above and says he will flip a coin to determine who gets which portion under each, expected utility maximization would yield unanimity. Expected utilities from a coin flip that yields teen 1 either 1.6 or 6.4 pieces is

$$E(U_1) = .5(2.53) + .5(5.06) = 3.80.$$

Similarly, for teen 2, (25.4)

$$E(U_2) = .5(2.53) + .5(1.26) = 1.90.$$

Hence, in this case each teen would opt for the first, equal allocation, since each gets higher expected utility from it than from the flip.

A Rawlsian Father. If the father could subject each of his teens to a "veil of ignorance" so that neither would know his or her identity until the pizza is served, the voting might be still different. If each teen focuses on a worse-case scenario, each would opt for the equal utility allocation since that ensures that utility will not fall below 2.53. But that may assume too much risk aversion. If each teen believes he or she has a 50–50 chance of being labeled "1" or "2," expected utilities are

(i) $X_1 = X_2 = 4$ $E(U) = .5(4) + .5(2) = 3$

(ii) $X_1 = 1.6$, $X_2 = 6.4$ $E(U) = .5(2.53) + .5(2.53) = 2.53$ (25.5)

(iii) $X_1 = 6.4$, $X_2 = 1.6$ $E(U) = .5(5.06) + .5(1.26) = 3.16.$

If the teens vote only on the basis of expected utility, each might now opt for the utilitarian solution (that is, iii).

QUERY: Might the degree of risk aversion exhibited by the teens change their voting in the Rawlsian situation, or has it already been accounted for in the calculation?

THE ARROW IMPOSSIBILITY THEOREM

The social welfare function, then, provides a useful tool for demonstrating particular aspects of the problem of social choice. We must recognize, however, that this tool is only a conceptual one offering little guidance for the development of practical policy. We have so far begged the question of how such a function is established or what the properties of the function are likely to be. Here we will examine the economic approach to such questions taken by K. J. Arrow and others.[6]

The Basic Problem

Arrow views the general social welfare problem as one of choosing among several feasible "social states." It is assumed that each individual in society can rank these states according to their desirability. The question Arrow raises is, Does there exist a ranking of these states on a societywide scale that fairly records these individual preferences? Symbolically, assume there are three social states (A, B, and C) and two individuals in society (Smith and Jones). Suppose that Smith prefers A to B (we will denote this by $A \, P_S \, B$, where P_S represents the words "is preferred by Smith to") and B to C. These preferences can be written as $A \, P_S \, B$ and $B \, P_S \, C$. If the individual is to be "rational," it should then be the case that $A \, P_S \, C$: The individual's preferences should be transitive. Suppose also that among the three states, Jones has preferences $C \, P_J \, A$, $A \, P_J \, B$, and $C \, P_J \, B$. Arrow's impossibility theorem consists of showing that a reasonable social ranking of these three states (call this ranking P) cannot exist.

The Arrow Axioms

The crux of this theorem is to define what is meant by a "reasonable social ranking." Arrow assumes that any social ranking (P) should obey the following six seemingly unobjectionable axioms (here P is to be read "is socially preferred to"):

1. It must rank all social states: Either $A \, P \, B$, $B \, P \, A$, or A and B are equally desirable ($A \, I \, B$) for any two states A and B.
2. The ranking must be transitive: If $A \, P \, B$ and $B \, P \, C$ (or $B \, I \, C$), then $A \, P \, C$.
3. The ranking must be positively related to individual preferences: If A is unanimously preferred to B by Smith and Jones, then $A \, P \, B$.
4. If new social states become feasible, this fact should not affect the social ranking of the original states. If, between A and B, $A \, P \, B$, then this will remain true if some new state (D) becomes feasible.[7]

---

[6] See K. J. Arrow, *Social Choice and Individual Values*, 2d ed. (New Haven, Conn.: Yale University Press, 1963).

[7] Condition 4 is sometimes called the axiom of the *independence of irrelevant alternatives*. More controversy has arisen over this axiom (and similar ones in the von Neumann–Morgenstern list) than any other. To see the sort of functions that are ruled out by the axiom, consider individuals voting for candidates in an election. Suppose that each individual can rank these candidates in

5. The social preference relation should not be imposed, say, by custom. It should not be the case that $A\,P\,B$ regardless of the tastes of individuals in society.

6. The relationship should be nondictatorial. One person's preferences should not determine society's preferences.

Arrow's Proof

Arrow was able to show that these six conditions (all of which seem ethically reasonable on the surface) are not compatible with one another: No general social relationship obeying Conditions 1 to 6 exists. Using the preferences of Smith and Jones among A, B, and C, it is possible to see the kind of inconsistencies that can arise in social choice. Since $B\,P_S\,C$ and $C\,P_J\,B$, it must be the case that society is indifferent between B and C ($B\,I\,C$). Otherwise, society's preferences would be in accord with only one individual (and against the other), and this would violate Axiom 6 requiring nondictatorship.

Since both Smith and Jones prefer A to B, Conditions 3 and 5 require that $A\,P\,B$. Hence, by transitivity Axiom 2, $A\,P\,C$. But, again, this is a violation of the nondictatorship assumption since $A\,P_S\,C$ but $C\,P_J\,A$. Thus, in this simple case an inconsistency arises in the attempt to construct a social preference relationship. Admittedly, this example is a bit contrived, but it does illustrate clearly the problems of trying to aggregate divergent patterns of individual preferences into some reasonable social pattern. The importance of Arrow's work is to show that any social decision rule that is chosen must violate at least one of the postulates embodied in Axioms 1 through 6.

Significance of the Arrow Theorem

Much research in social choice theory has been focused on Arrow's fundamental result and on whether it continues to hold under potential revisions in the set of basic postulates.[8] In general, the impossibility result appears to be rather robust to modest changes in these postulates. Systems with fewer basic axioms and systems under which some of Arrow's axioms are relaxed continue to demonstrate a variety of inconsistencies. It appears

---

order of their desirability. An election somehow combines these individual lists into a societywide list. According to Axiom 4, the social list must have the property that if candidate X is preferred to candidate Y, this should remain true even if other candidates enter or leave the race. The most common election procedure in which each person votes only for his or her most preferred candidate may not obey the axiom because of the presence of "spoilers" in the race. For example, it is conceivable that the presence of George Wallace in the 1968 presidential election caused Hubert Humphrey to lose (Richard Nixon was shown to be "socially preferred"). With the "irrelevant alternative" Wallace out of the race, Humphrey might have won. The presidential election system therefore would not obey Arrow's Axiom 4. Many authors have examined the consequences of relaxing the axiom.

[8] For a survey see D. H. Blair and R. A. Pollak, "Rational Collective Choice," *Scientific American* (August 1983): 88–95.

that to expect methods of social choice to be at the same time rational, definitive, and egalitarian may be to expect too much. Instead, compromises are inevitable. Of course, where to make such compromises is a very difficult normative question.

Despite the negative nature of Arrow's conclusion, it should be remembered that all societies do in fact make social choices. The U.S. Congress manages to pass a budget (often at the last minute); college faculties establish curricula; and Alaskan Eskimos decide how to improve upon their communal fishing methods for the next year. Rather than examining the normative question of how such choices might be made in a socially optimal way, it may be more productive to examine how these choices are actually made so that positive predictions can be made about what outcomes are likely in various situations. In the final sections of this chapter, we take such an approach in a brief review of aspects of what has come to be called "public choice theory."

DIRECT VOTING AND RESOURCE ALLOCATION

Voting is used as a social decision process in many institutions. In some instances individuals vote directly on policy questions. That is the case in some New England town meetings, many statewide referenda (for example, California's Proposition 13 in 1977), and for many of the national policies adopted in Switzerland. Direct voting also characterizes the social decision procedure used for many smaller groups and clubs such as farmers' cooperatives, university faculties, or the local Rotary Club. In other cases, however, societies have found it more convenient to use a representative form of government in which individuals vote directly only for political representatives, who are then charged with making decisions on policy questions. For our study of public choice theory, we will begin with an analysis of direct voting. This is an important subject not only because such a procedure applies to many cases, but also because elected representatives often engage in direct voting (in Congress, for example), and the theory we will illustrate applies to those instances as well. Later in the chapter we will take up special problems raised in studying representative government.

Majority Rule

Because so many elections are conducted on a majority rule basis, we often tend to regard that procedure as a natural and, perhaps, optimal one for making social choices. But only a cursory examination should suggest that there is nothing particularly sacred about a rule requiring that a policy obtain 50 percent of the vote to be adopted. In the U.S. Constitution, for example, two-thirds of the states must adopt an amendment before it becomes law. And 60 percent of Congress must vote to limit debate on controver-

TABLE 25.1

PREFERENCES THAT PRODUCE THE PARADOX OF VOTING

	POLICY			
	A	B	C	A
	LOW	MEDIUM	HIGH	LOW
VOTER	SPENDING	SPENDING	SPENDING	SPENDING
Smith	>		>	<
Jones	<		>	>
Fudd	>		<	>

sial issues. Indeed, in some institutions (Quaker meetings, for example), unanimity may be required for social decisions. Our discussion of the Lindahl equilibrium concept in the previous chapter suggests that there may exist a distribution of tax shares that would obtain unanimous support in voting for public goods. But arriving at such unanimous agreements may be very time-consuming and may be subject to strategic ploys by the voters involved. Examining in detail the forces that lead societies to move away from unanimity and to choose some other determining fraction would take us too far afield here. We instead will assume throughout our discussion of voting that decisions will be made by majority rule. Readers may wish to ponder for themselves what kinds of situations might call for a decisive proportion of other than 50 percent.

In the 1780s the French social theorist M. de Condorcet observed an important peculiarity of majority rule voting systems—they may not arrive at an equilibrium but instead may cycle among alternative options. Condorcet's paradox is illustrated for a simple case in Table 25.1. Suppose there are three voters (Smith, Jones, and Fudd) choosing among three policy options. For our subsequent analysis we will assume that the policy options represent three levels of spending on a particular public good [(A) low, (B) medium, or (C) high], but Condorcet's paradox would arise even if the options being considered do not have this type of ordering associated with them.[9] Preferences of Smith, Jones, and Fudd among the three policy options

The Paradox of Voting

---

[9] The "public good" being voted on might represent "equality" brought about through income transfers, so that this analysis is relevant to voting on equity matters as well.

are indicated by inequality signs. That is, the signs indicate that Smith prefers option A to option B, that Jones prefers option B to option A, and so forth. The preferences described in Table 25.1 give rise to Condorcet's paradox.

Consider a vote between options A and B. Here option A would win, since it is favored by Smith and Fudd and opposed only by Jones. In a vote between options A and C, option C would win, again by 2 votes to 1. But in a vote of C versus B, B would win and we would be back where we started. Social choices would endlessly cycle among the three alternatives. In subsequent votes, any choice that was initially decided upon could be defeated by an alternative, and no equilibrium would ever be reached. In this situation the option finally chosen will depend on such seemingly nongermane issues as when the balloting stops or how items are ordered on an agenda rather than being derived in some rational way from the preferences of voters.

Single-Peaked Preferences and the Median Voter Theorem

Condorcet's voting paradox arises because of the presence of a degree of irreconcilability in the preferences of voters. One therefore might ask whether restrictions on the types of preferences allowed might yield situations where equilibrium voting outcomes are more likely. A fundamental result about this probability was discovered by D. Black in 1948.[10] Black showed that equilibrium voting outcomes always occur in cases where the issue being voted upon is one-dimensional (such as how much to spend on a public good) and where voters' preferences are "single-peaked." To understand what the notion of single-peaked means, consider again Condorcet's paradox. In Figure 25.4 we illustrate the preferences that gave rise to the paradox by assigning hypothetical utility levels to options A, B, and C that are consistent with the preferences recorded in Table 25.1. For Smith and Jones, preferences are single-peaked—as levels of public goods' expenditures rise, there is only one local utility-maximizing choice (A for Smith, B for Jones). Fudd's preferences, on the other hand, have two local maxima (A and C). It is these preferences that produced the cyclical voting pattern. If instead Fudd had the preferences represented by the dashed line in Figure 25.4 (where now C is the only local utility maximum), there would be no paradox. In that case, option B would be chosen since that option would defeat both A and C by votes of 2 to 1. Here B is the preferred choice of the "median" voter (Jones) whose preferences are "between" the preferences of Smith and the revised preferences of Fudd.

Black's result is quite general and applies to any number of voters. If choices are unidimensional and preferences are single-peaked, majority rule will result in the selection of the project that is most favored by the median

---

[10] D. Black, "On the Rationale of Group Decision Making," *Journal of Political Economy* (February 1948): 23–34.

FIGURE 25.4

SINGLE-PEAKED PREFERENCES AND THE MEDIAN VOTER THEOREM

This figure illustrates the preferences in Table 25.1. Smith's and Jones's preferences are single-peaked, but Fudd's have two local peaks, and these yield the voting paradox. If Fudd's instead had been single-peaked (the dashed line), option B would be chosen as the preferred choice of the median voter (Jones).

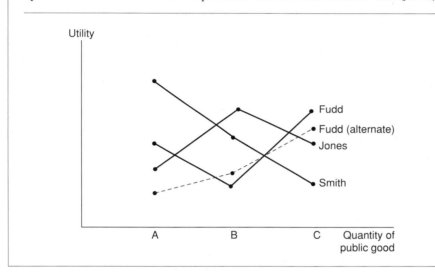

voter. Therefore, that voter's preferences will determine what public choices are made. These choices may not necessarily be efficient, however. The tax-spending package favored by the median voter might be quite different from a Lindahl equilibrium depending on the extent to which other voters favor the tax-spending combinations assigned to them under the plan.

Unfortunately, Black's median voter result may be of only limited importance since many issues of public choice are not one-dimensional. Consider, for example, choosing among alternative general environmental policies that involve varying levels of spending, locations of activities, and types of pollution permitted. In such a case, individuals' preferences are likely to be both varied and quite complex. In these situations the single-peaked notion loses much of its intuitive appeal, and there are no simple median voter theorems. Whether equilibrium voting choices exist in such instances and what the characteristics of such choices will be have proved to be very difficult questions to address in any general way. Still, the "median voter theorem" has intuitive appeal and has been used in many empirical analyses of public choices.

TABLE 25.2

INTENSITY OF PREFERENCES AND LOGROLLING

	PROJECT		
VOTER	A	B	C
1	−5	2	2
2	−5	6	6
3	3	2	10
4	3	−5	−5
5	3	−7	−7

(Figure shows utility gain or loss from each project.)

EXAMPLE 25.2

LOGROLLING, THE PORK BARREL, AND PARETO OPTIMALITY

Voters may sometimes be able to trade votes to get what they want. Table 25.2 provides an example of such logrolling. It records the preferences about three projects (in terms of utility gains or losses) for five individuals. If all the projects are voted on individually, all will pass—always by a vote of 3 to 2. That this may not be a desirable outcome can be seen simply by summing the utility levels (assuming that can be done) for each project; by this criterion, only project C is "worthwhile." Both A and B yield a net negative utility level to society as a whole.

Projects A and B might be blocked through logrolling. Suppose individuals 1 and 5 agree to "trade" votes; that is, individual 1 agrees to oppose project B, providing individual 5 will oppose project A. Such a trade makes both individuals better off than they would be should both projects be adopted. With the vote trading, both projects fail by 3–2 votes. Notice that this trade imposes a negative externality on voters 2 and 3 (who are worse off without both projects than with both) and a positive externality on voter 4.

Pareto Efficiency.   Simple vote trading does not guarantee that all projects that are, on the average, beneficial will be accepted and that those that are harmful will be turned down, however. Consider now a two-way choice between projects A and C. In that case individuals 1 and 5 can still profitably trade votes ensuring that both project A (undesirable) and project C (desirable) are defeated. As this example suggests, there is no very close connection between the concept of free trading in votes and choosing efficient resource allocations. No general efficiency theorems similar to those in Chapter 17 are possible. Nevertheless, "back scratching" and "pork barrel" politics are prevalent in legislative bodies.

QUERY: Why does voluntary trading of votes not result in Pareto optimality here, whereas voluntary trading of goods usually does in our exchange examples?

REPRESENTATIVE GOVERNMENT

In representative governments, individuals vote for candidates, not policies. Successful candidates then vote directly in legislative bodies for the policies they prefer. Politicians' policy preferences are molded by a variety of influences, including their perceptions of what their constituents want, their view of the "public good," the forcefulness of "special interest" groups, and, ultimately, the desire to ensure their own reelection. Once such policies are chosen, representatives must vote in the legislative bodies to which they have been elected. Modeling these votes raises many of the same issues of consistency, procedure, and logrolling that were described in the previous section. Despite these complications, economists must pay attention to the political process since it is an important allocator of resources in all modern economies. In this section we examine one tractable model of the political process which, though an obviously simplified picture of reality, may actually reflect some important features that guide such allocational questions.

Probabilistic Voting

In our model of representative government, we will assume there are only two candidates for a political office. Prior to the election each candidate announces his or her "platform"—a complete listing of the policies to be followed, if elected. The candidates' platforms will be denoted by Θ_1 and Θ_2. To simplify things further, we will assume that candidates, once elected, actually seek to implement the platform they have stated. Of course, in reality, candidates often go back on election promises, but to study the issue of credibility would take us too far afield.

Each of the n voters in society observes the candidates' platforms and decides how to vote. If π_i represents the probability that voter i will vote for candidate 1, we will assume that

$$\pi_i = f_i[U_i(\Theta_1) - U_i(\Theta_2)] \tag{25.6}$$

where $f' > 0$ and $U_i(\Theta_j)$ represents the utility that the voter expects to obtain from the platform announced by candidate j. Since there are only two candidates[11] in the election, the probability that voter i will vote for candidate 2 is given by $1 - \pi_i$.

The Candidate Game   Candidate 1 chooses Θ_1 so as to maximize the probability of his or her election:

$$\text{expected vote} = EV_1 = \sum_{i=1}^{n} \pi_i = \sum_{i=1}^{n} f_i[U_i(\Theta_1) - U_i(\Theta_2)]. \qquad (25.7)$$

Similarly, candidate 2 chooses Θ_2 to maximize his or her expected votes:

$$\text{expected vote} = EV_2 = \sum_{i=1}^{n} (1 - \pi_i) = n - EV_1. \qquad (25.8)$$

From the perspective of game theory (see Chapters 10 and 20) our voting model is therefore a *zero-sum game* with continuous strategies (the platforms, Θ_1 and Θ_2). The fundamental theorem of zero-sum games assures that such a game will have a Nash equilibrium set of strategies for which

$$EV_1(\Theta_1, \Theta_2^*) \leq EV_1(\Theta_1^*, \Theta_2^*) \leq EV_1(\Theta_1^*, \Theta_2). \qquad (25.9)$$

That is, candidate 1 does best against Θ_2^* by choosing Θ_1^*, and candidate 2 does best against Θ_1^* by choosing Θ_2^*. Considerations of the strategic aspects of elections, therefore, suggest that candidates will be led to equilibrium platforms and that the properties of elections can be studied by examining how these platforms are affected by changing situations.

EXAMPLE 25.3

NET VALUE PLATFORMS

Although it is generally difficult to quantify the various dimensions of candidates' platforms, one simple illustration is provided by "net value" platforms under which each candidate promises a unique dollar benefit (that is, value of government services less taxes paid) to each voter. For example,

---

[11] Here we also assume that all voters do, in fact, vote. The study of voter "turnout" is obviously quite important in the study of actual elections.

candidate 1 promises a net dollar benefit of Θ_{1i} to each voter. The candidate is bound by a government budget constraint:

$$\sum_{i=1}^{n} \Theta_{1i} = 0 \qquad (25.10)$$

(or, in the all too familiar context of congressional voting, the constraint consists of whatever deficit the voters will tolerate). The candidates' goal is to choose that set of Θ_{1i} which maximizes EV_1 against Θ_2^*. Setting up the Lagrangian for this problem yields

$$\mathcal{L} = EV_1 + \lambda \left(\sum_{i=1}^{n} \Theta_{1i} \right)$$

$$\qquad (25.11)$$

$$= \sum_{i=1}^{n} f_i[U(\Theta_{1i}) - U(\Theta_2^*)] + \lambda \left(\sum_{i=1}^{n} \Theta_{1i} \right).$$

The first-order condition for the net benefits promised to voter i is given by

$$\frac{\partial \mathcal{L}}{\partial \Theta_{1i}} = f_i' U_i' + \lambda = 0. \qquad (25.12)$$

If the function f_i is the same for all voters, Equation 25.12 implies that candidate 1 should choose Θ_{1i} so that U_i' is the same for all voters. Interestingly, this is the same policy that would be adopted by an omniscient philosopher king who sought to maximize the "utilitarian" social welfare function:

$$SW = \sum_{i=1}^{n} U_i(\Theta_{1i}). \qquad (25.13)$$

In this simple model, then, there is a connection between the strategic outcomes from voting for representatives and optimal resource allocations that might be suggested by specific social welfare functions. Competition among candidates in the public arena may to some extent complement Smith's invisible hand in private markets.[12]

QUERY: Does candidate 2 also select a utilitarian optimal platform? How would this result change if f_i differed among voters?

---

[12] Other normative properties of probabilistic voting models are discussed in P. Coughlan and S. Nitzan, "Electoral Outcomes with Probabilistic Voting and Nash Social Welfare Maxima," *Journal of Public Economics* (February 1981): 113–121.

Money and Politics

Since money has come to play an increasingly important role in elections, economists have sought to generalize the previous model to take account of campaign contributions and other types of political payoffs. There are two routes by which such payments can affect the allocation of resources through political channels. First, money spent on media advertising or on get-out-the-vote efforts may affect voters' decisions (that is, such spending may affect the function f_i introduced in the previous section). Second, the promise of campaign contributions may cause candidates to alter their platforms so as to appeal to special interest group contributors. Ultimately, then, the platforms chosen by candidates may not represent the pure Nash equilibrium choices implied earlier. Instead, actual platforms may represent complex trade-offs between candidates' needs to obtain campaign funding and their needs to appeal to a majority of voters. Modeling these trade-offs and inferring how various "reform" proposals might affect observed outcomes is a difficult problem in general equilibrium analysis.[13]

RENT SEEKING

Special interest groups attempting to influence elections through campaign contributions is one aspect of a more general phenomenon—seeking to use the political system to obtain economic returns that are not available through normal market transactions. The making of such expenditures has come to be known as *rent-seeking activity.*

DEFINITION

Rent Seeking   Economic agents engage in *rent-seeking activities* when they make expenditures that are intended to influence political choices in a way that provides economic rent to the agent.

For example, suppose a firm in an otherwise competitive industry can obtain a monopoly franchise for itself by bribing a set of governmental officials. The result will be monopolization of the industry, together with a transfer of some of what would have been the monopolist's profit to the officials. This bribe itself would not pose a welfare cost to society since it simply transfers what was already a transfer from consumer surplus (see Figure 18.3). But the

---

[13] See, for example, J. B. Kau, D. Keenan, and P. H. Rubin, "A General Equilibrium Model of Congressional Voting," *Quarterly Journal of Economics* (May 1982): 271–293.

allocational loss from the monopoly itself, together with whatever real resources were used in accomplishing the bribe, would constitute a welfare cost from rent seeking.

The political process poses a number of additional avenues for rent-seeking activity. Firms in an industry may lobby for tariff protection, thereby leading to the types of welfare losses examined in Chapter 15. Special interest groups may seek to have regulations introduced that enhance their returns, perhaps at the expense of other groups. This gives rise to the possibility that interest groups may in fact compete for regulatory favors. In many respects, this competition may result in gains that are largely redistributive—the regulations may involve only minor welfare costs—but may involve substantial transfers from one group to another. Finally, groups may seek rents through their direct contractual relationships with the government. Defense contractors may charge exorbitant prices, suppliers of equipment may provide low-quality service, and government workers may succeed in gaining especially favorable employment contracts. All such activities may have important impacts on the allocation of resources.

EXAMPLE 25.4

RENT DISSIPATION

If a number of actors compete in the same rent-seeking activity, it is possible that all available rent will be dissipated into rent seekers' costs. Suppose, for example, a monopoly might earn profits of π_m per period and that a franchise for the monopoly can be obtained from a pliant government official for a bribe of B per period ($B < \pi_m$). Risk-neutral entrepreneurs will offer bribes so long as the expected gain exceeds the costs of the bribe. If each rent seeker has the same chance of winning the franchise, the number of bribers (n) will expand to the point at which

$$B = \pi_m/n. \tag{25.14}$$

Hence, the total rent available will be dissipated through the bribes paid by all contestants for the franchise. If rent seekers were risk averse, or if government officials stop short of receiving the maximum bribes possible, some rent may remain for the franchise winner, however.

QUERY: Would rent be completely dissipated in this example if n were capped at lower than the number needed to satisfy Equation 25.14?

SUMMARY

In this chapter we surveyed some of the concepts from the economic theory of public choice. We showed that public choice mechanisms are intrinsically more difficult to evaluate than market mechanisms. Even in relatively simple situations, Pareto inferior results may occur. For complex situations (such as voting in Congress), developing explicit models of behavior may be very difficult and evaluation must be by less formal means. In examining these issues we showed that:

- Choosing equitable allocations of resources is an ambiguous process because many potential welfare criteria might be used. In some cases achieving equity (appropriately defined) may require some efficiency sacrifices.

- Arrow's impossibility theorem shows that, given fairly general assumptions, there is no completely satisfactory social choice mechanism. The problem of social choice theory is therefore to assess the performance of relatively imperfect mechanisms.

- Direct voting and majority rule may not always yield an equilibrium. If preferences are single-peaked, however, majority rule voting on one-dimensional public questions will result in choosing policies most favored by the median voter. Such policies are not necessarily efficient, however.

- Voting in representative governments may be analyzed using the tools of game theory. In some cases candidates' choices of strategies will yield Nash equilibria that have desirable normative consequences.

- Economic actors may make rent-seeking expenditures in order to gain returns not available through usual market mechanisms.

PROBLEMS

25.1

There are 200 pounds of food that must be allocated between two sailors marooned on an island. The utility function of the first sailor is given by

$$\text{utility} = \sqrt{F_1},$$

where F_1 is the quantity of food consumed by the first sailor. For the second sailor, utility (as a function of his food consumption) is given by

$$\text{utility} = \tfrac{1}{2}\sqrt{F_2}.$$

a. If the food is allocated equally between the sailors, how much utility will each receive?
b. How should food be allocated between the sailors to assure equality of utility?
c. How should food be allocated so as to maximize the sum of the sailors' utilities?
d. Suppose that sailor 2 requires a utility level of at least 5 to remain alive. How should food be

allocated so as to maximize the sum of utilities subject to the constraint that sailor 2 receive that minimum level of utility?
e. Suppose that both sailors agree on a social welfare function of the form

$$W = u_1^{1/2} u_2^{1/2}.$$

How should food be allocated between the sailors so as to maximize social welfare?

25.2

In the 1930s several authors suggested a "bribe criterion" for judging the desirability of social situations. This welfare criterion states that a movement from social state A to state B is an improvement in social welfare if those who gain by this move are able to compensate those who lose sufficiently so that they will accept the change. Compensation does not actually have to be made; it is only necessary that it could be paid. If the compensation is actually made, this criterion reduces to the Pareto definition (some individuals are made better off without making anyone worse off). Hence, the criterion is novel only in that compensation is not paid by the gainers to the losers. In such a situation, does the bribe criterion seem to be "value-free," or does the criterion seem somehow to favor those who are initially rich? Can you give some simple examples?

25.3

Suppose that an economy is characterized by a linear production possibility function for its two goods (X and Y) of the form

$$X + 2Y = 180.$$

There are two individuals in this economy, each with an identical utility function for X and Y of the form

$$U(X, Y) = \sqrt{XY}.$$

a. Suppose that Y production is set at 10. What would the utility possibility frontier for this economy be?
b. Suppose that Y production is set at 30. What would the utility possibility frontier be?
c. How should Y production be chosen so as to ensure the "best" utility possibility frontier?
d. Under what conditions (contrary to those of this problem) might your answer to part (c) depend on the point on the utility possibility frontier being considered?

25.4

Suppose that seven individuals constitute a society in which individuals cast votes for their most preferred social arrangement and that the arrangement with the greatest number of votes is always chosen. Devise an example of individual rankings of the three states A, B, and C such that state A is chosen when all three states are available but that state B is chosen if the "irrelevant" alternative C is not available. (This amounts to showing that the constitution of this society does not obey Axiom 4 in Arrow's list.) How reasonable is your example? What does it indicate about the nature of Arrow's axiom?

25.5

Suppose that there are two individuals in an economy.

Utilities of those individuals under five possible social states are shown in the following table:

STATE	UTILITY 1	UTILITY 2
A	50	50
B	70	40
C	45	54
D	53	50.5
E	30	84

Individuals do not know which number (1 or 2) they will be assigned when the economy begins operating. Hence, they are uncertain about the actual utility they will receive under the alternative social states. Which social state will be preferred if an individual adopts the following strategies in his or her voting behavior to deal with this uncertainty?

a. Choose that state which assures the highest utility to the least well-off person.
b. Assume that there is a 50–50 chance of being either individual and choose that state with the highest expected utility.
c. Assume that no matter what, the odds are always unfavorable such that there is a 60 percent chance of having the lower utility and a 40 percent chance of higher utility in any social state. Choose the state with the highest expected utility given these probabilities.
d. Assume that there is a 50–50 chance of being assigned either number and that each individual dislikes inequality. Each will choose that state for which

$$\text{expected utility} - |U_1 - U_2|$$

is as large as possible (where the | . . . | notation denotes absolute value).
e. What do you conclude from this problem about social choices under a "veil of ignorance" as to an individual's specific identity in society?

25.6

Suppose there are three individuals in society trying to rank three social states (A, B, and C). For each of the methods of social choice indicated, develop an example to show how (at least) one of the Arrow axioms will be violated.

a. Majority rule without vote trading.
b. Majority rule with vote trading.

c. Point voting where each voter can give 1, 2, or 3 points to each alternative and the alternative with the highest point total is selected.

25.7

In an economy characterized by a hierarchy of government units (for example, federal, state, and local governments), what criteria might be used to determine which public goods are produced by which level of government? How would economies of scale in production affect your answer?

25.8

The demand for gummy bears is given by

$$Q = 200 - 100P,$$

and these confections can be produced at a constant marginal cost of $.50.

a. How much will Sweettooth, Inc., be willing to pay in bribes to obtain a monopoly concession from the government for gummy bear production?

b. Do the bribes represent a welfare cost from rent seeking?

c. What is the welfare cost of this rent-seeking activity?

25.9

How does the free rider problem arise in the decision of eligible voters to vote? How might voter participation decisions affect median voter results? How might it affect probabilistic voting models?

25.10

Suppose voters based their decisions on the ratio of utilities received from two candidates—that is, Equation 25.6 would be

$$\pi_i = f_i[(U_i(\Theta_1)/U_i(\Theta_2)].$$

Show that the results from a game involving net value platforms would in this case maximize the Nash Social Welfare function

$$SW = \prod_{i=1}^{n} U_i.$$

SUGGESTED READINGS

Arrow, K. J. *Social Choice and Individual Values.* 2d ed. New Haven, Conn.: Yale University Press, 1963.
Classic statement of the impossibility theorem. Extensive discussion of its general meaning.

———. "Some Ordinalist-Utilitarian Notes on Rawls's Theory of Justice." *Journal of Philosophy* 70 (May 1973): 245–263.
Arrow's criticism of Rawls's welfare criterion, essentially because of excessive risk aversion.

Black, D. "On the Rationale of Group Decision Making." *Journal of Political Economy* (February 1948): 23–34. Reprinted in K. J. Arrow and T. Scitovsky, eds., *Readings in Welfare Economics.* Homewood, Ill.: Richard D. Irwin, 1969.
Early development of the "median voter" theorem.

Buchanan, J. M. "An Economic Theory of Clubs." *Economica* (February 1965): 1–14.
Develops an economic theory of the size, function, and internal operations of "clubs."

Buchanan, J. M., and G. Tullock. *The Calculus of Consent.* Ann Arbor: University of Michigan Press, 1962.
Classic analysis of the properties of various voting schemes.

Inman, R. P. "Markets, Governments and the 'New' Political Economy." In A. J. Auerbach and M. Feldstein, eds., *Handbook of Public Economics*, vol. 2. Amsterdam: North-Holland Publishing Co., 1987, pp. 647–777.
Extensive review of recent literature on the topics covered in this chapter. Interesting use of game theory to illustrate some concepts. Good discussion of theoretical role for tax limitation provisions.

Mueller, D. *Public Choice II.* Cambridge: Cambridge University Press, 1989.
Extends the analysis of probabilistic voting in this chapter to explicitly consider political contributions and a number of other issues.

Olson, M. *The Logic of Collective Action.* Cambridge, Mass.: Harvard University Press, 1965.

Analyzes the effects of individual incentives on the willingness to undertake collective action. Many fascinating examples.

Rawls, J. *A Theory of Justice.* Cambridge, Mass.: Harvard University Press, 1971.
Basic philosophical text. Makes wide use of economic concepts, especially Pareto efficiency notions and the contract curve.

Sen, A. K. *Collective Choice and Social Welfare.* San Francisco: Holden-Day, 1970.
Complete, formal analysis of collective choice issues. Has many literary sections among the more mathematical analyses.

BRIEF ANSWERS TO QUERIES

The following brief answers to the queries that accompany each example in the text may help students test their understanding of the concepts being presented.

CHAPTER 1

1.1

If $P = 5$, $Q_D = 950$, and $Q_S = 500$. There would be excess demand, and some type of rationing would be required.

1.2

If $X = 9.99$, $Y = 5.040$; if $X = 10.01$, $Y = 4.959$.

$$\frac{\Delta Y}{\Delta X} = \frac{-.081}{-.02},$$

which is close to -4. Calculus results can only be approximated by discrete changes.

CHAPTER 2

2.1

Since $\pi = 2,000\sqrt{L} - 20L$, profit maximization requires $1,000/\sqrt{L} = 20$. So $L = 2,500$, $q = 100$.

2.2

These would be concentric circles centered at $x_1 = 1$, $x_2 = 2$. For $y = 10$, the "circle" is a single point.

2.3

For different constants, each production possibility frontier is a successively larger quarter circle centered at the origin.

2.4

$\partial y^*/\partial b = 0$ because x_1 would always be set at b for optimality.

2.5

With $x_1 + x_2 = 2$, $x_1 = 0.5$, $x_2 = 1.5$. Now $y^* = 9.5$. For $x_1 + x_2 \geq 3$, the unconstrained optimum is attainable.

2.6

A circular field encloses maximal area for minimum perimeter. Proof requires a limit argument.

2.7

The local maximum is also a global maximum here. The constancy of the second derivative implies the slope of the function decreases at a constant rate.

2.8

This function resembles an inverted cone that has only one highest point.

2.9

This is a quasi-concave function. It has no unconstrained optimal value. Since contour lines are rectangular hyperbolas, critical points of the Lagrangian are local maxima.

CHAPTER 3

3.1

The derivation here holds utility constant to create an implicit relationship between Y and X. Changes in X also implicitly change Y because of this relationship (Equation 3.11).

3.2

The MRS is measured in units of Y per unit of X. In calculating MU_X/MU_Y, the units of utility measurement cancel out, leaving a "Y per X" measure (here hamburgers per soft drink).

3.3

For homothetic functions, the MRS is the same for every point along a positively sloped ray through the origin.

3.4

The indifference curves here are "horizontally parallel." That is, for any given level of Y, the MRS is the same no matter what the value of X is. One implication of this (as we shall see in Chapter 4) is that the effect of additional income on purchases of good Y is zero—all extra income is channeled into the good with constant marginal utility (good X).

CHAPTER 4

4.1

With three goods, the budget constraint is a plane given by $I = P_X X + P_Y Y + P_Z Z$. Solving for Y gives

$$Y = \frac{-P_X}{P_Y}X - \frac{P_Z}{P_Y}Z + \frac{I}{P_Y}.$$

Hence, I/P_Y shows Y purchases if $X = Z = 0$ and the coefficients of X and Z reflect their prices relative to that of Y.

4.2

Constant shares imply $\partial X/\partial P_Y = 0$ and $\partial Y/\partial P_X = 0$. Notice P_Y does not enter Equation 4.23; P_X does not enter 4.24.

4.3

Budget shares are not affected by income, but they are affected by changes in relative prices. This is the case for all homothetic functions.

4.4

Since a doubling of all prices and nominal income does not change the budget constraint, it will not change utility. Indirect utility is homogeneous of degree zero in all prices and nominal income.

4.5

Yes, all expenditure functions are homogeneous of degree one in prices since a doubling of all prices would precisely double expenditures required to reach U. Because relative prices would not change, this person would choose the same commodity bundle before and after the price rise.

CHAPTER 5

5.1

The shares equations computed from Equations 5.4 or 5.6 show that this individual always spends all of his or her income regardless of P_X, P_Y, and I. That is, the shares sum to one.

5.2

If $X = .5\ I/P_X$, $I = 100$, $P_X = 1$ implies $X = 50$. In Equation 5.11 $X = .5(100/1) = 50$ also. If P_X falls to .5, the Cobb-Douglas predicts $X = .67(100/.5) = 134$. Hence, the CES is more price responsive.

5.3

Since proportional changes in P_X and P_Y do not induce substitution effects, holding V constant implies that X and Y will not change. That should be true for all compensated demand functions.

5.4

A change in P_Y would have equal substitution and income effects in the demand for Y. The effect on X demand would be income and substitution effects of the same size, but opposite in sign.

5.5

One might assume $X = 0$ for P_X sufficiently high. If, for example, it is assumed that $X = 0$ for $P_X > 4$, then total consumer surplus is derived from Equation 5.51 by integrating from .25 to 4. Total surplus is 6. Still, it might be better to stick to analyzing small changes since the total measure is dependent on what upper-limit price we choose.

CHAPTER 6

6.1

Since $\partial X/\partial P_Y$ includes both income and substitution effects, this derivative could be zero if the effects offset each other. The conclusion that $\partial X/\partial P_Y = 0$ implies the goods must be used in fixed proportions would hold only if the income effect of this price change were zero.

6.2

Asymmetry can occur with homothetic preferences since, although substitution effects are symmetric, income effects may differ in size.

6.3

Since the relationship between P_Y, P_Z, and P_H never changes, the maximization problem will always be solved the same way.

CHAPTER 7

7.1

If I_1 were always in a constant ratio to I_2, the demand would be a stable function of $I_1 + I_2$. Here, differing coefficients for P_Y would not affect the stability of the market demand curve.

7.2

Use Equation 7.39. With $\alpha = \beta = .5$, $e^s_{X,P_X} = e^s_{Y,P_Y} = -.5$. With $\alpha = .3$, $\beta = .7$, $e^s_{X,P_X} = -.7$, $e^s_{Y,P_Y} = -.3$. Since the uncompensated price elasticity is unity for both goods in the Cobb-Douglas, the smaller income effect when $\alpha = .3$ must be

balanced by a larger substitution effect and vice versa.

7.3

Since expenditures increase for a fall in P when demand is elastic, expenditures are as large as possible when $e_{Q,P} = -1$. Equation 7.44 shows this occurs when $P = 6$.

7.4

This is homogeneous of degree zero since the sum of the elasticities (exponents) is zero. See also Equation 7.31.

CHAPTER 8

8.1

If $ln\ X_i = 2^i$, the paradox can be regenerated.

8.2

With linear utility, the individual would care only about expected dollar values and would be indifferent about buying actuarially fair insurance. When utility U is a convex function of wealth ($U > 0$, $U'' > 0$), the individual prefers to gamble and will buy insurance only if it costs less than is actuarially justified.

8.3

The risk aversion parameter (A), the size of the gamble, and the insurance cost (F) all enter the exponential utility function in a multiplicative way.

8.4

Willingness to pay is a declining function of wealth (Equation 8.42). With $R = 0$ will pay 50 to avoid a 1,000 bet if $W_0 = 10,000$, but only a 5 bet if $W_0 = 100,000$. With $R = 2$ will pay 149 to avoid a 1,000 bet if $W_0 = 10,000$, but only a 15 bet if $W_0 = 100,000$.

8.5

The actuarially fair price for such a policy is $.25 \cdot 19,000 = 4,750$. The maximum amount the individual would pay (X) solves the equation

$$11.45714 = .45 \, ln(100{,}000 - x)$$
$$+ .25(99{,}000 - x).$$

Solving this yields an approximate value of $x = \$5{,}120$. This person would be willing to pay up to \$470 in administrative costs for the deductible policy.

CHAPTER 9

9.1

Although price is uncertain, the model here allows the individual to buy more hamburgers when he or she encounters a low price and fewer when a high price is encountered. Because V is a convex function of P_Y, the mean of V for two different values of P_Y exceeds the value of V at the mean of P_Y. This has no relationship to risk aversion, which concerns choices among options with the same expected value.

9.2

Now insurance costs \$5,300 with no device and \$3,300 with a device. Utility with insurance and no device is $ln(94{,}700) = 11.4589$ so the individual prefers to install the device but buy no insurance.

9.3

Assuming only full coverage policies are offered, we need to find the value of X for which $ln(97{,}000 - X) = 11.4794$ (the value of utility for low-risk individuals without insurance). Solving this equation yields $X = 297$. To find what a forged certificate must cost (Y), we use

$$ln(97{,}000 - Y) \le 11.4616$$

(the utility from full coverage under a high-risk policy). Solving this inequality yields $Y \ge 2{,}003$.

CHAPTER 10

10.1

None of the strategies is dominant. Separate vacations are not Nash equilibria because both spouses have an incentive to switch.

10.2

Expected utility is two-thirds for each player with the mixed strategies—lower than that promised by either of the other Nash equilibria. This would not be a cooperative outcome.

10.3

See Example 10.4.

10.4

$\delta > .43$ seems quite likely unless very long periods are involved. With annual periods, a δ of .43 is equivalent to an annual interest rate of over 100 percent.

CHAPTER 11

11.1

Now with $K = 11$

$$q = 72{,}600L^2 - 1{,}331L^3$$
$$MP_L = 145{,}200L - 3{,}993L^2$$
$$AP_L = 72{,}600L - 1{,}331L^2.$$

In this case, AP_L now reaches its maximal value at $L = 27.3$ rather than at $L = 30$.

11.2

If $K = L$, since K and L enter f symmetrically, $f_K = f_L$, $f_{KK} = f_{LL}$. Hence, the numerator of Equation 11.21 will be negative if $f_{KL} > f_{LL}$. Combining Equations 11.24 and 11.25 (and remembering $K = L$) shows this holds for $K = L < 20$.

11.3

Since the Cobb-Douglas is a homogeneous function no matter what the sum of the exponents, it is always homothetic—the isoquant map is a radial blowup of the unit isoquant. With increasing returns to scale, the isoquants for given increments of output get closer together as output expands, whereas with decreasing returns they get further apart.

11.4

Using Equation 11.55, $q/L = 16.5(K/L)^{.5}$. If $K = 10$, $q/L = 52.2/L^{.5}$. If $q/L = 10(K/L)^{.5}$, would need $K = 27.2$ to get the same average productivity function.

CHAPTER 12

12.1
Now $RTS = MP_L/MP_K = 4/12 = 1/3 = K/L$. With $L = 3K$, $q = 40 = 10K\sqrt{3}$ so $K = 4/\sqrt{3}$, $L = 12/\sqrt{3}$, $MP_K = 5/\sqrt{3}$, $MP_L = 5\sqrt{3}/3$.

12.2
Each elasticity is one-half because each input constitutes only one-half of total cost.

12.3
Since capital costs are fixed in the short run, they do not affect short-run marginal cuts (in mathematical terms, the derivative of a constant is zero). Capital costs do, however, affect short-run average costs. In Figure 12.15 an increase in v would shift MC, AC, and all of the $SATC$ curves upward, but would leave the SMC lines unaffected.

CHAPTER 13

13.1
If $MC = 5$, profit maximization requires $q = 25$. Now $P = 7.50$, $TR = 187.50$, $TC = 125$, and $\pi = 62.50$.

13.2
An increase in v would not shift the short-run marginal cost curve and would not alter short-run supply decisions (though it might affect the decisions of the firm to stay in business). An increase in w to \$5 would shift short-run marginal cost to $SMC = q/40$.

13.3
An increase in F would shift the short-run supply function outward—more output would be supplied at each price. Optimal F would be found via an envelope procedure similar to that used in Example 12.3.

13.4
Equation 13.40 derives the short-run supply function as $q = 100P$. If $P = 1$, $\pi = 50 - R$ and short-run producer surplus is $PS = \pi + R = 50$.

Integration of the supply function gives $PS = 50P^2$; if $P = 1$, $PS = 50$; if $P = 1.5$, $PS = 112.5$.

13.5
Increasing q from 30 to 50 increases revenue but reduces profits. A utility-maximizing choice would consist of opting for the preferred pair among these options.

13.6
In this case the owners would have to structure a contract based on their assessment of the probability of inappropriate jet usage given the observed value of profits.

CHAPTER 14

14.1
Here the supply curve is linear and passes through the origin. It will always have unitary elasticity since changes in the wage only change the slope. In cases where the supply curve has an intercept (a shutdown price) or is nonlinear, the supply elasticity may not be the same at all points, and it may be affected by input costs.

14.2
The shift in demand causes a move along the supply curve—a 20 percent rise in price results in a 20 percent rise in quantity. The shift in supply implies that the demand elasticity is approximately –1.0—an 11 percent rise in price results in an 11 percent fall in quantity. For the cases described in the footnote, however, $e_{Q,P}$ is approximately –2 in case (i) and approximately –0.2 in case (ii).

14.3
Following steps similar to those used to derive Equation 14.32 yields

$$e_{P,\beta} = \frac{-e_{Q,\beta}}{e_{S,P} - e_{Q,P}}$$

Here $e_{Q,\beta} = e_{Q,w} = -.5$ so $e_{P,\beta} = \frac{-(-.5)}{2.2} = .227$. Multiplication by .20 (since wages rose 20 percent) predicts a price rise of 4.5 percent, very close to the figure in the example.

14.4

The short-run supply curve is given by $Q_S = .5P + 750$, and the short-term equilibrium price is $643. Each firm earns approximately $2,960 in profits in the short run.

14.5

Total and average costs for Equation 14.56 exceed those for Equation 14.43 for $q > 15.9$. Marginal costs for Equation 14.56 always exceed those for Equation 14.43. Optimal output is lower with Equation 14.56 than with Equation 14.43 because marginal costs increase more than average costs.

CHAPTER 15

15.1

Losses from a given restriction in quantity will be greater when supply and/or demand is less elastic. The actor with the least elastic response will bear the greater share of the loss.

15.2

An increase in t unambiguously increases deadweight loss. Because increases in t reduce quantity, however, total tax revenues are subject to countervailing effects. Indeed, if $t/(P + t) \geq -1/e_{Q,P}$, then $dtQ/dt < 0$.

15.3

Total transfer to domestic producers is (in billions) $.5 \cdot (11.7) + .5(.5)(0.7) = 6.03$. This would be gained as rents to those inputs that give the auto supply curve its positive slope. With a quota, domestic producers may also be able to gain some portion of what would have been tariff revenue.

CHAPTER 16

16.1

Set $RPT = dY/dX = 1/4$. Hence, $X/4Y = 1/4$ so $X = Y$. Substituting into Equation 16.6 yields $X = Y = 20$.

16.2

Clearly, $X = 10$, $Y = 0$ or $X = 0$, $Y = 5$ are inferior since for these $U = 0$. With $X = 5$, $Y = 4.33$, $U = 21.67$, which is also inferior to the maximum utility.

16.3

Now $MRS = Y/3X$. Equating this to the RPT and substituting into the production possibility frontier yields $X = 5$, $Y = 4.33$. The relative price of guns falls to $P_X^*/P_Y^* = 0.28$.

16.4

Walras's law ensures that the silver market is in equilibrium. Recalculating Equation 16.40 gives

$$ED_1 = 2(P_2/P_1)^2 + 2(P_3/P_1)^2 - 4P_2/P_1 - 7P_3/P_1$$

or, at the new relative prices,

$$= 2(3)^2 + 2(2)^2 - 4(3) - 7(2) = 0.$$

CHAPTER 17

17.1

Because each production function exhibits constant returns to scale, any allocation of capital will be efficient if labor is allocated appropriately.

17.2

Any output combination for England short of complete specialization results in loss of both outputs. With concave frontiers, complete specialization would be unlikely since the relative marginal cost of either good increases as more resources are devoted to it.

17.3

Inefficiency could be measured by the utility loss involved (assuming utility measurement is meaningful). For $X = 8$, $Y = 3$, the loss is $5 - \sqrt{24} = 0.10$. For $X = 5$, $Y = 4.33$, the loss is $5 - \sqrt{21.67} = .34$.

17.4

In this case, the sequence of prices would be $P_2 = 2.11$, $P_3 = 1.93$, $P_4 = 1.99$ so the convergence to equilibrium, while different, is not much slower than in Table 17.2.

17.5
The indifference curves are relatively flat here, implying that these individuals are quite willing to substitute one good for another. This flexibility implies a relatively narrow range of mutually beneficial trading opportunities at point A. With less flexible preferences, the number of opportunities is increased because the individuals may start trading from widely differing marginal rates of substitution.

CHAPTER 18

18.1
The increase in fixed costs would not alter the output decisions since it would not affect marginal cost. It would, however, raise AC by 5 and reduce profits to 12,500. With the new TC function, MC would rise to $.15Q$. In this case, $Q^* = 400$, $P^* = 80$, $TC = 22,000$, and $\pi = 10,000$.

18.2
With $e = -1.5$, the ratio of monopoly to competitive consumer surplus is 0.58 (Equation 18.18). Profits represent 19 percent of competitive consumer surplus (Equation 18.20).

18.3
If $Q = 0$, $P = 100$. Total profits are given by the triangular area between the demand curve and the MC curve, less fixed costs. This area is $.5\,(100)(666) = 33,333$. So $\pi = 33,333 - 10,000 = 23,333$.

18.4
Yes, output is the same since marginal revenue curves are linear too. Because output does not expand under the two-price policy, welfare cannot be increased by such a policy.

18.5
Profits would be maximized by setting marginal price equal to MC in each market and charging an entry fee of 36 in market 2 and 162 in market 1.

CHAPTER 19

19.1
With $q_2 = 40$, the residual demand facing firm 1 is $q_1 = 80 - P$. Hence, $MR = 80 - 2q_1$ so for $q_1 > 40$, $MR < 0$. Clearly, it is marginal revenue, not price, that matters for the chiseling decision.

19.2
In Example 19.1, q_2 was assumed to be constant. Now firm 2 is assumed to respond to firm 1's increase in output by reducing its own output.

19.3
Constant marginal costs would not change the nature of the problem. Increasing marginal cost would drive the firms toward more equal shares of the marketplace than result from the strategic interactions in the constant-cost case.

19.4
Efficiency requires $P = MC = AC$ unless the differentiated goods exhibit little substitutability.

19.5
Consumer surplus is as large as possible given the no-subsidy constraint. Marginal cost pricing ($P = 100$) would increase consumer surplus but would require a subsidy to cover fixed costs of $8,000.

CHAPTER 20

20.1
The higher is δ, the greater the present value of the future share of monopoly profits. Hence, higher discount rates favor tacit collusion. With $\delta = .8$, at most five firms will support a collusive agreement. With $r = .10$, up to 10 firms will collude tacitly.

20.2
Repeated Follower—Follower strategies might be enforced by retaliation whenever one firm chooses leader.

20.3
If A does not have the advantage of moving first, the situation of both firms is symmetrical, and

the model returns to the Stackelberg case. The analysis here differs from contestability because of the sunk-cost assumption.

20.4

Linear demand and marginal costs result in q_A^* being a linear function of q_{BH}^* and q_{BL}^*, which in turn are linear functions of B's marginal cost. With nonlinear demand or, more importantly, marginal costs, q_A^* would not be based on $E(MC_B)$.

20.5

Yes, a reservation price would change bidding strategies to raise bids so long as R (reservation price) $< V_A, V_B$.

CHAPTER 21

21.1

Hiring rises to $L = 36$ because the marginal revenue product function has shifted outward.

21.2

In this short-run problem, F is held constant. Increases in the variable inputs L and K encounter sharply diminishing marginal productivities.

21.3

Using Equation 21.43 yields $e_{Lw} = -(1 - .5)(1) + .5(-1) = -1$.

21.4

Now $MRP = \$30$ per hour. In this case, the monopsony will hire 750 workers, and wages will be $15 per hour. As before, the wage remains at only half the MRP.

CHAPTER 22

22.1

Here full income is $w + N$. Spending half of this on leisure would require $H = 1/2 + N/2w$ since leisure "costs" 2 per hour. Hence, $L = 1 - H = 1/2 - N/2w$ as was calculated directly.

22.2

With a flat N of $2, Equation 22.22 shows $L = 3/10$ (assume $w = 10$). Substituting the new formula for N into Equation 22.20 and solving for an optimum yields $L = 1/10, N = 7/2$. Institution of an implicit tax on earnings reduces labor supply.

22.3

The monopsonist wants to be on its demand for labor curve; the union (presumably) wants to be on the labor supply curve of its members. Only the supply-demand equilibrium ($L = 583$, $w = 11.67$) satisfies both these curves. Whether this is indeed a Nash equilibrium depends, among other things, on whether the union defines its payoffs as being accurately reflected by the labor supply curve.

22.4

If the firm is risk neutral, workers risk averse, optimal contracts might have lower wages in exchange for more stable income.

CHAPTER 23

23.1

If δ is the same for two individuals, but individual 1 can obtain a higher interest rate than individual 2, $U'(C_0)/U'(C_1)$ will also be greater for individual 1 than for individual 2. Hence, C_0/C_1 will be lower for individual 1 than for individual 2.

23.2

With an inflation rate of 10 percent, the nominal value of the tree would rise at an additional 10 percent per year. But such revenues would have to be discounted by an identical amount to calculate real profits so the optimal harvesting age would not change.

23.3

Would just raise the optimal price path by marginal cost of extraction.

CHAPTER 24

24.1
Production of Y would have a beneficial impact on X so labor would be underallocated to Y by competitive markets.

24.2
The tax is relatively small because of the nature of the externality that vanishes with only a relatively minor reduction in Y output. A merged firm would also find $Y = 38,000$ to be a profit-maximizing choice.

24.3
The roommates' separate allocations are $X = 1$, $Y = 1,000$ so they would achieve the efficient allocation if they moved in together. This results from the simple additive nature of the MRSs in the Cobb-Douglas case and would not be expected to hold generally.

CHAPTER 25

25.1
Each utility function here exhibits diminishing marginal utility. Each teen is therefore risk averse. The degree of risk aversion could only be altered by changing the assumed utility functions.

25.2
Voluntary vote trading is constrained because each person has only a single, binary vote. No such constraints occur in the exchange case.

25.3
Candidate 2 also selects a utilitarian optimal platform. If f_i differs among voters, candidate strategies need not maximize any simple function of utilities. A Nash equilibrium still exists, however.

25.4
Some profits might remain, or perhaps officials will raise the requested bribe to $B = \pi_m/n$.

SOLUTIONS TO ODD-NUMBERED PROBLEMS

Only very brief solutions to most of the odd-numbered problems in the text are given here. Complete solutions to all of the problems are contained in the *Solutions Manual*, which is available to instructors upon request.

CHAPTER 2

2.1
a. $x = 1, f(1) = -8; x = -1, f(-1) = 8.$
b. $x = 2$, a minimum.
c. Inflection at $x = 0$.

2.3
a. $t = 5/4$ second and $H = 25$ feet.
b. $t = 7.3$ second and $H = 145$ feet.
c. $\partial H/\partial g = -1/2(t^*)^2$ depends on g because t^* depends on g.

2.5
a. $8x, 6y$
b. $8, 12$
c. $8xdx + 6ydy.$
d. $dy/dx = -4x/3y.$
e. $x = 1, U = (4)(1) + (3)(4) = 16.$
f. $dy/dx = -2/3.$
g. $U = 16$ contour line is an ellipse.

2.7
a. $q = 10, \pi = 100.$
b. $\pi'' = -4 < 0$
c. Yes, $MR = 50 = MC.$

2.9
b. $X_1 = KX_2^{-\beta/\alpha}$
$K = C^{1/\alpha}$
$\dfrac{dX_1}{dX_2} < 0, \dfrac{d^2X_1}{dX_2^2} > 0$
c. $\alpha + \beta > 1,$
$f_{11} = \alpha(\alpha - 1)X_1^{\alpha - 2}X_2^{\beta}$
$f_{22} = \beta(\beta - 1)X_1^{\alpha}X_2^{\beta - 2}$
$f_{12} = \alpha\beta X_1^{\alpha - 1}X_2^{\beta - 1}$
$f_{11}f_{22} - f_{12}^2 = \alpha\beta(1 - \alpha - \beta) < 0$

CHAPTER 3

3.1
a. $U = 40, 30 = W + 3C.$
$U = 70, 60 = 2W + 3C.$
b. $MRS = \dfrac{\partial U/\partial W}{\partial U/\partial C} = \dfrac{2}{3}.$
c. $U = 40, 20 = 2W + 3C.$
$U = 70, 50 = 2W + 3C.$
$MRS = 2/3.$

3.3
a. Fixed proportion, perfect complements.
b. $U = 10M.$ $M = $ spending on hot dogs.
c. $U = 7.5M.$ Given M provides less utility.

3.5
a. No
b. Yes
c. No
d. No

e. Yes

f. Yes

3.7

The shape of the marginal utility function is not necessarily an indicator of convexity of indifference curves.

3.9

It follows, since $MRS = MU_x/MU_y \cdot MU_x$ doesn't depend on Y or vice versa. 3.5b is a counter-example.

CHAPTER 4

4.1

a. $T = 5$ and $S = 2$.

b. $T = 5/2$ and $S = 4$. Costs $2 so needs extra $1.

4.3

a. $C = 10$, $B = 3$, and $U = 127$.

b. $C = 4$, $B = 1$, and $U = 79$.

4.5

b. $G = I/(P_G + P_V/2)$; $V = I/(2P_G + P_V)$.

c. Utility $= M = V = I/(2P_G + P_V)$.

d. $E = M(2P_G + P_V)$.

4.7

a. Following the hint, since income tax is not tangent to indifference curve, improvement is possible.

b. Both constraints are tangent to indifference curve at same point.

c. Yes

4.9

a. Set $MRS = P_X/P_Y$.

b. Set $\delta = 0$.

c. Use $P_X X/P_Y Y = (P_X/P_Y)^{\delta/(\delta - 1)}$.

CHAPTER 5

5.1

a. $U = X + 2\frac{2}{3}Y$.

b. $X = I/P_X$ if $P_X \le 2\frac{2}{3} P_Y$

$X = 0$ if $P_X > 2\frac{2}{3} P_Y$.

d. Changes in P_Y don't affect demand until they reverse the inequality.

e. Just two points (or vertical lines).

5.3

Show budget constraint not tangent.

5.5

a. It is obvious since P_X/P_Y doesn't change.

b. No good is inferior.

5.7

a. $E = K^{-1}UP_X^3 P_Y^7$.

$U = KIP_X^{-.3} P_Y^{-.7}$.

b. $X_C = \partial E/\partial P_X = .3K^{-1} UP_X^{-.7} P_Y^7$.

c. Hint: It is easiest to show Slutsky equation in elasticities.

5.9

No

CHAPTER 6

6.1

Substitution and income terms in the Slutsky elasticity equation are +.5 and −.5, respectively.

6.3

a. $P_{BT} = 2P_B + P_T$.

b. Since P_C and I are constant, $C = 1/2 P_C$ is also constant.

c. Yes—since changes in P_B or P_T affect only P_{BT}.

6.5

a. $P_2 X_2 + P_3 X_3 = P_3(KX_2 + X_3)$.

b. Relative price $= (P_2 + t)/(P_3 + t)$.

Approaches $P_2/P_3 < 1$ as $t \to 0$.

Approaches 1 as $t \to \infty$.

So, an increase in t raises the relative price of X_2.

c. Does not strictly apply since changes in t change relative prices.

d. May reduce spending on X_2—the effect on X_3 is uncertain.

6.7

Show $X_i \cdot \dfrac{\partial X_j}{\partial I} = X_j \cdot \dfrac{\partial X_i}{\partial I}$ and use symmetry of net substitution effects.

6.9

a. $U_{XY} = 0$.
b. Assured by $U''_i < 0$.
c. No conclusion possible. Depends on $P_X X$.
d. $X^\alpha Y^\beta$ is not separable, $\alpha \ln X + \beta \ln Y$ is.

CHAPTER 7

7.1

Market demand for X

$$= \frac{\left(\sqrt{I_P} + \sqrt{I_B} + \sqrt{I_A} + \sqrt{I_R}\right)\sqrt{P_Y}}{2P_X}.$$

a. $X = 11.5$, $e_{X, P_X} = -1$, and $e_{X, P_Y} = \frac{1}{2}$. $e_{X,I}$ cannot be computed without knowing distribution of changes.
b. 5.75, 10.91, 10.04, and 16.26.
c. $X = 10$.
d. $X = 56.5$. If $P_Z = 2$, $X = 31.5$.

$$\text{Market demand} = \frac{I_R P_Y}{2P_X P_Z}$$

$$+ \frac{\left(\sqrt{I_P} + \sqrt{I_B} + \sqrt{I_A}\right)\sqrt{P_Y}}{2P_X}.$$

7.3

a. **P**	**Q**
50	0
35	50
25	135
10	300
0	410

d. Notice the kinks in the market demand curve.

7.5

Use $e = \dfrac{\partial Q}{\partial P} \cdot \dfrac{P^*}{Q^*}$.

$Q = a + bP$.

$X = P^*$ and $Y = -Q^*/b$.
$e = b\,(P^*/Q^*) = -X/Y$.

7.7

Apply the various definitions.

7.9

a. By Slutsky equation and Engel's equation
$e_{X, P_X} + e_{Y, P_Y} = -\sigma - 1$.
b. Results for a and b follow immediately.
c. $\sigma > 1$; elasticities are big.
$\sigma < 1$; elasticities are small.
For n-goods, $\Sigma e = -(n - 1)\sigma - 1$.

CHAPTER 8

8.1

$P = .525$.

8.3

a. one trip: expected value $= .5 \cdot 0 + .5 \cdot 12 = 6$.
two trip: expected value $= .25 \cdot 0 + .5 \cdot 6 + .25 \cdot 12 = 6$.
b. Two-trip strategy preferred because of smaller variance.
c. Adding trips reduces variance, but at a diminishing rate. So desirability depends on the trips' cost.

8.5

a. $E(U) = .75 \, ln(10,000) + .25 \, ln(9,000) = 9.1840$.
b. $E(U) = ln(9,750) = 9.1850$—insurance is preferable.
c. $260

8.7

a. Plant corn.
b. Yes, a mixed crop should be chosen. Diversification increases variance, but takes advantage of wheat's high yield.
c. 44 percent wheat, 56 percent corn.
d. The farmer would only plant wheat.

8.9

a. Use Figure 9.5.
b., c. Examine the curvature of the constant RRA function.

d. It follows, since the constant *RRA* function is homothetic in *W*.

CHAPTER 9

9.1
a. Yes
b. $50
c. 0

9.3
Cost = $1,750.
Now expected utility = $.5U(18{,}250) + .5U(14{,}750)$, which may exceed $U(15{,}000)$.

9.5
a. No
b. $20,000. It must cost low-ability workers more to provide no incentive to buy it, too.

9.7
a., b. $P_{min} = 300 + 100/(n + 1)$.
c. Set $-dP_{min}/dn = 2$, $n^* = 7$.

9.9
Use a constant *RRA* function for illustrations.

CHAPTER 10

10.1
a.

	HEADS	TAILS
HEADS	1, −1	−1, 1
TAILS	−1, 1	1, −1

There is no Nash equilibrium since at least one player has an incentive to change his or her strategy.
b. Use mixed strategies.

10.3
a. Stag-stag and hare-hare are both Nash equilibria.
b. If p = probability A plays stage, B will choose stag if $p > \frac{1}{2}$.
c. Require $p^{(n-1)} > \frac{1}{2}$ for cooperation.

10.5
Following analysis of problem 10.2, mixed strat-egy Nash equilibrium is $s = 1/(K + 1)$, $r = K/(K + 1)$.

10.7
Parents' maximum requires
$$-U_B' + \lambda U_A' = 0. \tag{i}$$
Kids' maximum requires
$$Y_A' = -dL/dr. \tag{ii}$$
Differentiation of (i) and substitution of (ii) shows $dL/dr = Y_B'$. Hence, $Y_A' + Y_B' = 0$ as was to be shown.

10.9
a. There are two Nash equilibria: *A:M, B:M* and *A:D, B:R*.
b. If game is played twice, both of the Nash equilibria are subgame perfect.
c. *A:U, B:L* is viable against *A:M, B:M* and against *A:D, B:R* if $\delta > \frac{1}{3}$.

CHAPTER 11

11.1
b. $AP_L = 100\sqrt{L}$.
c. $MP_L = \partial q/\partial L = 50/\sqrt{L}$, so $MP_L < AP_L$.

11.3
a. $K = 10$ and $L = 5$.
b. $K = 8$ and $L = 8$.
c. $K = 9$, $L = 6.5$, $K = 9.5$, and $L = 5.75$ fractions of hours.
d. The isoquant is linear between solutions (a) and (b).

11.5
a. $e_{Q,L} = \partial q/\partial L \cdot L/q = \alpha$.
b. $MP_L = \partial q/\partial L = \alpha K^\beta L^{\alpha-1} > 0$.
$\partial^2 q/\partial L^2 = (\alpha - 1)(\alpha)K^\beta L^{\alpha-2} < 0$.
c. $RTS = MP_L/MP_K = (\alpha/\beta)(K/L)$.

11.7
a. $\beta_0 = 0$.
b. $MP_K = \beta_2 + \frac{1}{2}\beta_1\sqrt{L/K}$; $MP_L = \beta_3 + \frac{1}{2}\beta_1\sqrt{K/L}$.
c. σ is not constant.

11.9
Apply the theorem to f_K, which is homogeneous of degree 0.

CHAPTER 12

12.1

The draftsman is right since the minimum of *SATC* curves occurs where the slope is zero. In the constant-returns-to-scale case, both are correct.

12.3

a., b. $q = 150$ $J = 25$ $MC = 4$
$q = 300$ $J = 100$ $MC = 8$
$q = 450$ $J = 225$ $MC = 12$

12.5

a. Set $RTS = w/v$. The expansion path is linear.
b. Use the hint.
c. It follows from b.
d. $MC = \dfrac{\partial C}{\partial q} = (1/\alpha + \beta)q^{1/\alpha + \beta - 1}w^{\beta/\alpha + \beta}v^{\alpha/\alpha + \beta}$

Elasticities are exponents.

12.7

a. $STC = 100 + q^2/100$ and $SAC = 100/q + q/100$.
b. $SMC = q/50$

     $q = 25$ $STC = 106.25$ $SAC = 4.25$ $SMC = .50$
     $q = 50$ $STC = 125$ $SAC = 2.50$ $SMC = 1$
     $q = 100$ $STC = 200$ $SAC = 2$ $SMC = 2$
     $q = 200$ $STC = 500$ $SAC = 2.50$ $SMC = 4$

d. $MC = SAC$ at $q = 100$. Lowest *SAC*.

12.9

a. $q_2 = 4q_1$.
b. 1.60, 2.00, and 3.20.
c. Because of constant returns to scale, it doesn't matter. $TC = 2q$ and $AC = MC = 2$.
d. If production functions are identical, $q_1 = q_2$.

12.11

a.

$$L = 0.5q\left(1 + \sqrt{\frac{v}{w}}\right); K = 0.5q\left(1 + \sqrt{\frac{w}{v}}\right).$$

b. $q = (0.5K^{-1} + 0.5L^{-1})^{-1}$.
c. $\sigma = 0.5$, $(\rho = -1)$, $\epsilon = 1$, and $\delta = .5$ generate this function.

CHAPTER 13

13.1

a. $q = 50$.
b. $\pi = 200$.
c. $q = 5P - 50$.

13.3

b. $mr = 8/\sqrt{q}$.
c. $q = 400$.
d. $P = .80$.

13.5

a., b. $q = a + bP$ $P = q/b - a/b$,
$TR = Pq = (q^2 - aq)/b$, $mr = 2q/b - a/b$, and the *mr* curve has double the slope of the demand curve, so $d - mr = -q/b$.
c. $mr = P(1 + 1/e) = P(1 + 1/b)$.
d. It follows since $e = \partial q/\partial P \cdot P/q$.

13.7

a. $q = 2P/w$.
b. $\pi = Pq - wq^2/4 = P^2/w$.

13.9

a. $q = 10$.
b. $\pi = 75$, $SFC = 75$, and surplus $= 100$.
c. $PS = \int_0^{P^*} q(P)dP = \int_0^{P^*} P/2dP = (P^*)^2/4$.

CHAPTER 14

14.1

a. $q = 10\sqrt{P} - 20$.
b. $Q = 1{,}000\sqrt{P} - 2{,}000$.
c. $P = 25$; $Q = 3{,}000$.

14.3

a. $P = 6$.
b. $q = 60{,}000 - 10{,}000P$.
c. $P = 6.01$, $P = 5.99$.
d. $e_{Q,P} = -600$
    a' $P = 6$.
    b' $Q = 359{,}800 - 59{,}950P$.
    c' $P = 6.002$; $P = 5.998$.
    d' $e_{Q,P} = -.6$; $e_{q,P} = 3{,}597$.

14.5

a. $P = 3$, $Q = 2,000,000$, and $n = 2,000$ farms.
b. $P = 6$ and $\pi = 3,000/$farm.
c. $P = 3$, $Q = 2,600,000$, and $n = 2,600$ farms.

14.7

a. $n = 50$, $Q = 1,000$, $q = 20$, $P = 10$, and $w = 200$.
b. $n = 72$, $Q = 1,728$, $q = 24$, $P = 14$, and $w = 288$.
c. The increase for the makers $= \$5,368$. The linear approximation for the supply curve yields approximately the same result.

CHAPTER 15

15.1

a. $P = 120$, $PQ = 48,000$, $CS = 16,000$, and $PS = 20,000$.
b. Loss $= 2,250$.
c. $P = 140$, $CS = 9,000$, and $PS = 24,750$.
$P = 95$, $CS = 22,500$, and $PS = 11,250$.
d. Loss $= 562.50$.

15.3

a. $P = 11$, $Q = 500$, and $r = 1$.
b. $P = 12$, $Q = 1,000$, and $r = 2$.
c. $\Delta PS = 750$.
d. Δ rents $= 750$.

15.5

a. $P_D = 140$, $P_S = 95$, $P_D - P_S = t = 45$; $Q = 300$.
b. Total tax $= 13,500$.
Consumers pay 6,000; producers pay 7,500. Producers pay 56 percent.
c. 2,250
d. $P_D = 129.47$; $P_S = 84.47$; $Q = 258$.
Total tax $= 11,610$, producers pay 79 percent.
e. $P_D = 150$; $P_S = 105$; $Q = 250$.
Total tax $= 11,250$; consumers pay 67 percent.

15.7

a. $Q = 250$; $r = 0.5$; $P_S = 10.5$; $P_D = 16$.
b. Total tax $= 1,375$; consumer tax $= 1,250$; producer tax $= 125$; loss of $CS = 1,875$; loss of $PS = 187.5$.
c. Loss $= .5(250) + .5(.5)(250) = 187.5$.

This is the total loss of PS in part b. Occurs since only reason for upward sloping supply is upward slope of film royalties supply.

15.9

The price rises to 9.6. Total tariff revenue actually falls to .462 ($ billion). $DW_1 = .315$ and $DW_2 = .234$. Hence, DW increases by .147, a 37 percent increase from Example 16.3.

CHAPTER 16

16.1

b. $C = 300$ and $M = 150$.
c. $P_C/P_M = 1/2$.

16.3

a. Efficiency requires $k_X = 2k_Y$.
c. $k_X = \dfrac{1}{1 + \alpha_X}$.
e. X is capital intensive.

16.5

a. Use the production possibility frontier, then the Edgeworth box.
b. If p doesn't change, the land-labor ratio must stay the same in each industry. This can happen only if production of the labor-intensive commodity expands.

16.7

a. Doubling prices does not change ED.
b. $P_1 ED_1 = -[-3P_2^2 + 6P_2P_3 - 2P_3^2 - P_1P_2 - 2P_1P_3]/P_1$.
c. $P_2/P_1 = 3$; $P_3/P_1 = 5$; $P_3/P_2 = \dfrac{5}{3}$.

16.9

a. Value of transactions $= 240 =$ income.
Wage $= 240/20 = 12$ per hour. Since $P_X/P_Y = 3/2$ and $P_X \cdot X + P_Y \cdot Y = 240$, $P_X = 6$ and $P_Y = 4$.
b. Wage is 18 per hour, $P_X = 9$, and $P_Y = 6$. Yes, the system does exhibit classical dichotomy.

CHAPTER 17

17.1
a. $C = F = 10$, $RPT = 1$, and $U = 10$.
b. $C = 2F$, so $C = 15$, $F = 15/2$, and $U = \sqrt{125}$.
c. $C = 5\sqrt{10}$, $F = \dfrac{5\sqrt{10}}{2}$, and $U = \sqrt{125}$.

17.3
a. $X_A^2 + Y_A^2 = 100$.
   $X_B^2 + Y_B^2 = 25$.
b. $RPTs$ should be equal.
c. $Y = 9$.

17.5
a. The contract curve is a straight line. Only equilibrium price ratio is $P_H/P_C = 4/3$.
b. Initial equilibrium on the contract curve.
c. Not on the contract curve—equilibrium is between $40H$, $80C$ and $48H$, $96C$.
d. Smith takes everything; Jones starves.

17.7
Changing endowments changes attractiveness of voluntary trade.

17.9
a. $P = 10$, $Q = 80$.
b. $P_0 = 8$, $P_1 = 11$; $P_2 = 9.5$; $P_3 = 10.25$ takes three periods.
c. Choose $E(P) = P^* = 10$.

CHAPTER 18

18.1
a. $Q = 24$, $P = 29$, and $\pi = 576$.
b. $MC = P = 5$ and $Q = 48$.
c. Consumers' surplus $= 1,152$. Under monopoly, consumer surplus $= 288$, profits $= 576$, deadweight loss $= 288$.

18.3
a. $Q = 25$, $P = 35$, and $\pi = 625$.
b. $Q = 20$, $P = 50$, and $\pi = 800$.
c. $Q = 40$, $P = 30$, and $\pi = 800$.

18.5
a. $P = 15$, $Q = 5$, $TC = 65$, and $\pi = 10$.
b. $A = 3$, $P = 15$, $Q = 6.05$, and $\pi = 12.25$.

18.7
a. $Q_1 = 25$, $P_1 = 30$, $Q_2 = 30$, $P_2 = 20$, and $\pi = 1,075$.
b. $P_1 = 26.66$, $P_2 = 21.66$, and $\pi = 1,058.33$.
c. $P_1 = P_2 = 23\frac{1}{3}$, $\pi = 1,008\frac{1}{3}$, $Q_1 = 31\frac{2}{3}$, and $Q_2 = 23\frac{1}{3}$.
d. $P_i = \alpha_i + mq_i$.
   Set $m = 5$, $\alpha_1 = 1,250$, and $\alpha_2 = 900$.

18.9
a. The government wants output to increase toward $P = MC$, but the lump-sum subsidy doesn't affect $MR = MC$ for the monopoly firm.
b. This will shift the MC curve downward.
c. Use $MR = P(1 + 1/e)$.

CHAPTER 19

19.1
a. $Q = 75$, $P = 75$, and $\pi = 5,625$.
b. $q_1 + q_2 = 50$, $P = 50$, and $\pi_1 = \pi_2 = 2,500$.
c. Under perfect competition, $P = 0$ and $Q = 150$.

19.3
a. Price leadership.
b. Price discrimination (by sellers), though Apple's strategy appears not viable in the long run. Why?
c. Probably incorrect accounting.
d. International competition.

19.5
Multiply by q_i/PQ—this shows that under Cournot competition, more concentrated industries are more profitable.

19.7
a. $P = 25$, $Q = 20,000$, and total $Q_s = \sum\limits_{1}^{1,000} q = 1,000P - 5,000$.
b. $P = 20$, $Q = 30,000$, and q (for leader) $= 15,000$.
c.

Price	Consumer Surplus
25	100,000
20	225,000
15	400,000

19.9

a. Yes, MC is declining.

b. $Q = 450$, $P = 11$, and $\pi = 3{,}341$.

c. $P = AC = 2.4$ (approximate).

CHAPTER 20

20.1

a. $P = 10 - \epsilon$, $q_A = 0$, and $q_B = 300$.

b. $\pi_A = 0$, $\pi_B = 600$.

c. Inefficient because $P > MC_B$.

20.3

Equilibrium with each stand at 50.

20.5

a. $P = 5$ $Q = 5{,}000$ $q = 250$.

b. If one firm sells $q = 251$, it increases its profits.

c. With 20 cartel members, only a very low price is stable ($P = .3$). With fewer members, a higher price is stable.

20.7

Trigger price strategy is subgame perfect providing $n < 1/(1 - \delta)$.

20.9

Follow procedure in Example 20.4. Gives $q_A^* = 30$ $q_{BH}^* = 40$ $q_{BC}^* = 20$.

CHAPTER 21

22.1

a. $w = 3$ and $L = 300$.

b. $w = 4$, $s = 3$, $L = 400$, and total subsidy = 1,200.

c. $w = 4$, $D = 250$, $S = 400$, and $u = 150$.

21.3

a. Hire 5: 3 at farm A; 1 at farm B; and 1 at farm C. Output = 34 and $MP_L = 4$.

b. $w = P = 4$, $wL = 20$, and $\pi = 14$.

21.5

a. $w = 10$ $L = 25$

  $w = 5$ $L = 100$

  $w = 2$ $L = 625$

b. $P = .1$ $Q = 500{,}000$

  $P = .05$ $Q = 250{,}000$

  $P = .20$ $Q = 100{,}000$

21.7

a. Factor shares constant.

b. Assumes $\sigma = 1$.

c. If $\sigma > 1$, capital is discouraged. If $\sigma < 1$, capital is encouraged.

d. If advanced firms have $\sigma > 1$, investment there is discouraged.

21.9

$L_m = 4{,}400$, $w_m = 20/3$, $L_f = 500$, $w_f = 5$, and $\pi = 3{,}833$.

If same wage, $w = 10$, $L = 1{,}900$, and $\pi = 0$.

CHAPTER 22

22.1

a. Full income = 40,000. $L = 2{,}000$ hours.

b. $L = 1{,}400$ hours.

c. $L = 1{,}700$ hours.

d. Supply is asymptotic to 2,000 hours as w rises.

22.3

a. Those with high values of time.

b. Desire to see event or low value of time.

c. Peanut vendor since the physician has high opportunity cost.

d. People with high time value will take transit if congestion worsens.

22.5

a. Both probably positive due to income effect.

b. Person 1 may work less in the market. Ions and comparative statics results.

22.7

$MR_L = 0$ if no unemployment benefits.

$MR_L = u$ if there is UI.

22.9

a. $w = 5$, $L = 2.5$, $U = 12.5$, $\pi = 6.25$.

b. With $w = 4$ and $L = 4$, $U = 16$. $\pi = 8$.

Therefore this is Pareto superior.

c. Will be sustainable if firm's $\delta > .36$.

CHAPTER 23

23.1
b. Income and substitution effects work in opposite directions. If $\partial C_1 / \partial r < 0$, C_2 is price elastic.

c. Budget constraint passes through Y_1, Y_2.

23.3
25 years.

23.5
a., b. See detailed solutions.

c. Here t^* is lower than in Example 23.2 because rotations involve additional opportunity costs.

d. $f(t)$ is asymptotic to 50 as $t \to \infty$.

e. $t^* = 100$ years. Maximum sustainable yield is not defined here since tree always grows. Notice that $f(t) = 25$ at the maximum, however, not 50.

f. $t^* = 104.1$.

23.7
PDV (whole life) = $6,304.

PDV (term) = $3,879.

Salesman is wrong.

23.9
Now *MR* should rise at the rate of interest. If demand is constant elasticity, however, $MR = kP$ so with same end price, price path will be same as in the competitive case.

CHAPTER 24

24.1
a. $P = 20$ and $q = 50$.

b. $P = 20$, $q = 40$, $MC = 16$, and tax = 4.

24.3
a. $N = 400$. The externality arises because one well's drilling affects all wells' output.

b. $N = 200$.

c. Fee = 2,000/well.

24.5
An essay question. Should consider: services are provided by parties, risks, information costs, incentives under the various contracts, and so forth.

24.7
a. Set $q_a = q_b$ and $Q = 90$.

b. Free rider problem might result in $Q = 0$.

c. Total cost = 10,800. If tax based on marginal valuation, *a* pays 900, *b* pays 9,900.

24.9
a. If each person is a free rider, utility will be 0.

b. $P = 5$, $G = 50$, $G/100 = 0.5$, and utility $= \sqrt{2.5}$.

CHAPTER 25

25.1
a. 100 each. $U_1 = 10$ and $U_2 = 5$.

b. $F_1 = 40$ and $F_2 = 160$.

c. $F_1 = 160$ and $F_2 = 40$.

d. $F_1 = F_2 = 100$.

e. $F_1 = F_2 = 100$.

25.3
a. $X = 160$; $(U_1 + U_2)^2 = 1,600$.

b. $(U_1 + U_2)^2 = 3,600$.

c. Max $2XY$ subject to $X + 2Y = 180$; $X = 90$; $Y = 45$; $(U_1 + U_2)^2 = 4,050$.

d. If utility possibility frontiers were to intersect, use the outer envelope of the frontiers.

25.5
a. *D*

b. *E*

c. *B*

d. *A*

e. Choice depends on criteria used.

25.7
Consider economies of scale and the regional homogeneity of demand for public goods.

25.9
Those with most to gain would vote. It could change Nash equilibrium strategies.

GLOSSARY OF FREQUENTLY USED TERMS

Some of the terms that are used frequently in this book are defined below. The reader may wish to use the index to find those sections of the text that give more complete descriptions of these concepts.

Adverse Selection When buyers and sellers have asymmetric information about market transactions, trades actually completed may be biased to favor the actor with better information.

Agent A person who makes economic decisions for another economic actor. A hired manager operates as an agent for a firm's owner.

Arrow Impossibility Theorem Fundamental result of social choice theory: any social decision rule must violate at least one of the axioms of rational choice that Arrow developed.

Bertrand Equilibrium Equilibrium in duopoly price-setting game.

Ceteris Paribus Assumption The assumption that all other relevant factors are held constant when examining the influence of one particular variable in an economic model. Reflected in mathematical terms by the use of partial differentiation.

Coase Theorem Result attributable to R. Coase: if bargaining costs are zero, an efficient allocation of resources can be attained in the presence of externalities through reliance on bargaining among the parties involved.

Compensated Demand Curve Curve showing relationship between the price of a good and the quantity consumed while holding real income (or utility) constant. Denoted by $h(P_X, P_Y, U)$.

Compensating Wage Differentials Differences in real wages that arise when the characteristics of occupations cause workers in their supply decisions to prefer one job over another.

Complements (Gross) Two goods such that if the price of one rises, the quantity consumed of the other will fall. Goods X and Y are gross complements if $\partial X/\partial P_Y < 0$. See also Substitutes (Gross).

Complements (Net) Two goods such that if the price of one rises, the quantity consumed of the other will fall, holding real income (utility) constant. Goods X and Y are net complements if

$$\left. \partial X/\partial P_Y \right|_{U = \bar{U}} < 0.$$

Such compensated cross-price effects are symmetric, that is,

$$\left. \partial X/\partial P_Y \right|_{U = \bar{U}} = \left. \partial Y/\partial P_X \right|_{U = \bar{U}}.$$

See also Substitutes (Net). Also called Hicksian substitutes and complements.

Composite Commodity A group of goods whose prices all move together—the relative prices of goods in the group do not change. Such goods can be treated as a single commodity in many applications.

Concave Function A function that lies everywhere below its tangent plane.

Constant-Cost Industry An industry in which expansion of output and entry by new firms has no effect on the cost curves of individual firms.

Constant Returns to Scale See Returns to Scale.

Consumer Surplus   The difference between the total value consumers receive from the consumption of a particular good and the total amount they pay for the good. It is the area under the compensated demand curve and above the market price, and can be approximated by the area under the Marshallian demand curve and above the market price.

Contestable Market   A market in which entry and exit are absolutely free. Markets subject to such "hit-and-run" entry and exit will produce where $P = MC = AC$ even if there are not a large number of firms.

Contour Line   The set of points along which a function has a constant value. Useful for graphing three-dimensional functions in two dimensions. Individuals' indifference curve maps and firms' production isoquant maps are examples.

Contract Curve   The set of all the efficient allocations of goods among those individuals in an exchange economy. Each of these allocations has the property that no one individual can be made better off without making someone else worse off.

Convexity Assumptions   Assumptions about the shapes of individuals' utility functions and firms' production functions. Based on the presumption that the relative marginal effectiveness of a particular good or input diminishes as the quantity of that good or input increases. Important because the conditions ensure that the application of first-order conditions will indeed yield a true maximum.

Cournot Equilibrium   Equilibrium in duopoly quantity-setting game. A similar concept applies to an *n*-person game.

Deadweight Loss   A loss of mutually beneficial transactions. Losses in consumer and producer surplus that are not transferred to another economic agent.

Decreasing Cost Industry   An industry in which expansion of output generates cost-reducing externalities that cause the cost curves of those firms in the industry to shift downward.

Decreasing Returns to Scale   *See* Returns to Scale.

Demand Curve   A graph showing the *ceteris paribus* relationship between the price of a good and the quantity of that good purchased. A two-dimensional representation of the demand function $X = D_X(P_X, P_Y, I)$. This is referred to as

"Marshallian" demand to differentiate it from the compensated (Hicksian) demand concept.

Diminishing Marginal Productivity   *See* Marginal Physical Product.

Diminishing Marginal Rate of Substitution   *See* Marginal Rate of Substitution.

Discrimination, Price   Occurs whenever a buyer or seller is able to use its market power effectively to separate markets and to follow a different price policy in each market. *See also* Perfect Price Discrimination.

Duality   The relationship between any constrained maximization problem and its related "dual" constrained minimization problem.

Economic Efficiency   Exists when resources are allocated so that no activity can be increased without cutting back on some other activity. *See also* Pareto Optimality.

Edgeworth Box Diagram   A graphic device used to demonstrate economic efficiency. Most frequently used to illustrate the contract curve in an exchange economy but also useful in the theory of production.

Elasticity   A measure of the percentage change in one variable brought about by a 1 percent change in some other variable. If $y = f(x)$, then the elasticity of y with respect to $x(e_{y,x})$ is given by $dy/dx \cdot x/y$. Most often used to describe how the quantity of a good demanded responds to a change in its price. For example, if $e_{Q,P} = -2$, a 1 percent rise in price causes quantity demanded to fall by 2 percent. The price elasticity of supply is defined in an analogous way.

Entry Conditions   Characteristics of an industry that determine the ease with which a new firm may begin production. Under perfect competition, entry is assumed to be costless, whereas in a monopolistic industry there are significant barriers to entry.

Envelope Theorem   A mathematical result: the change in the maximum value of a function brought about by a change in a parameter of the function can be found by partially differentiating the function with respect to the parameter (when all other variables take on their optimal values).

Equilibrium   A situation in which no actors have an incentive to change their behavior. At an equilibrium price, the quantity demanded by individuals is exactly equal to that which is supplied by all firms.

Euler's Theorem A mathematical theorem: if $f(X_1, \ldots, X_n)$ is homogeneous of degree k, then

$$f_1 X_1 + f_2 X_2 + \cdots + f_n X_n$$

$$= kf(X_1, \ldots, X_n).$$

Exchange Economy An economy in which the supply of goods is fixed (that is, no production takes place). The available goods, however, may be reallocated among individuals in the economy.

Expansion Path The locus of those cost-minimizing input combinations that a firm will choose to produce various levels of output (when the prices of inputs are held constant).

Expected Utility The average utility expected from a risky situation. If there are n outcomes, $X_1, \ldots, X_n$ with probabilities $P_1, \ldots, P_n$ ($\Sigma P_i = 1$), then the expected utility is given by

$$E(U) = P_1 U(X_1) + P_2 U(X_2)$$

$$+ \cdots + P_n U(X_n).$$

Expenditure Function A function derived from the individual's dual expenditure minimization problem. Shows the minimum expenditure necessary to achieve a given utility level:

$$\text{expenditures} = E(P_X, P_Y, U).$$

Externality An effect of one economic agent on another that is not taken into account by normal market behavior.

First-Order Conditions Mathematical conditions that must necessarily hold if a function is to take on its maximum or minimum value. Usually show that any activity should be increased to the point at which marginal benefits equal marginal costs.

Fixed Costs Costs that do not change as the level of output changes in the short run. Fixed costs are in many respects irrelevant to the theory of short-run price determination. *See also* Variable Costs.

General Equilibrium Model A model of an economy that portrays the operation of many markets simultaneously.

Giffen's Paradox A situation in which the increase in a good's price leads individuals to consume more of the good. Arises because the good in question is inferior and because the income effect induced by the price change is stronger than the substitution effect.

Homogeneous Function A function, $f(X_1, X_2, \ldots, X_n)$, is homogeneous of degree k if

$$f(mX_1, mX_2, \ldots, mX_n) = m^k f(X_1, X_2, \ldots, X_n).$$

Homothetic Function A function that can be represented as a monotonic transformation of a function that is homogeneous of degree one. The slopes of the contour lines for such a function depend only on the ratios of the variables that enter the function, not on their absolute levels.

Income and Substitution Effects Two analytically different effects that come into play when an individual is faced with a changed price for some good. Arise because a change in the price of a good will affect an individual's purchasing power. Even if purchasing power is held constant, however, substitution effects will cause individuals to reallocate their expectations. Substitution effects are reflected in movements along an indifference curve, whereas income effects entail a movement to a different indifference curve. *See also* Slutsky Equation.

Increasing Cost Industry An industry in which the expansion of output creates cost-increasing externalities, which cause the cost curves of those firms in the industry to shift upward.

Increasing Returns to Scale *See* Returns to Scale.

Indifference Curve Map A contour map of an individual's utility function showing those alternative bundles of goods from which the individual derives equal levels of welfare.

Indirect Utility Function A representative of utility as a function of all prices and income.

Individual Demand Curve The *ceteris paribus* relationship between the quantity of a good an individual chooses to consume and the good's price. A two-dimensional representation of $X = d_X$ (P_X, P_Y, I) for one person.

Inferior Good A good that is bought in smaller quantities as an individual's income rises.

Inferior Input A factor of production that is used in smaller amounts as a firm's output expands.

Input Demand Function Function showing the firm's demand for an input (say, labor) that depends on input costs (w, v) and on the level of output (q):

$$L = L(w, v, q).$$

Isoquant Map   A contour map of the firm's production function. The contours show the alternative combinations of productive inputs that can be used to produce a given level of output.

Limit Pricing   Choice of low-price strategies to deter entry.

Lindahl Equilibrium   A hypothetical solution to the public goods problem: the tax share that each individual pays plays the same role as an equilibrium market price in a competitive allocation.

Long Run   *See* Short Run–Long Run Distinction.

Marginal Cost (*MC*)   The additional cost incurred by producing one more unit of output: $MC = \partial TC/\partial q$.

Marginal Physical Product (*MP*)   The additional output that can be produced by one more unit of a particular input while holding all other inputs constant. It is usually assumed that an input's marginal productivity diminishes as additional units of the input are put into use while holding other inputs fixed. If $q = f(K, L)$, $MP_L = \partial q/\partial L$.

Marginal Rate of Substitution (*MRS*)   The rate at which an individual is willing to trade one good for another while remaining equally well off. The *MRS* is the absolute value of the slope of an indifference curve. $MRS = -dY/dX \big|_{U = \overline{U}}$.

Marginal Revenue (*MR*)   The additional revenue obtained by a firm when it is able to sell one more unit of output. $MR = \partial P \cdot q/\partial q = P(1 + 1/e_{q,P})$.

Marginal Revenue Product (*MRP*)   The extra revenue that accrues to a firm when it sells the output that is produced by one more unit of some input. In the case of labor, for example, $MRP_L = MR \cdot MP_L$.

Marginal Utility (*MU*)   The extra utility that an individual receives by consuming one more unit of a particular good.

Marginal Value Product   A specific case of marginal revenue product that applies when the good being produced is sold in a perfectly competitive market. If the competitive price is given P (= *MR* in this case), then marginal value product = $P \cdot MP_L$.

Market Demand   The sum of the quantities of a good demanded by all individuals in a market. Will depend on the price of the good, prices of other goods, each consumer's preferences, and on each consumer's income.

Market Period   A very short period over which quantity supplied is fixed and not responsive to changes in market price.

Marshallian Quantity Adjustment   The assumption that markets are cleared through quantity adjustments in response to excess demand or supply.

Monopoly   An industry in which there is only a single seller of the good in question.

Monopsony   An industry in which there is only a single buyer of the good in question.

Moral Hazard   The effect of insurance coverage on individuals' decisions to undertake activities that may change the likelihood of incurring losses.

Nash Equilibrium Strategies   A set of strategies (a^*, b^*) in a two-player game such that a^* is optimal for A against b^* and b^* is optimal for B against a^*.

Normal Good   A good for which quantity demanded increases (or stays constant) as an individual's income increases.

Normative Analysis   Economic analysis that takes a position on how economic actors or markets should operate.

Oligopoly   An industry in which there are only a few sellers of the good in question.

Opportunity Cost Doctrine   The simple, though far-reaching, observation that the true cost of any action can be measured by the value of the best alternative that must be foregone when the action is taken.

Output and Substitution Effects   Come into play when a change in the price of an input that a firm uses causes the firm to change the quantities of inputs it will demand. The substitution effect would occur even if output were held constant, and it is reflected by movements along an isoquant. Output effects, on the other hand, occur when output levels change and the firm moves to a new isoquant.

Paradox of Voting   Illustrates the possibility that majority rule voting may not yield a determinate outcome but may instead cycle among alternatives.

Pareto Efficient Allocation   An allocation of resources in which no one individual can be made better off without making someone else worse off.

Partial Equilibrium Model A model of a single market that ignores repercussions in other markets.

Perfect Competition The most widely economic model: there are assumed to be a large number of buyers and sellers for any good and each agent is a price taker. *See also* Price Taker.

Positive Analysis Economic analysis that seeks to explain and predict actual economic events.

Present Discounted Value (*PDV*) The current value of a sum of money that is payable sometime in the future. Takes into account the effect of interest payments.

Price Discrimination Selling identical goods at different prices. Requires sellers to have the ability to prevent resale. There are three types: first degree—selling each unit at a different price to the individual willing to pay the most for it ("perfect price discrimination"); second degree—adopting price schedules that give buyers an incentive to separate themselves into differing price categories; third degree—charging different prices in separated markets.

Price Taker An economic agent that makes decisions on the assumption that these decisions will have no effect on prevailing market prices.

Prisoner's Dilemma Originally studied in the theory of games but has widespread applicability. The crux of the dilemma is that each individual, faced with the uncertainty of how others will behave, may be led to adopt a course of action that proves to be detrimental for all those individuals making the same decision. A strong coalition might have led to a solution preferred by everyone in the group.

Producer Surplus The additional compensation a producer receives from participating in market transactions rather than having no transactions. Short-run producer surplus consists of short-run profits plus fixed costs. Long-run producer surplus consists of increased rents earned by inputs. In both cases the concept is illustrated as the area below market price and above the respective supply curve.

Production Function A conceptual mathematical function that records the relationship between a firm's inputs and its outputs. If output is a function of capital and labor only, this would be denoted by $q = f(K, L)$.

Production Possibility Frontier The locus of all the alternative quantities of several outputs that can be produced with fixed amounts of productive inputs.

Profit Function The relationship between a firm's maximum profits (π^*) and the output and input prices it faces:

$$\pi^* = \pi^*(P, v, w).$$

Profits The difference between the total revenue a firm receives and its total economic costs of production. Economic profits equal zero under perfect competition in the long run. Monopoly profits may be positive, however.

Property Rights Legal specification of ownership and the rights of owners.

Public Good A good that once produced is available to all on a nonexclusive basis. Many public goods are also nonrival—additional individuals may benefit from the good at zero marginal costs.

Quasi-concave Function A function for which the set of all points for which $f(X) > k$ is convex.

Rate of Product Transformation (*RPT*) The rate at which one output can be traded for another in the productive process while holding the total quantities of inputs constant. The *RPT* is the absolute value of the slope of the production possibility frontier.

Rate of Return The rate at which present goods can be transformed into future goods. For example, a one-period rate of return of 10 percent implies that foregoing 1 unit of output this period will yield 1.10 units of output next period.

Rate of Technical Substitution (*RTS*) The rate at which one input may be traded off against another in the productive process while holding output constant. The *RTS* is the absolute value of the slope of an isoquant.

$$RTS = -\frac{dK}{dL}\bigg|_{q = q_0}.$$

Rent Payments to a factor of production that are in excess of that amount necessary to keep it in its current employment.

Rent Seeking Economic actors using the political process to obtain rents that would not be available from market transactions.

Rental Rate   The cost of hiring one machine for one hour. Denoted by v in the text.

Returns to Scale   A way of classifying production functions that records how output responds to proportional increases in all inputs. If a proportional increase in all inputs causes output to increase by a smaller proportion, the production function is said to exhibit decreasing returns to scale. If output increases by a greater proportion than the inputs, the production function exhibits increasing returns. Constant returns to scale is the middle ground where both inputs and outputs increase by the same proportions. Mathematically, if $f(mK, mL) = m^k f(K, L)$, $k > 1$ implies increasing returns, $k = 1$ constant returns, and $k < 1$ decreasing returns.

Risk Aversion   Unwillingness to accept fair bets. Arises when an individual's utility of wealth function is concave [that is, $U'(W) > 0$, $U''(W) < 0$]. Absolute risk aversion is measured by $r(W) = \dfrac{-U''(W)}{U'(W)}$. Relative risk aversion is measured by $rr(W) = \dfrac{-WU''(W)}{U'(W)}$.

Second-Order Conditions   Mathematical conditions required to ensure that points for which first-order conditions are satisfied are indeed true maximum or true minimum points. These conditions are satisfied by functions that obey certain convexity assumptions.

Shepherd's Lemma   Application of the envelope theorem, which shows that a consumer's compensated demand functions and a firm's (constant output) input demand functions can be derived from partial differentiation of expenditure functions or total cost functions, respectively.

Shifting of a Tax   Market response to the imposition of a tax that cause the incidence of the tax to be on some economic agent other than the one who actually pays the tax.

Short Run–Long Run Distinction   A conceptual distinction made in the theory of production that differentiates between a period of time over which some inputs are regarded as being fixed and a longer period in which all inputs can be varied by the producer.

Signaling   Actions taken by individuals in markets characterized by adverse selection in an effort to identify their true risk categories.

Slutsky Equation   A mathematical representation of the substitution and income effects of a price change on utility-maximizing choices:

$$\partial X/\partial P_X = \partial X/\partial P_X \bigg|_{U = \bar{u}} - X\frac{\partial X}{\partial I}.$$

Social Rates of Transformation and Substitution   When externalities are present, private rates of trade-off and social rates of trade-off will differ. To study the optimal allocation of resources, it is necessary to examine social rates.

Social Welfare Function   A hypothetical device that records societal views about equity among individuals.

Subgame Perfect Equilibrium   A Nash equilibrium in which the strategy choices of each player do not involve noncredible threats.

Substitutes (Gross)   Two goods such that if the price of one increases, more of the other good will be demanded. That is X and Y are gross substitutes if $\partial X/\partial P_Y > 0$. *See also* Complements; Slutsky Equation.

Substitutes (Net)   Two goods such that if the price of one increases, more of the other good will be demanded if utility is held constant. That is, X and Y are net substitutes if

$$\partial X/\partial P_Y \bigg|_{U = \bar{u}} > 0.$$

Net substitutability is symmetric in that

$$\partial X/\partial P_Y \bigg|_{U = \bar{u}} = \partial Y/\partial P_X \bigg|_{U = \bar{u}}.$$

See also Complements; Slutsky Equation.

Substitution Effects   *See* Income and Substitution Effects; Output and Substitution Effects; Slutsky Equation.

Sunk Costs   One-time investments that must be made in order to enter a market.

Supply Function   For a profit-maximizing firm, a function that shows quantity supplied (q^*) as a function of output price (P) and input prices (v, w):

$$q^* = q^*(P, v, w).$$

Supply Response Increases in production prompted by changing demand conditions and market prices. Usually a distinction is made between short-run and long-run supply responses.

Tacit Collusion Choice of cooperative (monopoly) strategies without explicit collusion.

Total Cost Curve The relationship between (minimized) total costs and output, holding input prices constant. Derived from the total cost function

$$TC = TC(v, w, q).$$

Utility Function A mathematical conceptualization of the way in which individual rank alternative bundles of commodities. If there are only two goods, X and Y, utility is denoted by

$$\text{utility} = U(X, Y).$$

Variable Costs Costs that change in response to changes in the level of output being produced by a firm. This is in contrast to fixed costs, which do not change.

von Neumann–Morgenstern Utility A ranking of outcomes in uncertain situations such that individuals choose among these outcomes on the basis of their expected utility values.

Wage The cost of hiring one worker for one hour. Denoted by w in the text.

Walrasian Price Adjustment The assumption that markets are cleared through price adjustments in response to excess demand or supply.

Zero-Sum Game A game in which winnings for one player are losses for the other player.

NAME INDEX

SUBJECT INDEX

Key terms and the page numbers on which they are defined are set in bold type.